49.95
③ 60C
259570-0
10-23-85

THE PROFESSIONAL MICROCOMPUTER HANDBOOK

THE PROFESSIONAL MICROCOMPUTER HANDBOOK

Ivan Flores

Computer Consultant
Professor of Computer
 and Information Science
City University of New York

Melvyn Feuerman

VNR VAN NOSTRAND REINHOLD COMPANY
———————————————— New York

Copyright © 1986 by Van Nostrand Reinhold Company Inc.

Library of Congress Catalog Card Number: 85-3139
ISBN: 0-442-22497-4

All rights reserved. No part of this work covered by the copyright hereon may be reproduced or used in any form or by any means—graphic, electronic, or mechanical, including photocopying, recording, taping, or information storage and retrieval systems—without permission of the publisher.

Manufactured in the United States of America

Published by Van Nostrand Reinhold Company Inc.
135 West 50th Street
New York, New York 10020

Van Nostrand Reinhold Company Limited
Molly Millars Lane
Wokingham, Berkshire RG11 2PY, England

Van Nostrand Reinhold
480 Latrobe Street
Melbourne, Victoria 3000, Australia

Macmillan of Canada
Division of Gage Publishing Limited
164 Commander Boulevard
Agincourt, Ontario MIS 3C7, Canada

15 14 13 12 11 10 9 8 7 6 5 4 3 2 1

Library of Congress Cataloging in Publication Data

Flores, Ivan.
   The professional microcomputer handbook.

  1. Microcomputers. I. Feuerman, Melvyn. II. Title.
QA76.5.F47 1985   001.64   85-3139
ISBN 0-442-22497-4

Preface

This new *Handbook* provides all that the professional and business person needs to know to be current about micros. Many broad-brush books get you started with generalities, but fall short of solutions to your special needs. Specialty books tell you how to use specific micros or application packages, but they assume the *prior* purchase of a system—often itself a mistake. In contrast, this *Handbook* explains fully how things work and how competitive features compare, leaving it to your own good judgement to choose what is best for your business or practice.

Like numerous books now on the market, this *Handbook* introduces the reader to many new technical topics; but is also encompasses numerous important details usually omitted from the introductory survey. Material for both the novice and the experienced is contained in this single volume. It is meant to be scanned for general content, but a section of immediate interest may be read selectively and intensively; each major division is therefore self-sufficient.

WHO WILL BENEFIT FROM THIS HANDBOOK?

- **Corporate Managers.** Managers at all corporate levels obviously can benefit from the word processing, budget manipulation, and data processing capabilities of microsystems. These proven tools can be put to work effectively within the corporate setting once we understand them.
- **Organization Directors.** America has thousands of public and private organizations: service clubs, chambers of commerce, religious and social groups, political and charitable organizations. Many are staffed by volunteers, adding to their directors' challenge to get the most out of their staffs, to get their organizations to run smoothly. All the powers of the microcomputer that so ably assist corporate managers can make the not-for-profit dollar work more efficiently.
- **Accountants, CPAs.** Small businesses are flocking to buy computer systems. Some acquire inflexible packages lacking needed features or requiring changes in the firm's accounting procedures. The accountant

needs to understand micros and packages to help clients adjust to them and to assist clients in a better initial selection. He or she can then establish proper audit trails to make records safe against damage or loss because of equipment malfunction, human error or improper use.
- **Vendors.** The sales for computer stores should have a technical background but they are rarely trained programmers or engineers. This book fills the knowledge and training gap so that new sales people can help customers to assess what equipment is best for them.
- **Business Students.** The curriculum in business administration now includes much exposure to computers, but usually larger systems. The new graduate now emerges into a computerized business world with an arsenal of knowledge; one who also knows about micros—the purpose of this *Handbook*—is a much more attractive employee.
- **Small Business Owners and Managers.** A business owner questions whether a potential system will be cost-effective, whether it will provide a hard dollar improvement. In some cases, the answer is obvious, once it's known what the system's technology can do; in other cases, alternative systems must be examined to make a better judgment. This book furnishes answers or else points to where more help is found.
- **The Professional Office.** Doctors, dentists, lawyers, other professionals and entrepreneurs get valuable help from the PC. While specific turnkey packages are available, tailored to each profession, they are expensive. The *Handbook* not only explains what computer essentials the professional needs but also thoroughly examines general packages like word processing and data base managers. Low risk experimentation will reveal whether computerization of any or all office functions is feasible and economic.

SURVEYING THE CONTENTS

I. Overview

Part I introduces the computer to the uninitiated. Chapter 1 outlines **how the computer works.** Micros look different but have similar parts; what are they? Next we take a peek inside one. The computer is only one part of the system; what are the other parts?

Chapter 2 expands on the **computer system.** A section describes each hardware component, its purpose and its principles of operation. A final section tells you what software is, why it is so important and what distinguishes the operating system from an application program.

II. Hardware

Part II examines computer hardware. Chapter 3 is devoted to **communication:** how we talk to the computer, how the computer talks to us and how it talks to other computers.

The wide variety of **printers** available on the market, spanning a range of cost, speed and quality, is examined in Chapter 4. Proper selection can save much time and money, especially in the long run.

All the information needed by the micro is kept on **magnetic storage media,** explained in Chapter 5. Although disk drives, the focus in this chapter, range widely in price, the differences in capacity are even greater. Which type of drive should you choose? How can you make sure you get good disks? How do you keep them safely?

Computer manufacturers provide a wide spectrum of machines. Chapter 6 describes most **types of micros and PCs**—how the micro is put together, what a printed circuit board is, the add-on boards available; the many forms of memory, the control subsystem, how the processor does arithmetic and manipulates alphabetic data; how a structure called a bus connects the components within the computer, and how the computer is tied by cables and wires to peripheral devices which display information, print out forms and store data. A section in this chapter introduces the IBM PC, XT and AT and their direct competitors.

III. Software, Programs and Data

Part III is about operating systems, programs and data. Sitting between an application program and the computer hardware is the operating system, a middleman. It is required to provide compatibility between program and computer. Chapter 7 explains the **operating system's function** and why a program must mate with it and the computer.

All application programs are written in some programming language. Languages differ in important ways: speed in running, ease for learning, power and simplicity of use. Chapter 8 examines **languages for micros** ranging from assembly language to higher level languages and why it is important for you to know about them. This chapter considers the major programming structures, using BASIC for examples, and outlines Pascal, the principal alternative to BASIC. It also examines a new choice, True BASIC.

Chapter 9 discusses **data organization.** External storage holds all the company's books as disk files. The organization of the file determines the time it takes to get back information you request or to process data, how easy it is to make requests and to alter and modify your "books." We contrast the principal file organizations and show how to use each in two dialects of BASIC.

IV. Applications

PART IV is devoted to applications and their software. Chapter 10 is an overview, examining the **features and limitations** of commercial application packages and looking at the important factors to review when considering them.

Chapter 11 looks at editing, formatting, printing and additional features of the **word processor** and examines a number of packages available to do the job.

A **data base** systematically stores many kinds of data quickly and easily and simplifies retrieval and entry, as shown in Chapter 12. It is also a way of systematizing small business and personal activity. Its applications for many purposes are closely examined through dBase II as a model in this key chapter.

A **picture** is worth many words but it costs something in terms of memory, space, computer time and initial investment. Still it may be worth the price to see graphs and visual images rather than to interpret numeric printouts. Chapter 13 looks at the potential and the tradeoffs.

Some executives have bought microcomputers solely for the facilities provided by **spread sheet packages.** They enable the executive to make important "what if?" projections which would otherwise take considerable time and money. Three generations of spread sheet packages, each with additional refinements and features over the previous ones, are the subject of Chapter 14. First generation examples are drawn from SuperCalc; the second generation examines Multiplan in detail. The third generation provides combination packages which include graphics, data base and other features; here Lotus 1-2-3 provides the detailed examples.

Two **advanced fourth generation spread sheets** packages appeared at the end of 1984. They have sold well and reflect the attitude that one produce can provide for almost all ones needs. Chapter 15 examines these highly complicated application programs, Symphony and Framework and contrasts their capabilities.

V. Putting It All Together

Part V brings it all together. Chapter 16 reviews the **entire system,** examines **the major choices** and how you might **acquire a system.** Because of IBM's dominance, a section is devoted to the IBM personal computer and its look-a likes, assessing the capabilities of the competition. Working with several application packages simultaneously by means of "windows" is described here. Then three sections examine emerging systems: Lisa, Macintosh, multiuser systems and high resolution graphics. Finally, for atypical applications, the purchase of a custom configured system from an original equipment manufacturer (OEM), who provides all system hardware, software, maintenance and service, is analyzed.

Appendices and Index

A large **Glossary** encapsulates "computerese" for both general scanning and specific reference; and an extensive **Index** shortens the search for topics of all levels of importance in the *Handbook*. Several other appendices give **common accronyms, command references** for several packages, contrast capabilities of selected **major spread sheets** and **word processors** and provide both a **bibliography** and a listing of further **reference resources**.

ACKNOWLEDGEMENTS

Melvyn Feuerman helped me with this project in many ways. His assistance in formulating the direction of the project was invaluable. Further, he helped evaluate its progress and made many contacts with others who also participated. Among these was Don Kabut, who reviewed much of the material as it was generated and also developed new material which integrated business and accounting methods as well as analysis. This effort was eventually broken off into another book. Let us hope that this fine start will materialize as a separate volume.

Several people assisted in the real work of converting ideas into an actual manuscript. I must especially mention Cecile Lumer and Ricki Sodokoff. I would also like to thank Dr. Naomi Mendelsohn, not only for her inspiration but also for her help in reviewing all the book and suggesting passages which were unclear and needed mending.

Finally, I would like to thank the staff at Van Nostrand Reinhold, not only for their assistance, but also for their support in tolerating my moods when things occasionally went wrong. I especially thank Larry Hager and Walter Brownfield. The book's great cover is the work of Arlene Abend, who never fails to come through with a new and meaningful creation.

IVAN FLORES
Brooklyn, N.Y.

Contents

Preface ... v

I. Overview

1. Introduction
- 1.1 Overview ... 3
- 1.2 The Nature of the Computer ... 3
- 1.3 The Computer from the Outside ... 8
- 1.4 From the Inside ... 11
- 1.5 What Is a System? ... 14
- 1.6 Computer Benefits ... 19

2. The Computer System
- 2.1 Overview ... 26
- 2.2 The CPU ... 28
- 2.3 Communicating ... 35
- 2.4 Printers ... 38
- 2.5 Storage ... 39
- 2.6 Software ... 42

II. Hardware

3. Communicating
- 3.1 Introduction ... 49
- 3.2 Keyboards ... 52
- 3.3 More about Keys ... 58
- 3.4 Displays ... 64
- 3.5 Character Storage and Generators ... 69
- 3.6 Communication between Computers ... 78

4. Printers
- 4.1 Introduction ... 84
- 4.2 Modified Typewriter ... 85
- 4.3 The Dot Matrix Printer ... 87
- 4.4 The Daisy Wheel Printer ... 95
- 4.5 The Line Printer ... 97
- 4.6 The Laser Printer ... 100
- 4.7 Motion in the Printer ... 101
- 4.8 Summary ... 108

xi

5. External Storage
5.1 Introduction	111
5.2 Magnetic Recording	114
5.3 Disk Drives	117
5.4 Diskettes	125
5.5 Disk Contents	134
5.6 Winchester Drives	141
5.7 Considerations	146

6. Computers
6.1 Introduction	152
6.2 The CPU	157
6.3 Memory	161
6.4 More PC Boards	168
6.5 New Chips	181
6.6 The IBM PC and XT	184

III. Software, Programs and Data

7. The Operating System
7.1 Overview	199
7.2 The Operating System	204
7.3 The Resident Operating System	207
7.4 Requesting Action	215
7.5 Nonresident Services	220
7.6 CPM Utilities	230
7.7 Other Utilities	236
7.8 PC-DOS, MS-DOS and Other Operating Systems	245

8. Programs
8.1 Introduction	258
8.2 How Programs Are Created	261
8.3 BASIC	278
8.4 Properties of Languages	294
8.5 Pascal	297
8.6 Other Languages for Micros	305
8.7 Advanced BASIC	311
8.8 True BASIC	318

9. Data and Files
9.1 What Is Data?	326
9.2 Data Representation	332

9.3 Sequential Files	338
9.4 Direct Files	350

IV. Applications

10. Application Software
10.1 The Choices	367
10.2 The Complete Application Package	369
10.3 Considerations	373
10.4 Selection Resources	380
10.5 Programming	383

11. Word Processing
11.1 Introduction	387
11.2 General Functions	389
11.3 Creating	393
11.4 Editing	397
11.5 Format	409
11.6 Printing	421
11.7 Portions of Documents	424
11.8 Editing Assistance	430

12. Data Base
12.1 Introduction	436
12.2 Data Entry	440
12.3 Simple Retrieval	448
12.4 Selective Retrieval	455
12.5 Facilitation	465
12.6 Update and Modification; Utilities	477
12.7 Command Files	487
12.8 Reports	503
12.9 Report Command Programs	514

13. Graphics
13.1 Introduction	526
13.2 The Graphic System	535
13.3 The Image and Its Display	540
13.4 The Screen	546
13.5 Making the Picture	551
13.6 Input Devices	560
13.7 Menu Driven Graphics	568
13.8 Output	577
13.9 IBM PC/XT Graphics	583

14. Spread Sheets
    14.1 Introduction   593
    14.2 Basics   597
    14.3 Simple Applications   607
    14.4 More Functions and Examples   615
    14.5 "What If?"   628
    14.6 Multiplan and the Second Generation   642
    14.7 Lotus and the Third Generation SS   658

15. Fourth Generation Spread Sheets
    15.1 Introduction   680
    15.2 Introduction to Framework   681
    15.3 Framework Menu Choices   690
    15.4 Tasks   700
    15.5 Symphony   717
    15.6 Assessment   722

V. Putting It All Together

16. Systems
    16.1 The Computer System   729
    16.2 The IBM PC and Its Clones   730
    16.3 The Operating Environment   733
    16.4 Lisa, Macintosh, Lisa 2 and Their Ilk   740
    16.5 Multiuser Systems   753
    16.6 Graphic System   762
    16.7 The System House   766

APPENDICES

A. **Abbreviations**   773
B. **Glossary**   775
C. **BASIC Commands by Type**   810
D. **BASICA Commands and Their Meaning**   815
E. **Word Processing Packages**   830
F. **DBase Commands and Their Actions**   834
G. **Spread Sheet Characteristics**   843
H. **Bibliography**   847
I. **Resources**   849

Illustration Credits   851

Index   853

I
Overview

1
Introduction

1.1 OVERVIEW

The overall aims of this chapter are to explain:

- why the computer is unique as an invention and must be viewed in a different light from other technical advances;
- what the computer looks like from the outside and how you deal with it physically;
- in general terms, what's inside the computer and what makes it run;
- the advantages (and disadvantages) the computer brings to the small business which it is supposed to help.
- how a computer fits into a small business;
- what is in the rest of this book and how you can best make use of it.

Bear with me and take a little time to examine ideas in the form that I view them. This may help us to avoid any misunderstanding later on.

1.2 THE NATURE OF THE COMPUTER

There are several points to keep in mind about the computer:

- It is a machine.
- An *electronic* machine works at extremely high speed.
- It may be used *conceptually,* working with ideas rather than physical quantities.
- It is a *restructurable* to take on different capabilities and roles.
- It is driven by a *program,* a set of directions which it follows immutably.

An Electronic Machine

The computer is a machine and a complicated one at that. Machines and computers seem to engender fear. But professionals have mostly overcome these fears, and so many of us have some contact with computers in our everyday life.

Children growing up now find a world filled with computers of all sorts. They see them as friends or peers with whom they compete often and hard. Still, it is important to examine some of the sources of fears that linger on.

An Alien Force

Machines of all sorts are a force to be reckoned with. They have power which may get out of control and be turned against us. If an automobile or an aircraft become defective, we can easily lose our lives.

Science fiction has not helped the matter; stories show robots who take over the world and subjugate us. There was a time when it was important to point out to the novice that a computer has no physical power to exert against us. It is incapable of locomotion; we turn it off by flipping a switch or pulling out the plug.

It's Our Competitor

A computer does many of the jobs which people were specially trained to do in the past. Furthermore, the computer is extremely accurate and not prone to human error. Won't it replace so many of us that many will become jobless?

Often the computer does a job more effectively than we do it ourselves. However, most of these jobs are repetitious and tedious. The computer frees us from these chores and lets us do more productive and inventive things. And then there are so many additional jobs created to service the computer and provide it with programs to work properly. The change is occurring gradually so that there is little perceptible effect on society.

Firms that buy small business computers find that they don't eliminate employees, who instead benefit from them. The firm runs more efficiently and productively, generates greater profits, but requires the work of all existing employees. Some are freed from routine to take on new creative tasks, which makes their job more enjoyable.

Too Complicated to Cope With

The computer is definitely a complex machine which requires years of study to know thoroughly. But so are many technological advances that we use without care. The automobile is highly engineered; the television set is beyond the comprehension of even many engineers but provides us with continuous entertainment, and even a child can master its simple controls.

We are confronted all the time with electronic marvels designed so that a youngster can cope with them. The small computers on the market, however, are much more complicated to learn about than, say, a television set. But they help us and facilitate our lives.

Computer system designers realize how complicated the machines are and have done much to simplify their use. Packages for the business computer system are becoming increasingly **user friendly** and some are almost self-teaching. Provisions are made to forestall mistakes which we *might* make; the system responds by preventing difficulties from arising.

A Catastrophe Could Easily Happen

There is a constant fear that something someone might do could foul things up so badly that the firm would be ruined or at least set back a few months or weeks. The same design which helps make computers simple to operate also makes them more reliable and tends to prevent uncontrolled failure. Of course, any machine operated incorrectly might be injured. If you put your car in reverse while it's going 60 miles an hour, who knows what might happen. A training period is required to learn the proper use of any expensive and powerful machine (driving school, computer training courses). During this period, you learn the "no-nos." For instance, you never turn off the computer until you know that data you have been working on has been put away safely.

If you think about it, you can mess up almost any set of books by not employing the proper procedures, whether manual or machine. Therefore, I stress the importance of *standard procedures.*

There is still the lingering question, "Well, if I do obey the proper operating procedures, could I hit the wrong button by mistake and still mess everything up?" Again, many systems are designed for use by novices and have safeguards built into them so that such mistakes are unlikely. Also, if proper backup procedures are employed, even when a mistake is made, recovery from it is not difficult.

A Conceptual Machine

The computer is the first machine in history that deals with *concepts* rather than *physical* phenomena such as motion, temperature and so forth. What distinguishes humans from other animals is an ability to deal with concepts and abstractions. This is just one more reason some fear the computer: it comes closer to our own sphere of influence than any other machine or creature we have known.

In the past, we have developed machines to deal with quantities and numbers. First, there were mechanical calculators, then slide rules, the only aids to calculation up to a few decades ago. Both these means for calculating have been supplanted by the pocket calculator; they are *obsolete*.

But quantity is only one concept. The computer can be directed to keep track of many different kinds of conceptual entities, such as

- identifier (name, employee number, vendor number, and so on);
- category;
- pattern;
- color;
- description.

to name but a few.

The computer deals with concepts because it can make **decisions** based on class membership, size or other criteria. A decision is the basis for further action. The computer can perform a number of different actions on conceptual entities, including

- making calculations;
- putting pieces of data together;
- taking apart and removing data;
- getting the attention of the operator;
- creating a pattern on paper or on a screen.

The Computer as a Professional

With the capability described above, the computer can perform compound routine activity such as we professionals do in the course of our jobs. Here are just a few examples of complex tasks it can help with:

- statistical analysis;
- letter writing, including checking spelling, hyphenation and organizing format;
- architectural and mechanical drawings;
- simple graphic displays, such as bar and pie charts;
- helping to lay out a floor plan;
- helping to analyze a malfunctioning machine;
- helping to diagnose human ailments;
- keeping track of long lists and large sets of data;

- accounting;
- billing, invoicing and inventory control;
- planning and budgeting.

What a wealth of skills!

The Program

The **program** is the set of directions which runs the computer and solves a particular problem. These directions could be simple, even trivial, such as to add a set of numbers and come up with their sum. You can add more and more talent to the directions, so that one program can select from a multitude of actions. As you add capabilities, the program grows. Eventually it takes on the status of a single-minded professional. For instance, a program might do all the activities that a bookkeeper would perform in doing the payroll for your staff. We now have a *payroll program*.

This program needs the same kind of information that the bookkeeper requires for each employee. It produces the same output, including a check, a statement to the employee, entries for various journals and lists of taxes and other monies withheld.

The computer, and the program which runs it, work on information provided for this payroll period and come up with the desired output. But note that the information must still be entered by someone. The computer cannot read, listen or interpret spoken English, nor can it move around the premises and collect the information. It relies on a human operator to enter the information. Thus we have not eliminated the human; an operator enters all data required for each payroll period. Perhaps that person may be less skilled than the original bookkeeper. Still circumstances arise which may require human ingenuity in settling what the program wants and needs.

The computer and payroll program have replaced the payroll bookkeeper. But for many years we have had bookkeeping machines which would perform similar actions at an equivalent cost. The problem with them was that they could *only* do payroll bookkeeping. They had little or no versatility.

Changing the Program

A long and complicated program provides the services previously rendered by the payroll bookkeeper. This program has to be available in the computer memory, as we examine later. To cause the computer to become a different professional, to do a different kind of task, we replace the existing program in memory with another one. Thus, by changing the program, the computer does engineering design, drafting, medical diagnosis, and so forth.

To replace one program with another in order to change the computer's role takes a mere minute or so. The computer has "changed hats."

What's in the Program

A program consists of many elementary operations which the computer performs. Each brand of computer has its own set of elementary operations. Many such operations may be required to answer what we humans consider a simple question, such as "Did this person work overtime during last week?" It is conceivable that the answer to this question might take forty or fifty **commands** (elementary operations). Hence to develop a complete payroll program may take one person one or more years, or a team of people a few months.

1.3 THE COMPUTER FROM THE OUTSIDE

The computer consists of units which have separate functions and often are physically separate. These functions are

1. Storage;
2. Communication;
3. The ability to produce written reports;
4. Capability to manipulate and process data.

We examine each of these and how they are used.

Storage

For the computer can be likened to the file cabinets in your office which contain many different kinds of written information. Usually we separate the file cabinets into groups: within a file cabinet we have drawers; within those drawers, folders; and so forth. A good system of classifying the information within cabinets is imperative if we are to find something quickly.

Information to be consumed by the computer is in a different form. The most popular form for storing information in computer systems is the **floppy disk.** It is a small black square of cardboard, 3 to 8 inches on the side; from looking at it you would have no idea that it contains tens or hundreds of pages of information. *You* cannot see the information. It is only readable by the computer, which can both read or alter the information.

1.3 THE COMPTUER FROM THE OUTSIDE   9

Not only can these disks keep all the contents of files we might use in our office, but they can also keep programs which solve problems for us.

Disks are compact and reliable. Information can be stored there indefinitely and recovered any time needed. It is as safe there as it would be in any office. Disks are *not* secure against fire or flood; catastrophes which would destroy paper would probably destroy these disks too.

To mount a disk and make the information it contains available to the computer is simple; school children have mastered it. The information is read by a mechanical device called a **disk drive**. It may be an integral part of your computer or it may be in a separate box. The disk fits into a slot. Close the door or snap the handle down and information is immediately available; the computer can extract a program or data or enter new information momentarily.

The sizes, capacities and specifications of these disks differ considerably; we examine these attributes in Chapter 5 to see how they influence system selection.

Communication

By **communication** I mean the way that you talk to the computer or it talks to you. *Talking* is a possibility but not economically feasible at this time. It takes a lot of computer talent to understand the human voice. It is somewhat easier to have the computer make sounds which resemble human speech. In any case, talking is not the way that people and computers communicate at present.

A program that runs the computer puts messages to its operator on the **terminal screen.** These screens, perfected for television, easily show letters put together into sentences so as to be meaningful to the operator. The characters are well shaped and easily readable from a reasonable distance. Thus the program can transmit messages which

- tell you of its progress;
- ask you to submit information of a particular kind;
- show a result that it comes up with;
- indicate that an error has been detected or that you seem to have made a mistake;
- and so forth.

The program creates a message and sends it to the display, where it appears in a fraction of a second. The terminal has a built-in beeper which the program can also activate to get your attention when you are not looking at the display.

Talking Back

As you operate the computer, you furnish the answers to the program's questions. Except for graphics input, the only way you "talk" is through the **terminal keyboard**. This is a conventional typewriter keyboard which has been expanded by almost doubling the number of keys. There has been resistance to terminals by business and professional people who say they are demeaning to use. But most of us have given in, since typewriters abound in the business world.

It is important to realize that all the data about your business—all its books, accounts, ledgers, journals and so forth—*have* to be entered via the keyboard. Products from computer manufacturers provided on disks contain programs and some marginal data readable by the computer. The data concerning your firm is *not* available in such a form. The only way to convert data for use by the computer is for someone to type it in at the keyboard. Therefore, any conversion from a manual to a computer system requires considerable data entry.

Reports

The computer sends transient messages and requests to the terminal screen; these disappear when a new message displays. Any information to be referenced when the computer is turned off should be printed on paper.

A **printer** is a device to put information on paper to be kept permanently, filed or distributed. A wide range of printers is available, attachable to most systems. Printers differ in these characteristics:

- speed;
- quality of printout;
- versatility;
- cost.

The printer attaches by a cable and connector to the computer box. Be careful to match your programs to the printer you buy, as emphasized in other parts of the book.

Intelligence

The capacity to do calculations, edit data and make decisions is available in the computer proper. Computers differ considerably in aspects of interest mainly at the engineering level. It is important to keep in mind that most computers can do most things. If they could not, they could not compete on the open market to satisfy most purchasers.

An important feature not seen from the outside is **compatibility**. Once you have chosen a particular computer type, *only* programs, software and application packages written specifically for that computer type work on it. (You wouldn't expect to be able to take a wheel from a Volkswagon and put it on a Ford.)

A package that works on one computer type may not work on another computer type. An entirely different design of that same program may exist which *does* work on the latter. It's up to you to verify that this is the case.

Interconnection

The storage unit, the terminal, the printer and the computer may be housed in different cabinets and connected with cables. At the other extreme, a single cabinet can hold all four units appropriately matched to each other. A more common occurrence is to find storage, the terminal (screen and keyboard) and the computer built into one cabinet and connected by a cable to a separate printer. *All the devices must match each other.*

1.4 FROM THE INSIDE

The purpose of this section is to see, in a general way, what happens inside the computer. Even a simplified idea will help you to understand which aspects are important and which can be ignored.

Subsystems

Figure 1.4.1 shows the four computer subsystems as boxes. At the top is a **memory**. It holds programs and information currently to be worked on by the computer. It is the internal equivalent of storage. At the left is the **control system**. It examines the program and interprets each instruction contained there. Then it delegates an action to one of the other two units. The program is a sequence of elementary operations called **instructions** or **commands**.

At the right is the **processor**. It receives data from memory, processes it by arithmetic or editing and returns results to memory.

The box at the bottom right is the device for bringing in new data to memory and for taking data from memory.

12 INTRODUCTION

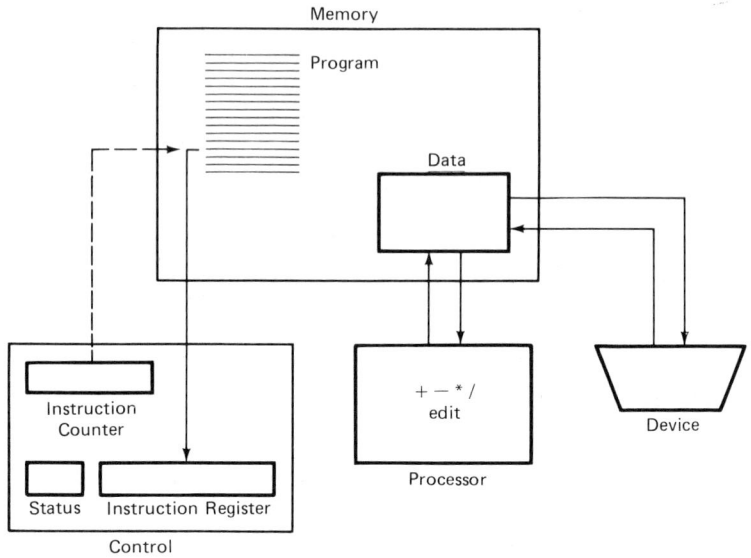

Figure 1.4.1. The computer subsystems.

Memory

Memory holds the program which runs the computer and part of the data being processed. Memory works only when the power is on. When you first turn the computer on, you find only garbage in memory. To get things started, a program is **loaded** from a disk into memory. The program can get **data** (what the program *processes*) from the same or another disk or request it from the terminal operator.

Because the computer is so fast, it needs the program readily available in equally fast memory. If we kept the program out on the storage medium, the computer would run much more slowly. Thus everything needed for current operation should be in memory as the program runs.

Control

The **control subsystem** sequences through the program and delegates commands to other units. Note three little rectangles in the control subsystem box. Each represents a **register,** a place where data is kept for rapid access by the hardware. The registers in the figure have these names and functions:

- The **instruction register** holds one instruction from the program as it is analyzed to be delegated to another unit.

- The **instruction counter** contains the location in memory of the instruction *currently* being executed.
- The **status register** contains information about the present state of the computer in general and the effect of one or more of the preceding instructions.

To see how the computer operates, we examine its two phases of operation called fetch and execute. The computer alternates between these two phases. It's like the pendulum shown in Figure 1.4.2, which swings back and forth between these two alternatives.

Fetch

Fetch acquires the next command to be executed; it begins when the command in progress is completed. The control subsystem recognizes command completion and enters the fetch phase of operation. The instruction counter gives the location of the instruction just completed. The next instruction is at the next consecutive location whose number is obtained by simply adding one to the instruction counter. That number, called an **address,** is sent to the memory. The instruction procured from that address in memory is sent to the instruction register. Now the control system has a new instruction to execute.

Execute

To **execute** an instruction, the control subsystem assigns it to some other subsystem to perform. First the control subsystem analyzes the instruction in its register to determine who gets it. Further analysis reveals where to find the *datum* to be acted upon (called the **operand**). The operands are routed from memory (or elsewhere) to the processor or input/output subsystem, which goes to work to perform the action.

Once an action is finished, signals go to the control subsystem, which responds by entering the fetch state. Program execution continues thus.

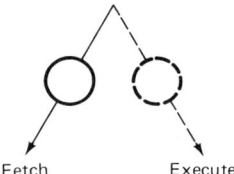

Figure 1.4.2. Two phases of computer activity.

Decisions

Decisions are made and acted upon by the control subsystem itself. They are based on previous actions the computer has taken. One criterion for decision might be whether the result just produced is positive or negative. This distinguishes a credit from a debit, causing different actions for each. Information about what has happened is kept in the status register.

The control subsystem is activated by a decision making command (often called a **branch**) just fetched into the instruction register. This command offers a choice to the control subsystem based upon the status register: continue the program by getting the next command; or go to another portion of the program located elsewhere in the memory.

1.5 WHAT IS A SYSTEM?

A **computerized system** is a combination of a number of different kinds of things. These include hardware, programs, people, ways of doing things and so forth. It is important to classify, examine and understand the components of the system. First off, let's simply list them in no particular order except perhaps in the order of their obviousness:

1. **Hardware**—you can't run a computer system without a computer.
2. The **operating system** is a set of programs which helps application programs to run.
3. The **application program** is one or more programs that does the work needed by your firm.
4. **Data** is the information entered and/or created by the system which replace the documents your firm uses.
5. **People** run the system, operate it, and alter it, should difficulties arise.
6. **Procedures** specify when people do what with the system.

Basic Components

Let us now examine the nature of these components and their importance to the overall system.

Hardware

Earlier we examined the computer hardware—how it looks from the outside and how it functions. The same principles apply to both the least and the most expensive systems. Useful microcomputers sell for a few thousand dollars; huge mainframes sell for several million dollars. Some small businesses can get most of their work done with one or two microcomputers. The amount of computing power needed is a function of the extent of the system, which we examine subsequently.

The Operating System

All general purpose computers can do a variety of jobs but require an operating system, a collection of programs designed specifically for a particular type of computer. The operating system does not solve a particular user problem. Instead, it helps the user operate the computer and helps the application programs use the computer's power more efficiently. For instance, one function of the operating system is to help you get the computer started and to load a program. Thus you specify whatever applications you need and get them running.

The Application Program

The application program (AP) solves a user problem. It is important to realize the large range of programs with respect to user specificity. That is, some programs have to be tailored to a particular business and its unique needs. Other application programs provide functions so general that any simple business can use them directly without modification.

To make this clear, consider a word processing program. It helps you create, edit, revise and print documents such as letters and reports. A good word processing program can satisfy most user requirements.

Even so, there are exceptions. For instance, the lawyer needs a word processing program which can handle several footnotes per page for preparing contracts or briefs. This function is important to the lawyer but not to someone mainly applying the word processor to correspondence.

At the other end of the spectrum, consider an order entry program. Each business has its own format for an order. The most effective program includes your order format and *only* your format. This makes the program more efficient and easier to use but requires specialized talent to create. You cannot expect to buy it off the shelf. Again, the exception is that some order processing programs can be tailored by the knowledgeable user to business requirements. When the program is put into use, the operator sees a display formatted to the company's order entry system.

Data

Every time an application program is run, data is brought in and results produced. Some APs are totally independent of previously existing data and only use new data. For instance, a word processing program for outgoing correspondence creates the correspondence from input keyed by the operator. A letter is kept on hand (in storage) only as long as revisions are required. When the letter is accepted in final draft form, it can then be printed and sent out. There is questionable value for keeing a machine-readable copy of this letter on hand if a paper copy exists in the file.

On the other hand, a payroll application package relies heavily on information stored the last time the program was run. Equal in importance to preparing the check and statement is the accumulation of taxes withheld for use at the end of the period or the year. Thus a master payroll file in storage is indispensable.

The data base program is an extreme case. A data base—information about the firm held in storage by the computer—facilitates managerial decisions. However, that information must already *exist* in computer-readable form. Hence a considerable amount of data entry precedes any realistic use of a data base.

From the extremes, it is clear that it is much easier to install a word processing system than a data base system, since no data preparation is necessary before useful work can be produced by the word processor.

People

Although computers are sometimes called *automatic,* that is a misnomer. Computers do not operate by themselves but need people to activate them. People must be trained to operate the hardware *and* to use the application programs. The importance of training cannot be overemphasized.

Consider the word processor. Many offices have bought specialized word processing computers; other small businesses, laboratories, and so forth, have bought micros with word processing application packages. In both cases, it is easy to receive a prompt return on their investment. Secretaries who have been using typewriters find that they need little training to get the same or greater productivity from the word processor. Hence they often receive no training. The training offered by the manufacturer or by manuals included with the package is circumvented to make the operators immediately productive. The prospect of further training gets lost in the shuffle.

But the advantage of a word processor *greatly* exceeds its replacement value as a typewriter. For instance, it is possible to transfer a paragraph or group of words from one place in a manuscript to another in a few seconds. But the operator has to know *how* to apply this function. There are progressively more productive measures provided in the advanced word processors described in this book. Although these features are easy to apply, one must know how. Without proper training, it is difficult, if not impossible, for the uninformed operator to use these really powerful features without frustration and anger.

To get the most out of your system, the people who use it must be trained!

Procedures

Good procedures can make or break a firm. A **procedure** is a set of rules describing how a given set of actions is done and in what sequence. It also includes rules for handling exceptions.

Firms differ widely in how procedures are stated. One firm has procedure manuals which state rules for all situations that might arise in many departments. (Whether the employees are informed of the manuals and trained in how to use them is another question.) At the other end of this spectrum, procedures are passed down by word of mouth and their rationale may only be known to the department manager, office manager or other official. When a problem arises, this is the source of the information.

The application program has hard and fast rules which it employs for making a decision and determining its alternatives. If the people who use the program are not equally well informed, they may apply the program improperly with unpredictable results.

Computerization offers an ideal opportunity for reexamining the procedures on record or in the minds of the managers, for stating them explicitly and for revising them to fit application packages and activities of the firm.

The Extent of the System

In bringing in a computer, consider the extent to which the firm's activities are affected. There is a range of alternatives. It might be possible to computerize all the activities so that they are integrated by a single computer or by a number of computers connected together. At the other extreme, one computer performs a single function, for example, word processing or spread sheet analysis of the budget. Similarly, a number of small computers can each provide a separate single function. Or one computer may be used for several functions by several people.

A business is constantly in a state of flux. A satisfactory solution at one point in time may be inadequate later. An adequate solution for one firm may be wholly optimistic or unacceptable for another. Applying computers to your firm depends on its nature, the way it does business, its form of management, and so forth.

Example

Let us take an example to see how a computer system may be phased into operation. Consider a green grocer distributor. This firm services small vegetable stores within an area of ten square miles in a metropolitan setting. Orders come in during the day from the stores for vegetables to be delivered the next day. Early the next morning, the company sends out its trucks to the wholesale vegetable market and buys produce to fill the orders. Produce is brought back to the warehouse, where it is divided and redistributed among the trucks. Orders are sent out to the stores. Some staples are warehoused on the premises and need not be picked up each morning.

To computerize the operations, we might do it in a single step and make everything automatic. Or it might be done in several stages, which can be variable. Let's break down the action into five steps.

Word Processing

The first and easiest computer function to install is word processing. The firm has some correspondence which it does on aging typewriters. Why not replace one or more of them with a computer, a printer and a word processor program. Little training is necessary and the computer is productive at once.

Payroll

The payroll for this firm is simple; there are only two kinds of employees: hourly and fixed salary. A payroll package is found and installed with no help from the outside.

Order Entry

Each customer calls on the phone to enter an order for the next day. Someone writes this order on a form. Later, orders are combined by type of produce to purchase by bulk from the wholesale market for the next morning. A satisfactory order entry program accepts the input data keyed by the clerk to create output files with totals for each bulk item by vendor. This program should be available off the shelf but may require modifications to fit into the procedure used by this firm; such modifications may require specialized help.

Composite System

The next step is to integrate other aspects of the accounting process into the system: accounts receivable, accounts payable and billing. This might be combined with the preceding step if an overall package seems to lend itself to the firm's operations.

Truck Dispatching

Here's a place where the computer can make a unique contribution. Each day is different for this distributor. Produce is placed on trucks according to what each customer needs and the store location. Some attention is given to automobile traffic patterns and the time of day. It is difficult to find the best combination of truck loads and routes because the amount delivered to each customer and the customer mix varies from one day to the next. A computer program could take into account all these factors. It is highly unlikely that such a program is available off the shelf. A programmer would need months of work to solve this problem. However, the payoff in the long run makes better use of the trucks and serves more customers with the same warehouse and truck configuration.

1.6 COMPUTER BENEFITS

What good will it do to computerize your business? It's always nice to get a simple answer to a simple question but this one is not so simple. Benefits are measured in costs and results, which, in turn, depend upon a number of factors, including

- which aspects of the business are computerized;
- the extent of the effort;
- whether application packages are used;
- how much custom programming is necessary;
- how effectively the programming is done.

To make more sense out of all this, we divide computerization into four different kinds:

1. Specific nonaccounting applications;
2. Accounting packages;
3. Integrated accounting systems;
4. Specialized application programs.

We now examine these four classes in that order.

Specific Nonaccounting Packages

The microcomputer revolution was brought about by five kinds of applications:

- spread sheets;
- word processing;
- data base;
- games;
- teaching and instruction.

Clearly the first two categories are responsible for businesses of all sizes going on a rampage to purchase personal computers for office use.

Word processing and spread sheet programs form the core of specialized packages which usually include several other types. Data base is of emerging importance. Each of these important package types has a chapter devoted to it in this book. Here are some of the features of the better programs:

- inexpensive;
- available for almost any micro or personal computer;
- easy to learn;
- easy to operate;
- effective;
- well documented;
- not prone to error;
- provide safe error recovery procedures.

Now let us look at two of them to see why business people have fallen for them.

Word Processing

Word processing is particularly effective when documents issued by the firm go through many revisions. With the typewriter, a few simple corrections still require that the entire document be reprocessed from beginning to end. With the word processor, a copy of the document is maintained in machine-readable form. This document can be altered in a few places with only a little bit of labor. Printing the document is automatic, with human intervention required only to start the process and to change paper in a less automated system.

The word processor lets you take a standard report form, contract or other fixed type of document and enter personalized information to get an immediate copy with little effort.

When word processing first entered the office environment, it used a specialized computer and software and the units sold in the $10,000 to $20,000 range. Now the same facilities are available on personal and microcomputers in the $1,000 to $5,000 range.

Spread Sheets

Managers spend a good portion of their time in planning and budgeting. They use columnar paper to set up current, historical and projected expenses, purchases and so forth. A lot of their work is cut and try, "what if": Let's change this figure or that figure and see what happens to all the others.

Along comes a useful tool, a computerized **spread sheet.** Set it up just like the paper model, except that you type the data into the spread sheet on the terminal screen. You don't have to fill in all the cells (spaces for amounts) in the model; simply tell the program how to do it. For instance, for 12% annual inflation, proceding from one column to the next increases the figures by 1% a month. Put the inflation rate in a simple formula in the applicable cells. All the cells in the spread sheet are automatically calculated for you as soon as you enter the first number.

But even better than that, you have control over all the resulting figures. You can change the inflation rate from 12% a year to 10% or 15% to see what happens throughout the spread sheet.

All of Chapter 14 deals with this topic. The important thing to understand is that the spread sheet is a tool aimed at management that really works. It has become so important that at some firms almost every manager has a computer with a spread sheet program for immediate access.

Data Base

Data base packages vary in scope from the simplest, which are nothing more than file handlers, to complex relational data base systems. The small packages are trivial and for the layman; they can be ignored. The large ones are indeed useful to the manager or business person.

Even the best DBs do not come near what is available for the mainframe. The major DBs for micros allow you to store large quantities of information in a compact form. They facilitate and verify data entry as well as expeditious retrieval.

Of most importance to the manager is the *query facility*. Sweeping questions get terse meaningful replies, if the file has been organized advantageously. Chapter 12 examines important DBs and demonstrates their power.

Others

A number of other nonaccounting packages with specific purposes are attractive to particular types of businesses. Let's just look at one example.

A **calendar program** keeps track of everyone's schedule for this and several succeeding weeks. A small legal firm might find this particularly useful. Each attorney has meetings with clients, court appearances and appointments. Occasionally it is necessary for the attorneys to get together to consider topics of mutual interest. They have to find a day and time which won't interfere with their other activities; a computer program can select an optimum time.

The same thing could be done manually though more laboriously. The big plus with the computer is that a procedure is built around it. When you invest money in a program, you want it to work properly. Someone enters everyone's appointments; each attorney gives this information to the designated person. The procedure and the program operate together to make the whole thing work right.

Accounting Packages

An **accounting package** does a single accounting function. For example, the grocery distributor cited above might purchase a payroll package to perform the payroll functions. There are a number of advantages to selecting a single package for each particular function to be computerized.

+1 There are many packages to choose from.
+2 There are few variables to consider in selecting a single package.
+3 Experience with one package helps later with a complex system.
+4 A mistake in selection costs less.
+5 Specialized packages offer more hand tailoring.
+6 Some functions are better done independently of the rest of the system, such as tax preparation.
+7 Specialized programs tend to be perfected and work effectively since they don't have to match other packages.

On the other hand, some disadvantages are inevitable:

−1 You don't have an integrated system.
−2 Packages *should* feed each other (such as order processing and accounts receivable). Packages provided by different vendors often do not mate properly.
−3 The data format produced by a package may not be appropriate to other programs.

—4 The overall system best for you might be incompatible with packages you have chosen earlier. Thus much or all of the work has to be redone to make an integrated system.

Still, starting with separate packages might be the best way to go, especially for the novice. The tax preparation package is an excellent example. Several vendors provide packages which prepare all the tax forms that a business needs. True, all the data must be hand entered (keyed) into the package. However, this is summary data which you probably want to go over in any case.

These packages produce control totals and include all sorts of precautionary features. They print onto the standard tax form or they will even print the form itself with the data on blank paper, acceptable to the IRS.

The Integrated Accounting System

The output of one accounting program is often an input to another such program. When books are kept manually, entries from one set of journals are transferred to another set. An **integrated system** simply means that all the programs talk to each other coherently and output from one is available as input to another. This is effected smoothly.

Programs from different vendors can be integrated. Or a single vendor can supply all the programs in a single package. The third alternative is a group of programs designed by a consultant or by an in-house programming team.

Single Vendor

For the simplest solution, one vendor supplies a complete package. The biggest restriction is the number of options supplied with respect to accounting procedures. Accounting compromises are always a necessity, even with a single application package. With several programs involved, this restriction is more severe since it forces compromises in several different areas.

One is reluctant to make procedural changes to suit a stock program although this may simply be a function of psychological inflexibility. Sometimes a change in accounting practice may produce an adverse economic effect. But the number of total packages on the market attests to the fact that small firms are willing to make the required compromises in return for

- a low price;
- immediate availability;
- ease of installation;
- a complete system.

The tradeoffs must be investigated thoroughly to make sure that the package does not lead to an economic loss or an investment which must be discarded later.

Where only one or two options are unacceptable, it may be possible to reprogram part of the package. It is important to understand how the programming language effects this if the original source input is available. This alternative is examined in Chapters 8 and 10.

Multiple Articulated Packages

Buying packages from different vendors that fit together is an attractive alternative. It allows the system to evolve naturally. That is, one package can be installed, put into operation and checked out thoroughly. Others are then added one at a time.

The biggest problem encountered is the possible incompatability of data format and organization. In other words, the output of one program may not be in the form expected as input to the second program. An additional program may be inserted between the two to reformat the data but this is inefficient and costly. Another alternative is to alter one or the other program or perhaps both so that they can talk to each other. These considerations are investigated in Chapter 16.

Specialized Requirements

Some businesses have special problems. When there are many such businesses, vendors see an opportunity to provide a complete system because of the large market it provides. Therefore, we find complete systems for pharmacies, dentists, physicians, restaurants and so forth. If such a complete package exists, *your* business needs, should be compared and contrasted with the system vendor's view. Should these two views be in close harmony, then the vendor's system might be right for you.

Some businesses do not fit into a pattern; there are too few businesses of this type or vendors have had little exposure to their requirements. The grocery distribution service described earlier falls into this class.

Truck Routing

The truck routing problem requires analysis and the application of mathematical and statistical principles. Further, observations are needed to determine traffic densities in the service area.

The problem may have a practical solution. For instance, for each customer it may simply be necessary to find routes between that customer and all of his neighbors. A route between two customers, A and B, may not be fixed; the best route may depend upon the time of day and the traffic concentration.

The point of this discussion is not to present the problem or provide solutions to it, but to indicate that it is highly unlikely that a package is available off the shelf to solve the problem. It is important to understand that there are people skilled in analyzing and others skilled in programming such problems. Further, when a solution is forthcoming, it may not only save time but increase operating efficiency.

Undoubtedly this involves an investment, perhaps even thousands of dollars, to examine the problem, analyze it and write a program to run on an affordable computer.

Anything can be done for a price. The shrewd businessman must gauge whether the solution is worth the eventual total investment—whether it will improve operating efficiency and pay back its cost and a good deal more.

2
The Computer System

2.1 OVERVIEW

Review of the Computer System

The ingredients of a computer system are of three types. First, the mechanical and electrical equipment is tangible; it can be touched and seen and sometimes even smelled when an electrical problem arises. It is called **hardware** in computer jargon, perhaps because of its tangibility.

Next is the set of directions to the hardware telling it *exactly* what to do, the **program**. While running in the computer, the program is not visible—it is less tangible and more easily modified than the hardware and hence is called **software**. Programs are written by **programmers** trained in the discipline called **programming**. A program is specific to an application and makes the computer behave as though it were designed to solve only this problem or class of problems.

The third element combines **people** and **procedures**. People operate terminals and keyboards and perform procedures to supply data to the computer system. The hardware, software and the people and procedures should fit together to produce the information and communication needed in the business environment.

This chapter introduces the computer system components and enables someone in a managerial position to understand their interaction. With this background, the decision maker may talk cogently to salespeople and engineers who propose to install or modify equipment to automate the business.

A First View of Hardware

Figure 2.1.1 illustrates schematically the components which comprise most computer systems and shows the flow of data (arrows) among them. The square box at the center represents the computer, often referred to as the **central processing unit,** or **CPU,** examined in Section 2.2.

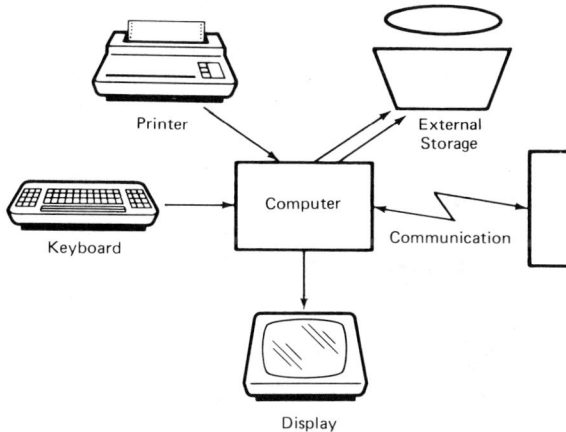

Figure 2.1.1. Devices attached to the computer.

At the left of the CPU is the **keyboard,** where an operator enters data and commands. At the bottom is the **display, video display terminal,** or **VDT,** with a screen, where the computer presents information to the operator. This is the same kind of screen you are familiar with in your television set; it works differently when used with the computer. The keyboard and display are described in detail in Chapter 3.

Sometimes a display and keyboard are built into a single box, a **terminal.** Although housed together, these units do not interact directly; each is connected separately to the computer. It seems as though what you key in is immediately displayed, but actually the data are first verified and accepted by the computer. You see *only* what the computer has accepted.

The **printer** (top) prints information onto paper. Printer speeds vary considerably from a few characters a second for a small system to many pages per second for very large and expensive computer systems. For most business purposes, a readable document produced at high speed and low cost is most desirable and preferable to a letter quality document, which costs more and sacrifices speed. Only when word processing for correspondence is part of the system is letter quality a necessity.

External storage (upper right) stores data safely, even when the computer is turned off. In the last few years, the cost of putting information on convenient magnetic disks has plummeted. Hundreds of thousands of characters can be stored on a flexible (or "floppy") disk that looks like a 45 RPM record and costs only a few dollars. It can store 50 to 200 pages of written material or business data. A new set of data becomes immediately available simply by changing disks. This may not be enough for the medium-size business; then hard disks of adequate capacity should be employed. More about this later.

Computers can be connected together to deliver messages, both written (electronic mail) and oral (electronic voice mail), from one office or part of an office to another. Either cables or regular telephone lines connect compatible computers (lower right). In this way, for example, you can send summary information directly from your terminal to your accountant's terminal or computer and save him or her a trip (and yourself a travel fee). You can also enter data and do business with a remote terminal.

The rest of this chapter provides a broad-brush description of the components of the computer system. Each component is then reconsidered in detail in a chapter of its own. The first of these, Chapter 3, is devoted to communication between a computer and you (the terminal), or another computer (modems).

Printers for micros are covered in Chapter 4, and includes a discussion of features which add to their power and flexibility. External storage is so important and large a topic that all of Chapter 5 is devoted to it. Chapter 6 looks deeper into the alternatives for the computer proper. Software is covered in Chapters 7 and 8.

2.2 THE CPU

The CPU in Figure 2.1.1 appears as the central block to which several devices connect. Each device, display, keyboard, printer, and so forth is shown as a trapezoid. The line between blocks represents a cable, a number of wires, which connects a device to the CPU. It could be a round cable such as used for hi-fi equipment; sometimes many wires are pressed into a flat ribbon like long lasagne. Figure 2.2.1 shows what is inside of the CPU:

- the **memory** stores either data or programs;
- the **processor** works on this information as directed by the program;
- the **bus** is a set of wires that interconnects all the units;
- the **interfaces** connect the bus to external receptacles into which device cables are plugged.

Data, Programs and Memory

Two kinds of things are stored in memory: programs and data (Figure 2.2.2). A **program** is directions to the computer about what actions to take. **Data** consists of letters, special symbols, spaces or blanks, numbers and punctuation—all called **characters**—to be processed by the computer.

Data

All data processed within the computer must consist only of **0**s and **1**s, or of *states* called **on** or **off**. These units of information are called **bits**, a con-

2.2 THE CPU   29

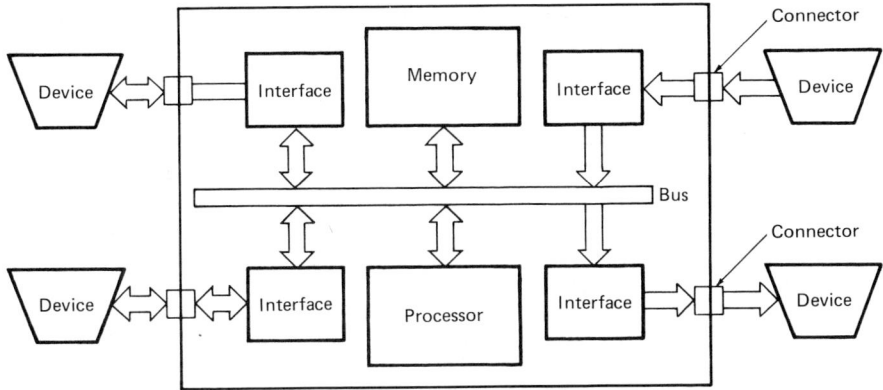

Figure 2.2.1. Inside the computer.

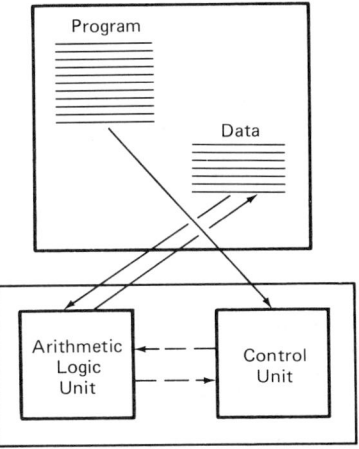

Figure 2.2.2. Two kinds of things in memory.

traction for binary digits. But the printed page has letters, symbols, numerals and punctuation on it. A sequence of bits called a **code** represents each input character on the keyboard. The number of bits in each *code* depends upon the number of characters or symbols in the **alphabet** incorporated into the computer by the manufacturer. For the small computer, each code usually consists of seven bits to provide 128 unique combinations.

A *code* is an assignment of a combination of bits to one character; for example, we could assign 1000001 to A. The collection of code assignments made, so that each character in the alphabet has a unique code, is called a

code set. There are several standard code sets. One of these, the American Standard Code for Information Interchange, or **ASCII** for short, uses seven bits. It is most often found in small business computers (minis or micros). Another code set you might encounter in large IBM computers is called **EBCDIC** for Extended Binary Coded Decimal Interchange Code.

Computers are designed to represent a character as a **byte**, a fixed sized unit of 8 bits. The ASCII 7 bit code is most popular; this is advantageous because it leaves an extra bit in each byte. This extra bit can check the transfer of data to make sure that the code has not been altered, that is, whether 1s are improperly changed to 0s, or vice versa, during transmission. Simply recording characters for manipulation within the computer is not enough. There must be some way to distinguish the beginning of one packet of data and the end of its neighbor. Several sizes of packets are needed. These are complex matters. The alternatives for representing and storing information are examined in Chapter 9.

The Program

Figure 2.2.2 shows a program and data in memory, each in a specific area. The computer gets its directions *only* from the program area—should it stray and try to interpret the data as instructions, trouble is bound to arise. A further look at programs is found in Chapter 8.

Memory

Memory is rated in *bytes*—eight bits which holds a single-character code. Since memories are large, we speak of **kilobytes**; here *kilo* means exactly 1024 or approximately 1000. Thus 16K bytes of memory means exactly 16,384 bytes. Note that a single spaced standard 8½ by 11 inch page can hold about 3 to 4K bytes (letters and spaces.)

Memory is divided into **cells**, each holding a piece of information. For micros this "piece" is usually one byte or two bytes (for 8 bit and 16 bit computers). Each cell has an **address**, a number, which identifies it. The memory will put a datum into a cell whose address is given, or bring out the datum it finds there on request.

Memory comes in several forms:

- **RAM** is **random access memory**. It can be read from or written into. The **access time** is the time to get at a piece of data; typical access time is 250 nanoseconds (billionths of a second). The memory is called **random** because cells take the same time to access, either for reading or writing, regardless of which cell was just examined. Data or a program, unless written over, is stored in RAM as long as the power stays on. When the power is turned off, data and programs in RAM disappear. Hence, RAM is called **volatile**.

ROM is **read-only memory,** which cannot be written into or modified except at the factory. But it is not volatile! Hence it is sometimes used to hold programs with the assurance that they will be there after turning on and off the computer. For the Apple II and the IBM Personal Computer, their BASIC programming language is immediately available because the translator is kept in ROM.

The CPU

The CPU consists of two smaller units shown at the bottom of Figure 2.2.2. At the left is the **arithmetic logic unit** or simply the **ALU,** which processes data with arithmetic or editing operations when requested by the program; at the right is the **control unit,** which finds out what has to be done next by examining the program in memory.

Control Unit

The control unit responds to the commands in the program by delegating them to other units. A **command** (or **instruction**) is a request to (1) move data about, (2) do arithmetic or (3) make a decision. One command after another is obtained from memory sequentially; this is called **fetching.** The control unit examines the command to figure out *what* must be done and then asks the ALU to do it.

A typical command might *move* data received from the keyboard into a memory work area. In this way, an accounting transaction is assembled in memory for posting to the computerized records. Sometimes a command directs a device such as the printer (to print the transaction) or the disk drive (to bring in a customer's record). For simplicity this is not shown in the figure.

The control unit delegates a request to the ALU or device to perform the action requested during the **execute** cycle. If data are required from memory, they are obtained as part of this cycle. The ALU (or device), when done, returns a signal to the control unit; indicating completion of its assignment. Now the control unit can fetch another command to continue the program.

Interface Control

As the control unit scans the program for directions, it encounters requests for processing which it delegates to the ALU; requests to send data out or bring them in are passed over to *devices.* All **input** and **output** requests, sometimes called **I/O,** the data and directions for where they go, are put on the bus. The **bus** is a group of wires, anywhere from 40 to 100 or so, which passes from one end of the computer cabinet to the other. Connected to the bus are several sockets at intervals, called **slots.** Each slot accommodates a printed circuit board. Some of these slots may be empty when you buy the computer. This allows for expansion. If you want to add another terminal to enter data more rapidly, another board may be needed to talk to it. The more extra slots you have, the easier it is to add terminals, special purpose devices and memory to your system.

In some computers, calculating and input or output may take place simultaneously. However, for most small computers processing is suspended while data come in or out of computer memory. When the device is done, it simply returns a signal to the control unit to proceed with the next fetch cycle.

The Computer

The computer proper consists of several parts:

- A box holds and protects the chassis.
- The chassis holds the bus, slots, power supply and connections to external devices.
- The power supply provides the required voltages.
- The motherboard carries the power to the slots which hold the cards and may have supplementary circuitry.
- The CPU card containing the ALU and the control unit is the driving force.
- The memory contains a program and data.
- Connectors for the ports provide an exit and entrance for data to or from the outside world (disks, printer, console).

The principal parts of the computer are examined now. Further detail about each part is given in Chapter 6 in relation to the particular types of computers used for business purposes.

The Chassis

The computer is housed in a box. It is built on a **chassis,** a metal frame, where the components of the computer are laid out and wired together. One of these is the power supply. Modern computers consume little power. A normal home or office circuit fused for 15 amperes accommodates most small business computers. The line cord plugs into the wall socket which supplies the standard 115 volts alternating current (AC). This voltage is too high for most transistor circuits. The power supply converts 115 Volts AC to the direct current (DC) voltage used by the computer circuits.

The power supply provides **regulated** voltage and current. There is noise on the line due to variations in voltage supplied by the power company and to surges and spikes created by equipment in the neighborhood. Most of these fluctuations are filtered and removed by the regulator and power supply so as not to interfere with computer performance.

Noise is less prevalent in the home; therefore many personal computers do not provide adequate voltage regulation and hence noise immunity for business applications. The purchaser should be careful to investigate whether the computer operates well on much noisier power lines found in the industrial requirements.

The S-100 bus computer is more rugged and immune to noise because, additionally, each card has its own regulator to isolate it from its neighbors and to filter out all electrical disturbances. The power supply provides regulated $+8$, -16, and $+16V$ to the bus; this is again regulated on the board to supply $+5$, -12, and $+12V$ to the chips and components.

Motherboard

The power supply feeds a set of components laid out on the **motherboard,** a printed circuit board permanently attached to the chassis. It feeds signals and voltages to a set of lines called a **bus**—connected to **slots.**

The Bus

The slots are connectors where **printed circuit boards** (**PC boards** or **cards**) are inserted. The cards may contain the CPU, the memory and auxiliary subsystems. This arrangement has two clear advantages. Extra slots make it easy to expand the computer functions as needed; for example, to add more memory simply plug in another card. Should the computer malfunction, and we can localize the trouble, the computer can be put back into use immediately by replacing a defective board with a good one. Later, the bad component on the removed board can be found by a service person and replaced without inconveniencing the computer user.

The bus design specifies which wires carry each kind of signal. This makes it possible for manufacturers to design and make available printed circuit boards for additional functions and tailored to the bus. There are only two or three bus standards; some manufacturers (IBM, Apple, Radio Shack) have their own bus design. This means that standard printed circuit boards do not fit into the slots of their computers. Third party vendors have seen the need for additional functions so that there are cards on the market to fit the TRS-80, Apple II and IBM PC as well as some from these machines' own manufacturers.

Boards

Most computers have separate boards for the CPU and the memory. Additional boards may be plugged in to provide disk controllers, modems and other functions, discussed in Chapter 6.

Peripheral Devices

The prefix *peri-* conveys that the **peripheral devices** are situated *around* the computer proper. It's hard to make a general statement about which devices are contained in the computer box and which are external. We almost always find that the printer is a separate unit. Most minis and a few micros provide a box reserved only for the computer. All other devices are attached by cables to this box as shown in Figure 2.2.1.

Let us now concentrate on the geometry of Figure 2.2.1. It makes no difference which of the peripheral devices are included in the computer box. We examine the computer itself, ignoring the peripheral devices for the moment.

Devices in the Cabinet

There is an advantage to putting devices in the computer box because power may be derived from its power supply. This reduces the cost of the system. Two disadvantages are apparent. First, if a difficulty arises, all parts of the computer are disabled. It is impossible to switch a device from one computer to another without making radical wiring changes. Second, once you have purchased a combination box, that combination is fixed and you cannot easily make substitutions to suit changing needs.

Categories of Computers

Twenty years ago, computers were expensive and therefore only affordable by large companies. Though they differed in internal design, they were similar in price and capability. As computers grew larger and able to do more functions, a new breed of computer arose, called **minicomputers**. This name designated them as costing much less than their larger cousins (**mainframes**) so they were accessible to the medium size company.

Technological progress has been relentless; within the past few years a less expensive class of computer has developed. They are small, inexpensive and with little power drain. They make computing power available to almost everyone. That is why they are called **personal computers** or **microcomputers.** Yet they can do nearly as much work as their predecessors of twenty years ago.

With such a vast number and variety computers on hand, it is indeed difficult to put them into neat categories. The boundary lines are hazy and it would be easy to conceive of six or seven categories. For this book, we consider only three categories.

- **Micros** cost between $1,000 and $20,000.
- **Minis** range from $10,000 to $100,000.
- **Mainframes** cost $100,000 or more.

2.3 COMMUNICATING

What and How

This section discusses the interchange of information between

- the operator and the computer;
- the computer and the operator;
- two computers.

The human operator and the computer talk to each other via the **terminal** which is actually two separate devices:

—The operator enters data and commands at the **keyboard.**
—A **display** shows information sent from the computer.

Computers, regardless of their size, can talk together over telephone lines using the **modem.** There are other ways they may be connected to converse but this is the most important. Even with a modem, talking is impossible unless the connected computers have compatible communication programs.

The Keyboard

The keyboard sends data to the computer in the form of bytes, which are character codes. The code produced by the keyboard corresponds to the character engraved on the key hit by the operator. The code appears on a set of lines emanating from the keyboard which connects by cable to the computer. Sometimes the terminal is included within the cabinet of the computer and the connections made internally.

Each time you hit a key, a code is transmitted to the computer. However, the computer ignores that code unless it is primed to accept it. That is, the program which is now running the computer must be asking for information from the operator. This request is made by a command issued by the program to the computer hardware. When that command is issued, the computer is primed to receive and accept bytes sent by the keyboard.

After receiving a byte, in most cases, the program stores it, interprets it and returns it to display on the screen. There appears to be a direct connection between the keyboard and the screen because hitting a key makes the character appear on the screen. But there is no *hardware* connection. If the program has not requested the information, the keyboard appears to be dead. Hitting keys has no effect on the display.

Key Arrangement

Keys on the keyboard are arranged like those on the typewriter for transfer of training. The touch typist can achieve normal speed without further training. However, there are a number of additional keys. Some produce codes for which no corresponding character is displayed. These codes tell an application program that some request is being made by the operator.

The computer terminal keyboard has twice as many keys as the typewriter. Some of them are simply duplicates of others. For instance, it is easier to key in numeric information with the **numeric key pad,** a duplicate set of numeric keys arranged in an adding machine pattern. The numeric key pad keys produce the same codes as the number keys on the top row.

Even with so many keys, there are more codes than keys. To produce the additional codes, there are two keys: the shift key; and the control keys, which are used as multipliers (described in detail in Chapter 3).

Display

The millions of terminals now in offices use the same type of tube found in your television set to display written data. Sometimes the tube is in a separate box called a **monitor.** When the tube is built into the terminal additional circuitry is provided, including memory called a **buffer.** The buffer is large enough to hold enough codes for all the characters which may be displayed simultaneously on the screen. A character generator contains circuitry to produce the shape for each character that can be displayed on the screen.

Information which displays is stored in the buffer. It is redisplayed many times per second. The technique for doing this is described in Chapter 3.

Additional capability can be provided in the terminal at additional cost for

- color.
- graphics.

Most displays show text as white (or some other single color) on a black background, or vice versa. For multiple colors, a special display tube is necessary along with circuitry to cause the separate colors to display. This facility goes to waste unless the computer and the program running it are capable of activating colors.

Graphics capability is something very special and can be provided with or without color. As in the case of color graphics capability goes to waste unless there is a program which can produce images.

The Modem

The modem allows a computer or a remote dumb terminal to talk with another computer. The modem is additional hardware at each computer which hooks into the telephone line or the telephone itself. It converts signals normally handled by the computer into a form that can be transmitted on telephone lines.

Micros Talking

In the small business environment, micros really have very little to say to each other. Yet it is important to have the facility to do this. The reason is the general incompatibility of different brands of micros and different disk sizes and formats. Even identical computers require a null modem, which is a special cable, and a communications program to talk to each other. It is so difficult to connect two micros directly that the telephone lines are a good alternative. Then two machines can talk to each other regardless of the format of the data or the kind of computer being used. The modem is a leveling force.

Micro and Mainframe

These days large businesses have a mix of mainframes and micros. The mainframes have many data bases with important information that we would like to get hold of in machine-readable form. The problem is how to access this information without endangering it. Many communication programs to permit the flow of information between micro and mainframe are in the offing. This is an important field to watch.

2.4 PRINTERS

Several types of printers are available for the business environment:

1. The augmented electric typewriter.
2. The dot matrix printer.
3. The daisy wheel and thimble printers.
4. The line printer.
5. The laser printer.

These are introduced in this section and examined more thoroughly in Chapter 4.

The earliest printers used for automating the office were based on the electric typewriter. In its original form, the operator hits a key activating a mechanism which is electrically propelled to cause printing. To make such a mechanism usable as an output device, a computer is interposed between the keyboard and the printing mechanism. The electric typewriter was designed for an operator whose maximum speed never exceeds 15 characters per second (**cps**). This is the limit for the output rate of the typewriter even when it is computer-driven.

The dot matrix printer is characterized by a relatively high speed obtained at a rather low cost. It prints from 40 to 500 characters per second and costs between $400 and $3,500. The Epson MX-80 is the most popular printer for micros. It prints 80 cps of fairly good quality and costs about $500 as of 1984. The MX-100 is similar, with a wider carriage.

Although the print quality of the low cost devices is low, it is acceptable for most business printouts, since they are used mainly within the company or furnished to government agencies. Higher quality is becoming available now and dual speed printers can turn out correspondence acceptable to most managers.

The **daisy wheel** printer is the most popular device for writing letters by computer and for other word processing needs. It provides high quality output at low to medium speed at moderate cost. It prints 12 to 160 characters per second (cps) and costs from $400 to $4,000.

The **line** printer is so-called because it prints a complete line at a time. Several copies of the complete alphabet on type slugs are imbedded in a moving circular arrangement alternatively called a **chain, train** or **belt**, according to its design. It covers the print area for one line, which can then be printed in a single operation. The line printer produces anywhere from 300 to 3000 lines per minute (**lpm**) with prices starting in the $3,000 range and extending up to hundreds of thousands of dollars. Its high speed makes it popular for larger organizations because all computer output can be produced on a single fast machine.

Laser printers are part of an emerging technology and have become available to the high end of the small business community.

2.5 STORAGE

Modern minis and micros are completely dependent on magnetic disks to store *all* their data, programs and application packages. The business manager should be knowledgeable about the properties of these media, the options for their use and the cost alternatives. Understanding how they work ensures that

1. Your storage method is reliable and remains so;
2. Down time and maintenance is kept at a minimum;
3. The system is not unnecessarily limited in speed by the choice of hardware;
4. You don't buy the most expensive item when a more frugal choice will do.

It's like owning a home. If you know about plumbing and wiring, it's easier to work with repair people and contractors.

Need

Data and the transactions of your firm must be in a work area of computer memory to be processed. Internal memory (see Section 2.2) for the modern computer is fast and much less expensive than it used to be. It has one big drawback; it is *volatile;* when you turn off the computer, whatever is in memory disappears. For just a one-shot document, which you prepare, print and never use again, that is all right. But business files are voluminous and must be stored safely, even when the computer is turned off. You must be able to get at them quickly, even if just to review them. The business system *demands* that you save your files on external storage, disk or tape. Then they are safe. It is even better to keep at least *two* copies of all files: the latest version and the one just before that. Better still, keep *another* copy of the latest version on a separate disk.

Main memory is limited in size for two important reasons:

1. It is not large enough to hold many records *and* the programs it needs to process them.
2. Main memory is more expensive than external storage.

External storage provides lots of comparatively inexpensive, reusable nonvolatile storage. It consists of two parts:

- a *medium*, the **disk,** on which electronic transactions or documents are written;
- a *mechanism,* the **disk drive,** for putting records onto the medium and recovering them from the medium any time later—a few minutes or years.

To **write** is to place a record on the medium; **read** recovers a record from external storage and puts it into memory. Reading is *nondestructive*: you copy the record from external storage (into memory), but the original record is still on the medium. It's like reading a book—after your read it, it's still there. The third action of external storage is to *hold* information; if you read the medium an hour, a day or a year later, the electronic document is probably still safe and sound.

I say *probably* because we have to take normal precautions to ensure the safekeeping of electronic files, just as with paper ledgers and journals. Neither floppy disks nor paper archives can survive a flood.

We now look into disk media. It is easy to talk generally about them because they all work in pretty much the same way; large or small, separate or built-in, floppy or hard, they are all quite reliable.

Medium Characteristics

Let us examine some of the characteristics which make the magnetic disk a good medium for external storage. (Section 5.7 provides information about choosing and buying them.)

Permanence

The medium should hold many electronic documents *securely* over long periods of time.

Capacity

The more electronic documents that a medium can hold, the more useful it is. A unit of a medium which may be installed on the drive at any given time is called a **volume**. Examples of a volume are a cassette, a floppy disk and a disk pack (several disks in a removable unit for a large hard disk device). For most hard disks, the volume is *permanently* mounted.

Difference in volume capacity is striking. A magnetic card holds a page of text; a floppy disk holds thirty to a hundred pages. Hard disks hold 5 to 300 million bytes. **Gigabyte** (one billion bytes) drives are on the market for mainframes. It is preferable to measure media capacity in bytes, kilobytes or megabytes, units more precise than "pages."

Size

The dimensions of the medium have an effect on its acceptability in the business office. All the above are small relative to their capacity in bytes (a fraction of a cubic foot to two or three cubic feet).

Reliability

If we cannot retrieve data without mistakes induced by the medium, then that medium is less attractive, if not totally useless. Reliability is measured by how many bits can be read, on the average, before one bit is read incorrectly. Reliability for the magnetic disk is in the order of 10^9 (1 error per billion bits read) to 10^{10}.

Reuseability

When we record on some media, such as paper, the medium is permanently deformed. Perhaps "deform" is a strong word, but when paper has holes punched in it or has been written on, it is difficult if not impossible to enter new information. Magnetic media can be erased and reused without affecting reliability.

Cost

Unit cost of the medium is important. This is less true when the medium is reusable, especially when its life is long. Most magnetic media are so inexpensive that their cost is hardly a factor, $3 to $5 for a floppy. The higher cost of hard disks (typically $1,500 to $3,000) is compensated for by their long life, reliability and speed for accessing programs and data.

Speed

If you can request a record and have it displayed on your CRT screen within a few seconds, then this storage medium is probably fast enough for the business environment. But your system may be too slow for many reasons which lie in

1. The application program;
2. The operating system;
3. Device limitations.

You can only be sure of the cause (and cure) if you know the part each plays.

Accessibility

Data may be stored on a physically sequential medium, such as paper or magnetic tape. Then you must pass through all the data from the beginning to the end if you need to get data at the end. A **random access file** (see Chapter 9) lets you go directly to the data you need without passing through intervening "garbage." *Disk* storage lets you access files thus.

Media Choices

There are really just two choices for physical media: paper and magnetic materials. Once a lot of paper was used with the computer to store information. It's still around today as punchcards and punched paper tape. The trouble with paper is that, once information is entered on it, it is impractical to recycle it.

Cards and paper tape get a grade of F because they are not reusable.

Magnetic materials hold full sway today because they are compact, easy to use, fast, inexpensive, reliable and, perhaps most important, they are reuseable. A floppy disk can be used hundreds of times before its performance degrades to the point that a character or two gets lost. Floppies are so inexpensive that we can throw them away when they become defective. Of course we want to copy off and revitalize the information first. Utilities described in Chapter 6 do this. Hard disks are durable and defects can be compensated for as described later.

2.6 SOFTWARE

Another component of the computer *system* is software. People spend years learning about this specialized field. What do you need to know about it and why?

Like many things in this life, software is something you may not need to understand until you encounter trouble. Then you really need to know!

2.6 SOFTWARE

Software is another name for *computer programs*. It should be clear by now how the program directs the computer in *all* its activities. What is not clear is the need for two kinds of programs:

- The **operating system** is a set of programs which assist the computer in fulfilling your needs but does not actually solve your problems.
- The **application program,** or package, is designed to replace manual business operations.

Operating System

The *operating system* is the mediator between the application program and the hardware. It lets the operator choose among a number of programs or tasks which may be performed. Only when the system is single-minded and serves just one purpose is it possible for the computer to function without an operating system. Then it is **dedicated.** An example of this is the elevator dispatching computer. Modern office buildings have many elevators which are programmed according to traffic, time of day, and other factors. Only this program runs the computer and hence no operating system is required.

Sometimes it is not obvious that there is an operating system (or even a computer). Users of office word processors may not be aware that they are dealing with a computer or that the computer has an operating system. But this word processor may be converted to do accounting, record keeping and other office tasks by swapping in the proper program. Indeed, that is the feature which distinguishes the computer from other machines which preceded it: the computer can become one kind of worker or another—a mathematician, an accountant, or a word processing agent—by installing a different program into its memory.

Simply stated, there are a number of actions which most programs may request. It would be silly to have to reproduce these directions in each program that needs them. Instead, they are already rolled up into a single package—the operating system. Either you build these common functions into each program at great cost or you rely on the operating system to supply them.

One more thing: an operating system is designed to run on one particular kind of hardware. An IBM PC operating system cannot run on Apple equipment; conversely, an Apple operating system cannot run on an IBM PC. Operating systems work on different computers only when the computers are **compatible.** This means that the computers act identically, but they are made by different companies and with somewhat different circuitry. The IBM PC has many look-alikes which *do* run the IBM PC operating system and most of the application programs intended for the IBM machine.

Application Program

The *application program* provides the skills that the computer system needs to perform particular tasks. One program lets the computer do accounts receivable; another program produces payroll checks; still another monitors inventory. The operating system enables you to switch from one application program to another.

An application program is designed to run with a particular operating system which, in turn, runs on a particular computer. It doesn't seem reasonable that a programmer solve an important application problem only to find that the program runs on only one particular computer system. For this reason, people have tried to design languages which are computer independent, hence **transportable**: programs written in such languages work on many different computer systems, provided the program is translated again. The truth is, there are few cases where a program or the data it uses is totally transportable; we examine this problem in greater depth in Chapter 8.

Some computer systems are designed to work without human intervention, but such cases are rare (the elevator-dispatching computer). However, the business computer system is run by an operator and is usually turned off at the end of the day. Someone comes in and turns it on; someone tells the computer what to do next.

Mating

Mating is getting the parts of the computer system to fit together. The larger parts of the system are the hardware, the operating system and the application program. If these parts do not mate, the computer system does not function.

An operating system is built for a particular type of hardware. There may be more than one operating system designed for that hardware. And one operating system may have several versions for different kinds of hardware.

For example, CP/M is an operating system that works on the Z80 (It is sometimes called CP/M-80 or simply CPM). There are other operating systems (such as Oasis and Turbodos) which work on Z80 hardware. Similarly, there are other versions of CP/M (such as CP/M-86) redesigned to work on a computer using other processor chips (such as the 8086).

2.6 SOFTWARE

The application program is written in one of many programming languages. Before the program can run on a computer, it must be **translated** into a machine language module. This module can then do useful work if the program has been properly written. But the module runs only on the computer for which it has been translated (Z80, 8086, etc.) and with the operating system for which it was designed to mate (CP/M-80, Oasis, etc.). This is illustrated in Figure 2.6.1.

In the figure, the hardware, operating system and application program are each represented as a form with a unique shape. A component does not work properly unless its shape and that of its mate fit, or **interface**, exactly: the application program mates with the operating systems; the operating system mates with the hardware.

There is more latitude with the application program. Programming languages are designed to be independent of the hardware and the operating system. Although a translated application module depends on the hardware, the program used to create this module may still exist. It may be translated again, this time for a different operating system and hardware configuration. Then the reprocessed module will work on that configuration but it will not work on another combination. This is an oversimplified but essential explanation of programs and their languages. A full explanation is postponed until Chapter 8.

Operating systems get full attention in Chapter 7. This important program goes between the hardware and the application program and talks with you too. When something goes wrong, it's hard to tell whether it's the application program (AP), the operating system (OS) or the hardware. Understanding what the OS does and its tools can help you discover and resolve *problems.*

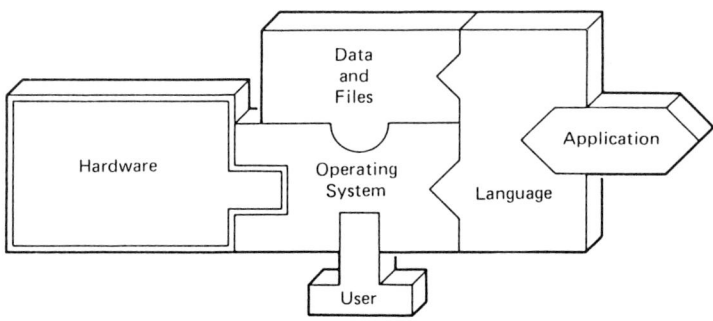

Figure 2.6.1. Mating the parts of the computer.

But why should you know these things if you don't want to be a computer repairperson? Here's why:

1. Even if you can afford a repair call, its more important to keep your computer available for normal business activities—it may take hours (days?) before someone comes.
2. The repairperson only fixes the *hardware;* if something is wrong with a program or the OS, you are still charged for the call though what's really wrong may not have been fixed.
3. If you can localize the problem to one program, you can still use your computer for other work.
4. Knowing the OS may let *you* figure out what to do when something goes wrong. Maybe all you need to do is revive a backup copy of a faulty program, copy a disk or reinstall the operating system.

I can't give you specific answers, just knowledge which some day you may put to work to save yourself money and aggravation.

II
Hardware

3
Communicating

3.1 INTRODUCTION

This chapter discusses how the computer talks and listens in three ways:

- human to computer;
- computer to human;
- computer to computer.

All original information enters the computer by one of these methods. Once in the computer, data can be placed on external storage as examined in Chapter 5. There it is safe and can be recovered more quickly than from a human or from another computer over telephone lines.

Three devices are responsible for communicating:

- The **keyboard** is the main data entry device.
- The **video display terminal,** or **VDT,** provides messages, prompts and queries to the user.
- The **modem** ties into the telephone lines to let the computer talk to other computers.

The computer itself may be fully integrated or modularized. On the one extreme, all of these three devices are built into the computer and at the other extreme they are separate.

Physical Alternatives

Hereafter we assume that the operator can converse with the computer via the keyboard and VDT. Most systems do not provide a modem except as an option since the ability to talk to another computer is not as important. How are the keyboard and VDT supplied?

Here are most of the alternatives:

- totally built into the computer cabinet;
- the keyboard in the cabinet and the monitor separate;
- the keyboard attached by cable to the computer and the monitor separate;
- the monitor built in and the keyboard attached by cable;
- a separate terminal housing both keyboard and display;
- a separate terminal housing the display with the keyboard attached by cable.

Some of these are now examined.

Built-In

Here the keyboard and the screen are an integral part of the computer, which keeps costs down for medium-range micros and personal computers. However, because of the recognized convenience of the detachable keyboard, this configuration is increasingly rare for full computers; the most prominent example today is Radio Shack's TRS-80 series.

Keyboard in the Cabinet

The least expensive computers such as the Commodore, Atari, and Apple II supply the keyboard integral with the computer but no screen. This certainly keeps costs low since you must supply your own screen. Usually a television set will do, but separate monitors are available. Then a switch is necessary to go between the computer and the normal antenna that you would use for television.

Separate Terminal

The **terminal** is a combination keyboard and display screen. There are millions of them in the field in a price range from $400 to $3,000. This combination is also used to talk to a mainframe.

The most primitive arrangement has a display and keyboard in fixed positions. This terminal can be moved about as a unit but is not adjustable. Since some operators spend considerable time at terminals, adjustability is an important factor. Some terminals allow rotation of the display around one or two axes or movement up and down. While adjusting the chair may help, only moving the screen and/or adding a non-glare panel can reduce reflections significantly.

If the keyboard is supplied as a unit attached by cable, once you adjust the position of the display, you can move the keyboard to suit your physical dimensions.

Some terminals include a modem. Its physical location has no bearing on its function.

Functional Alternatives

The three *functional* alternatives to the fully independent small system in terms of increasing capability are

- the dumb terminal;
- the smart terminal;
- the intelligent terminal.

The Dumb Terminal

This combination is a keyboard and display which are separate entities and which communicate on separate parallel lines with the computer. **Full duplex** operation allows two devices to talk separately and simultaneously over a set of lines—the typical mode of operation for the micro and personal computer.

What you key at the terminal does not display directly but instead is sent to the computer. Unless the program has asked the computer to activate the keyboard, it seems dead. That is, as you hit keys there is no apparent response. This is because

- there is no program running,
- or the program that is running is busy and does not pay attention to the keyboard.

In the first case, if you have not set up the system or program and there is none in the computer as you turn on the power, then hitting the keyboard has no effect. There is no program to accept the data.

In the second case, a program which has been activated and running has something to do and does not pay attention to data entered at the keyboard. Sometimes it notifies you of this by putting up on the screen a message such as "system working." In any case, the keyboard is ignored.

The Smart Terminal

The **dumb terminal** is so-called because there is no processing capability built into it. The **smart terminal** does have processing capability and can be switched from full duplex to **half duplex** operation. In the latter mode, what you key into the terminal goes into the terminal's memory and displays directly on the screen. This mode is not normally available for micros or PCs. It is used for communicating with mainframes and minis.

For the smart terminal in **local mode,** you enter information and fill up the screen without involving the computer. Should you make a mistake, you can backspace over it with control keys provided at the terminal. You have editing capability much like that provided in the word processor. When you have composed a full screen, those data are passed over to the computer. To transmit the entire screen and terminal memory contents to the computer, use **block mode** for a block transmission. This is handy in multiple-user operations. Editing and data entry does not tie up the computer. Only when you are done is the computer involved and then for a short period of time, since the block of information is transmitted much faster than you can key it.

The Intelligent Terminal

This name is sometimes used for the personal computer when it communicates with a network. Now the "terminal" is actually a computer and has full processing capabilities within it. *Note:* Smart and intelligent terminals are generally associated with mainframes, *not* micros or PCs.

3.2 KEYBOARDS

Purpose

The **keyboard** is the only way (except for graphics and analog input devices) to talk directly to the computer. You give all directions from the keyboard. You also use it to key in all transactions and changes in the "books."

The computer manipulates data in bytes, sets of 8 bits; each byte represents one letter or number internally. The keyboard generates these bytes or codes as input to the computer. Each key, when pressed, produces the code for the character engraved on the key top; this code is passed onto the cable to the computer. Figure 3.2.1 shows the characters and their ASCII codes.

We all know from experience with typewriters that an alpha key top (for alphabetic letters) has a *capital* letter engraved on it. If you hit an alpha key on the typewriter, a lower case letter prints. This is so for the terminal

3.2 KEYBOARDS 53

b_7					0	0	0	0	1	1	1	1
b_6					0	0	1	1	0	0	1	1
b_5					0	1	0	1	0	1	0	1
Bits b_4	b_3	b_2	b_1	Column → Row ↓	0	1	2'	3	4	5	6	7
0	0	0	0	0	NUL	DLE	SP	0	@	P	`	p
0	0	0	1	1	SOH	DC1	!	1	A	Q	a	q
0	0	1	0	2	STX	DC2	"	2	B	R	b	r
0	0	1	1	3	ETX	DC3	#	3	C	S	c	s
0	1	0	0	4	EOT	DC4	$	4	D	T	d	t
0	1	0	1	5	ENQ	NAK	%	5	E	U	e	u
0	1	1	0	6	ACK	SYN	&	6	F	V	f	v
0	1	1	1	7	BEL	ETB	'	7	G	W	g	w
1	0	0	0	8	BS	CAN	(	8	H	X	h	x
1	0	0	1	9	HT	EM	)	9	I	Y	i	y
1	0	1	0	10	LF	SUB	*	:	J	Z	j	z
1	0	1	1	11	VT	ESC	+	;	K	[	k	{
1	1	0	0	12	FF	FS	,	<	L	\	l	:
1	1	0	1	13	CR	GS	-	=	M	]	m	}
1	1	1	0	14	SO	RS	.	>	N	ˆ	n	~
1	1	1	1	15	SI	US	/	?	O	−	o	DEL

Columns 0–1: COMMUNICATION CODES. Columns 2–7: PRINTABLE CHARACTERS.

Figure 3.2.1. The ASCII code set.

keyboard: hit an alpha key and it produces the code for a *lower case* character, as shown in columns 6 and 7 of Figure 3.2.1. To get the code for the upper case letter, press the shift key *and* the desired letter. Then codes for upper case characters, columns 4 and 5 of the figure, are sent out on the cable.

Key Action

Press a key and the keyboard electronics

1. Determines the code to produce;
2. Creates a *sequence* of 1s and 0s;

54 COMMUNICATING

3. Puts this sequence of signals on a pair of wires in the cable connected to the computer.

This is called a **serial** signal because it consists of a *sequence* of bits. The signals occur at a rate, bits per second (**bps** or **bauds**), adjustable at the terminal to match the computer.

Hit a key and you produce a code, a string of bits; hold the key down and you get **repeat action.** Nothing more happens for a second. Then codes are produced, *repeated* at a fixed rate, usually between 5 and 10 times per second.

A glance at the ASCII code set of Figure 3.2.1 shows a number of combinations at the left labelled communication codes. There is no corresponding character on the printer for those codes. Therefore each of these is also called a **nonprinting code.** They can represent operator requests, which are then easily distinguishable from data.

A **control code** is a nonprinting code which represents an operator *request,* not *data.* If it also represented a character, a conflict might easily arise.

Keyboard Requirements

It is important *not* to confuse the keyboard with the display, which may be part of the same terminal. The terminal is a *combination* of two devices, one to send—the keyboard—and the other to receive—most commonly a display screen. Usually the screen is placed directly above the keyboard and fixed in a cabinet. However, detachable keyboards connected to the terminal box by a cable are becoming more popular. This lets you move the two separately around your desk to the most comfortable position.

When you use the terminal, characters you type immediately appear on the display; it seems that what you type is sent directly to the screen. Actually, there is no *direct* connection; all characters entered at the keyboard go first to the computer before they are sent back to the screen to display.

The essential requirement for the keyboard is that, when you strike a key, the 8 bit code for the character engraved on the key top is transmitted to the computer. Shift and control keys effectively multiply the number of codes produced.

There are several other characteristics of the keyboard which we examine

- keys and key placement;
- control keys and control information;
- rollover.

Keys and Key Placement

Alphanumeric keys, namely those for letters and numerals, have an established place on the typewriter which is carried over to the computer input keyboard. That is, the numbers appear in order in the keyboard's first row: 1, 2, 3, . . . ; the next row has the letters q, w, e, r, . . . ; and so forth. These positions maintain a transfer of training from the typewriter which also has the so-called QWERTY keyboard (from the keys covered by the left hand's fingers "at rest").

Occasionally manufacturers, especially in the personal computer field, make changes with regard to the position of punctuation and special symbols. This simplifies engineering design and reduces the keyboard cost. Thus for some keyboards, such things as the colon, exclamation point, etc., may turn up in odd places. This *detracts* from the transfer of training and lowers your typing speed initially.

The physical position of a key, its distance from its neighbors, the tilt of the keyboard and its feel are all factors in operator comfort and work efficiency. Some keyboards also produce clicks to tell the operator that a key is fully depressed. These factors vary from one keyboard to the next; the most preferred keyboard is closest in appearance and feel to the common typewriter. Because of similarity of arrangement, touch, appearance and sound to the IBM typewriter model, some are called "Selectric" keyboards.

Most users do not seem to be influenced by these design factors—shape of each key, layout of the keyboard, slant of each row, spacing of the keys, their touch and springiness or the sound they make. There has been much criticism of the IBM PC keyboard, which varies from the much-praised Selectric "standard," yet sales continue to soar.

Shift

Typewriters have a shift key and a shift lock. On a manual typewriter, the **shift key** actually moves the carriage vertically so that a different part of the type bar hits the paper—the part with the upper case letter.

When you press the shift key along with a character key, the terminal keyboard generates the code for the upper case character. When you press a key with two symbols on it, such as punctuation, and the shift key, this sends the code for the upper symbol to the computer. The **shift lock** on the conventional typewriter, once set, causes any key to print as though the shift key were also pressed. Some business computer keyboards (but few micros) have a shift lock while others have an alpha lock.

Alpha Lock

The off-the-shelf commercial, micro and PC terminal keyboard both have an **alpha lock**. When it is set, all letter keys produce upper case character codes. However the numerical and punctuation keys are not affected. When you hit keys with the alpha lock set, these codes are produced:

- upper case codes for a letter;
- number codes for a number;
- for punctuation keys, whatever is on the *lower* part of the key.

Shift still works with the alpha lock set. If you hit a number on the top row of the keyboard and shift, the code for the symbol at the *top* of the key is reproduced. The numeric key pad is not affected. The purchaser of a business system which includes a personal computer should note carefully whether it has a shift lock, an alpha lock or something different.

Standard, Nonprinting and Control Codes

Several keys have no corresponding symbols on the printer or typewriter. The number and function of these keys vary from one keyboard design to another. Here is a list of four types of control keys with examples of each:

Typewriter oriented	return
	tab
	rub
Screen oriented	clear
	home
	break
Special multiplier	control
	code
	escape
Editing	delete
	insert, etc.

Names for such keys appear underlined throughout the text.

Return, tab and backspace (called rub on some keyboards) perform mechanical or electrical functions on the typewriter. For the terminal keyboard, each produces a code sent to the computer. The ASCII code, respectively 0D, 09 and 7F, informs the application program that you have finished a paragraph, wish to tab, or to backspace to eliminate the last character typed.*

Screen-oriented **command keys** produce codes which the program interprets in connection with the display. Clear blanks the screen and affects only the terminal, no code being sent to the computer; the effect of home depends on the application program; break creates a **communication code** which most programs do not recognize. It is needed when transmitting data over telephone lines to alert the receiving communication program.

Control Keys

Some keys, like escape, produce a **control code**—a single nonprinting code (there is no character on the printer or for the display corresponding to this code.) A control code is often used as a command to the application program: it tells the program what to do; it is not data. When you hit the key, the active program gets the control code, but does not send it back to the display since it is a request for service. If the control code were sent back, the display could not produce a character for it anyway.

You are concerned with how easy it is to tell the program what to do. Most business packages provide *menus* or structural questions—see Chapter 10. Another means to instruct the application program is a separate key on a specially designed keyboard for each function you might need—a **function key**. This is the case for software packages such as word processors designed for computers with function keys, for example, the IBM PC.

Still another approach involves a **multiplier key** (code or control on most keyboards). Hit this key in conjunction with one or more alphanumeric keys and you give a command. The command depends on the letter you hit. And that's the catch. You have to remember which letter or number is associated with which function. Some manufacturers inscribe the name for the *additional* function on the **skirt,** the vertical edge facing you on each such key; others use a plastic overlay on the keyboard. This method is used in some operating systems.

When a function is described in an operator or reference manual, control is often referred to as CNTRL or by a caret (^). Thus control C might appear as CNTRL C or ^C. (Note that the TRS-80 has no control key.) To get some systems to stop what it is asked to do (such as processing data, printing a report, etc.), you might press control C (^C), for instance, for some systems.

---

*For an explanation of the two-digit description of ASCII codes; see Section 9.2.

3.3 MORE ABOUT KEYS

Types of Keys

Let us take a closer look at control codes. Several types of control codes and the way that they are produced deserve attention:

- **Universal keys** appear on *most* keyboards and produce a fixed code.
- A **control key, code key** or **alternate key** may be pressed *with* another key to create a control code.
- **Fixed function keys** on some keyboards produce unique control codes or control sequences.
- **Programmable function keys** on some keyboards are set to a single code or a sequence of codes by software, mechanical adjustment, key entry at the terminal or downloading by the program.

Universal Keys

An example of a universal key is rub. The screen is not a carriage and does not move backwards. When you hit rub, the *program* receives the ASCII code 7F. It usually removes the last character from the command or field you are entering and shows this action on the screen. Rub produces a universal (nonprinting) code.

Escape

Most keyboards have an **escape key,** esc. It is used either alone, or as a **prefix** is hit *before* another key. Alone, it is often used to cancel or "escape from" the last request, as with the word processor Benchmark, or the data base program dBase II. If you press esc and some other key simultaneously, the results are uncertain; hence for programs which use it as a prefix, hit esc *then* a letter to transmit a command. Esc produces a code as soon as you hit it. Thus if you hit esc h, two codes are produced, one for each key.

Control Keys

Most keyboards have a key labelled control, CONTROL CNTRL, cntrl or code, which multiplies the action of the other keys similarly to shift.

As Multiplier

Cntrl (like shift) produces no code when hit alone; if it is pressed along with one letter or symbol key, a control code is generated. You *always* hit control first, then the additional key right after, holding it down a moment. If you hit cntrl, then h̲, you get cntrl h̲; if you hit h̲ then cntrl, you get the code for h̲ and nothing more.

For example, consider the H̲ key.

- h̲ alone produces the code for h;
- shift h̲ produces the code for H;
- cntrl h̲ produces a control code different from the code for h or H.

You may wonder if there is a fourth case—what happens for cntrl shift h, or for control h with the alpha lock on? The former requires some finger acrobatics but the result depends on the keyboard; it usually produces ^H.

Alternate

The IBM PC has a key called **alternate**, alt, which is also a multiplier. Press alt and a letter and a totally different code results, different from that generated when shift or cntrl is used. Alt is used with BASIC to provide shorthand for the commands in that language.

Combination

Many packages use a combination of these techniques:

- a typewriter keyboard for alphanumerics;
- special function keys and a plastic overlay for frequent requests;
- code or control as a multiplier for less frequent action requests.

Numeric Key Pad

Most terminals for micros and minis provide a **numeric key pad,** a set of eleven or more keys arranged in the standard adding machine and calculator format as shown in Figure 3.3.1. This provides ten digits and a decimal

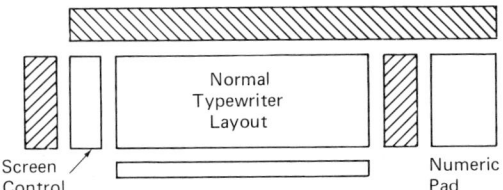

Figure 3.3.1. Typical general keyboard layout.

point. Sometimes additional keys may include a comma, enter, plus (+) and minus (−). They *duplicate* keys on the alphanumeric part of the keyboard.

Note that the keys on the Touchtone telephone are in a *different* pattern. This means that you must reorient as you go from one to the other, a *negative* transfer of training.

Programmable Function Keys

A **programmable function key (PFK)** can be set to produce any *single* code or *sequence* of codes. You enter and set up the sequence of one to ten or more codes from the keyboard. In some cases, codes for other function keys can be chained together to produce 50 or 60 codes. Pressing one PFK can display a disk directory, start a program, boot your system, and so on.

Downloading

Some keyboards have a set of ten or so function keys at the left of the keyboard. These may be set by an application program, called **downloading**. The program transmits a set of codes to the terminal. Their purpose is not to display something on the screen; rather, these are instructions to the keyboard about what code(s) each function key produces when hit.

This is a powerful labor saving function. Even IBM's operating system makes use of it to assign commands to these keys labeled F1 through F10. Entirely different codes can be assigned to the keys by the next program that gets control of the computer. Thus a word processor might assign F1 to its delete code, which is ^G; ^QA for search-and-replace to F2; and so forth. A plastic overlay supplied by the WP vendor can be placed over the function keys as a reminder of their current assignment.

There is a IBM PC function key, F10, assigned when the OS comes up with the code used to reassign the function keys. Thus if *you* want to reassign the keys, hit F10 and enter a key sequence which describes the new code sequence and the key to which to assign it.

Cursor Keys

The **cursor** is a distinguishing mark on the screen which shows the active data entry point and is given full attention in the next section. You need to be able to move this entry point around the screen at will. Four **arrow keys** are supposed to cause the cursor to move left, right, up and down respectively: Since there is no *direct* connection between the keyboard and the CRT pressing an arrow key with a program active will *not* cause the cursor to move. An arrow is engraved on the key top pointing in the direction the cursor should move. Each arrow key produces a distinctive code.

But cursor codes are not standard. Each terminal manufacturer has its own set of cursor codes. Of course, these codes must be different from the letter, numeral or punctuation codes and from each other. But these are the only limitations. Some cursor keys even produce a sequence of codes.

Actually, there is a standard established by ANSI (the American National Standard Institute). That standard provides **escape sequences,** a series of nonprinting codes always *beginning with* an escape code, esc. Only a few manufacturers have included this standard in their terminals; Visual Technology is an example. The IBM PC also uses the ANSI terminal code.

Installation

Some programs require that the operator tell it where to move the cursor. Hence these programs have to respond to the control code produced by arrow; that is, determine what it means and then send a code sequence to the terminal to move the cursor. Neither the cursor codes to send to the display nor the *arrow* codes received from your keyboard will be known to the application program unless the dealer from whom you buy it has prepared the program for you. Otherwise you have to install this information into the terminal driver (this is discussed in more detail in Chapter 7). The object of *installation* is to let the program know what control codes to expect from the cursor keys on your terminal. Then it can respond accordingly by directing the screen cursor to move to the proper position by sending it the proper cursor motion code(s).

Rollover

A keyboard should provide a unique code whenever you press a single key. But the operator is human. What if more than one key is pressed at once or if a second is pressed before the first is released? How should the keyboard respond?

Unless the keyboard is specially designed, pressing two keys produces a code different from what is expected from either. This is not acceptable. The solution is called **rollover** and works like this. When two keys are pressed together, nothing happens until *one of them* is released. The keyboard generates the code for the key released first. When the next key is released, its code is generated too. This is an effective solution for an important problem.

Occasionally three or more keys may be pressed at the same time. Some keyboards handle this case the same way. The solution is called **multikey**

rollover. A code is always produced as a key is *released*, not when it is pressed. When several keys are pressed at once, a code is produced as each successive key is released. The manufacturer may or may not specify the maximum number of keys for which the multikey rollover applies. It is up to the purchaser to find this out.

Note that control and shift are not subject to rollover since they are *multipliers*. But esc is a prefix key and *is* subject to rollover. If you hit esc and another key, the one released first produces the code.

Most keyboards have rollover these days.

The IBM PC Keyboard

The IBM PC keyboard is different and innovative in several respects. The most obvious difference from the conventional keyboard is the key arrangement shown in Figure 3.3.2, which has been the object of much criticism. A user with experience on a typewriter or another micro may find it disconcerting that the left shift key is an extra position to the left, the shift lock and alternate keys are in odd places and special keys are in new positions. After a few days, one gets used to this.

It is the operation of the keyboard which is truly innovative. It contains much circuitry and its own Intel 8048 microprocessor chip. The keyboard does not transmit the ASCII code for a symbol as described above.

Keyboard Function

Each key is assigned a number as displayed in Figure 3.3.2. This number is transmitted by the keyboard to the operating system (OS), which in turn creates the proper code for the symbol as now explained.

The key number has been determined arbitrarily but somewhat system-

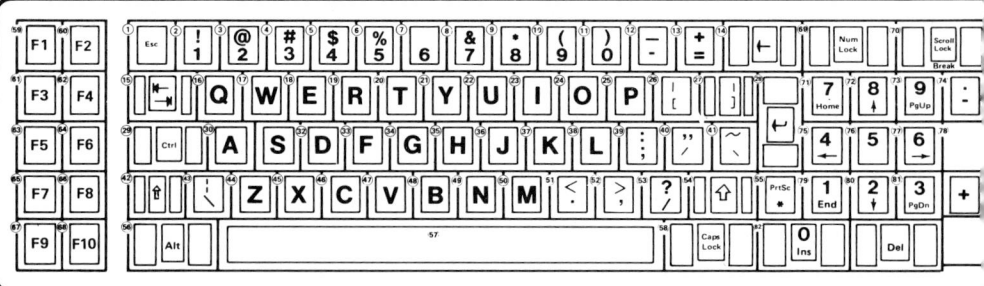

Figure 3.3.2. IBM PC keyboard with key numbers shown. (From Peter Norton, *Inside the IBM PC*: *Access to Advanced Features and Programming*. Bowie, MD: Robert J. Brady Co., 1983)

atically, as the figure shows. Each time you *hit* a key, its binary number equivalent is generated. This fits into the seven bits of a byte; the first bit is set to 0, and this is transmitted to the computer to be picked up by the OS.

Now, when you *release* that key, its code is also sent to the OS, but this time with a 1 in the first bit. Hence, at any moment, the OS knows the exact position of every key on the keyboard, whether pressed or released.

Upper and Lower Case

The OS notes when you hit a key; only when you release it does the OS send the ASCII code for the alpha character to the application program (AP). To get an upper case letter or symbol, usually generated by a key and shift, you first hit shift and then hold it down as you hit the other key. The OS has a record that the two keys are depressed and generates the proper code only when you release the nonshift key (but no code when you release shift).

Caps lock has an action which is strange to most people—it does not have the feeling of being locked nor does its action show as a light. When hit and released, the action is recorded by the OS. Thereafter, when you hit letter keys, upper case codes are sent to the AP for them. When caps lock is hit and released again, the action is reversed.

Control Codes

If control is depressed, the OS notes this and creates the ASCII control code for the second key pressed, after it is released. Thus ^A is transmitted to the AP as ASCII hex 01.

Two Byte Codes

IBM wanted to provide more than 256 codes. This was achieved by setting up for the AP to receive two bytes for any key hit. This seems wasteful; now the AP has to interpret two bytes. But, if the first byte is all 0s, only then is the second byte significant. This alleviates the problem. Here's how the plan works:

- All standard 7 bit ASCII codes work identically, except for nul, since that designates a two byte code.
- The remaining 128 combinations beginning with a 1 are assigned to special printing characters and graphics.
- If the first byte is all 0s, the next byte designates a special control character.

Graphic Characters

Graphics can display on the screen and on most dot matrix printers. An AP can use these codes to create pictorial displays by sending them to the VDT. But there are no keys for them on the keyboard. If you need to enter such codes, you can use the alternate-numeric method—hit alt, followed by the decimal equivalent of the code for the graphic. These keystrokes and number equivalents go to the OS, which prepares the proper code. These combinations, together with the 7 bit codes make up the extended ASCII, or 8 bit ASCII, code.

Special Codes

IBM *created* a number of special codes, but only those that it thought necessary, as described above: the first byte is all 0s; the second is shown in Table 3.3.1 by its decimal equivalent. Forty of these combinations use the ten function keys thus,

- alone;
- with shift;
- with control;
- with alt.

Other combinations are shown in the table.

When the designated combination of keystrokes is observed by the OS, it prepares the two proper code bytes and places them in the two microprocessor registers, AL and AH. When the AP gets control, it examines the AL first. If AL is not 0, then it contains the standard 8 bit ASCII code and is complete; otherwise AH has the second byte of a special code.

3.4 DISPLAYS

This section describes how the terminal displays text but neglects graphics entirely, since Chapter 13 is dedicated to that topic.

Physical Appearance

The display consists of a **cathode ray tube (CRT)** such as in the home TV and the associated electronics in a neat housing such as shown in Figure 3.4.1. The visible portion of the CRT is referred to as the **screen**. The effectiveness of the display depends to a large extent on the physical appearance of the CRT as well as how the characters display on the screen. You

Table 3.3.1. Second Byte of Special Codes

CODE	KEYS
3	Nul
15	shift tab
16–25	alt q w e r t y u i o p
30–38	alt a s d f g h j k l
44–50	alt z x c v b n m
59–68	F1 - F10
71	home
72	up
73	pgup
75	left
77	right
79	end
80	down
82	ins
83	del
84–93	shift F1 – shift F10
94–103	^F1–^F10
104–113	altF1 - altF10
114	^prtsc
115	^left
116	^right
117	^end
118	^pgdn
119	^home
120–131	alt 1 2 3 4 5 6 7 8 9 0 – =
132	^pgup

may spend many hours at the terminal, so it is important that you are comfortable and content with the physical surroundings. The description which follows considers the qualitative aspects of the display.

Size and Shape

CRTs are rated according to their diagonal size—the distance along the diagonal from one corner to the other. There is a standard **aspect ratio,** the ratio of height to width, which is usually about 3:4. The common TV CRT is rectangular with the width being greater than the height—just the opposite of the conventional printed page.

CRTs are manufactured with a diagonal size anywhere from 3 to 26 inches. The former is tiny and useful only in portable TVs that you might take to the seashore; however, you do find them on portable micros such as the Osborne (5 inches). The latter size is immense and might be found

Figure 3.4.1. A typical terminal.

in a den in an impressive TV console. CRTs for most computer displays range from 7 to 15 inches in diagonal size. Most commonly, they are 9 and 12 diagonal inches. Clearly the size of the characters depends on the overall size of the screen. It is easier to read text on a 12 inch screen than on a 9 inch one.

Because of its aspect ratio, only a portion of a document can be displayed on the *standard* CRT. Even if it is turned on its side, the tube does not provide the proper height for the desired width. (Now you can get a terminal that can rotate 90 degrees to give either a wide or long display.)

Some word processor displays present a full page of text at once. CRTs for today's micros to provide 16 or 25 lines of 40 or 80 characters. Special business displays provide lines of 132 characters, which would appear on a standard computer printout.

Phosphor

The beam of electrons produced within the CRT is directed by the electronics to hit the screen at a spot which then glows. The inner surface of the glass is coated with a **phosphor** which *fluoresces*—emits light—when the electron beam hits it. The light produced by a single phosphor is **monochromatic,** a spectral color. This color may be green, blue, orange; a mixture of phosphors produces a white light. Opinions differ about the most pleasant and least tiring phosphor despite many psychophysical studies.

Another quality of the phosphor is **persistence.** After the beam of electrons is turned off, the spot continues to emit light. For a **low persistence** phosphor, the spot seems to disappear immediately. For a **high persistence** phosphor, the spot may continue to emit light for minutes or even hours. Thus it would be impossible to change the display immediately. Hence we do not see high persistence phosphor in business applications.

Though very low persistence phosphors are useful in some kinds of work, we do wish the light to continue for several milliseconds so that the operator does not see much **flicker** (but still classified as low persistence).

The image of the text is created on the screen just like a movie at the movie house. It is made by projecting many, almost-identical frames. If the rate is too slow, the result is annoying flicker, perceptible changes in brightness which make some people jittery. This effect can be cured by increasing the number of frames per second, which increases the cost of the display.

Other Factors

These factors should also be considered in selecting a display:

- A display that tilts can suit the physique of the operator.
- Brightness and contrast should be adjustable by knobs to the operator's preference and the lighting.
- Some displays have less distortion, especially near the edges of the screen.
- A chemically treated CRT or one with a filter installed reduces glare considerably.

Black on White

Some vendors contend that black print on white paper is what we are used to and the display should conform to this. Studies seem to show a benefit to black print on a white background. Hence, for example, the TRS-80 and Apple Macintosh personal computers make the CRT background white and the letters appear black, as with white paper and black print. Most vendors, however, supply the conventional terminal where white or colored letters appear on a black background. Recent offerings let you choose either alternative.

Display Layout

Figure 3.4.2 shows a typical CRT screen layout. For discussion, imagine that the screen is divided into horizontal rectangular **rows** and vertical **columns.** Where a row and a column intersect is a **cell,** one screen position where a letter or a character may display. Screen **capacity** is the number of cells, the number of rows times the number of columns.

Displays for some small personal microcomputer systems, such as the Apple II, Commodore 64 or PET 4016 have a capacity of 16 × 40 (16 lines of 40 characters, or 640 characters). This is too small for most business applications. Standard screen capacity is 24 × 80 = 1920. Eighty columns is about the right width for most text documents. A printed circuit board is available for the Apple, Osborne and others to provide this screen capacity at a small additional cost.

A standard 8½ × 11 sheet of paper at 10 characters per inch would be 85 characters wide without margins. With a one inch margin on each side, we get 65 characters or columns per line. Twenty-four rows provide for about a third to a half of a text page. Even for word processing, this is all you need to enter and edit efficiently.

Business reports are usually larger. Standard mainframe printout 14 inches (wide) by 11 inches (long) has found universal favor in the business community. The width provides space for a line of 132 characters. It does not all show on the standard 80 by 24 display. Therefore the software breaks

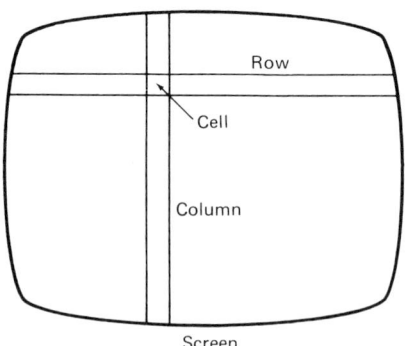

Figure 3.4.2. The screen layout.

wide text vertically into two parts, left and right. You move, or **scroll**, from left to right and back; there is no need to display information in the same manner that it is printed. But vendors have noted this deficiency and it is now possible to get terminals which display the 132 position line.

3.5 CHARACTER STORAGE AND GENERATORS

The Cell

A **cell** is a small area on the screen within which a full character can display. The character is formed in one of two ways:

- a matrix of dots;
- a set of strokes.

When a number of small dots are placed close together in the cell, this array of dots, called a **dot matrix,** produces a clearly recognizable character. This method is pervasive in commercial terminal displays and gets full attention below.

Another technique puts a number of **strokes**, or line segments, into the cell to compose the letter. This method is used for some **graphic displays** to create sketches and graphs and is discussed in Chapter 13.

Definition

Definition, the presence of detail in the character, is determined by the number of horizontal and vertical dots in each fixed size cell. Typical dot matrix sizes are 5×7 (5 dots wide by 7 dots high), 7×9, 7×11 and 9×14. Larger matrix size provides more detail in the letter on the screen but requires more expensive technology. This additional definition (and cost) is necessary for the high resolution graphic display but not for business application. Displays in the $500–$1000 terminal use matrix sizes up to about 7×9. For simplicity we examine only the 5×7 matrix.

The matrix is a grid of horizontal and vertical lines; a dot of light may or may not appear at the intersection of two of the grid lines. If light appears there, it is referred to as a **dot**; if no light appears at the intersection of a horizontal and vertical line, I call this an **undot**. Hence a letter or numeral is composed of *dots* and *undots*.

At any cell on the screen where a horizontal line intersects a vertical line (a spot), the electron beam is turned *on* to create a dot or *off* to create an undot.

The electron beam sweeps out each horizontal line of the cell and is turned on or off as it reaches each spot to create the dots and undots which make up a letter. The motion of the beam as it sweeps over the *entire* screen is called a **scan**.

At the left of Figure 3.5.1 we see a 5 × 7 grid and dots and undots which make up the letter E.

The Character

Displays and printers used to put both lower and upper case with the bottom of the letter at the bottom of the cell. Lower case letters do not look right when displayed this way. Part of the letter should go below the imaginary line where the letter sits. The tail of a letter such as p or g, which usually goes below the line, is called a **descender**. To include the descender, the matrix has to be lengthened.

A full 5 × 7 matrix actually consists of *ten* horizontal lines as shown on the right on Figure 3.5.1. At most, seven dots may appear in any vertical. The top seven lines are for upper case letters, lower case letters without descenders and numbers. Two additional lines are for descenders; the tenth line separates the bottom of characters in one row from the top of characters in the next row down. Better displays and printers show characters with descenders.

Display Memory

Display memory holds one byte, 8 bits or one character code for each cell on the screen. The standard display with 24 rows of 80 characters has 1920

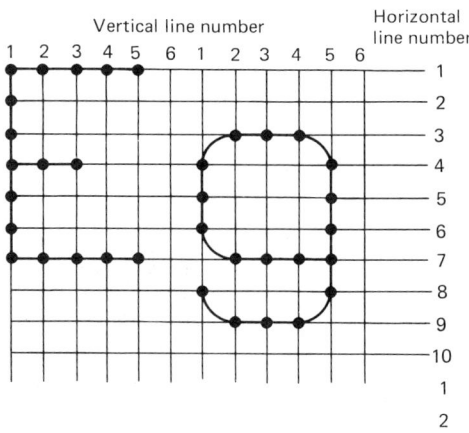

Figure 3.5.1. Forming letters on the grid.

3.5 CHARACTER STORAGE AND GENERATORS 71

bytes of display memory. When the display is turned on, each byte of display memory is set to the **null code** (00 for ASCII) for the **null** or blank character. The blank consists only of undots; hence the whole display appears blank.

The computer transmits a character code to the display by sending it over the connecting cable. Normally, codes received are placed into successive positions of display memory. In most cases, display memory is loaded sequentially, as the discussion below reveals.

Memory-Mapped Video

Less expensive micros, such as the Commodore and the Atari, include a keyboard but no display. The display memory is actually a portion of main memory. The computer hooks up to a TV set or a separate monitor, not included to keep the sale price low.

Since main memory is needed to drive the screen, its size is kept small, resulting in a low display capacity, 16 to 24 lines of 40 characters. In Osbornes or Apples which work this way, a display card that fits into a slot in the bus includes its own display memory and provides a 24 × 80 display. The IBM PC and its clones and Lisa and Macintosh also use memory mapped video, described in more detail in Section 6.6.

Cursor

The cursor is a distinguishing mark which appears in one cell to show where the action is—where to enter data, where to delete text, where the response to a message appears, etc. There are several ways to make the cursor cell stand out:

- Underline it.
- Show it in reverse video.
- Make it blink.
- Use an underline that blinks.

This applies whether the cursor cell is blank or contains a character. The cursor *always* appears in *some* cell.

As you key a character, the cursor moves to the right to the next cell along the line. When you *edit* text, you move the cursor into existing text and usually over an existing character. Reverse video shows the cursor clearly, yet does not obliterate the letter it sits on. A plain "white" rectangle would blot out the character. **Reverse video** makes the square appear white and the character within it black. Some displays let you choose how you want the cursor to appear.

Reverse Video

Reverse video for the white-on-black display presents a black character on white in the cursor cell. Foreground and background are reversed. Suppose the matrix for a character stores 1s for dots (white) and 0s for undots (black background). To get reverse video, the display electronics simply changes the meaning of bits: use 1 for undots (black) and 0 for dots (white).

Reverse video applied to black-on-white achieves a similar effect: the cursor shows a character as white-on-black.

Display Procedure

Text displays employ low persistence CRTs. Characters written on the display fade in a fraction of a second. To maintain the text on the screen, all characters must be **refreshed**—rewritten many times a second. A common refresh rate is 60 times a second (60 Hz [hertz]). This is the same frequency commonly found at the wall plug in the home or office. You do not notice that the screen is being rewritten, even when a new character appears, since the refresh rate is well past the flicker rate.

The screen is always rewritten in the same order. Scan starts at the upper left hand corner and writes the characters in the first row from left to right; then the beam returns to the left and the second row is written; scan continues thus until the whole screen is written; then the scan starts all over again.

The center of Figure 3.5.2 shows **display memory** for the standard display, 24 × 80. Each byte contains the 7 bit code for the character which should appear in the corresponding position on the screen. Where a blank space appears on the screen (between words or at the end of the last line in a paragraph), a space, null code or nonprinting code is recorded in memory.

During the scan, a **display counter** keeps track of the cell where the next character should be, its row and column number. This counter also points to the position in display memory—its **address**—where the corresponding character code is stored.

As the scan reaches a cell, display memory is consulted and the recorded character code is brought forth. Now the character is created on the screen in the cell where it belongs; dots and undots are written in the cell in the form of the desired letter.

3.5 CHARACTER STORAGE AND GENERATORS 73

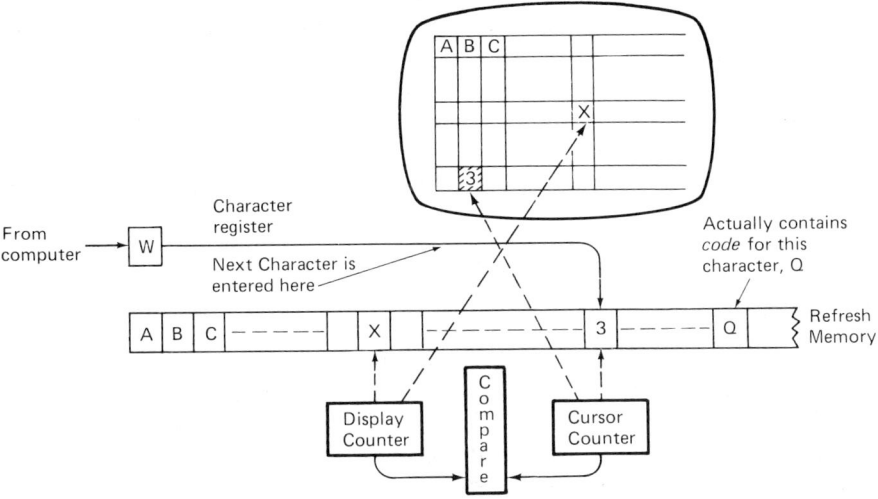

Figure 3.5.2. Display memory drives the screen.

Creating a Character

The foregoing description is actually oversimplified. Characters are not displayed a cell at a time. Instead, one line segment from each character in each cell of the row is written all the way across the screen. A **scan line** is one complete horizontal beam motion across the screen from left to right. A *row* of characters is 10 *scan lines*. The top dots and undots of all the 80 characters in one row is written by the first scan line of that row. Then the beam goes back and writes the second set of dots and undots for each of the 80 characters; this continues for all 10 scan lines of the row (the last line being blank).

Cursor Position

The cursor is presented by one of the techniques mentioned earlier. A **cursor counter** records the position of the cursor relative to display memory and corresponding to its row and column. During each refresh cycle, before each character is presented, the display counter is incremented by 1. Then it is compared to the cursor counter. When the two are equal, this position should display the cursor.

When the cursor and display counters point to the same cell, the presentation method for the cell is altered so that the cursor appears as

- an *underline*: display the character as usual but add a horizontal segment in the eighth line;
- *reverse video*: interpret 0s and 1s from the character generator for each horizontal line segment of the character as 1s and 0s respectively so that black and white are reversed;
- as a *blink*: cause the character (or underline) to appear for a while (typically 60 cycles/second) and disappear for another such period.

Entering Data

What happens when you hit a key at the keyboard to enter a character? If this is a data code generated during a data input sequence, the program should display it on the screen. After verifying it, the program sends the same code to the display. The display receives the code and puts it in the **character register** shown at the upper left of Figure 3.5.2. The code remains there until the scan reaches the right position. The code in the character register enters display memory and is simultaneously displayed on the screen, *only* when the cell pointed to by the cursor counter is reached by the scan.

In Figure 3.5.2, the code for W is now stored in the character register. The display counter points to where X is being displayed. Scan and display continues; soon the display counter and the cursor counter are equal. They both point to the cell where W should be shown; it is now put in the display memory cell pointed to and simultaneously presented on the screen.

Thereafter the cursor counter is advanced by one position and a **flag**, a hardware indicator, is set to tell the computer that the character register is free and a new character may be sent to it if the program should wish to do so.

More Data

When you hit the next key, the same thing happens. The fastest typist might hit ten or twelve keys in one second. But the refresh rate is 60 per second. So the next character is always sent one scan later.

However, the program might want to put up a whole new screen. This would be the case as you browse brough a document you edit. The word processor sends a signal to clear the screen and memory and move the cursor to the upper left corner. It has the new screen contents in memory and sends them over a character at a time. New characters are written to the screen and to display memory as fast as the transmission rate between the computer and the terminal permits. When the terminal signals that it is free,

3.5 CHARACTER STORAGE AND GENERATORS

the computer sends the next character. It is picked up at once on this refresh cycle if possible.

Transmission Rate

The **transmission rate** of data between the computer and the terminal (the display in particular) is given in **bauds**, which are approximately equal to bits per second (**bps**) in this case. Both computer and terminal rates are adjustable either by hardware (a switch on the terminal) or software (the operating system) but *must* be the same during any transmission. Rates vary between 300 and 19,200 (even 38,400) but 9600 is most common. When rates are altered normally, the software must also be informed.

At 9600 baud, 1200 bytes per second are sent, so it takes about two seconds to put a new screen. This happens twice as fast at 19,200 baud!

Cursor Movement

Cursor positioning may be requested at most keyboards using **arrow keys** (keys marked with arrows): up, down, left and right. When you press an arrow key (designated arrow here regardless of which way it points), a control code goes to the computer. It is picked up by the program which notes which directional cursor key was pressed. The program then calculates the new position for the cursor, which is now transmitted to the display as a control code or a control code sequence to distinguish it from data. The display receives the sequence, converts it to a number corresponding to that position and enters it into the cursor counter.

Example

Thus each time left is pressed, a nonprinting code is sent to an application program, such as a word processor, which *de*crements the position counter that the WP program keeps. The new cursor coordinates are sent to the display and to the cursor counter, which causes the cursor to move. Pressing up decrements the WP position counter by 80 instead of 1. The program transmits a code for this position to the display. When this is put in the cursor counter, the cursor jumps up by one position. *Repeat action* applies to the cursor key and is particularly useful. After you hold down arrow a second or so, the cursor moves rapidly in the proper direction.

It is common, while editing text or screen information, to move the cursor from one part of the screen to another to make changes. A character you enter at the terminal when you stop the cursor is picked up by the program and put into its text in memory at a position corresponding to the cursor. The character code is also transmitted to the display to enter the code into the display memory at the cursor position. In this way, a single character may be altered in the middle of the text. The rest of the text remains unchanged. The cursor advances one position because the cursor counter is incremented automatically by this action.

If data update were done directly at the display without a signal going to the computer, then the program would not record the new cursor position.

Fonts and Alphabets

Except when memory mapped video is used, the pattern for each character of the display alphabet is stored in ROM (read only memory) within the terminal called the **character generator**. For the more elaborate displays, where several different fonts are provided, each font requires its own ROM character generator. Such an expense is not justified for the business computer display.

Graphic Symbols

A code for which there is no character on the printer is a nonprinting code. However this code may call forth a pattern from the character generator in the display. When this pattern does not correspond to a letter, number or punctuation mark, it is called a **graphic**; examples of the graphic are the triangle, square and circle.

Graphics are often used by the application program to show special functions you have called for such as return on text editors or symbols for **prompts**, requests for a response from an accounting program, for example. Graphics can be used (as with the IBM PC) to build charts and graphs. The form of the graphic is built into the ROM; if there are several ROMs, all need the same graphic patterns included.

Display Functions Provided by the Program

Your display may provide functions to show two or more kinds of data such as:

1. A **split screen** enables you to view two electronic documents at once and move information from one to the other.
2. A **menu** provides a choice of alternative functions to request.

3. A **status line** shows the document name, page number, and so on, for word processing or the customer number, name, and so forth, for accounting applications.
4. Special marks show protected fields which are skipped as you enter data.

These functions *seem* to be provided by the display. Some are not (1,2) and depend entirely on the program which is currently in the computer. Others require both special display features and program participation (3). This section only describes facilities provided *within* a display. Other functions invoked from the keyboard are implemented in the application program which fabricates and presents the altered display.

Display Control

For simple use of the terminal where information is displayed as entered from the keyboard or from a file, little direct control of the display is necessary. More sophisticated programs do such things as:

- clear the screen and put the cursor in upper left corner;
- move the cursor to a particular cell without altering the display;
- insert a blank line on the display;
- **highlight**, put in reverse video, a set of characters.

These actions are requested by the program sending a **control sequence**, a sequence of codes, to the terminal. The terminal notes the presence of control codes in the sequence (esc) and *responds* to them instead of trying to display them.

The trouble is that each manufacturer has its own control sequence. This means that terminals are *not* compatible for many special applications, such as word processing. The ADM-3, SOROC IQ120, TeleVideo 950 and DEC VT-100 all have different control sequences.

The program needs a **driver**, a routine which directs the terminal, tailored to the particular terminal type. Remember this if you decide to buy a new terminal. For the new terminal,

A. Does the display or program vendor supply drivers?
B. Does the display or program vendor supply an *install* program to convert the driver to the program?
C. Or must the computer retailer install it for you?

Graphics

There are applications which present charts, graphs and drawings at the display. Most of the work is done by the program and this is described in Chapter 13. Graphic applications require that the display have graphic support capability, namely

- dot addressability;
- adequate definition in lines per screen and dots per line.

Some systems compensate for deficiencies in these areas by providing graphic symbols which can be strung together, but this is adequate only for simple things like charts.

3.6 COMMUNICATION BETWEEN COMPUTERS

Need

For a small business, a personal computer or a single micro may suffice. When there is sufficient work to keep a number of work stations busy, a larger system is needed. For a large business, it becomes useful to have several complete systems which can converse with a supermini or a mainframe. A company with two or more branches, each with computers, might want these computers to communicate. For all but the smallest facility, communication of some kind is an important consideration.

Complex systems consist of several computers; the one in command is the **host**, or **master**, computer. Other computers report to it and are known as **satellites** or **slaves**. There is a need for the host and its satellites to talk.

Where a number of computers are equal in status, as in a network of small business computers, we call them **peer** computers. When any two of the computers can talk, this is called **networking.**

A personal computer such as the Apple or TRS can tie into the telephone lines, which is a boon to the entrepreneur. It gives access to commercial analysis services for quotations on stocks in the firm's portfolio. Data can pass to and from branch offices. Summary reports can go to a distant accountant. Electronic mail becomes possible: between offices; with associates; with vendors or salesmen.

Most minis and micros can communicate to mainframes using telephone lines. Special software makes the micro look like a terminal to the mainframe computer. For example, using software, the Apple II+ looks like or **emulates** an IBM 3270 display terminal or a DEC VT-100 terminal. Thus a low priced micro can serve two functions:

3.6 COMMUNICATION BETWEEN COMPUTERS

- a low priced calculator, word processor or a data base manager;
- a terminal for a mainframe computer.

Furthermore, when acting like a terminal, it can save the information sent by the mainframe (in a buffer area); this information can later be written to external storage attached to the micro. Similarily, data files created on the micro can be shipped to the mainframe by telephone.

All is not bliss though! Micros use ASCII for data representation and mainframes usually use EBCIDIC (see Chapter 9). So data from mainframes must be converted by the micro to be used and then reconverted for transmission in a form acceptable to the mainframe.

Distance

The way that components are connected depends upon the distance separating them. We discuss communication according to three distance ranges:

- a few feet;
- within the same office or building up to a few hundred feet;
- long distances over public telephone lines.

Method

The simplest way data flow between components is by a direct connection—wires pass between the components. A character or symbol is represented by a code; the aggregate of bits which compose the code is a byte. When a separate wire is furnished for each bit of the byte, this is **parallel** transmission. If we convert each byte into a *series* of bits so as to transmit one bit at a time sequentially on a pair of wires, this is **serial** transmission. Although bits are transmitted one at a time, which is slower, only two wires connect the components.

When the transmission distance is long, for private lines around an office or building, cables need *amplifiers*. Finally, there is the public carrier, or telephone line.

Short Distance

Only a few feet separate components in the typical system. The terminal may be on top of a desk while the computer may be underneath the desk or in a different box. A number of signals pass in parallel between the two. A cable consisting of a separate wire for each signal is acceptable for distances of up to about ten feet.

80 COMMUNICATING

When components are separated by greater distances, even though still in the same general area, a simple cable is no longer viable. The signals are degraded by the resistance of the wire and become susceptible to all kinds of electronic and magnetic noise present in most business settings.

One solution provides an amplifier for each wire; it boosts each signal as it leaves the computer to travel unmolested through the noisy environment. But this is costly.

Another solution **serializes** the signals—converts them from parallel to serial form. Then only two wires are needed to carry them. A single amplifier provides noise immunity. This arrangement is shown in Figure 3.6.1. The receiving equipment converts the serial signals back to parallel form using a **deserializer.** If signals pass in both directions, then amplifiers are required at both ends of the line. Also, each end must have its own serializer and deserializer.

Medium Distance

Consider data transmission among components or computers in a large office or building. Although slow communication is tolerable between a computer and a component such as a terminal, computers should talk to each other more rapidly. The technique described for short distances is not satisfactory at faster rates when longer distances are involved. It is still necessary to serialize the signals or to use other techniques, but transmission must take place rapidly and over a special line.

Medium distance transmission lines which connect several computers are called **local area networks (LANs).** There is no standard LAN. Examples are the Ethernet, marketed by Xerox, and the Wangnet, by Wang. Transmission uses a coaxial cable such as brings in cable television signals to your home. Each computer or component is hooked into the cable through a **gateway.** When the cable is not busy, a station may send a message which bears the identity of the receiver. The message on the line is available to all other stations. However, like a party line telephone, only the intended receiver picks up the phone and accepts the message. This is illustrated in Figure 3.6.2.

The gateway puts other senders on hold while the line is in use. The line

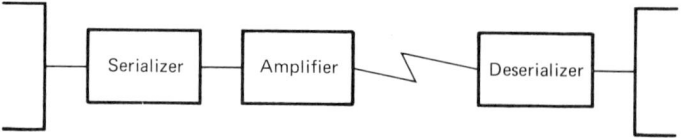

Figure 3.6.1. The serializer and deserializer.

3.6 COMMUNICATION BETWEEN COMPUTERS

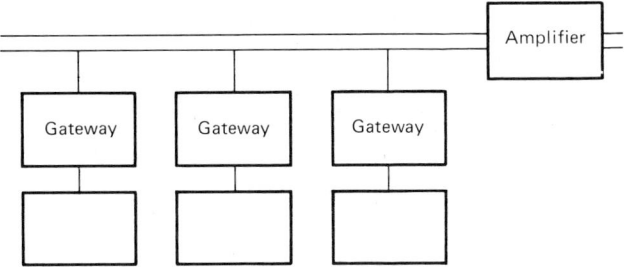

Figure 3.6.2. The local network uses gateways.

becomes available to requesters by priority. This system is suitable for distances up to about a mile. It is also possible to add amplifiers as shown in the figure to double or triple this distance.

Long Distance

It is possible to transmit data around the world using telephone and microwave lines, optical fibers and satellites. Communication over distance uses *serial* signals.

Line capacity is the rate at which information is transmitted; greater capacity costs more. To transmit large amounts of information fast requires expensive lines such as coaxial cable. Given their high cost, these lines are used only in special cases.

Telephone lines cost the same whether they carry voice or digital communication. Line capacity is limited to a few hundred characters per second. With low priced modems (explained shortly) costing $200 to $500, you can transmit 300 to 600 bits per second (**bps** or **baud**). This amounts to 30 to 75 characters per second (**cps**). With more expensive equipment, you can transmit 1200 and on up to 9600 baud.

Conversion

Telephone lines do not carry on/off (binary) information directly. One technique converts binary information into the presence or absence of a **tone** (or pitch). But when no tone is present, the line is susceptible to noise. Hence, a better method employs two tones: one tone stands for a 1; the other stands for 0.

Figure 3.6.3 shows equipment to tie into a telephone line. The computer data in parallel form goes to a serializer which converts the data to a series of 0s and 1s. These pass to a **modem,** a device which converts pulses into one or another tone of a tone pair; this process is called **modulation.** The opposite action of converting tones into bits is **demodulation.** *Modem* is a

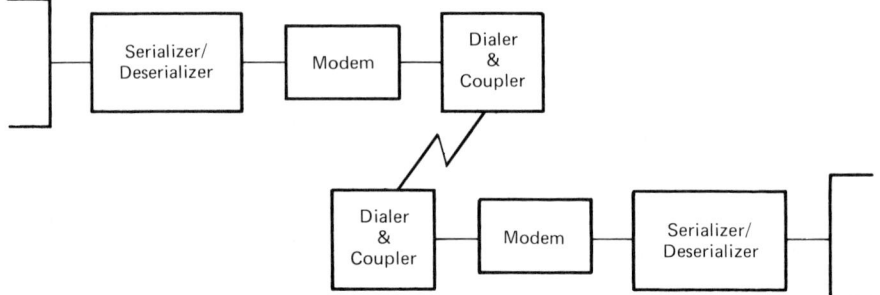

Figure 3.6.3. How to connect to a telephone line.

contraction for *modulator-demodulator*. The final box in the figure shows the dialer and the coupling from the transmitter to the telephone line.

It is best for two stations to be able to talk and answer simultaneously. One pair of lines could be used in each direction between the stations (call them A and B): one pair is to talk on A and listen at B; the other pair is to talk on B and listen at A. This is **full duplex**.

A terminal and a computer can manage with a single line. One talks while the other listens until such time as the roles reverse. Then the computer switches the hardware around. This is called **half duplex**.

Full duplex operation with a *single* pair of wires is possible and the most common method. *Two pairs* of tones a total of four tones, (like notes on a piano) are provided. Before communication begins, decide which tone pair applies to each direction. The station which uses the lower frequency pair is in **originate mode**. The other station is in **answer mode**. The tones used are standard:

- The low frequency pair is 1270 hertz for mark and 1070 hertz for space.
- The high frequency pair is 2225 hertz for mark and 2025 hertz for space.

Mark is communication jargon for *on* (1), **space** means *off* (0).

In a **dial-up** network, there is one host computer which one of the many remote users may dial into via the telephone. It is customary for the remote user to be in *originate* mode. It is less expensive to get a modem which only accomodates one mode. For only a slightly higher cost, one can get a switchable modem.

Rates

The rate at which data are sent or received may be given as *bits per second* (bps). Another common term in communication circles is the baud, the number of marks and spaces per second. In **synchronous** operation, bps and Bauds are the same. Bits of the characters are sent at fixed time intervals, in accordance with a clock. This is common when two computers talk to each other.

When data are generated by a human operator at a keyboard, key strokes occur irregularly. Additional pulses are required to indicate the *start* and *end* of a character; this is called **asynchronous** communication. Now a character consists of the code byte plus from one to three additional bits for synchronization. Thus the character uses 9 to 11 bits. Hence 1200 baud may be equivalent to 900 or even 600 bps if this were synchronous operation, because of the extra bits required.

To reiterate, the baud and bps are equivalent. To get the cps, divide bps by the number of bits per character, usually 8, for synchronous operation. For asynchronous operation, you have to know how many bits are transmitted for each character; extra bits are always needed to keep the receiver in step with the transmitter—from one to three. Then divide bps by bits per character to get cps.

It is important that data are received accurately. Various techniques are used to assure this; one of them is called **parity**. An additional bit is appended to each byte so that the number of 1s is always odd (or even, whichever the rule). Upon receipt, each character is checked to make sure that its code contains an odd number of 1s. All characters received are so checked. For seven bit ASCII, the remaining bit of the byte is used for parity and the transmission rate per character is hence unaffected.

Another technique, called **check sum**, verifies the accuracy of a group of characters. A check sum is calculated as a block of data is transmitted; the check sum is added to the block transmitted; it is calculated at the other end as the data are received. Then the check sum transmitted at the end of the block should agree with what is calculated on the *receive* end. Otherwise the receiving computer requests a retransmission of the block.

Parity *and* check sum used together improve accuracy.

Protocol

For two systems to talk with each other, each must follow a sequence of steps that the other is acquainted with and verifies. This fixed procedure, called a **protocol**, assures that data are transmitted correctly and interpreted properly. A protocol works by stating when a block stops and starts and by demanding that a block which contains an error is retransmitted so that eventually a correct transmission is achieved—not withstanding hardware failure. Several transmission protocols are described in the literature but there is no standard.

4
Printers

4.1 INTRODUCTION

Section 2.4 introduces printers. Now we examine how they fit into the business world. But first we examine a combination not mentioned before, the printer terminal.

The Printer Terminal

The **printer terminal** consists of two parts: a printer and a keyboard. It is the antecedent of the video display terminal. It has been around a long time and is also called a **teletypewriter.** It communicates with a computer: it sends information keyed into the keyboard; the computer returns information to the printer.

The terminal printer is often a computer-activated typewriter with output rate restricted to 15 characters per second (cps). Such a machine is aggravating to someone experienced with a faster terminal, but it has served for a long time in the computer world.

The keyboard connects directly to the printer by throwing a switch. Then keyed information prints directly and is not sent to the computer. This has the advantage that, when the computer is inoperative, the terminal becomes a typewriter.

Both the **dot matrix** and the **daisy wheel** printer can have a keyboard incorporated at an additional cost of $500 or so. The printer terminal is rarely found in the small business or office environment, although they are encountered in large businesses with mainframe installations.

The Modified Typewriter

An electric typewriter modified for computer output is rarely found in the small business environment. It is slow, prone to mechanical difficulties and should be avoided. However, an understanding of its principles of operation (Section 4.2) is helpful and aids in understanding how other printers work.

Dot Matrix

This fast and economical printer is also reliable. The part most prone to wear, the print unit, can be easily replaced by anyone with mechanical ability. Print quality is satisfactory for all business use, except correspondence: invoicing, billing, even payroll. If you are willing to spend a bit more, you can get a printer with correspondence quality at lower speed and business-report quality at a high speed.

Another kind of printer, based on the dot matrix principle is the ink jet printer. The differences are described later.

Daisy Wheel

The daisy wheel produces high quality correspondence output, often better than an electric typewriter. The output rate is restricted to about 65 cps, half that of an inexpensive matrix printer. Such high quality is not necessary for business reports but is the best for word processing.

Line Printer

This printer is most applicable to a firm which produces a lot of reports (where paper is not such an important product, the matrix printer is quite serviceable). A line printer for $5,000 to $10,000 provides speeds ten times greater than a dot matrix printer.

Laser Printer

This printer is priced beyond the means of most small businesses. However, this technology is improving rapidly, and its cost is declining. It is discussed because in the next decade it will become accessible to the small business market: its price should drop to that of a line printer; it will definitely take most of the market away from them. It combines both print quality and speed.

4.2 MODIFIED TYPEWRITER

The typewriter was adapted for computer use many years ago. Early micros used them because little else was available. With few exceptions, this device is *not* recommended for use in small business applications. It is discussed here because

86 PRINTERS

- You may encounter one.
- The principles are important to help understand other kinds of printers.

Figure 4.2.1 shows the Selectric™ typewriter. A **platen**, present in all printers, is the horizontal rubber cylinder against which the paper is held by the **paper bail** so that it does not get out of line during printing. Platen rotation advances the paper (**line advance**) upwards past the carriage when one of its knurled knobs is turned or when a line advance signal is sent by the computer. The **carriage** (sometimes called the **carrier**) holds the ribbon cartridge, the print element and part of the print mechanism. As each character is printed, the carriage moves to the next print position and stops.

The removable **print element** does the printing and is dubbed a **golf ball** because of its shape, Figure 4.2.2; four rows of characters are arranged at different "latitudes" parallel to its "equator." The ball moves in three ways:

- it turns halfway round on its vertical axis to get to upper case characters and symbols;
- it also turns around its vertical axis to one of many character positions in either direction *in addition* to the half revolution required for upper case characters, when present;
- it tilts forward or backward on a horizontal axis to one of the four rows.

Entry

Hitting a key, perhaps accompanied by a shift, causes the ball to position so that the desired character is above the paper; then an electrically energized hammer hits the ball. The type bangs against the ribbon to leave an ink impression at this position on the paper.

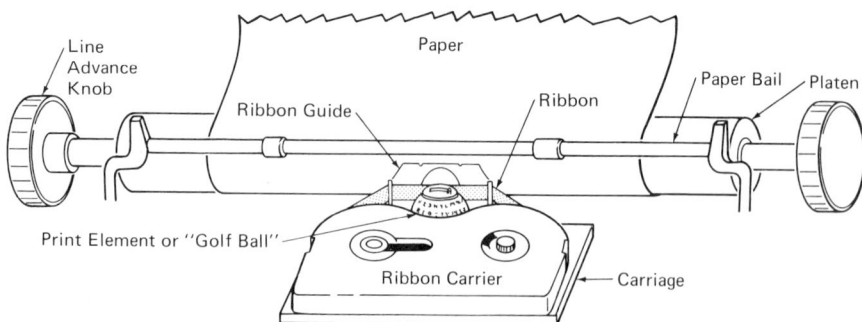

Figure 4.2.1. A typical electric typewriter.

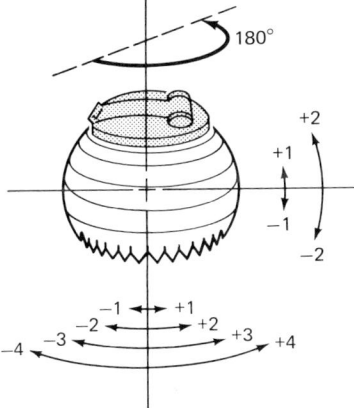

Figure 4.2.2. Typewriter print element.

This typewriter can be "computerized" in two ways. The first approach is an add-on solenoid arrangement which is cheap, but unreliable and unsuited to the business environment.

The second method incorporates circuitry in the modified typewriter to convert the character codes sent by the computer into impulses which substitute for those created by the operator when a key is pressed. But the machine was designed for human use and has an inherent speed limitation of about 15 characters per second (cps). When run at top speed, higher than any realistic continuous human output rate, it is prone to frequent mechanical failure.

4.3 THE DOT MATRIX PRINTER

Each character is printed as a set of dots by this device. The pattern of dots for the printer is stored in a **character generator** just as for the CRT display (described in Section 3.5). The print carriage sweeps out *one row of characters* at a time. The layout of the dots and undots (see Section 3.4) for each character is kept in binary in a ROM (read-only memory) in the printer. The print head consists of wires arranged vertically. As the carriage sweeps continuously across the paper horizontally, print wires are activated to print dots which make up portions of each character. Thus a character is printed one vertical column of dots at a time. For the 5 × 9 dot matrix, each character consists of five vertical columns, each with up to 9 dots in it.

A character consists of dots laid out in a matrix. Although there are many varieties of matrix design, we discuss only the 5 × 9 matrix displayed in Figure 4.3.1. The top seven rows (horizontal) are used for upper case letters

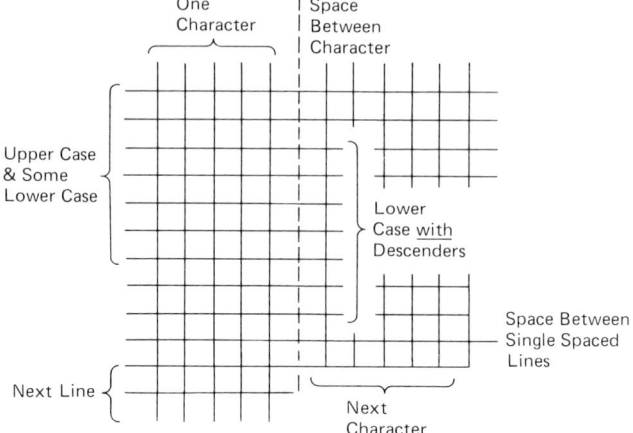

Figure 4.3.1. Dot matrix print grid (5 × 9).

and lower case letters without descenders. Rows 3 through 9 print lower case letters with descenders; the tenth row (not shown) is a nonprinting separator between single-spaced lines.

The carriage shown in Figure 4.3.2 carries a ribbon cartridge and a **print element** which consist of nine rigid **print wires** arranged *vertically*. Behind each wire is a tiny fast-acting hammer which may be activated to hit that wire against the ribbon to make an ink dot on the paper. These wires are shown from the side in Figure 4.3.3 as they print the third vertical of the

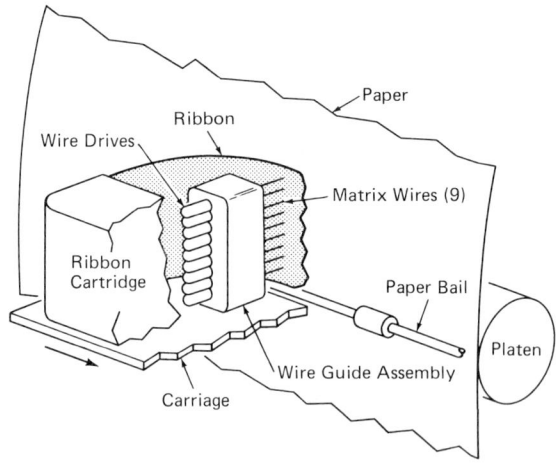

Figure 4.3.2. Dot matrix printer carriage.

4.3 THE DOT MATRIX PRINTER   89

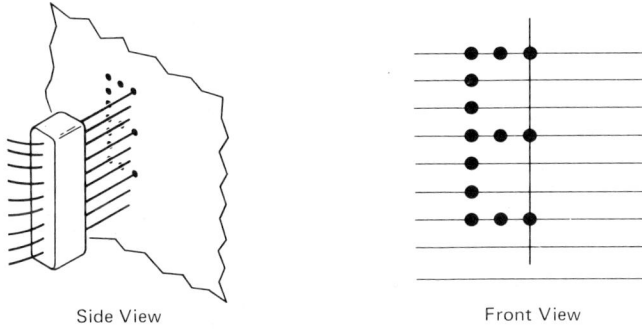

Side View   Front View

Figure 4.3.3. Dot matrix printing an "E."

letter E. This action, as it appears from the front, is shown at the left of the figure.

Figure 4.3.4 shows how the print head is positioned in front of the paper. Figure 4.3.5 shows the ballistic print head manufactured by Lear Siegler Inc; at the left are magnets. When one is energized, it pulls down the hammers sharply to send the wire (center) to hit the ribbon and make the impres-

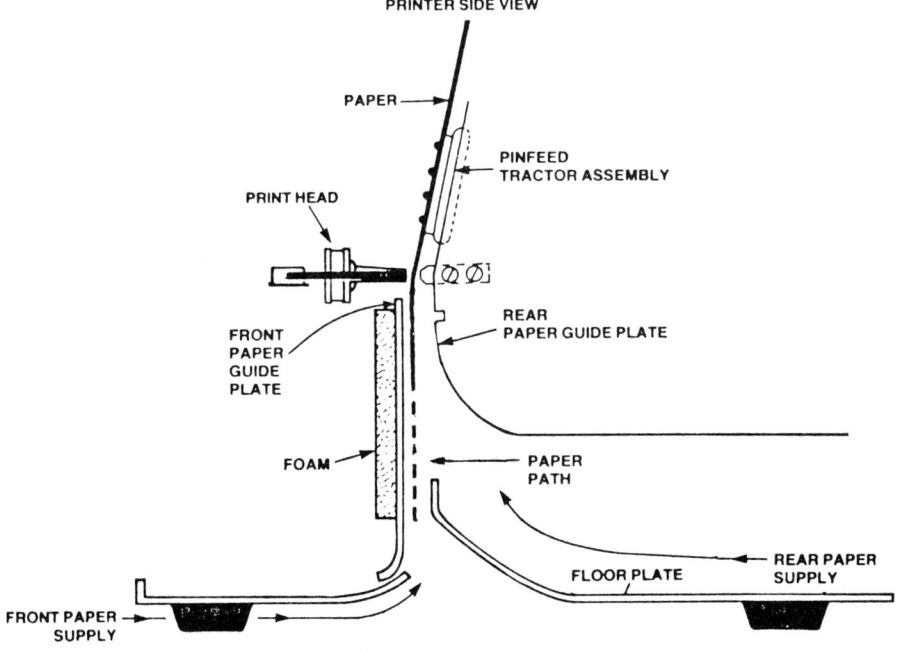

Figure 4.3.4. Dot matrix printhead in position.

Figure 4.3.5. Dot matrix ballistic printhead.

sion of a single dot. In Figure 4.3.6 we see that the print needle is spring loaded away from the paper (a) until the electromagnet is energized to move the clapper to hit the needle and make a dot on the paper (b). Figure 4.3.7 shows the print head installed in the printer and actively printing.

All the codes for characters to be printed on this line are sent by the computer program to a **print buffer,** a small memory in the printer. Printing does not start until the buffer is full. The computer cannot send over another line until this one is printed. The printer, in turn, must wait for the buffer to fill before it can print again. That is why some printers have two or more buffers: one can fill while printing from the other.

External buffers now on the market can hold 16K of text for the printer to work on. You attach an external buffer between the computer and the printer as shown in Figure 4.3.8; the vendor supplies an extra cable. The program fills up the external buffer for the printer to get text from when the print buffer runs out. The computer is then often free to do other jobs while printing goes on.

Printing

The carriage starts its fast horizontal trip across the paper; it does not stop until it reaches the other side (or the end of short line). As the carriage arrives at each character position, the circuitry gets the character code for that character from the print buffer. Figure 4.3.7 shows the printhead in

4.3 THE DOT MATRIX PRINTER 91

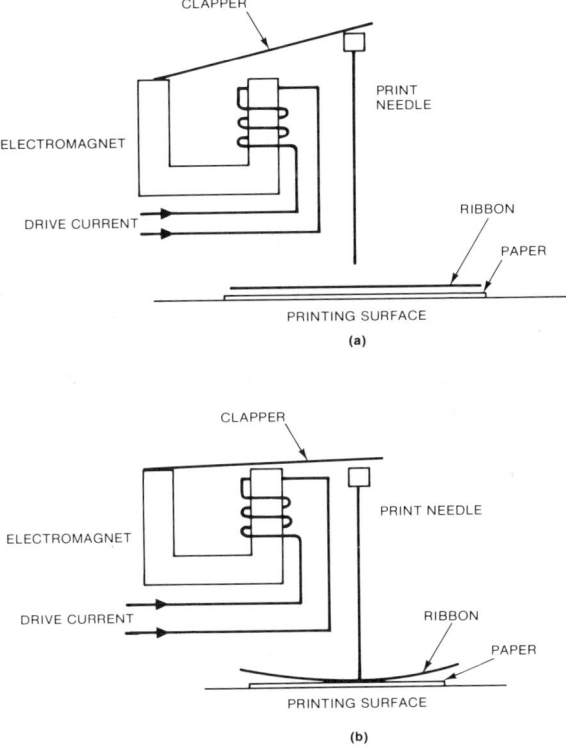

Figure 4.3.6. Dot matrix printhead in both positions.

action. The character generator produces a description of the first vertical position, a set of 9 dot sites. There are five such verticals for the 5 × 7 dot matrix. The ROM supplies a set of 1s and 0s corresponding to the wires to hit to make the first vertical segment of this character.

This set of bits from the character generator is put into a 9 bit **hammer register.** The carriage arrives at the first column of the character. Where there is a 1 in the hammer register, a hammer hits the corresponding wire. Thus the hammers print the first set of vertical dots for this character. The carriage moves through four more vertical positions. At each position the character generator is interrogated. A set of nine bits for the dots which make up this vertical of the character is put into the hammer register. Hammers hit the print wires as those positions are swept out. The result is a rectangle containing dots which look like the character requested for this position.

Figure 4.3.7. Dot matrix actively printing.

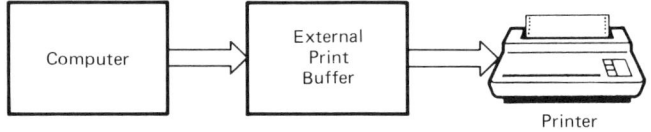

Figure 4.3.8. External print buffer.

Characteristics

Dot matrix printers produce draft quality output at 50 to 500 cps. Prices vary from $500 to about $3000. Less expensive models provide only one type face but this can be printed in compressed or expanded format (fewer or more characters per inch) as shown in Figure 4.3.9. More expensive models (such as manufactured by Malibu) have several fonts as well as multipass capability. This produces higher quality printing at a slower speed.

4.3 THE DOT MATRIX PRINTER

NORMAL

!"£$%&'()*+,-./0123456789:;<=>?@ABCDEFGHIJKLMNOPQRSTUVWXYZ
[\]^_`abcdefghijklmnopqrstuvwxyz{|}~
!"#$%&'()*+,-./0123456789:;<=>?ÉABCDEFGHIJKLMNOPQRSTUVWXYZ
ÄÖAÜ_éabcdefghijklmnopqrstuvwxyzäöåü

NORMAL ELONGATED

!"£$%&'()*+,-./0123456789:;<=>?
@ABCDEFGHIJKLMNOPQRSTUVWXYZ[\]^_`
abcdefghijklmnopqrstuvwxyz{|}~
!"#$%&'()*+,-./0123456789:;<=>?
ÉABCDEFGHIJKLMNOPQRSTUVWXYZÄÖÅÜ_
éabcdefghijklmnopqrstuvwxyzäöåü

PROPORTIONAL

!"£$%&'()*+,-./0123456789:;<=>?@ABCDEFGHIJKLMNOPQRSTUVWXYZ
[\]^_`abcdefghijklmnopqrstuvwxyz{|}~
!"#$%&'()*+,-./0123456789:;<=>?ÉABCDEFGHIJKLMNOPQRSTUVWXYZ
ÄÖÅÜ_éabcdefghijklmnopqrstuvwxyzäöåü

PROPORTIONAL ELONGATED

!"£$%&'()*+,-./0123456789:;<=>?@ABCDEFGHIJKL
MNOPQRSTUVWXYZ
[\]^_`abcdefghijklmnopqrstuvwxyz{|}~
!"#$%&'()*+,-./0123456789:;<=>?ÉABCDEFGHIJKL
MNOPQRSTUVWXYZÄÖÅÜ_éabcdefgh
ijklmnopqrstuvwxyzäöåü

Figure 4.3.9. Dot matrix printing.

Multipass

There are a growing number of **multipass** printers on the market in the $2,000 to $4,000 range and it is even a feature of inexpensive printers such as the Epson MX-80. They produce printing approximating letter quality. The printhead moves back and forth across the *same* line several times. For each **pass**, one scan of the same line, the paper is advanced only slightly.

Figure 4.3.10. Dot matrix multipass printing.

The set of dots printed in the first pass of a character is offset from the second set of dots produced. The result is overlapping images which produce a cleaner and sharper result with a blending of the dots. More passes provide greater improvement. Good quality is thus achieved, but at one-half or less of maximum speed. Speed for draft quality is 150 to 400 cps; good quality printing is produced at 40 to 200 cps.

Several different typefaces are built into some printers or supplied as additional ROMs and selected by switch or by the computer program. Figure 4.3.10 shows samples produced on such a printer manufactured by Malibu. Besides alternative fonts in ROM, some matrix printers provide for **downloading** (sending data from the computer.) A program gets font information from disk and sends it to a RAM in the printer. This is then referenced by the character generator. Sometimes you can even create you own fonts, but this is tedious and usually unnecessary.

The Ink Jet Printer

IBM has manufactured an ink jet printer for its Office System 6 since the late 1970s. The IBM 6640 sold for $23,000. Now the technology has become available at reasonable prices for the micro.

The character is formed by a matrix of ink dots which are sent to the paper as a jet. Because the ink is liquid, it tends to spread out more and characters look better than those produced by the mechanical matrix printer.

There is one jet for each dot, which appears along one of the vertical lines constituting a character. An electronically driven generator to create an ink jet includes an ink supply and a tiny crystal which vibrates because a high frequency voltage is applied to its sides. This breaks off tiny droplets, which are then ejected toward the paper.

As each ink jet travels toward the paper, it passes through a charged grid. For an undot, the grid is charged with a voltage to deflect the jet into a reservoir; it never hits the paper. If the grid is uncharged, the jet reaches the paper as a dot.

As with the matrix printer, the print line is stored in a buffer. As the print element approaches a new print position, the code for the character to be printed is sent to the ROM and the pattern of 1s and 0s for one of the vertical segments is extracted. This pattern is stored in a buffer and 0s activate the corresponding grid while 1s do not.

4.4 THE DAISY WHEEL PRINTER

The **daisy wheel printer** is so-called because its print element is a small disk from which spokes radiate. At the end of each spoke is a circular area on which is stamped a raised character as shown in Figure 4.4.1. The print element looks like a flower; the petals are type slugs. There are as many petals as characters that may be printed, usually 96. Figure 4.4.2 is a photo of a daisy wheel made by Qume.

The print element is centered in a carriage which also carries the ribbon. The print buffer stores codes of characters in the line to be printed. The carriage is in motion while a line is printed. As the carriage is on its way to the next position, after printing this character, the code is brought from the next position of the print buffer. Then the daisy wheel is rotated to the position which has that character.

Print Wheel Rotation

One petal on the daisy wheel is defined as **home.** A **petal table** stores a petal number for each character, counting its position from home.

Distance to Rotate

A microprocessor in the printer has a **petal register,** which stores the petal number of the last character printed. The number of petal positions to ro-

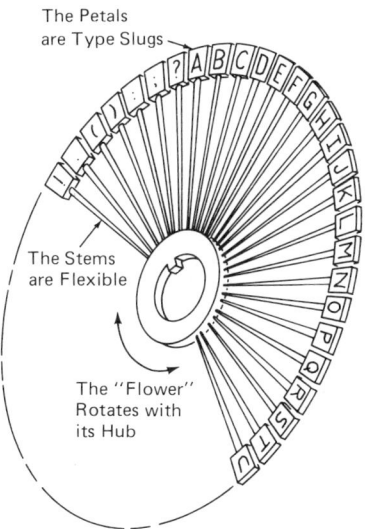

Figure 4.4.1. Typical daisy wheel configuration.

Figure 4.4.2. Daisy wheel by Qume.

tate the daisy wheel to the next selected petal is the difference between the number in the petal register and the number of the desired petal. The microprocessor finds the petal number for this code in the petal table and then calculates the difference, call it D.

Suppose the number in the petal register is 27 and the number in the petal table for next character to print is 41. Then the wheel should rotate $41 - 27 = 14 \ (= D)$ positions forward.

The printer's electronics sends 14 pulses to the motor to rotate the daisy wheel. The selected petal is positioned while the carriage moves. When the carriage arrives at the next print position, the hammer hits the chosen petal against the ribbon to make the ink impression.

Other Direction

Suppose the described petal number is 20. With 27 in the petal register, $D = 20 - 27 = -7$. Thus the print wheel should rotate 7 positions in the *other* direction. Since the petal motor is **bidirectional** and rotates in either direction, the microprocessor simply tells it *how many* positions to go, and in *which direction*.

Optimizing

Assume the petal register still contains 27, but the destination is 90. Subtraction yields $D = 90 - 27 = 63$. If the maximum rotation is 96, this represents more than half a revolution. It is quicker to rotate a smaller distance in the other direction. The microprocessor compares each distance (63 here) to half a revolution (48). If smaller (D less than 48), that quantity is used; if larger (D equal or greater than 48, the case here) then it is subtracted from 48 $(48 - 63) = -15$ and the wheel moves in the opposite direction by this number of petals (15).

Daisy wheel printers are made by Ricoh, Diablo, Qume and NEC (the last using a thimble, instead), to name a few, and sell for $1,800 to $4,000. They produce letter quality output at between 20 and 60 cps. More economical (Brother) but slower versions (13–16 cps) have recently dipped well below the $1,000 barrier, down to $500. A small firm with little correspondence might make good use of such a product.

An external printer buffer as shown in Figure 4.3.7 for the dot matrix printer, may also be used with the daisy wheel printer.

Print Wheel

The daisy wheel is removable; it comes in a variety of type faces and is made in different materials. Plastic wheels are less expensive and print at top speeds, but wear out after several million impressions, degrading in the process. Metal wheels provide a better impression from the start and last several times longer than plastic but cost more. A metal wheel does not print at as high a speed as a plastic wheel because it is heavier. Plastic wheels seem good enough for business use and have taken over the market.

It takes only a few seconds to remove one daisy wheel or thimble and mount another. Italics or a different font can be employed several times on the same page for word processors with operator intervention twice for each change. Smaller type faces can be used to print wide reports.

4.5 THE LINE PRINTER

The **line printer** is so-called because it seems to print a line at a time. Its printing rate is generally much higher than printers discussed so far and is measured in **lines per minute (lpm).** Printing speeds range from 300 lpm to 2,000 lpm or more. (High end dot matrix printers are becoming competitive.) Line printers found in medium and large computer installations usually print only upper case; they print faster this way. They *can* print lower case too, at a sacrifice in speed, if you change the chain.

The central component of the line printer is a carrier for a set of engraved type slugs. There are several ways to mount and carry the slugs along the paper, named the chain, train, and belt.

For both the **chain** and **train,** each metal or plastic type slug is independently mounted and hooked together with a pivot arrangement. At the top and bottom of each slug is a sprocket hole. The result looks like a chain, and is moved by two sprocket drives as shown in Figure 4.5.1.

For the **belt,** each slug is cemented to a polyeurethene and fiberglass belt. This moves at high speed, driven by spindles, one at either end.

Printing

The printing arrangement is shown in Figure 4.5.2. The "endless" circular belt of type slugs moves continuously at high speed. Behind the belt is an inked ribbon the length of the paper, then the paper.

Within the belt is a set of hammers, one for each print position along the paper. Each hammer is separately activated. When a character on the belt is aligned at a print position where it should print, the hammer behind it hits the slug sharply against the inked ribbon to print the desired character.

Transmitting the Line

Character codes representing the print line are transmitted from the computer, received by the printer and put in the **print buffer** shown in Figure 4.5.2. Printing does not begin until the complete line image is there.

A **character buffer** records the code for each character slug which momentarily occupies each position on the belt. As the belt moves, this buffer

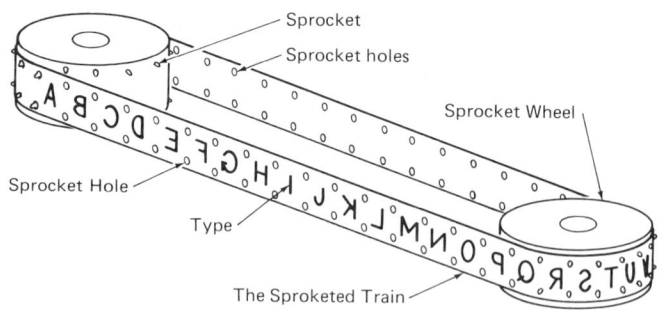

Figure 4.5.1. The print chain.

4.5 THE LINE PRINTER

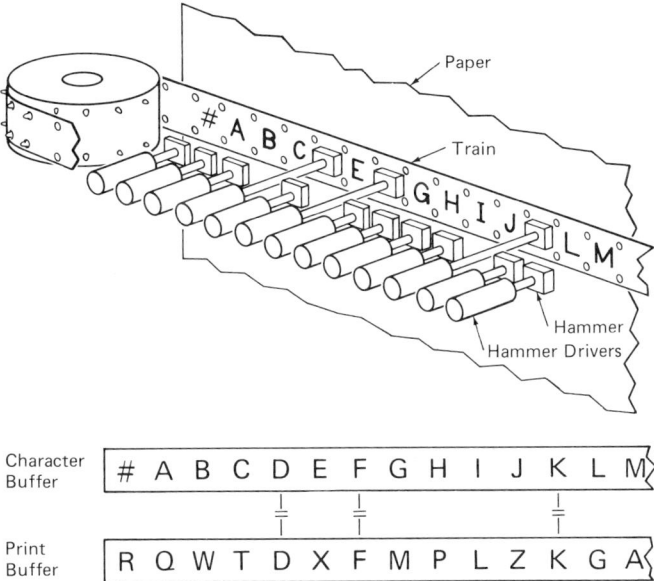

Figure 4.5.2. The character and print buffer.

is updated to record which slug is at each position. As the chain reaches a print position boundary, the print buffer and the character buffer are compared. Where the character codes in the two coincide, the corresponding hammer drivers are set. At the proper instant they are activated, the hammers hit those slugs and an impression of *only* those characters is made.

In the figure, the hammers are printing D, F, and K. Slugs on the chain are of fixed widths and should only strike at fixed print positions along the paper. Note that each time the slugs get to a print position, none, one, several or all the slugs may be hit simultaneously.

Print Complete

The maximum time to print a line occurs when, for some print position, the proper letter is just passing by. Hence we have to wait for another copy of that character to appear at this print position. However, the chain may have several copies of the alphabet on it, so that the maximum time to print a line might be a half or a quarter of a revolution.

The maximum time to print a line is the time for one set of the alphabet to pass by. Usually the message is printed in less than that. To determine when the printer is available to print the next line, we keep track of whether each character in the message has been printed with an extra bit in the print buffer. Printing is complete when this bit is on for *all* characters in the print buffer.

When properly maintained, the line printer produces good quality printing at high speed. Line printers cost from $5,000 to several hundred thousand dollars, according to speed and size.

4.6 THE LASER PRINTER

Like the electron beam for the CRT display, the laser beam in this printer sweeps from one side of the paper to the other. It is turned on and off to produce dots and undots as with the dot matrix printer and has the dot matrix printer's flexibility regarding characters and buffers. The beam prints by putting a charge on a drum much like xerographic copiers. The charged area picks up pigment particles which are transferred to the paper. The paper is then chemically fixed so the pigment does not scrape off. This action is shown in Figure 4.6.1.

This was an expensive device costing hundreds of thousands of dollars and found only in large computer environments. However, it is now within reach of the larger small business. We have the IBM 6670, the Xerox 5700 (under $29,000) and Hewlett Packard has a product for its minicomputer. By this book's publication, models costing under $5,000 should be available for use with micros. A number of different character generators can be referenced for boldface, italics and additional character fonts to be mixed in the same line. Graphics, such as charts and drawings, can be mixed in.

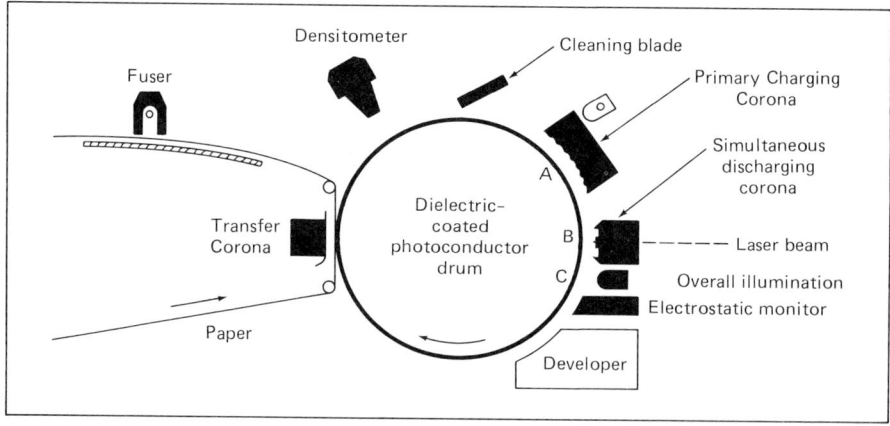

Figure 4.6.1. How the laser printer works.

4.7 MOTION IN THE PRINTER

Motion is required to put the right character on the paper in the right position. What moves?

1. The print element moves along the paper horizontally;
2. The paper moves up (or down) vertically from one line or page to the next;
3. The ribbon passes beneath the print element to provide fresh ink.

These motions are examined in that order.

Print Element Advance

During printing, the paper is held fixed between the platen and the paper bail as shown in Figure 4.2.1. The carriage moves the print element to the desired print position. The print element creates an image of the correct character. For some printers, printing occurs only at fixed positions along the line, while, for the others, character positions may be varied in discrete increments.

Fixed

The golf ball, dot matrix and chain/train printers usually position the type at fixed column positions along the width of the paper. The golf ball advances one position after each strike. For the chain, the proper slug is aligned in a column position before the hammer strikes it.

Variable

For the daisy wheel and some dot matrix printers, the carriage moves in **increments,** usually $1/120$ inch. The number of increments that the carriage moves is controlled by the computer. **Horizontal pitch,** or simply **pitch,** is rated in characters per inch (**cpi**). There are three standard pitches: 10, 12 and 16.5. Sometimes pitch is controlled locally within the printer and may be set by a switch on the front panel. Pitch of 10 and 12 cps correspond to elite and pica type respectively and are standard typewriter sizes; they are used for correspondence. The narrow pitch of 16.5 is harder to read but good for business applications. Thus you can squeeze down a standard 132 column printout to print on 8½ by 11 paper. **Justification**—all lines the same width—is controlled by the print program by varying the spacing between print positions. Proportional spacing (see below) may also be under program control.

Some dot matrix printers provide **compressed** (narrow characters) and **expanded** (wide) type (see Figure 4.3.7). The former prints a full size computer printout (132 columns) on 8½ by 11 paper, across the 11 inch width. Expanded type is for titles and emphasis. Also, to supplement the more usual fixed width character, some printers provide for **proportional spacing,** in which, for example, "i" occupies less space than "m."

Bidirectional

The typewriter moves the carriage rightward as each key is pressed; It returns to the left margin when you hit *return*. This full line reverse motion of the carriage takes only a fraction of the time spent moving forward—and besides, who can type backwards?

Since the daisy wheel and dot matrix printer speed are so fast, the time for the return of the carriage is now a large fraction of the forward printing time. That reverse time can be put to use if the carriage prints also from right to left during its return trip. And why not? The print mechanism itself couldn't care less which way the carriage is moving.

But you keyed in each line from left to right. That is the way the application program stores it, displays it and records it on disk. To improve print speed, the program or print driver can reverse alternate text lines as it sends them to the printer. This takes advantage of the speed gained by **bidirectional printing,** printing alternate lines in alternate directions. Some printers (Epson for example) have this capability built into them; they reverse the scan direction of the print buffer as the carriage moves from right to left while printing. Then the program can send *all* lines as though scanned left to right.

Line Advance

Line advance is vertical paper movement to position the next line on the paper for printing. There are three types of paper feed mechanisms:

- friction feed;
- pin feed;
- tractor feed.

Friction Feed

Friction feed is found on typewriters and used for manual feed on most printers. The paper is held between the platen and the paper guide. The platen is made of rubber or a similar compound with a rough surface. The metal paper guide is slippery; when the platen moves, friction takes the paper for a ride.

Friction feed is used with separate hand-fed pages. However, when it comes to continuous stock, friction does not maintain proper alignment of the paper for more than a few pages.

Pin Feed

A **pin feed** printer requires a platen with pins projecting radially at both ends, as shown in Figure 4.7.1; continuous stock has holes punched in both margins. The pins on the platen fit into these holes. The platen advances the paper positively, maintaining its alignment indefinitely. But the pins in the platen are set a fixed distance apart and can be used with only one width of stock.

Tractor Feed

The **tractor feed** handles many different widths of stock. Figure 4.7.2 shows an adjustable tractor which handles forms from a couple of inches to the maximum width of the platen.

In Figure 4.7.3, as the paper emerges from the paper guide, it passes over the tractor feed. Two sprocket hole guides at opposite ends of the feed may be moved horizontally in either direction and clamped in place with thumb screws. In this way it can handle narrow label stock (3") and wide (14") accounting paper.

Continuous paper is inserted so that the pins in the guides fit into the holes in the paper. A hinged clamp holds the paper against the guide and keeps the pins in the sprocket holes. When the printer gets a line feed signal,

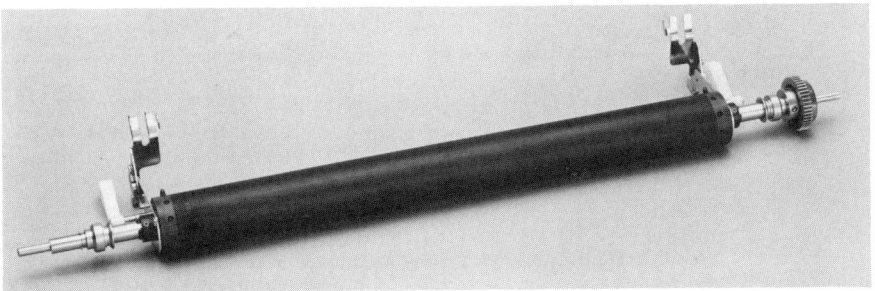

Figure 4.7.1. The pin feed platen.

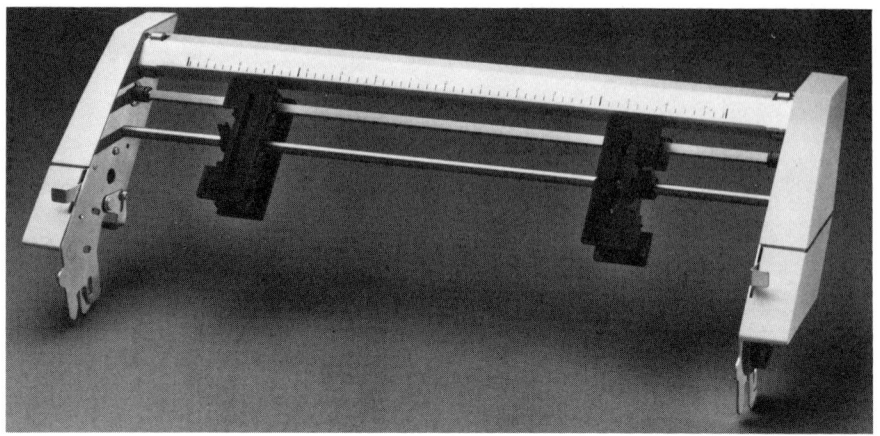

Figure 4.7.2. The tractor feed.

Figure 4.7.3. Adjusting the tractor feed.

a **stepping motor** geared to the sprocket wheels advances the paper by as many notches as set on the printer control panel or dictated by control signals from the program.

> *Note:* The friction feed should always be disengaged when either the pin feed or tractor feed is in use. Otherwise, the feed holes in the paper get mangled and alignment is altered or feeding interrupted.

The tractor is removable (in about 15 seconds) so that single sheets may be handled with the friction feed. Some paper suppliers take single sheets, such as your letterhead, or envelopes and paste them on a continuous backing with feed holes to be handled like continuous forms. These may be alternated, letter head then envelope, to associate the two.

Quantity and Direction

The number of lines per inch (**lpi**) for vertical paper advance (**line advance**) has two standards, 6 lpi (elite) and 8 lpi (pica) as on the typewriter. **Line spacing** describes one or more extra lines inserted between text lines; **single spacing** provides no *extra* space between lines of print; **double spacing** provides one empty line between printed lines; **triple spacing** two empty lines, and so forth. However, the daisy wheel and some dot matrix printers provide a finer granularity of paper advance with 48 vertical units per inch being common. The number of vertical units per line advanced is under program control. A word processing program may allow you to select intermediate line spacings to achieve more attractive page makeup. With almost continuous control of line spacing, you can get, for example, 1½ (a half line space between lines) or 1¼ line spacing.

If the computer can control the *direction* of line spacing and the printer can also move the paper backwards, a number of important WP features can be easily implemented, including **subscripts** and **superscripts** (for example, a^2 [the "two" is a superscript] and a_2 [subscript]).

Feeding Paper

Paper is fed by the printer in different ways. For continuous **fan fold** paper with small holes on each side, the printer has either a pin feed or a tractor feed. The pin feed is built into the platen and handles paper of fixed width. The tractor feed is detachable and adjustable. For manual feed you insert the paper, align it and clamp it. The printer advances the paper and ejects the page when it is printed.

Continuous roll feed moves paper from a roll mounted on pivots into the printer by friction. The paper tends to get out of alignment and there are often no perforations for separating one sheet from the next. It is not recommended.

Tractor Feed

The tractor (and pin feed) have two advantages:

- No stopping is required between pages.
- The printer can work continuously unattended.

The main disadvantages of the tractor feed are (1) limitations on the kind of paper stock which can be used and (2) the processing which is necessary after printing—tearing apart the sheets of paper, called **bursting**; trimming the half inch with the feed holes from each side of each sheet. After this is done, the page still has slightly ragged edges on each of its four sides.

A large number of preprinted continuous forms are available for invoices, purchase orders, telex forms, payroll checks and so forth. You can select from these and the vendor will add your letterhead or logo at a small additional charge.

Manual

The manual feed has the advantage that it takes most shapes of paper. You can use your letterhead or any kind of paper, form or stock. On the other hand, the manual printer requires the presence of an operator to

1. Put the paper into the printer and turn the platen to align the paper;
2. Watch for completion;
3. Remove the printed sheet and stack it.

Automatic Sheet Feed

This feature is important for word processing but not for other business applications. The sheet feeder has one and sometimes two hoppers where you place paper commonly used in your office. Some feeders also take envelopes. Printed sheets move to an output stacker.

Ribbon

The line printer uses a wide ribbon of a single color. The other three impact printer types use ribbon cartridges. Figure 4.7.4 shows how a cartridge is inserted into a dot matrix printer. Ribbons come in three varieties:

- Inked cloth ribbon of one color winds from one spool to another until the end is reached. The spool mechanism resets automatically to wind in the other direction. The ribbon is thus reused many times until someone notices that the impressions are faint and changes it.
- Inked cloth of two colors works the same way, but the print color can be changed between black and red by the program. You can print debits in red!
- The "multistrike" cartridge contains Mylar plastic ribbon coated with carbon which makes an excellent dark impression when struck, but this ribbon cannot be reused. With each strike the ribbon is advanced a fraction of a character width. When the spool is wound completely to one end, an alarm notifies the operator to change the ribbon.

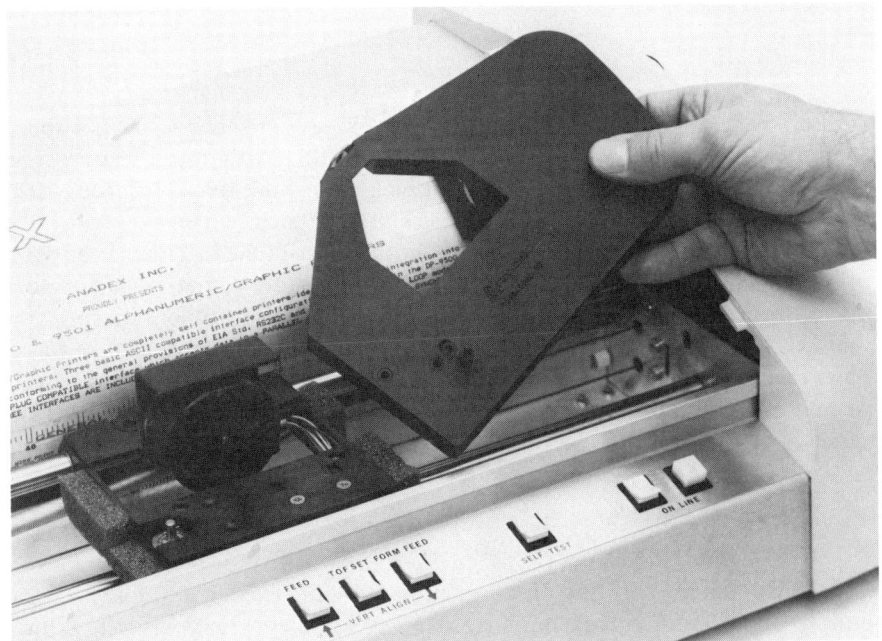

Figure 4.7.4. Installing a ribbon cartridge.

Cartridge

Except for the line printer, ribbon is furnished in a cartridge (much like the typewriter ribbon cartridge) which you can quickly load without touching it or dirtying your hands. There is no standard shape or size for cartridges and they are *not* interchangeable between different manufacturers or models. Cartridges can cost from $5.00 to $50.00 each and seem to disappear quickly. Because of their expense, an industry has risen which replaces or reinks the ribbon in used cartridges for about 60% of the cost of a new one. Some vendors now seal their cartridges to prevent reuse.

4.8 SUMMARY: CHOOSING A PRINTER

This section summarizes the factors to consider in acquiring a printer. Then it examines the needs of various classes of users.

Factors

Print Speed

Printers vary in speed from 15 cps to many pages per second. Output speed for business applications is important. No printer with speed less than 50 cps should be considered except for supplementary use for word processing. Speed costs money. High speed printers are the most expensive.

There are transition points which should be watched. That is, as your printer needs increase, you may consider going from a matrix printer to a line printer. You should also consider the alternative of purchasing two matrix printers. Since printers are the component most prone to need repairs (see below), two matrix printers that do the job might be preferable to one line printer. In this way, should one printer fail, during repair the other is available.

Quality

The daisy wheel and the laser printer provide excellent quality—good enough for all your correspondence. However, unless you *do* use the printer for correspondence, that quality goes to waste. All the printers described are satisfactory for documents for internal consumption.

Print Refinements

Refinements in printing are somewhat different than print quality. **Print quality** refers to the uniformity of the printing, how well each letter is formed and the final appearance of the document on the paper.

Here are some of the features which are referred to as **print refinements:**

1. A small *character* advance increment permits complete line justification and proportional spacing for documents hard to distinguish from the printed page.
2. A small *line* advance increment and the ability to move paper downwards can create subscripts and superscripts.
3. Interchangeable type wheels let you print in different type faces, including those for foreign languages.

Operating Attention

It is important in the business environment to have a printer which operates with little human attention. This need demands continuous form feed. A tractor feed is best except where correspondence is concerned. This device lets you attach a box of 3000 sheets of fan fold paper for computer activated feed through the printer.

Where correspondence is concerned, letter head is most frequently used. When fed by hand it slows down operation considerably. An automatic sheet feed overcomes this.

Cost

The least expensive dot matrix printer costs about $500; the most expensive laser printers cost over $300,000. A great variety of printers exists between the bottom and top of this range.

Maintenance

The printer works hard in your system. It is mechanical and its parts are subject to considerable wear. It is the system component most liable to fail. Even the cheapest printers can operate reliably over a period of a few months, but if you have just one printer and it fails, you won't be able to get out any reports, invoices or correspondence until it is fixed.

A maintenance call without a **maintenance contract** is hard to come by.

Without one, you may have to wait days. Therefore it is highly advisable that you have a maintenance contract with a reliable firm. Chapter 10 discusses maintenance of computer equipment and indicates ways that you can verify that your contractor is reliable.

Your Needs

You have to balance your needs and the availability of the various types of printers against your budget. Here are some examples of alternatives.

If you are a small business seeking to automate operations without introducing word processing, then choose an inexpensive dot matrix printer such as the Epson MX-80, Okidata 92 or the Epson MX-100. The medium quality low cost devices in this category can print at 80 to 100 cps and have a low breakdown record. As you gain confidence in your system, you may wish to acquire a more reliable and more expensive additional printer, retaining the first printer as a backup should difficulty arise. Or if this one seems to produce adequately, your alternative might be another of the same type.

For a small business which also wants word processing, two printers are advisable: a dot matrix printer provides for your business needs; a low cost daisy wheel produces high quality correspondence at low speed and is back up for the dot matrix printer.

As your print output increases, you may wish to migrate to a line printer, with high speed and medium quality output.

5
External Storage

5.1 INTRODUCTION

Importance

The importance of external storage cannot be overestimated. Computer memory is volatile—whatever is there disappears when you turn the power off. The only safe place for information is on an external medium.

All media of any importance to modern computing use magnetic recording principles. You might think that such materials would be prone to loss by exposure to magnetic fields except for intentional vandalism. Experience with audio and video tapes tell us this is highly unlikely.

Still, some precautions should be taken when handling these media. Considerable information is concentrated in a little floppy disk; some can hold a good size book in machine readable form. Carelessness could destroy all or part of a valuable document stored on it.

This chapter tells you all you need to know about the most important computer subsystem, the disk drive, and the disks that it uses, what specifications for the drive mean and the differences among disks. These topics require the technical background provided in Section 5.2. Some of it you may skim through; you can concentrate on other parts when you need particular information.

A lot of the computer's resources are devoted to handling data stored on external storage. This includes both hardware and software. We examine these facilities in the next part of this section. Then we preview the rest of this chapter.

Data Flow

Figure 5.1.1 shows the flow of data and control signals with respect to the exchange of data between a program and an external medium. In the figure, data is exchanged with the floppy disk shown at the extreme right. Data

112 EXTERNAL STORAGE

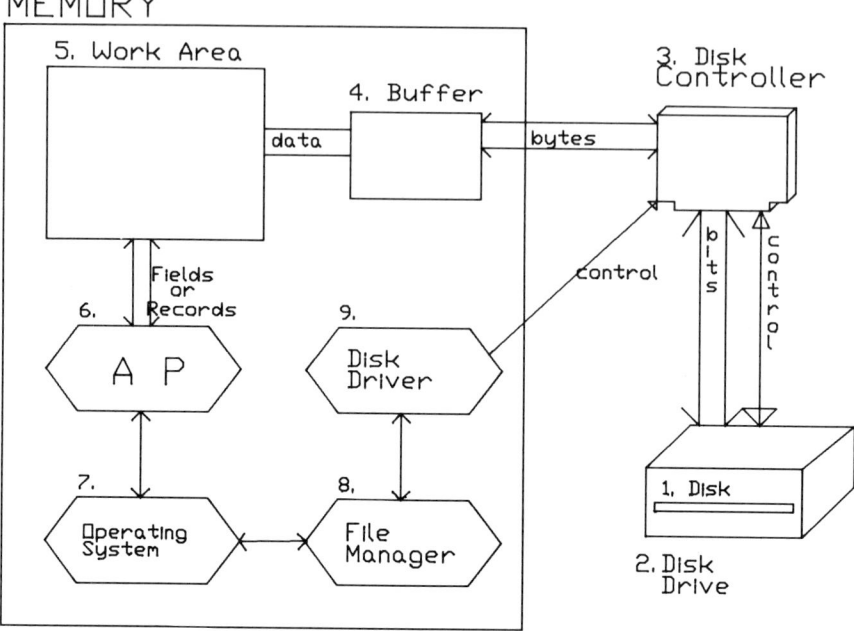

Figure 5.1.1. Data and control flow in disk I/O (drawn on AutoCAD system described in Chapter 16).

flow is shown by wide arrows, double headed because information can flow in either direction—from the program to the disk or from the disk to the program.

Input

Input brings information from external storage to the program. Let us examine input data flow using the numbers in the figure to help the discussion. Data are stored on the disk (1) When directed by the drive, data flow from the disk to the drive (2) which places signals on the cable, sending them to the **disk controller** in the computer. This is usually a PC board in a slot of the computer chassis (3). The disk controller puts the data in memory in a **buffer** (4). The **File Manager** is the operating system component which moves the data from the buffer to a work area in memory (5) where it is available to the application program (6).

Output

Output sends data from the program's work area to the device; it occurs in the opposite sequence. The application program (6) puts information to be written on the disk into the work area (5). The File Manager puts chunks of this data into the buffer (4). These pass to the disk controller as needed (3). Data are sent to the disk drive (2) when the proper place on the disk (1) is found.

Software

Software is shown in Figure 5.1.1 as hexagons. Requests for input and output come from the application programs (6) and go to the operating system (7). A request is interpreted by the operating system and in the case of **I/O** (input or output) is forwarded to the OS component, the File Manager (8). The File Manager gets a request in relative terms and converts it into a **physical request,** a command to move data with respect to an exact physical location on the disk. The File Manager forwards a physical request to the operating system component called the **disk driver** (9). The disk driver converts it into a sequence of computer commands which goes to the disk controller (3) to run the disk drive (2).

Information passes between software components in the form of control messages. These are shown in the figure as single lines pass in either direction.

Chunks of Data

For later reference, the figure shows the quantity of information between various points in this system. Examine this with respect to input. Data comes from the disk as a stream of bits (1–2). This stream is picked up by the drive and passed over, again as a stream of bits, to the disk controller (2–3). They accumulate here and are passed as bytes to the buffer (3–4). The buffer holds a block of information which is put into the work area (4–5). The application program views the data in terms of records further divided into fields (5–6). These are standard terms which have not been introduced but are explained in this chapter or Chapter 9 on data structure.

Chapter Overview

Section 5.2 describes in simple terms how magnetic recording takes place and the general structure of magnetic media. Although it is not too technical, you may skip it without impairing your understanding of the rest of the chapter.

Section 5.3 describes the disk drive and how it acquires data from the disk or records information in the proper area of the disk. The next section describes the diskette itself and what its specifications mean. Then section 5.5 examines the form of data on the disk. Here we look at the file and get an initial impression of its structure. We see how files are found and how the software keeps track of available empty space.

Hard disks are important to business applications because they store lots of information and do it quickly; this gets attention in Section 5.6.

With some concept of the technical aspects of disks and drivers, Section 5.7 looks at some of the considerations: buying, storing and using disks of various kinds.

5.2 MAGNETIC RECORDING

Principles

The principles of magnetic recording apply to all magnetic media, regardless of their form: magnetic cards, floppy diskettes, magnetic tape (cassette or reel-to-reel) and hard disk drives with fixed and removable packs.

Medium

Data are stored on a very thin uniform coating of magnetic material. This coating is mainly iron with other metals like cobalt and manganese mixed in to get an attractive set of magnetic properties. The coating is applied to a plastic disk (sometimes metal for hard disks) called the **substrate,** which may be rigid or flexible. Most magnetic media on the small business scene are flexible Mylar, such as tape and floppy disks. (Hard disks are rigid.)

The important property of the coating is that it is magnetizable by a magnet placed on or near the disk surface. The coating area near the magnet retains the magnetism indefinitely after the magnet is removed. Yet the medium can be remagnetized to hold new data. It is reusable.

The Data

Magnets are **polarized:** one end of a bar magnet is the **North pole** and the other end is the **South pole.** It is easy to distinguish one pole from the other by using another magnet. Opposite poles attract; like poles repel. (A small compass tells you which pole is which.)

In the simplest system, the polarity of the magnet is the means for recording data. But we want to use the magnets to record 1s and 0s. The polarity of the recorded magnet lets us tell a 0 from a 1. The North pole of the magnet points one way for a recorded 1 and in the opposite direction for a 0 as in Figure 5.2.1.

Simplified, entering bits is writing little magnets pointing in one direction or the other. The medium has to be in motion to recover the data. The

5.2 MAGNETIC RECORDING   115

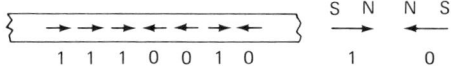

Figure 5.2.1. Magnets have North and South poles.

tape, mag card or floppy disk is moved at a *constant* speed to extract data from or enter data onto the medium.

A single head to both read and write is a fraction of an inch wide. As the medium passes beneath, it sweeps out a thin long area called a **track.**

Read

The **head** is a soft iron bar bent so that one end almost touches the other, as shown in Figure 5.2.2. It is a circular horseshoe. The space between the ends of the horseshoe is the **gap**; the iron horseshoe is called the **core**. Wire wound around the middle of the core is called the **coil.**

When a magnet on the medium sits beneath the gap, its magnetic field, shown in the figure as lines of force, prefers to go through the soft iron rather than through the air. Many lines of force coming out of the North pole are detoured through the core to return to the South pole of the magnet. They pass through the top of the core and through the coil of wire. As long as these lines of force remain constant, they have no effect on the coil of wire. If they change intensity, they generate a voltage in this coil.

When the little magnet on the medium sits still in the gap, nothing happens. Move the medium and the number of magnetic lines passing through the core changes and produces a voltage in the coil. This voltage is picked up and amplified by the electronics which also extracts the 0 and 1 information originally recorded on the medium.

Since the coil responds only to a changing magnetic field, you see how important it is for the medium to move. If the speed of the medium past the gap is kept constant, it is easier to extract 0s and 1s from the voltages produced in the coil.

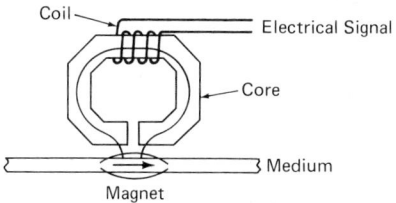

Figure 5.2.2. The recording head.

116 EXTERNAL STORAGE

Writing

To write on the medium with the same head, write electronics is switched in to replace the read electronics. The medium passes below the head at a constant speed. A current sent through the wire produces a magnetic field in the core. When the field reaches the gap, it is easier for it to travel through the metal coating on the medium then across the gap. When the electrical current stops flowing, this removes the magnetic field. The magnet recorded on the medium remains there and can be read back later.

The direction of flow of the electric current determines the direction of the magnetic field and whether the magnet on the medium has a North pole which faces right or left (0 or 1).

Shape of the Medium

Figure 5.2.3 shows three important shapes for the medium. In the middle we see a long, thin tape. At the left is a disk; at the right is a flat rectangle.

The tape in the middle may contain a single track or a set of seven or nine tracks (Figure 5.2.4). The disk has two surfaces on which many circular tracks may be placed. The rectangle represents the mag card containing many parallel tracks going from one side to the other (for word processing but of little use in the business world).

Magnetic Tape

Magnetic tape was the first external erasable computer-controlled storage medium. Tapes between ½ and 1 inch wide store large quantities of infor-

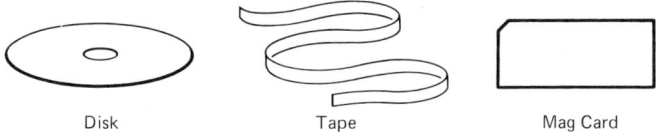

Figure 5.2.3. Magnetic medium shapes.

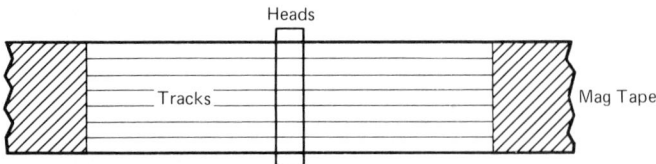

Figure 5.2.4. Tracks on a magnetic tape.

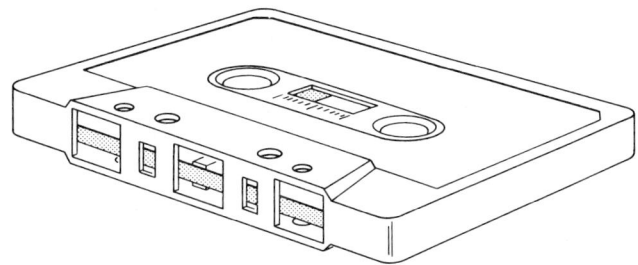

Figure 5.2.5. The cassette.

mation. Such tapes are of little importance in the small business world because the drives are expensive—$20,000 or more, well above the price of a full microsystem.

Tape was one of the first media to be associated with personal computing. The **cassette** shown in Figure 5.2.5 contains several hundred feet of magnetic tape, ⅛ to ¼ of an inch in width. One head both records and reads the tape. Mass-produced cassettes for audio equipment are inexpensive. For computing, a form of digital recording writes and reads from these cassettes. Cassettes are still used with the home computer. You can get games and home application programs on them, but they are not adequate for business applications.

The floppy disk and the hard disk are so important for the small business computer that separate sections are devoted to them.

5.3 DISK DRIVES

Physical Features

The **disk** *is* the medium; the **disk drive,** is a mechanical and electrical device which holds and rotates the disk, and reads from or writes onto the disk. Some disk units accommodate more than one drive. The disk(s) on one drive automatically accessible without operator intervention is called a **volume.** For floppy drives, the volume is a single floppy, which is **removable.** A volume is built in and cannot be removed from some rigid drives.

The Disk

Figure 5.3.1 shows a floppy disk; it looks like a 45 rpm phonograph record without grooves. Data is on invisible tracks. A small rectangle in the figure represents the head, which moves in both directions horizontally. A head positioning mechanism moves precisely to one of many horizontal posi-

118　EXTERNAL STORAGE

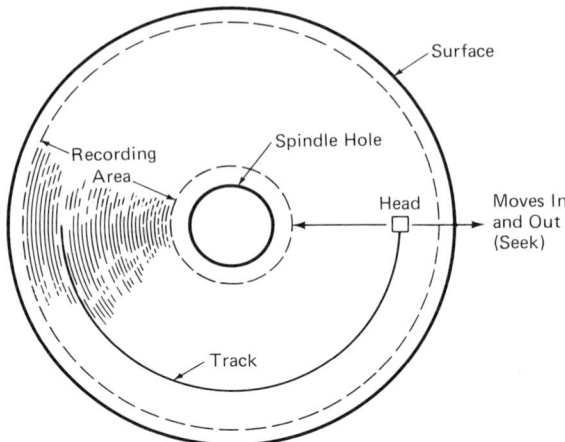

Figure 5.3.1. The floppy.

tions. Here, with the head motionless, as the disk rotates, a thin circular band the width of the head gap called a **track** passes beneath the head. One track is defined for *each* of the possible positions the head can take.

The recording area where data may be stored starts at the outer edge of the disk but does not go to the center. The center area of the disk is not suitable for recording because it moves too slowly, just as with a long playing record. Between the outer edge and the inner recording limit, a number of tracks are defined by the discrete spots where the head may stop. This number, the **tracks per surface,** is fixed. It can vary for different kinds of drives from a total of about 35 to 96 tracks on minifloppies and 77 on floppies to 400 or more on large disks.

Multiple Surfaces

A volume, for hard drives, may consist of more than one disk. Each disk consists of two **physical surfaces,** its top and bottom. The volume shown in Figure 5.3.2 has four disks and eight physical surfaces. All surfaces are

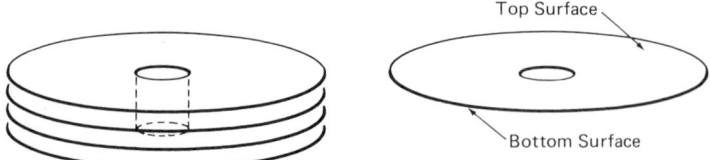

Figure 5.3.2. A disk pack has several disk with two surfaces.

coated with magnetic material. Sometimes not all surfaces are used for recording. The four disks shown in the figure may have only six **recording surfaces.** There is one head for each recording surface and this is called a **head-per-surface drive.**

One (or more) head is mounted on an **arm** which moves in and out horizontally, at the request of the computer. Called **seeking,** this operation positions the head accurately to a selected track. The time to position the head to the desired track, the **seek time,** is proportional to the distance between the tracks; it takes longer to go from track 1 to track 21 than to go from track 5 to track 10.

With multiple surfaces, a single arm has fingers holding two or more heads and moves between adjacent surfaces. The arm positions all heads at once: if the head on the first surface is on track 10, the heads for all the other surfaces are also on track 10. The set of tracks defined by each position of the arm is called a **cylinder.** Cylinder 16, for a six surface volume, contains track 16 on surface 1, 2, 3, etc., here a total of six tracks.

Timing

The disk has circular tracks which have no beginning or end. To make it possible to find specific areas of data, a timing signal originating on the disk itself establishes the start of each track, designated as **home.** This is a synthetic beginning for each track to which all data is referenced.

Sectors

Secondary markers reference smaller amounts of data. **Sector markers** at fixed positions along the track separate the data into sectors as shown in Figure 5.3.3.

A track is easier to visualize when cut apart at the home position and spread it out along a straight line, as in Figure 5.3.4. A track begins at home and contains a number of **sectors,** data between two consecutive sector markers. Sectors are numbered sequentially from home; the first sector is numbered 0, the second is numbered 1, and so forth.

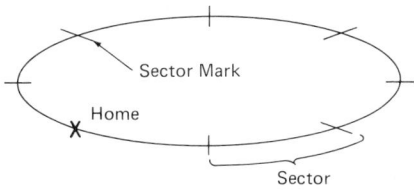

Figure 5.3.3. A track is divided into sectors.

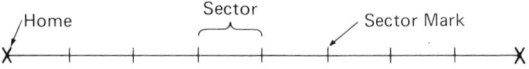

Figure 5.3.4. A track begins and ends with home.

Marking

There are two ways to mark sectors. **Hard sectoring** marks sectors by the position of small holes in the floppy disk. The disk spins between a light source and a photocell. When a sector hole passes, the light hits the photocell to produce the sector signal.

A **format program** is another way to mark sectors; it writes identifiers at the beginning of *every* sector on the disk. Before a new volume is used, this program must be run to **format the volume.** The program writes identifiers for each sector at fixed intervals along every track. These identifiers may be rewritten later, should the format program be rerun. They are not permanent; that is why disks used this way are called **soft sectored.**

Usually the format program also

1. Checks the disk to see if it can write and read back successfully on *all* tracks;
2. Creates a directory to keep track of your files;
3. May write a copy of the operating system, as with Apple II.

The two methods of sector marking are equally reliable.

Data

The drive reads and writes data in units of one sector. Commands to request reading and writing come from the computer. Each sector read or written and every function performed needs a separate command. Reading or writing takes place only when the head is over the desired track *and* the sector arrives beneath the head. To identify the sector we ask

1. If there are several surfaces, which surface is desired?
2. Which track?
3. Which sector on the track?

The Sector

Figure 5.3.5 shows the general makeup of a sector. At the left, for hard sectoring only, the sector is announced by an optically sensed timing signal.

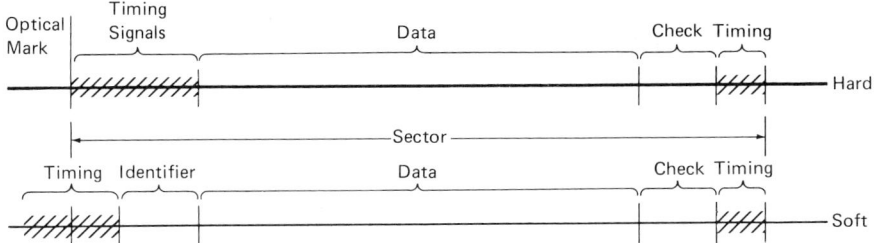

Figure 5.3.5. A sector is different for hard and soft sectoring.

Following this (or at the beginning of a soft sector), a number of timing pulses are written to make sure that the electronics is in synchronism with the signals coming from the head. Next, an identifier, provided only for soft sectoring, lists this surface, track and sector number. Data follow and consist of bits grouped into bytes. A sector usually holds 128, 256 or 516 bytes of data.

After the last data byte are two additional bytes for checking, called the **cyclic redundancy check** or **CRC,** discussed shortly. Following the CRC, timing pulses fill the area up to the beginning of the next sector. This compensates for slight variations in speed when the disk is moved to another drive.

Checking

It is essential to insure data accuracy. The electronic document or customer record that you wrote yesterday should be the same when you edit it or refer to it today. Two kinds of checking may be provided:

- a parity check bit in each byte;
- a CRC at the end of every sector.

Parity

A parity bit checks each byte. Odd parity is standard. (It is possible to use even parity.) For **odd parity,** one bit is added to the seven bit ASCII code for every character. This eighth bit, the **parity bit,** is set to 1 or 0 so that there is always an *odd* number of 1s in the byte. If a character code is read with an even number of 1s, this is a **parity error** (since it was *written* with an odd number of 1s. What the system does when a parity error is found usually depends on the operating system (see Chapter 7).

CRC

A standard but complex operation is performed with the bits of the data sent to the disk drive as the unaltered data are *written* into the sector. This operation comes up with a set of sixteen bits for the sector data being written and is next written as the last two bytes of the sector, the **CRC (cyclic redundancy check).**

Later the disk drive *reads* data from the sector and performs this same set of operations on them. The result is another set of 16 bits, the **calculated CRC.** If the *calculated CRC* is the *same* as the CRC bits *recorded* at the end of the sector, there is an excellent chance that the data is absolutely correct.

Although many disk systems do not use parity, almost all use the CRC.

Drivers, Blocks and Sectors

The disk drive is run by the hardware **disk controller** shown in Figure 5.1.1. After a sector is read or written, control goes back to a program called the **disk driver.** This is part of the operating system which runs the disk drive (see Section 7.2). The disk driver tells the disk drive each action it should make.

It takes times for the disk driver program to make a decision. In the meantime, the disk itself continues to rotate. The situation is shown in Figure 5.3.6. Here sector 3 of some track has just been written. While the disk driver is making a decision, the disk rotates to sector 5. To enable the use the next data sequentially appearing on the track after sector 3, almost a full rotation is required before sector 4 appears again.

The Block

A **block** is the *quantity* of data held by one sector on the disk. The software which manages your file, the File Manager, sees a file as sequential blocks. Keeping blocks in corresponding sectors, block 0 in sector 0, block 1 in

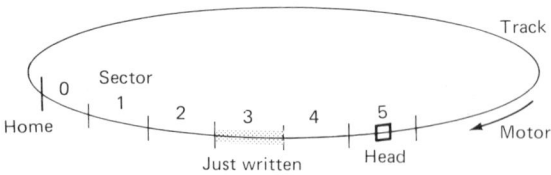

Figure 5.3.6. The next sector is gone before it can be used.

sector 1, and so forth, reduces the timing efficiency of the hardware. To write into four sequential sectors might take four revolutions. By the time the driver reaches a decision, one (or more) sector has passed beneath the write head; it takes a full revolution for the right sector to return.

Skewing

Skewing, or **interleaving,** reduces the time to read or write a full track. *Skew* is another word for *offset.* Instead of sequential blocks being put in sequential sectors, they are **offset.** The amount of the offset takes into consideration the longest decision making time required by the disk driver program.

Figure 5.3.7 shows a skewing scheme for an eight sector track. Sectors are numbered sequentially 0 to 7 (the first is numbered zero). Blocks are numbered 1 to 8, a more natural numbering system. Writing (reading) several sequentially numbered blocks into (from) the sectors assigned to them is definitely faster when skewing is employed.

Here's how to write blocks 2, 3, 4 and 5 in two revolutions. On command, the disk drive finds the desired track (the head seeks). After writing block 1 in sector 0, the controller watches for sector 3 to write block 2. Then the disk driver program determines that block 3 goes in sector 6. Meanwhile the disk turns. Perhaps the head is in the middle of sector 5 when the disk drive is activated. That is fine, because sector 6 is coming up next. Both blocks 2 and 3 can be written on the same revolution of the disk; blocks 4 and 5 are written on the next revolution.

Disk Software

There is considerable division of labor with respect to the tasks which are performed for **input** and **output** (other terms for reading and writing for the disk). Figure 5.3.8 shows the agencies involved in simple input and output activity. In memory we find two rectangles which represent work areas to hold transactions. There are three hexagons, each representing a program. The left hexagon is for an application program such as a general ledger or accounts receivable program. The other two are parts of the operating system.

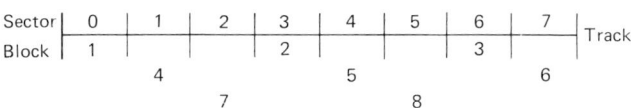

Figure 5.3.7. Interleaving.

124 EXTERNAL STORAGE

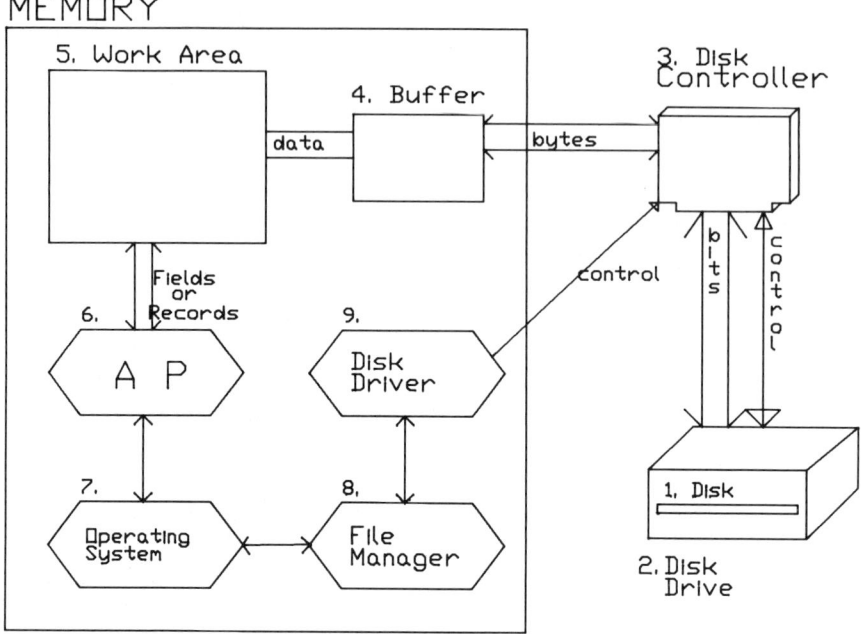

Figure 5.3.8. The software and hardware involved with the disk.

The hexagon labeled File Manager accepts a request from the application program in general terms such as by record number and converts it into specific terms such as block and track number for the disk driver. This driver program converts the request from the File Manager into commands which cause head movement, data acquisition and checking in the disk drive.

The disk controller is a hardware component. It accepts commands for physical motion and electrical action. It supervises actions in the mechanical disk drive. Signals from the disk drive tell the controller what is happening and it issues further signals to complete the action.

Finally, there is the disk itself. It contains the data. It is moved by the disk drive so that data can be either copied from or entered onto the disk.

The disk controller accepts only one command at a time from the computer. The hardware command may involve a number of simple mechanical actions within the drive. Signals may go back and forth between the controller and the drive during the course of this command. An area in memory, called a **buffer,** is set aside for data acted upon by the drive. A hardware command may either fill or empty this buffer (Figure 5.3.8). The device controller carries out the sequence of commands required to fill or empty the buffer. More details about file management are forthcoming (Section 7.3).

5.4 DISKETTES

The most popular external medium for the micro is the diskette. It is important to understand how the diskette is used and what the disk and drive specifications mean.

Physical Description

The **diskette** has several other names: sometimes it is called a **floppy disk** or simply a **floppy;** a smaller diskette is a **minifloppy** (5¼ inches) or **microfloppy** (3½ inches). We simply call it a **disk** or **floppy** for brevity. A sandwich consisting of a thin coated plastic disk between two sheets of cardboard is usually referred to as the diskette, since the disk and its container are never separated. It comes in three sizes: 8 inch, 5¼ inch and 3½ inch. The most popular size used to be the largest, the floppy; the middle size, the minifloppy, has overtaken it. The microfloppy is a new product not yet standardized. It is used by the Macintosh and by the Hewlett-Packiard 150. It gets one line in the table.

Floppies are made of thin plastic coated on both sides with a magnetizable material. The disk is inside a square envelope of thin cardboard, usually black on the outside. A label bears the vendor's name; there may be room here for you to give the disk a name to tell it from others.

Both the disk and the envelope have a large center hole; the disk hole is smaller than the envelope hole. The drive mechanism grasps the disk and rotates it within the envelope, which is coated with smooth plastic on the inside to reduce friction.

Figure 5.4.1 shows a floppy and a minifloppy and their envelopes.

Holes and Slots

There are several holes and slots in the envelope and disk.

Spindle Hole

A tapered cylinder in the disk drive, (A) in Figure 5.4.2, fits into the hole in the center of the disk (B) to position it precisely, so that its center *is* the center of rotation and it doesn't wobble. When the disk is seated properly and the head is positioned over a track, all of that track passes beneath the head. If the disk were off center, the track would wobble back and forth beneath the head like an off-center record on a turntable. If you put the disk into the drive so that the disk is slightly off center, then close the drive door or locking bar, the cylinder moves in and centers the disk properly.

126 EXTERNAL STORAGE

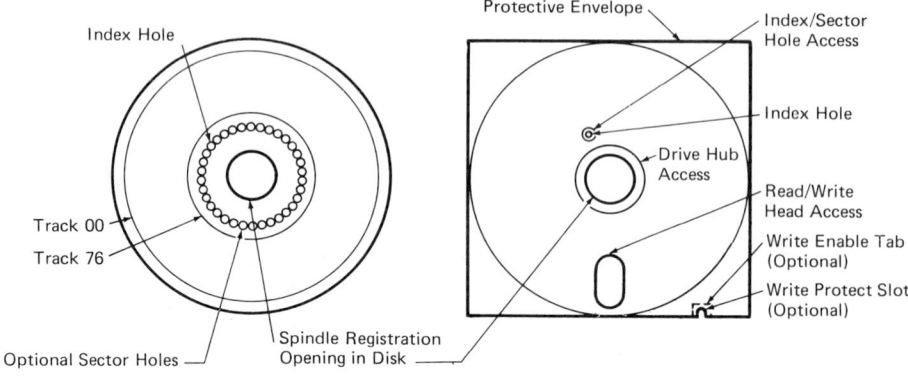

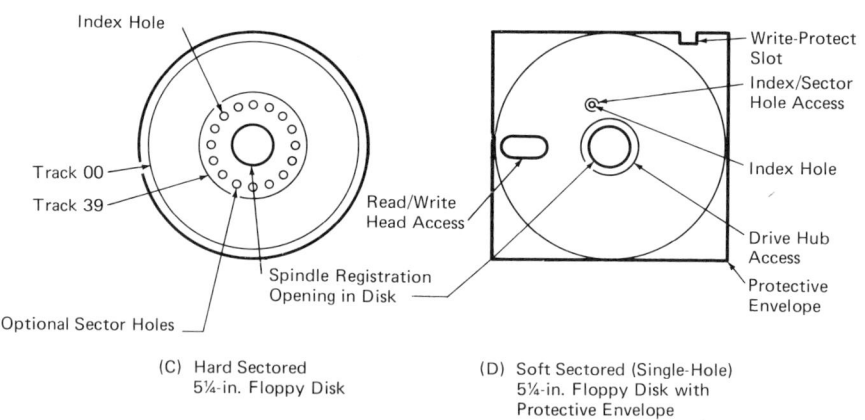

Figure 5.4.1. Floppy geometry.

It is amazing how well this works. Still, the area around the center hole is subject to wear:

1. You should watch carefully that the disk is centered in the envelope before you insert it in the drive;

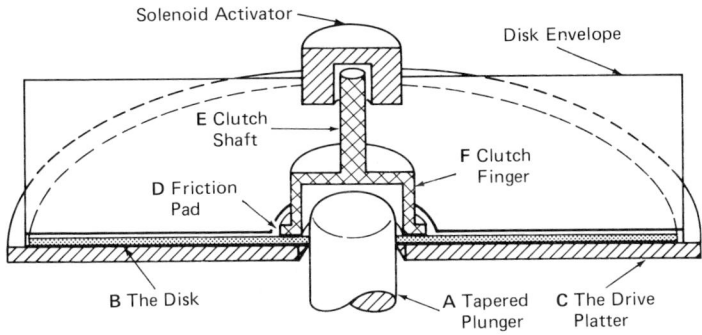

Figure 5.4.2. The plunger centers the disk on the drive platter and the clutch gets it up to speed.

2. You could apply a plastic reinforcement ring made for this purpose to each side of the disk. This protects the hole, just like the little "life savers" you put on paper held in a three ring binder.

The hole in the envelope is larger than the hole in the disk to leave some of the disk showing. When the drive is turned on with a disk inside, a clutch is electrically activated. On one side of the disk is a continuously running drive platter, (C) of Figure 5.4.2; on the other side is a friction pad (D) attached to a shaft (E) which is free to rotate in a bearing. The clutch finger (F) moves the shaft and pad to push the central hub portion of the disk (B) against the drive platter (C). This starts the disk moving. The motion of the rotating platter is imparted to the flexible disk and brings it rapidly up to speed within its envelope—the disk must be moving at a uniform speed for it to be read or written accurately.

Head Access Slot

A **slot** along one diameter of the disk (labeled *head access* on Figure 5.4.1), exposes the recording surface. If the disk is oriented properly as it is inserted, the head is above this slot. All the tracks are available to the head as it seeks back and forth. The head moves in *fixed steps;* the discrete positions where it may stop define the tracks. Figure 5.4.3 shows the disk with the envelope removed to show the head positioning mechanism moved by the stepping motor.

Before the head can read or write it is placed in contact with the disk. When no information is being transferred, some drives keep the head away from the disk to prevent wear. **Loading** the head pushes it towards the disk to make contact.

128 EXTERNAL STORAGE

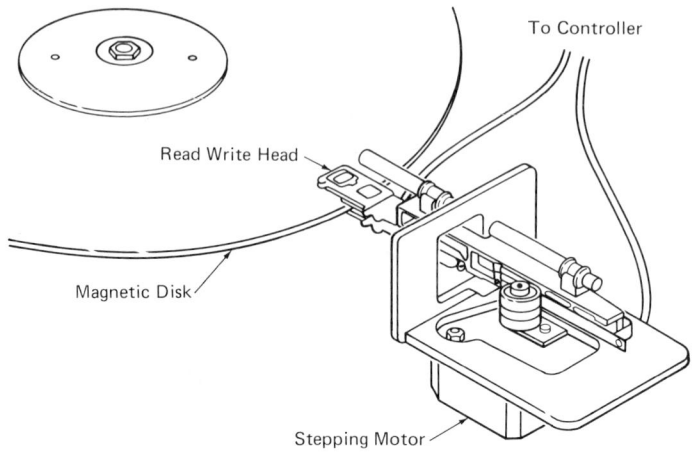

Figure 5.4.3. Head positioning mechanism.

Index Hole

There is a small hole in the envelope called the **index hole**. There is at least one hole in the disk at the same distance from its center. When the disk index hole passes beneath the hole in the envelope, it signals the beginning of each track. When the index hole in the disk and the envelope are aligned, light passes from a light source to a photocell as shown in Figure 5.4.4, producing a timing signal, indicating *home* on all tracks. At other times the disk interferes with this ray of light and no signal is produced.

Sector Holes

All disks have one index hole to designate home. Only hard sectored disks have additional but smaller **sector holes** at the same radius as the index hole. The same photocell and light source produce a **sector signal** as each sector hole passes, as shown in Figure 5.4.4.

Centering Notch

There is a pair of small notches at the rear of the disk on the edge that should enter the slot first. Two matching projections in the drive fit into these notches and help to center the disk.

Protect Notch

There may be a slot or notch in the cardboard envelope. No part of the disk lies beneath this slot; there is a clear path for light to pass through.

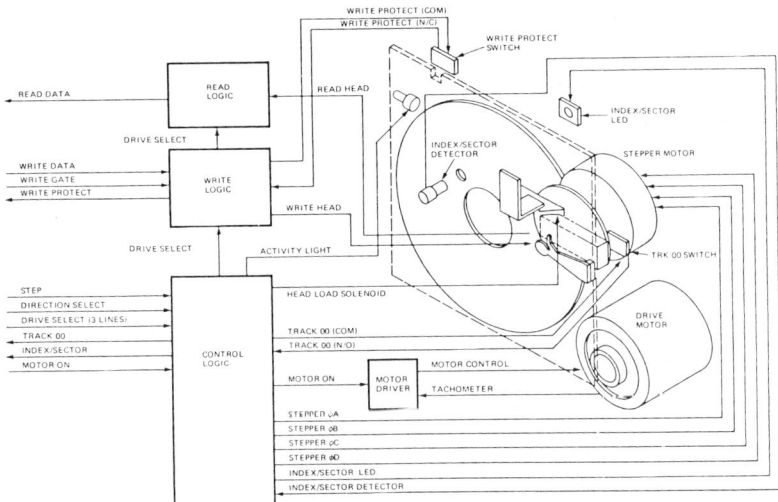

Figure 5.4.4. Sector detection.

Another light source and photocell detect whether the slot is covered or uncovered.

For some reason the standards are different:

- For the minifloppy, you *cover* the slot to *protect* the disk from being written on and uncover the slot to write on the disk.
- For the floppy (8"), you cover the slot to enable the disk to be written on and uncover the slot to protect the disk.

Operating the Drive

Inserting the Disk

Your computer has one or sometimes two slots (**dual drives**), each of which can receive a disk. The slots may be vertical or horizontal. For this description assume a horizontal slot. There are eight permutations for inserting the disk, determined by

- which side of the disk is up;
- which edge of the disk goes in first (of course, there are four edges).

Follow the directions given by the vendor: inserting the correct surface facing up makes that surface available to the head; putting the proper edge in first aligns the head slot to expose the surface of the disk to the head. The other seven positions will not allow the head to contact the surface of the disk.

After inserting the disk, close the door or move the closure bar to activate the drive mechanism. If your drive has neither, a microswitch in the back of the drive turns on the drive when the disk is seated.

Activating the Disk

For the floppy disk, closing the door or pushing the disk in firmly activates the drive mechanism, engages the clutch and causes the disk to get up to speed. The drive circuitry may check out the disk to make sure that it can be read, align the head to track 0 and read in the first track, if you are "booting" the system. As long as the door is closed and the computer is on, the disk rotates. When the computer needs to write or read, it issues requests to the controller to position the head to the right track, load the head and check for home position. When the desired sector arrives, the controller begins to read or write information.

The minifloppy in many drives is driven by a DC motor which gets up to speed quickly. When the disk is not in use, the motor is off—the disk is not revolving. To access the disk, the controller starts the motor; the disk needs time, several hundred milliseconds, to get up to speed. During this delay, the heads may position; then they are loaded. Transfer of data is possible when the right sector arrives.

Another time delay in the minifloppy drive keeps the disk rotating for a few seconds, since you may use the disk again shortly. To use the disk within that interval, the mechanism simply loads the head, a matter of 50 to 100 milliseconds.

Positioning Time

How long does it take to find the data? It depends upon where you are. Let's start with the 8 inch floppy. If the disk has not been used recently, the head is not loaded; the head is sitting above the disk. Take the simplest case: to read data on the track where the head is sitting, it takes the load time plus latency. **Head load time** is the time needed to push the head against the disk, about 40 ms (milliseconds).

Once the head is loaded, you wait until the data appears beneath the head. The floppy disk revolves at 360 revolutions per minute or 6 revolutions per second. One revolution therefore takes 167 ms. On the *average*, you wait for ½ revolution. **Latency**, the average waiting time for the block containing the data to rotate into position beneath the head, is about 83 ms.

To seek, the drive stepping motor moves the head past one track at a time. **Track to track positioning time** to move to an adjacent track is between 10 and 15 milliseconds. If the heads had been just used, a seek is performed *while* they remain loaded. Otherwise, the seek is done *as* the heads are being loaded.

When the head arrives at the right track, it is still shaking because of the start and stop motion of the stepping motor. **Settling time** allows for the head to stop vibrating before use and is about 35 to 40 ms.

How long does it take to access data? The **average access time** is based on positioning the head over approximately one third of the tracks on the disk. It consists of time to

- seek over one third of the tracks;
- settle down;
- load;
- wait for the right block (latency).

This calculation of time in a typical case is illustrated in Table 5.4.1. The **track to track average access time** is calculated using the time to move to an *adjacent* track.

Specifications

Manufacturers and vendors provide quantitative figures about what their drives can do. What does each parameter mean?

Sides

Disks are manufactured with a coating on both sides. Presumably, all disks *could* be recorded on either side. However, if they are only checked out on

TABLE 5.4.1 Time for Floppy Activities

ITEM	RANGE	TYPICAL	TIME IN MILLISECONDS
Track-to-track seek	3–8	6	
Seek 26 tracks	78–208		156
Settle time	10–15	13	13
Load	35–40	37	37
Latency at 360 rpm	83	83	83
Track-to-track access time		139	
Average Positioning time			289

one side they are called **single sided disks** and are intended for a **single head drive**.

When the disks are checked on both sides, they are called **dual sided disks** for use in a **dual head** or **dual sided drive**. It has two heads on the arm, one to read or write on *each side* of the disk. This provides double the storage capacity of a single head disk and drive.

Density

Density refers to the number of bits packed per square inch of recording surface. Recording density depends on the chemical composition of the coating, the design of the read/write head and the recording technique. The smaller the gap in the head, the smaller the spot where a bit is written. Figure 5.4.5 shows the evolution of the read/write head to the present day thin film head.

Information is packed differently *longitudinally*—along the track created by the path of the read/write head—and *laterally*—between tracks. Hence there are two measurements of density. The size of the head gap determines how close tracks can be packed to one another without interference from its neighbor, called **tracks per inch.**

How close are bits written within the track? **Bits per inch** determines the number of **bits per track** and consequently the number of **characters per track**. Since the outermost track is longer than the innermost track, bit density is limited by the length of the innermost track. The track density in bytes per track applies to every track, regardless of its position on the disk.

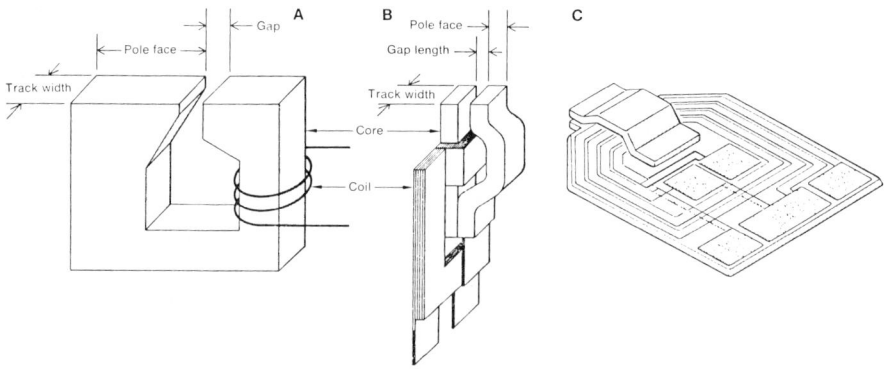

[1] Read/write heads are basically electromagnets (A), and conventional heads are made of a ferrite core (B). Much higher densities are achieved by thin-film heads (C), which are made through photolithographic processes, and have higher resolution, higher permeability, and less noise.

Figure 5.4.5. Evolution of the read/write head design.

Speed

The speed of rotation for the disks is standard: 8 inch disks rotate at 360 rpm or 167 ms per revolution. Minifloppies rotate at 300 rpm or 200 ms per revolution.

Transfer Rate

Given the speed of rotation and the number of characters on each track, the **transfer rate** is the rate data pass between the disk and the computer. It is the product of revolutions per second and characters per track.

Capacity

The amount of data that a disk can hold, **disk capacity,** is the number of tracks times the number of characters on each track. Disk capacity is rated in kilobytes (KB) per disk. Soft disks need to be formatted with sector marks. The capacity after formatting is the **formatted capacity. Unformatted capacity** is a useless figure.

Summary

Table 5.4.2 gives capacity information for disks currently available, including microfloppies and high density minifloppies by Tandon.

TABLE 5.4.2 General Floppy Disk Specifications

Diameter:	8"		5 1/4"				Tandon	3 1/2" Hewlett-Packard
Tracks/side	77		35		35		80	80
Sectors/track	26		HARD=10		SOFT=26		10	
Density	S	D	S	D	S	D	D	
Bytes/Sector	128	256	256	512	128	256	512	
Sides	1 | 2	1 | 2	1 | 2	1 | 2	1 | 2	1 | 2	2	2
Capacity, K	256|512	512|1024	89 |179	179|358	71|143	143|287	819	1000
			Old IBM PC		New IBM PC		IBM AT	
Tracks/side			40		40		80	
Sectors/track			8		9		15	
Bytes/sector			512		512		512	
Sides			2		2		2	
Capacity, K			328		369		1228	

5.5 DISK CONTENTS

At least 80,000 characters of text can be stored on a minifloppy. This could be one file or many. Commonly, there are several files on each volume. Each file may be a program; a ledger; a group of transactions; a word processing document; or so forth.

The File

The **file** is information on the medium, allocated and named by its creator. The file is not available until an application program asks the File Manager to **open** it. When you are finished with it, the application program asks the File Manager to perform an opposite action, to **close** the file.

All data and programs on the disk are in the form of files. There are different kinds of files; their organization is postponed to Chapter 9. For word processing, the electronic document (ED) comprises a file; for accounting, one set of books or a set of transactions is a file. Each application program is stored on a volume as a file. Some parts of the operating system, before they get into memory, are stored as files.

The Volume

There is a lot of room even on the smallest volume. It is important

- to keep track of all empty space,
- and to be able to find a desired file immediately.

First, let us make some order out of the space. Begin with cylinders and number them from the outside in, starting from 0. Within a cylinder there is one (single sided), two (double sided) or more (hard disk) tracks; number them according to the surfaces on which they appear, starting from surface 0. Within a track, number the blocks starting with 1. If there is only one surface, number tracks and then blocks within the tracks.

Blocks and *sectors* do not correspond exactly because of skewing (Section 5.2). The disk driver program converts the block number requested to a sector number.

Counting Extents

With the help of the driver, blocks (and tracks) numbered consecutively *seem* to be adjacent. A number of consecutive blocks on consecutive tracks is called an **extent**. It is a solid data area with no "holes" belonging to

5.5 DISK CONTENTS

another file. It is simpler to address a file which is in one solid area, a single extent. But if that were a necessity, it would interfere with the growth of the file as you add material to it during updating. Hence, for most operating systems, a file may occupy several extents (noncontiguous areas on the disk).

The File Manager keeps track of the area occupied by each file, the extents it occupies. The File Manager also monitors unoccupied space to provide for growth of existing files during processing and for creating new files.

Allocation Directories

Two directories are on each volume to monitor:

- **free space** which is not allocated;
- **occupied space** allocated to existing files.

The disk is an unwieldy shape. Let us view it as a rectangle. Think of the disk as made of flexible material that can expand or contract at will. In Figure 5.5.1 we cut this disk along the home position and make a separation. Now we reform the disk, contracting the outside and stretching the inside so that it becomes a rectangle as shown at the bottom of the figure. Blocks numbered 1 through 8 maintain the same relative position. Track 0, on the outside of the disk is at the top of the rectangle. The last track on the inside of the disk now appears at the bottom of the rectangle.

A **bit map,** shown in Figure 5.5.2, keeps track of all space on the disk, telling whether it is allocated or not. For simplicity, that map shows space monitored by track. An actual map may keep track of sectors or groups of sectors. In Figure 5.5.2, the large rectangle shows which tracks are assigned to different files on this disk. At the right, a column consists of rows of one bit each, set to 1 if the track is assigned to some file and to 0 if the space is free. At 1 bit per track, only 34 bits are needed for the minifloppy. At 8 sectors per track and 77 tracks, a floppy needs 77 bytes for a sector bit map.

The **file directory** describes each file by name and the space assigned to it. One organization (used by the CP/M operating system) is shown in Figure 5.5.3. Each entry begins with the name of the file consisting of up to eleven characters. The name is divided into two parts: the first is the actual name; the second is called an **extension** and conveys the type of file. It is often omitted—you can simply call your file X, for instance. Bytes which follow may hold a number (in binary) of each sector or track in the order each is assigned to this file. A file may have one or many sectors allocated. To indicate that no *further* sectors have been allocated to this file, the next byte position continues. Thus HELP.TXT is assigned only sector 8.

136 EXTERNAL STORAGE

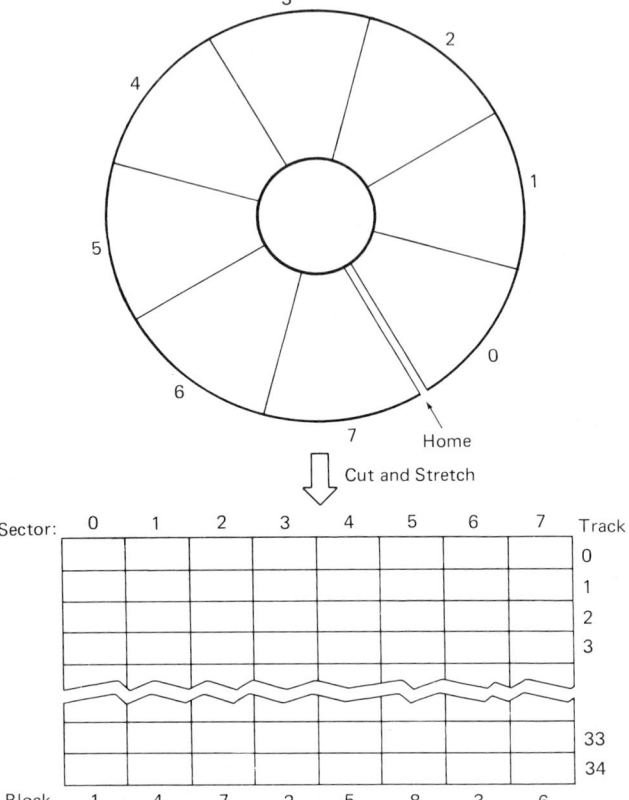

Figure 5.5.1. Tracks, sectors and blocks.

Allocation Strategy

There are at least two **allocation strategies**—ways to assign space to files:

1. Provide a separate utility program called by a user to create and destroy files.
2. Have the File Manager allocate more space automatically as files grow or contract.

For (1), a user who needs a file calls upon the allocation program to create the file entry and allocate space to it. The application program uses the file with the help of the File Manager. When the space assigned is used up, the File Manager cannot call the allocation program to expand the file.

5.5 DISK CONTENTS   137

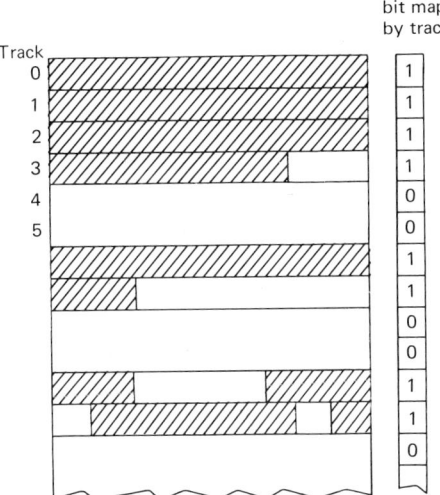

Figure 5.5.2. Bit map.

LTR.1	18	19	0	0	0	0
PROG3.BITS	2	3	4	0	0	0
HELP.TXT	2	0	0	0	0	0
SCHED.COM	23	0	0	0	0	0
RPT3	12	13	14	15	0	0

Figure 5.5.3. Allocation table.

To get more space, the user must copy the file into a new, expanded area requested from the utility program. This strategy is obsolete and unsatisfactory for most applications; but you still find it around (in the North Star DOS, for instance). When you create a file, you should not be expected to know its size.

With the second strategy, when you open a file, this only establishes a directory with *no* sectors assigned. The File Manager servicing your data requests is also in charge of allocation. When you first need space, or any time thereafter when you reach the limit of your current allocation, the File Manager immediately gets more space and your file grows *automatically* (until there is no more space left on the volume). This action of the File Manager is unknown to you. In computer jargon, it is **transparent** (until the disk is full).

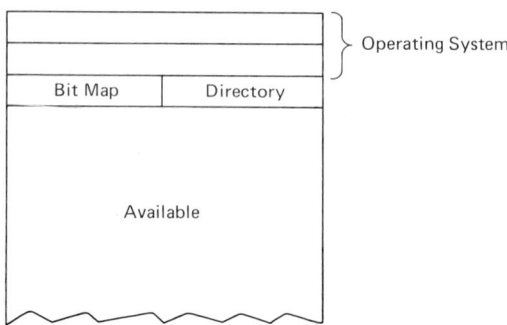

Figure 5.5.4. Occupants of the beginning of the disk.

Disk Layout

Figure 5.5.4 shows how the space on the disk might typically be used. It is standard to have the operating system at the beginning of a (system) disk. This facilitates bringing in the operating system (Chapter 7). At a standard position near the beginning we find the bit map, followed by the file directory, part of which is unused with empty entries to add new file descriptions as files are created. The rest of the disk stores the files: programs, text or other data.

Using the Directory

The File Manager uses the directory for

1. Creating a new file;
2. Finding parts of an existing file;
3. Deleting (destroying) an existing file.

Creating a File

When an application program needs a new file, it makes a request of the File Manager (FM). The bit map of the disk is in memory. The FM goes through the file directory on the disk to see if a file with this name exists; if so, the creation request is invalid and the program is informed.

Otherwise, the File Manager finds a free track on the disk, from the bit map, to allocate to this file. The FM sets the bit for this track in the bit map to 0 to show that it is in use. Then the FM creates a directory entry in memory using the name supplied by the application program and puts the location of the first track allocated there.

From time to time, the AP sends data to the File Manager to write to the disk; it accumulates data in a buffer until a complete block arrives. The File Manager sends the block and its physical address to the disk driver, which activates the disk drive to write the block to the medium.

The File Manager keeps a close check on how much data go to the disk. When an allocation is used up, the File Manager refers to the bit map, makes another allocation, sets that bit in the map to 0 and enters the track location into its copy of the file directory entry in memory.

The File Manager keeps track of file space thus until the application program has finished adding to the file. When the program CLOSES the file, the File Manager has an updated bit map and a completed directory entry in memory. Both must be rewritten onto the disk at their assigned location to keep an accurate record of space allocation.

The new directory entry goes into the directory to replace a currently unused entry. If there is no empty entry in the directory, additions to the disk cannot be recorded. An unused entry in the directory left over from a deleted file is marked with a special character, a **flag**. It shows that the entry can be reused to keep track of a new file. The File Manager writes the directory entry it has created in memory for this new file, putting it into the first flagged blank entry encountered. The next time someone needs this file, it's listed in the directory.

Expanding Files

When an existing file is needed, the File Manager finds its entry in the directory which it brings to memory when the AP opens the file. During processing, the application program may add data to the file beyond its present allocation. The File Manager notes that and acquires new space. It

- examines the allocation bit map (in memory);
- finds the closest empty space;
- marks it as assigned;
- alters the memory directory entry to show new space;
- writes new material to the blocks so acquired.

This procedure recurs whenever an allocation is used up. When the application program is done and closes the file, the File Manager returns the augmented bit map and directory entry to the disk.

Large Files

The file directory entry has room to record the file name, its status and a number of fixed size extents. This is usually enough to keep track of 16K of space. But what if the file grows larger: we have run out of room in the entry! That has been thought of. There is room for another flag in the entry to give its ordinal number. The File Manager sets the flag to indicate that this is the first of several. Then the FM returns it to the directory, gets another empty entry from there and finds empty space in the bit map. Now the FM acquires this space, recording it in the entry and setting the flag to mark it as the second entry until its capacity is used up. And so on. When a file is closed, as long as the current entry has room to record more extents, it is also flagged as the *last,* so that the FM does not look for more when sequencing through the file the next time it is used.

To restate this situation, large files have several directory entries, flagged by number. As the AP sequences through a file, when the FM finishes with one entry it finds the next entry. The directory is at the beginning of the disk; some drives make a characteristic sound as they seek over the long distance from the file to the directory and back again. Now you know why.

Using a File

Consider a program which reads a file but does not alter it. The program to print a text file reviews (reads) the file from beginning to end without adding or deleting text. When you start a print format program, it requests the name of the file to print. The AP passes this to the File Manager, which gets the text file entry from the directory and puts it in a memory area.

As requests come from the print program, the File Manager directs the disk driver to get blocks of data. The File Manager notes the track and block used. The last block in the file ends with an **end of file mark.** This tells the File Manager that no more data is forthcoming. This goes to the print program, which stops printing and returns control to the operating system.

Deleting a File

Either the File Manager or the erase utility gets a request to delete a file. *A file is never really destroyed* until new data is written into the space that it occupies. Instead, its entry in the directory is flagged as empty and all the space it occupies is marked as available in the bit map. If there is no directory entry, the file does not exist and can't be deleted!

When space is needed at some later time for another file, the bit map lists the space occupied by the old file as available. It is then written over by another user under another file name. If you use a utility program to print out the entire contents of a disk right after you delete a file, you will see that the file is actually still on the disk.

Since this is the case, utilities can be purchased which restore a deleted file, as long as its space has not been written over. POWER is such a product (see Section 7.7). It finds directory entries which contain a name and are flagged as empty. It can check whether the space has been used from the bit map; if not, you can choose to revive it.

5.6 WINCHESTER DRIVES

The amount of **online** storage—storage immediately available to the computer—required for a particular application depends on the number of customers, account information, kind of stock, and so on, and the data needed to be recorded for each. Often the space available on a floppy does not suffice, even for a small business. This has led to user frustration over poor system performance. The need for more storage has spurred technological development and now an economical solution is here.

Winchester drives, hard disk drives or **rigid disk drives** fill the bill for small business because they have several advantages:

- They store large amounts of data—from 5 megabytes to 200 megabytes or more.
- The transfer rate is about ten times faster than for floppies so that an electronic document, once found, can be brought into memory much more quickly.
- They are physically small yet reliable.

The main disadvantage of the hard drive is that it is more expensive than floppies, costing from one to several thousand dollars. But note that the cost per megabyte (MB or million bytes) is *less* than for the floppy! And the cost is going down every day. Another difference is that the volume is usually fixed, not removable. (Removable volume drives are becoming available but tend to be less reliable.)

Characteristics

Let's see what they are like.

Fixed

There are a large variety of hard disks available, yet there are few real standards. However, most such drives and the disks are sealed together in a single unit so that the disk is not removable. Only filtered air is allowed to enter to keep out tiny dust particles. Reliability, packing density and speed of transfer are high.

Rigid

One or more disks are mounted on one spindle. These disks are **rigid**. Before data can be transferred, the disks must get up to speed. They revolve continuously at a high rate, commonly 3000 rpm (revolutions per minute) or 50 rps (revolutions per second). It takes a minute or so to get the disk up to speed because the motor is small to keep the units compact and the price down. A time delay prevents access to data while the disk is getting up to speed.

Hard drives have one head for each recording surface. For a three disk drive we need up to six heads. All the heads are mounted on an arm which moves them as a unit so that they all position to the same cylinder.

Air Cushion

Since the disks are sealed within the drive, it is important to keep wear at a minimum. To protect the disks, the heads are *not* in contact with the surface during reading or writing. They are kept a tiny fraction of an inch from the surface. This would seem hard to achieve, since both the head and the disk are rigid; and the disk cannot be made totally flat economically. Hence the distance between the two would vary as the disk rotated if the head's position were rigidly fixed. A relatively small surface irregularity could strike the head, crashing the whole system.

When the disk is up to speed, a thin film of air forms above each surface. Lower the small light heads and let them float freely on this air film, staying a uniform distance from the surface regardless of small irregularities. Thus for the hard disk, head loading gently releases the heads.

Specifications

Two characteristics of hard disks make them attractive to the user: their high data capacity and high transfer rate. The transfer rate improves the response time of the program because data are moved between the disk and memory at ten times the speed of the floppy. Transfer rates similar for most drives are from 500 to 800 kilobytes or higher per second.

Size

The first hard disks for small business applications were furnished by manufacturers of large commercial computers. Frills were removed to make them affordable. These disks were 14 inches in diameter. (A 14 inch drive may be housed in a cabinet which is 25 or 30 inches in its largest dimension.)

During the last several years, a race has developed in the electronics industry to see who can make the smallest hard drive with the largest capacity and the lowest price. Disks of 8 inches and 5¼ inches seem to be winning the battle. They are small enough to fit into a desktop console, yet they can hold 5, 10 and even up to 200 or more megabytes.

Electronic Specifications

Table 5.6.1 displays the range of characteristics for hard disk drives. Heads are much smaller and have a tiny gap, and because dust is no problem, information may be packed at a much higher density than for the floppy drive. This is responsible for the tremendous improvement in capacity. Also, the disks rotate at 3000 rpm, ten times faster than the floppies, to yield a higher transfer rate. The table contrasts specifications of disk drives for the larger mainframe computers.

Other Considerations

Besides having greater capacity, larger drives differ from the smaller ones in these respects:

- They consume more power to keep the larger disks rotating at the high speed.
- They produce some heat.
- Large ones may produce noise.

Hard disks are generally reliable because they are hermetically sealed. Dust and abrasion which inflict harm to the disk surface are kept minimal. Still, errors arise and are coped with as is discussed shortly. Hard disks

TABLE 5.6.1 Hard Disk Drive Characteristics

	SIZE				
ATTRIBUTE	$3\frac{1}{2}$	$5\frac{1}{4}$	8	$10\frac{1}{2}$	14
Transfer rate MB/s	.5–2	.5–2	1–2	1–2	3–5
Density, Kb/inch	7–15	7–15	6–18	9–15	8–20
Density, Tpi	250–500	250–500	200–500	700–800	600–900
Surfaces	2–4	1–8	1–11	4–8	4–19
Capacity, MB	6–13	5–150	7–110	85–475	10–1250
Price, K$	.8	.8–8	2–15	4–8	4–40

make much more data available, often to several users. This capability also presents a problem—how to keep track of a larger number of files. If the vendor does not furnish a good means for cataloging files, difficulties arise.

Drivers

The structure, format and circuitry of Winchester drives are different from those for floppies. So to speak, they talk a different language. The floppy driver cannot talk to a hard disk (see Section 7.2). A different driver program lets the application program give the same kind of requests to both types of disks. A different (hardware) controller is also needed. It is a printed circuit board which fits into an available slot. The hard disk driver (program) accepts application program commands and activates the controller properly to run the hard disk.

File Directory

The method for keeping track of files and empty space described in Section 5.5 is still applicable with reservations. The hard disk has much more space and holds many more files. Hence its directory is substantially larger.

As with the floppy, the track is divided into sectors. But 256 byte sectors are inefficient. Track capacity, even for 5¼ inch disks, ranges from 8K to 14K bytes. For the 14 inch drive, a track holds 20K or more. Hence, it makes sense to use 1K, 2K or more as a sector size. The bit map and the file directory space are larger. The amount of unused space allocated to a file increases, but is unimportant relative to the volume available.

Backup

What is something should happen to the hard disk? Would *all* those files be lost? This is a scary thought. Hard disks are *more* reliable than floppies, yet there is still a slight possibility of losing data.

Backup, making another copy of a file, is always an important consideration—it never hurts! But how do you back up hard disks? Some drives have backup devices, such as tape cassettes or streaming tape, built in. Otherwise, the system has at least one floppy drive to write out hard disk files to several **archive disks.** Backup can be selective or total. For **selective backup** only altered files are copied. This effecient procedure is often neglected. Since only a few files are altered at the normal session, few need be copied. The Turbodos operating system can mark the directory to show when a file has been altered and should be archived. The mark is removed during archiving.

Total backup, writing *all* hard disks files to floppies, may take an hour or more. The activity must be watched, since someone has to insert and remove the floppies. Hard disk manufacturers have sought alternatives:

- **Streaming tape** is a cartridge of ¼ inch tape to which you can copy an entire hard disk in a few minutes. (But, since it is a *sequential* medium [see Chapter 9] the tape itself is of no use for normal applications.)
- The **video cassette recorder (VCR)** can be used with additional hardware and software for selective or total backup.
- A system may provide a *duplicate* hard drive. All writing is done on *both* drives. The two copies are constantly compared during reading. Should one disk drive fail, the other is automatically put into service and the first withdrawn.

Error Detection and Recovery

Not like Floppies

Hard disks are not like floppies simply because the medium is permanently attached. When you encounter difficulties with a floppy disk and you find that the disk is at fault (by trying others), the remedy is simple. Copy all the files from the bad disk onto another disk. Then make sure that the file giving difficulty has been corrected and brought up to date. Now you may throw away the bad floppy.

Floppies do go bad because head contact with the disk causes wear. Particles of the magnetic material are scraped away. When material is missing from the disk, you cannot write or read at that spot. Although damage to hard disks is less frequent, you must know how to detect and correct errors of any sort.

Detecting Hard Disk Errors

When you cannot read a file properly, this is *not* proof that the disk is at fault. Many parts of the hardware and the software may malfunction. To verify that an area is faulty, write and read back from it, then check that what is read is what was written. The application program does not usually make this **read after write** check. As a consequence it is advisable to check a hard disk periodically as now described.

Hard Disk Checkout and Error Prevention

The first step in this procedure is to back up the *entire* hard disk. Write all files to a backup medium—a set of floppy disks or streaming tape. Use a utility which verifies that the copy is accurate.

Now the hard disk is thoroughly and totally checked by another utility. It writes a fixed pattern onto each sector of the disk, reads it back and compares it with the original pattern. This is repeated many times with different patterns to check every bit site on the disk. This may take a full day. However, it need not be attended; the computer can run it over the weekend to find all bad sectors.

The utility makes a table of all the sectors which do not perform perfectly. Another utility now combines the noted sectors into an invisible file. This file is listed in the directory but flagged so that the user does not see it. The space this file occupies (the bad sectors) is listed as allocated in the bit map; no user file will be assigned those sectors. They are thus taken out of service.

A final utility takes the backup information and rewrites it on the hard disks to make the best use of the available good space and to provide the most free space. You are now guaranteed that the files are in good sectors and that space assigned to new files will come from sectors that have been thoroughly checked out.

5.7 CONSIDERATIONS

This section summarizes the chapter by reviewing the paramount issues.

Choice of Floppy Drive

Suppose you are free to choose any floppy drive without regard for cost. Which type is most reliable, fastest and so forth? The floppy drive is mechanical equipment made on an assembly line and fabricated to tight tolerances. Vendors maintain quality control. Most drives perform excellently and there is little difference among them. As with any mass-produced item, there is statistical variation. You may get a lemon which gives you constant trouble or you may get a perfect item which never goes bad. The probability of either of these cases is very small.

Also, there is very little difference in performance and reliability between single and double density and between single and dual sided disk drives. There *is* a difference in price. But the price difference is not directly proportionate to the quantity of storage that you get. That is, for twice the price you may get four to eight times the storage capacity.

Most floppy drives work approximately the same. Disks with greater storage capacity cost only a little more. The best buy in drives uses double sided, double density 8 inch disks with a capacity of a million bytes per disk.

Larger capacity means that you can store more files on each disk. Less physical space stores all the disks needed for your firm. But the advantage is much greater. Now a single disk may store an application program and all the data files you need. This reduces and even eliminates the need for removing disks while a processing program runs—an important consideration.

Another inducement: the system and a couple of APs use up a large fraction maybe half of the space; double disk space and you *triple* the room for data.

Two Drives

A system with only one floppy drive is almost impossible to use. Most utilities require two drives for smooth operation. I recommend against any system with a single drive only: to copy a disk requires inserting and removing both disks involved many times.

If there is any standard format among floppy disks, it is the single density, single sided, soft sectored 8 inch floppy for the exchange of text and programs. If you have an 8 inch drive which handles double density, double sided disks it can read and to write single density, single sided floppies for the interchange of information.

Buying Floppies

There is a wide price variation, at least two to one, among floppies of a particular format from different manufacturers and through different sources. There is not nearly that kind of variation in quality. Vendors at the low end make their money from occasional users who can stand a less reliable product. The vendors on the upper end sell their disks relying on their name and service. There are very few solid facts available about disk quality. The longevity of disks is more dependent upon how they are handled than the vendor quality control. An improperly adjusted drive can wreck more than one disk.

Mail order houses advertise in the microcomputer magazines and sell name brands at a lower than "official" retail price. Are these the same disks? Yes, they are bought in great quantities at a high discount and resold at a small markup in retail quantities. Name brands bought thus are backed by the original manufacturer.

Care of Floppies

Your floppies may "be" the firm's books when your system is computerized. They should be treated with due respect. Your accountant would reprimand you if he found your ledgers stained with coffee or spaghetti sauce. At least you could read these stained books; you couldn't read similarly spotted floppies.

Disks come in envelopes which cover slots and holes of the otherwise exposed magnetic coating; disks are shipped in cardboard boxes of ten. Some people keep their floppies in these boxes. I prefer rigid plastic containers which can hold fifty or so floppies, all I might ever need for a particular set of applications. There are many other kinds of holders, for example, clear plastic flexible pages with three holes punched to keep a collection of floppies in a loose leaf binder. This makes it convenient to put the binders on a shelf like books, labelled to show what is inside.

Never leave exposed floppies lying around where they can collect dirt, be scratched or have garbage fall on them.

Mounting Disks

How you put the disk into the drive, **mounting** the disk, is important. If inserted incorrectly, information may be improperly read or written. Before mounting the disk, make sure that its center hole is centered within its envelope. If not, the drive mechanism will center it for you at the expense of wear to the inside edge of the disk. This centering action hurts the disk.

You can purchase nylon grommets and a special applicator to reinforce the center hole of your disks. This is a good idea and well worth the cost. Some brands provide grommets in place on new disks.

Insert a disk gently. Be sure that it seats correctly before you close the door or otherwise engage your drive. *Never turn on* the equipment with the disk mounted in the drive. Always, *insert all disks* **after** turning *on* the equipment, and *remove all disks* **before** turning *off* the equipment. Switching the power on and off creates voltage surges in the drive. Even when the head is not loaded, these voltage spikes may record noise and obliterate information on your disk if it is in place when the power goes on or off. If the head is positioned over the directory and the head is loaded, there is great danger that you may lose records in the directory. This means that the files on your disks cannot be found even though they are intact.

Full Disks

All disks have a maximum capacity. You can keep putting files on your disks until this maximum is reached. Then beware! If you try to create or enlarge a file beyond the capacity of the disk, you may be in trouble; the AP may not be able to cope with it and current records may be destroyed. If you have two drives, you can put an empty disk on the second drive and perhaps save this morning's work. This is not always possible, however.

It is important to realize an AP's limitations. The AP may not be able to recover when the disk it is using is full, that is, to save this morning's work as a separate file on another disk. It is wise to check APs for error recovery capability and verify that you have spare space before you go ahead with an application.

Backup

When you send a letter to someone, you keep a copy. Every important document has a spare in some file if you are a cautious person. This policy should extend to disk files. Every time you run an AP which creates a new file or alters an existing file you should note this. Before turning off the computer, make copies of them on other disks, even when the AP produces a backup file on its disk. This ongoing process should take place at every sitting. Should trouble arise during the sitting and files get messed up, perhaps due to negligence, computer malfunction or power failure, you have an alternate set to fall back on. You may lose today's work but not the work for the past month.

Files tend to accumulate at an alarming rate. Your business should have two kinds of directories:

1. A printed directory for each disk on its envelope.
2. A directory of all files identifying the disk which contains them.

Utilities discussed in Chapter 7 make both kinds.

Hard Disks

Hard disks have larger capacity and are more reliable than floppies. Any business with more than a couple of employees keeps a large number of records. To provide room for them and the many programs required to meet accounting standards, a hard disk is mandatory. Even the smallest of them holds 5 million characters. On a cost per byte basis, they can easily be justified.

Semidisk

A high speed "electronic" disk has been developed, called a **semidisk, m-drive, virtual disk, RAM drive** and other names. It consists of a printed circuit board holding a large main memory and software which makes it appear like a disk. *It is volatile.*

This PC board contains 500K to 2000K (½M to 2M) of RAM. At high memory speed, retrieving or writing information is very fast. Files kept there are available almost instantaneously. You can switch between two programs in semidisk without a perceptible wait. The new program is simply moved from semidisk to main memory at memory speed.

A big RAM alone is not sufficient. A program package supplied by the semidisk vendor or other supplier hooks the device into the operating system. This makes the additional memory *look like* a disk drive to the operating system, with the drive location you name. If you call it M, then all operations for semidisk are addressed to drive M. All the disk actions are maintained for M, including keeping a directory, a bit map, accessing data in sectors and so forth.

Semidisk is merely extra RAM put to work and made to look like another drive. A software package hooked to the OS does this. The IBM PC, XT, AT and compatibles have large *optional* RAM available. Packages you can purchase let you install a RAM drive and vary its size according to the AP you are now running.

The main advantage of semidisk is its high speed. It works twenty times faster than floppies and twice as fast as most hard disks. Hence you can find data and bring them into main memory at that speed. But it is volatile. Anything left on disk M disappears when you turn off the computer. (Now some vendors provide backup battery power to protect you from power outages.)

Here is how to work with semidisks. Start up the system and ask the supplied program to attach the driver for semidisk as drive M. Next transfer a group of files to this semidisk drive M using a utility (such as PIP or POWER described in Section 7.5). Now you can access all programs and files on disk M as with any other disk, but twenty times faster. You process files, create them, run programs and do translations. This especially saves time when using data bases.

When you are done, you *must* remember that anything on disk M disappears when the power goes off. Therefore, you must transfer all the files that have been *created or changed* back to some *real* disk before you turn off the power. Program files *need not* be copied since the originals are still on their source drives. That is the only precaution to be observed with a device which really speeds up operation.

Observations

There are many APs for which disk speed is unimportant, for example, word processing. Minutes of overhead are needed to transfer files back and forth, which may result in a net loss in time instead of a gain. Semidisk is *not* appropriate here.

For program development, on the other hand, much time is spent on

- modifying the source program;
- compiling it;
- linking it;
- testing it.

Often, more time is spent on bringing in each of the four programs involved than in running them. This program access time is virtually eliminated when both the programs and the source file are in semidisk.

Data base applications, sorts and programs, such as spelling checkers which require considerable disk access, are also facilitated by using semidisk.

6
Computers

6.1 INTRODUCTION

The Computer System

Earlier chapters examine the computer system, viewing it as a hierarchy, like boxes within boxes. Now we make an analogy with the audio system.

The Audio System

Figure 6.1.1 shows a total audio system. An audiophile tells you that your system sounds different depending upon how you arrange it. Performance depends upon the shape and size of the room, the placement of the speakers and furniture and the kind of drapes. Also, the system sounds different according to how many people are in the room, how much noise they make, whether an air conditioner is running or the window is open. This is the *total* sytem; none of these factors in the listening area can be ignored when you make your purchase.

The audio system consists of audio hardware and software. The software, the media, include phonograph records, tapes and radio stations. (There is a considerable difference in sound quality from one station to the next.)

Audio hardware consists of components which can be modular and purchased separately or as a single unit in one cabinet. It used to be that good systems were only modular but now total systems are quite competent. In good systems the speakers are in their own cabinets (just as is the printer for the computer system). The purchaser is faced with a choice of whether to get separate modules or a single cabinet containing an amplifier, phonograph and receiver. A similar choice faces the computer system purchaser.

6.1 INTRODUCTION

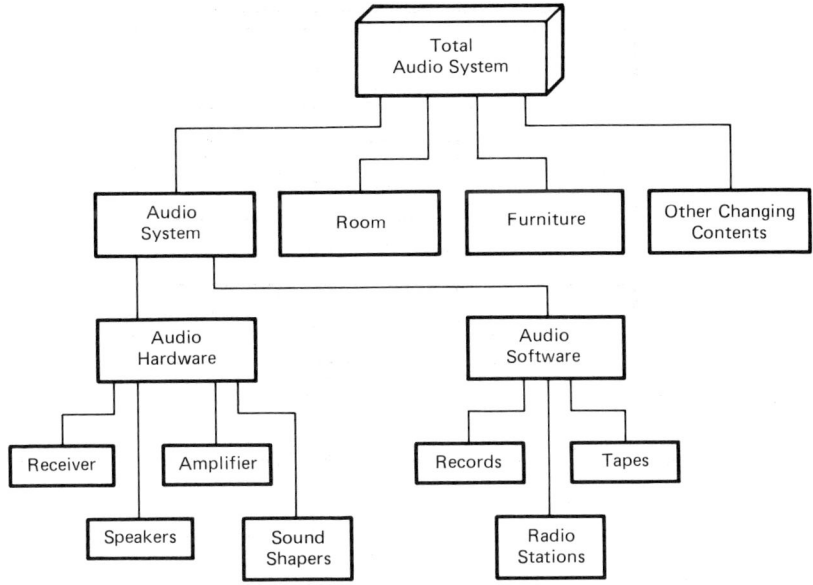

Figure 6.1.1. Total audio system.

Business Computer Systems

Figure 6.1.2 shows a *business* computer system, consisting of accounting procedures and people, the first level. The computer system consists of hardware, the operating system and the application packages, the second level. The latter two, the boxes at the left and right on the third level, are discussed in succeeding chapters.

At the fourth level is the computer cabinet and bus, storage, terminal and printer. These have been given attention. The dashed line indicates that those components are often found in one cabinet. We now turn our attention to the computer itself.

The computer cabinet contains a **chassis**. On it are a power supply, a motherboard and a bus with slots where printed circuit boards plug in. The bus on the fifth level shows boxes which represent the CPU, memory, the device controller and other boards. Discussion of these four boxes comprises the bulk of this chapter.

The CPU consists of a number of parts, shown on the sixth level. But the microprocessor determines the characteristics of the computer. Other boxes on the sixth level are for circuitry to support the microprocessor at the heart of the CPU.

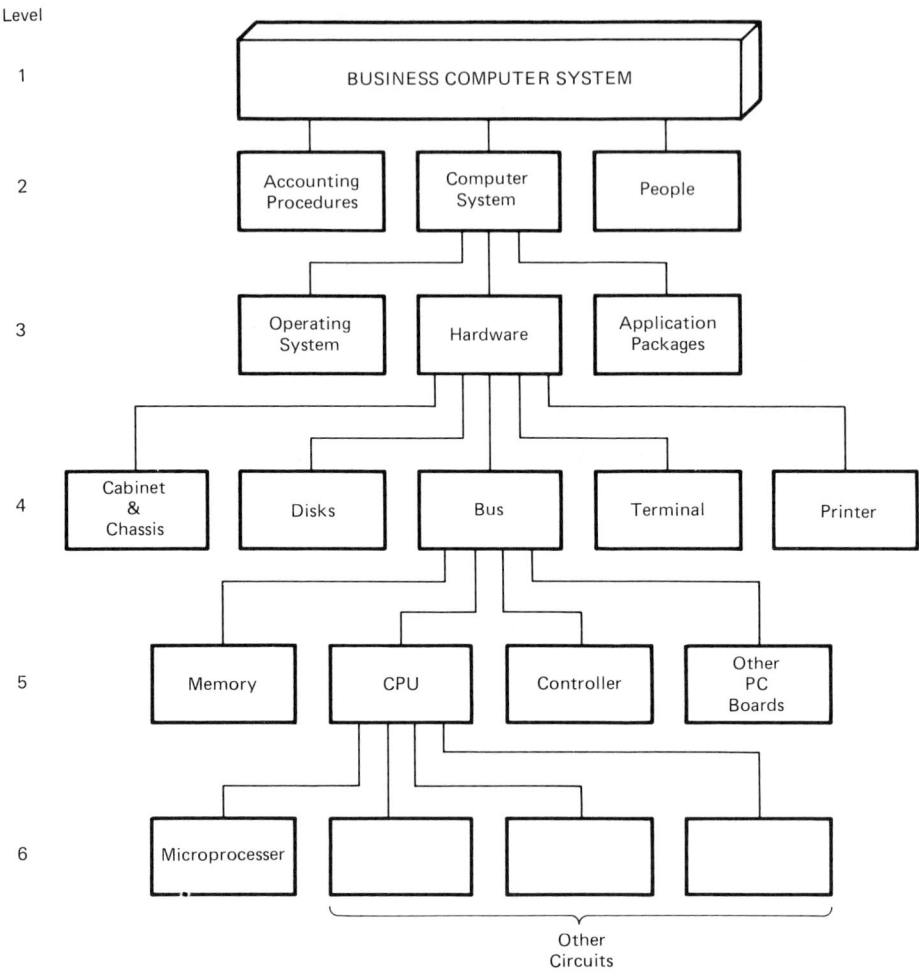

Figure 6.1.2. Total computerized business system.

Brands of Computers

Today many computers come as a *package deal* which includes hardware and a number of software packages. A given brand and model number has a microprocessor chip associated with it. The microprocessor has a set of commands which it executes from machine language programs furnished. An operating system is part of this package; there may be other operating systems that also work with this computer. Application packages may be included in the deal. If you switch to another operating system, you must make sure that the application programs work with it.

The best way to computerize a business is to consider its *accounting method* and choose packages most suitable. *Then* determine the operating system and computer under which those packages function best. Some packages have versions that work on almost any computer and operating system. For instance WordStar, a word processor, has been around for several years and has versions which operate on all the big brands.

We now examine some brands of micros, big and little, and some of the considerations associated with them.

Famous Brands

The three most popular manufacturers of micros for professional use are Apple, Radio Shack (Tandy Corp.) and IBM. Each has its own *groups* of computers; each is based on a different chip. Apple features MOS Technology's 6502 on the Apple II and Motorola's MC68000 on the Macintosh and Lisa; Radio Shack has a group of computers called the TRS-80 based on Zilog's Z80 chip, the Model 16B based on the 68000 and the Tandy 2000 based on Intel's 80186 chip; IBM uses a relative of the Z80, Intel's 8088 chip, on its PC and XT and the 80286 on the AT.

Each uses its own nonstandard bus structure. Most contain spare slots where PC boards fit. But only PC boards specifically designed for that brand (or "compatibles" in the case of the IBM PC) fit into its slots. Something intended for the standard S-100 bus group of computers is not compatible with any of the big three.

Look-Alikes

There are two kinds of **look-alikes:** carbon copies and modified duplicates.

A **carbon copy** is identical to the original down to the last detail. The printed circuit boards are exact duplicates. Carbon copies are manufactured in Taiwan and Korea. Reputable magazines do not take their ads. Information is passed by word of mouth or xerographic copies of literature. There are bans on their importation. An order by mail that gets by the U.S. Customs Service arrives within two or three weeks. You can even purchase software this way, although it is also illegal.

Some American companies have taken a different strategy, **modified copies,** or **compatibles.** Chips on the free market can be bought fairly by any manufacturer. These are put on printed circuit boards for the same slot design. Slots go on a chassis of different design but which meets the essential specifications of one of the big three. This is totally within the law. And that's the catch. A product that does not exactly duplicate the specification of the known brand may not run all application programs properly.

Some companies have gone through several stages in producing their compatibles. For instance, Eagle has come out with three models compatible with the IBM PC. The latest version *will* run the operating system and most application programs without a hitch, it seems. If you buy a lookalike, be sure that all application programs you want to use run on this machine by getting a demonstration from the dealer.

Portables

By the end of 1981, a few companies, notably Osborne, had come out with portable computers with small screens that could be folded up into a unit the size of a small suitcase and toted around the country. They had most of the qualities of larger computers except for a small screen. They are not recommended for small office business applications because:

- their power supply is usually inadequately filtered for heavy commercial use;
- the screen is too small to expect an operator to use for long periods of time.

That is not to say that these computers don't have their place. If you have salespeople who travel and enter data on route, this is ideal for them. Floppy disks can be brought back to the office and data transferred from the small system to a large one by

- providing a drive compatible with the portable;
- using data lines and modems to let the computers talk.

Some have been specifically designed for this function, such as the Hewlett-Packard Portable with its LCD display, and the earlier Model 100 from Radio Shack. These are truly *portable,* rather than simply *transportable* as in the case of the "suitcase" models.

Lesser known Firms

There are a number of lesser known firms which have high reputations and have been in the business for several years. They manufacture equipment which tends to be sturdier and designed for the commercial environment. These include Altos, Cromenco, North Star, Televideo, Sage, Compupro and a host of others. Many rely on a standard S-100 bus, and printed circuit boards purchased from a number of vendors can be used in this equipment.

Applicability

If computers vary so much from one brand to the next, is there any point in trying to discuss the whole range of computers? This chapter uses the standard S-100 bus computer as an example but everything said here applies equally well to most micros, regardless of bus structure, chip used, board layout and physical characteristics. This chapter should give you some feel of how modular designs help in the business environment.

6.2 THE CPU

The heart of the computer is the **central processing unit,** or **CPU.** Modern technology places most of the CPU circuitry on a tiny chip. This is put in a package with a number of small pins projecting. The package fits into a socket on a printed circuit board that fits into a slot on the bus on the computer chassis which is in the computer cabinet. This section discusses the chip, the chip package and the CPU printed circuit board, in that order.

The CPU Chip

The *circuitry* for the CPU (Figure 6.2.1) is on a tiny chip, a quarter of an inch in diameter. The design of the chip is a long, laborious and quite costly process. But, once the design is completed and the chip is mass produced, its cost drops drastically.

The chips are tiny and delicate; before they can be handled, they are encased in a plastic package with a number of pins projecting from two of its parallel edges. A typical package is shown in Figure 6.2.2. Once the chip's wires are connected to the pins, the package is filled with plastic. This hardens to make a solid free of air and moisture, which protects the chip from the atmosphere and makes it easy to handle.

Although a chip package contains a large number of circuits, it is not a complete CPU. A number of supporting chips are required. All the package for the CPU is assembled on a single **printed circuit board.**

A typical board is about 6 × 9 inches. Sockets are mounted on each board (see Figures 6.6.3 and 6.6.4 for examples). Wires are "printed" or deposited on this board to connect sockets to each other and to components fastened to the board. A set of printed wires is brought to one edge which plugs into the slot of the bus where information and electrical current pass

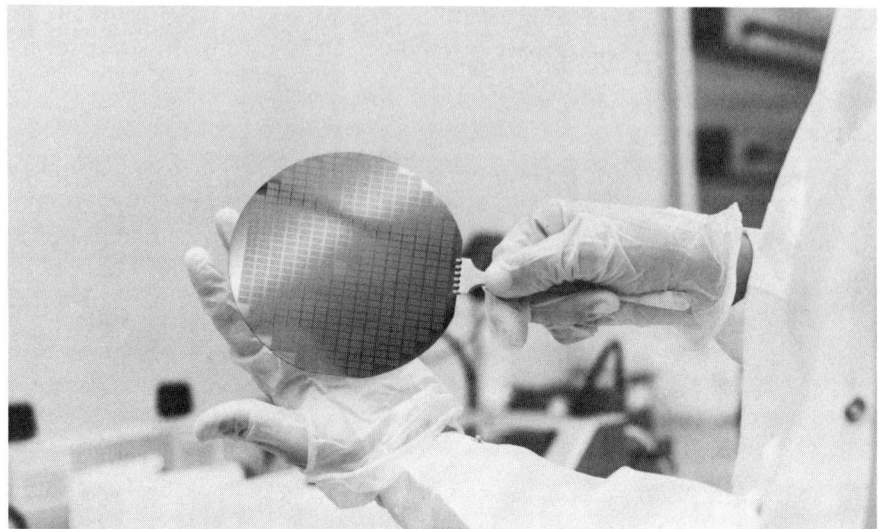

Figure 6.2.1. A 4 inch wafer containing many fabricated integrated circuit chips.

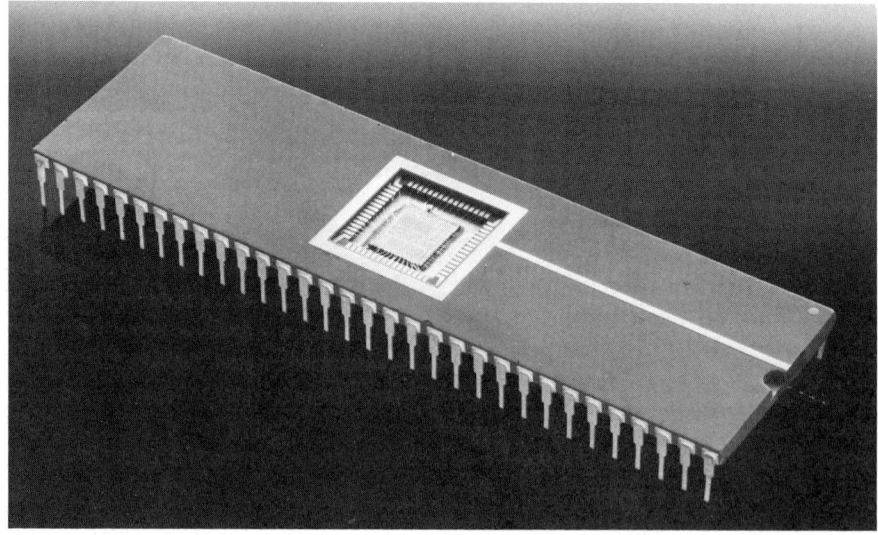

Figure 6.2.2. The Motorola 68000 chip package cut away to expose the mounted chip.

to it. This terminating edge is often gold plated to insure good contact with the slot.

CPU chips differ in many respects; most important are the instructions which the computer executes. An **instruction** or **command** is one elementary action that the computer can perform on data or one decision that it can make. The collection of all the instructions the computer can perform is the **instruction set**.

A datum accessed by the CPU for an instruction is called an **operand**. Operands are in memory or in **registers**, temporary fast storage in the CPU. CPUs differ in how many registers are available and how they are used. CPU instructions differ from one chip to another in

- length, the number of bits occupied by each;
- the function each performs;
- places where operands may be found by the instruction;
- the kind of data manipulated;
- the way to make a decision.

A CPU chip design is created by a semiconductor manufacturer, such as Intel, National Semiconductor, Motorola, Zilog or Fairchild. The company assigns a number to its chip, patents its design and regulates its production and distribution. It may license other companies to fabricate and market chips which bear this same number.

Family of Chips

Semiconductor companies are constantly improving old designs and creating new ones. Improvements are usually **upward compatible:** the new chip design runs programs written for the older chip but not the other way around. Programs written for the new chip may not work on the old chip.

Upward compatible CPU chips make a **family**. A popular family began with the 8080 chip from Intel. Improvements in this chip—labeled the Z80, Z80A, Z80B and Z80H from Zilog; and 8085, 8088, 8086, 80186 and 80286 from Intel—all form a *family*. Differences among the chips consist of

- additions to the instruction set;
- the speed at which the CPU operates;
- the ability of the CPU to be interrupted to give attention to other actions.

The CPU chip is the heart of the computer. The chip designation describes the computer. Computers with a design based on one chip family do not execute language programs or software designed for any other chip family.

The CPU Printed Circuit Board

Many additional circuits are required to turn the chip into a functioning CPU. They are designed into other chips in their own packages. A physical support holds all the chip packages, the **printed circuit board** (or **PC board**). The board designer finds chips to make a good CPU, lays these out on a PC board and, with computer aided design, connects the chip packages together with wires printed onto the board.

The additional chips

1. Provide timing signals to coordinate the CPU activities;
2. Shape signals so that the output of one chip can properly feed another chip;
3. Amplify the signals so that they are of the magnitude proper to drive other chips;
4. Reorganize the signals to make many from few or few from many;
5. Match the signals to the bus.

A CPU printed circuit board fits and can be put into any slot on the bus, the set of wires over which components talk to each other. Like the telphone, you can call "home" from any one of them. The bus also provides power for the PC boards. We find plugged into the bus

- the CPU;
- the memory board;
- the disk controller;
- other assorted boards for additional needs.

The Bus Design

The bus contains four kinds of wires:

1. Power wires bring voltage to each of the boards.
2. Control wires carry signals telling each board what to do.
3. Address lines name a location in memory.
4. Data lines pass data between memory and the CPU.

A bus design designates

- which wires are assigned for each purpose;
- the physical position of each wire on the bus;
- the nominal voltage signal on each line;
- the voltage tolerance for each line.

The bus specification can be determined in two ways. The first is by a **standard,** usually developed by a **standards committee.** There are several standard buses. One of these is the **S-100 bus** for micros (also called the **IEEE-696 standard**); others are the **Multibus** and the **Q-bus** for minis. Then there are individual bus specifications developed by computer manufacturers.

The Computer Manufacturer

The computer chassis, the printed circuit board and chip may be fabricated by different companies. The computer vendor chooses a design based on a CPU chip, a bus design and a set of printed circuit boards. It may fabricate these boards or subcontract them to another manufacturer.

PC designers and manufacturers jump on the bandwagon when the computer sells well. They design boards not offered by the computer vendor or at a lower price which mate with the bus. (Quadram makes a composite memory board which costs less than IBM's memory extension board for its PC.) This gives you a wide choice for additional boards.

6.3 MEMORY

Typically, memory for the micro is on a separate printed circuit board. (There are a few exceptions.) This section examines how the CPU calls for data from memory and other topics related to the PC memory board: the memory chips from which the PC board is fabricated, the structure of the PC board, how memory is expanded to satisfy today's insatiable needs.

Addressing

The 8 bit microcomputer CPU can address any byte in memory. The number of bytes accessible to the CPU is called the **addressability** of the CPU. Without special provisions, the Z80 based CPU addresses a maximum of about 65,000 bytes (64K). An address is 16 bits (See Chapter 9 for a further explanation of bits, bytes, and data).

Figure 6.3.1 shows a memory PC board plugged into the bus. Wires on the bus convey the address (16) and others receive or transmit the datum (8). One control signal says *recall* information *from* memory; another says *memorize* information *into;* one more says *start*.

In Figure 6.3.1, the address goes to a **decoder** which selects exactly one byte in memory. It is retrieved and sent through amplifiers (which increase the signal to useable level) to the bus data lines to be picked up by the CPU when a *done* signal from memory appears.

Chips

Fabrication of the memory board begins with printing wires on it. Then chip package sockets are soldered to the board. After IC chips are placed in the sockets, the board is tested.

Chapter 2 introduces two types of memory:

- **ROM** is read-only memory which cannot be altered.
- **RAM** is random access memory which may be read from or written into.

We confine this discussion to RAM.

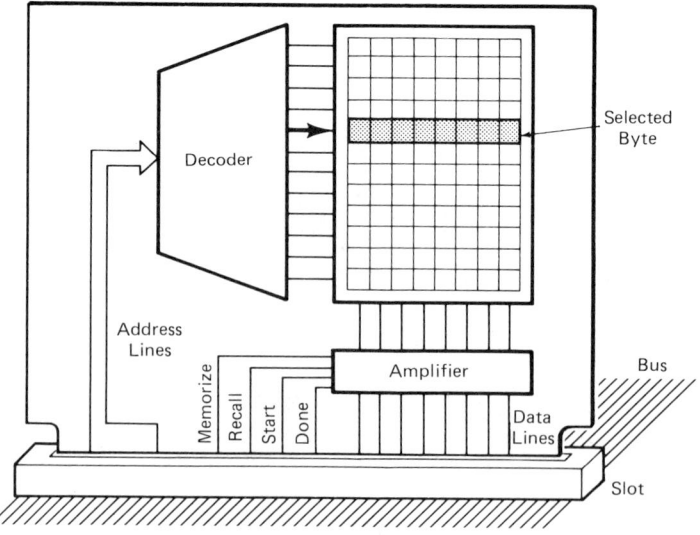

Figure 6.3.1. Memory board (diagrammatic).

Dynamic

Dynamic RAM stores bits as a voltage on **capacitors**; the voltage gradually leaks away. Circuits on the board restore the information periodically, an operation called **refresh**. Dynamic RAM must be refreshed continuously.

Static

Static memory stores information on semiconductors. Each device either is or is not conducting current according to whether it represents a 1 or a 0. Current continues to flow indefinitely for 1s and not at all for 0s (or vice versa in some designs) until new information is written into that portion of the memory (or until the power is turned off). No refresh cycle is required. Hence, the memory is called static.

Contrast

Because current flows for each bit in the memory which is set to 1, a static memory incurs greater power drain. Dynamic memory needs refresh circuitry. Nevertheless, the cost of the dynamic memory is less because its components are simpler and less expensive. Thus the dynamic memory board is cheaper and requires less power drain. The advantage of the static memory is that it *seems to be* more reliable where there are fluctuations in the power lines and can operate at a higher speed.

Memory chips come in different sizes and configurations. Dynamic RAM chips are readily available in packages which contain from 4K to 64K bits.

Bits

Vendors are at work trying to manufacture 128K and 256K bit chips; the former has become available in 1984 and the latter is expected in quantity in 1985. Dynamic RAMS are one bit wide and have a decoder on the chip to select the desired bit. A 4K RAM has twelve input leads which select one of the 4K bits, with one output lead for the bit accessed. Control leads tell it whether to *memorize* or *recall*. To write into a selected bit, select and control lines are activated. A one bit data register holds the value to be entered for *memorize;* it receives the value read for *recall*. Since this chip can choose one out of 4K bits, it is sometimes designated as a 4K x 1 chip.

In 1984, the largest RAM in use in micros is 64K x 1. Sixteen input lines select one bit. RAM speed is rated in **access time,** the minimum time between uses. Access time ranges between 150 and 500 nanoseconds (150-500 ns). A **nanosecond** is a billionth of a second. Hence the computer can access the 200 nanosecond chip approximately five million times in one second. Another way to describe speed is in **access rate:** 200 ns is 5 megahertz (5 MHz).

It is not possible to pack as many bits on the *static* RAM chip which has 4K or 8K *bits* of storage. Frequently static RAM is configured four bits wide. For instance, a 4K static RAM chip is designated as 1K × 4: Ten input lines select one of a thousand *4 bit slices;* there are four output lines, one for each bit of the slice you select. Static RAMs operate faster and have a larger speed range, anywhere from 30 to 500 nanoseconds. Hence, the fastest of these can access memory 30 million times per second (30 MHz).

Package

The chip is placed into a package, connected to the pins, encapsulated and tested. Pin configurations are fairly consistent over the large range of memory sizes. Pins are required for

- multiple select input, which chooses a (set of) bit(s);
- data input or output (one or more lines);
- function and control inputs;
- one or more voltage sources;
- a refresh signal in the case of a dynamic memory chip.

The Memory PC Board

Size

Memory boards sizes range from 8K to 512K bytes (1984). Dynamic RAMs can be packed at a high bit density (bits per square millimeter). *Static* memory boards have a maximum of 64K bytes.

Configuration

The number of chips used and how they are organized depends on chip family. For the 64K dynamic memory board, we might use eight chips, 64K × 1 with sixteen select wires connected and one data lead to each chip.

To make a 32K byte static RAM memory, we might use 1K × 4 memory chips. We need 64 of these packages. Five of the select bits from the address bus select two of the packages accessed for this request. The remaining 10 select lines choose a 4 bit slice from each of the two selected packages.

Other Chips on the Board

The memory board is crowded with memory chips. Additional packages perform selection for static RAMs. Other chips provide timing and refresh for the dynamic RAM. Signals from the bus have to be shaped to provide driving voltage to each memory chip. Output to the data bus must be amplified because memory chip output is low. Two way switches are needed for all memory PC boards: to recall (read) data go *from memory* onto the data bus; to memorize (write), data go *from the data bus* into the memory.

Boundary Selection

More than one memory board may be used. For 48K bytes of memory composed of three 16K memory boards, each board holds a different memory section:

1. 0 to 16K;
2. 16K to 32K;
3. 32K to 48K.

Each board has a **DIP switch** (for **dual in-line pins**) to fix the lower memory boundary (and automatically the upper boundary), which is setable in 4K increments; i.e. you can set the boundary to 12K or 16K but not to 17K.

Disable

You may **disable** part of memory, to use ROM in place of RAM for these addresses, for instance. You could remove memory chip packages physically from the board; but then if you were to change your mind later, you would have to reinsert them. Removing and inserting chips requires dexterity—chips are delicate. A better way is a disable switch on the board.

Why would you do this? A ROM containing part of the operating system or a translator may use addresses 0 to 4K. The RAM board may use addresses 0 to 32K. You cannot have two identical segments of memory represented; something has to give. Disable the 0 to 4K segment of RAM to make room for the ROM addresses.

Phantoms

A common way to bring in the operating system is a loader program in ROM on the disk controller board (described later) occupying addressable memory space. If ROM occupies a memory address segment permanently, this segment cannot be used for RAM to hold data or programs, even if RAM has the physical space.

Some RAM boards provide a **phantom** lead to disable part of RAM *temporarily* while the system is loading. When the phantom signal is removed and ROM is disabled, that portion of RAM is restored and becomes addressable.

Expanding Addressable Memory

Earlier CPU chips and designs seemed adequate. Most CPUs provided a maximum memory of 64K. Since then, applications needs have expanded tremendously (along with the exploding technology). But a lot of software and programs were written for older CPUs. If we were to go to another CPU organization and command structure, these programs would be lost.

Another reason for larger memory is *multiple users.* The personal computer was once truly *personal,* used by one person at a time with adequate processing capability. But for business needs it should be available to more than one person at a time. Do you want to stop entering sales invoices while payroll checks are being prepared? You would have to organize the day to suit the various separate uses of the computer. Some businesses can put up with this; others will not.

To make the computer available to several users requires more memory, additional terminals and a suitable operating system to handle several terminals and two or more programs running concurrently. For now we examine only the problem of adding more memory. Instead of 64K, we can get 128K or more with bank switching or extended addressing.

Bank Switching

Bank switching organizes memory into several **banks:**

1. Each can be of maximum size (64K for the Z80);
2. Each has a **bank number;**
3. Only one is accessible at any moment;
4. The CPU can turn any bank on or off.

The bank number on each board is set by a DIP switch. There is an input port for turning a bank on or off.

Ports

Input and output devices attached to the computer, such as the printer, are addressed by numbered **ports.** Before information is sent to the printer, the

CPU puts its port address on the lower address byte of the bus; this half of the address bus is called the **port lines.** Only the printer responds to its port address (if the memory line is turned off) and picks up the data transmitted on *the data lines.*

The console has two ports assigned: input from the keyboard and output to the display. The CPU looks at the input port to pick up codes for keyed characters. The CPU sends characters to the output port for display on the screen. There are many spare port designations; one may address the input port for banked memory. All memory board signals are set to the same input port designation (by still another DIP switch on each) shown in Figure 6.3.2.

Switching

Suppose all of three memory boards are set to input port number 10. To switch to bank 1, the CPU addresses port number 10, asking for bank number 1. All three boards receive this request. A *bank on* **register** on each board records whether the board is *on* or *off.* The board responds by comparing the number in the message to its switch setting. Bank 0 and 2 set their *bank on* registers *off,* while bank 1 goes *on.* Hereafter all requests are ignored by banks 0 and 2 and honored by bank 1.

Extended Addressing

Extended addressing is faster to use and easier to program than bank switching. It requires a simple change in both the bus design and the CPU function, but this alteration is upward compatible.

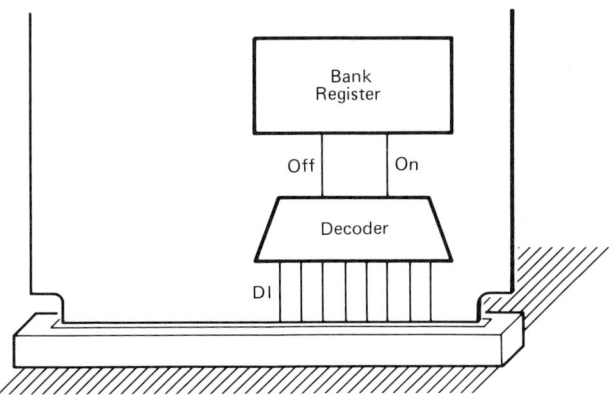

Figure 6.3.2. How the bank select works.

The bus is altered with 8 more address bits The new S-100 standard (IEEE-696) uses previously unused bus positions to address 16M bytes of memory. The CPU must put 24 bit addresses on the bus; old boards still work but limit memory to 64K. The CPU board is redesigned with

- additional address lines;
- additional commands for extended addressing;
- circuits to send the additional byte to memory boards so each can determine whether to respond.

The 8088 chip found in the IBM PC and XT uses a form of extended addressing which employs internal segment registers and can accommodate memory up to 1MB.

6.4 MORE PC BOARDS

The Bus Again

Figure 6.4.1 shows another view of the computer. At the left on the chassis is the power supply, the motherboard and the bus with slots where printed circuit cards fit. Wires go to connectors where cables attach, one for the terminal and another for the printer. At the top are the CPU and memory boards. At the bottom are several more boards described in this section.

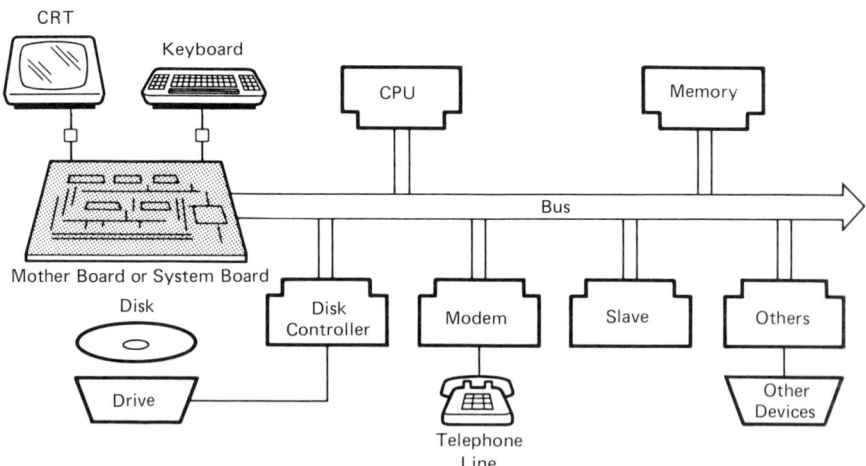

Figure 6.4.1. PC boards fit into the bus.

Activation

Figure 6.4.2 shows the bus—wires printed onto a plastic base with **slots**, which are female receptacles mechanically attached and electrically connected to the wires. A printed circuit card is pushed firmly into the slot so that all its connections make good contact. A **guide rail** on each side guides the board into the off-center slot; the board (or PC card) can only be inserted one way. The figure shows groups of wires for power, control, address and data. The wires are not grouped together *within* the bus as pictured here only for clarity.

Addressing

How is it possible to direct a request to one of the many boards on the bus? A separate control wire for each board would be wasteful. Instead, one control wire indicates whether memory is addressed. If not, the lower address byte placed on the bus selects one of 256 possible ports; one or more is associated with each board.

Typically the computer can send either an input or output command to each board. I/O commands for the Z80 computer, OUT and IN, include a register designation and a port number. First the program fills that register with one character for output. To execute the I/O, the CPU

1. raises the control lead which **deselects** (turns off) memory;
2. puts the port address on the lower address byte;
3. applies the datum from the register to the data outline.

This applies to the 8088, 80186 and so on.

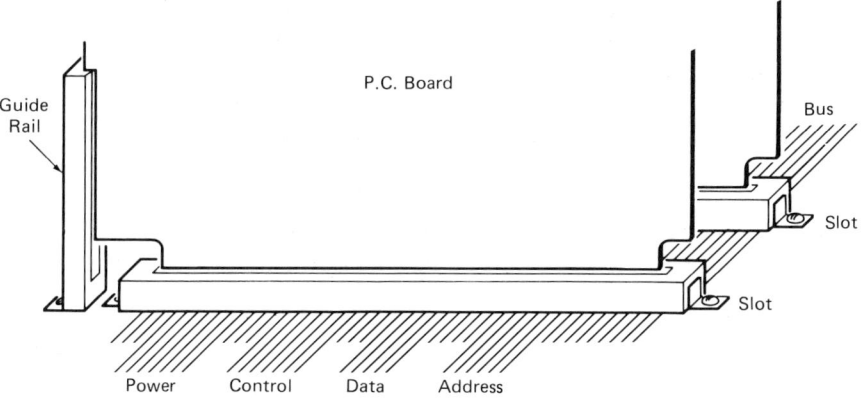

Figure 6.4.2. The physical bus slot arrangement.

Clock and Calendar

A few personal computers have a clock and calendar function built in; otherwise a PC board can provide it. The clock and calendar are setable, just like your wrist watch. With this "time stamp," all printouts and files can be dated if your operating system handles this feature. (Modem PC boards often provide multiple functions. The clock and calendar may come as a bonus with a memory or graphics board, for instance.)

Registers on the board store the current time and date from its crystal controlled clock. A nickel/cadmium battery keeps the clock running accurately for up to two years. One small program provides an interface to set the time into the board when you first install it. An application program must have a module to request, interpret and format the time for output.

Getting the Time

A calendar/clock board has an output port to furnish the date and time and input port to set the time or date into the board when it is first put into use. Registers keep track of seconds, minutes and hours as a binary number. A program can interrogate these registers at the output port. The program must convert binary time and date into decimal and formats it (1 becomes January, etc.). To access a register (for second, day, month, or year), put its number on the data line and direct it to the board's input port. The board puts the byte for the value of that date function on the data bus.

Disk Controller

The **disk controller** is electronics which operates the disk drive as described in Chapter 5. It issues control signals in sequence to the drive to read or write a sector. (See Figure 5.1.1.) Controllers for floppy and for hard disks differ considerably. But their objective and the basic means for achieving it are similar. We examine only the floppy disk controller.

Controller boards made by PC board manufacturers fit a standard S-100 bus or a nonstandard bus for the Apple or the IBM Personal Computer. At the top of the board are connectors for cables which go to the disk drives. Either there is a separate cable for each drive or a cable goes from the controller to the first drive, another from the first drive to the second, and so forth.

Matching

The controller matches the drive to the computer. The computer bus and the drive lines differ in several respects:

- The drive expects and transmits control signals to and from the controller.
- Data come from and go to the disk as a sequence of *bits*.
- Data appear on the bus as a byte, a character code.
- Data come from the disk drive at a fast rate.
- Once data begin to pass from the disk to the computer, they continue unabated and could easily be lost if the timing is not just right.

Multiple Drives

A disk controller controls up to four disk drives but there is never more than one drive active at any time. Designs are versatile and the same controller may handle minifloppies or floppies, either single or double density and either single or double sided. Some controllers can intermix disk types.

Addressing

One or more port address is assigned to the disk controller where input and output commands are directed, naming a unit, one of the four physical drives.

Section 5.1 describes how the AP talks to the File Manager, which in turn talks to the **driver**. The driver then gives commands to the controller. It is important to distinguish the *driver*, which is software, from the *drive*, the mechanism that operates the disk. A simplified chain of events is this:

1. To read or write, an AP talks to the operating system;
2. The operating system calls in the File Manager;
3. The FM talks to the driver;
4. The driver talks to the controller;
5. The controller activates and directs the disk drive.

This is shown on Figure 5.1.1.

DMA

For *slow* output devices, the computer is directly involved with the transfer of characters between memory and device. For instance, when you type into the keyboard, the computer collects characters one at a time. The application program asks for the next character before you hit the key. Then it continually checks to see when you hit a key. It picks up the code, enters it into a memory buffer and asks for the next one. Essentially the computer has nothing to do while you enter information.

The disk is so much faster. It can send hundreds of thousands of characters per second through the controller and onto the bus. If the computer gets involved with each character delivered to the bus, this materially reduces the maximum speed for information interchange between disk and memory.

Direct memory access (DMA) allows a controller to take over the bus completely. After receiving the directions for the disk driver, a controller with DMA sends a signal requesting possession of the bus to the CPU, which surrenders the bus to the controller. Now the controller talks directly to memory. Each time it assembles a byte, it places

- the memory address where the byte goes on the address lines;
- the byte on the data lines;
- signals on the control lines to tell memory to write information at that address.

The controller gets bytes from memory for output in the same fashion: It puts an address on the address bus and asks memory to recall the next byte, which is delivered to the bus.

Serialization

Disk data is read and written as a *series* of bits. For *reading,* the drive transmits bits which the controller distributes to an internal register. When eight bits accumulate in the controller's register, it puts the byte on the data bus for memory. This is **deserialization.**

For *writing,* bytes acquired from memory are placed in the same controller register and bits are sent one at a time to be written by the driver to the floppy. This is **serialization.**

CRC

Validity checking for data blocks on the disk uses the **CRC (cyclic redundancy check.)** As a block is written, a complex procedure is performed by the controller on the bits to construct an additional pair of bytes, the CRC, which is written at the end of the block.

During reading, as the bits of a block are brought from the disk, the controller does the same complex procedure. The result, the **calculated CRC,** is put in a register. As the two remaining bytes are read—the **written CRC**—they are compared, bit for bit, with the *calculated CRC* in the register. If the two are identical, the data is valid. Otherwise, a CRC error has occurred and the data is invalid.

Sectors

As described in Chapter 5, for hard sectoring, holes at intervals around the floppy disk produce timing signals photoelectrically; for the soft sectored disk, sector information is written onto the disk. The drive sends these signals to the controller:

- for the hard sectored disk, a pulse for each hole;
- for the soft sectored disk, the entire data stream from which the controller finds the end of one sector and the beginning of the next.

The drive sends a *home* signal, detected photoelectrically from the disk, which marks the beginning of all tracks. This causes the controller to reset a **sector counter** to 0. When the drive sends the controller a sector pulse (hard sectored) which marks a change from one sector to the next, the controller adds 1 to the count in the sector counter; then it increments the sector register. For soft sectoring, the controller must monitor the data stream to find the next sector.

The driver converts the block number to sector number to make requests of the controller. The controller watches for this physical sector, which is ready when its number is in its sector counter.

Track Position

The controller monitors track position with one **track register** for each drive. The controller initializes each drive as directed by the OS when the OS is loaded. The controller positions to track 0 with a control signal to the drive and sets the track register to 0. When the controller sends *seek* signals to a drive, it alters the track register; when it moves the head inward one track, it adds 1 to the track register; when it moves the head outward, it subtracts 1 from the track register.

Clock

Accurate timing enables us to write data on a floppy using one drive and read it back from a different drive. The controller includes a crystal controlled time source to write characters at exact intervals along each track. It also times incoming pulses and segregates bits for one character from those for the next.

Typical Input Action

Typically, the disk driver interprets each disk request and puts a description in a control block (such as to move information between the disk and memory as portrayed in Figure 6.4.3). A block read from disk goes to a location in memory called a **buffer**.

The disk driver (program) records the request parameters in an **I/O block**. The driver now transmits, a byte at a time, these "directions" to the controller from the I/O block. A final byte tells the controller to take over.

The controller (hardware) now interprets the parameters sent from the I/O block. Often one parameter requests mechanical motion of the disk drive to seek to a track; another parameter requests a sector number. While disk activity is going on, it might be possible for the computer to carry on useful work. In single user operation, there is only one AP in residence. Since it is waiting for data no other useful work can be done. Eventually, for DMA, the controller asks for ownership of the bus and the CPU gives the controller sole access to it.

After the drive positions to the desired track, a stream of bits comes from the head through the drive to the controller. The controller determines when the requested sector is reached and then accumulates bits to make a byte in the **data register**. It sends the address of the next vacant position in the memory buffer to memory along with the data byte. This continues until the entire block is transmitted. Then the CRC is checked to complete this controller action.

The controller now sends a signal to the CPU on a control line to release the bus. Thereafter the CPU repossesses the bus to continue to execute its program, namely the driver. The next command (in the driver) checks the status of the controller to see whether the block is in the buffer and if it is valid. If so, the driver gives control to the File Manager.

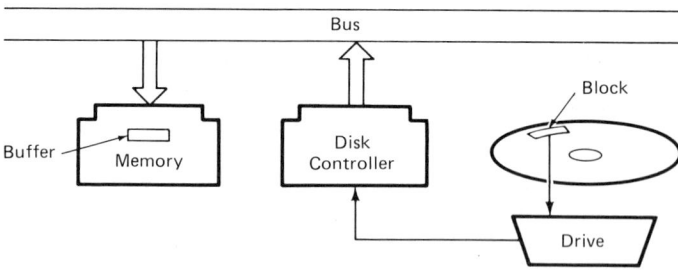

Figure 6.4.3. The disk driver IO block.

Complete Computer On A Board

It is now possible to put an entire computer on one printed circuit board: the CPU chip and associated circuits, a complete memory of 64K and with chips and ports to support a keyboard, display and printer.

Need

The old method of providing one CPU board and memory on separate boards seems to work fine. But for a system with several simultaneous users entering information, the operating system becomes large, involved and occupies considerable memory. This makes the system inefficient and slow. An attractive alternative provides each user with a CPU and has one more computer which runs the entire system. The user gets a **slave** and the separate CPU which runs the slave is called the **master**.

Operation

Each user gets a computer and video terminal. The printer and external storage may be shared; they are used infrequently during data entry or retrieval. When they are required, the master provides access to them.

It is impossible for several users to run the printer simultaneously. Output is **spooled**—sent to a disk file, where it accumulates until the printer is free.

Each user has a terminal to operate one slave. The slave runs autonomously until it needs the printer or external storage. The slave asks the master, which provides the services and then returns control to the slave to continue. This slave may have to wait a fraction of a second, but other slaves are not detained.

The Slave Board

Figure 6.4.4 shows the block layout of a typical slave computer PC board to fit into a slot on the system bus, a complete CPU, including

- the chip and additional circuitry;
- a memory of 64K or more;
- an interface which mates to a video screen and a keyboard.

An *internal* bus on the slave lets board components talk to each other.

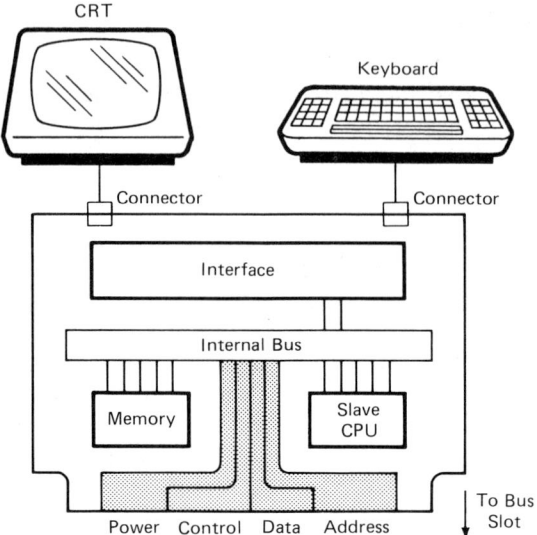

Figure 6.4.4. A slave PC CPU board layout.

The board fits into a slot on the master bus and works independently from the master computer except when service is required. Then the slave CPU makes an interrupt request.

The Interrupt

The **interrupt** is the key to complex operations in the modern computer. Think of the computer as an administrator with a number of devices under its control. It is time consuming for the administrator to constantly check the activities of the devices to see if they are running smoothly. A better alternative is for the device to request attention when service is needed.

This is like the manager who stops what he or she is doing when a telephone call comes in. The call gets attention, is dispatched and the manager returns to the job at hand. The administrator must know where to resume the activity without repeating a lot of chores in between.

This same philosophy is used in computing. When an interrupt request occurs, the computer finishes the command now executing—like putting the last few words on a sentence you are writing. Then the computer marks its place: it puts the instruction counter in a safe place where it can be recovered later. Now the computer finds out which device needs service and of what kind. The appropriate OS program is run to provide the service.

When the service is finished, it returns control to its original task if appropriate.

Data Request

Let us examine the master/slave operation where the slave needs data from a disk file. The slave and master talk to each other via a segment of the operating system sitting in each of their memories and the port hardware in the slave. When the slave needs data, it sends an interrupt request to the master with a control signal on the bus.

The master checks which slave is making the interrupt request and sets aside a place in its own memory for a message. The master then asks the slave to put a message there.

The master picks up the message and determines, for example, that the slave needs a block from a designated disk drive. The master activates the disk drive and assigns a buffer for the block. A DMA transfer of data to the master's memory occurs without attention. The slave in the meantime has nothing to do without the data, but the master can serve other slaves or devices as required; other slaves are unaffected.

Once data arrive in memory, the master is notified by a DMA interrupt and passes the block along to the slave. The master notifies the (idle) slave that data are coming. The slave now provides a buffer in *its* memory for the block which the master then transmits from its buffer through the port to the slave. This transfer happens extremely fast.

The Modem

A modem board sometimes has an external attachment which holds the telephone receiver. This allows the telephone to be activated without actually tying into the phone jack. Tones generated by the device are picked up by the telephone receiver and transmitted over the telephone lines. For reception, sounds received by the telephone are transmitted to the small speaker in the headset, picked up by the microphone in the cradle, passed to the modem board and translated.

Modern modems hook directly into the phone jack. Marked on the modem are the FCC number and other information which should be registered with the telephone company.

The modem lets you talk to other computers and computer service bureaus which furnish information or transmit your messages to distant users. The modem will not operate properly unless you provide a *program to run it*.

Modes

The modem operates in several modes:

1. As a dumb terminal so that a host computer thinks that you are at a terminal instead of a computer.
2. To send or receive a file to or from another computer.
3. To send multiple files in either direction.
4. For callup so that another computer or dumb terminal may call in and use this computer even when no one is there.

Functions

Let us examine modem functions as they apply to the *transmission* of information from the micro to some distant point. The action is the reverse for the reception of information.

The computer activates the modem by addressing the modem's port. It sends a byte at a time to the modem, which serializes it into a stream of bits. A clock on the modem board times these bits and converts each into one of a pair of standard tones. The selected tone is applied to the telephone line for a fixed duration determined by the baud rate for transmission. For some modems this is adjustable and under program control. The communication program sends the modem the parameters of transmission. The modem emits a different tone according to whether the outgoing bit is 0 or 1.

Software

The modem is *hardware* for transmitting, receiving and converting bits of information; a **communication program** is the *software* that does the **handshaking,** enforces a **protocol**—the transmission rules—and does all error checking, both parity by character and a check sum for each block of information transmitted.

Other Boards

Here are a few of the many additional boards that might go into bus slots.

Console and Printer Ports

Micros come with ports for a console (a display and keyboard) and printer. When additional devices are needed, a PC board with extra ports and connections hooks to the added devices. Thus a micro might accommodate several users if it has the proper OS.

A console is connected to the computer by a serial line; it sends or receives characters one bit at a time. The console needs two ports, one for sending, the other for receiving. For data entry, as you hit a key, the code is sent to the computer and picked up by the OS for the application program (AP). The AP accepts the character and returns that character code to the screen for you to verify. Since you type much slower than the computer can react, there is no timing problem.

When you review records in a file or pages from a document, data are sent to the screen as fast as they can be absorbed by the terminal. The limitation is the **baud rate,** the transmission rate between the computer and the terminal. This limitation is governed by the speed of the terminal electronics and the rate selected for the transmission between the computer and the device. The faster character codes are transmitted, the quicker the information appears on the screen.

A common upper limit to transmission, mainly because of the electronics in the terminal, is usually 19,200 baud. At this rate, the contents of the whole screen can be totally replaced in less than a second. A more common figure is 9600 baud. At this rate it takes about two seconds to replace the screen contents completely. The difference is appreciable when you sit at the terminal all day. Be well advised to check the maximum transmission rate of equipment you purchase.

Printers attach to the computer either through serial lines just like the console, called the **RS-232 connection,** or through a parallel line, sometimes called a **Centronics connection.** There is really no significant difference in operation between the two. However a parallel connection to the printer may be somewhat less expensive and hence more desirable.

Interface Board

An **interface board** connects two or more consoles and/or printers to the CPU. Switches on the board set up port number(s) and establish the baud rate for each device. They are also needed to connect pen plotters, tablets and mice.

In some micros, components on the motherboard or chassis are wired to connectors which accept mating cable connectors and tie into consoles and printers. In a multiuser environment, an interface board is needed to provide for the additional terminals. Of course, the board alone is not sufficient; a multiuser operating system is absolutely necessary.

The PC interface board has connectors for cables to bring signals either to other connectors on the computer chassis or for direct attachment.

Video Board

Inexpensive computers such as the Sinclair, Atari and Commodore come with a keyboard but no display. You hook up the computer to a television set. To save expense in these tiny computers, frequently the display only provides capital letters on 16 display lines, each of 40 characters. This is unsatisfactory, especially for word processing. Lines to be displayed use up part of computer memory. A **video board** plugs into a slot and overcomes these obstacles by providing 24 lines of 80 characters, upper and lower case, and onboard memory, which releases valuable program space.

Analog to Digital Converter

A computer can control things in the real world if you give it the means: sensors to detect sound or light, output devices to move or control things. Attach a photocell to one port and a relay to another port, and a program can note when it gets dark outside and turn on lights in your absence. That is a simple example. Microcomputers control complex test equipment and large industrial processing equipment.

Information from sensors is analog: an electronic thermometer produces a voltage proportional to temperature. To be processed by the computer, this voltage must be converted into 0s and 1s (on and off quantities)—digital signals. The **analog to digital PC board** (or simply **A/D board**) converts an analog signal into a train of pulses. There are often several convertors on a board.

A medical monitor attached to a sick patient checks pulse, breathing rate and other vital signs. One sensor makes each kind of measurement and connects to an analog to digital converter which goes to the computer. At frequent intervals, the computer checks these inputs. When any one measurement, or a combination of them, goes beyond a safe limit, the computer automatically notifies the authorities.

The computer can send a digital signal to the port of a **digital to analog converter**. It produces a proportional voltage. For instance, a program can derive a digital pitch which the D/A converts to a voltage to drive a sound source.

A digital cruise control for your car might work thus: speedometer readings are digitized and sent to the computer. If you are not travelling at the desired speed, the program produces an output, converted to a signal applied to the accelerator to reduce or increase the speed of the car to put it in range.

An office computer can monitor windows and doors after your facility closes. With a modem, a tape recorder and additional equipment, the computer can initiate a call to the police or an executive and play a recorded message, should there be indications of an intruder.

Computer on a Board

It is now possible to get an entire computer on a board, a master, with its own disk controller. Teletek makes a PC board with the CPU chip and all its electronics, 64K of memory, I/O ports for the console and printer, *and* a disk controller. One slot on the chassis holds the master; remaining slots are free for slaves and accessory equipment boards.

6.5 NEW CHIPS

Many new chips, 16 and 32 bits wide, are on the market. All are advertised as the hottest thing around, destined as the wave of the future to obsolete all 8-bit computers. If this is so, why does the IBM Personal Computer run BASIC programs slower than most 8 bit micros? This section should provide some answers.

What Are They?

Newer computer chip designs are based on a 16 (or 32) bit structure. Most are upward compatible from 8 bit families. For instance, the Intel 8086, 8088, 80186 and 80286 are similar in many respects to the Z80 and 8080 computer chip; the Motorola 68000 and 68010 are similar to the Motorola 6800.

Start with a 16 bit chip and design the CPU board around it. The board fits into a bus, existing design or a new one. Some 16 bit CPU boards use the S-100 bus.

Basics

The true 16 bit chip can handle twice as much information with a single instruction as its 8 bit equivalent. Operations for the former are based on the **word**, a data unit of two bytes. All registers on the chip are of word size. Instructions pass words back and forth, add or subtract words and so forth. Data is read or written from memory in units of words.

Improvement

The later you design a chip, the better it should be. Technology moves rapidly and newer chips have these improvements:

1. The CPU handles 16 or 32 bit words instead of bytes.
2. Given a fixed memory speed, the CPU can get instructions faster and store and retrieve results faster.
3. Because it operates on words, the CPU does arithmetic with larger numbers in the same length of time.
4. More powerful instructions are added to the instruction set.
5. Since circuitry is faster, chips, both CPU and memory, function faster.

With all these advantages, how could a new computer possibly be slower than one built with older 8 bit chips?

Bus Compatibility

The same bus structure can be a little modified to accommodate the new computer chip. *It is very important to note that bus compatibility does not imply any other kind of compatibility.* A machine language program for a computer with an 8 bit chip will absolutely *not function* on one with a 16 bit chip or a different 8 bit chip. A program written in a higher language for one computer may be recompiled or reinterpreted for the newer computer, but the program may not function faster, as we will see.

Let us see how an existing bus can accommodate a PC board with a new chip using the S-100 bus as the example.

Data Lines

The S-100 bus provides two sets of eight **data lines,** one called **DO,** for data output, and the other **DI,** for data input. The CPU always looks at the DI line for information from memory or a device. Information *to* memory or a device goes on the DO lines.

There is really no need for unidirectional lines. For this pair of lines to transmit *or* receive a word at a time, put the 8 bit lines together and you have one 16 bit data line, Figure 6.5.1.

Address Lines

New computers may have full 20 or 24 bit addressing as shown in Figure 6.5.1.

Control Signals

Two additional control signals let memory operate in either 8 or 16 bit mode: one sent by the master says that it is working with 16 bit data; the other

6.5 NEW CHIPS 183

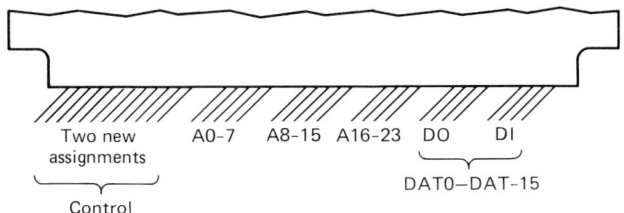

Figure 6.5.1. The 16 bit S-100 bus layout.

signal is sent by the memory or slave confirms that it is operating with 16 bit information.

Memory Redesign

New memories work in both modes: a memory of 32K bytes also operates as 16K words.

Word Oriented

To access new memory in terms of words, the following action takes place. To *recall,* a 24 bit address is put on the address bus and the master control signal is asserted. When the memory receives the address, recall request and control signal, it puts a word on the 16 bit data bus and asserts that it is operating in 16 bit mode.

To *memorize,* the CPU sends a word on the combined data bus. This is picked up by the memory board and written into the addressed word.

Byte Mode

When an 8 bit CPU uses the bus to recall information from memory, it *does not* assert the 16 bit mode signal; it sends a 16 or 24 bit address to the memory. Memory responds by *not asserting* its 16 bit response signal and puts one byte on DI.

Memorizing is similar: The CPU sends the address and places the datum on DO. Since no control signal for sixteen bits is sent, memory looks for only eight.

Performance

There is no question that the 16 bit computer accesses memory much faster. Then why doesn't it perform better?

Probably the most important fact about the IBM PC is that, while its 8088 chip *can* address up to 1M of RAM by extended addressing, it *does not* access full words. It passes one byte between RAM and the CPU. This cuts its speed in half.

Existing programs for 8 bit machines cannot be used in their current form, so they must be translated. The old translator is rewritten to use the same commands on the new computer and does not take advantage of the new commands. Hence only slight improvement in performance, if any, is seen with the same program operating on the faster computer. Some benchmark BASIC programs when executed on three 16 bit computers and a typical S-100 8 bit computer actually performed best on the latter.

I/O Limitation

Programs designed for business applications or word processing are limited by the speed of I/O devices. Clearly when you enter information at the console, it doesn't matter how fast the computer runs; it can keep up with your slow typing.

Transferring information between the program and floppy disks is independent of CPU speed. A business program speed is limited to how fast the floppy operates. To find a record, a program scans a file at the speed of the floppy disk. A faster CPU does not help.

Faster CPUs may affect calculation speed but have little effect on business applications, except where large spread sheets are concerned.

6.6 THE IBM PC AND XT

Importance

Section 6.5 was first drafted shortly after the IBM PC was introduced and emphasizes its shortcomings. But IBM is no laggard in marketing. It knows how to get a strong foothold and immediately sought out prospective application program vendors. At the time of its introduction, there was practically no software for the 8088. Within a matter of a year, many new programs were being written *exclusively* for the IBM PC. The software scene has shifted and now there are a considerable number of APs for this machine. One should carefully consider the advantages of a system so well supported, advertised and marketed and with such a wealth of software.

The PC and XT have become popular and offer much, hence deserve special attention.

6.6 THE IBM PC AND XT

- This section examines the hardware, its layout and special considerations.
- Section 7.8 is about operating systems for the PC, XT and AT.
- Section 8.4 examines versions of BASIC designed for use with the IBM PC.
- Parts of Chapter 16 are devoted to the PCjr and look-alikes.

The Hardware

The IBM PC, XT and the AT look almost exactly alike. They have what the industry calls a **small footprint,** which means that the system occupies very little desk space. This makes it appealing for the office.

By now the appearance of the IBM PC is familiar to all. The main computer box shown in Figure 6.6.1, has two rectangular areas at the right for the disk drives. Slots permit loading the floppies. In the XT, one of the rectangles has no slot since the hard disk is housed there. Above the box is the monitor, attached by cable to the computer box; the monitor may be moved about to provide a better view and to reduce relections. A 6 foot

Figure 6.6.1. The IBM PC XT.

cable attached to the back of the box leads to the keyboard, giving freedom of placement. You may even hold the keyboard on your lap. Still another cable goes to the printer, which may be placed conveniently, even under the table if desired.

Figure 6.6.2 is a photograph of the IBM PC XT with the cover removed and the front at the bottom of the page. At the left you see the **system board** and seven expansions slots—the XT has more slots than the PC. In the center at the bottom is the floppy drive with only its built-in circuit card showing. At the bottom right is the totally enclosed hard drive.

Figure 6.6.3 is a photograph of the same view, this time with printed circuit boards plugged in. Notice how they vary in size. Some of the slots are actually unavailable because their boards supply needed functions for normal use. Here you see one cabled to the disk drive—it is the disk controller board. Also at least one video board is needed.

The System Board

Figure 6.6.4 shows the IBM PC system board diagramatically. At the rear are two connections to the cassette drive and the display. At the upper left,

Figure 6.6.2. Inside the IBM XT with no PC boards.

6.6 THE IBM PC AND XT 187

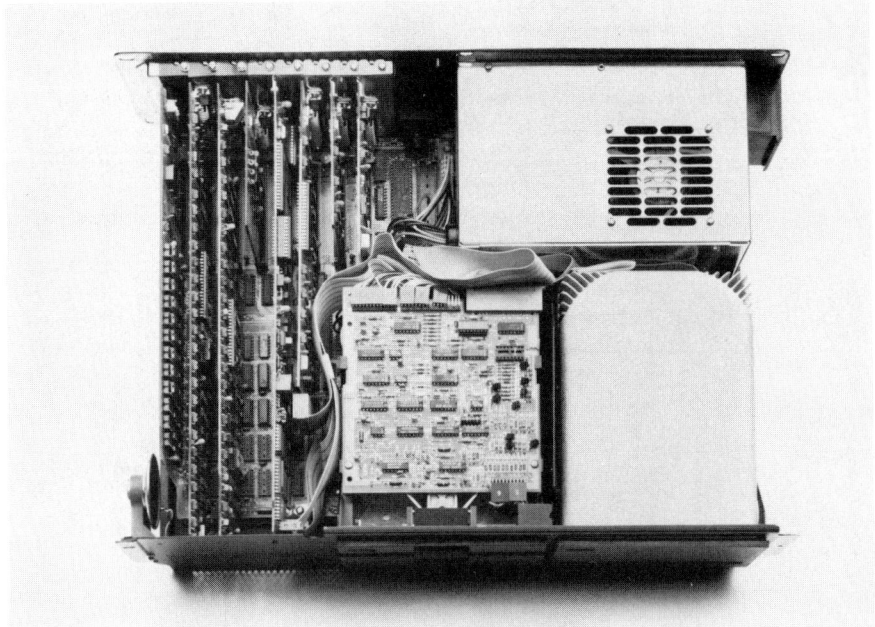

Figure 6.6.3. Inside the IBM XT showing the PC boards.

five **expansion slots** are wired into the bus to accept PC boards. Going rightward, we encounter the main microprocessor chip, the 8088. Next to it is a socket, usually supplied empty, where you can plug the 8087 coprocessor. This additional chip speeds up calculations. Its effect is not evident unless you execute programs which mainly do arithmetic processing. At the right a connector hooks the board to the power supply on the chassis (not shown).

Near the center of the system board are a number of sockets, some loaded with ROM chips. Their use is discussed shortly. Below are sockets for RAM chips and a connector where the speaker at the front of the computer plugs in. The speaker can be programmed to emit musical noises.

Memory

As noted, the PC contains both ROM and RAM memory. It is important to understand why two types of memory are used and how much of each is available.

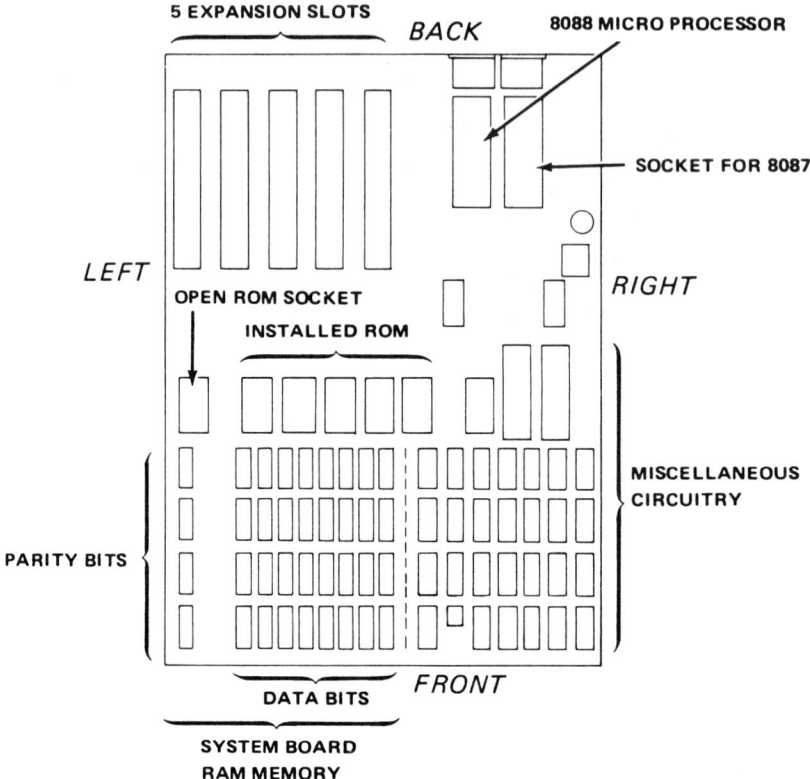

Figure 6.6.4. IBM PC system board. (From Peter Norton, *Inside the IBM PC: Access to Advanced Features and Programming.* Bowie, MD: Robert J. Brady Co., 1983)

RAM

The newer Intel chips, the 8088, 8086 and later revisions of this microprocessor, the 80186 and 80286, have 20 bit addressability. Theoretically these microprocessors could be used with one megabyte (1MB) of memory, either RAM or ROM. Of this over 600 kilobytes (KB) can actually be installed in a PC (or XT).

A PC minimum configuration comes with 64K of RAM. There are sockets on the system board (Figure 6.6.2) which accommodate an additional 192K of RAM to a maximum of 256K. These additional chips are usually plugged in by the dealer. This is a simple operation. (As long as you know the right place to put them, it is cheaper to get them from a parts dealer and plug them in yourself.)

There are slots on the bus for expansion PC (printed circuit) cards. One card provides additional memory. It is sensible to expand to 512K or 640K but only if you have programs which can use the additional memory. Otherwise it uses up a slot which might go for some other purpose. If you are wise, you can put memory to use as a "semidisk"; files kept there are accessible at ten or more times the speed for floppies.

ROM

ROM stands for read-only memory. It is **nonvolatile**—information and data stored there is immediately available when you turn the computer on. Hence four important programs are kept there:

- the **bootstrap loader,** which brings nonresident portions (those which are on disk) of the operating system into memory;
- the main device drivers, known as the **basic input/output system** or **BIOS;**
- the **checkout program,** which checks memory, the processor and the devices on startup;
- the **BASIC interpreter.**

There is space on the system board for 64K of ROM. This is a huge amount. Chips for 40K of ROM are provided. The remaining 24K sockets are left empty and may be used for expansion in the future.

Every system requires a bootstrap loader. We have seen that it may be located on the disk controller board. Another place for it is in the main memory ROM, but this was not possible in earlier computers which did not have this large amount of memory addressability.

Putting the BASIC interpreter into ROM has dubious advantage for a computer of this size and price, since disk drives are almost standard and it's easy to bring the interpreter from them. However, the original design considered use with only a cassette as input and output. When such is the case, it takes considerable time to bring in the interpreter. A ROM interpreter is immediately available and makes good sense.

In my judgment, the most important ROM feature is for holding part of the operating system. Whether this facilitates the operating sytem is doubtful, but its effect is to bury part of DOS in ROM. Software is not patentable; however, what is wired into the hardware or put in ROM is subject to copyright. IBM has copyrighted their ROM contents, which makes copying by its competitors illegal. Companies have pirated Apple software. The makers of the Eagle, and Corona systems copied or closely adapted part of IBM's ROM software and were sued by IBM. They settled out of court and agreed to rewrite their BIOS. The BIOS in ROM is given more attention in Section 7.8, where software compatibility is examined.

Addressing

A 20 bit address is required to reach all of memory. However the 8088 and comparable microprocessors deal with numbers as words of 16 bits. A command can refer to an **operand,** a datum to be processed, using a 16 bit word or two of them as a 32 bit word: the former is insufficient to reach all of memory; the latter is extremely wasteful.

The answer is a special register in the 8088 chip called the **segment register (SR).** It holds a portion of an address, the high order (left hand) few bits. All information, data and instructions, is referenced with respect to this particular segment whose address is stored in the SR. Relative addressing with respect to the SR may reach a maximum of 16 bits.

The actual address of a datum is 20 bits and is called its **effective address.** The method for software to reach a particular datum is illustrated in Figure 6.6.5. The program first sets the segment register. That setting may remain in effect as long as the program does not stray out of a 64K area called a **segment.** That is a simple demand. Now all information is addressed relative to the segment address.

The address in the SR has a final nibble (4 bits) of 0 implied. The SR only holds the first four hex nibbles of the address (hex, for hexadecimai, is explained in Section 9.2). The offset register, shown in the figure as OR, contains some hex address within the 64K segment (here 4444). The effective address is calculated by adding the SR and the OR, assuming that the last nibble of the SR is 0. The result is shown in the figure (the contents of the registers are in hex and in hex addition, 4 + 9 = D, not 13).

Assignment

Portions of memory are assigned to particular functions. The most popular unit for assignment is 64K. This is exactly 10,000 bytes in hex. Thus assignments are often made in terms of the most significant hexadecimal digit. This chunk of 64K, called a **paragraph,** is named by its leading hex digit. Thus the bottom of memory is paragraph 0.

Figure 6.6.6 shows the standard memory assignments. Minimum mem-

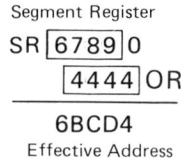

Figure 6.6.5. Forming the effective address.

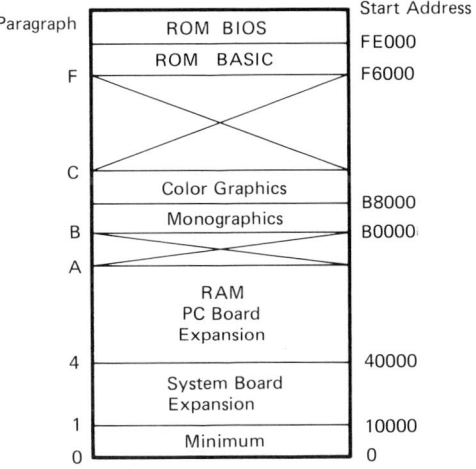

Figure 6.6.6. IBM PC memory assignments.

ory, paragraph 0, is always supplied to the purchaser on the system board. Expansion sockets on the system board account for paragraphs 1 through 3, a total of four paragraphs or 256K. Directly above this are addresses for more memory. This can be purchased on PC expansion boards which fit into slots on the bus and may occupy paragraphs 4 through 9.

Paragraphs A and B are assigned for graphics. Use is not currently made of paragraph A. All graphic memory is provided in paragraph B but physically situated on graphic boards inserted in slots, as discussed in detail in Section 13.9.

ROM occupies the top of memory, paragraph F, not all used. The figure shows the top of memory used for BASIC and the BIOS from F6000 on.

Figure 6.6.4 shows that IBM has designated that paragraphs C through E are not available nor addressable.

Disk Drives

The PC uses disk drives developed by Tandon, including one or two floppies according to whether you opt for an additional disk. Each floppy has 40 tracks of eight 512 byte sectors. Thus the capacity of the floppy is 164K per drive. The optional dual sided floppy doubles this to 328K.

Floppies for newer versions of the PC and all of the XTs now record nine sectors of 512 bytes per track. Thus single sided disks hold 184K bytes with dual sided disks hold 368K.

Disks are soft sectored. Hence the same disks may be used with either sytem. The nine sector system can also *read* eight sector disks but can only *record* in nine sector mode. The XT comes equipped with one double density floppy drive and one hard Winchester drive which stores 10 megabytes (10MB).

The **IBM PC AT** has several combinations of external storage. The Model 68 comes with a single 1.2MB double sided quad density floppy disk drive. It achieves this high capacity in two ways. It uses 80 tracks per side instead of 40. Each track has 15 sectors instead of 9. Special floppies for the drive cost about $8 a piece at this writing. The drive can also read disks written at the lower 320K/360K densities used for the PC and XT, but cannot write at the lower density.

The Model 99 has both a 1.2 MB floppy and a 20MB hard disk. A second 20MB hard disk can also be handled by the controller if ordered. An important feature of these hard disks is their higher transfer rate, which is at least twice that of the XT hard disk drives.

The use of the expansion slots to add a hard disk drive either to the PC or to the XT is explained shortly.

Keyboard

The IBM PC (and XT) keyboard has received considerable criticism. One would expect the ultimate from the company which developed the Selectric typewriter, the de facto standard. Here are the major complaints:

1. The touch and feel of the keyboard is not the same as the Selectric.
2. The shift key is on a different horizontal level from the space bar. There are other keys in positions usually occupied by the shift keys; this takes getting used to.
3. The carriage return key is called enter and has a strange arrow on it.
4. The number lock key (numloc) changes the function of the numeric key pad, but there is no way of knowing whether the lock is on (until you see that keys on the key pad provide a different function than you expect). Other keyboard vendors, including PC compatibles, provide light emitting diodes (LEDs) on locking keys which light when they are locked.

The keyboard certainly has a large number of keys which provide flexibility in entering information. Some improvements have been made for the AT keyboard, including lights for the key locks and a better feel to the keys.

Function Keys

At the left of the keyboard is a group of ten function keys, as described in Chapter 3. They generate fixed codes whose meaning is set by the OS, BASIC and by most APs. The operating system sees them as requests to perform specific OS functions. BASIC uses them as described in Chapter 8. An AP such as a word processor responds to codes from the function keys as specific WP functions. Up to 40 codes result from using function keys alone or in combination with alt, shift and control. (See Section 3.3)

Numeric Key Pad

The key pad, found at the right of the keyboard, has the conventional numeric keys which function to enter numerals, plus and minus signs and the decimal point in numeric mode when numloc is locked. When numloc is released, the keys position the cursor to different parts of the screen as noted by the symbols inscribed on the keys. It is difficult to see which purpose the keys have, since there is no way to tell whether numloc is set, except by its feel, or when you have an AT.

Monochrome Display / Printer Adapter Card

The hardware and circuitry to drive both the printer and a black and white display are incorporated in one PC card which fits into a bus slot. The card contains memory which is directly addressable by any program or the operating system. Thus data stored in particular positions in memory on the graphics board can be processed directly by the program and displayed simultaneously on the screen. This board contains circuitry to *refresh* the screen many times per second.

Circuitry usually kept in the terminal is found on the board: the display memory and the character generator. Since the display buffer is directly addressable, characters entered or altered need not be retransmitted to a separate terminal buffer. In some instances, this saves time.

The character generator consists of 8K of ROM. Monochrome display memory consists of 4K of RAM. Two consecutive bytes are assigned to each screen character:

- first is the code for the character to be displayed;
- next is the **attribute code,** which indicates whether a character is to be displayed directly, in reverse video, flashing directly or in reverse video, or invisible.

The display provides a twenty-fifth line which may be used by application programs for status.

Color Graphics Monitor Adapter

This PC board plugs into the bus and is necessary for color graphics. It operates in two modes:

- **alphanumeric (A/N),** or text mode where the screen displays text;
- **all points addressable (APA),** which is graphics mode.

The board is set when the AP or OS sends a command to enter one or the other mode.

Devices

The board can drive one of four different devices:

1. A black and white monitor.
2. A color monitor.
3. A RGB color monitor.
4. A television set.

An RF modulator is required to connect the PC to a television set. It converts the video signals into the proper form for one channel on your TV set, and attaches to the antenna lead of the set. The TV display is restricted to 25 lines of 40 characters each.

The graphics board provides a video output connected directly by cable to a monitor: a B/W monitor displays only black and white, but is not recommended, since such monitors do not handle color signals well. Either type of color monitor is possible, with the RGB monitor providing the best kind of display.

A/N Mode

An A/N mode, you get 25 lines of 40 characters each when the color board is hooked to a TV set, which acts as a low resolution or medium resolution monitor. Only with the high resolution monitor—RGB—do you get lines of 80 characters, as with the monochrome adapter card and its display. A blink or change of intensity is provided for the monochrome display. With color, associated with each character is a choice of eight background colors and sixteen foreground colors. These are fixed combinations of the primaries: red, green and blue.

APA Mode

APA mode provides dot addressable graphics. It can be set to three qualities of resolution depending upon the monitor provided. More about this is in Section 13.9.

Expansion Slots

Both the PC and XT include expansion slots; the PC has five slots and the XT has eight. These slots get used up very quickly. One is necessary for the floppy disk controller; another is required for the monochrome display and printer board; color graphics requires a third board. The XT comes with the asynchronous communications adapter and the hard disk controller, each requiring a board.

Of the eight slots in the XT, only six accept full size accessory cards. The other two accept only smaller cards, such as the game controller, printer or asynchronous communication cards.

The AT has 8 full size slots for the same cards as those the PC and XT use. Each slot has 8 additional conductors to accomodate special PCs with full AT memory addressability.

Expansion Unit

One can purchase an expansion unit for the PC which contains a 10MB hard disk and an additional expansion bus with a number of slots. The expansion unit plugs into one of the PC or XT slots, and you get a hard disk and room for further expansion.

III
Software, Programs and Data

7
The Operating System

7.1 OVERVIEW

Definitions

Software consists of programs. One program, of which there are several types, is in control of the computer whenever it is running. An **application program (AP)** usually solves a single user problem; it

- does text editing;
- makes numerical calculations;
- prints out a report;
- keeps track of money and materials;
- does forecasting, and so forth.

There are APs (i.e., Lotus, Context MBA) which combine several such functions.

Another group of programs helps run the computer: the **operating system** (or **OS**) lets you choose what AP to run next. It provides services to all APs; it does not solve a user's problem directly. It is important to understand the *need* for the operating system and the function of its *components,* introduced here and described in more detail in the next sections.

Parts of the Computer System Must Match

The overall computer system consists of a number of parts, all of which must match exactly for it to work, shown pictorially in Figure 7.1.1.

At the left is the hardware. A shape with double lines conveys that it cannot easily be altered; to change it you have to open it up and add new boards or solder new connections.

The only way you talk to the hardware is through the operating system.

199

200 THE OPERATING SYSTEM

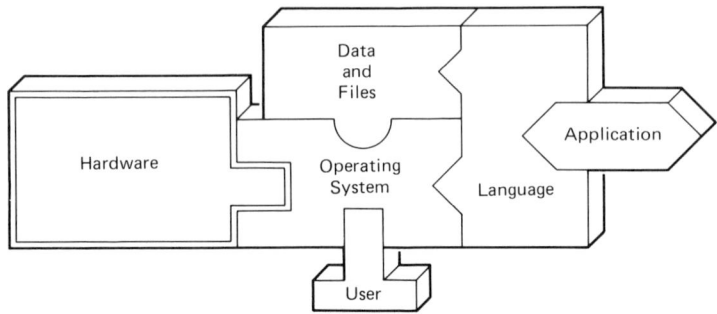

Figure 7.1.1. Mating the parts of the computer.

The OS is, both figuratively and actually, at the center. It is the mediator and provides communication with

- the hardware;
- the operator;
- data and files;
- the programming language;
- the application.

Hardware

An OS is designed for one hardware family. Figure 7.1.2 shows this pictorially. The Radio Shack TRS-80 microcomputer has its own OS, called the TRS Disk Operating System (TRSDOS). The TRS-80 cannot reasonably operate without any OS. It cannot use IBM's MVS, which is a large mainframe operating system that would not fit into its memory; the TRS-80 cannot use RSX-11 for DEC's mini, its PDP 11 series; it cannot even use CP/M-80 for the S-100 bus computer, though the two hardware systems use similar components and are comparable in other ways.

To use an OS on a machine other than one for which it was designed, two approaches are taken. Each involves considerable cost and labor.

One approach, shown in Figure 7.1.3, alters the hardware to make it look like what the OS was designed for. CP/M, a major microcomputer OS, does not work on the Apple II. But you can purchase an AppleCard printed circuit board that fits into a slot in the Apple and makes it look like the S-100 computer for which CP/M was designed. You might do this to use the many application programs (APs) that work with CP/M but would not otherwise run on the Apple.

The other approach, Figure 7.1.4, redesigns the OS to fit different hard-

7.1 OVERVIEW 201

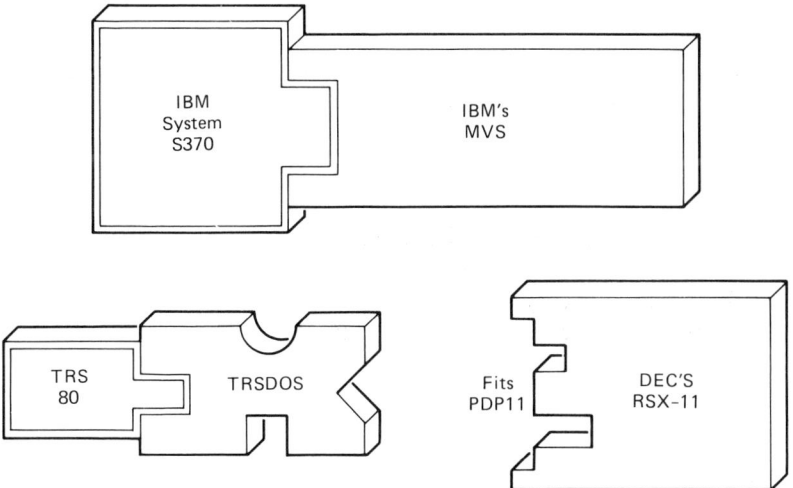

Figure 7.1.2. An OS is designed for a particular computer.

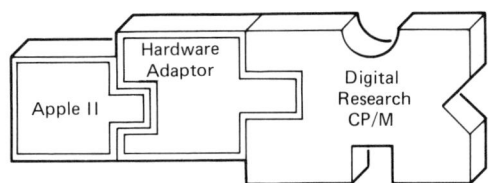

Figure 7.1.3. A hardware adapter can mate an OS to a CPU.

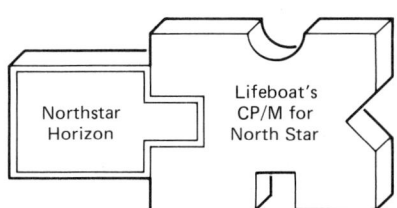

Figure 7.1.4. An OS can be adapted to a different computer.

ware but otherwise remains the same. CP/M was reworked by Lifeboat Associates to match the North Star Horizon, with which this new OS mates exactly. CP/M-86 from Digital Research runs on the IBM PC.

The "personality" of the computer system resides in the operating system.

User

OS contact with the user arises when you boot the computer or when an application completes. The OS issues a **prompt,** a visible request to ask you what to do next. You now can ask the OS to

1. Start an AP;
2. Find out what files are on the disk;
3. How much room is left for new files;
4. Look at a file quickly;
5. Use a maintenance routine to check the hardware;
6. Employ utilities to copy, create, destroy or rewrite a file;
7. Do any of many other things.

Data

Data arrives and departs in different ways:

- entered at the keyboard;
- viewed on the screen;
- printed on paper;
- from a file on disk or tape;
- stored into a file.

Whichever the source or destination, a small program, or **routine,** is needed to handle the data. It is redundant for every application program to have its *own* routine for *each* activity. Instead, the OS has **drivers** which the AP calls on to provide the service.

The Working System

Figure 7.1.5 shows a computer system with several devices and memory in the center. A hexagon represents a program or part of one. The user cares only about the **application program,** or **AP.** All the other components shown are parts of the OS.

Three hexagons are labeled *driver*. A **driver** runs one device attached to the system. At the bottom of memory is the **control program.** It accepts requests from the operator, the application program and other operating system components. The **File Manager** manages the files and data on external storage.

OS components which are **resident** remain in memory after the OS is loaded and hence give immediate service to an AP. They do not have to be

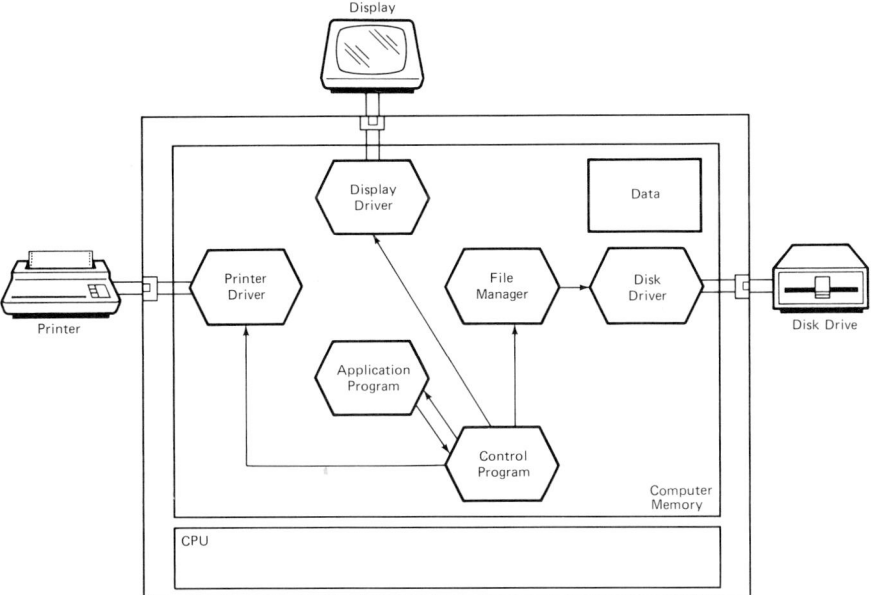

Figure 7.1.5. A computer system with hardware, devices and the components of the operating system.

loaded from the disk. A copy of larger OS components, which cannot be stored conveniently in memory is on the **system diskette:** translators and utilities for creating and copying programs and data.

Data used by the program is also in memory, Figure 7.1.5. Some programs only need a little data—a few numbers, perhaps. For the word processor (WP), one or more pages of text is in memory as you edit it: records processed by an accounting program are temporarily held in memory.

One Piece Software

The computer is sometimes run by a single package. You do not know what is on the disk or in memory while the package runs. But an OS *is* there and consumes memory, which limits the amount of space available for program, data and working storage. So is it really necessary to understand the operating system? When the supplier provides a complete system with little or no choice for the devices supplied, it is virtually impossible to alter the software without the help of the manufacturer.

However, understanding software requirements can help you make choices among systems and make it possible to talk more effectively with sales people regarding the current and future capabilities of systems. It also lets you consider putting together your own system from components and making knowledgeable choices.

7.2 THE OPERATING SYSTEM

An operating system component works rapidly and effectively when resident. But then the portion of memory it occupies is unavailable to application programs or as a work area. Thus some components remain on disk to be brought in only when needed. This includes utilities, translators, special programs for math, sorting, etc.

Resident OS

Three parts of the operating system are resident:

- the control program;
- device drivers;
- the File Manager.

ROM

How do resident portions of the operating system get into memory? The manufacturer can supply them in ROM (read-only memory), which is **nonvolatile**—its contents do not disappear when the machine is turned off. Programs in ROM are permanent and always available. But to revise and update the ROM portion of the operating system, the manufacturer must design and fabricate a new ROM; you must buy it and plug it in. Changes in ROM OS are expensive and difficult to make.

Booting from Disk

The other alternative keeps a copy of resident OS components on disk. The hardware automatically "brings in the system" each time the computer is turned on: you **boot** the system. This signifies that the system is pulling itself up by its own bootstraps. The OS components are written in fixed positions on disks called **system disks.** The disk controller which runs the disk drive may have its own small ROM. When you turn on the power, the disk controller program in ROM reads in the OS to a preassigned position in memory.

ROM gives control to the OS which displays a sign-on message and issues a prompt to enter the first request. A **turnkey system** is self-contained and its operating system has built-in instructions to bring in the AP and give it control. The AP then prompts for the first action, often with a menu.

Control Program

The **control program** simplifies the job of all APs, which need to

- get data and commands from the keyboard;
- put information on the display;
- operate the printer;
- use a disk file.

The control program uses the device drivers extensively. Data typed at the keyboard passes through the keyboard driver to the AP. The control program transmits messages from the AP to the display via its driver.

Your requests are handled initially by the control program when you ask to

- run a chosen program;
- display the contents of a disk which is mounted;
- erase or copy a named file.

The control program uses the drivers directly; its File Manager finds files or loads a program from the disk. The resident operating system consists of all the programs displayed in Figure 7.1.5 except the AP.

Drivers

Each device connected to the computer needs a driver routine *tailored to it*. For each action it might perform there is a small program, a **subroutine**, in the driver. The AP through the OS makes a simple request for a specific device action; the driver chooses the proper subroutine. The saving derived is this:

- all driver routines are prewritten and in memory;
- they are available instantly;
- they need not be rewritten for each application;
- a simple request activates each.

Functions performed by the device and run by subroutines in the driver are standard. But devices differ from one manufacturer to another. A driver must be tailored to a particular device; it gives control signals expected by *that* device and interprets signals returned from *that* device.

Consider the printer. The AP assembles a line of text to send to the printer driver. It accepts the identical AP request, regardless of the physical device. Printers differ, not only in how they print a line and their speed, but also in the control signals they receive and generate. The driver for a Qume printer, for instance, is adjusted to the data and **control signals** for that printer and does not work with an Epson or Printronix. Control signals determine character spacing, line spacing, carriage return, and so forth.

Availability

The driver is available (because it is resident) to both the application program and the control program; to reach the driver, the AP calls the control program, passing along a number. The control program finds the driver using a table giving its locations. The number passed tells the driver what service is needed.

Tailoring

Since a driver is device specific, it is important to provide proper routines for a particular physical device. Sometimes a system vendor does this tailoring for you. However, you may buy a package such as VisiCalc for your Apple and find that *you* have to install the printer (see page 205). This is because the package talks directly to the printer instead of using the system driver.

When it is necessary to tailor a driver, whether for the system or an AP, there is a special program included with either you call up. It has a large table listing the codes required by most common devices that you may have purchased. It then presents a menu to you listing these devices by vendor and model number. You hit a key to name your device. The program looks up the codes for that device and alters a "prototype" driver accordingly. Then it writes the driver back to the disk. Now whenever access is needed to that device, the altered driver is employed.

If you have an uncommon device not listed in the table, the program may ask you for the codes required to activate it in various ways. Then you must refer to the device's technical manual to determine them and answer the questions. The program enters the codes into the prototype driver as above.

Summary

Some application programs, such as word processors and data base managers, have special requirements. Sometimes they include their own driver(s) to manage a device more efficiently or in some special way. Still, the OS must include its own device drivers for the use of other programs and to communicate with the user directly.

There must be one driver for every device attached to the system. It is tailored by the user, vendor or supplier to match that device.

7.3 THE RESIDENT OPERATING SYSTEM

Source

The **resident operating system** is in memory while programs run. It's important to distinguish services of the OS from those supplied by the AP. The operating system is there to serve you. It can do so only if you know how to tell it what you need. For instance, it can show the names of all the files on the floppy disks now in your drives.

Example OS

Since OSs differ considerably, even for micros, it would be foolhardy to try to cover all of them. I use CP/M as an example of a typical system because it serves a wide variety of compatible computer systems. It is also the basis for *both* MS-DOS and CP/M-86, the two principal OSs for the IBM PC. Although OSs differ in where modules go in memory and what commands activate them, they are similar in the *kind* of services they provide. Hence knowing one OS well lets you extend this knowledge easily to other OSs.

Later, in Section 7.8, the pertinent missing details of PC-DOS are filled in.

Program Space

Figure 7.3.1 is a map of memory after CP/M is brought in. The area available to application programs is called the **transient program area,** or **TPA.** It extends from 100 hex to an upper boundary labeled CBASE in the figure. Numbers for memory addresses are **hexadecimal** (base 16). They consist of the digits 0 to 9 and the letters between A and F. This is explained in Chapter 9.

Upper Limit

The transient area must begin at a fixed and known location memory where APs are designed to be loaded. In this way, the loader for all application

208 THE OPERATING SYSTEM

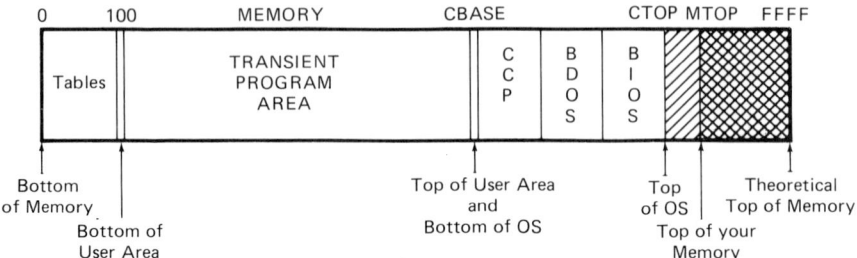

Figure 7.3.1. Map of memory showing the position of the operating system components.

programs and utilities can be kept simple. (An AP has to be altered to be run at another address.)

The upper limit of memory available to the AP is shown symbolically as CBASE. It depends on how much hardware memory is in the computer.

The more memory you have bought, the more is available for APs. The amount of memory occupied by the operating system is "overhead"; it depends on the devices in the system (and hence the drivers) and not on memory size. CP/M is about 3K and can operate in a minimum of 24K. In 64K, CP/M leaves 61K as a transient area. The IBM PC has a minimum of 64K. Its transient area size depends on the amount of memory you have and can be 500K or more, if you have a 640K memory.

Rationale

Let us examine the rationale for the arrangement of Figure 7.3.1. First, why not put all the OS at the bottom of memory and make the TPA a fixed area right above it? That would be fine if the OS were fixed in size. But the more devices you have, the more drivers you need and this takes up more room. If you make the OS big enough to serve any system, you waste valuable memory.

Then why not start the TPA at the bottom of memory, at 0? Then the operating system could occupy whatever it needs up to the top of memory. The problem with this alternative is that entry points to the operating system and the drivers would then depend upon the OS size.

The position of the operating system varies from one computer configuration to the next. For CP/M (and PC-DOS), a table of reference points is put at the bottom of memory in a fixed position, and is easily referenced regardless of where the rest of the operating system is. The tables occupy the positions between 0 and FF hex (**hex** is an abbreviation for **hexadecimal** described in Section 9.2). The TPA begins at 100 hex for both CP/M and PC-DOS.

7.3 THE RESIDENT OPERATING SYSTEM

Other Boundaries

At the right of Figure 7.3.1 is the theoretical top of memory, 64K or hex FFFF. The actual top of your memory is called MTOP in the figure. The locations between MTOP and FFFF *do not exist* in your system (but could be present in others).

The operating system lies between CBASE and CTOP. It starts at a round binary number; a few bytes between CTOP and MTOP are unused, shown shaded in the figure.

CP/M Components

The operating system consists of three main resident routines examined in more depth in this section:

CCP—the **console command processor** examines characters you enter at the keyboard and furnishes services you request if your command makes sense.

BIOS—the **basic input/output system** provides the drivers for all devices attached to your computer, tailored to their specifications.

BDOS—the **basic disk operating system,** the File Manager, provides control and access to files on floppies or hard disks.

Booting the System

Bringing in the operating system is *booting* the system. In some systems, all or part of the operating system is resident in ROM. In others, the system is usually on the first and second track of a floppy disk. We examine that case.

The Loader

Loading starts when you

- turn on the system or
- press the reset button.

Both activate the ROM boot loader.

The ROM loader is in read-only memory; the physical location of this ROM may either be on the disk controller or CPU board. Occasionally the ROM loader is found on the RAM board (IBM PC). In old systems, the ROM loader occupied addressable memory space which then could not

210 THE OPERATING SYSTEM

be occupied by RAM. In the North Star Horizon, for example, the memory segment occupied by the ROM loader is in the middle of RAM and breaks up memory so that an AP cannot be loaded contiguously.

Today, most 8 bit computers use the phantom line described in Chapter 6. Then the ROM address space is unavailable *only* during booting, when the phantom line is turned on. After booting is completed, the phantom signal is removed and the space just occupied by the ROM is now available for RAM addressing.

The ROM loader itself is not capable of bringing in the operating system; all it does is bring in a **loader module** to do the job. The loader is located at the very beginning of the system disk, track 0, sector 0. Figure 7.3.2 shows the ROM on the controller board. The dashed line indicates that the ROM temporarily occupies some portion of the memory address space. The boot ROM reads the first sector from the disk which passes through the controller to the bottom of memory. The sector read *is* the loader. The ROM program gives control to this loader program and turns off the phantom signal.

The System Loader

The loader now at the bottom of memory brings in the **nucleus,** the resident OS, from the remaining sectors of the first and second tracks (track 0 and track 1). The loader has the starting address of the nucleus, CBASE, and activates the controller to read those sectors into memory as shown in Figure 7.3.3 between CBASE and CTOP.

The tables associated with *this* copy of the operating system go at the bottom of memory, where the loader is now. The last act of the loader brings in one more sector from track 1 of the disk and writes it into the

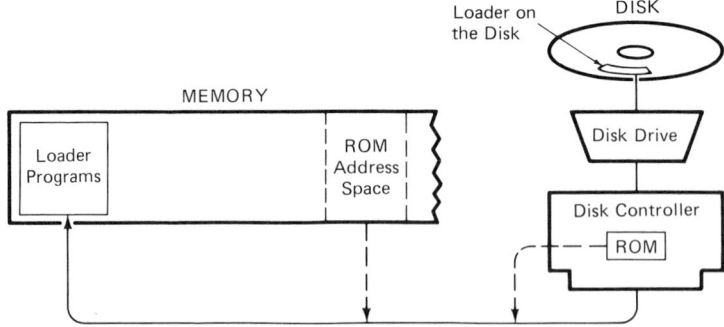

Figure 7.3.2. The first step of booting is for the disk controller ROM to bring in the loader.

7.3 THE RESIDENT OPERATING SYSTEM   211

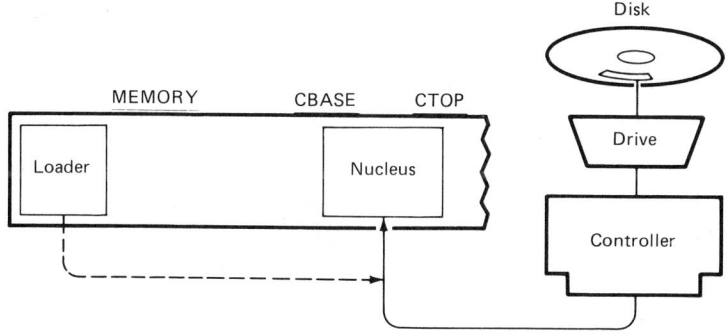

Figure 7.3.3. The loader brings in the nucleus.

bottom of memory as shown in Figure 7.3.4. This overwrites the loader except for one or two commands at its end. These commands now execute to give control to the CCP routine in the nucleus. The CCP issues a prompt to the user. The operating system is now running!

Sign On

Turn on the power or press the reset button to boot the system, called a **cold boot**. This takes a few seconds, more or less. A **sign on** message appears. It identifies the operating system, presents a license number and a caution about selling or duplicating it. A prompt line follows. A **prompt** is a symbol presented by the system (or AP), a request to enter a command. Until you answer the prompt, the system (or AP) remains idle. The CP/M prompt is,

A>   (7.3.1.)

The prompt assures you that the system is there and has finished the last request, probably successfully.

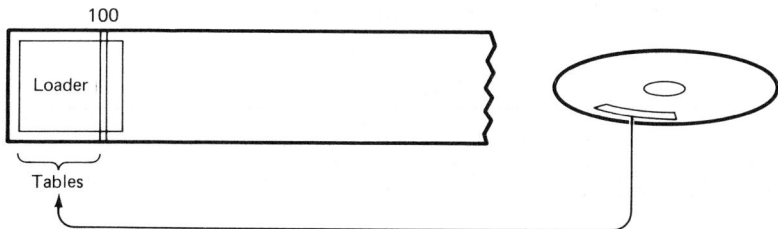

Figure 7.3.4. The loader brings in the tables and self destructs.

Warm Boot Entry

When an application program or a utility completes satisfactorily, the operating system is re-entered to return a prompt. This asks you, "What's next?" The console command processor (CCP) provides the prompt and analyzes your reply. Upon program completion, the CCP shown in Figure 7.3.1 is entered. All terminating programs execute a jump to location 0, called the **warm boot location.** It contains a jump to an entry point of the CCP which does not present the cold boot message. The CCP issues a prompt and waits. The location of the CCP depends on the amount of memory in your system; the table at the bottom of memory contains the entry points to the system.

I/O Byte

The **I/O byte** (Figure 7.3.5) specifies where output data goes and where input data comes from. This byte can also direct information which appears on the screen to print on the listing device.

Default Drive

The **default drive byte** (Figure 7.3.5) records the designation of the currently active drive called the **default drive.** You boot the system from the first drive, called drive A. This remains the default drive until you say otherwise. Requests for files with no drive prefix are directed to the floppy mounted in the default drive. Should the requested file be on some other drive, the system does not find it and reports this to you. This is clarified shortly.

Jump to BDOS

An AP can use OS services. It gets a service by performing a subroutine jump using location 5 which contains a jump to the BDOS. BDOS determines the service required from a number passed to it in a register by the AP, performs it and returns to the requestor.

0	3	4	5	8	3B	5B	80	MEMORY	100	
Warm Boot Entry		IO byte	Default Drive	Jump to BDOS	Interrupt Locations	Unassigned	Default FCB	Console and Disk Buffer Area		TPA

Figure 7.3.5. CP/M memory below 100 hex.

Interrupt Locations

When an event occurs which requires special service, an interrupt request activates the computer. Interrupt locations direct CP/M to the applicable routine. For most versions of CP/M, the interrupt locations go unused.

FCB

A fixed size **file control block (FCB)** describes the file now in use; it holds the directory entry for the active file.

Buffer Area

A buffer area of 128 bytes (80 hex) holds either a block of information from the current file being accessed or a line typed at the console.

Making Requests

When the prompt appears, you tell the system what you want done. First, you must know how to name and describe files.

File Name

File names take the form

[disk:]name[.ext] (7.3.2)

where

disk refers to one of the drives and can be a single letter from A through P;
name is a file name which must begin with a letter, and consists of not more than eight characters;
ext is an extension which describes the kind of file that is called for, may be absent and consists of not more than three characters.

The square brackets enclose items that may be omitted.
All application programs and system utilities are **command files,** with the extension COM. Other files have required suggestive extensions. For instance, a BASIC program uses the extension BAS, which the interpreter recognizes as valid.

Starting a Program

In response to the prompt, enter characters which describe the program or service you need, in this format,

    A>service [file1 file2]   (7.3.3)

Information in the brackets may sometimes be omitted. We have that

    Service is the name of a program, service or utility;
    File1 is a file or descriptor required for the service;
    File2 is another file or descriptor which may be necessary.

Here are examples of requests:

    A>AR   (7.3.4)

requests the accounts receivable program named **AR.COM** but supplies no file nor parameter names to that program.

    A>WS DATA   (7.3.5)

This requests the WordStar word processing program, called **WS.COM**, and asks that the text called **DATA** be obtained by WS to work on.

    A>PASCAL MYPROG NP   (7.3.6.)

is a request for the Pascal compiler, **PASCAL.COM**, asking it to work on a program called **MYPROG**; the last characters convey an option, **NP**, telling the Pascal compiler not to produce a printout.

Response

Let us see the *effect* of the command. *How* it is achieved is examined in Section 7.4.

The OS examines the request to see whether it is a resident service, a utility or a program. A resident service is found and supplied at once. A program or utility command file is sought and if found, is brought into the transient area. If the command file cannot be found, the system returns a message followed by a prompt:

A>GONE

?GONE

A>   (7.3.7)

If the program file is found, it is installed in the transient area and the file name and parameters which follow are loaded into the default FCB at the lower part of memory, 5C (see Figure 7.3.5). Then the program in the transient area gets control from the OS and begins to run.

7.4 REQUESTING ACTION

Entry Action

After the CCP sends a prompt to the console, it enters the BIOS keyboard routine, which activates the keyboard and waits for codes to arrive. As you hit keys, the keyboard transmits codes to BIOS, which places them in the console buffer starting at location 80. They are echoed to the screen. Should you make a mistake, you correct it by pressing backarrow. BIOS moves the cursor and the console buffer pointer back one character and you can rekey. (Rub works too, but instead of backspacing, the CCP echoes the character erased and this is confusing.)

CP/M is not sensitive to case; it sees upper and lower case as equivalent. Codes entered are checked for case; if lower case, they are echoed as such but converted to upper case in the buffer. Hence all new file names are entered in the directory in upper case. When you OPEN a file later, the name you enter is converted to upper case to match against names in the director.

BIOS accepts keystrokes until you enter return. Then BIOS returns control to the CCP. The complete command you enter is available to the CCP in the console buffer. The characters up to the first blank indicate a service. These characters are checked by the CCP against a table of resident services. If they match, the service is supplied immediately. Otherwise CCP assumes that this is a nonresident service. These two alternatives are now examined in that order.

Resident Services

When the name of the resident service described below is found in the CCP table, this causes a jump to the corresponding CCP routine. We now examine typical requests.

Directory

An important OS function is to provide a list of all files on a volume mounted on one of the drives. Simply issue

    A>DIR   (7.4.1)

and the directory of files on the default disk displays. For the directory of files on some other drive, you either switch drives, as discussed next, or issue the directory command naming the drive thus,

    A>DIR B: (7.4.2)

Change Drives

Changing the default drive directs all unprefixed requests to a different drive; reply to the prompt with the name of the new (existing) drive (a letter from A through P followed by a colon). To change the default drive from A to B, issue

    A>B: (7.4.3)

Thereafter all files are sought on B unless their name is prefixed with a file designator.

Delete a File

To delete a file, use **ERA**. The directory entry with this name is flagged to make it inaccessible. The file remains on the disk, until the space is reassigned to another file and data are entered in the physical space occupied by the *erased* file. To erase BAD, issue

    A>ERA BAD   (7.4.4)

Rename

Sometimes an existing file needs a new name. Thus, if you make changes in a file and keep a backup copy, rename **MYFILE** as an old version, MYFILE.OLD. Issue this command,

    A>REN MYFILE.OLD=MYFILE   (7.4.5)

Saving from Memory

A program in memory may be altered with a utility such as DDT, described in Section 7.5. This is an advanced technique. An altered program in the transient area is moved from memory to disk with **SAVE**. Indicate the number of blocks (128 byte units) to save and the name of the file. To save 10 blocks from the TPA to a file called **NEWPROG.COM**, give this command,

    A>SAVE 10 NEWPROG.COM   (7.4.7)

Note that you must give the extension explicitly.

Display File Content

To inspect a text without an editor, use **TYPE**. (For a *program file,* you get strange results, beeps, and symbols thrown all over your screen because many bytes in the file are nonprinting control characters.) Enter **TYPE**, followed by the name of the file; display a file called **LTR.TXT** with

    A>TYPE LTR.TXT   (7.4.7)

Halt the Display

CP/M displays text as fast as it can be transmitted, much faster than you can read it. To stop display, press ^S before it starts the display. The CCP sends a request for the next character from the keyboard before it starts the display. Thus keyboard characters can act as commands during display. Most characters stop display action dead and bring forth a prompt. However, ^S simply directs the CCP to stop for a while. The next time you press ^S, more text begins to display again.

Print Output

You can direct all output going to the screen to print with ^P. With **TYPE**, ^P prints and displays a file at the same time. But when finished, the prompt which goes to the screen also goes to the printer. And the reply that you make, and so on, until you tell the CCP to stop printing by pressing ^P again. (Hence ^P is a toggle.)

Warm Boot

The execution of some system services and most programs can be stopped if you press ^C. This directs an immediate warm boot which returns a prompt to start something new. This works while running a program with BASIC and halts most any other program, unless there is something wrong with it. The only hope then is to press the reset button for a *cold* boot. When you change disks, you must also hit ^C for CP/M to get the directory for the new disk instead of using the old one.

User Identification

When several users have programs and documents on various disks, these can be kept private from each other to a certain degree. A user number can be associated with each file. Then when a directory is requested by user number, only files for that user display.

Program Loading

Any command which begins with characters not in the CCP resident utility table represents an externally stored program or utility. CCP requests a command file with the extension COM. BDOS searches the directory on the *default* disk for a file with the name entered and the extension COM. If it is *not* found, CCP displays the command file name with ? after it and then the prompt

    A>WS

    WS?   (7.4.8)

With the program on another drive, prefix its name with the drive name. For example, with WS on drive B, say

    A>B:WS   (7.4.9)

For PC-DOS the CCP (called COMMAND) also checks for files with extension EXE and BAT.

Work for BDOS

When the program name *is* found, the directory entry describes the file's extents. A large program may consist of extents. An **extent** is a group of contiguous blocks. The directory entry contains the disk location of each extent of the file. This is needed by the file manager but does not display when DIR is issued.

The CCP issues a BDOS call to read the program from the listed extents to memory, starting at location 100. After loading the first extent, BDOS finds the next extent on disk and loads it following the first in memory, continuing thus until the whole program is in memory. BDOS reports this to the CCP, which then gives control to the program.

The name of any data file associated with the program is in the **default FCB,** 5C. If a second file name or a set of parameters is included, this is loaded from the console buffer by the CCP into the second half of the default FCB. That part of the FCB is free, since the FCB itself has not yet been recovered from the directory. The AP knows where to find the FCB if it chooses.

Service to Application Programs

The OS provides services directly or through BDOS to APs on request thus:

1. The AP describes the service with a number;
2. It provides a location in memory;
3. It passes control to the service routine;
4. The service is rendered;
5. The calling program gets control back;
6. The AP can check a register to see the status of the service.

Identifying the Service

CP/M identifies services by number as the AP puts this number in the C register (a Z80 hardware register).

Memory Location

The AP assigns a place in memory for

- output for the terminal;
- the FCB for a disk file;
- the file name sought in the directory.

The AP puts two bytes which give this memory location in registers D and E for BDOS.

Calling BDOS

The program fills the D and E registers and passes control to BDOS with a subroutine call to location 5. That location contains the entry point to BDOS (see Figure 7.3.5). The jump via 5 gives control to BDOS at the location peculiar to your system.

Return Code

BDOS tries to perform the service requested but may not succeed. What if the AP asks for a file that's not listed in the directory? The AP can tell if services were provided from a result byte which BDOS puts in the A register. A value of 0 signifies that the request has been serviced; another number indicates why the service was not provided (e.g. unlisted file name).

Return to Caller

When control goes to BDOS, the return point in the original program goes into the **system stack.** This is a repository for information, just like a bulletin board. When BDOS finishes its work it gives a *return* command. The return address is popped out of the stack and control goes back to the program. Its first action should check the A register to check the service request.

7.5 NONRESIDENT SERVICES

Description

CP/M comes with a number of utilities. Others to serve additional purposes can be purchased: translators, compilers, interpreters, word processors and so forth, might also be considered utilities. **Nonresident services** are programs which run in the transient area and are found on the disk with the extension COM. When you create a system disk, you may include or exclude any of these services. To call for a service, type its name after the prompt. The extension COM is implied.

Any command is first reviewed by the CCP. When its name is absent from the internal service table, the CCP program looks for the program in the default volume directory. The service program is located and loaded into the transient area. If the name is absent from the directory, the CCP returns a message and issues a new prompt.

STAT

STAT is an abbreviation for "statistics" or "status". When invoked, it provides information about devices and volumes currently attached to the computer.

File Names

We have examined the **unambiguous file name,** up to eight characters which begins with a letter. Names can be supplied in either upper or lower case characters, but are always written into the directory as upper case characters. Translation from lower to upper case is done by the program or utility which accesses the directory. This is a convenient feature. Some programs (such as MBASIC) enter the name in the directory *exactly* as you supply it; upper and lower case letters are mixed. Some services like TYPE won't be able to find it because the CCP translates your entire request to upper case. Hence for TYPE Myprog, the CCP records this as TYPE MYPROG; but Myprog is actually in the directory. You must use the right mix of case to refer to a file from MBASIC for it to be found. File names may have an extension.

In requesting information or asking for services with respect to files, an **ambiguous file name** may be used. Its first form uses a question mark as a **wild card.** Characters in names are matched exactly except for the wild card. Where a question mark (?) appears in the file name, any character is accepted by STAT. For instance, a request for files with names CHAP? turns up all of the following: CHAP ; CHAP3; CHAPX.

The second form of the ambiguous file name uses * as either a name or an extension. For instance, a request to find files with *.COM turns up all names of program files such as: STAT.COM; PIP.COM; ASM.COM; and so forth. The symbol * may be used as the extension: A request for XYZ.* may turn up XYZ.BAS, XYZ.INT and XYZ.COM. Thus you make multiple requests by typing one ambiguous request.

Request for STAT

Table 7.5.1 shows how to issue status requests described briefly below and keyed by number.

A request without any parameter (1) returns the number of bytes of unused space on volumes currently mounted on disk drives. To know about a specific drive, supply its designation (2).

Table 7.5.1 Commands to Illustrate STAT

1. STAT
2. STAT B:
3. STAT FILE
4. STAT B:FILE
5. STAT WP????
6. STAT *.BAS
7. STAT B:*.BAS
8. STAT *.*
9. STAT WS.COM$R/O
10. STAT WS.COM$SYS
11. STAT WS.COM$SYS
12. STAT WS.COM$DIR
13. STAT DSK
14. STAT USR
15. STAT DEV:

Find out about a particular file by using its unambiguous name (3). STAT displays the name, the file size in bytes, the number of records and extents and whether it is a read/write or a read/only file. If the file is on another drive, prefix the file name by the drive (4).

Using wild cards, it is simple to ask for

- all files with a partial name (5);
- those with any name and a given extension on the default drive (6);
- those with a given extension on a particular drive (7);
- *all* the files on the default drive (8) with the result provided as in Figure 7.5.1.

A disk can be protected against writing by either *applying* a protect tab for the minifloppy or *removing* the tab for the floppy. STAT can protect a file on an *unprotected* disk against writing by the system or an AP by **flagging** it in the directory: use the file name followed by $R/O (9). To restore a file to be written on, issue STAT, the file name, then $R/W (10). You may hide files from users by making them so-called system files (11). Another command restores them to visibility (12).

Other commands describe the characteristics of all disk drives (13), the users attached to the system according to their user number (14) and what kind of devices are used for each system purpose (15).

```
A>stat b:*.*

    Recs   Bytes   Ext  Acc
       0      0k     1  R/W   B:-MW.113
     128     16k     2  R/W   B:EDIT.COM
     237     30k     2  R/W   B:SBC6C
     238     30k     2  R/W   B:SBC7A
Bytes Remaining on B: 87k
```

Figure 7.5.1. A STAT request and its product.

COPY and DISKCOPY

COPY is a utility to copy any disk to another disk, including the operating system, the file directory, the bit map, the existing files and empty tracks. COPY duplicates the source disk and obliterates the former contents on the destination disk. This utility is called DISKCOPY for PC-DOS.

An application program or utility you purchase comes on a disk with a directory, bit map and one or more files but no operating system. Don't use it directly; *make a backup copy first*. The disk may be inadvertently written on; even when you write-protect the disk (which you should do immediately), a sudden change in line voltage or other anomaly may cause information on the disk to be altered and irreparable damage is done. You make a copy of the OS on the active disk as described shortly.

Some computers (Apple) provide hardware and software protection to *prevent you from copying disks* either for yourself or your friends. Some software suppliers give you two disks and provide another original if you return a damaged disk (for a fee).

Use

Simply answer COPY to the prompt. An example of a typical COPY dialog is shown in Figure 7.5.2. The CCP finds the utility on the default disk, places it in the transient area and asks where to find the source and destination disk. It may ask more questions about the density and number of sides.

At the prompt, remove the system disk (COPY is now in memory) and put in the source and destination disks. COPY does not examine the destination disk at all. *Exercise caution* to be sure that you either place a *new* disk in the destination drive or that the old disk you place there holds *nothing* of value. (Consult your utility manual for whether the destination disk must be formatted.)

COPY informs you of each track duplicated successfully and then verifies that it can read that track. Once in a while, the destination disk proves faulty and COPY tells you. If COPY cannot duplicate a track successfully, you should discard that disk. When COPY is done, it asks you if you wish to copy something else. You can use the old parameters or enter new ones and to swap disks.

PIP and COPY

PIP stands for the Peripherial Interchange Program, coined by Digital Equipment Corporation for their utility. PIP transfers files between disks and pastes files together. PC-DOS calls this simply COPY.

COPY

COPY Version 5.5
(C) 1981 Lifeboat Associates

Disk copy for CP/M2 on North Star — SD and DQ.

```
****** O P T I O N  T A B L E ******
  "A"   =   Copy ALL tracks.
            This option also FORMATS a new disk.
  "M"   =   Copy MOST until empty (0E5H) track.
  "V"   =   VERIFY the disk by reading all data.
  "E"   =   EXIT and return to CP/M.
```

Enter you selection from option table. - A

Enter SOURCE drive name: (A B C or D)
or <CR> makes default copy from A to B. - A

Enter DESTINATION drive: (A B C or D). - B

Insert SOURCE in A, DESTINATION in B
  and then press <CR> to copy the disk
  .or any other key to reset options. -

Copy in progress - Press ESC to abort.
Each * is a track copied and verified.

Source disk is double density, single sided.

****

Copy complete. NO errors were detected.

```
****** O P T I O N  T A B L E *******
  <CR>  =   Run again with same parameters.
  "A"   =   Copy ALL tracks.
            This option also FORMATS a new disk.
  "M"   =   Copy MOST until empty (0E5H) track.
  "V"   =   VERIFY the disk by reading all data.
  "E"   =   EXIT and return to CP/M.
```

Enter your selection from option table. —

Figure 7.5.2. A COPY dialog.

7.5 NONRESIDENT SERVICES

Table 7.5.2 Commands to Illustrate PIP

1. * D.D=S.S
2. * B:OLD.COM=OLD.COM
3. * B:=OLD.COM
4. * B:NEW.OLD=OLD.COM
5. * B:=OLD
   OLD NOT FOUND
6. * DATA.TXT=B:DATA.TXT
7. * DATA.TXT=B:
8. * B:=*.COM
9. * C:=*.*[V]
10. * WP=B.WP1,B:WP2
11. * LST:=PROG.PAS
12. * LST=P2.PAS[N]
13. A>PIP TEXT=B:

PIP accepts ambiguous file names. Table 7.5.2 shows typical commands. Any PIP command may include **options,** one or more letters enclosed in square brackets. Table 7.5.3 lists options and their meaning. Personally, I rarely use any option except verification, [V], where PIP reads back the copied file, comparing it byte for byte with the original file.

Invoking

The first way to invoke PIP is by answering PIP to the prompt. PIP prompts you for its first command using *. PIP accepts a properly formatted request; it rejects a bad request by repeating it on the display followed by ? and putting * on the next line. After completion, PIP prompts for another

Table 7.5.3 Option Letters Used with PIP
[Put in square brackets like this]

B	Block mode transfer
Dn	Delete all characters past column n
E	Echo all transfers to console
F	Filter form feeds
Gn	Get file from user n
H	Check for Intel hex format
I	Ignore 00 records in hex format
L	Translate upper case to lower case
N	Add line numbers as each line is transfered
O	Object file — ignore end of file
Pn	Put it page ejects every n lines
Qs^z	Quit copy when ^z is found
R	Include system files
Ss^z	Start copy at ^z
Tn	Expand tabs to every nth column
U	Translate lower to upper case
V	Verify
W	Write over read-only files
Z	Zero parity bit

```
A>pip
* b:=ws.com
* b:=wsmsyg.ovr

NO FILE:=wsmsyg.ovr
*
```

Figure 7.5.3. Using PIP.

request with *. Hit return and control goes back to CP/M, which issues its own prompt. Figure 7.5.3 demonstrates this.

The Command

A command to PIP is in the form of an equation. On the right side of the equal sign is the name of an existing file from which a copy is made; on the left is the name for the new file created. If neither file name is prefixed, then it is assumed that source files are on the default volume; a prefix distinguishes a volume on a nondefault drive.

File Duplicate

To request another copy of an existing file, S.S on the same volume but with a new name, D.D is simple, as in Table 7.5.2 (1). PIP will not produce files with duplicate names on the same volume.

To Another Volume

To make a copy from a file on the default volume, no drive prefix is required on the right of the equal sign (2), to place it on the volume in drive B. A faster way drops the name of the destination file (3). You may copy and rename a file (4). PIP searches for a file with the name you supply. If you misname the source file or leave out its extension, PIP cannot find it and returns an error message (5) and a new prompt.

Copy to the Default Drive

When the default volume is the destination for the copy, no drive prefix is necessary on the left (6). For the same source and destination file, the name can be omitted from the nondefault file name (7).

Multiple Files

Ambiguous file names make it possible to copy sets of files. It is easy to copy all program files from the default drive to the B drive (8) or *all* the files on a disk to another (with verification) (9). As each file is copied, a statement appears on the screen (and printer if you hit ^P) so you'll know where PIP leaves off, should something happen.

PIP only has access to files listed in the directory, so it does not copy the operating system. The destination disk *must* be formatted. Files can be copied from one disk to an empty, but formatted disk but not to an unformatted virgin disk.

Concaternation

For **concaternation,** two or more files named on the right are pasted together, copied and the resulting single file is given the name on the left. The source files designations are separated by a comma (10).

To Another Device

A file is printed by sending it to the system list device (11). PIP can do special tasks for you, like number the lines of your program (12).

Single Request

Instead of calling PIP and waiting for the PIP's prompt to give the command, an action can be stated on a single line following the CP/M prompt (13). PIP does its thing, then returns directly to CP/M.

How PIP Works

PIP uses BDOS services to set up a destination file. BDOS finds space and creates a directory entry for it is written on the destination disk. If this entry were to use the actual name of the destination file, a problem might ensue.

Suppose that PIP is copying a file called X to B:X. During copying, the space on B becomes exhausted. Suppose X is 20K, but there is only 10K space available on B. When PIP gets half way through, it has created an incomplete file, X, of 10K. Even though PIP informs us that an error has occurred, the file B:X exists. This is BAD! It might be used mistakenly.

Actually PIP gives any new file the extension $$$, a temporary file. Above, A:X is copied to B:X.$$$. If the process goes to completion, then B:X.$$$ is renamed B:X. Should a difficulty arise, the file is *not* renamed. There is no B:X, only B:X.$$$.

SUBMIT

When CP/M issues a prompt, your reply requests a single program. When that program terminates, it returns control to CP/M by jumping to the warm boot location in low memory. To run a set of programs, start each separately after the previous one concludes. SUBMIT is a program which runs a **batch** of programs.

Setup

Set up a sequence of commands in a text file with the extension SUB, the **submit file**. It contains one line ending with *return* for each program to run. The programs are executed in this sequence. Prepare the *submit* file with a text editor, such as ED or a word processor like WordStar. Name the file with the extension SUB, for example, JOB.SUB.

Running

Issue SUBMIT followed by the name of the *submit* file, but omitting the extension, SUB, thus,

A>SUBMIT JOB   (7.5.1)

As you watch, a new prompt appears and the first command in the *submit* file is issued automatically. Then the program executes. On terminating, the prompt appears followed by the second command in your file. This continues until all the commands have been executed. Then a final prompt appears on the screen and stays there until you enter a new command.

Action

As you key the *submit* request, the character codes are placed in the console buffer by the CCP. When the CCP receives *return,* SUBMIT.COM is brought from disk and placed into the transient area where it executes. SUBMIT immediately moves itself to the top of the TPA to make room for incoming programs. SUBMIT finds the file JOB.SUB for (7.5.1), brings it into a work area and writes a new file called $$$.SUB to the disk. $$$.SUB contains all the items in the file except the first (for the first batch program). It puts the name of the first program in the console buffer. SUBMIT changes the warm boot address to point to an entry point within SUBMIT so that it regains control when the first AP terminates. Then SUBMIT gives control to the CCP.

CCP puts the program named in the console buffer in the TPA. That program executes and, upon completion, tries to perform a warm boot. Since the warm address has been altered, control goes to SUBMIT. It acquires the intermediate file, $$$.SUB, peels off the name of the top program, places it on the console buffer and rewrites the file with one less item. Action continues thus until the last program is to run.

SUBMIT notes when there is only one program to run, places its name in the console buffer area, but writes no $$$.SUB file. SUBMIT restores the warm boot address, so that the CCP really gets control when the last program terminates.

Parameters

SUBMIT runs a sequence of programs; here is a file for PL/I compilation called COMP1.SUB,

    PLI PROG
    LINK PROG
    PROG   (7.5.2)

This set of programs compiles PROG, then links it to all the routines it needs and finally runs the program. But it only works for a program called PROG. To fix this, you may supply the program name when you issue SUBMIT.

Use parameters formatted as $n and numbered consecutively in your SUB file. Replace them with a parameter you supply when you submit the job. Here's COMP2.SUB,

    PLI $1
    LINK $1
    $1   (7.5.3)

Issue it for MYPROG thus,

    A>SUBMIT COMP2 MYPROG   (7.5.4)

The result is almost identical to (7.5.2).

Several parameters may be used. Put them anywhere in the SUB file. Name them in order in the SUBMIT command which has the format,

    A>SUBMIT LIST [$1 $2 . . . $n]   (7.5.5)

What if trouble arises? If SUBMIT can't find a file or the CCP detects an error, the file $$$.SUB is erased and a warm boot occurs.

If you want SUBMIT to stop, hit <u>rub</u>.

XSUB

The SUBMIT facility is expanded to include a further capability, called XSUB. Once a program begins to run, it may need directions. With XSUB, you put commands and responses in your SUBMIT file, which then consists of

1. The statement, XSUB;
2. The name of the first program to run;
3. Directives or replies for that program, one per line;
4. A continuation of this list containing programs and a single line for each directive or reply.

Operation

XSUB is first loaded into memory and moves itself up to the top just below CBASE, so as not to interfere with programs brought in later. Then each request or prompt from the executing program, instead of going to the CCP, is intercepted by XSUB, which gets the directive or reply from the *submit* file.

This powerful technique is little understood and infrequently used. Parameters may also be used with XSUB.

DDT

When you write a program, it is never perfect the first time. Difficulties become apparent, called **bugs**; getting rid of them is **debugging**. Tools help. DDT stand for Dynamic Debugging Tool.

When you include its name on the command line, DDT loads your program into the transient area as though it were going to execute. DDT loads at the top of memory, where it helps you examine and alter the program *in machine language* in the transient area. How to do debugging is beyond the scope of this book. However Table 7.5.4 displays some DDT commands.

Once the program is fixed and available in the TPA, put it away using SAVE.

7.6 CP/M UTILITIES

This section discusses utilities for setting up the operating system and initializing disks, necessary before they can be used. These programs can be called *only* from a working system.

7.6 CP/M UTILITIES

Table 7.5.4 DDT Commands

A	Enter assembly language code into memory
D	Display memory in hex and ASCII
F	Fill memory with a constant
G	Go to location and start executing
I	Identify file and set up FCB
L	List memory as assembler mnemonics
M	Move segment within memory
R	Read file into memory
S	Substitute values into memory
T	Trace program
U	Execute designated program steps
X	Examine and alter CPU registers

FORMAT

A fresh floppy disk out of the package is not immediately usable. It needs:

1. A formatted file directory with empty entries;
2. A bit map showing empty space;
3. For soft disks, track and sector marking.

Figure 7.6.1 shows a typical format dialog; a new asterisk is displayed as each track is formatted.

The program called FORMAT does the chores (1-3 above). It also checks that each track may be written on and successfully read back.

A freshly formatted disk has no operating system. Purchased software comes on a formatted disk but without an operating system.

```
FORMAT ver 2.6 for CP/M2 on North Star.
(c) 1981 Lifeboat Associates.

Drive   (A B C D or E for Exit) ? B
Single or Double DENSITY (S or D) ? D
Drive allows single sided operation only.

Press <cr> to format DOUBLE density, SINGLE sided in drive B
or "E" to EXIT, "N" for NEW parameters.

Press "ESCAPE" at any time to ABORT.
[Side one now being formatted]
******************************

RUN again, EXIT or NEW parameters (R E or N). E
```

Figure 7.6.1. A FORMAT dialog.

Suiting the System to Memory

The location of the nucleus of CP/M and some other OSs depend upon the size of physical memory in your system. Suppose you have 32K of memory now and you get an additional 16K. The system which worked in 32K also works with the additional memory. However, you need to move the nucleus so it occupies the *new* top of memory.

The program called MOVCPM (see Figure 7.6.2) relocates the operating system to sit at the top of physical memory. There may be two sets of two alternatives for MOVCPM:

1. Tell it the size of memory, or let *it* find out;
2. Put the new OS into use immediately or set it up for copying onto a system disk.

Memory Size

To determine memory size, MOVCPM writes a pattern at address boundaries and reads it back. If there is no such address in your computer, then 0s come back instead of the pattern.

```
A>MOVCPM * *
Constructing 63K CP/M

CP/M2 on North Star
63K Vers 2.23a DQ
(C) 1981 Lifeboat Associates

Do you have a Horizon computer (Y/N) ? Y
CONFIG.COM not required on disk.

New CP/M in memory at 900H (sysgen image)
is ready for "SYSGEN" or "SAVE 40 CPM63.COM"
SYSGEN

SYSGEN Version 3.0
Distributed by Lifeboat Associates
for CP/M2 on quad North Star.

Source drive NAME (or RETURN to skip)

CP/M image in RAM at 900H is ready to write
or reboot and "SAVE 40 CPMxx.COM"

Destination drive NAME (or RETURN to reboot)B
Place DESTINATION disk on B, then type RETURN
FORMAT
```

Figure 7.6.2. A MOVCPM dialog.

If instead you give this command,

A>MOVCPM 50   (7.6.1)

then MOVCPM creates a 50K version of CP/M. You may give MOVCPM a smaller number than the actual amount of memory. This lets you place additional drivers on top of those supplied by CP/M, sometimes done for a hard disk.

Now or Later

The CP/M created by MOVCPM is installed, entered and immediately issues a prompt. There are two disadvantages to that. First, you haven't saved a copy of the system. Second, if the program gets into trouble, you have to reboot the system. Since you don't have a copy of the system on the disk, the boot does not work and you have to employ MOVCPM again. The alternative is to call CP/M in one of these forms,

A>MOVCPM 50K*   (7.6.2)

A>MOVCPM * *   (7.6.3)

In both cases, CP/M is prepared at 900 in memory but not put into use. You can use SAVE to put CP/M in a named file or you can write it in the first two tracks of a system disk with SYSGEN explained below.

You might wonder about the very first time that you use CP/M after you uncrate your computer. A 24K CP/M is on a disk. It works immediately in all computers which might use CP/M. However, it is not tailored to the actual size of memory; that is the purpose of the MOVCPM.

Making a System Disk

You cannot simply *copy* an OS onto another disk. The OS is put on the first two tracks of the disk with SYSGEN. There are three ways to do this.

Directly from This Disk

A system volume with a copy of SYSGEN can copy CP/M from that disk to another disk, when requested as shown in Figure 7.6.3.

SYSGEN asks you where the source is. To use the OS on the system disk in drive A, respond A. The program captures another image of CP/M from drive A to copy, putting it at location 900. Now it asks for the destination

```
SYSGEN Version 3.0
Distributed by Lifeboat Associates
for CP/M2 on quad North Star.

Source drive NAME (or RETURN to skip) A
Place SOURCE disk on A, then type RETURN
Function complete

CP/M image in RAM at 900H is ready to write
or reboot and "SAVE 40 CPMxx.COM"

Destination drive NAME (or RETURN to reboot) B
Place DESTINATION disk on B, then type RETURN
Function complete
```

Figure 7.6.3. A SYSGEN dialog.

drive. When you reply, B, SYSGEN makes a copy of the system in memory in the first two tracks of the disk in drive B.

From Another Disk

The second method copies the system from one disk to another, but to use the SYSGEN program on a third disk which is initially booted up. The dialogue is exactly the same. You remove the current floppy and replace it with another containing the copy of the CP/M you want to use, because that disk does not have SYSGEN on it.

Generated

This is used after MOVCPM tailors a system and puts it at 900. When SYSGEN asks for the source disk, reply return and SYSGEN finds the copy at location 900. Tell it the destination drive and you are in business.

Autoboot

Some operating systems have provision for **autoboot,** whereby the system steps automatically through the prompt stage and initiates a program previously designated.

An area is reserved in CCP for the name of the program, files and parameters to start after a cold boot. A knowledgeable system programmer can put CP/M in memory and alter it with DDT so that it has autoboot. Here are the steps:

1. Use MOVCPM to put a tailored copy of CP/M at 900.
2. Bring in DDT to modify CP/M.

3. Give commands to DDT to insert the program name and parameters to run when booted in the CCP autoboot area.
4. Leave DDT and return to the current operating system.
5. Issue SYSGEN, noting that the new system is in memory by replying to the first prompt about where the system is with return.
6. SYSGEN copies the autoboot CP/M to the disk.

Use

Autoboot is particularly helpful for the naive user. Place the autoboot disk in the drive and press reset. The system boots and produces the prompt but the CCP notes the autoboot. The automatic response to the prompt displays. CP/M finds, loads and runs the program.

By combining SUBMIT with the autoboot, several programs run as a batch when you power up.

SETCPM

Lifeboat Associates provides a version of CP/M for certain computers which includes a program called SETCPM. It calls up a version of CP/M and you set in an autoload designation by answering prompts (Figure 7.6.4). This version of CP/M can then be placed on a disk with SYSGEN.

```
       SETCPM v2.2 for Lifeboat CP/M2 on North Star   (c) 1981 M. Dubno

   Auto message           :  "AUTO"
   Activate on            :  No boot set      FOUR drives
   Interrupt enable       :  OFF       Read after write : OFF
   Printer on : Right serial port

                Drive A      Drive B      Drive C      Drive D
                =======      =======      =======      =======
      Speed:    slow         slow         slow         slow
      Sides:    one          one          one          one

                    ----- O P T I O N S  M E N U -----
              Q    QUIT with no changes
              A    Change AUTO command
              D    Change number of DRIVES in system
              I    Change INTERRUPT enable status
              P    Change PRINTER assignment on Horizon
              R    Change READ AFTER WRITE status
              S    Change SPEED & SIDES of the drives
              E    EXIT this program

     Select option: [ Q,A,D,I,P,R,S,E ]:
```

Figure 7.6.4. SETCPM.

Drivers

Every device attached to your computer must have a driver in the operating system. If you add new PC cards or devices, or both, they cannot be reached without a corresponding software driver. Sometimes the hardware manufacturer supplies a driver on a disk and outlines the procedure to put it in your operating system. This is the case for semidisk and hard disks.

Not all device manufacturers are so responsible. Before you purchase devices, you should determine how difficult it is to make that device operational in your own system. Adding a hard disk and its controller to an existing system may require professional intervention.

Some utilities can put drivers furnished on disk into an existing operating system or tailor existing drivers to suit added devices. For instance, CP/M issued by Lifeboat can tailor the printer and console drivers to suit most devices you might purchase. Similarly, Apple provides a program to tailor its drivers.

7.7 OTHER UTILITIES

Need

Operating systems provide a number of services mainly for manipulating files. These are essential to any user. Regardless of the size of your disks, you soon accumulate a vast number of files. You need to move files about and to keep good records of which files are on which disks. Such facilities are not always supplied with an operating system. Consequently, other sources have arisen for compact and friendly utilities.

One source is from users themselves. They have formed users' groups classified according to the operating system which they use. There is, for example, a North Star Users Group, NSUG; the one of interest to us here is the CP/M Users Group, called CPMUG with mailing address at Lifeboat Associates, New York. They have amassed a collection of more than a hundred disks containing applications and utility programs. What is more remarkable, all these programs are in the public domain and are free. For a few dollars—only the cost of the disk, putting the programs on it and shipping and mailing—you can obtain a number of such utilities. If you have a modem and a communication program, you can call up various services that supply programs absolutely free (outside of the cost of the telephone call).

There are many agencies which supply free public domain software. In New York City there is the NY Amateur Computer Group and NYPC Inc. for IBM programs. A dealer in your region can direct you to such local groups.

Some vendors have seen a need for good utilities and have refined them, put them in a package and placed them for sale. They are quite reasonable for the functions they perform. This chapter gives four examples of utilities, two of which are free. Only those available for CP/M are discussed here. However, other versions or different utilities are available for other operating systems.

POWER

POWER (Computing Inc., San Francisco) provides most of the CP/M utilities and the debugging facilities of DDT and more and is much easier to use. I personally use POWER frequently and recommend it highly. It has additional functions which are invaluable, such as RECLAIM which lets you bring back a file that has been inadvertently erased. A version is also available to work with both PC-DOS and MS-DOS.

Start-Up

To get POWER going, call it forth from the prompt. Since it is something I use a lot, I have renamed it POW to make it easier to request. After a sign-on message, it issues a prompt which consists of the drive name, the user number and an equals sign as at the top of Figure 7.7.1. Reply with a directive, many of which are described below.

Once POWER is resident, it remains in memory even if you change disks. After acting on a request, POWER regains control and issues another prompt.

Each time you change a disk, tell POWER by hitting control C (^C) just as with CP/M. Directions you issue apply to the current default drive. Change drives by giving the drive letter, a colon and return.

    A0 = B: (7.7.1)

COPY

A most useful routine of POWER is COPY, which copies selected files from one disk to another. The command, illustrated in Figure 7.7.1, is issued by keying COPY. The response is a numbered directory of the files on the default disk. *Read-only* files are followed by an asterisk; they cannot be erased without changing their status.

To copy any file, respond to the prompt (at the bottom of the figure) with its number in the screen directory, followed by return. POWER asks the drive to copy the file(s); as soon as you key the drive letter (without return), copying begins.

238 THE OPERATING SYSTEM

```
A0 = copy
A0:    1 = -TSYS       .001    | 2 = AUTOLOAD   .COM* |  3 = BACKUP     .COM
A0:    4 = BUFFERS     .COM*   | 5 = CATALOG    .COM  |  6 = CATALOG4   .DAT
A0:    7 = CHANGE      .COM*   | 8 = CONSYS     .COM  |  9 = COPY       .COM*
A0:   10 = CP          .COM    |11 = CPM60      .COM  | 12 = CPM64      .COM
A0:   13 = DATE        .COM*   |14 = DDT        .COM  | 15 = DELETE     .COM*
A0:   16 = DIR         .COM*   |17 = DO         .COM* | 18 = DRIVE      .COM*
A0:   19 = DUMP        .COM*   |20 = ED         .COM  | 21 = EDIT       .COM
A0:   22 = ERASEDIR    .COM*   |23 = F          .SYS  | 24 = FIXMAP     .COM*
A0:   25 = FORMAT      .COM    |26 = FORMATM    .COM  | 27 = FORSYM     .COM*
A0:   28 = GEN         .COM*   |29 = I          .COM  | 30 = INSTALL    .COM
A0:   31 = LABEL       .COM*   |32 = LOAD       .COM  | 33 = LOGOFF     .COM*
A0:   34 = LOGON       .COM*   |35 = M          .     | 36 = M1         .
A0:   37 = M1          .BAK    |38 = M2         .     | 39 = MASTER     .COM*
A0:   40 = METASOFT    .OP1    |41 = MODEM      .COM  | 42 = MW         .COM
A0:   43 = MWHELP      .DAT    |44 = O          .COM  | 45 = OSMASTER   .SYS
A0:   46 = OSSLAVE     .SYS    |47 = P          .COM  | 48 = PASS       .
A0:   49 = PIP         .COM    |50 = POW        .COM  | 51 = POWER      .COM
A0:   52 = PRINT       .COM*   |53 = PRINTER    .COM* | 54 = PWRETOOL   .COM
A0:   55 = QUEUE       .COM*   |56 = RELCVT     .COM* | 57 = RENAME     .COM*
A0:   58 = S           .SYS    |59 = SET        .COM* | 60 = SHOW       .COM*
A0:   61 = SMCP/M      .$$$    |62 = SOSMASTER  .SYS  | 63 = SPELSTAR   .OVR
A0:   64 = STAT        .COM    |65 = SYSGEN     .COM  | 66 = T          .SYS
A0:   67 = TYPE        .COM*   |68 = USER       .COM* | 69 = VERIFY     .COM*
A0:   70 = WSMSGS      .OVR    |71 = WSOVLY1    .OVR  | 72 = WSU        .COM
A0:   73 = WSV         .COM    |74 = WSV1       .COM
select?
```

Figure 7.7.1. POWER's prompt and copy display.

The beauty of COPY is evident when duplicating a number of files. Instead of separately entering the name of each as with PIP, simply enter numbers from its directory, separated by blanks. To copy files listed as 11, 31 and 14, use the following (Select? is a prompt),

Select? 11 31 14 (7.7.2)

Hit return and copying begins when you enter the destination drive letter.

To copy a contiguous group of files, say from 11 to 27, enter 11-27 separating the number with the keyboard hyphen. To get all files copied, simply type 1-. To copy the files up to 50, say -50. Use any combination of these.

COPY Alternatives

Contingencies arise which COPY can solve. You have considerable choice in what the utility does:

1. Put a character within square brackets before or as you issue a command.
2. Use **LOG** as in Figure 7.7.2 to see the alternatives in force for the duration of the session.

For (2), at the left are the alternatives and the toggles now set; on the right, their meaning. Explanations below are keyed to the numerals on the far left (in the discussion).

What should COPY do if a file to copy exists on the destination disk? The alternatives are indicated by the first four letters of the alphabet:

A-overlay and replace the old version with the new one.
B-give the old file the extension BAK, and make the copy.
C-prompt the operator.
D-do not copy the source file at all.

PIP always makes a copy. An old file would be destroyed. Choose that alternative by entering [A] at the prompt.

The next alternative (2, Figure 7.7.2) determines the number of columns for the directory display (2, 3 or 4). A large directory can show continuously or as a number of pages (the current choice). There are many more alternatives; the few that we have examined should indicate how powerful this utility is.

SIZE

Figure 7.7.3 shows how **SIZE** displays the size of a group of files. The wild card option is specified (ws*.* requests all files whose name begins with

```
        A0 = log
 1.     C            If file exist A-overlay, B-back up, C-ask, D-skip
 2.     3            columns
 3.     P (ON)       paging
 4.     R (OFF)      request Y/N on current file   (C-request new
                     name)
 5.     V (ON)       read after write
 6.     S (ON)       show system files
 7.     t (OFF)      stop if disk is full
 8.     M (OFF)      Mark copied files
 9.     X            list drives A-P if on line
10.     U            list users 0-15
11.     $ (ON)       submit $$$.SUB - A:POWER
12.     +/-          1-8 or (R)ead/write, (S)ystem/dir, e(X)tra
13.     POWER        0100H - 3C89H
14.     TPA          3D00H - D9FFH   314 sectors
```

Figure 7.7.2. POWER's log display.

```
A0 = size ws*.*
A0:     1 = WSMSGS   .OVR  |  2 = WSOVLY1 .OVR |   3 = WSU   .COM
A0:     4 = WSV      .COM  |  5 = WSV1    .COM
select? 1 —

A:WSMSGS    .OVR  -  218 sectors   6 empty   28K    28K
A:WSOVLY1   .OVR  -  266 sectors   6 empty   34K    62K
A:WSU       .COM  -  124 sectors   4 empty   16K    78K
A:WSV       .COM  -  124 sectors   4 empty   16K    94K
A:WSV1      .COM  -  124 sectors   4 empty   16K   110K

A0 =
```

Figure 7.7.3. POWER's size request shows details about space occupied by a file.

WS). The directory which results shows only these files. Now you may request one, several or all of these files. All are requested here; the display which follows gives the file name, the number of currently used and empty sectors assigned, the size of the file in kilobytes and finally the cumulative size of all files listed.

RECLAIM

The reclaim function alone is worth the price of this package. Should you inadvertently erase a file that you really need, it is inaccessible but actually exists: the directory entry is flagged. RECLAIM finds flagged entries for files which *are* still intact. RECLAIM presents each file name in sequence and asks if you want to reclaim it. If so, the flag is removed and the file becomes a *read-only* file.

TEST

TEST checks the entire disk to find bad sectors. This is a nondestructive test, using the CRC at the end of each block. Bad sectors are grouped together in an invisible file so that the remainder of the disk can be used. For an existing file, bad sectors can be brought out and fixed.

Others

POWER provides many other functions to rename and erase files, to run programs and return to POWER, to type out files and to get help should you forget the meaning of the commands.

MODEM7

MODEM7 is a modern program in the public domain written by Ward Christiansen and distributed by CPMUG. It mates with the PMMI hardware modem but can be tailored to work with almost any other modem. The program lets you talk with other computers that have that program. It and a variation called XMODEM are also available for the IBM PC.

Dumb Terminal

The simplest use for MODEM7 makes your computer a **dumb terminal,** a slave for a larger computer or computing service. Call **MODEM**, issue T at its prompt and the computer becomes a terminal. I can dial up the City University computer. It responds with that peculiar tone telling me that I am "speaking" to a modem. With my computer functioning as a terminal, I enter my identification and other accounting information and can operate the computer from my micro. Now I have the services of this large computer do such things as

- run a designated program;
- compose text and programs in my own files at the remote computer;
- get access to data bases;
- leave messages for staff members.

I can also dial up computing services such as The Source for access to any number of data bases such as airline schedules, cultural events in my city, lists of restaurants, current events, stock market reports, a file of recipes and so forth. I can use the **electronic mail** facilities. I am assigned an electronic mailbox. I can write messages at my terminal and deposit them in other people's mailboxes who use the system. They can reply, leaving messages in my mailbox.

Connecting to such a service is done on a local telephone line which costs me only a local phone call. I also pay **connect charges** by the minute to The Source; these are charged to my credit card and billed by the month. Electronic mail is much cheaper and as fast as a long distance call across the country. Further, both the recipient and I have a record.

Between Micros

Two micros that have modems and similar modem programs can talk: I can send copies of programs or text across the telephone line at relatively high speed and low cost. Thus, in a minute or two a company could send summary information to their accountants at low cost and whenever required. MODEM7 can send single or multiple files, once the computers are attached.

Transmission is reliable because a **retransmission protocol** is built into the program. The sending program calculates a **check sum** for each block it sends, adding it to the end of the block. As a block is transmitted, the receiving modem program creates another check sum. This it compares against the one at the end of the block to verify the transmission. If the information should be corrupted on route, the receiving station sends back a message to ask the transmitting station to repeat transmission of the faulty block.

Auto Dial

My PMMI hardware modem has a dialer. MODEM7 has an automatic dialing facility. Thus to connect to a computer which I use frequently, by choosing option 6 I tell MODEM7 to "dial 6, the CUNY computer." It applies the proper dial tones to the telephone line.

Remote Dial-In

After you set up your computer installation and furnish it with the modem and a modem program, it is possible to use these facilities remotely and unattended. For instance, salespersons in the field can report summary information during the night. This is especially useful for staff on the West Coast and a central office on the East Coast. Provide salespersons with small, portable computers which include modems. They record activities on the keyboard at the customer's office; the data are placed on a small self-contained disk. When they get back to the hotel in the evening, they dial and transmit the information on the disk to your computer at the main office.

Catalog (Public Domain)

Ward Christiansen has developed programs in the public domain, obtainable through CPMUG, to catalog all your files. It places their names and disk identifications in a catalog file on a master disk. Disks to be cataloged must have an empty file with a name consisting of two parts: a file name beginning with a hyphen and a numeric extension between 0 and 999, such as —LETTERS.134. These are respectively the disk name and the disk number. This empty file occupies no space on your disk, gets its name in the directory and is prepared with this command:

SAVE 0 —LETTERS.134 (7.7.3)

Figure 7.7.4 illustrates the programs and files that are used and how you catalog a disk. The master list has the name MAST.CAT. To recatalog a disk, run the program FMAP. It copies the directory of the disk you are cataloging to NAMES.SUB.

Next, UCAT compares the items in NAMES.SUB to those in MAST.CAT listed for disk name. It adds names in NAMES.SUB which are missing from MAST.CAT; it deletes names which are in MAST.CAT absent from NAMES.SUB. When done, UCAT eliminates NAMES.SUB.

The program CAT accesses the catalog on your request by ambiguous names (page 221), by disk identification and in other ways to produce a listing either on the screen or printer.

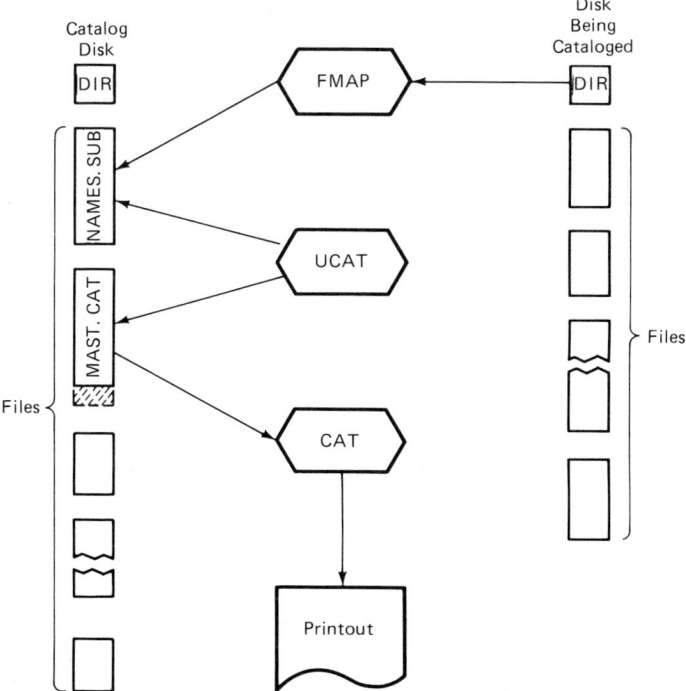

Figure 7.7.4. Files and actions for Ward Christiansen's catalog utility.

CATALOG

CATALOG, a product of SRX Systems, has several features which make it stand out:

- it is a single program;
- one command catalogs a disk and updates the catalog file;
- an annotation of up to 63 characters can be provided for each file and disk, *describing* its purpose;
- the file number need not be established as a directory entry on the disk.

To use the utility, simply call it up by name. You can list files from the catalog using ambiguous names. To update the catalog, insert the source disk in a drive and key in the drive designation and the disk number.

Copy Protected Programs

Vendors want to protect their software products from unauthorized duplication. They build all kinds of complicated schemes into the program command file so that it cannot be copied by normal methods. This is especially prevalent with Apple and IBM PC APs. You cannot even make a backup copy; instead, you register the product and must get the vendor to send you another copy if you ruin yours.

This inconvenience is unwarranted. Specialized vendors make *copy* products to "break the code" and copy *anything* that can be put on disk. These products are both popular and useful; no one yet has been prosecuted for using one, nor have the vendors been chided. One of the best products for this purpose is COPY II Plus for the Apple II Series and COPY II PC for the PC and its clones. Both are products of Central Point Software, Inc.

RamDisk

In a number of ways, via hardware and software, you can provide high speed storage for programs and data which appears to the OS as though it were a disk.

Hardware

You can buy a board from Semidisk Inc. which provides 500K, 1M or their latest, 2M of RAM. It plugs into a PC slot and works like a disk when the driver supplied with it is installed into your system. This gives the advantage of not detracting from existing memory, for example, you may have 640K and need most of it because you are running Framework. Your Semidisk would have no effect on this memory.

Software

If you have a lot of memory but are running comparatively small programs, why not put the extra memory to work? Several firms provide a driver which converts part of your main memory into a virtual disk. You can usually predetermine the division of RAM between normal use and RamDisk to make optimum use of memory for a session. Here is a list of such products:

- Insta-Drive 3.00 by Persyst at $50.
- RAM Driver 2.0 by DataSource Systems at $79.
- RamDiak II by Rensin Communications at $59.95.
- Smart Cache by EKC Inc. at $39.95.

7.8 PC-DOS, MS-DOS AND OTHER OPERATING SYSTEMS

There are a number of other operating systems. Indeed, there is a different operating system for each important micro: Apple, Radio Shack, Hewlett Packard, Fortune and so forth. They are important to the owner of the hardware. They all perform their interfacing function, letting the user and operator talk to the application program and hence the hardware. I would not say that the differences among these proprietary systems are slight, but it is beyond our scope to discuss them.

There are operating systems besides CP/M which claim to be universal. Unix is one of these. There are several versions of Unix which work on micros. It is derived from a larger version which works on Digital Equipment Corporation's minicomputers. This makes it an attraction, especially for those who have used the mini version of Unix. However, it is difficult to understand, unfriendly and can invoke catastrophic errors, such as destroying a file if you are not careful.

I have stressed CP/M because it not only runs on Z80 computers but a board can be added to an Apple or other computer to superimpose this operating system on that micro. A second reason for studying CP/M is that it is a precursor for the operating sytem used by IBM for its PC, namely PC-DOS.

History

Work began on an operating system for the Intel 8086 chip long before IBM's hardware needed an operating system. Seattle Computer Products (SCP) needed an operating system for the hardware they were designing around this chip. They had hoped for a version of CP/M which was under development by Digital Research, the originators of the CP/M system. It soon became clear that the new version of CP/M would not be available in time. Hence SCP went forward with their development of what they then called SCP DOS-86. It was ready in the middle of 1980 and was issued with their new computer.

Meanwhile, Microsoft saw what was happening and became interested in this new operating system. Their main market was application programs. They also developed Microsoft Basic (MBASIC). They witnessed the evolution of the Z80 into the new chips and expected an immense market to develop. They bought SCP's DOS-86. They made changes to come up with a version which is now available from Microsoft, called MS-DOS and works with micros based on the 8086 and 8088 architecture.

IBM was completing their hardware, which needed an operating system. They wanted to put part of the OS into ROM and to add new features. They contracted with Microsoft to develop a version now available from IBM as PC-DOS. The first version for the PC differs only slightly from the original concept of CP/M. It was modified by Microsoft to operate with the hard disk; this modification has since been replaced by Release 2.0. This augmented version of PC-DOS handles hard disks and imposes a tree directory structure on the files, which helps multiple users considerably to keep track of their own files. At the end of 1983, another version was issued for the PCjr, Release 2.1.

Compatibility

An important question that immediately arises in the user's mind is compatibility of APs for the IBM PC and for its look-alikes. What exactly does one mean by compatibility? This is discussed at the end of this section and also in Chapter 16.

A Name

Let us simply call the system DOS because the Microsoft and the IBM product differ so slightly. The rest of this section is devoted to the examination of DOS.

Components

The components of DOS fall into three categories according to their location when the operating system is up and running:

1. **ROM resident**—in the read-only memory, which is part of the hardware;
2. **RAM resident**—at the upper bounds of random access memory;
3. **Disk resident**—on the disk and brought into memory as needed.

7.8 PC-DOS, MS-DOS AND OTHER OPERATING SYSTEMS 247

The only part of the operating system resident when the computer is turned on is in ROM (discussed in Section 6.6). The rest of DOS is missing and must be made available before action can proceed. A copy of RAM resident routines is either on a floppy for the PC or the hard disk for the XT.

Disk Context

We find these components on the disk:

1. The boot record;
2. The RAM resident components;
3. The utilities.

The three resident components which are discussed shortly are:

- IBMDOS.COM;
- IBMBIO.COM;
- COMMAND.COM.

Start-Up

To see how DOS is established, let's trace the process from power-on.

Power-On

Flipping the power switch generates a pulse which gives control to the **self-check routine,** a small program in ROM and part of the BIOS. This routine mainly checks memory (which can be truly extensive), by writing into it and reading back to verify its function. The more memory in the computer, the longer this takes—you can have more than 600K.

This routine also checks the processor and other circuitry to verify that arithmetic and logic is working.

Booting

To **boot the system** is to bring in the **boot record** located at the beginning of the system disk, which in turn brings in the rest of the system. The ROM boot in ROM BIOS activates the disk to find and bring in the boot record and give it control.

Boot Record

The boot record checks to see the extent of memory, finds the three RAM resident components on the disk and puts them at the top of RAM.

RAM Components

The RAM components do some preliminaries and announce to the user that the system is available. How this happens is explained shortly.

Memory

DOS runs in memory. Therefore it is important to understand memory in two ways: as physical memory and its distribution; and as memory in use and how it is allocated to various components and programs.

Addressing

As discussed in Section 6.6, up to one megabyte of memory is addressable. Twenty bits are needed to specify this many distinct addresses. In hexadecimal notation this 20 bit address is given by five nibbles: the bottom of memory is at 00000; the last addressable byte is FFFFF.

The Physical Memory

Figure 7.8.1 is a map of physical memory. The lowest addresses are at the bottom and the highest at the top. Location 0 to 0FFFF, the first 64K, is *minimum* memory. If you order the PC with additional chips installed on the system board, these occupy addresses 10000 to 3FFFF. With expansion

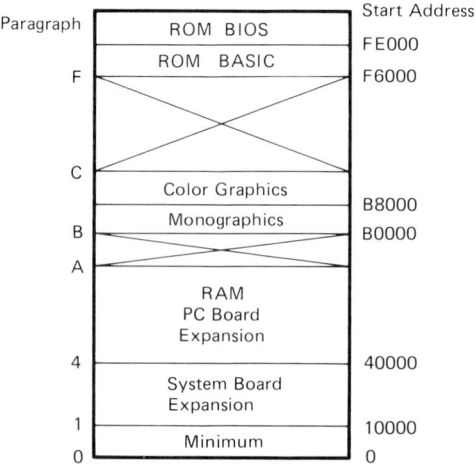

Figure 7.8.1. IBM PC map of memory assignments.

7.8 PC-DOS, MS-DOS AND OTHER OPERATING SYSTEMS

PC boards, additional RAM up to 640K is situated, when provided, at locations from 40000 to 9FFFF.

Addresses from A0000 to AFFFF have been reserved for expansion of graphics. The locations from B0000 to BFFFF are actually on the mono and color graphics boards. The basic interpreter is in ROM starting at location (address) F6000. The BIOS, also in ROM, begins at location FE000.

Note that the actual RAM available starts at location 0 and can reach up to 10000 to 9FFFF. This is called **active RAM.**

Memory Allocation

Figure 7.8.2 shows how memory is allocated. At the bottom, from 0 to FF (hex), are tables and vectors. Application programs are loaded in the transient area beginning at 100 hex. The resident operating system is placed at the top of memory. At the top of active RAM is IBMBIO with the others loaded just below it.

Loading

Resident components are loaded somewhat differently from those of CP/M. For the latter, all are on the first tracks of the system disk, right after the boot record and are loaded as a unit into the top of memory. DOS keeps each component as a file which is listed in the system disk directory. These files are not apparent to the normal user because they are made "invisible" by setting bits in the directory.

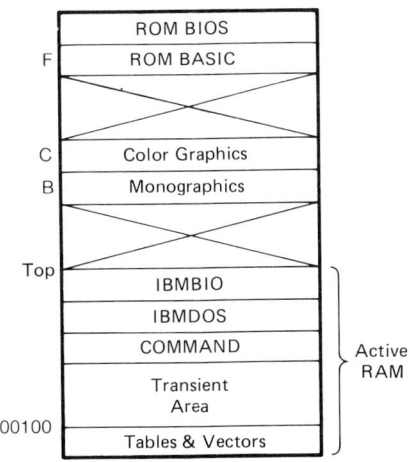

Figure 7.8.2. IBM DOS components in memory.

Resident Components

During startup, the resident components, IBMBIO, IBMDOS, and COMMAND, are found, brought in and situated on top of RAM as displayed in Figure 7.8.2. Startup is not complete until the first of these components gets control and performs its initial function.

IBMBIO

IBMBIO gets control immediately after loading. This module has three functions:

- make updating modifications and extensions of BIOS in ROM;
- provide interfacing required for other operating systems;
- find and incorporate drivers for additional devices not provided for in BIOS.

A ROM chip is fabricated at the factory and inserted in the computer before you get it. The programs in ROM have been checked innumerable times, but sometimes slight changes would make them more effective. It would be indeed expensive to create new ROMs and distribute them to all PC owners. A new software module is much easier to design and distribute. When small changes are in order, it is easy to write extensions to ROM BIOS, placing them in IBMBIO. The first function of IBMBIO is then to connect its extension to ROM BIOS.

BIOS can be expanded by adding additional drivers for other devices and for extension routines which make it possible for the computer to work with other operating systems. Drivers and extensions are incorporated into a configuration file which you, the user, construct with DOS commands. IBMBIO incorporates this file into the BIOS by altering pointers in the tables below 100 hex. Calls to BIOS are hence rerouted to IBMBIO extensions instead of going to ROM BIOS.

Then IBMBIO activates the disk to seek configuration files of drivers. If these are found, they are brought into memory and linked with resident modules. Thereafter these drivers are available for AP to activate the additional devices or to talk to a foreign operating system.

IBMDOS

This module is almost identical in function with CPM's BDOS. It provides an intermediate level of file management functions. These are required by all services and utility routines and are used extensively by APs.

The principal difference between IBMDOS and BDOS is the means for invocation. A DOS service is requested by an AP by issuing the INT com-

7.8 PC-DOS, MS-DOS AND OTHER OPERATING SYSTEMS

mand. This command causes an interrupt which gives control to DOS by means of interrupt vectors established at the bottom of memory: a number associated with the interrupt is established in a register where the hardware looks to give control to DOS; the set of locations which are examined is called the **interrupt vector.** The AP may also insert a number in an internal register. This gives DOS more information about the request. IBMDOS then uses both the interrupt number and the number in the register to determine the exact service required.

COMMAND

The command processor, COMMAND, is the DOS module to get control after the three modules are loaded. It presents the system prompt to enter the first command. It works similarly to the command processor for CP/M.

Type command letters, finishing with return to give control to COMMAND, which "analyzes" the characters in its buffer. First it determines if the command asks for a resident service by looking in an internal table for the name you furnished. If found, COMMAND issues the request to IBMDOS using the INT command.

If not a resident service, then this is probably the name of a program to run. As with CP/M, most programs have the extension COM. But there is another program format with the extension EXE. These two must be sought on the default disk drive. A third kind of file is automatically sought, a batch file with the extension BAT. We examine this feature shortly.

Summary

To reiterate, if you have not requested a resident service then you probably need a program or batch file. This file is sought on the default disk and, if found, the action is initiated. Otherwise, COMMAND displays a question mark and repeats the system prompt.

You invoke most resident and nonresident services essentially as described in Sections 7.3 through 7.6.

Directories

CP/M and early PC-DOS use the same directory structure. A directory is viewed with the command DIR. All file names display. You can pack a lot of files onto a 1MB double sided, double density 8 inch floppy. IBM floppies only provide one-third or one-sixth of this space. Keeping track of files on the floppy does not present a problem.

However, the IBM XT provides one or more 10MB hard disks, each of which can hold several hundred files. DOS Release 2.0 and later provide software support for the hard disk. The directory structure adequate for floppies would provide problems to hard disk users and perhaps the quad density disk for the IBM AT.

When a disk holds fifty to a hundred files, it's not too difficult to examine its contents on a directory readout. Even if you have forgotten a file name, a screen review should jog your memory. But with several hundred files to contend with, this becomes difficult. CP/M has a method of dividing the directory into up to 15 groups by user number. This is effective, even with one user, as it hides the other files and makes it easier to find the one you want in this group.

A new directory system supplied in Release 2.0 and higher allows you to break up a directory into parts called **subdirectories** using a tree structure.

Trees

A **tree** is an abstract entity consisting of **nodes** and **edges.** Pictorially, points represent nodes and line segments represent edges. The result is shown in Figure 7.8.3. The terms used are defined precisely in a discipline called **graph theory.**

A tree is a particular kind of graph, an example of which is shown in the figure. The most important node, the **root,** is the starting point of the tree. All nodes are at some level but the root is the only one at level 0. It is at the top or bottom of the tree, depending upon your viewpoint.

Every node is associated with an edge which connects it to some other

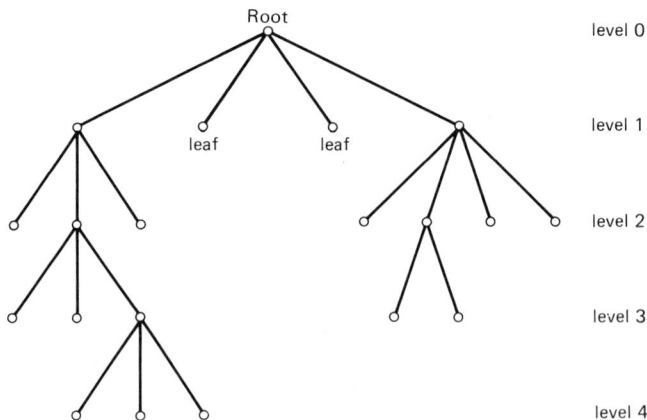

Figure 7.8.3. The tree.

7.8 PC-DOS, MS-DOS AND OTHER OPERATING SYSTEMS 253

node. Now let's define **level:** nodes at level 1 are all connected by an edge to the root; nodes at level 2 are each connected by an edge to exactly one node at level 1; nodes at level 3 are each connected by an edge to exactly one node at level 2; and so forth. A node is always connected to another at a lower level, except the root itself; a node may be connected to one or more nodes at a higher level. A node which does not connect to a higher level is a **leaf.**

The tree contains exactly one more node than edge: every time we add a node, it brings with it an edge connecting it to exactly one lower level node. Note also that there is no direct connection between any two nodes *at* a given level.

Subdirectories

Let's see what the tree has to do with the directory. It is a scheme to break up a directory into smaller parts so that files are easier to find. A **subdirectory** is a portion of a directory which lists only some files on the disk. We could break up the directory into a group of subdirectories, each listing a number of files, and let it rest at that. But there is no reason a subdirectory cannot list another subdirectory instead of referring immediately to files. That's what this tree structure does. We have that

- the root is the main directory and the default when DOS is started;
- files are leaves: they point to nothing else;
- a subdirectory is a node at any level which is not a leaf and therefore contains entries listing either files or other lower level subdirectories.

Example

Figure 7.8.4 is an example of a minidirectory in tree form. We enter the directory at level 0 and have the same access as previously. That is, to start a program listed at level 1, we give its name followed by the name of a file that we want to access. Thus, to sort the file in the figure called ABC, issue this command:

A>SORT ABC   (7.8.1)

We get a listing of the directory as with CP/M by using DIR to display all files and subdirectories in an appropriate order.

The **default directory** is the subdirectory currently in use. When you start the system, the root directory is the default. You can access only first level files from the root directory. You make a lower level subdirectory available

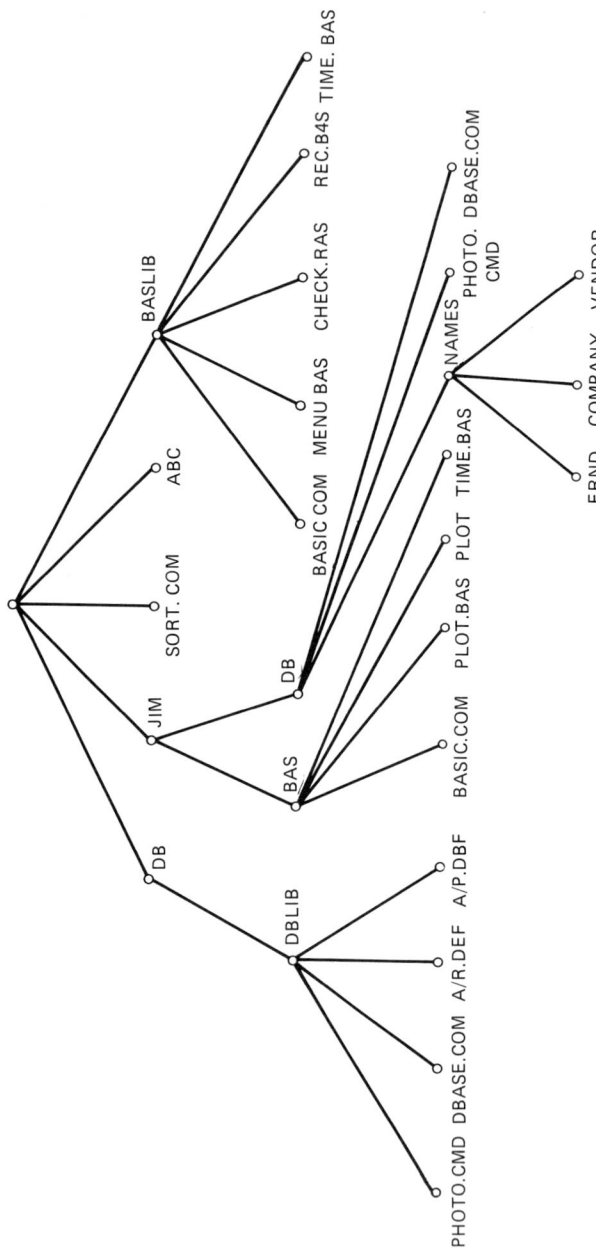

Figure 7.8.4. Typical DOS directory tree.

7.8 PC-DOS, MS-DOS AND OTHER OPERATING SYSTEMS

by using the **change directory** command, CHDIR, which then becomes the default directory. For instance, to access the BASIC library shown in the figure, you can make it the current directory with:

A>CHDIR\BASLIB (7.8.2)

Now you have available only those files which are listed in BASLIB. After the command above, you could issue this command to execute a BASIC program:

A>BASIC TIME (7.8.3)

Paths

A **path** is a sequence of nodes in which any two consecutive nodes must be connected by an edge in the directory tree. Wherever a file name could appear in a command, a legal path can be substituted. Node names in the path are separated by the backslash character. A disk drive specification may precede the top directory level to indicate the use of a different disk drive. Here is how to request one of JIM's BASIC programs (Figure 7.8.4) from the root directory:

A>JIM\BAS\BASIC TIME (7.8.4)

However, if (7.8.2) had been issued, JIM should be preceded by \ to direct DOS to start from the root directory thus,

A>\JIM\BAS\BASIC TIME (7.8.5)

A path usually goes from a lower to a higher level. However, there is a way to backtrack. A pair of dots in a path indicates a request to move to the next lower level, the **parent.** Thus, while executing programs from the default subdirectory called BAS, we could issue a command to execute a dBase program by using a path stated thus,

A> ..\DB\DBASE PHOTO (7.8.6)

Here the two dots take us from BAS down to JIM; \DB takes us up to the directory DB and then on to the dBase program to use the file PHOTO.CMD.

Directory Commands

We now discuss the commands for manipulating the tree directory structure with reference to Figure 7.8.4:

- MKDIR, also abbreviated MD, creates a new subdirectory in the default directory. If you wish to create a subdirectory in another directory, make it the default directory first, with CHDIR or use a path description.
- CHDIR, abbreviated CD, changes the default directory. To return to the root directory, use the backslash,
  A>CHDIR \ (7.8.7)
  To move from any subdirectory, such as BASLIB to DB, first return to the root with \, then give the path from there,
  A>CHDIR \JIM\DB (7.8.8)
  To move up from this subdirectory, omit the \. To go from DB to NAMES say
  A> CHDIR NAMES (7.8.9)
- RMDIR, abbreviated RD, removes a directory only if it is empty. Files should first be deleted with ERA; subdirectories are removed with RD, providing they have been emptied.
- TREE produces a listing of the tree. It does not show the tree itself but lists a level and then the next subdirectories reporting to that level.
- PATH sets up alternate paths to find command or batch files. That is, if the command file is not found in the default directory, then these paths are searched in the order provided in the PATH command. Entering PATH without an operand displays the current alternate paths available from issuing PATHs previously.

Notes

The tree directory structure described does not permit you to share command files among several subdirectories. Figure 7.8.4 shows two copies of the BASIC interpreter, one in JIM's BASIC library and the other in BASLIB. This certainly facilitates different users getting to their own files and not having to worry about other people's files. Still, it results in duplication.

Note that there is no easy way to move a file from one directory to another. Thus, to combine two subdirectories and make them part of a new larger directory, take the following steps:

1. Create the new directory with MKDIR.
2. Create new subdirectories under this directory corresponding to the two you are combining with MKDIR.

3. **COPY** files from the two old subdirectories to the new subdirectory.
4. Erase the old copies of the files with **ERA**.
5. Remove the old directories with **RMDIR**.

If one of these subdirectories contains a higher level subdirectory, the process becomes more complicated.

Batch Files

DOS provides a facility like **SUBMIT** (Section 7.5) to set up a list of programs to be executed in sequence, along with the files which they process. This list has a name with the extension **SUB**. **SUBMIT.COM** is invoked to examine the list and send off the programs to be executed in turn. For instance, you make such a request thus;

    A>SUBMIT LIST   (7.8.10)

where **LIST** is the name of the list of files.

DOS has no separate program to run a sequential group of programs; instead, the DOS command processor, **COMMAND.COM**, schedules the programs in sequence from a list having the extension **BAT**. Thus with list called **GROUP.BAT**, simply issue the command **GROUP**; **COMMAND** finds **GROUP** and dispatches each program in turn. There are three simple ways to prepare the batch file called **GROUP.BAT**:

1. Type the file at the console after issuing this command: **COPY COM: GROUP.BAT**.
2. Use the line editor, **EDLIN**.
3. Use any word processor.

You can leave spaces for parameters supplied at call time with %1 instead of $1 as with CP/M's **SUBMIT**.

8
Programs

8.1 INTRODUCTION

Programming is very complicated; why do *you* need to know about it? A businessperson provides a product or service about which he or she is most knowledgeable. Still, an understanding of accounting procedures and principles is necessary to run the firm effectively and profitability. Although it may take time away from the business, the good manager is aware of how books are kept. Even with the best product, if a company is not profitable, it cannot survive.

Since you have taken this opportunity to investigate how computers can add to your profitability, you realize that a large part of the cost of a computer system is in software. Projects have failed and companies gone bankrupt because their projection of the labor to produce a program and its eventual cost was incorrect.

There is no question that computers can make a contribution to your firm. However, the computer industry is expanding explosively. Those who advertise, sell and service computers may be either unscrupulous or ignorant, or both. They unknowingly or willfully make claims that they cannot back up. When the dust settles, you may be left holding the bag, unless you can separate the chaff from the wheat.

Dependence on the Program

The computer only does what is requested by the program which drives it. If the program does not do your accounting as you, your customers and the IRS want, then it is of little use to you. If you can get *no* program to function the way you need it, you might as well throw away your computer.

The program has to make decisions the way you want it to. Do not make the all too common error; the computer is not going to make decisions *for* you. *You* tell *it* how you have set up the simple decisions your staff usually makes, such as when to order paper clips before they run out. Then the computer program does that task in the same way. This means you have to examine *how* you make your decisions, what exceptions might arise and how you handle these exceptions.

Interdependence of Factors

There are a number of related factors to consider when evaluating a program. However, if you understand the basics you can predict qualitatively how alternative designs might satisfy your need. Here are some factors to consider:

1. The initial cost of the program, whether purchased as a package or written by staff;
2. The speed at which it runs;
3. Its **response time,** the time the program takes to react to data entry or to answer questions;
4. How to make minor modifications, such as the FICA ceiling for a payroll program;
5. How to make more substantial changes, such as to add a new payroll deduction for union dues;
6. What can be done if unpredicted difficulties arise (**error recovery**);
7. How easy it is to use and understand;
8. How well it relates with your other programs, especially with regard to its input and output.

There are many more considerations, but this list should give some idea of things this chapter examines.

Language

The program consists of directions to the computer: what to do and how to do it. We give directions in English to those who work for us. A program is a set of directions conveyed in a programming language.

It would be convenient to talk to the computer just as you do to someone who works for you. The trouble is, the computer is not a human worker; it has no resourcefulness, inventiveness, ingenuity or intelligence. Every request must be unambiguous and precise.

A **natural language,** a language for conversation such as English, is ambiguous. It is full of double meanings and lack of meanings. For instance, if I say, "I want this tomorrow," it is unclear *when* tomorrow—in the morning or by the end of the day?

Just take the little word "or." If I tell you that Jim *or* Alan will come to the conference tomorrow, you're not at all surprised when they *both* show up. On the other hand, when Reagan and Mondale were running in 1984, you knew that one *or* the other would become President for the next term, definitely not both candidates. Although it's easy for a human to see these distinctions, it is impossible for the computer to predict which is the intended use of **or**.

That is why programming requires a **formal language**. Each word in such a language has an exact meaning. Two words never have the same meaning. Rules of grammar, **syntax,** govern which words can follow other words.

More Than One Language

It would be nice if there were just one standard **programming language** to write programs. But there are hundreds of natural languages in use today. The move to create a universal language, Esperanto, made little headway. It is not surprising that there are actually hundreds of programming languages. Fortunately, like natural languages, there are only a few popular ones and these get you around well in the "programming" world.

Programming languages differ: here are some features which distinguish one language from another:

1. Ease in learning it.
2. Terseness—you give directions in a few words.
3. Readability—its easy to understand its statements.
4. Ease for writing.
5. Speed in converting to a running program.
6. Speed in running the resulting program.
7. Ease in altering the program.

This chapter examines several programming languages and their advantages and disadvantages for small business applications.

Mode of Operation

There are two modes of program operation. Each has advantages and disadvantages. However, you cannot assess the usefulness of either for any particular application unless you know how each works.

It's like the difference between typing and word processing. The end product of each is a printed page which is neat and acceptable for written communication. Yet there are differences between each process. You can make a proper judgment only when you understand them.

The two main modes of operation, **compilation** and **interpretation,** are introduced now and examined in more detail in Section 8.2.

Compilation

In both modes, you write the program in a formal programming language. The statements which comprise the program, the **source code** or **source program,** are the directions that hopefully solve the application problem. But the source program cannot run the computer directly.

The source code can be processed in a number of steps to produce **machine language code,** the directions translated into a form that *can* run the computer directly. In this form, it is sometimes called a **load module,** a command file on a floppy disk (with the extension COM for CP/M or PC-DOS). The OS loads it into the transient program area (TPA) as described in Chapter 7.

A number of computer programs, together called a **compiler,** are provided by a vendor. These are run in sequence, using the source code as input, to translate the source program into the load module as described in Section 8.2.

Interpretation

For some languages, some machines and some operating systems, a program called an **interpreter** can run a source program. You first load the interpreter into the TPA (see Chapter 7). You provide the file of source code as input to the interpreter. The interpreter scans the source code a line at a time (a single directive). It figures out, or *interprets,* what to do in response, and does it. For each kind of statement you might write, the interpreter contains a **subroutine,** a tiny program which runs the computer to perform the action described in the statement.

8.2 HOW PROGRAMS ARE CREATED

Programming

Programming is the art of writing a program in some program language. Some programs are really small and require only a few statements. With a little experience, one can sit at the terminal and write a simple program in a language like BASIC and, when it doesn't work, fix it, all in a matter of minutes. An example is a program to calculate extensions for items on your order, where you are prompted to enter the price and quantity of each.

Then you can improve on it to calculate the net total, sales tax, add in the shipping and handling and show the grand total.

At the other extreme is the program which automates all your business activities. You wouldn't expect to write this at one sitting! It takes a lot of planning and investigation. Here are some of the steps you would take:

- Divide the company's activities and take on only one at a time.
- For a single activity, review the current procedure.
- Document the following kinds of information:
  - *Input:* what new information is brought in?
  - *Processing:* how are data altered and merged with existing data?
  - *Output:* what documents and files are produced and what does each contain?
- Put it into pictorial form as in Figure 8.2.1.
- Check with those involved to see that this is really what is happening.
- Convert this into a data flow diagram, such as Figure 8.2.2.
- Make a rough sketch of program flow.
- Refine this into a program flow diagram with statements in English about what happens at each stage.
- Convert this into actual programming language statements.
- Prepare files and sample data.
- Manually act on them as required to produce test results.
- Run the program against the files and data.
- Check out what is going wrong.
- Go back one or more steps to alter the charts and program and run the program again.
- Repeat as often as required to get it to work.
- Do the same for the other activities.
- Integrate all of the foregoing activities into a system.

This outline should give you some idea of the extensiveness of a programming job and why they are so often contracted out to professionals.

Again, you should be aware the principles of programming because you can put them to work to do simple tasks for you and you can appreciate what is involved in the larger business automation task. Thereby you can work with programming staff and talk intelligently with them.

An important consideration is the organization of the data in files. Files are a replacement for the books that the company now keeps manually. Everything that is now on the books, if it is still needed, should also be found in one or another of these files. When setting up and specifying these files initially, you should determine what additional information might be needed in the future so that it may have a place in some file. The importance

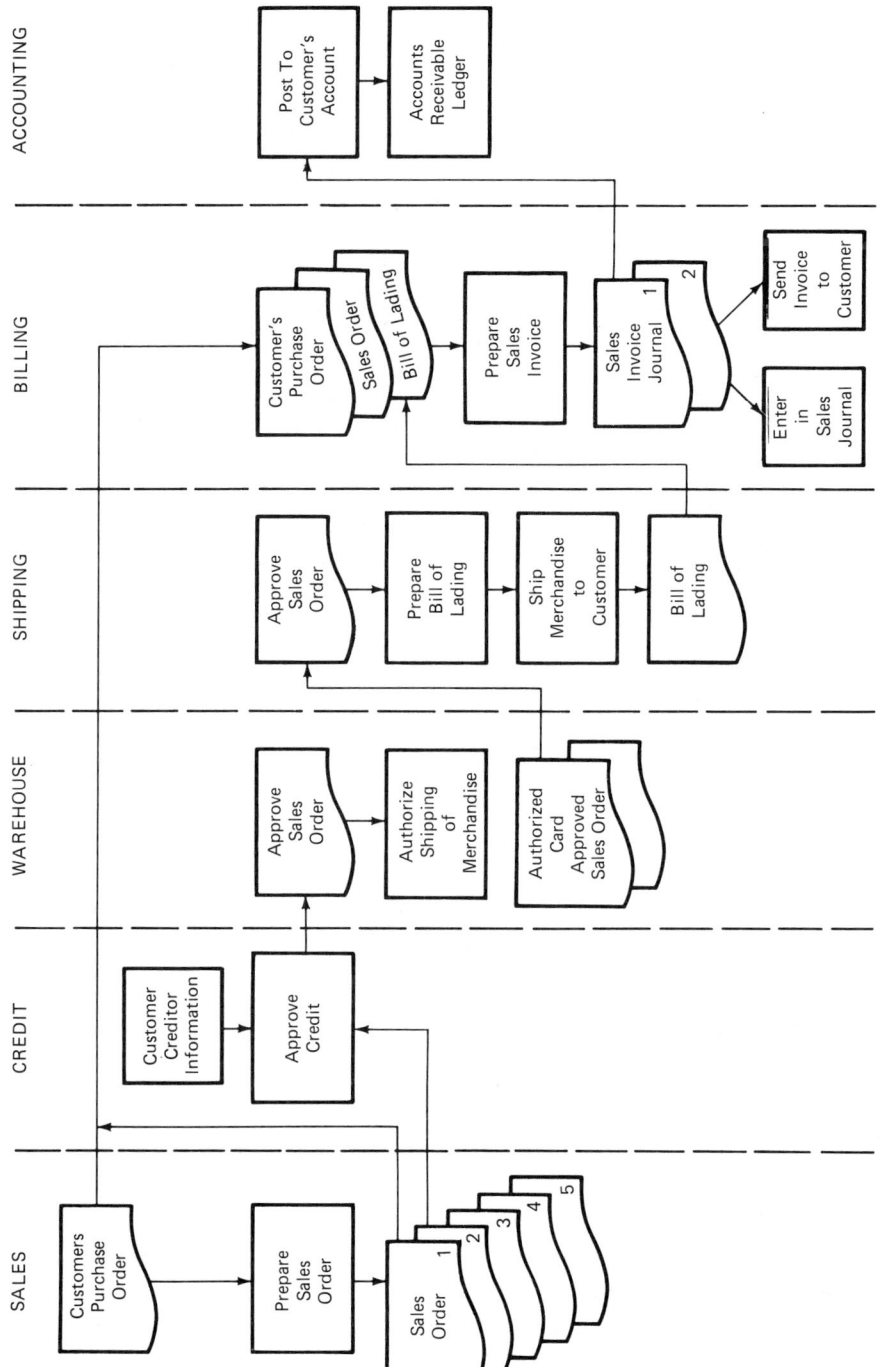

Figure 8.2.1. Flow and processing of documents.

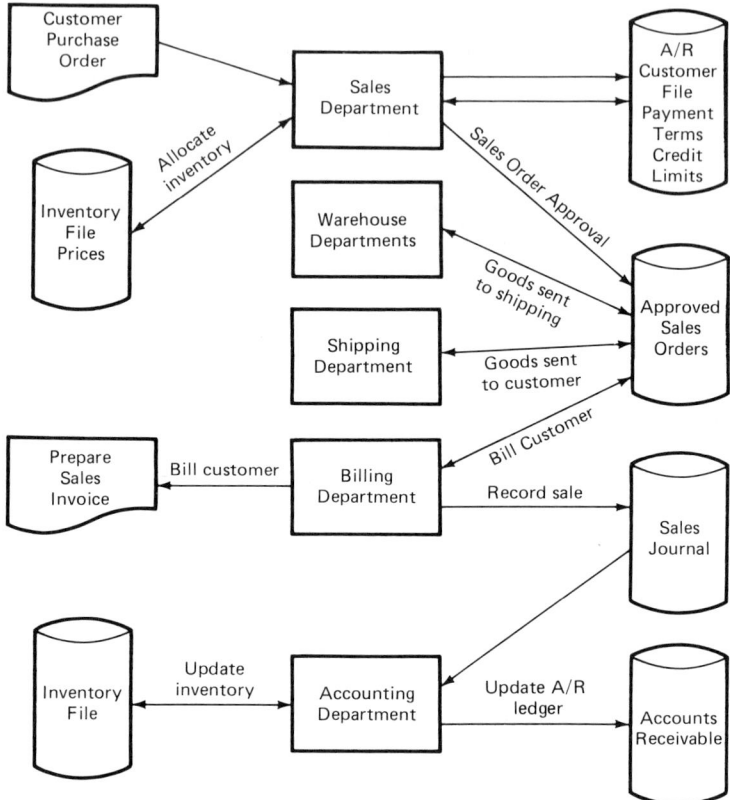

Figure 8.2.2. Data flow diagram for program analysis.

of file design cannot be overemphasized. Once a file design is fixed, it is difficult and inconvenient to change it since you would have to alter all existing files to comply with the new specifications.

After the files are designed, information flow diagrams can be converted into a set of procedures to be further expanded into the source program.

Entry Modes

The **entry mode** is the method by which the source program is entered into the computer to be translated into a form to be executed. Note that entry mode is distinct from *translation mode* (Section 8.1). The two entry modes are called batch entry and terminal entry.

8.2 HOW PROGRAMS ARE CREATED

Batch Entry

For **batch entry,** the source program is keyed manually and converted into machine readable form without involving computer time. Batch entry is useful only when there is access to a mainframe either directly or via communication lines. The steps for batch entry are:

1. Write the program.
2. Key into machine readable form (punchcards).
3. Let the computer access this medium at *its* convenience.

Even at large computer centers, batch entry is giving way to terminal entry.

Terminal Entry

The source program is keyed directly into a terminal and simultaneously displayed on the screen for terminal entry. Some programmers *create* the program at the same time that they enter it, but usually they are not trained typists and make frequent mistakes. They could not easily program at a keypunch, where correction is difficult. An **editor** (program) makes terminal entry feasible. Personally, I find a word processor ideal for writing programs. You can go *directly* to any line and alter it. The word processor is sometimes referred to as a **screen editor** when used for creating a program, because you can move around the screen at will to make corrections.

The alternative is a **line editor.** It numbers (often automatically) each line. Call for a line by number to alter it. Enter combinations of letters at the keyboard to manipulate the line, as described in the manual for your line editor. Some interactive translators (MBASIC and BASICA) have line built-in editors which make them even easier to use.

Compilation

Software manufacturers, such as Digital Research, produce language processors called **compilers** for micros; Pascal/MT+ and FORTRAN 80 are examples. The processor includes all programs required to translate a source program into executable machine language code. The package also includes **utilities** to help find out what's wrong with a program when it doesn't work, and to do other useful things.

Three Steps

Most compilers require three steps, that is, three programs to run before translation is complete and checked out:

1. The compiler;
2. The linker;
3. The translated program.

The *compiler* translates the source program, which may take from several seconds to a minute. It detects and displays errors in syntax, which must be corrected before the program can be run. A program may be translated many times before all the **syntax errors**, violations of the rules of the program language, are removed. The first step (translation) is most significant; if errors occur here, there is no reason to continue with the other steps. Therefore its designer should minimize the time taken by the translator.

Compilation time is reduced significantly by having the compiler produce only a skeleton. The additional "flesh and muscles" to make a "readable" program, called **subroutines,**—preprogrammed, oft-used units of code, are kept in a **library** on a disk supplied by the vendor. When compilation finishes successfully (no syntax errors), the **link program** is called in to find the missing subroutines in the library and paste them together with the **object module** created by the compiler. It *links* library modules to the object module to make the **load module,** a machine language program which should now run. These actions are shown diagrammatically in Figure 8.2.3.

Request the editor (1) at the OS prompt. Write the program with it. When done, return control to the OS (2). Now ask the OS for the compiler (3), which goes to work. When done, it displays messages describing syntax errors it has encountered. Then it returns to the OS (4).

Return to the editor (1) to correct errors and recompile (2-4). This sequence of steps must be repeated until you get a message indicating success.

Next enter the **linker** (5), which finds the subroutines in the library, pastes them together to the object module, then copies this **load module** to disk. (6). Now the program should be tested (7) with prepared data and its results compared with the answers *you* have calculated (8). If it seems to be functioning badly or not at all, the program has to be revised (1-8).

To Translate

Figure 8.2.4 shows what is in memory at each stage and more detail about each phase, keyed to the text with numbers. First write a source program (1) with a text editor (2) to create the source statements in memory (3) which

8.2 HOW PROGRAMS ARE CREATED 267

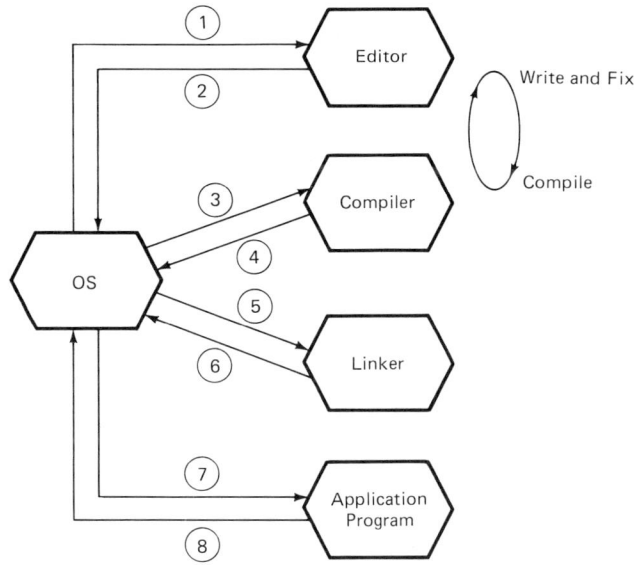

Figure 8.2.3. Actions for compiling a program.

it puts into a source file (4) when they seem correct to you. To translate them, call in the compiler in response to the prompt (5), naming the source program file thus:

>C80 MYPROG (8.2.1)

You ask for the CBASIC compiler, C80 here to work on a file of source statements called MYPROG.

The OS brings the compiler into the TPA (6). The compiler performs a number of steps; their order and how they are combined is peculiar to each compiler.

The compiler brings in the source program (7) and scans it (8) to validate each statement. A **valid statement** conforms to the programming language rules, its syntax. A statement which does not conform is flagged as an error and printed or displayed (9). You must put all statements into the proper syntax before the compiler will compile the program, instead of just checking syntax.

A datum to be manipulated by a program is named. In some languages (viz Pascal), every name must be defined to describe the *kind* of data that it represents. A compiler flags an undefined data name as an error. To facilitate fixing the program, the *entire* program is scanned, regardless of

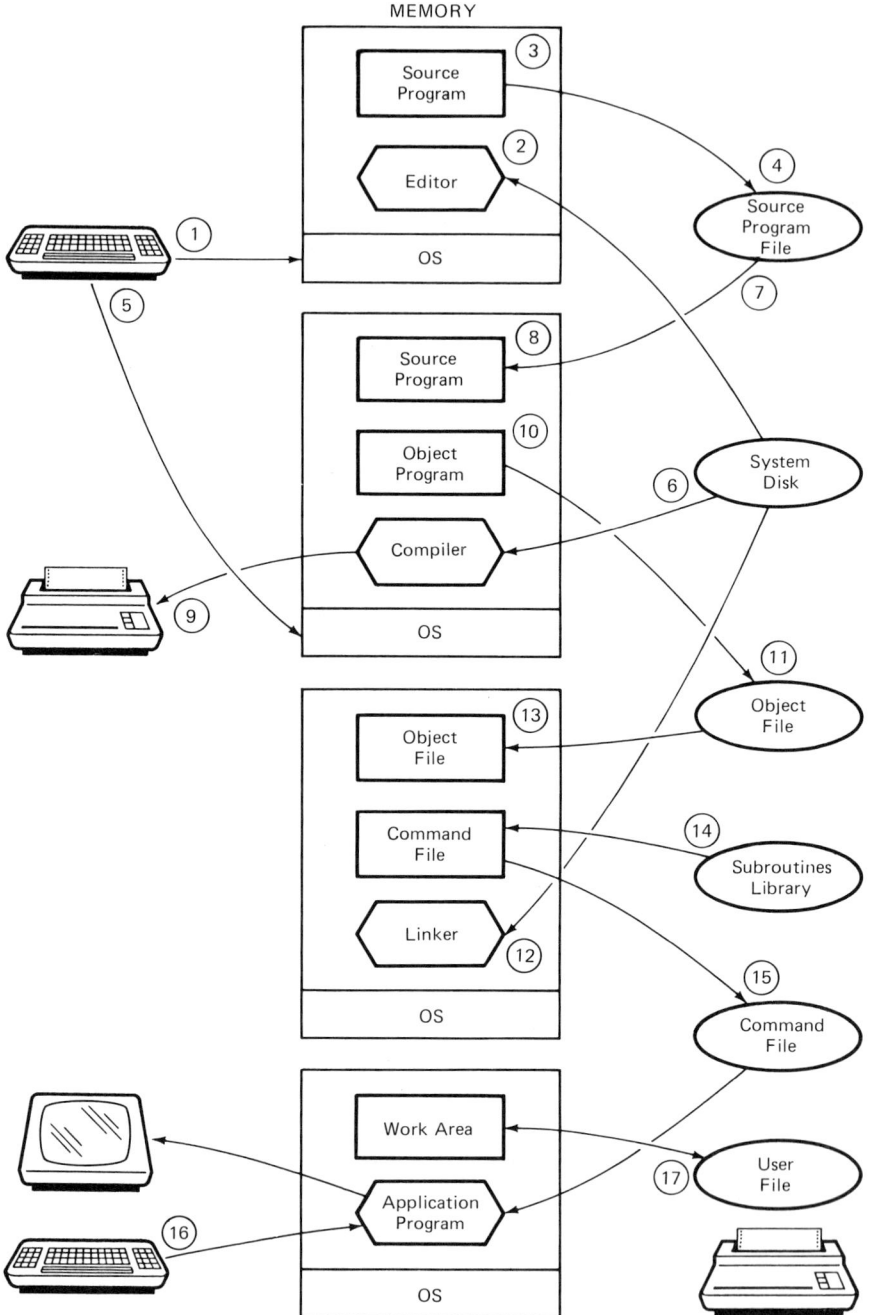

Figure 8.2.4. Detailed outline of compilation.

how many errors are found, and *all* syntax and data errors are displayed on the screen as an **error listing** and printed out on your request (9).

When the compiler finds a source program with **no** severe errors, it **translates** the statements. Each statement is converted into one or (usually) more machine language commands, which carry out the prescribed action when the computer executes them (10). The **object program** is then written to a file (11), usually with the same name as the source file but with a different extension.

To accelerate performance, some statements are not translated; rather, they are converted into subroutine requests. At the prompt, ask the OS to find the **linker** and put it in memory to replace the compiler (12). The linker brings in the object module (13) and each named subroutine module from the library (14). The result is written to a **command file** (15).

Once the program compiles, it will probably run; getting it to do *exactly* what you want is another story. Fixing errors in a program is called **debugging.** To help you, the compiler may produce a number of aids in the form of printouts:

1. A list of syntax errors encountered;
2. Variable names and where each appears in the source program. (called a **cross-reference list**);
3. Library modules to be attached to the link program;
4. Intermediate assembly language commands that the machine language code represents (of use in debugging the program).

Link

The object module created by the compiler is often incomplete; it is only a skeleton. The modules needed to make a load module are in a **subroutine library,** a group of modules from which the linker, a utility program, chooses the required ones.

In most cases, the programmer must invoke the link program at the prompt. LINK is called using the name of the source program as the parameter. All versions of a program usually have the same name but different extensions. For PL/I, the source code has extension PLI, the object module, REL and the command file, COM.

LINK loads the object module into memory. As each reference to a library module is noted, it is copied into memory. The program in memory is "opened up" by moving pieces of it around to make room for each new module. After LINK pastes in all needed modules, a complete load module is in memory. As its last chore, LINK writes the load module as a disk file with the extension COM.

Execution

The compiled and linked program is now available as a command file (15). When the OS prompts, call the program by name (16) to run it. Provide test data or the duplicate of a real file (17). Compare the actual results produced by the program with test results prepared (by hand) earlier (18). If they do not correspond, the problem in the source code must be located and fixed (1-18). The program must be debugged.

The Interpreter

The interpreter is, by far, the most popular means for writing and using programs on micros. It is so popular because you get almost instantaneous feedback. Examples of interpreters are TRS BASIC, Apple BASIC, MBASIC and BASICA (the last two are products of Microsoft). BASIC interpreters differ, as we see in Section 8.3.

Some interpreters are built into ROM (read-only memory). When you turn on an Apple II computer, the interpreter in ROM is immediately available. Others, such as MBASIC, are on disk and are invoked by a simple command from the prompt.

Most interpreters have three main components:

1. Direct command interpretation;
2. An editing facility built in;
3. A program interpreter.

These are discussed in that order for MBASIC under CP/M. The discussion applies equally to BASICA under PC-DOS. Enhancements found only in BASICA are described in Section 8.7.

Direct Commands

Request the MBASIC interpreter thus,

    A>MBASIC   (8.2.2)

CP/M brings BASIC into the transient area in a few seconds. It prints Ok on one line of the screen and the cursor drops down to the next line, ready for you to enter the first command. Ok is the MBASIC prompt and appears on the line above the cursor.

In **direct command mode,** you give directions to the interpreter which it checks and carries out *immediately,* if they make sense. Use this facility to print the results of arithmetic, just like a calculator. Here is a sample dialogue, with your input in italics.

PRINT 39.75/2.5
75.9
Ok   (8.2.3)

The result displays, followed by another prompt. To keep a record, get the printer going with ^P.

Sometimes the calculations are complicated. It may be easier to set up variables and assign values to each on its own line as a separate command. In the dialogue below, you assign values to X and Y separately. When you are ready for the calculation, display the result with PRINT.

X=57.8
Ok
Y=6.6
Ok
PRINT (3*X)/1.7*Y +4.85
20.304545
Ok   (8.2.4)

If you use a variable in a print request which you have not defined, the interpreter responds by printing a question mark:

PRINT Y+Z
?
Ok   (8.2.5)

The Editor

The editor helps you construct *and* alter a program. At any point you can submit it to the interpreter for execution by typing RUN. It executes statements in line number order and produces results. If it finds an improper statement, it stops to display an error message about the bad statement.

Statements in the MBASIC program must be numbered, but can occupy more than a single screen line. Usually you enter the statements in line number order. If you assign them *consecutive* ascending numbers, such as 16, 17, 18, etc., then there is no room to add a new statement between 16 and 17, say; a fractional line number such as 16.5 is **illegal.**

The editor has an automatic numbering facility which assigns sequential line numbers in multiples of 10 (unless you say otherwise). To set this facility into motion, simply issue the AUTO command thus,

    AUTO
    10 [ ]   (8.2.6)

The editor responds with 10, leaving the cursor (shown by the pair of brackets) on the *same* line, but does *not* say Ok. Now type a statement followed by return. The editor drops down to the next line (scrolling the text if you are at the bottom of the screen), produces the next number (here, 20) with a space and the cursor after it, ready for you to enter the next statement.

Notice in (8.2.6) that the editor responds with 10, not 1. Unless otherwise instructed, it produces multiples of 10. This lets you add several new lines between each original pair of statements, if you need to later. Thus, to add two statements between 130 and 140, you could number them 133 and 136, for instance.

Running the Program

Once you have "completed" a program with numbered lines, you can try to run it. The statements are still in memory. First, exit the editor, which is done differently for different interpreters. For MBASIC, exit with ^C (control C). When you leave the editor, you receive the prompt, Ok.

To run the program, simply type RUN. If the program runs smoothly, then answers directed to the display with PRINT now appear. If the program runs to completion you receive a new prompt. Here is a sample dialogue,

    RUN
    36.66
    Ok   (8.2.7)

When the interpreter encounters a statement with incorrect syntax or if interpreting the statement causes an error, the interpreter stops. It displays an error message including the troublesome statement number and perhaps a description of the type of error. It might even give you a complete diagnosis.

Listing

As you key in a command, it displays. When you have a long program, as you enter new commands at the bottom of the screen, old commands are pushed off the top of the screen. Therefore, you see only about twenty commands of your program.

The editor contains a listing facility invoked with LIST. It shows you the program in one of several ways:

1. The entire program displays continuously the earlier parts being pushed off the screen by scrolling with

    LIST (8.2.8)

2. A designated segment of the program displays (statements 100 through 300) with

    LIST   100-300 (8.2.9)

3. The entire program prints with

    LLIST (8.2.10)

4. A portion of the program prints with

    LLIST   100-300 (8.2.11)

In all cases, you can stop and restart (toggle) the display with ^S.

With the editor you can alter a command selectively. Include the statement number after EDIT thus:

EDIT 320 (8.2.12)

The editor finds line 320 and responds to keystrokes (see your BASIC manual), letting you add or delete characters where necessary.

At any time you may add a new command by first typing its number and then the statement after the prompt,

Ok
135   X=X+5 (8.2.13)

If 135 already exists, the new command replaces it. To *remove* a command, just type its number,

Ok
120 (8.2.14)

Operation

Figure 8.2.5 shows the contents of memory when the BASIC interpreter is loaded. You direct the operating system to MBASIC at the system prompt (1). The OS loads the interpreter from the system disk into memory (2).

Directions to BASIC entered at the keyboard (3) are received by the BASIC **executive,** which echoes them to the screen (4). They also go to the memory program area, where they are stored (5).

For a direct command, characters go to a work area (5). Hit return and the executive examines and checks it and selects a routine to make the calculations (6). Results are returned from the routine to the executive, which displays them on the screen.

Numbered statements pile up in the program area (5) until you are ready

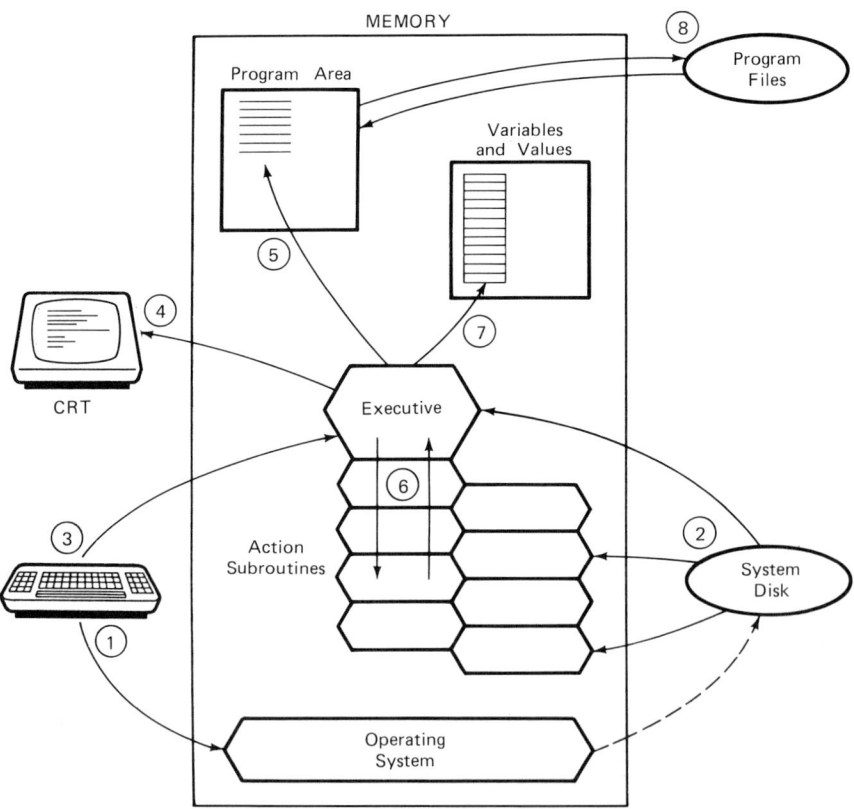

Figure 8.2.5. How the MBASIC interpreter works.

to run them. If you are using AUTO to number the program, exit the editor (with ^C) and issue RUN. The executive scans the program area, "interpreting" one statement at a time. Each is delegated to one subroutine, hexagons in Figure 8.2.5. A subroutine may alter or return one or more values to the executive, which places them as variables in a data area (7). PRINT uses variable values from this area in an expression and displays the result (4).

When the executive cannot make sense of a statement, it displays an appropriate message from its error table.

The LOAD (SAVE) command moves a program to(from) the program area in memory from (to) a program file on a designated disk (8). For instance, MBASIC saves a program you have just written or altered to a disk in the B drive with

SAVE "B:MYPROG" (8.2.15)

To be able to read and alter it later when you LOAD it, add ,A to (8.2.15) so that the program is stored in ASCII.

Mixed Mode

We have examined the two methods of program translation: compilation and interpretation. Their advantages and disadvantages are summarized in Section 8.4. Software creators have combined features of each method into **mixed mode**.

How It Works

For mixed mode, you prepare a program at the terminal, usually with a text editor. When it seems correct, submit it for translation. The entire program is scanned and syntax errors are displayed or printed. If *any* errors are detected, translation aborts and the translator returns control to the OS, perhaps displaying bad statements and error messages.

When your source program is free of errors, the translator produces an **intermediate code file** in a form unique to the language. This is not machine code and cannot be executed. The code runs the interpreter; the language of the code is not humanly comprehensible.

The translator's output file has the extension INT, for intermediate. To run it, call the interpreter (at the OS prompt), brought into the TPA (transient program area). Include the name of the intermediate file (with no extension). The interpreter finds it and brings in all or part of it and begins to interpret it.

The most popular mixed mode translator is CBASIC. A large number of business packages are available in this dialect of BASIC. Other popular mixed mode languages are PASCAL/M (a product of Sorcim) and the UCSD p-system.

Rationale

With the mixed mode method, two separate programs work on your source program: the compiler translates it into intermediate code; the interpreter interprets the intermediate code and produces results. The interpreter runs on a particular machine; it is **machine dependent.** In contrast, the source code and the intermediate code produced by the translator does *not* depend upon the machine; it is **machine independent.** A program can be translated and debugged on a different machine. Therefore program development for micros can be done on high speed mainframes. This reduces program development time, an important advantage to software manufacturers.

The development process is expedited for another reason. Complete translation requires three steps, compilation, linkage and execution. For mixed mode, the only two steps are translate and interpret.

Software vendors copyright their products for legal protection so users do not swap and copy packages; the purpose and procedure are similar to those for copyrighting books. But software copyright is hard to enforce. A purchased source program for interpretation (in CBASIC, for instance) can be copied by a utility. It can easily be altered, removing copyright messages and changing a couple of lines. Then it is difficult for the vendor to claim that the product was stolen.

Compiled programs are sold as machine language code which is transportable among machines of the same type. It is extremely difficult to alter unless you are a knowledgeable assembly language programmer. Mixed mode application packages are sold in translated (intermediate) form, which is equally difficult to alter.

The mixed mode translator falls between the full interpreter and the compiler. It requires an extra step to produce the intermediate code. But this code runs faster than an interpreted source language program.

It is more difficult and tedious to debug a compiled program. An interpreter acts directly with the source language which contains your symbolic variables and can be debugged directly.

A mixed mode translation also has to be debugged. As with the compiler, it is difficult to identify the faulty symbolic variables. However, debugging tools supplied with some mixed mode interpreters can identify symbolic references which appear in the source programs, to facilitate debugging.

Thus it is easier to write programs correctly and to alter them in the mixed mode than with a full compiler, but not as easy as with an interpreter.

Operation

Figure 8.2.6 illustrates how the mixed mode interpreter works. Prepare the source program with an editor. For the CP/M system this could be ED, a line oriented editor provided with the operating system, but a word processor is superior (see Chapter 11).

Activate the editor from the operating system (1) to write statements which comprise the source program stored to disk (2). Leave the editor (3) and request the "compiler" for the source file (4). Statements in the program file are checked by the compiler for syntax. Should it find an error, it puts a message into an error list and continues. If no errors are found, the compiler creates an intermediate file on disk with the source file name and extension INT (8). Otherwise it displays error messages and returns control either to the operating system (6) or editor (7) for correction.

If the compiler returns to the operating system with a screen message indicating success, call the interpreter giving the program name (9). The interpreter accesses the intermediate file (10) and runs the program as de-

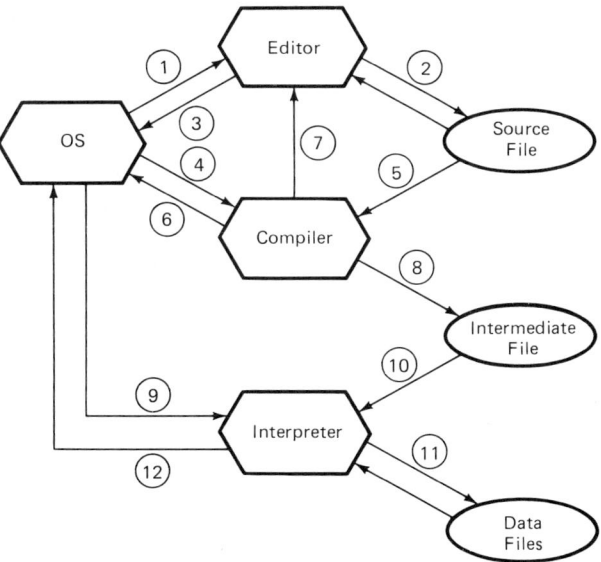

Figure 8.2.6. The mixed mode interpreter.

scribed earlier (Figure 8.2.5). The interpreter accesses files for you (11). When the program is done, the OS gets control (12).

The program which has been successfully compiled is without syntax errors but still may *not* do the job that you want it to do. Therefore, it must be debugged.

8.3 BASIC

Significance

BASIC is the most popular language for microcomputer systems; for minis it is outdistanced only by FORTRAN. BASIC is infrequently used for mainframes.

There are many **dialects** (variations) of BASIC. Each may have advantages such as;

1. Simplicity;
2. Added powerful statements;
3. Speed to run.

BASIC is the choice for most micro applications because it is easy to use and fast to learn. It has many features of more complicated languages, yet it is **friendly**—easy for the novice to use. A message supplied by a friendly system indicates the exact nature of each mistake; an *unfriendly* processor only gives an error number to guide you to an error description in a language manual—most inconvenient, to say the least.

BASIC is so easy, it's possible for the novice to do productive work in a few hours. Few other languages have a direct mode to let you do calculations *without* programming.

As a final motivation, every micro has a BASIC language facility. They differ in minor respects, enough to prevent you from running BASIC source programs on different micros. But, as with automobiles, it is easy to shift from programming one micro in BASIC to another.

To get the *flavor* of what the programmer does, the rest of this section looks at features of BASIC. We examine various *types* of statements to see what a program does and how the programmer requests them.

Types of Statements

We now examine different kinds of statements, taking examples from BASIC.

The Assignment Statement

The **assignment statement:**

1. creates a variable;
2. gives it a name;
3. assigns a value to it;
4. lets you refer to the variable later by name and consequently to find out its current value, change it and use it.

In BASIC, you name a variable *and* assign it a value at the same time. Other languages (such as Pascal—see Section 8.5) require one statement to *define* a variable and another to *assign* a value to it. This makes it less friendly.

For assignment, a variable name appears at the left, and the value given it at the right of an equal sign (=). A **variable name** is a set of characters beginning with a letter. Dialects restrict size and composition of variable names. Originally, BASIC variable names were only one or two characters. MBASIC used for most of our examples allows up to eight.

A value in a **simple assignment** is a number,

$$X = 3 \tag{8.3.1}$$

or a string of letters surrounded by quotes,

$$N\$ = \text{``HARRY''} \tag{8.3.2}$$

Alphabetic variable names are followed by $.

For a **compound assignment,** the value is obtained by evaluating an **expression,** a combination of variable names, arithmetic signs, numbers and strings. Here is an example,

$$X = Y + 3 \tag{8.3.3}$$

The value of Y is added to 3 and the result is assigned to X. If Y is not defined, (8.3.3) is an error.

The assignment statement is *not* an equation. The expression on the right may include the variable for which assignment is made. The equal sign should always be read as "assigned to." For example,

$$Y = 4*Y + 7 \tag{8.3.4}$$

requests that the current value of Y is multiplied by 4 (it is common to use * for "times"); 7 is added to this which becomes the *new* value for Y.

Sometimes we need words or sentences to appear on the screen or print in a report. A **string variable** contains a set of letter symbols: a sentence, a series of words or a set of letters, and may include numerals, punctuation and special symbols. This is called a **string**. Versions of BASIC require that string variable names end with a dollar sign ($). Here is a typical string assignment:

    N$ = "NAME"   (8.3.5)

Note that the *specified* string value *must* appear within quotes.

Remarks

The **remark statement**, REM, is a most important tool for **documenting** programs, telling, or commenting on, what each part of the program is supposed to do. REM can appear in numbered statements anywhere in the program. BASIC ignores it as a command. Here is an example,

    10   REM *** CHECK to post checks 1/8/83 ***   (8.3.6)

This remark at the beginning of the CHECK program tells its purpose and the last revision date. Should you revise the program again and/or keep several versions of it, this comment tells you just which revision you are using when you LIST it (if you keep REM up to date). It has no effect on performance.

Later you or someone else may want to make changes in a long program. It's helpful to know what each section does,

    580   REM ****** Check if FICA should be deducted ***   (8.3.7)

and where the section ends,

    660   REM ****** End of FICA check *****   (8.3.8)

You may document an individual command by entering a blank, a *single* quote and then a remark thus,

    710   I = I + 1 'Increment the index   (8.3.9)

Numbering Statements

In BASIC, *every* statement in a program must be numbered. Numbers are created automatically with AUTO (8.2.6). When you test your program, you may find that it needs an additional statement. Put a new statement between statements 20 and 30 thus,

    25   Q=X/9+27   (8.3.10)

As you add statements, numbers get closer together and it becomes difficult to add more. They are no longer "neat." Have the statements renumbered in multiples of 10 by using RENUM, the **renumber command:**

    RENUM   (8.3.11)

Given in direct mode, RENUM renumbers all statements using increments of 10, so that the new statement numbers are equally spaced. RENUM handles GOTOs and their targets properly, too.

Printing

PRINT sends information to display on the terminal; LPRINT (L for the system List device) sends information to the printer. They can be used in both program and direct mode. Display the current value of a variable thus,

    PRINT X
    33   (8.3.12)

Ask for the values of X and Y:

    PRINT X Y
    33   185.6   (8.3.13)

For brevity, ? replaces PRINT (in MBASIC) thus:

    ? X Y Z
    33   185.6   173.8   (8.3.14)

PRINT displays values assigned to several variables and can intersperse text so that the printout is more comprehensible. Here is an example,

    PRINT "X=" X " AND Y=" Y   (8.3.15)

which prints as,

    X=33 AND Y=185.6   (8.3.16)

Text between quotes is a **literal** and is printed verbatim, while variable names are replaced by their value. Use quotes only in *matched pairs*. (Note in 18.3.9) that the lone single quote signals a remark, not a literal.)

PRINT displays character information now stored in a string variable, as with

    PRINT "CLIENT NAME IS: "; N$ (8.3.17)

When printing a report, to leave blank lines, use PRINT alone, once for each blank line.

Editing

LIST with no operand displays all the BASIC program; stop and restart the display with ^S. Display line 90 with

    LIST 90   (8.3.18)

Edit a faulty statement by issuing EDIT with the statement number:

    EDIT 330   (8.3.19)

Now combinations of keystrokes cause the cursor to move to a particular letter, and delete one or more letters or insert characters. The characters to activate the editor are presented in Table 8.3.1 for MBASIC; they are different in other BASIC dialects.

Table 8.3.1. MBASIC Edit Keys and Results

KEY	EFFECT
blank,	Duplicate next letter.
L	Finish line "as Is" and start to edit line again.
D	Delete next character.
nD	Delete next n characters.
I	Enter insert mode; thereafter characters key go into line.
esc,	Leave insert mode.
iS	Search for next occurrence of i in the line.
nC	Replace next n character by those typed.
X	Move to end of line and insert until esc.
iK	Like search but delete intervening text.
return,	Finish line and leave edit mode.
A	Restore line and restart editing.

Instead of deleting or editing a statement, you can rewrite it. The old statement is eliminated and the new copy replaces it, as in this dialogue,

```
LIST 330
330    X=X+Y
330    X=X-Y
LIST 330
330    X=X-Y
```
(8.3.20)

Saving and Running Programs

The BASIC program is kept in memory while you create and run it. If you don't SAVE it, when you turn off the computer, the program disappears. SAVE, in direct mode, writes this program to the default drive, giving it a name you assign thus,

```
SAVE "PROG1",A
```
(8.3.21)

The terminal A saves it in ASCII so that it is readable by TYPE or when returned to memory. This move establishes a file with the name PROG1 and writes the BASIC program there. There is still a copy of the program in memory. You may change the memory copy and run it again.

Later, to run the program again, either to produce results or to alter it, first bring in BASIC. Then LOAD reads the program into memory thus,

```
LOAD "PROG1"
```
(8.3.22)

With PROG1 in memory, start it with RUN:

```
RUN
```
(8.3.23)

You can do both at once with

```
RUN "PROG1"
```
(8.3.24)

If you make changes in the program, the copy in memory and that on the disk will differ. SAVE the altered program; otherwise, when you LOAD it later, you'll get the old version.

If you SAVE a revised program with the *same* name, then the old version is destroyed. This is all right, if you are sure *this* is the version you want to keep. SAVE an altered program under a *different* name and both versions are available later.

Stopping the Program

A running program continues to run until the interpreter encounters END. END stops the interpreter and the prompt, Ok, appears on the screen. It is possible to write a program that, by mistake, runs forever.

You can stop a running program with a control code. For MBASIC, press control C; the program stops and the prompt appears. The interpreter waits for the next directive. PRINT may be used in direct mode to show the value of variables when the program quits. You *cannot* resume where the program stops; begin from the beginning with RUN.

When debugging a program, it is useful to stop the program to find out the status of results, and then continue. STOP does this:

```
10   PRINT "I am going to stop"
20   PRINT "Enter CONT to continue"
30   X=X+83
40   STOP
50   PRINT "I am running again"
```
(8.3.25)

After executing the first two commands, displaying the messages at 10 and 20, the interpreter stops and prints out a message, such as STOP in line 30. Now use PRINT in direct mode to view the present value of variables. Continue the program by typing the **continue command,** CONT. The program resumes for (8.3.25) at 50.

Instead, when you find difficulties, you can ask the editor to make changes in the program or add new commands and then have the program run from the beginning by simply issuing RUN.

When you are finished with a BASIC session, leave the interpreter and reenter the operating system with an **exit command,** which depends on the dialect: QUIT, EXIT, BYE, or SYSTEM (MBASIC).

Condition

To take an action which depends on the result of a calculation or the kind of data encountered. BASIC provides a **conditional statement:**

IF condition THEN action (8.3.26)

Condition is a **relation** which *may* exist between named variables and constants and is expressed with **operators.** Table 8.3.2 lists operators. *Action* is an assignment, PRINT or I/O statement, done when *condition* is true.

Table 8.3.2 Relations in MBASIC

=	for equals	< >	for not equals
<	for less than	< =	for less or equal
>	for greater than	> =	for greater or equal

For instance, a payroll program does different things according to whether the employee has reached the FICA limit for deductions; an A/R (accounts receivable) program takes different steps for a customer credit or debit. Consider the case in which the tax for the year, TAX, should be zero if gross pay, GP, is less than a particular amount, TOP. Such rules are common. This one is incorporated into your program as

IF GP<TOP THEN TAX=0 (8.3.27)

Sometimes an action is taken only when a *combination* of conditions exists. AND and OR combine relations in an IF statement. Income tax is calculated using a range of values. When net income, NI, lies between one pair of values, an applicable formula for TAX is used. Suppose net income is between $18,000 and $20,000; TAX is calculated thus:

IF (NI> =18000 AND NI<20000) THEN TAX=1960
   + 0.18* (NI−18000) (8.3.28)

For IF, *action* is performed when *condition* is true. Suppose the condition is false. For (8.3.26) nothing happens; instead, the *next* higher numbered statement is executed.

The IF statement is extended to provide for the *false* alternative:

IF condition THEN action ELSE alternative (8.3.29)

If *condition* is false, then *alternative* is executed instead of *action*. To assign the value 3 to X if a variable T has the alphabetic value Y and assign X the value −3 otherwise, enter

IF T="Y" THEN X=3 ELSE X=−3 (8.3.30)

With BASIC, *action* or *alternative* is only a single statement. Sometimes for a given condition, we would like a number of actions to be done. Branching is the only BASIC way to do this.

Branches and Subroutines

Lines in a BASIC program are executed in numerical sequence. However, sometimes it is necessary to **branch**—to continue execution of the program at some statement other than the next sequential one. Here are several reasons why branching is needed:

1. The statements that follow are not required for the record being processed.
2. Processing lines specified earlier should now be repeated.
3. A series of statements listed elsewhere should be executed at this point in the program.

You direct the program to perform a statement out of sequence with GOTO. For instance,

    520   GOTO 300   (8.3.31)

requests the interpreter to examine the statement in 300 next instead of 530. GOTO gives control to the designated line. Successive statements following 300 are then used.

Sometimes the same group of statements should be executed at different places in the program, a **subroutine.** When that series of statements has been interpreted, control goes back to the line after the one which asked for the subroutine. A subroutine is requested thus with

    160   GOSUB 550   (8.3.32)

GOSUB does line 550 next, then 560 and so forth. The interpreter notes that 160 causes the *branch* to the subroutine. Statements starting at 550 are interpreted until RETURN is encountered. This ends the subroutine and BASIC resumes execution at 170 (just after GOSUB). Here are statements making up the subroutine:

    550   ONHAND = ONHAND − WITHDRAW
    560   IF ONHAND < 10 THEN ORDER = 1
    570   IF ORDER = 1 THEN PRINT "ITEM IS LOW"
    580   RETURN   (8.3.33)

GOSUB can be incorporated in an IF statement:

    IF BALNC > = 0 THEN GOSUB 600 ELSE GOSUB 800   (8.3.34)

Loops

FOR repeats a *set* of statements called a **loop**:

    FOR limits
        statements
    NEXT   (8.3.35)

Limits provides an index or variable name and a range of values for which the set of statements that follows is repeated. *Statements* is a set of one or more BASIC lines followed by NEXT. *Limits* has this form:

    var = num1 TO num2   (8.3.36)

where *var* is a symbolic name, *num1* is its **initial value,** and *num2* is its **final value.** The set of statements is performed repeatedly, first using *num1* as the value for the variable, *var*. Then 1 is added to the value of *var* and the set of statements is performed again. This continues, using successive values for the variable. The statements are done one last time when *var* reaches the value, *num2*. NEXT simply marks the end of the group of statements to be repeated.

This loop prints out a number, its square and its cube on the same line:

```
300    FOR I = 1 TO 17
310        PRINT I,
320        PRINT I^2,
330        PRINT I^3
340    NEXT
```
                                                                                                                   (8.3.37)

I is varied between 1 and 17 in steps of 1. The three statements (310–330) occupy one line each. The caret after I indicates exponentiation. A comma at the end of each PRINT statement in lines 310 and 320 suppresses the line feed, causing printing in *columns* (use ; instead to suppress spacing between variables). The result of (8.3.37), for the first three repeats of the loop, displays thus:

    1   1   1

    2   4   8

    3   9   27

    . . . .   (8.3.38)

Variable Increment

A complete form of the loop is

    FOR var = first TO last STEP inc
        statements
    NEXT   (8.3.39)

Var is assigned the value *first* and *statements* are done. Then *var* is assigned the value *first* + *inc*. Here *inc* is an increment added instead of 1 in (8.3.31). Next *first* + 2∗*inc* is used; this continues up to, but not including the first n for which

    first + n ∗ inc > last   (8.3.40)

Input and Ouput

Input and **output** (together called **I/O**) are functions to:

- bring in data from the keyboard or from a file;
- move data to the display or to the printer;
- create, add to or amend an existing file.

PRINT directs output to the console and **LPRINT** directs it to the printer. Now let us examine, in a general way, how file input and output are specified. Actions depend upon *file organization,* discussed in detail Chapter 9.

OPEN and CLOSE

Before *any* disk file can be used, **OPEN** must be issued; in MBASIC it takes this form,

    OPEN "mode",#num,"filename"   (8.3.41)

Here *mode* is a single letter which describes the file's use: I for input; O for output; R for random. Each I/O request uses *num,* a number instead of the full file name. *Filename* is the name of the file as listed in the disk directory; it may include a drive designation and an extension (such as B:MYFILE.DAT). Hence OPEN names a file, gives it a reference number and says how it will be used.

    Immediately the interpreter tries to find the file; if the file for input (or random) cannot be found, there is no use to continue with the program.

BASIC displays an error message and stops with a prompt. Therefore, OPEN should appear early in your program so that nothing is done unless the file is available.

For a *mode* of O, the file should not exist. If it does, the contents will be destroyed and replaced by what the program now generates.

Here is how you tell the interpreter to look for an existing inventory file, INVEN:

    OPEN "I",3,"INVEN"   (8.3.42)

When you finish with the file, issue CLOSE thus:

    CLOSE #num   (8.3.43)

where *num* is the number you assigned with OPEN.

When you OPEN a file, the interpreter assigns a work area—a **buffer**—to hold records brought from the device or to hold data to be written out. CLOSE releases buffers, providing more space for the program and results.

Input

A program needs data. One source is the keyboard. INPUT tells BASIC to put values keyed at the keyboard in one or more named variables. The general form is,

    INPUT ["prompt",]v1,v2, . . .   (8.3.44)

Here *prompt* is a string of characters (in quotes) which displays first. *Prompt* tells the operator or user what type of information should be entered. When *prompt* is omitted, MBASIC shows a question mark instead. In that case, INPUT should be preceded by a PRINT statement, which performs the function of *prompt*.

INPUT (8.3.44) includes variable names, *v1, v2,* etc. If only one variable is requested, the operator enters digits or letters for a string to assign a value. For a mistake, hit left (the left arrow) or backspace to move the cursor backward and overwrite the bad character(s) with the proper new one(s). When entry of the single variable is complete, the operator hits return to give control to MBASIC to record the value provided for *v1*.

Here is an example of a single variable INPUT request:

    INPUT "Enter client name: ",NAME$ (8.3.45)

and here is what displays when INPUT is encountered by MBASIC, together with operator input in italics, return being omitted,

 Enter client name: *Brooklyn Letter Company*   (8.3.46)

INPUT can request several values. Numeric values entered are separated by commas. The program requests several data in this example:

 INPUT "Enter date as mm,dd,yy", MONTH,DAY,YEAR (8.3.47)

where MONTH, DAY and YEAR are the name of the MBASIC variables to hold the values entered. This might be the resulting dialog,

 Enter date as mm,dd,yy *12,25,83*   (8.3.48)

INPUT cannot be used to enter multiple strings because the comma itself is a proper string character. Hence BASIC could not tell if a comma is being used a separator. INPUT can bring in several numeric values and one string if the string is the *last* value to be furnished, as with

 900 INPUT "Enter employee number, S.S. number and name"

 ENO,SSN,ENAME$ (8.3.49)

When a line does not fit on the screen (or paper), BASIC breaks it where necessary, skips a line and continues.

File I/O

Now suppose that the information needed is in a file on a floppy or a hard disk. The programmer knows the order that the variable values are found in the record and what these variables are. An OPEN statement such as (8.3.41) appears in the program. Assume that the file is positioned at the desired information. A request is directed to *num* in OPEN, followed by the variable names for values to be brought in:

 INPUT#num,v1,v2,v3, . . .   (8.3.50)

This input command references a vendor file:

 INPUT#3,VEND$,VADR$,VCITY$ (8.3.51)

Information is written to a file with

    PRINT#num,v1,v2,v3, . . .   (8.3.52)

Tables

One more feature deserves mention, a neat way to establish and refer to tables. A **table** is a set of values, sometimes called a **vector** or an **array**. You can name a table just as you would any other variable. Put the item number—the numeric position of the item in the table—within parentheses following the table name thus,

    tablename(itemnumber)   (8.3.53)

for which this is an example:

    MYTAB(21) = 87.1   (8.3.54)

which assigns 87.1 to the twenty-first item of MYTAB.

You can manipulate a table variable just like any other. Here are examples:

    Y = 3*TAB(6) − 2*TAB(3)   (8.3.55)

    NAME$ = T$(7)   (8.3.56)

where TAB is a numeric table and T$ is an alpha table.

As with all variables in BASIC, as soon as you need a table, make up a name for it and put that name in a statement; BASIC sets up the table with room for *ten* items. If you need more than ten items, give the exact number with a **dimension statement** (DIM). That way, BASIC does not set aside a lot of table space that won't get used. Here you ask for an array called TABLE with 85 entries:

    DIM TABLE(85)   (8.3.57)

Dialects

A formal language is a set of rules and a method for stating how the computer solves a set of problems. But a language is no good unless a translator exists which converts it into machine language or intermediate code that the computer or interpreter can execute. Every time a new hardware design comes out, a new translator is required for each language. The designer, the system programmer, makes the translator obey the rules of the language and issue error messages.

Translator writers should know the language well and be familiar with its deficiencies. Often they have strong feelings about new rules or more powerful statements to incorporate into the language. There is a great temptation to do just that, to say "What if I had a feature which. . . ." Then they go right ahead and incorporate it into the translator and the language. When a natural language or a programming language is altered thus, it becomes a **dialect**.

BASIC is a very popular language with many dialects. We now examine some of them and their differences.

Symbolic Names

Each variable in a program must have a unique name so that the interpreter can tell one from the next. The language may limit the size of these names. One restriction in some BASICs is that variable names are designated by a *single* letter which may be followed by one digit and/or a suffix such as a dollar sign ($) for a string variable. This suffices for small programs which do simple things.

Two character variable names will not do for professional programmers. Languages such as MBASIC and CBASIC allow longer names, so that you can call a variable by a suggestive name such as TAX or GRPAY to convey its function in the program. They also have commands (DEFSTR, DEFINT) to define variable types so that you need not use a suffix such as $. Thus

    20   DEFSTR C-F   (8.3.58)

says that variable names beginning with C, D, E or F are always defined as strings.

Line Numbers

Line numbers do not aid the programmer and if you move statements around with a word processor, they have to be renumbered. CBASIC requires no line numbers.

There is still a requirement to label points to branch to (GOTO, GOSUB). For CBASIC, this label may be a number. In fact, all CBASIC statements *may* be numbered (for compatibility) but the numbers are ignored, except where a statement is the object of a branch.

More Statement Types

A language is limited by the kind of statements available. Some vendors have enriched the BASIC language by providing additional powerful statement types.

As an example, MBASIC's ON branches to one of many different places depending on the value of an integer variable and is written thus,

ON var GOTO line1,line2, . . . (8.3.59)

Here *var* is a variable with whole number values 1, 2, 3, and so forth. *Line1, line2,* and so on, are statement numbers. BASIC continues execution at one of these lines as determined by the value of *var:* if *var* is 1, execute the statement with number *line1* next; if *var* is 2, then do *line2;* and so forth.

In an accounting program, we wish to separate processing into classes according to the type of record encountered. For instance, let CR be the credit rating for this vendor. Then

ON CR GOTO 380,740,1120 (8.3.60)

chooses a processing routine according to the credit rating.

File Handling

BASIC dialects and translators vary in how they handle different kinds of files; this is also a function of the operating system. More information is found in Chapter 9.

Translation Mode

BASIC translators come in all flavors, from resident ROM interpreters to full compilers as discussed in Section 8.6. There are some dialects for which there is both an interpreter and a compiler. This permits you to develop and test a program with an interpreter at a slower execution speed but faster elapsed time for program development, since you work interactively. When you get it working properly, you can then compile the program so that it executes much faster. The interpreter is easier to use, but speed gain using a compiled program may justify the additional cost of the compiler.

MBASIC has both an interpreter and a compiler called M80; the two form a fine combination.

8.4 PROPERTIES OF LANGUAGES

BASIC is not the only language in the micro world. It is, however, *the* most popular language and that is why I gave it so much space. Sections 8.4 through 8.6 cover other micro languages.

This section discusses languages features. Section 8.5 is devoted to Pascal. Other micro languages are examined in Section 8.6 in relation to packages you might buy and programming you might do. Now we look at features which a language might have.

Ease of Learning

BASIC is a great success because it is the easiest language to learn. Designers have tried to develop easier languages, but with little success.

Laypersons contend that you should be able to tell the computer what you want just as you would one of your workers—give it an assignment and let it report when the job is done. Vendors have tried to develop program generators which use simple English statements as input and generate a program in a language such as BASIC. None of these generators really work.

The ambiguity and redundancy of English is the problem; a formal program language is necessary. There is no getting around it. How many times have you told an assistant just what you want and the next day you find that you were misunderstood? The problem is communication.

I have put these remarks right after the section on BASIC because the examples there show how easy it is to say exactly what you want in BASIC despite rules.

Friendliness

A language is **friendly** when it seems to cooperate. If you make a mistake and it can guess approximately what you meant, it can do what you seem to want and let you know how it has corrected your error. It is forgiving. BASIC is friendly; Pascal is unfriendly. When most Pascal compilers find a place where you have omitted a semicolon, they report it, but make no attempt to correct the error.

As an example of the tolerance of some versions of BASIC, they accept both **GOTO** and **GO TO**.

Another example concerns numbering. Each statement must be numbered in most versions of BASIC and a blank placed between the number and the statement on the line. But some versions are forgiving here: when they note that a character appears immediately after the number, they assume that you meant to leave a space.

Compactness

A program requires a lot of writing. Programmers know what they want to say and like to abbreviate things. Some languages permit shortened forms of various verbs. Other languages, APL for instance, provide special symbols which stand for a word. But it is difficult for even a mathematician to make sense of an APL program because it often uses esoteric symbols instead of words or letters. It is so terse and compact that most programmers cannot read it. BASICA lets you use single keys plus alt for important verbs (8.7.1).

Readability

If a competent programmer can understand a program somebody else has written, then a language is **readable**. This is opposite from abbreviation and shorthand. When it is easy and quick to jot the program down, (in a language like C) the program is often difficult to decipher. In contrast, Pascal is more readable than BASIC, and both are more readable than APL.

Data Checking

Some languages, such as COBOL, require a complete picture of each data component (the fields of a record as discussed in Chapter 9). The program checks that incoming data satisfy the picture: length, size and type of character in each field.

While COBOL automatically does this, a program in another language will need special statements for the checking function. You thus have to write more statements, which is an inconvenience.

Chopping It Up

There are reasons to chop a program into smaller pieces:

- It is large, requiring several programmers.
- It includes procedures, each needed in several places.

It should be possible to paste these portions together to make the complete unit.

Subroutines

A group of statements used repeatedly at different places in a program is a **subroutine**. When a subroutine is needed, it is **called**. After it executes, the subroutine returns control to the main program or even to another subroutine, whichever is its **caller.** Programming languages provide mechanisms for establishing and calling subroutines, which are referred to as **procedures** in Pascal and COBOL. The procedure is called by its name when needed in the program. BASIC lacks this facility, providing only the **function call,** a single statement defined by name.

File Management

A comprehensive file manager is a necessity for business applications. FORTRAN has only a rudimentary capability.

A full capability is sometimes added to a version of the language, as for MBASIC and CBASIC. We see in the next chapter how to activate and manage files.

COBOL and PL/I have advanced file functions so that, regardless of the processor vendor, the user is sure to get what is needed.

Richness

Richness for a programming language is similar to that for a natural language; a language is rich when there are several ways to say the same thing with somewhat different nuances.

For instance, DO . . . WHILE. . . and REPEAT. . . UNTIL. . . are quite similar but perform in slightly, but significantly, different ways. The point is, it is preferable to have a choice. The features which enrich languages are beyond our scope; they often bewilder the novice. Hence there is a tradeoff between richness and simplicity.

Correcting Errors

A program is not translated completely until it is correct syntactically; it then obeys the rules of the language. As noted, a proper translation is no guarantee that the program will do what you want it to do. When it fails to perform correctly after successful translation, it is said to be **logically incorrect.** Logic is much more difficult to correct than syntax. Some language processors provide tools and mechanisms to help you correct program logic (see TRON and TROF, Section 8.7). Again, these kind of tools and their use are mostly beyond the scope of this book. It is important to know that some versions of languages have them, while others do not.

Efficiency

Efficiency is how quickly things get done. Of primary importance is being able to

- write the program quickly;
- have it translate quickly;
- alter it readily so that it really works.

Efficiency is generally not a function of the language but of its translator.

For production programs which handle lots of data and are run many times during their lifetimes, program speed and response time are important. The biggest limitation for business application of micros is the time to get information to or from the disk. Even a slowdown by a factor of ten in using an interpreter, instead of a compiled program, has little effect because disk access is the significant limiting factor.

8.5 PASCAL

Pascal is the second most popular language for micros. There are several good Pascal compilers in a price range of $49.95 to $500, but no interpreters (except for a special implementation for Apple's Macintosh). Pascal is not a favorite vehicle for purchased packages, which are often written in assembly language. (CBASIC is popular for business application packages.)

Features

Pascal's features distinguish it from BASIC:

1. Pascal has a built-in block structure which helps produce structured programs.
2. It is both rich and powerful.
3. It is self documenting—you can often understand a program written by someone else.
4. It is unforgiving but precise.
5. It is strongly typed—every variable *must* have a type associated with it.
6. Pascal can eliminate branching (**GO TO**) almost entirely, a mark of good programming.

Structure

Pascal has many rules which you *must* obey. This consumes time in writing and recompiling and slows down program development. If your program has an error, the compiler rejects it. But in the end, your program is easier to use, understand, debug and alter.

Statements

The first rule, that I (and other programmers) often forget, is: a statement must end with a semicolon (;). Next, Pascal distinguishes clearly between *assignment* and *equality*. An assignment statement uses an **assignment sign,** a colon followed by an equal sign (:=). The calculated value on the right is assigned to the variable at the left:

$$x := y + 7; \qquad (8.5.1)$$

where x is given the current value of y to which 7 is added. Further, the current value of a variable may be used in determining its new value,

$$a := a + 3*b; \qquad (8.5.2)$$

No line numbers are needed.

Relations

Equals without the colon conveys equality, the **relation.** An expression is evaluated to determine whether it is true or false. Then an action is performed or omitted according to whether the relation is **true** or **false.** **Reserved words,** those with a particular meaning and which cannot be used as variable names in the programming language, are in boldface below.

An **if-then** statement performs an action when the stated relation prevails, as,

$$\textbf{if } x = 3 \textbf{ then } y := y + m/2; \qquad (8.5.3)$$

Here, if the variable x has the value 3, a new value is given to y as described by the expression following **then.** The semicolon ends the statement. If x is not 3 (the relation proves false), no assignment for y is made unless **else** is present.

Blocks

The **block structure** combines several statements so that they can be substituted anywhere a single statement would be used. The block is a set of statements bracketed by two of the reserved words, **begin** and **end.** The block, a **compound statement,** contains one or more secondary statements and *always* terminates with a semicolon. Here is the model:

$$\textbf{begin } s1; s2; s3 \textbf{ end}; \qquad (8.5.4)$$

Notice that **begin** and the last internal statement, *s3*, do *not* have semicolons after them; *s3* is associated with **end**.

Indenting

To increase readability, often **begin, end** and each statement are placed on a separate line and indented thus:

    begin
        s1;
        s2;
        s3
    end;   (8.5.5a)

However, I prefer this form:

    begin s1;
        s2;
        s3 **end;**   (8.5.5b)

because each line ends with a semicolon which I am hence less likely to omit.

Using

The block replaces any single statement. Thus one compound statement causes many actions:

    if vacation = "NO" **then**
        begin
            pay: = hours*rate;
            tax: = pay*taxrate;
            netpay: = pay − tax
        end;   (8.5.6)

There is nothing comparable in BASIC.

Another example is the **case statement,** similar to ON in BASIC but more powerful in Pascal. **Case** chooses from different actions according to the value of a named variable. Suppose that a record contains a field called **tag**. We want to do a different action or sometimes a *set* of actions according to the value of **tag**. For BASIC with ON, we could *only* jump to another program area, depending on **tag**'s value, which has to be a whole number. For Pascal, either a single statement or a block of statements bracketed by **begin** and **end** is specified and done at once:

 case tag **of**
   1: payee:="ABC Bolt and Screw";
   3: **begin**
    payee:="Elton Stationary";
    code:=345;
    amount:=36.72
   end;
   2: payee:="Computer Supplies Inc."
 end; {case}   (8.5.7)

Observe that

1. No order is required for the appearance of values for **tag** (which need not be numeric), a most powerful feature. Thus **tag** could also have a value XYZ if it is a string variable.
2. There is an **end** associated with **case**.
3. The last **case** alternative does *not* have a semicolon but *is* followed by **end;**.
4. Comments are in braces ({}) so that the last line of (8.5.7) identifies this **end** as being associated with **case** to distinguish it from the previous **end** associated with **begin**. Comments, which are not active parts of programs, serve solely to aid understanding.

Variables and Types

Types are big in Pascal. *Every* variable must be identified by type *before* use. Type statements are collected and placed in the front of the program or the block where used.

Defining Variables

A sequence of statements, the first preceded by **var** enumerates, *all* variables that appear in the program (or block):

 var choice,coat,stop,ok:char;
    code,date,x,prsw :integer;
    amount,balance :real;
    merchant   :string[16];
    out,inp   :file of rec;   (8.5.8)

Variables of the same type may be listed along a line separated by commas; a colon and the applicable type follow and *always,* a semicolon. One (or more) line describes each type.

There is no automatic type transformation. You cannot simply put variables of different types into an expression. A special function may be called when it is possible to transform from one type to another. There are many **classes of types;** three are discussed below.

Types

The **standard types** are **char** (for character) **real, integer, boolean (true, false)** and **string** (a common extension found in most implementations of Pascal for micros of the type **char**), all declared as in (8.5.8).

The language includes **structured types,** such as **record, array** and **file** (for internal files), which are less common in other languages. Each must be defined in terms of its component parts with **type.** Type definitions precede variable declarations. Here the record rec is defined:

type   rec = **record**
             a,b:real;
             c,d:integer;
             m :string[16]   **end;**   (8.5.9)

The components of a variable of a special type are variables of a declared type and must *also* appear in the **var** list, An example appears soon. Components of the same type appear on one line as above; each line ends with a semicolon.

User Definition

The programmer may also define variables of **user type,** usually defined by *enumeration*—name all the *values* which the variable might have. Pascal checks that you use a variable correctly, i.e., that the value corresponds to one in the list. Here is an example of user type declaration:

type   day = (sun,mon,tue,wed,thu,fri,sat);   (8.5.10)

Here variables are declared to be of **type** day;

var   weekday,offday,sabbath: day;   (8.5.11)

Now a value of the proper type may be assigned:

sabbath: = sun (8.5.12)

A **range,** or subset, may be defined also using **type:**

type   weekday = mon..fri;
             offday = sun,sat;
             sabbath = sun; (8.5.13)

The **ellipsis** (. .) indicates inclusion of all values in the original list between the two cited. Relations can be evaluated with reference to the original **type** list. These relations are **true:**

    mon < fri
sabbath = sun
   sat > sun 8.5.14

Order is evaluated with respect to the **type** list.

Procedures

Definitions

A **procedure** provides important shorthand for a set of statements, a subroutine. It names a set of statements which operates on parameters that you pass to it. Procedures must be named *and* defined *before* the main program and *after* the **type** and **var** declarations.

Let's start slowly: a procedure which *always* does the same thing is not too useful but it is easy to explain. The model for such a procedure is

procedure PROCNAME
VARIABLES
begin
        STATEMENTS
end; (8.5.15)

Here the things *you* supply are shown in (8.5.15) in capital letters: The name of the procedure, PROCNAME, the variables used within the procedure, VARIABLES and several statements which appear instead of STATEMENTS.

Here's a procedure to display three blank lines on the screen:

procedure blank3:
begin
        writeln ('   ');
        writeln ('   ');
        writeln ('   ');
end;   (8.5.16)

Parameters

A procedure becomes valuable when you pass it data and get back results. Two types of data passed are:

- **variables,** which are changed by the procedure
- **values,** which are examined and used by the procedure but never altered by it.

Both are represented by **formal parameters (variable parameters, value parameters)** which are put in parentheses after the procedure name in the procedure definition. Variables are named first and are grouped by type in one or more statements. Here is the prototype:

procedure PROCNAME (**var** V1,V2,..:TYPE; **var** V5,V6:TYPE;...);
                                                                                             (8.5.17)

Value parameters, which do *not* change, then follow and are itemized similarly except that **var** does not precede the items in this list.
    Then **local variables**—internal to the procedure only—are defined. The set of statements which comprise the procedure is bracketed by **begin** and **end.** This is the complete model:

procedure PROCNAME (VARIABLES; PARAMETERS);
LOC VARIABLES;
begin
        STATEMENTS
end;   (8.5.18)

Here is a procedure, **deposit,** from my check handling program to let me enter a code for the type of deposit. Variables for the formal parameters m and c are defined *outside* the procedure, but they may be reassigned values within the procedure. The payee's name, m, is entered or simply chosen in the case of recurring deposits. The local variable, **dtype**, which ranges from 1 to 8, records the operator's entry choice entered while the procedure runs.

```
procedure deposit(var m:string; var c:integer);
    var dtype: integer;
    begin
    writeln('Select type of deposit');
    writeln('1 Baruch');
    writeln('2 VNR');
    writeln('3 Prentice-Hall');
    writeln('4 Consulting');
    writeln('5 Medical');
    writeln('6 Dividend);
    writeln('7 Interest');
    writeln('8 Misc');
    readln(dtype);
    case dtype of;
        1:  m:=:'Baruch                    ';
        2:  m:='Van Nostrand Reinhold      ';
        2:  m:='Prentice-Hall              ';
        4,5,6,7,8 : begin writeln('Source:  ');
        readln(m) end {4-8} end; {case}
    c:=9000+dtype;
    writeln(m,c) end {deposit};                                    (8.5.19)
```

There are three pairs of **begin** (or **case**) and **end**; the title in the braces following **end** says which **begin** it matches.

Procedure Call

Whenever you need a procedure either in the main program or in another procedure definition, you **call** it by using its procedure name as a verb in a statement. For (8.5.16), the call is simple because no parameters are needed.

```
blank3;                                                            (8.5.20)
```

For deposit (8.5.19), the **actual parameters,** merchant and code below, provide operational names for the formal parameters (m and c) for *this* call. They *replace* formal parameters where they appear in statements of the procedure. Put them in parentheses after the procedure name; as with, deposit(merchant,code);   (8.5.21)

where merchant replaces m and code replaces c. They are **positional parameters** since the position of an actual parameter in the call dictates which formal parameter in the definition it replaces.

A procedure can be called in a compound statement:

if choice = 'D' **then** deposit (merchant,code)   (8.5.22)

But great power can be achieved by **nesting** a call within another procedure definition thus

procedure setchoice (**var** choice:char; **var** merchant:string;
    var code:integer; **var** amount:real);
begin case choice **of**

    'D': deposit (merchant,code);
    ----
end end;   (8.5.23)

Setchoice includes a call to deposit. Now the main program can be reduced in size and each procedure checked out separately.

8.6 OTHER LANGUAGES FOR MICROS

FORTRAN

FORTRAN, one of the earliest programming languages, is an acronym for FORmula TRANslation; its main use and origin is in the scientific community.

Advantages

I see no advantage to FORTRAN over BASIC, especially for the less experienced user. Many existing FORTRAN programs, most scientifically oriented, might be altered to your needs. FORTRAN graphic packages do complex things such as show various views of a three dimensional object.

There are few FORTRAN packages that apply to business: determine the best route for a salesperson to take to visit the cities in his or her territory; determine the most strategic location for goods among a number of warehouses and shipping points.

You cannot use a machine language version of a FORTRAN program which runs on a mainframe. You can only compile the program from the original source statements. These can be transmitted from a mainframe to your micro, if you have a modem and the proper communication package on both micro and mainframe, and convert from EBCIDIC (if an IBM mainframe) to ASCII. The source code and a compiler may produce a running program if the dialects are compatible.

Disadvantages

For existing source programs, you must make certain that the dialect of the compiler matches that of the program. FORTRAN has many dialects, but it has been subjected to much standardization. A late version compiler should compile earlier programs.

One deficiency of FORTRAN is meager print formatting and file handling, both essential to business data processing. Therefore FORTRAN is not a good language for writing a program for a business system.

COBOL

COBOL is THE business language. Most organizations in the business community use COBOL for all their business applications—that is what it was designed for, and it works very well. It was devised many years ago and it has been upgraded many times since. The acronym stands for COmmon Business Oriented Language.

Discussion

Few business packages for micros were designed in COBOL. Still, there are a large number of existing COBOL source language programs in large installations. There are several compilers available for micros. It would seem possible to recompile programs to run on your micro. But this is not so; the programs must be altered.

All COBOL programs have an Environment Division which specifies the hardware and software with which the program runs. The Environment Division of a source program from a large company is incorrect for a micro. This part of the program must be altered and the dialect of COBOL and the micro compiler must mate.

If you are writing packages from scratch, COBOL is a possibility. It is easy to find programmers, but they don't come cheap. COBOL programs tend to be long and word y as compared to other simpler languages like BASIC. It does not seem advisable to use COBOL for new programs where BASIC is available.

PL/I

PL/I was devised by IBM more than a decade ago. The acronym stands for Programming Language #1. PL/I includes most features that the designers could think of. Consequently, it is a very rich language containing many alternatives.

Discussion

Few programmers know PL/I thoroughly. However, the Digital Research PL/I compiler for micros, although small, provides most of the original functions (subset G). It is effective and has been used by software manufacturers to develop packages which they supply in machine language only. It is not possible to alter the packages, unless you get the source statements and permission from the vendor.

As for programming from scratch with this language, the same comments apply as those made for COBOL. But Digital Research's PL/I is more accessible and easier to use than COBOL. I have used the former to create a graphics "paint" program and found it easier to master than Pascal. Its main deficiency is in port accessing. But Digital Research's compiler is fast and excellent.

Assembly Language

What Is It?

An advanced programming language used by expert programmers, assembly language is both difficult to learn and use. It is the **lowest level language.** This means that it is closest to machine language, the language it which programs must exist in machine memory for them to be executed directly by the computer.

Each assembly language (**AL**) command represents exactly one machine language command. However, some AL processors provide a facility for **macros:** name a *sequence* of assembly language commands and call them at any point in your program (like the PASCAL procedure).

You write an AL program with a text editor or a line editor. To make changes in the source program, use the same editor. When the program seems satisfactory, the translator, an **assembler,** converts the source code in assembly language into a matching language object module. However, for many assemblers the program is still not executable in this form. It must be **linked** with a **link program** (Section 8.2) and converted into absolute form as a **load module** (Section 8.2) to be executable.

Since assembly language is so close to machine language, it is **machine dependent**. In many cases, this is undesirable. Remember that a language with a particular dialect such as MBASIC is **machine independent,** which means that a program you write for your Televideo computer *can* be used on a TRS-80 (with a comparable interpretor or compiler). This is *not* so for assembly language; an AL program for the Televideo machine does not run on your Apple, or is not likely to on a different make or model of machine even with a comparable processor.

Why Is It Needed?

With these difficulties, what is the need for assembly language? It is always the first language developed for a new computer. Original software is developed in AL, including the assembler itself, other language processors and the operating system. Hence you must work with assembly language to make changes in this basic software.

But then why a change the operating system? It usually works properly. There are some conveniences that can only be included by altering it. For instance, the consider the advantage of an **autoboot**—the capability to put in a disk, start the system and have it begin to execute a particular application program immediately without any prompts to the operator. You can make this simple **patch** alteration in your operating system if you know the rudiments of its assembly language.

Consider a more urgent change. You decide to get an additional (or a replacement) printer which requires a driver to run it. Some operating systems have a menu driven patch program which makes it simple to include a driver supplied by the vendor. With other operating systems, you use a utility written is assembly language to remove the old driver and put in the new one.

Advantages

Are there any real advantages to assembly language program segments? Indeed there are! An assembly language program is more compact and works more efficiently.

What Is It Like?

Let's take a very superficial look at assembly language. Here is the format for most assembly languages:

    label mnemonic operand ;comment   (8.6.1)

8.6 OTHER LANGUAGES FOR MICROS

Central to the command is the **mnemonic** a set of letters, usually one to four. *Mnemonic,* derived from the Greek root for *memory,* consists of letters which jog one's memory to recall their meaning. For instance, in Z80 assembly language, LD is the mnemonic for load and ADD is the mnemonic for add. There is one mnemonic for each machine language command.

The next field, *operand,* (8.6.1) locates data manipulated by the command. High level languages refer to operands by name and request operations on them directly. But additional commands are actually performed to move these operands into registers before they can be operated on. Hence almost all AL commands name one or more registers. There are many registers in the Z80 computer which hold temporary results and bear letter labels: A, B, C, etc, but often used in pairs (as we see shortly) since each single register holds only one byte.

The label field, not always used, labels a command or datum so that it can be referred to by another command such as *branch.* At the right, *comments* may document the command but has no affect on the machine language generated. It is helpful for altering or debugging your program.

Example

Let us now look at a simple example to add two 16 bit numbers, NUM1 and NUM2, and place the result at NUM3 with four commands:

```
LD    BC,NUM1
LD    DE,NUM2
ADD   DE,BC
LD    NUM3,DE
```
(8.6.2)

The first two commands load the first number into the register pair B and C, and the second into D and E (16 bit numbers). The third command adds the registers, putting the result in D and E. The fourth stores the result in DE at *location* NUM3.

Contrast this with the simple BASIC statement

```
1000   NUM3=NUM1+NUM2
```
(8.6.3)

The Disassembler

Most vendors supply application packages in machine language. There is seldom a source assembly program provided or any other help in case you wish to alter it. In fact, you are not supposed to, but the need may arise.

A **disassembler** uses a machine language program as input and produces a printout which is an approximation of the assembly language program. These are the results:

1. Mnemonics are accurately translated.
2. Symbolic references are necessarily different; the disassembler has no way to determine original variable names and makes up its own, which then appear in the listing.
3. Commands are labeled only when referenced by others in the program. Labels are created.
4. Data in the program is similarly identified with made-up names.
5. Comments are absent.

I hope I have conveyed that assembly language is difficult to work with. You can imagine how much more difficult it is to use the disassembled assembly language program!

C

The **C language** is closely associated with UNIX. It's a professional programmer's language, just one step above assembly language. Some developers of APs for micros design them in C. The best reference to the language [*The C Programming Language* by Brian Kernighan and Dennis Ritchie, Prentice-Hall, 1978] states,

> C is a relatively "low level" language. This characterization is not pejorative; it simply means that C deals with the same sort of objects that most computers do, namely characters, numbers, and addresses. These may be combined and moved about with the usual arithmetic and logical operators implemented by actual machines.

It is difficult language and one which I would not encourage you to program in from scratch because, as Kernighan and Ritchie note,

> C provides no operations to deal directly with composite objects such as character strings, sets, lists, or arrays considered as a whole. There is no analog, for example, of the PL/I operations which manipulate an entire array or string. The language does not define any storage allocation facility other than static definition and the stack discipline provided by the local variables of functions. . . . Finally, C itself provides no input-output facilities: there are no READ or WRITE statements, and no wired-in file access methods. All of these higher-level mechanisms must be provided by explicitly-called functions.

8.7 ADVANCED BASIC

This section is about BASIC for the IBM PC and XT. Three versions are supplied.

- **Cassette BASIC** is for a system without disks. It lacks many MBASIC features.
- **Disk BASIC** is similar to MBASIC but lacks BASICA's keyboard and screen features.
- **Advanced BASIC,** or **BASICA,** includes commands to control graphics display and the small speaker in the PC and XT.

Cassette BASIC is ignored here because few people purchase this configuration. MBASIC is **upward compatible** with Disk BASIC and BASICA: an MBASIC program functions properly on the PC or XT.

New features in BASICA can be grouped thus:

- Keyboard and screen features make it easier to enter, edit and use a program.
- Graphics commands control the color and monochrome display and let you draw lines and circles and so forth.
- Sound and audio commands let you control the little speaker and make "music".
- Communication commands facilitate talking with other computers.

Facilitation

BASIC is relatively easy to use on the PC and XT. The designers took advantage of keyboard and screen capabilities with these features:

1. **Function keys** give commands in direct mode with one keystroke.
2. A large number of the extra keys are put to use to help you edit and move through your program, almost like a screen editor.
3. With the alternate key, alt, single keystrokes put commands into your program.
4. You have better control of screen presentation through extra commands, for instance, to clear the screen.
5. A group of miscellaneous commands helps, too.

Function Keys

The ten function keys are labeled F1 through F10. BASIC assigns them particular functions. Key assignment displays on the twenty-fifth line of the screen if you issue the direct mode command KEY ON (you turn off the function key display with KEY OFF). Here is how they are allocated when BASICA comes up:

    F1: LIST   F4: SAVE   F7: TRON   F10: SCREEN
    F2: RUN   F5: CONT   F8: TROFF
    F3: LOAD   F6: LPT1   F9: KEY   (8.7.1)

The first five functions are familiar. Where return usually follows, it is included. F5, for instance, after a program encounters **STOP** is the same as CONT return.

Trace action is also available in MBASIC to help you to **debug** your program, that is, to find out what's wrong with it, to put a trace on a group of commands. Insert **TRON** before and **TROFF** after the group of commands to be traced. When you run the program, besides displaying answers as directed by the program, every time this group of commands executes, their line numbers also display brackets.

LPT1, a new command, prints what is on the screen. KEY displays the current meaning of the soft keys and can alter their setting. To reset a soft key, use this form of KEY.

    KEY   num,string   (8.7.2)

For instance, this command alters the first soft key so that it now means LPRINT:

    KEY   1,LPRINT   (8.7.3)

SCREEN is a graphics command discussed later.

Editing

EDIT, as with MBASIC, still calls forth a line for you to edit in the conventional way. With BASICA, you can use other keys to make alterations in the program you are constructing and to move around the screen. Here are some edit commands:

home	cursor to upper left
^home	cursor to upper left and clear
up/down	cursor up/down
left/right	cursor left/right character
^left/^right	cursor left/right word

end/^end	erase/erase to end of line
insert	toggles insertion
delete	deletes cursor character
break	like rub
esc	erases current line
^break	returns to command level

(8.7.4)

Create your program by typing in a line number, a space and then the statement. You can also number commands automatically with AUTO. As you type commands, the screen fills up. At any point, if you see something that you want to correct, simply enter command mode and use the keys (8.7.4) to position the cursor and to make alterations.

Abbreviation

Instead of typing four or five characters for a reserved word, use abbreviations by holding down alt and hitting just one key. For instance, instead of typing AUTO, hold down alt and hit A. There are about twenty such abbreviations, which appear in Table 8.7.1.

When you make the entry, the full word appears on the screen and in your program in upper case letters. The alternate key is also used to enter ASCII codes. Hold alt and enter three digits, the corresponding nonprinting ASCII character is entered into your program. This is done when you want the program to control a device directly by sending it control codes, such as to make the printer generate italics.

Table 8.7.1 Letters (with Alt) to Enter Reserved Words, BASICA

A	AUTO		N	NEXT
B	BSAVE		O	OPEN
C	COLOR		P	PRINT
D	DELETE		Q	(no word)
E	ELSE		R	RUN
F	FOR		S	SCREEN
G	GOTO		T	THEN
H	HEX$		U	USING
I	INPUT		V	VAL
J	(no word)		W	WIDTH
K	KEY		X	XOR
L	LOCATE		Y	(no word)
M	MOTOR		Z	(no word)

Screen

PRINT displays information on the screen sequentially a line at a time. BASICA has commands to clear the screen, position the cursor to a designated position and begin presentation there. You can also do this with MBASIC by sending control chracters to your terminal, if you know what it uses. BASICA was written for the IBM terminal and screen, using standard ANSI screen control characters.

CLS clears the screen and leaves the cursor in the upper lefthand corner. LOCATE moves the cursor to the named row and column number.

Miscellaneous

Additional commands are available for unique PC and XT facilities. DATE$ and TIME$ set and read data and time. In assignment statements, their function is determined by whether the command appears on the left or the right. For instance, to enter the date:

DATE$ = 1/1/84   (8.7.5)

and display the time:

PRINT TIME$ (8.7.6)

A list of miscellaneous commands appears in Appendix D; here is a partial list of a few interesting ones:

- MOTOR starts or stops the cassette motor.
- PEN enables or disables the light pen.
- ON KEY sets up a **trap routine** for a specified function key. A trap routine is a subroutine which gains control when a special event occurs (here, hitting a specified function key).
- ON PEN GOSUB enables a trap for the light pen.

There are also commands which enable the joystick, and so forth.

Sound

The PC and XT can make sounds. Let's look at them from the simplest to the most complex.

BEEP

The simplest sound is initiated with BEEP and causes the speaker to make a tone while executing a program, mainly an alarm in case something wrong happens.

SOUND

The SOUND command makes a sound of a specified frequency and duration. You can make sequences of such sounds by giving a sequence of commands. Frequencies correspond to specific notes on the scale or tones in between.

PLAY

This is by far the most complex sound command and lets you actually play compositions from a BASIC program. You can store a tune as a string of characters. A note is designated by the letters C through B, the notes of the scale. A flat or sharp is indicated by a minus or plus following the note letter. Let us look at an example,

```
10  REM little lamb
20  MARY$ = "GFE-FGGG"
30  PLAY "MB T100 O3 L8; XMARY$; P8 FFF4"
40  PLAY "GB-B-4; XMARY$; GFFGFE-."
```
(8.7.7)

The tune is defined in 20. The tone E flat is designated by E-. Line 30 plays the tune with PLAY. In the quotes are directions for playing.

MB	asks that the tune be played in background mode, which means that the program can continue as the tune plays;
T100	sets the tempo at 100 notes per minute;
O3	determines that the tune is played in the middle octave;
L8	says that the notes defined in the tune are eighth notes;
XMARY$	asks for the tune defined at 20 to be played;
P8	asks for an eighth note pause (where no note is played);
FFF4	plays three F notes, the last given the value of a quarter of a note.

Line 40 plays another tune which includes MARY$.

Graphics

Bit map graphics is quite powerful, as explained in Chapter 13. BASICA provides a number of commands to take advantage of these features.

SCREEN

SCREEN sets up the mode, whether color is on or off, and determines the display page and the active page. Pages in graphic mode are discussed in Section 13.9.

COLOR

To keep only a small amount of main memory tied up in graphics, color choices are kept to a minimum. COLOR for text mode sets the foreground, background and the border. Of course, it only works if you have a color monitor. PRINT thereafter shows text with these specifications.

For graphics, COLOR chooses one of 16 background colors and a palette. There are two palettes. Each has three colors for drawing objects. Thus color graphics displays one background color (out of 16) and gives color alternatives (4) for objects that appear there.

Points

It is difficult and tedious to draw a figure a point at a time. Still this capability is useful. A point is set with the PSET command given thus:

PSET p1[,color] (8.7.8)

where *p1* is the *x* and *y* coordinates of the point; *color* is a number between 0 and 3 which chooses a color from the current palette. The coordinate *y* specifies a line from 1 to 200 from the top to the bottom of the screen. The coordinate *x* is some dot along that line and the number depends on whether we are in medium (320) or high (640) resolution.

PRESET, which has the same format, (8.7.8), resets the point to the background color. This erases a point.

Lines

The LINE command not only draws lines but makes boxes and colors them. It has this format

LINE p1–p2[,color,box,style] (8.7.9)

Here *p1* and *p2* are the coordinates of the end points of the line in absolute or relative form; *color* chooses one of four colors from the palette; *box* can be B or BF for a box or a filled box, where *p1* and *p2* are the end points of a diagonal which determines the box; *style* describes a choice of line style (for monochrome only).

A point (*p1* or *p2*) is specified by its x and y coordinates in that order within parentheses. A point may be defined relatively as STEP (x,y), where x and y are offsets in rels from the current point. You draw a line from the current position by leaving out p1 in (8.7.9) above. Here is an example:

$$\text{LINE } -\text{STEP}(20,-5),3 \tag{8.7.10}$$

which draws a line from the current position to the right 20 and up 5 in color 3.

Ellipses

The CIRCLE command draws and colors ellipses. It has this form,

$$\text{CIRCLE } p1,r[color,start,end,aspect] \tag{8.7.11}$$

where *p1* is the absolute or relative coordinate of the center of the ellipse; *r* is the major axis or radius (in pixels) in the case of a circle; *color* is evident; *start* and *end* are the angles in radians, the starting and ending point for the curve (for an arc); *aspect* is a number or expression less than one which gives the ratio of minor to major axes and draws a circle if omitted.

Fill

The PAINT command fills a closed area:

$$\text{PAINT } p1,[color,boundary,tile] \tag{8.7.12}$$

P1 is a point inside the figure; *color* is a choice from the current palette; *boundary* is another color chosen for the boundary of the figure; *tile* is the pattern to fill the figure. If the *tile* is omitted the figure is filled with a solid color.

Saving an Image

GET and PUT in graphic format converts a graphic image into an array to store in disk file. You may also transfer the image from the array back to the screen. GET has this form:

$$\text{GET } p1-p2,\text{name} \tag{8.7.13}$$

where *p1* and *p2* are the diagonal of a rectangle, the area being saved, and *name* is the name of an array which stores the information. The array must be declared large enough to hold the image in the area defined. The manual for BASICA gives a formula to calculate the space required.
PUT has the form

    PUT p1,name,[action]   (8.7.14)

where *p1* is a point to enter the image on the display and *name* is the array name; *action* describes how the array is to display. With PUT, you can make a copy of an object anywhere on the screen. Remove an object by duplicating it in the background color. *Action* alternatives help you make animation. Thus you can obliterate an object and reproduce it in a nearby position. Doing this several times makes the object appear to move.

8.8 TRUE BASIC

Introduction

Professors Kemeny and Kurtz of Dartmouth developed BASIC in 1964. It was designed for an interactive system. That is, students learn to program in BASIC by working at terminals which connect to a mainframe. The terminal looks to each user just like a modern micro, except that often a printout may be provided at a central location.

Since 1964, many forms of BASIC have evolved for the micro. Section 8.7 examines the most advanced form of BASIC available for the IBM PC to date. However, anyone who has used BASIC is familiar with its strengths and weaknesses: its great strength is its friendliness; its greatest weakness may be its lack of control structures.

It is always important to standardize a programming language, if possible. Then you can write a program on one machine and translate it and execute it on others. The program becomes **transportable**. A standard version of BASIC has been approved by ANSI (The American National Standard Institute) based on an early version produced at Dartmouth. It does not include the many features of either MBASIC or BASICA.

ANSI is working on a new standard which includes many of the control structures associated with True BASIC. True BASIC is a new form of the language being created by the two Dartmouth professors. They have formed a firm called True BASIC to market the product and a translator for it.

Since True BASIC has the stamp of approval of the originators of BASIC and will probably bear a similar stamp from ANSI, it may be the BASIC of the future.

The rest of this section is devoted to examining the structure of the language, particularly improvements that have been made over the other revisions. Finally we look at the translator and the screen editor and how they work.

The Language

Evolution has produced a number of extensions to the original language as we have already seen. However, the control structure left something to be desired. BASIC programs tend to be liberally sprinkled with GOTOs. There is little possibility to make structured programs because of the reliance on the GOTO statement. To me, the most attractive feature of True BASIC is its set of new control structures; we examine them shortly.

Symbols and Labels

Variable names are now permitted to have up to 32 characters. This is nice, but not particularly appealing to me. I try to keep variable names short so that they are easy to type.

Variables are assigned values with the assignment statement for which LET is mandatory. Assignment is expanded, so that several variables may be given a single value in one statement thus,

LET a,b,c = 1.35 (8.8.1)

Remember how all statements had to be numbered? This was so that GOTO could make reference to a statement by number. Since the new control structures get rid of most GOTOs, numbers become less important and are eliminated entirely. Instead a **label**, a name followed by a colon, *may* precede a statement.

Substrings

Recall the three functions required to describe properly all combinations of substrings? A standard notation has made this unnecessary. Any substring can be described in this form,

string$(start:end) (8.8.2)

where *string$* is the name of the string into which we enter a substring or from which we extract a substring; *start* is the position in the string where the substring begins; *end* is the position in the string where the substring terminates.

To clarify this, consider a string containing "Mr. Harris." We can change the name of the man from Harris to Jones thus,

    LET name$ = "Mr. Harris"
    LET name$[5:10] = "Jones"   (8.8.3)

Hence now name$ = Mr. Jones

Matrices

The ability to handle arrays has been expanded. Any upper and lower bound may be set with a DIM statement; the lower bound need not be 0 or 1. There is a complete set of commands to read an input matrix, as well as to print and output it. There are also standard transformation functions, such as the determinant, dot product, inverse, transposition and so forth.

Control Statements

The most important advances in True BASIC are control statements and the function definitions. These indeed extend the power of the language.

Loops

IF and WHILE have been incorporated very usefully into MBASIC and BASICA. In True BASIC, the termination of all loops has been made uniform. A loop takes this form,

    DO condition
        statements
    LOOP   (8.8.4)

where *condition* provides the means for terminating the loop and *statements* includes one or more statements, the processing performed during the loop. LOOP marks the end of the loop.

    The WHILE form is
    DO WHILE condition
        statements
    LOOP   (8.8.5)

The UNTIL form is

    DO UNTIL condition
        statements
    LOOP   (8.8.6)

An important variation of UNTIL permits *condition* to be put after LOOP so that testing is performed *after* processing instead of before the next loop.

IF

Almost all the existing implementations of the IF statement pose problems for me because only one statement can be included for execution. The exception is MBASIC, which permits several clauses separated by semicolons within a single statement. Even this is unwieldly.

True BASIC provides for multiple statements terminated by END IF. The general form is this:

    IF
        statements
    END IF   (8.8.7)

In its complete long form, it is possible to include ELSE and ELSEIF, where the meaning should be obvious:

    IF...ELSEIF...ELSEIF...ELSE...END IF   (8.8.8)

Case

MBASIC provides ON whereby the integer value of a variable determines which line to jump to. This is useful, but leaves much to be desired, since it makes true structured programming impossible.

True BASIC provides SELECT, shown in its general form here:

    SELECT CASE var
    CASE valist
        statements
    CASE valist
        statements
    ...
    END SELECT   (8.8.9)

The first statement leads in to a series of selections and names the variable, *var*. Then, below this, each instance of CASE includes *valist*, which gives an integer alternatives for the variable and then statements to be performed when *var* had one of the values in *valist*. Here is an example of the value list statement,

valist: x = 3,7,9   (8.8.10)

Thus when *var* is 3, 7, or 9, the statements below are executed. The benefit of this technique should be obvious: selection and processing are specified in one place.

To visualize this better, here is an example* from a forthcoming book by Kemeny and Kurtz which illustrates these principles,

```
FOR game = 1 TO 10
          LET die1 = int(6*rnd + 1)
          LET die2 = int(6*rnd + 1)
          LET dice = die1 + die2
          PRINT dice;
          SELECT CASE dice
          CASE 2,3,12
                    PRINT "You lose"
          CASE 7,11
                    PRINT "You win"
          CASE ELSE
                    LET point = dice
                    DO
                          LET die1 = int(6*rnd + 1)
                          LET die2 = int(6*rnd + 1)
                          LET dice = die1 + die2
                          PRINT dice;
                    LOOP UNTIL dice = 7 OR dice = point
                    IF dice = point THEN
                          PRINT "You win"
                    ELSE
                          PRINT "You lose"
                    END IF
          END SELECT
     NEXT game
     END                                              (8.8.11)
```

Here rnd produces a random number between 0 and 1.

---

*As given in George Stewart, "True Basic," *Popular Computing*, Vol. 4, No. 1 (Nov. 1984), p. 106.

Subroutines and Functions

Here is perhaps the most valuable feature that True BASIC incorporates—the ability to name a multiline subroutine or function. The format is

    DEF name (parlist)
        statements
    END DEF   (8.8.11)

where *name* is the name for the subroutine or function, *parlist* is a list of none, one or more parameters to be passed and *statements* consists of a number of BASIC statements, as many as you need. The final line, END DEF, tells the translator that the definition is complete. Two simple examples are in order.

Subroutines

Let us define a simple subroutine which finds the hypotenuse of a right triangle thus,

    DEF hyp(a,b,c,)
        LET c = sqr (a**2+b**2)
    END DEF   (8.8.12)

Call this subroutine anyplace in your program thus,

    CALL hyp(x,y,z)   (8.8.13)

Function

Let us make a function call out of (8.8.12):

    DEF hyp(a,b)
        LET hyp = sqr (a**2 + b**2)
    END DEF   (8.8.14)

To use, an expression such as this appears in the program,

    LET z = hyp(x,y)

where the value from calculation is assigned to the variable z.

Branches

GOTO is eliminated from True BASIC. It is possible to branch to any statement preceded by a label—a symbol followed by a colon. A means is also provided to exit a loop thus,

IF cond THEN EXIT FOR (8.8.16)

which requests a jump just past LOOP, the end of the FOR loop.

Mixed Mode

A mixed mode interpreter is planned for True BASIC. We have seen this feature earlier in the chapter. You submit an edited program to the compiler, which creates an intermediate translation. This translation, in turn, is submitted to the interpreter which uses it as directions by which the program simulates the action you want. This philosophy has been altered and improved as follows.

Resident Editor

Both the editor and compiler are resident during compilation. The compiler reviews source code, translating it into intermediate code at the same time, which is held in memory. Should the compiler encounter a syntax error, it stops and gives control to the editor. The editor creates a screen window where the statement in error displays in context. Now you can alter the errant statement with the editor and then return to the compiler.

Interactive correction and compilation continue thus until the program is translated in full (or until you give up).

Execution

When compilation completes, an object module results, kept in memory. Hence interpretive execution can begin at once without disk activity. The program executes the memory module and results display, according to the commands in the program. If you note an error or unpredicted result, the source program is *also* present in memory and available to be corrected. You can halt the interpreter at any time and return to the editor to make changes in your source program.

Since all three components—editor, compiler and interpreter—are resident in memory, along with both the source program and the object code, the time for bringing the components from disk to memory is eliminated.

Saving the Programs

The source program and the object code may both be resident at the end of a session. One or both may be saved. Then the original source program may be reworked and recompiled at another session. However, if your program is working satisfactorily, there is no need to bring in the source code to run it. Simply bring in the True BASIC object module to be interpreted.

The True BASIC package is being designed for micros with at least 128K of memory, which allows all components and both versions of the program to be in memory. Because of the extensive use of memory, it is unlikely that a version will be available for CP/M.

9
Data and Files

9.1 WHAT IS DATA?

Need for Computerized Information

There are many reasons to computerize the books for your business. Here are just a few:

1. It's easier to get information into the system because you set up a uniform entry procedure for the computer.
2. Reports are printed quickly with little labor involved.
3. It is easy to retrieve information about particular client items, inventory, cash flow, bills due and so forth.
4. The relationship between people, objects and accounts within the company is clarified.
5. You improve your accounting methods and tailor them to your operation as you computerize.
6. It is easier to make changes in a computerized system.

Data are machine readable information kept in the computer. Since space to store information and time to enter it cost money, data are a *compressed* form of information, a kind of shorthand.

You keep your books in a methodical way. All transactions of the same kind are kept in one book or ledger. Each transaction occupies a row of its own. The page is divided into columns, each with its own meaning. Usually the columns are labeled at the top to show what each contains.

You use a kind of data compression to keep the books—you don't repeat the labels for each transaction or each item of the transaction. Instead, the transaction is identified at the left of the row and the meaning of the entries is found at the top of the column.

For instance, in an order entry ledger, each order might be identified at the left by an order number and perhaps the order date. There are separate columns for each pertinent item associated with the order: customer name, customer number, part number, part description, part price, part quantity, extension and so forth.

You avoid repetition by having labels appear only once. Data is managed in the computer in a similar way so that unnecessary room is not devoted to repetitious material. Keep this example in mind as we examine how data are organized.

Some attention is required to understand how data are managed by the computer just as it takes study to read ledgers and books kept by your firm. If you don't know the alternatives for arranging and organizing data, you cannot make the best use of the computer.

There are many things to keep track of in your business: employees, parts you manufacture, orders that come in and shipments that go out, bills that come in and payments that go out. Each comes from a different class. Employees are one class and Jane Lerner, the purchasing manager, is one employee. I refer to the *collection* of similar items as a **population:** it consists of the same type of individual (employees); an **individual** (Jane Lerner) is one *member* of this population.

The employee population consists of people: Jim the accountant, Bernie the secretary, Harriet the saleswoman, and so forth. Individuals of a population needn't be people. They can be

- parts your firm manufactures and distributes;
- orders for raw materials;
- checks issued to your vendors;
- the vendors themselves;
- banks you deal with.

Each individual has properties: some are of interest; others are not. A personnel file records each employee's social security number and pay rate but not the kind of car the family owns or excellence at tennis.

Data Terms

Data in the computer represent a portion of the real world *of interest* to your business, called the *population* and describe *some properties* of its members. Terms to describe units of data are presented in Figure 9.1.1. At the left, the population in the closed form consists of individuals who appear there as people.

Attributes

An individual has characteristics of interest called **attributes.** For illustration, the figure shows physical attributes; the arrow to the right of one individual shows height. An attribute has an **attribute name.** The same name is used for the attribute regardless of which individual it applies to.

There is a value for each attribute which describes an individual. The man, Ken, in the figure is 5'10" tall. This is the **attribute value** for Ken—*his* height. Also, every person has a weight: Ken's weight is the value recorded for him—*his* weight.

For each attribute we monitor the data has a value, a **field value,** which is always in a particular position of the data called a **field.** The value describes an attribute of this individual. In the earlier description, this is the value on the books in a fixed position in each row. The name for the place in the data where each value is recorded is the **field name;** this is the column title for the books.

A value in a data field *corresponds* to the attribute value for that individual. However, this may not be an *exact* correspondence. For instance, the scale might measure a value of 162.3 pounds, whereas it is actually recorded simply as 160 pounds. Also, your weight varies from day to day, month to month, and so forth. Yet there is only a single value recorded in the data kept in your personnel file for the day you were weighed.

Record

Data about one individual are kept together in a **record** with fields for each attribute monitored. This corresponds to the row for the ledger. The box at the right of Figure 9.1.1 represents a record, data about one individual. It is divided into fields, each for one attribute of the individual.

Key

How do we know which record relates to an individual? Some field uniquely identifies an individual. This is the **key field,** or simply the **key.** The key for a personnel file is either the employee number or the social security number. A name is rarely used since common names might produce duplicates. The key for a ledger corresponds to the left hand column(s) used for identifying an entry or row not the row label.

File

A collection of records is a **file** and corresponds to the population. Since the *population* only contains *individuals* of importance to the business, the

9.1 WHAT IS DATA? 329

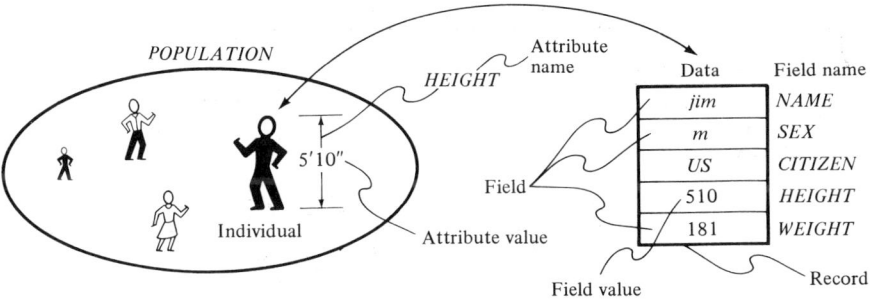

Figure 9.1.1. How data describe a population.

file only contains *records* for these individuals. Figure 9.1.1 shows a file on the right which represents the population at the left. The two are equivalent because

- there is exactly one record in the file for each individual in the population;
- there is one field in each record for each attribute of interest.

The key associates an individual with the record which describes it.

A file corresponds to a complete ledger.

File Types and File Storage

In this section we examine files to store data. Three kinds of files have been encountered so far but not explicitly described:

1. A **data file** stores information about the business as described above.
2. A **program file** contains a program which directs the computer to carry out a task.
3. A **text file** contains a document, report or letter.

Because computer memory is volatile, anything put there is gone when the power is turned off. A file is kept securely on an external medium: a floppy or hard disk.

Using Data Files

There are several alternatives for how records appear in a file. These are described in the rest of this chapter. Now let us examine the major ways to *use* information in a data file, shown pictorially in Figure 9.1.2.

330 DATA AND FILES

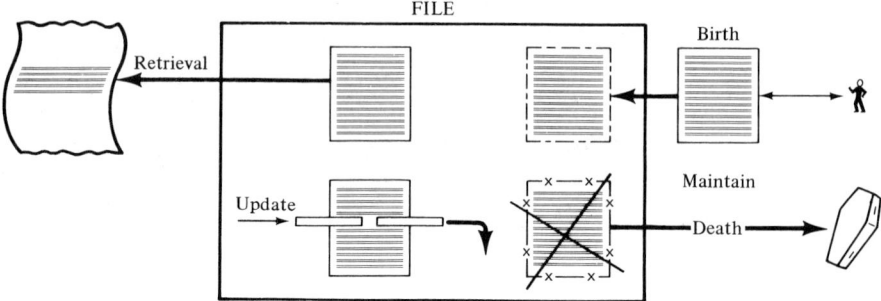

Figure 9.1.2. Ways of using a file.

Retrieval

To **retrieve** information about an individual, find its record in the file. Retrieval alters neither the record nor the file. For example, to find the status of an account, *retrieve* the record by key and display it on the screen or print it as a report.

Update

To **update** (or **post**) a file is to *change* records to show the *current* status of the associated individuals. It is important that data are up to date. Some populations do not change; their files are referred to as **archives**.

The information for most business applications is constantly in flux. Each time a customer orders a new item and it is shipped, a record in the file is updated to reflect this. When an employee receives another pay check, a payroll record is updated to show YTD taxes withheld. When stock is withdrawn to ship to customers or comes in from a vendor, an inventory record is updated to show what is actually on the shelf.

To update a file, the key of the active individual is supplied and the record obtained from the file. When it displays, the change is entered at the keyboard: fields are altered to reflect changes. Then the record is rewritten to the file.

In updating, a *record* is altered, not the file. There is still the same number of records in the file.

Maintenance

Maintenance alters the *file* because individuals are *added* to or *removed* from the population that it represents. Maintenance is a change in *file* makeup.

9.1 WHAT IS DATA? 331

Birth *adds* a record for a new individual. Here are examples:

• An employee joins the company.
• A part is added to our inventory.
• A customer begins to trade with our company.
• A vendor begins to sell us goods.

These actions increase the population size and each requires an additional record.

For **death,** an individual leaves the population. Here are examples:

• An employee leaves the company.
• We no longer stock an item.
• A customer has not bought from us in a long time or has a low credit rating and we remove that record.
• We no longer buy from a vendor.

In these cases, we don't seem to need that record in the file because this individual has left the population.

Be cautious before you delete a record from the file. For instance, when an employee leaves there are funds in the bank representing taxes withheld. At the end of the year, this money must be turned over to the government. You must keep track of it; you will be fined if you fail to submit it.

Another action which I call a **change** alters a field that does *not normally change.* For payroll, a field which does not *normally* change is the number of dependents. But when a child is born or an employee gets divorced, it may change. The *file* does not change—only a field in the record does.

Combined Actions

For **batch processing,** when a number of changes are made at the same time, update and file maintenance can be combined and often are. **Transaction records** representing birth, death, changes and update records may be interspersed. A **transaction** is the information required to alter the individual's record. **Transaction files** may be prepared at multiple stations, then combined and sorted.

Other Considerations

Most small business computer applications use **real time processing,** or **random entry,** so called because transactions are entered in no particular order. An operator enters each request by record key. The record is found, displayed and then altered on the spot.

332 DATA AND FILES

For **batch processing** in large installations, information is entered, collected, but not acted upon. A **transaction record** is created for each entry to be processed against the main file and placed in a **transaction file.** This is **sorted,** that is, placed in key order, so that posting is more efficient. The transaction file is used as a *batch.* Records read one at a time are posted to the master file. Then the transaction file may be discarded. Accounts payable lends itself to batch processing because it is updated periodically and consistently.

Frequency is how often batch processing is performed: payroll is done weekly, biweekly or monthly; billing monthly; and so forth. **Turnover** or **activity ratio** is the average percent of the file which changes. Turnover for payroll is close to 100%; for billing it may be 30–50%; for library file maintenance, where new books are entered into the card file and cards for stolen books are deleted, turnover may be 1% or less.

9.2 DATA REPRESENTATION

Bits

The computer deals only with digital information. Digital circuits are produced inexpensively by mass production, yet are accurate and reliable. They use only **on** or **off** signals.

Information is transmitted and recorded in the **binary** system. The prefix **bi-** means two, as with *bicycle* and *biped.* Binary counting uses two states. For the binary computer, the symbols 0 and 1 represent the two states, off and on. These are **binary digits,** called **bits** for short. Digital computers work with bits.

The Nibble

Long strings of bits written as 0s and 1s are hard to figure out. It is easier to break the strings into sets of four bits, **nibbles.**

The nibble is not really a unit of information; it is a convenient way to talk about it. Since each bit of a nibble is either 0 or 1, there are exactly sixteen different instances of a nibble, as displayed in Figure 9.2.1.

Think of the nibble as a binary number. When all bits are 0, the number has the value 0; when all bits are 1 the number has the value 15 (second column of the figure). Represent the first ten nibbles, equivalent in value to 0 through 9, by those symbols. Nibbles with values 10 through 15 are represented by the first six letters of the alphabet, A through F respectively. This is the **hexadecimal** system (or **hex** for short), which uses 0 through 9

9.2 DATA REPRESENTATION

```
Bit        Binary    Memory
             0         off
             1         on

Nibble
            Hex      Decimal
0 0 0 0      0         0
0 0 0 1      1         1
0 0 1 0      2         2
0 0 1 1      3         3
0 1 0 0      4         4
0 1 0 1      5         5
0 1 1 0      6         6
0 1 1 1      7         7
1 0 0 0      8         8
1 0 0 1      9         9
1 0 1 0      A        10
1 0 1 1      B        11
1 1 0 0      C        12
1 1 0 1      D        13
1 1 1 0      E        14
1 1 1 1      F        15
```

Figure 9.2.1. The hexadecimal code.

and A through F to represent the sixteen nibbles. Hex is used widely to represent the machine form of data.

Codes

A **code** is an assignment of a set of bits to represent one character or symbol in the computer's alphabet. The order of the bits in the code is important: 0001 is different from 1000.

There is one code for each character in the alphabet. The number of bits used determines the size of the alphabet it can represent. The number of different unique codes is a power of 2 of the number of bits. Six bits represent 64 different characters, which suffice in many instances. Line printers for data processing applications have fewer than 64 different characters in their print chain. The **byte** is a standard unit of 8 bits. It provides 256 different combinations for up to 256 different symbols.

A **code set** is a collection of assignments, one code for each symbol in the alphabet. Where no confusion arises, sometimes **code** is used instead of *code set*.

Standard Codes

There are several standard code sets: ASCII-8 and ASCII-7, for 8 and 7 bit codes (American Standard Code for Information Interchange); and

334 DATA AND FILES

EBCDIC (Extended Binary Coded Decimal Interchange Code), in use by IBM and on most large mainframes. The standard microcomputer data code is ASCII-7. Since each code occupies one byte (8 bits), the extra bit is important for checking purposes (see page 83).

The ASCII Code

Table 9.2.1. displays the 7 bit ASCII code. A byte is two nibbles; since the first bit of the byte is not used "X" appears there. The column heading indicates the first 4 bits and the corresponding hex (hexadecimal) form as though the first bit were 0. Thus codes for the characters in column 3 begin with the bits, X011; this column has all numbers and some punctuation.

TABLE 9.2.1 The ASCII Seven Bit Code Set

SECOND (RIGHT) NIBBLE			FIRST (LEFT) NIBBLE							
BINARY	HEX	*Binary* *Hex*	000 0	001 1	010 2	011 3	100 4	101 5	110 6	111 7
0000	0		NUL	DLE		0	@	P	'	p
0001	1		SOH	DC1	!	1	A	Q	a	q
0010	2		STX	DC2	"	2	B	R	b	r
0011	3		ETX	DC3	#	3	C	S	c	s
0100	4		EOT	DC4	$	4	D	T	d	t
0101	5		ENQ	NAK	%	5	E	U	e	u
0110	6		ACK	SYN	&	6	F	V	f	v
0111	7		BEL	ETB	'	7	G	W	f	w
1000	8		BS	CAN	(	8	H	X	h	x
1001	9		HT	SUB	)	9	I	Y	h	y
1010	A		LF	SUB	*	:	J	Z	j	z
1011	B		VT	ESC	+	;	K	[	k	{
1100	C		FF	FS	'	<	L	\	l	|
1101	D		CR	GS	-	=	M	]	m	}
1110	E		SO	RS	.	>	N	^	n	~
1111	F		SI	US	/	?	O	_	o	DEL

The second nibble of the code is at the left: all codes in that row have the binary and hex representation shown there. For example, 6, F, V, and the ampersand all end with hex 6—binary 0110.

Find the Code

To get its code, first find the symbol in the table. Its first nibble is at the top of the column; the second nibble is at the left of the row. For instance, M is in column 4 and row D. Hence its hex code is 4D, or 1001101 in binary.

A few properties of the ASCII code are:

- All numbers begin with hex 3.
- All upper case letters begin with either hex 4 or hex 5.
- All lower case letters begin with either hex 6 or hex 7.
- The upper and lower case equivalents of a letter end in the same 5 bits.
- Punctuation begins with nibbles between 2 or 7.
- Special characters and control codes begin with hex 0 or 1.

Data Codes

Data in memory and on disk is represented by the codes in Table 9.2.1. Codes in the first two columns are nonprinting: they are control or communication codes not normally found in data files.

Codes in the remaining five columns represent printing characters (for the most part), properly included in text and data files. The exception is 7F (lower right hand corner) created by rub or delete. It tells a text editor or application that the last key struck was in error and its code should be deleted from its work area. It sends back a code to the terminal to move the cursor left one position and deletes the last code received from the work area.

The space bar generates hex 20 for a space or blank between words in text and a filler in alphabetic fields. Other bytes in the right hand five columns are generated by hitting a key with the symbol on the top.

Nonprinting Characters

Nonprinting codes in the first two columns of Table 9.2.1 cannot be created by pressing a single key nor in combination with shift. All *can* be created by a combination of control and another key. This is shown in Table 9.2.2 where ^ is the control or code key. These codes are insensitive to case, so that both ^C and ^c produce 03.

TABLE 9.2.2 Control Codes

First Nibble	0	1
Second Nibble		
0	^@	^P
1	^A	^Q
2	^B	^R
3	^C	^S
4	^D	^T
5	^E	^U
6	^F	^V
7	^G	^W
8	^H	^X
9	^I	^Y
A	^J	^Z
B	^K	^[
C	^L	^\
D	^M	^]
E	^N	^^
F	^O	^_

Note: "^" means *code* or *control*, and is insensitive to case. For example, ^M is the same as to ^m.

Command Functions

The interactive business program may prompt you to tell it what to do. You respond by hitting single keys for a menu or by entering a **mnemonic**, a set of letters. The program expects one or a sequence of characters.

You type text for word processing. Characters for the keys you hit are presented on the screen. This is *text,* not commands. Some word processors distinguish *directions* from text letters by means of control or nonprinting codes found in the first two columns of the chart. APs which run on the IBM PC and its clones can get control signals generated by function keys and other combinations translated by the OS as explained in Chapter 3.

Codes in these two columns have another use. The computer sends a stream of information to a device, such as a printer, to do mechanical functions—to feed a new line, start a new page, set a different character height and width, and so forth. Device directions are in the text stream as control codes.

Communication codes used in the communication *protocol* are listed with the control codes. They direct the receiving device that a transmission begins or ends, that a block of information begins or ends, etc. The receiving device sends one code to the transmitting device when it receives and validates information; another code says information appears to be incorrect. Communication codes are not confused with text characters.

Parity

Accurate transmission of data between the computer and its devices helps to guarantee that your books are kept properly. The computer is extremely accurate because many checks and balances make sure that *all* data is valid. One important technique, called **parity**, puts an extra bit in each code to make sure that it is written and read back correctly; this bit is called the **parity bit**.

Odd Parity

Two schemes may create and check the parity bit, called odd parity and even parity. We examine the most popular, **odd parity**.

Creation. Every device or subsystem which creates or sends information to another device may put a check bit at the beginning of each byte. There is a simple rule for *odd parity:* set the bit so that there are always an *odd* number of 1s in the character. Here is the rule:

- If the code contains an odd number of 1s, the parity bit is 0.
- If the code contains an even number of 1s, the parity bit is 1.

When you hit a key at the console, it creates the 7 bit code and an *additional* parity bit, as above. When that code arrives at the computer, the program checks how many 1s are in the code. For an even number of 1s the code is viewed as **invalid**. When a record is created or altered and is written to the disk, CRC characters are added to the block (See Chapter 6).

Checking. When information is written or read back from a medium, *every* character is checked to see that it is valid. To do this, the number of 1s in each byte is counted. If that number is even, this is a bad character. If the number of 1s is odd, then it is assumed that the information is valid.

There are many ways that data may be corrupted during transmission. Data lines may pass near power lines and may pick up voltage spikes which are erroneously received as 1s. Disks become faulty, flecks of the magnetic material come off, so that nothing may be recorded in these spots. When this is the case, bytes erroneously recorded are detected by this parity scheme and the code noted as invalid. Sometimes the data can be corrected by simply having it retransmitted. When information is improperly recorded on the disk, the data cannot be recovered automatically. Correction requires human intervention.

9.3 SEQUENTIAL FILES

Origin and Definition

The **sequential file** (sometimes called a **serial file**) is based upon the organization of the **sequential medium,** where reading and writing *must* proceed sequentially from one end of the medium to the other. To make this clear, Figure 9.3.1 displays a tape reel. The tape unwinds from the hub of one reel and passes over to the other reel where it is wound up from the inside out.

Spread out the tape along a straight line as in Figure 9.3.2. When positioned the head is at the beginning of the tape, to read a record at the other end you must pass over *all* intervening records in sequence. This medium is hence *sequential*.

Not all media are sequential. The disk consists of concentric tracks shown in Figure 9.3.3. If we cut the disk along the home position and stretch it out, the tracks appear as in Figure 9.3.4. Track 0, the outermost, is at the top and the innermost track, is at the bottom.

With the head positioned on track 0, you can move it directly to a record on track 19. The head skips over the intervening tracks. Since the head goes *directly* to the desired track, this is called **direct access** (it is also called **random access**). Clearly it takes much less time to go directly to a track than to examine the contents of each track along the way. This alternative is examined in detail in Section 9.4.

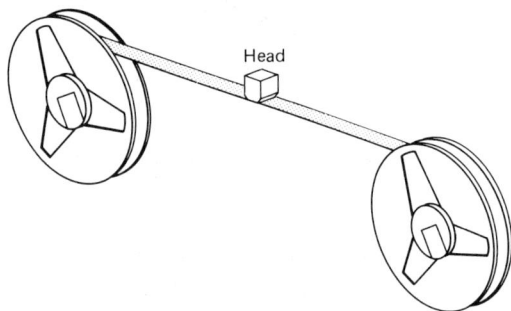

Figure 9.3.1. A reel of tape is sequential.

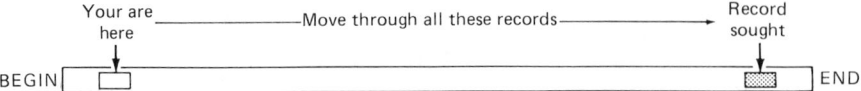

Figure 9.3.2. The tape stretched out.

9.3 SEQUENTIAL FILES 339

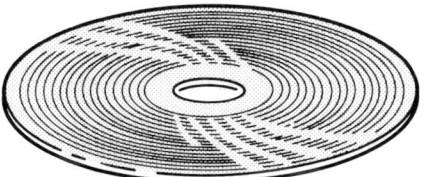

Figure 9.3.3. A disk has tracks.

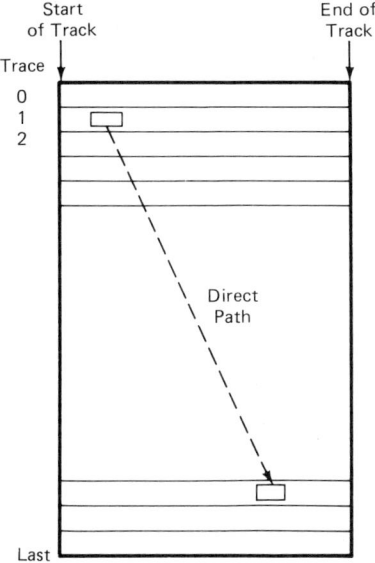

Figure 9.3.4. A direct path from one track to another.

A *sequential file* may be kept on a disk. Now the organization, *not* the medium, limits the way you use the file. You cannot normally move *backwards* within a sequential file.

File Space

The operating system and the language processor may limit how your files can grow. It is important to understand this so that the system that you acquire does not unduly limit the way that you do your accounting.

Fixed File Space

Once you get space for a file, some systems, such as North Star DOS, make this the maximum file size. If space runs out while executing a program

340 DATA AND FILES

which adds records to the file, you get an error message and the program terminates.

It is possible to live with this limitation. Suppose you try to add a record larger than the space remaining in the file, as in Figure 9.3.5. The system prevents this; instead, an error occurs, a message appears and the program terminates. To recover, call a utility to allocate an area larger than this file to another empty file. Copy the old file into the new, larger quarters. Finally, destroy the old file and give its name to the new file. Now restart the application, adding records to the new file. Make sure that the last record which was entered but not successfully stored is now reentered.

Modern micro OSs do not have this restriction.

Expanding Files

In most micro OSs, the file manager allows files to grow. CP/M and PC DOS note when a request exceeds the current allocation and acquires more space. You do *not* specify size, because files expand automatically.

Field Format

A program keeps track of fields by symbolic names and writes them in a fixed sequence for consistent processing, since they appear in the same relative position in every record. A field is classified by the **type** of information it stores:

- **character** or **string**—a set of symbols;
- **integer**—a whole number;
- **real**—a number which has a fractional or decimal part and includes a decimal point for proper display.

A **processor** is a combination of a programming language and a compiler or interpreter. It determines the way that information is written to the medium. We examine how processors handle different field types.

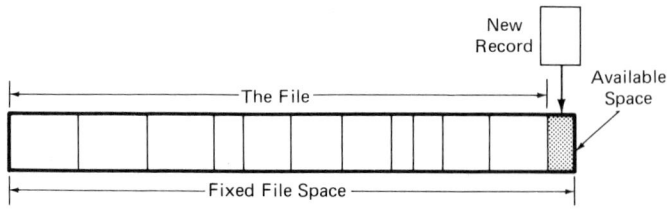

Figure 9.3.5. A file assignment.

Numeric

Both real numbers and integers are represented and processed in the computer as binary numbers of 1 to 4 bytes. There are two ways a processor may write a number on the disk:

1. In binary, prefixed with a length flag;
2. As converted by the processor into its ASCII decimal equivalent (which can be displayed or printed directly from the medium).

Binary numbers may be used for arithmetic immediately as read from the medium without conversion and reconversion. Further, a binary number occupies less space and is more compact than its ASCII equivalent: six digit decimal numbers require six bytes in ASCII and only three bytes in binary.

But binary numbers are not in standard format for utilities and service routines and have to be converted to ASCII to display or print. This is no problem in a self-contained turnkey system provided by a single supplier; it is a problem if data is to be shared by different packages, which is more common.

Character Data

Character data is manipulated by a processor in ASCII. But how does a routine tell where one field ends and another begins? Field separators determine this. With North Star BASIC (BASIC for the North Star computer) character fields have a prefix which describes its length. This field is not properly interpreted by the CP/M TYPE utility. Only ASCII format approaches a standard. It is used by CP/M, MS-DOS and PC-DOS utilities and processors.

ASCII Format

The processor can write output to disk in **ASCII format** (not to be confused with the ASCII code set) for BASIC compilers and interpreters, including MBASIC and CBASIC:

1. Fields are separated by commas.
2. A record terminates with return (a carriage return code) followed by line (the line feed code).
3. A file terminates with control Z (^Z).

The processor records different field types thus:

- *Integers* are ASCII numerals.
- *Reals* are ASCII decimal fractions; the decimal point is a period.
- *Strings* are ASCII characters surrounded at each end by double quotes (''). You may omit quotation marks when no comma appears in the field (it would be interpreted as a field separator).

ASCII format is directly readable by operating system utilities like TYPE. It is also accepted by other programs which expect data in this format. Thus data may be exchanged among MBASIC, CBASIC, WordStar, SuperSort and many other conforming packages. **Interchangeability** is a definite asset.

Streamed Records

If you request, the processor **streams** records on the medium:

- characters of fields are written in sequence to the medium;
- fields are written in the order they appear in the output command in the program;
- the length of each field is the number of characters it holds and can vary from one record to the next.

Thus 3 requires one byte while 15,000,000 requires eight bytes. (No commas appear *within a numeric field*.)

Variable length is more apparent with string information. For instance, JOHN DOE requires 10 bytes while ALBERTA ROCKERFELLER uses 20 bytes.

The alternative to streamed records is fixed size records. These are less efficient and more trouble to manage. Then why use them at all? They are needed for direct files, discussed in Section 9.4.

Creating a File

How do you create a sequential file? Here we use MBASIC as an example. (Regardless of the language, the procedure is almost identical). Near the beginning of program, open the file with **OPEN** (See Section 8.3 and (8.3.16)). There is no sense in proceeding any further if the file already exists or if there is no room on the disk for a new file. **OPEN** checks this.

Next, assemble one record at a time. New information is entered, often from the keyboard. The program might prompt an operator to enter each field. A better program also **validates** data; that is, it makes sure only numeric information is entered for numeric fields, and so on. For example, the program would reject an amount in dollars of "ABC".

Once fields of a record are collected and verified, it may be written to disk. MBASIC writes a record with a *single* PRINT# command; *two* PRINT#s create two separate records.

Now the program inquires whether the input session is over. If not, the program prompts for data again, gets the fields, produces the next record and writes it to the file. When you run out of data, the program closes the file and returns to the processor or OS.

Here is a portion of such a program:

```
10   OPEN "O",2,"VENDOR"
     assemble fields of a vendor record
300  PRINT#2 VNAME$,VAD$,VCITY$,VCLASS,...,VRATE
     check if there are more records to come
600  IF MORE="YES" GOTO 30                              (9.3.1)
```

Intervening actions omitted are in lower case Roman.

Retrieval

There are two ways to retrieve information from the streamed file:

- Review the entire file and present each record on the screen, either on demand or automatically.
- Present a single record requested by the operator.

File Review

There is little to a program which presents records one at a time on the screen. Simply open the file, read a record, present it on the screen and continue to loop. A WAIT command might be inserted so that the observer has time to look at a record before the next appears.

Request by Key

Once the file is open, the program asks the operator to identify a record. A search loop scans the file sequentially for the desired record. Here is a segment which does this:

```
190  INPUT "Enter employee number:",KSRCH
200  WHILE NOT EOF (1)
```

```
210          INPUT#1,KEY,NAME$,DEPT,RATE
220          IF KSRCH = KEY THEN GOTO 500
230     WEND
240     PRINT "Record not found"
250     CLOSE 1
260     INPUT "Enter YES to do another search:",YES$
270     IF YES$ = "YES" THEN GOTO 100
290     END                                                    (9.3.2)
```

The loop between 200 and 230, encompassed by **WHILE** and **WEND**, searches for the requested record by comparing the key furnished (**KSRCH**) with the key (**KEY**) of successive records read. If the two are equal (220), a branch to a **PRINT** statement at 500 displays the record and returns to 250. Should the loop complete unsuccessfully, a message appears (240).

After each search, the file is closed (250). The *streamed* file is *sequential* and must be closed to be reused. The operator is asked if another search is required (260). If so, the program loops back (100) where **OPEN** resets the file to its beginning.

Posting

Posting finds a record and alters it to reflect the present status of the individual it represents and is done in two ways. For random update, the operator makes requests in any order. The program searches the file from its beginning to find and alter that record.

For batch update, each request is transformed into a record which is put in a transaction file, but the master file is not affected until later. During the second phase, the transaction file is matched against the master file and alterations put in the master file.

One at a Time

Figure 9.3.6 shows random posting to the streamed file. Note that *each* posting request rewrites the entire file because the record size may change. The record size *is* the sum of the sizes of its fields which may vary from one record to the next. Posting may cause field size to change. Suppose a customer's current balance is $3.99; posting a new large purchase changes this balance to $5,379.26.

The posting program opens the old master file for *input* and a new master file for *output*. A transaction record menu displays and the operator keys the record identification and values for fields to be changed.

When the operator enters the record key, the program copies records

9.3 SEQUENTIAL FILES

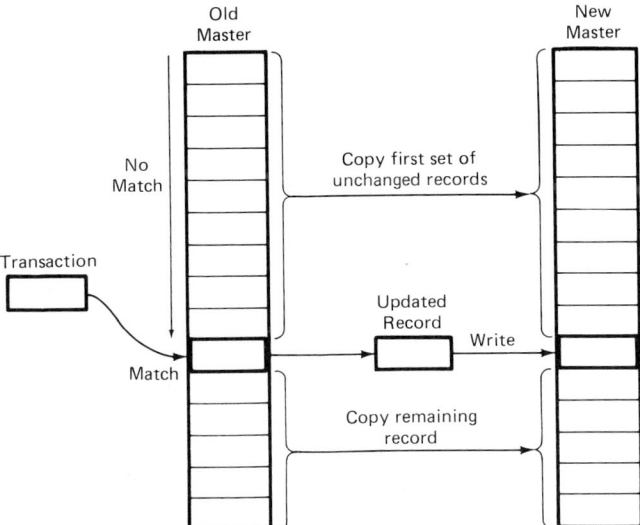

Figure 9.3.6. Posting one record at a time.

from the old master file to the new until the designated record is found. Meanwhile, the operator enters values for the transaction, checks the fields and signals when done. The program updates the record and displays it.

After the operator's approval, the record is written to the new master file. The remaining old master records are transferred to the new master and the two files closed. The old master file becomes a backup file and the new master file is renamed. The program does not end. The new master is opened and becomes the old master as above. The user is prompted for another transaction or may quit and return to the OS.

No Match

When the transaction key matches *no* record in the file, no update is possible. But during the search, the entire file is copied. One copy must be destroyed. The operator is told that the key is missing and is asked to furnish another key.

Batch Processing

Batch processing is recommended when the old master is in key order, is comparatively long and periodic update is acceptable. Accounts receivable or payable are examples. In Figure 9.3.7, a transaction file is prepared.

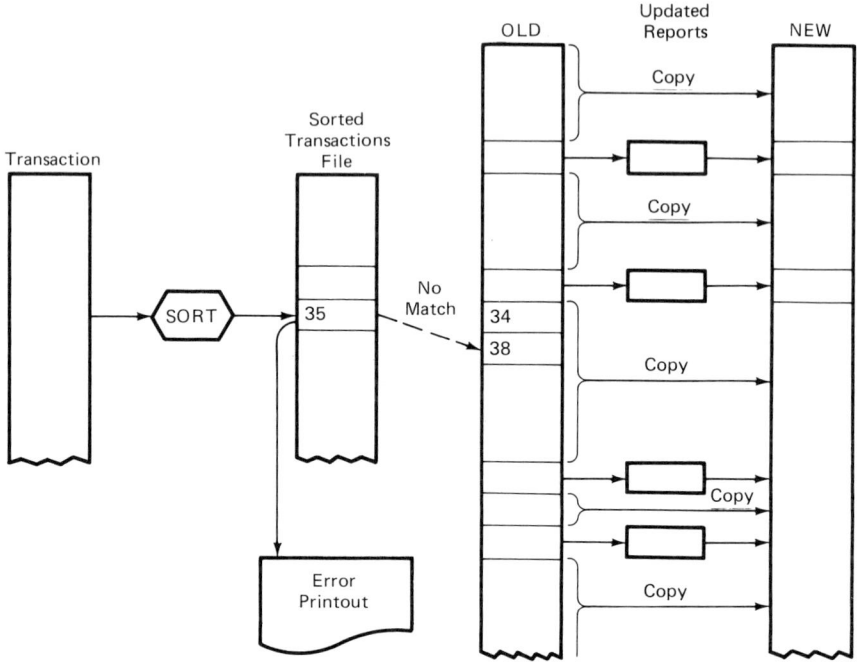

Figure 9.3.7. Batch posting.

Where a lot of data are entered, separate and independent transaction files are generated by different operators.

Before posting, transaction files are passed to a sort program which puts records in key order in a single merged and sorted output transaction file. Since the old master file is ordered by key, one posting pass examines both files simultaneously: the ordered transaction and master file are opened for input. A new master file is opened for output.

The first record from the transaction file is read and the key extracted (TKEY). Then an old master record is read. The transaction key and the master key (MKEY) are compared. If the transaction key is lower (TKEY < MKEY), copy the old master record to the new master file until a match occurs (TKEY = MKEY); posting now takes place.

The next transaction record is read and its key is sought on the old master. Its key must be greater than the last TKEY, since the file is sorted. Intervening records (TKEY < MKEY) are copied from the old to the new master. This process continues until the last transaction record is read. The remaining records are copied to the new master from the old, which is deleted or labeled as backup. The new master becomes the current master.

The batch posting program should take into account all eventualities. When a record with the transaction key is *not* found in the old master file (TKEY>MKEY), it cannot be posted. Instead of stopping, it is preferable to print out the transaction record for later verification and reposting, as shown in Figure 9.3.7.

Key order for both the transaction and master file makes it easy to detect a bad transaction record (a missing master). Figure 9.3.7 illustrates an attempt to post a transaction against record 35. No match is made with master record 34 nor 38. Since 38>35, a matching master is missing. The search for record 35 is discontinued at once and the next transaction key is compared with 38. However, the transaction record with key 35 is printed.

File Maintenance

File maintenance involves three activities:

- **Birth** creates records for individuals added to the population.
- **Death** eliminates records for individuals who leave.
- **Change** causes alterations in some records in those fields not used for posting.

Appending birth records at the end of the file is examined first.

Appending

Appending at file end is done when

- the file is *not* kept in order; or
- the file *is* in key order but the new individuals have keys higher than any on the file.

Some processors can append to an existing file. With CBASIC, after you OPEN the file for *both* input and output, it can read the file to the end, discarding record images as they are acquired. New records are simply added as in Figure 9.3.8.

MBASIC does not permit file use for *both* input and output. Hence the original file must first be copied to an output file as in Figure 9.3.9, then closed. The output file is kept open and new records are added at its end. Then the old file may either be deleted or archived (renamed with extension .BAK). The existing output file should be renamed after it is closed.

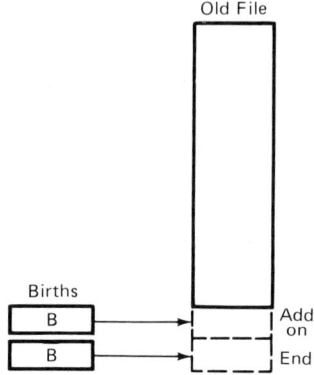

Figure 9.3.8. Adding births at the end of a file.

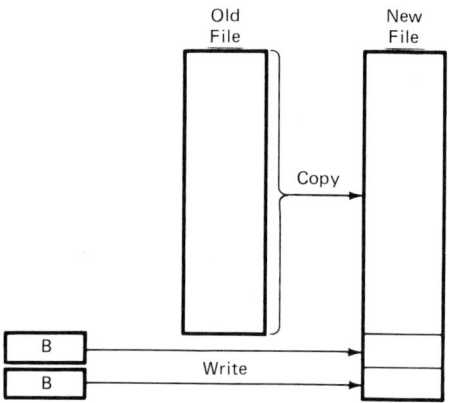

Figure 9.3.9. Adding births as a file is copied.

An example should make this clear. Start with a master file, **MAST**, with an existing backup copy called **MAST.BAK** (a common backup extension). First copy **MAST** to **MAST.$$$**, with intermediate status. Then add new records to **MAST.$$$**. Now treat the three "master" files as follows after they are closed:

- MAST.BAK is deleted with KILL "MAST.BAK";
- MAST now becomes the backup copy with NAME "MAST" AS "MAST.BAK";
- The new file becomes the current master with, NAME "MAST.$$$" AS "MAST".

BASICA

BASICA has improved OPEN and, while (8.3.35) is still acceptable, there is another form:

OPEN filename [FOR mode] AS [#]num   (9.3.3)

where a *filename* and a number is always provided by *num*. *Mode* may be INPUT, OUTPUT or APPEND. In the last case, the file is positioned to the end of data to add new records. An intermediate file is unnecessary if only births are to be handled; simply issue

OPEN #MASTER FOR APPEND AS 3   (9.3.4)

to add new records to MASTER.

Batch Maintenance

There are several alternatives in maintaining files. For batch maintenance, you enter changes at the terminal using a maintenance transaction file creation program as shown in Figure 9.3.10. You can create transaction rec-

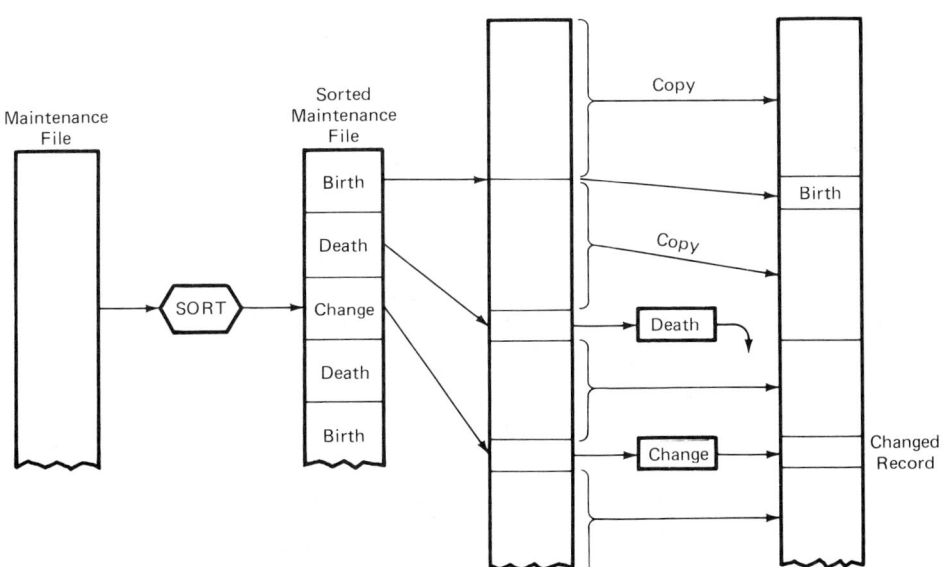

Figure 9.3.10. Maintaining a sequential file.

ords in any order, one record for each change in the population. Information entered varies with the kind of action. For

- *deletion,* only the record key is required;
- *change,* the individual and the attributes changed are identified together with their new values;
- *birth,* the entire record must be supplied.

The maintenance file is sorted as in Figure 9.3.10 to simplify review of the master file.

Birth

As shown in Figure 9.3.10, a birth transaction record is read and its key sought in the old master file. Inactive records are copied from the old master up to where the birth record goes to the new master file. A birth record should *not* have an equivalent record in the old master file. Put the birth record where it should appear (TKEY>MKEY) on the new master file and copy the remaining records after it.

Death and Change

For a *death,* copy records until the dying master record is found: do *not* copy it to the new master. For a *change* record, new field values replace old ones in the corresponding old master record and then the change record is copied to the new master file.

The maintenance program checks for errors which are printed or displayed so that the transaction may be reprocessed after human intervention has corrected the difficulty. Here are examples:

- A birth record appears for an individual listed in the master file.
- For a death record, there is no existing equivalent master record.
- For a change record, there is no existing record.
- For a change record, a field which is recorded in the transaction record has that value in the master record.

9.4 DIRECT FILES

The Concept

The file manager finds a record much faster in the **direct file** (MBASIC and BASICA call it a **random file**) than in a sequential file. The disk drive head takes the most direct route instead of passing through intervening data. The drive must be told precisely where to go. Since program time is mostly consumed in file manipulation for business applications, anything that reduces I/O time is advantageous.

It would be absurd to expect the operator or program to know the physical track and block number where data is located. There must be a better way! As an intermediate step, use the relative record number of the desired record.

Relative Record Number

The directory on the floppy keeps track of where the file is. How can the program identify a record without using its key? Use its *relative* position in the file: first record, the second record, the fortieth record or the fiftieth; this is its **relative record number**.

The application program can calculate the exact physical position of a fixed size record from its relative number. This is simple because the AP

- gets the beginning location of the file from the File Manager;
- knows the record length (for all records).

When records vary in length, it is impossible for the File Manager to calculate a record location without a table of record lengths. Hence direct access requires **fixed record size;** all records must have the same length. Together, BASIC and the FM have the track size, block size, number of blocks per track and the record size. From this they calculate a track and block number.

Use

The program has to get the record number. Conversion from the record key to the relative for the record with that key number is discussed shortly. First we examine how to create a direct file with fixed size records.

Establishing the File

Commands to establish a direct file depend on the processor. We now discuss briefly the two important BASIC processors.

CBASIC

For direct CBASIC files, put the fixed record length in OPEN:

OPEN name RECL length AS num [BUFF nb RECS 128]   (9.4.1)

352 DATA AND FILES

Here *name* is the file name and the record *length,* follows RECL. *Num* is a number to reference this file. The other parameter, often omitted, *nb,* gives the number of **buffers,** work areas where the records are kept as they arrive or depart. More of these *may* hasten the program.

MBASIC

Establishing a direct file with MBASIC is more complicated. This scares people away. MBASIC requires that *you* (the programmer) handle the buffers instead of the processor doing it. *You* have to provide additional names for fields in the buffer. But this only *seems* difficult until you get used to it.

Open an MBASIC or BASICA direct file with,

OPEN "R",#num,"fname",len   (9.4.2)

Here "R" tells MBASIC that this is a random (direct) file and

- *num* is a number to refer to the file;
- *fname* is the file name;
- *len* conveys record length.

I/O for a File

MBASIC establishes a buffer of size *len,* but you divide it into fields to receive variables with the FIELD statement:

FIELD #num, ln1 AS b1, ln2 AS b2,...   (9.4.3)

where *num* is the file number and there is an AS statement for each field. On the left of AS is the length of a field (*lnl*); on the right is the name assigned to the field *within the buffer*—b1. Here is how FIELD is used:

FIELD #1, 20 AS BNAME$, 1 AS TYPE, ...   (9.4.4)

which provides an area of 20 bytes with a name BNAME$ for the first variable, an area of one byte called TYPE for the second, and so on.

Put Values in a Buffer

You cannot enter values directly into buffer variables; instead, use the command LSET;

LSET b1 = value1   (9.4.5)

where *b1* is a field name from a **FIELD** statement and *value1* is a value or expression to assign to it. Here is an example:

 LSET BNAME$ = VNAME$ (9.4.6)

This copies **VNAME$** at the left of the field **BNAME$** and puts blanks on the right end. Remember that the size of the buffer field (**BNAME$**) is a *maximum* length and usually is not completely filled by **VNAME$**. Put the value at the right of a field in the buffer for a number with **RSET**. Fill the buffer by putting values in all of its fields. Then **PUT** writes the record to disk:

 PUT #num,rnum   (9.4.7)

where *num* is the file number (in **OPEN**) and *rnum* is the relative record number. Write the record in the buffer to file 2, record 35, with

 PUT #2,35   (9.4.8)

Input

GET is issued for input in the same way:

 GET #num,rnum   (9.4.9)

GET places a record in the buffer. You can use buffer variable names (assigned with **FIELD**) to print information from the buffer (such as **PRINT BNAME$**). An assignment moves a value from a buffer field into a named variable; the buffer field name is on the *right* of the equal sign:

 VNAME$ = BNAME$ (9.4.10)

Altering in Place

A direct file may have any record updated or altered in place. Here are the steps:

1. **GET** the record by relative number;
2. Move values from the buffer to a program variable;
3. Make calculations and alter variables;
4. Replace buffer areas with new values;
5. **PUT** the altered record back in the file.

Finding Records

Each record in the direct file has a relative number. However, the terminal operator cannot be expected to furnish the record number. A key which identifies the individual (employee, part, account, etc.) suffices. The *program* converts this into a number by one of two means:

- a formula.
- a table for lookup.

It is important to understand each, for the method chosen determines the efficiency and responsiveness of the program.

The Formula

A **formula** to convert the key into a record number can be quite simple. For instance, if the employee numbers assigned to workers range from 1 to 50, then the record number can be the employee number. If outstanding purchase orders begin at 750, then subtract 750 from the purchase order number to get the record number.

The complexity of the formula depends on how close we have to get to the exact record number. If it gets us to an approximate area, the program can search sequentially from there. **GET** without *rnum* gets the sequentially next record. The search key can be checked against the next few records quickly.

Here is another example. To look up a record by an alphabetic key, use the first letter in the name to divide the file into 26 groups. The first letter is converted into a number to tell whether to look, for instance, in group 1, 5, or 26 (for names starting with A, E or Z). From there, you start looking sequentially. The program compares the key sought with that of each record in this group.

Tables

A table may list the keys of records in the same order in which they appear in the file; Figure 9.4.1 is an example. Each entry could show the relative number of the record and its key. But the record number is not necessary; the entry number *is* the record number. Hence a table can simply be a string array containing records keys. For a table called TAB(I), the key of the third record in the file is at the third entry, TAB(3).

Where is the saving if the program searches the table instead of the file? Searching the small table in memory takes a few microseconds whereas

1	Abel
2	Amber
3	Anderson
4	Bison
5	Blake
6	Bogan
7	Bragh
8	Carlton

Figure 9.4.1. Table showing relative record position by key.

searching the file takes milliseconds per record, giving the table an advantage of a factor of 1000 or more.

A formula may be simple and quick only if the relation among the keys in the file is simple and rigid; when records are assigned irregular keys and there are missing records in the file, a formula becomes complicated.

A **complete table**—one entry for each record in the file—points to the record by giving its number.

Storing the Table

Note these alternatives to having a conversion table in memory:

A. Keep the table in the program.
B. Incorporate the table in the direct file to which it applies.
C. Keep the table as a separate file.

If the table is in the program, whenever the file changes, the table changes and you must alter the program by reviewing it manually. This is not desirable.

The table could be part of the same direct file which it manages. However, the table has a different format from that of the records. This makes it more difficult to design and access the file.

The final alternative is best: provide a separate file for the table. Bring in the table file first. If a program alters the table because records were added or deleted, the table file must be rewritten. If the main file is not modified (retrieval only), the table file on disk is still correct. The examples below assume that the table is a separate file.

Creating a Direct File

Consider a sequential file, a streamed file with fields separated by commas; records are of unequal size, separated by return and line to be converted to a direct file. Variable size records have to be converted into fixed size records. First *you* must examine the file to determine the maximum size of each field. Then you create a structured buffer with FIELD.

At the top of Figure 9.4.2 is a sequential streamed file. The buffer reflects the largest record consisting of the maximum size for all fields. An unused blank area in a field is shaded in the figure.

A streamed record is read with INPUT# and its fields put into named variables. Fields are transferred into the direct file buffer with the LSET command. A record thus prepared is written to a fixed size record area of the direct file. Fixed records in the new random file are retrieved by relative record number.

Example

Let us take a vendor sequential streamed file which contains the vendor name, address, city, contact and other information. Convert it to a direct file and make a table to facilitate lookup.

Initialization. Figure 9.4.3 is a partial MBASIC program to illustrate the features of file conversion. First OPEN

- the sequential file, SEQ, for input (10);

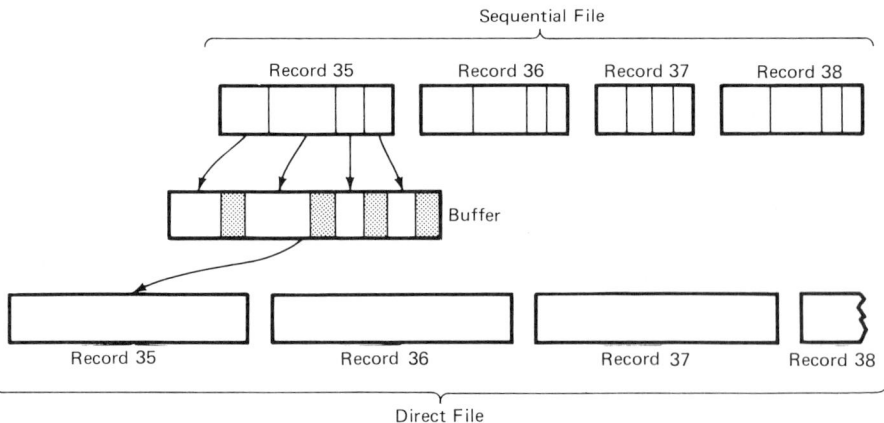

Figure 9.4.2. Converting a sequential file to a direct file.

```
10   OPEN "I",1,"SEQ"
20   OPEN "R",2,"DIR",200
30   OPEN "O",3,"DIRTAB"
. . . . . . . . . . . . . . . . . . . . . . . . . . . . . . . . .
80   FIELD #2 30 AS BVNAME$,30 AS BVADR$,30 AS BVCITY$,...
90   I=1
100  WHILE NOT EOF(1)
110      INPUT#1,VNAME$,VADR$,VCITY$,...
120      LSET BVNAME$=VNAME$
130      LSET BVADR$=VADR$
. . . . . . . . . . . . . . . . . . . . . . . . . . . . . . . . .
180      T$(I)=VNAME$
190      I=I+1
200      PUT #2
210  WEND
. . . . . . . . . . . . . . . . . . . . . . . . . . . . . . . . .
400  I=I-1
410  PRINT#3,I
420  FOR J=1 TO I
430      PRINT#3,T$(J)
440  NEXT
```

Figure 9.4.3. Converting a sequential to a direct file.

- the direct file, DIR, indicating that it is a random file (R) (20) with record length 200;
- another file for output, DIRTAB, to receive the table that associates a record with its relative record number (30).

Reading and Writing Records. Set up a buffer with FIELD (80) to assemble each random record. Name each field in the buffer and give its size. I keeps the number of a record transcribed (90). All the fields of a record are read (110) and each is placed in the buffer (120, 130) with a separate LSET.

Now prepare a table entry for this record. I is the record number *and* the entry number. T$(I) is the table entry which gets the vendor name, the key for this record (180). Then the index, I, is advanced by 1 (190). Finally the fixed size record is written from the buffer to the direct file with PUT (200).

Note that no record number is supplied with PUT. If the record number is omitted, PUT uses the *next* successive record number. When the file is opened, the current record number is automatically set to number 1. It is advanced by 1 with each PUT (200). A loop (100 to 210) reads records until the sequential file is exhausted (EOF(1)).

Writing the Table. The table is prepared one entry at a time in memory (180). After the records are copied to the new file, the table is complete.

However, the index, I, is 1 greater than the size of the file (190), since it points to the next entry which *might* be brought in. Reset it to the number of records in the file by subtracting 1 (400). The table file, DIRTAB, is sequential and each record consists of just one field. The first record is a numerical value giving the table size. Each subsequent record contains the key of the next record in the direct file.

First write out the number of records in DIR (410). Then write all subsequent records, putting the keys into the table T$(I) with a loop (420-440). After a few housekeeping tasks, the two files are ready for use.

Retrieval

Retrieval for the direct file is fast because the disk head moves directly. The more records in the file, the more efficient is direct access. The three phases for retrieving information are:

1. Bring in the sequential table file which describes record position in the direct file.
2. Check a request by key against this table.
3. Go *directly* to the record position given by the table to retrieve the record.

We now examine MBASIC program segments which perform these actions.

Set Up and Get Table

The program segment in Figure 9.4.4 opens the direct file DIR (10) and table file, DIRTAB (20). The first record from the table file is put at TSIZE (30) and it contains the size of the table. Set up space for the memory table (40). (You have to *declare* an array of more than 10 items.) Next, loop once for each entry in the table (50): bring in an entry (60), put it in the table (70) and continue (80).

```
10   OPEN"R",2,"DIR",200
20   OPEN"I",3,"DIRTAB"
30   INPUT#3,TSIZE
40   DIM T$(TSIZE)
50   FOR I=1 TO TSIZE
60       INPUT#3,T$
70       T$(I)=T$
80   NEXT
```

Figure 9.4.4. Set files and get table.

Search Request

The next program segment, Figure 9.4.5, prompts for a record key (190), VIEW$. The loop (200) examines all the entries in the table from the beginning for one that matches (210). If found, the routine at 500 (shown later) displays the record. Should there be no match with the table, a message displays (240). Then the loop is restarted with the prompt for another request (250, 190). When the record key is in the table, the index, I, contains its number since NEXT is not reached to advance I.

```
190   INPUT "View record for which vendor?",VIEW$
200   FOR I = 1 TO TSIZE
210       IF VIEW$ = T$(I) THEN GOTO 500
230   NEXT
240   PRINT "Vendor name not found"
250   GOTO 190
```
. . . .

Figure 9.4.5. Finding the number of a record.

Get Record and Display

The program segment, Figure 9.4.6, shows how a record is found by number and displayed: issue GET with the index I (500), its relative record number. This brings the record into the buffer which has been set up with FIELD. PRINT (510-570) displays fields directly from this buffer. A prompt (580) maintains the display unit you hit C (590); if you hit another key, (600) closes all files and the program ends (610).

```
500   GET #2,I
510   PRINT "Vendor:            ",BVNAME$
520   PRINT "Address:           ",BVADR$
530   PRINT "City, state, zip:",BVCITY$
```
. . . .
```
580   INPUT "Hit C to continue",HIT$
590   IF HIT$ = "C" THEN GOTO 190
600   CLOSE
610   END
```

Figure 9.4.6. Get record and display.

Posting

Posting enters new information about an individual by altering one or more fields. **Interactive posting** is possible for a direct file, rewriting one record instead of the whole file. There is room in each record to accommodate altered fields up to the maximum length. Indicate the record to be posted by key and supply new information as prompted. The record is assembled with its new values and written back to its old spot in the file.

Example

A small inventory program is an example. The stockperson enters actions taken at a stockroom terminal. We examine only a stock change for the inventory file. Actually, a stock change should affect the shipping invoice and the sales order files, too.

Identify the Stock Data. The program, Figure 9.4.7, prompts the stockperson (300) for the stock number for a part removed or put on the shelf.

Assume that two tables are in memory:

- PIT$ is the part identification table;
- PDT$ is the part description table.

These two tables are correlated: the fifteenth entry in PIT$ is the identification for a part; the fifteenth entry in PDT$ is the description of that same part. The program loops through the part identification table, PIT$, looking for the part number supplied, P-ID$ (310-340). If absent, a message

```
300   INPUT "Enter part number:      ",P-ID$
310   FOR I=1 TO TSIZE
320        IF P-ID$=PIT$(I) THEN GOTO 370
340   NEXT
350   PRINT "Part number not found!"
360   GOTO 300
370   PRINT "Part description:      ",PDT$(I)
380   GET #2,I
390   INPUT "Hit A to add to stock, R to remove from stock",ST$
400   INPUT "Enter amount added or withdrawn",AMT
410   Y=CVD(BOH$)
420   PRINT "Amount on hand is      ",Y
430   IF ST$="R" THEN AMT=-AMT
440   Y=Y+AMT
450   PRINT "New amount on hand is      ",Y
460   LSET BOH$=MKD$(Y)
470   PUT #2,I
490   GOTO 300
      . . . . . . . . . . . . . . . . . .
```

Figure 9.4.7. Part of a posting program.

(350) and prompt appear (300). When the part number is found in PIT$, the part description is printed from the matching entry in PDT$ (370) and the inventory record is obtained with GET (380).

The tables are complementary: enter the part number and the program finds the part description; enter the part description and get back the part number for verification. Since shelves in the stockroom are marked by part number, this is the usual entry by the stockperson.

Posting the Change. Now indicate the kind of change made in the stock (390): stock is removed to be shipped to a customer (R); incoming stock shipped by a vendor is put on the shelf (A). Then (400) tells how many items are to be added or removed.

The stock record requested (380) is in the buffer and shows the stock on hand before this transaction, BOH$. However, BOH$ is in ASCII (which accounts for the $ suffix); to convert it to a double word number variable, Y, for arithmetic, use CVD (*convert to double*) (410), then display the conversion (420).

If stock is removed, AMT is made negative (430). The new number of items on hand (Y) is the change in the number of items (AMT) plus the current amount on hand, Y (440). This result is then displayed (450).

Rewriting the Record. Convert the quantity on hand (Y) from binary to ASCII (BOH$) (460) with the *make double ASCII* command, MKD$(Y) as you put it in the buffer. Write the updated record (from the buffer) with PUT to the I'th (470). The program now asks for the next transaction (480).

Maintenance

Changes

A change is handled like posting: identify a changed individual and the program looks for the record. It asks for new values, perhaps with the aid of a menu. Respond by pressing a key associated with the attribute. The old and new values for the field are presented. The menu is presented again when you alter several fields. When the display properly shows the individual's attributes, the program writes the record back to the file.

Death

A death means that a record is to be deleted. The action depends upon the program philosophy adopted. Some keep a compact file: when a record is withdrawn, the ranks close up; there must be no holes—empty records—

in the file. And the order of the records within the file should be maintained. For most applications this is "overkill."

The alternative procedure deletes a record by flagging it, leaving garbage in the record space in the file or by clearing it to blanks. This is quick and is generally acceptable. Let us focus on this philosophy.

To delete a record is a serious matter. Once removed, it is no longer available and is difficult, if not impossible, to recover. Therefore, why not give the operator a chance to reconsider? The program looks up the key in the table, locates the record in the file and displays it for verification.

Once approved, the program removes the record from the file *and* its key from the table. Filling the table entry and the record with blanks leaves little room for human error. A simpler alternative allows for reconstruction: put a special nonprinting character in the first position of the record *and* in the table entry. Hex FF is popular for flagging a deleted record.

Births

For the sequential file, births are handled by rewriting the file completely, inserting the new record where it belongs in key order. This facilitates batch processing and is easy. For the direct file, the table leads directly to any record requested. Hence there is no reason to keep the file in order if the directory can be searched in a reasonable time. In fact, the speedy processing of a birth is impeded when the master file *is* kept in order.

There are two ways to handle births. The first writes the birth record at the end of the master file. Three features of the direct file make this simple:

1. The file directory is in memory and is quickly checked to ascertain that the birth key is not in a master file record.
2. The number of an entry in the directory (and hence in the file) tells where the birth record goes.
3. It is possible to write anywhere in the file *or* into empty space at the end of the file.

The second method provides even further improvement. It stems from the fact that we delete records by marking both the directory and the dead record. For a birth, the maintenance program looks through the directory for the birth record key, which *should* be absent. At the same time, it looks for an empty (flagged) slot in the directory. If one appears, its number is noted; it corresponds to a "hole" in the file. If the birth record key is missing, write the birth record in the first hole in the file. This keeps the file compact. The record key is put in the corresponding empty slot in the table.

Table Rewrite

During *maintenance,* the population changes due to births and deaths. Record additions and deletions in the table. Then the table in memory is different from that on the disk and must be rewritten to reflect accurately the contents of the file. This is the final step in the maintenance program.

Partial Key

Reference to the file need not require a *full* key. For instance, for a personnel, customer or vendor file, you may not be sure how to spell a name. If you use just the first few letters, the program can look up and display all entries which begin with these letters. Then you can choose the proper one.

When files are sufficiently small and there is little ambiguity, it saves time to enter only a few key strokes instead of the entire key. If the key is ambiguously defined, the display which follows presents all the alternatives.

IV
Applications

10
Application Software

10.1 THE CHOICES

There are thousands of application packages available for the micro. For some of them, hundreds of thousands of copies have been sold. That's a lot of software!

Application packages (**AP**) vary considerably in a number of factors, including price, what they do, their support and so forth. This chapter discusses what the factors are and how you can find out how packages for a particular purpose stack up against each other.

First we look at the ways that you can acquire a package and what you do with it thereafter:

- Buy an advertised AP and use it without modification.
- Buy the AP but modify it so that it performs specialized functions to suit you.
- Write the AP yourself or subcontract it to a qualified vendor to do what you want the way you want it.

Fixed AP

A **fixed application program** provides all the services that you need without *any programming*. It may require tailoring and other modifications as described in Section 10.2, but the means for altering the program are provided in the package. Instructions are usually complete and menus and prompts make tailoring easy for even the novice.

Chapters 11 through 14 discuss four distinct types of package, the most representative and most popular. Other less popular and more specialized packages include calendars, ticklers, communication programs, compilers and so forth. Utilities such as POWER (Chapter 7) and shells which fit on top of operating systems to make them easier to use are another group of facilitating packages. A popular program for the business person prepares a tax return.

Modified Packages

Some packages do not do exactly what you want. They provide no way for you to alter them directly. If you acquire one, since you cannot change it, you must change you method of doing things, hardly an attractive prospect.

Modification consists of getting inside the program and adding, deleting or altering its commands. If there is one class of programs where this tends to be done, it is those that do the accounting for your business, such as general ledger, payroll, accounts receivable and so forth.

It has been my experience that even when a business finds that only a small alteration in a program is necessary to conform to current procedure, it usually underestimates the extensiveness of the changes required in the program. The trouble it takes to modify an existing package is often not worth the effort as compared with starting from scratch and writing a new program to do the job.

Programming

This path incurs considerable costs but reaps appreciable rewards. It involves two kinds of services:

- A programming analyst should review the firm's entire operation and find out how data flows to meet all the accounting requirements.
- A programmer then creates a group of programs to work on a complete system and thus to meet your needs.

Although costly, the analysis phase reveals how the company's accounting actions function to benefit or hinder the firm. Old procedures may consume unnecessary time and involve labor which is redundant. Instituting a new system may eliminate much extra work and cost by revamping outmoded procedures. This alone pays for installing the new system.

A computerized system designed to suit you needs can provide all kinds of reports that you never thought possible. It also gives you the means to act on these reports and include additional programs with little or no trouble.

10.2 THE COMPLETE APPLICATION PACKAGE

The Total Package

A **total package** performs a complete function. Examples are the word processor, spread sheet and data base programs. They were not meant to be altered. They may have to be *tailored*. The need and how it is done is discussed shortly.

Characteristics

Although some total packages are simple, brief and inexpensive, most of them are quite complicated. The simple package is small and inexpensive; it provides a function which is fixed but requires no programming. At the other end of the scale is the very complicated package. The micro word processor for instance, demands several man years of programming. It is an exceptional bargain at current prices.

In the rest of this book, we are mainly concerned with the large complicated total package. It has been carefully designed so that

- the uninitiated can start it up easily and get some useful work done immediately;
- the beginner quickly learns new tricks and expands his or her repertory of skills;
- the advanced professional has available tremendous power combined with speed and friendliness.

Unfortunately, not all packages are so well designed. However you can find several excellent examples in each category examined in this book. Since there are so many, it is important to select wisely. Even though most packages are inexpensive for what they do, still one would not like to waste money and time learning how to use a package less effective than others available. For this reason, Section 10.3 examines resources for selecting among large numbers of packages.

The Operating Environment

Several computer systems and specialized programs allow you to do different tasks *at the same time* and coordinate them. This is a very important area. A lot of vendors are putting their money into these systems. You find two of these systems discussed in Chapter 15, on spread sheets; and in Chapter 16, general systems are examined.

Tailoring

Most application packages need tailoring. Exceptions are language processors; an interpreter such as MBASIC can be used immediately without tailoring on any computer and devices because it uses the operating system drivers.

An AP is tailored to activate properly the devices associated with it: the terminal, the printer, the keyboard and anything else it might use. There are dozens of manufacturers of such devices. Each vendor has several models and styles which differ. **Tailoring** makes the package fit the device.

The **install** routine is provided with the package. The package instructions tell you how to employ this routine. It alters the program so that the devices react properly to the commands used.

There is need for tailoring for three principal types of devices. The requirement is discussed in the applicable chapter but is reviewed here for continuity.

The Keyboard

Most keys on the keyboard produce standard codes. This includes all the letter, number and punctuation keys and some special function keys such as escape and rub. Keys like arrow and home are most troublesome. On some terminals, these keys produce a single code while on other terminals they produce a code sequence. Arrow keys for most packages move the cursor in the indicated direction. If they cannot be mated to the program, the result can be achieved through a control sequence, but this is less appealing.

CRT

Packages control the screen display by sending control codes or control sequences to the CRT circuitry; these codes or sequences differ from one terminal to the next. The ANSI (American National Standard Institute) standard is used for DEC's VT-100, the Visual Technology 300, the IBM PC terminal and its compatibles. Some packages don't even provide tailoring for these particular terminals.

Here are some of the actions which the program wants to control on the terminal screen:

10.2 THE COMPLETE APPLICATION PACKAGE 371

- clear the screen;
- move the cursor to a particular line and column;
- delete a complete line, a line up to the cursor or a line from the cursor to its end;
- insert a line or a portion of a line;
- and so forth.

This partial list shows how important it is to match the terminal to the program.

The Printer

There are two categories of printers: dot matrix and daisy wheel. For each type, there are a number of vendors and each vendor has many different models. Some packages are insensitive to printer type. Others merely need to know whether the printer has the standard serial or parallel connection. (This information is sufficient for instance for a data base program or a spread sheet.)

But when it comes to a word processor which provides bold face or underline emphasis, fine control of printer motion is necessary. A sophisticated word processor can do proportional printing when attached to a daisy wheel printer with a proper print wheel. The output is equivalent to an expensive typewriter or a typeset page, done by printer character width control.

Print control is again achieved by control codes or sequences sent by the program to the device. The install program sets up a character width table for the package so that it activates the device correctly.

The Install Routine

The AP manual gives the name of the install routine and whether it is requested directly from the operating system (OS) or from a menu of the AP. The program presents a sign-on message telling you that you are installing a particular package.

The install routine creates tables or selects them from a file provided, as needed for the terminal, the printer or both. Then these are incorporated into the main program so that this process need be done only once.

Most install routines present a menu which lists terminals, for instance, where you should be able to find your own terminal manufacturer and model number. When you do, press the indicated key and the routine finds the corresponding table in its library and inserts it into the program.

A package may match so many devices that one menu panel may not suffice. If your terminal is not on the first panel, you press another key to get a new menu containing a list of more devices. You may have to go through three or four menus to find your particular device.

Even so, there are so many devices on the market that yours may not be provided for. There is an entry on the menu for that. Now you will have to do more work. You customize the routine by providing your own table from prompts or menu requests. The install routine asks for the code used by your terminal for doing various activities. To find out this code, you refer to the manual supplied with your terminal. You might expect that all the information is gathered in one place in the terminal manual, but this is not usually so. It may be aggravating, but you have to search through the manual and find all the requested codes. The same procedure is required to install your printer.

No Installation

Packages for most systems are installed as described. However, some versions of a package are intended for a fixed computer and configuration. The IBM PC is such a configuration. Its terminal has the ANSI standard control codes. If you are going to use a package like Lotus 1-2-3 on the IBM PC, the system disk from the vendor works at once for the PC; no installation is required.

Purchasing Your Package

There are several alternatives regarding how you might obtain packages for your micro:

1. Some dealers sell a combination hardware/software package which provides a computer, several important devices and a number of packages.
2. When you buy your computer system, either bundled as in (1) or as separate components, you may want additional packages, which might be purchased from the dealer at an advantageous price at the same time.
3. After owning and using your computer, you may decide that an AP suits your needs and purchase it from the same dealer.
4. Mail order sales, with a very low markup, are advertised in many computer magazines.

These purchase alternatives are arranged in order of approximate system integration. When you buy a bundled package (1), you can expect that all the APs work properly as soon as you bring them up and that they are tailored to the devices that you purchase. With (2) and (3) you may arrange with the dealer to put in extra work to match the hardware to the programs for you. You pay for this in one way or another. With the mail order package (4), you are on your own and it is up to you to get the package working with your equipment. But that's really not much of a problem with a well-established product such as WordStar of dBase II.

Support

Support is another word for the assistance that you get from various sources. The first source is the dealer from whom you purchase the equipment or package. (Mail order houses provide little, if any, support.) **Initial support** is help with getting a package to work with your system and is usually supplied by the dealer unless you buy the package by mail.

With **extended support,** you get help in problems you encounter with the advanced facilities. You cannot be expected to test these facilities when you first purchase the item. The vendor often provides a **hotline.** When you have a problem in a product that you have purchased (even by mail order), a call to the vendor gets help usually from a technical expert. Depending on the vendor, you can often get extremely good service in this fashion.

New Releases

The application package has a registration certificate which you should fill out and mail in. The vendor keeps these on file and notifies customers of the release of new versions of the package. When this occurs, you return the original disk along with a small fee, somewhere around $25 or $50, and receive an updated disk within a couple of weeks. If the package requires installation, you have to go through that procedure again.

10.3 CONSIDERATIONS

Compared to software for mainframes, that for micros is a real bargain; the price of a micro word processor, for instance, is a few hundred dollars at most, while one for a mainframe is several thousand dollars. Even so, most people have the attitude that the package cost is a substantial investment, especially since it is a large fraction of the computer cost, perhaps as much as 20 percent. Often, a good way to obtain software is through a deal where you get the computer, an operating system, peripheral devices, along with several application packages, for a fixed price much lower than that for the same components purchased separately. However, you are tied in to the specific packages supplied in the deal.

374 APPLICATION SOFTWARE

This section examines factors to consider when purchasing APs:

- performance;
- friendliness;
- error recovery;
- documentation;
- maintenance.

These are ordered in the approximate importance I give to them.

Performance

Performance, how well the package does what it is supposed to, is composed of a number of elements which we now examine in the approximate order of their importance.

Basic Capabilities

By **basic capability** I mean whether the package can do simple actions we expect. Packages which have met the test of time, designed by a reputable software house, generally pass with flying colors. You expect a word processor to provide a basic search and replace function, for instance. Whether it provides enough options is another story. Some do not have discretionary search and replace; if you need that feature, you should be sure that your package contains it.

Responsiveness

Responsiveness describes how fast the package reacts to instructions, the time it takes to perform an action after you initiate it. Responsiveness, of course, depends upon computer speed. But despite the propaganda, there is little difference in processing speed among popular micros and PCs. Therefore most of the time differential is in the *software* package design.

A few programs do extensive calculations while you wait. One such program is the spread sheet, used for "what if" projections. You may change one value, which causes most of the other values on the spread sheet to be recalculated. If you do this frequently, it may be aggravating to wait a number of seconds for each recalculation.

Another cause for waiting is access to disks, important when working with a large data base. If the file is organized sequentially, finding an item you need may take considerable disk time. Sorting a file also takes time, which depends on some degree on your disk mechanism and whether you have hard or soft disk. However, there are also *program* considerations. For instance, Human Soft provides a sort utility for dBase which is five times as fast as that for dBase II.

Terminal responsiveness is most noticeable to the operator. How quickly does a new screen of information appear? The limit here is hardware terminal transmission speed. But a program may acquire new screen information from disk, which contributes to slowing down the action.

In word processing, inserting a few characters may require a complete reorganization of the screen, which may take several seconds. Characters you type meanwhile may not show immediately on the screen. This worries the novice but is of little consequence, since none of the characters are lost and the program eventually catches up when one stops typing.

Print speed is not solely dependent on the printer itself and can be expedited by providing a print buffer or spooling, either in the program or as a separate utility.

Extensiveness

By **extensiveness** I mean the *amount* of information that the package handles: how many records, files, fields, and so on. What is the maximum size of a file, a record, a field? For the casual and managerial user, these amounts are of little importance. The tasks to be done are not that extensive. But for an accounting application, in which all the firm's books are kept on the computer, it is important to know, for instance, the maximum number of accounts that the package can handle.

Advertising tries to hook you any way it can. I have seen advertisements for data base managers which are truly extensive and can handle large amounts of information. What you don't see from the ad is that the package has fewer *capabilities* than you would like.

Advanced Features

Advanced features are those that other similar packages may not possess. For example, integrated graphics for spread sheets is an advanced feature; for word processing, advanced mail merge capabilities are uncommon. If you recognize early that you need advanced features, then certainly you should purchase a package which has them. However, for a first-time package user, general basic capabilities may suffice. The field is advancing rapidly. Today's advanced features may be commonplace tomorrow, with even newer features vying for your attention. Hence if you settle on a simple package now, the advanced package you get later will provide more features than those presently available.

Friendliness

Friendliness is the ease with which you can both *learn* and *use* the package. I emphasize *two kinds* of friendliness because you are in a different position as you learn the system from that when you really know it. WordStar is an example of a word processing package which is difficult to learn but not nearly so difficult to use (though I wouldn't call it easy to use). Its performance makes up for lack of friendliness.

Friendliness breaks down into a number of factors which we now examine.

Ease of Invoking

The easiest way for the novice to make requests is by menu. Selection amounts to hitting a key or a key with return.

As the novice learns, more and more complicated actions become available. Generally this is accomplished with a sequence of menus wherein a choice on one menu brings forth a second menu. Menus are helpful in learning a complex procedure. However, once you get to know the sequence of operations, you become impatient when you have to wait for the next menu to appear. Some packages have overcome this by letting you anticipate the next menu and type ahead before it is presented; this works well.

The second way to invoke an action is to hit a key or a command, no menu being presented. This is quickly mastered by the constant user. However, the occasional user forgets what the commands are from one time to the next, especially after a lapse of a week or so. It is time consuming and annoying to have to refer to the reference manual.

Help Screens

Many package vendors provide **help screens,** which display a list of available commands together with the actions they perform. It has almost become a convention that you bring forth a help screen by hitting ?. For instance, most spread sheet programs use a set of commands with the mnemonics displayed on a status line. However, you may forget that V stands for "Enter a numerical value," for instance. To bring forth this information, you simply hit ?.

Error Recovery

There are many actions you might perform which could lead to trouble. A good package anticipates as many of these as possible and provides remedies of one sort or another. **Error recovery** consists of

- preventing problems;
- detecting problems and letting you know when they arise;
- detecting and eliminating problems.

All three should be provided if possible.

Consider creating or editing a document, when the document disk is almost full as an example (there is very little room left on it). What should a good word processing program do?

Preventing a Problem

For **prevention,** the word processing program reacts to your request to edit a document by first seeing how much space is on the disk. When the WP program finds that there is very little room left, it projects a message on the screen, something like "Warning, there is 1K left on this disk".

Detecting a Difficulty

A different word processor might accept your request unconditionally. After you edit your document, it tries to write the revised version onto the disk. However, as it gets part way through, the File Manager tells the WP that there is insufficient space for the rest of the document. The bad WP fails and your document is lost.

The good WP flashes a message and gives you a chance to remedy the situation. You can now eliminate either the backup copy or the original draft of what you have just revised, the latter being text now in memory but not yet rewritten to disk. However, if you decide to keep both the original and the modified copy, you can select another file on the disk to eliminate. You might even be able to change disks and put the text in memory on the new disk. When you have made your decision and eliminated some file, the word processor regains control and continues to write text from memory to its file.

Remedying the Situation

After determining that the file cannot be properly be written to the disk, as a third alternative, some word processors eliminate the original or backup copy without asking. The screen notifies you of the action. This is a fairly intelligent solution and does not produce any harmful aftermath.

No Remedy

Some word processors start to write back a file and find in the middle that there is insufficient space; they terminate the job, which is unforgivable.

You have lost the text on which you have worked for minutes or hours to edit. Try to avoid such a product.

Documentation

Documentation is written material supplied with the package which instructs you on its use and describes all its features. The factors described below contribute to the effectiveness of documentation.

Extensiveness

Extensiveness when applied to documentation means the kind and nature of the documents furnished. The material is usually supplied in a loose leaf binder so that it can be updated by the vendor for mistakes in the documentation or changes made in the package. One or more kinds of documents may be supplied; all may be in the same binder. The more kinds of documentation provided, the more useful the material usually turns out to be. I divide documentation into six classes:

1. An **introduction** tells the new user what the package is about, how to get started, what functions it performs in general and what these functions accomplish.
2. The **installation guide** tells how to prepare the package to work on your computer configuration, including how to use install routines for getting the printer and terminal to mate with the software.
3. **Guided lessons** are *written* instructions which provide lessons in how to use each of the features and are often geared to sample files provided on the original disk. A lesson asks you to operate on one of the sample text files to delete or insert characters, giving the correct result and showing how it looks when printed out. If you follow the instructions, you should get the intended result.
4. A **programmed learning tutorial** on disk provides an interactive program which teaches you how to use the package. Instructions are brought up to the screen. If you follow them, you should get the desired results. If you make a mistake, the program detects this and may go back to a new starting point and to tell you what to do again. Usually either a tutorial or a set of guided lessons are supplied, not both.
5. The **operator's manual** contains sections on each function and its options. It describes how to employ the function. You can look up a procedure which you have forgotten to find out what to do to put it into play.

6. A **reference manual** describes in detail each function and all the options which apply. It is arranged by function name (which varies from one vendor to the next). It is intended for the experienced user who wants to know if there is a better way to do a particular operation.

Quality

There are considerable differences in how well an explanation is understood by readers. Technical manuals should be written by technical writers who have users of varying abilities in mind.

User Aids

Good documentation contains a number of items which help you use it:

- a table of contents;
- a generous index;
- a glossary explaining jargon and terms the user may be unfamiliar with;
- tables showing similar functions, command codes and so forth. These can be invaluable and are sometimes pasted to the terminal or user's desk.

Updates

Perhaps the microcomputer field is changing faster than any other high tech area. New and better software is constantly emerging. When making improvements, the manufacturer often will inform registered users (who have returned the warranty card). A new release of a product is usually offered for a minimal fee. Updated documentation is also required, to be inserted by the user with the original documentation.

Importance of Documentation

I put this topic at the end of the section because I think other factors are more important in selecting a product. When documentation is deficient, but the AP itself is popular, within months or a year, texts more fully or clearly explaining the program will appear. Witness the number of books on CP/M and WordStar. These are complicated, powerful, widely used products with less than optimum (though improving) documentation.

10.4 SELECTION RESOURCES

How Do You Choose?

How do you find a product to suit your needs? For starters, this book should whet your appetite for packages which seem to fulfill your expectations for services. This is not a software encyclopedia; its purpose is neither to list all the packages available nor to compare how they perform in relation to each other. It would be out of date before it ever got published.

Then what resources do you have to find suitable products? This section examines resource alternatives in this order:

- this book;
- the package manual itself;
- specialized books on particular packages;
- subscription services;
- magazine reviews;
- a trial package;
- friends.

Books And Manuals

This Book

Major packages in several classes of software are examined in this book. They give you the features of the packages and contrast a number of specific packages. If you choose one of them, you know what to expect. Products discussed here are reliable and their vendors stand behind them. Appendices E and G contrast capabilities of major APs.

The Manual

As you look through computer magazines you find that mail order houses often give separate prices for a full package and a separate manual. One good way to find out about a package is to purchase the manual. Usually its price is rebated if you do decide to purchase the software.

The manual tells you everything the vendor believes valuable. If the documentation is inadequate, you will find that out, too. Although the software itself is missing, you get a good idea about what it can do.

Manuals comprise fifty to several hundred pages. They are not all well written. It takes a couple of hours to wade through one to determine if the product is for you, which may be time well spent in the long run.

Specialty Books

All the important programs have books published about them if they are more than six months old. You can get books on WordStar, Multiplan, VisiCalc, Lotus 1-2-3 and so forth. Not all are well written. Still they give an "objective" view of the product and are available in computer dealer's book displays or in a good bookstore. You save the time of ordering a manual and waiting for it to arrive. A book is also a useful supplement to the manual, should you decide to buy the product.

Subscription Services

Keeping track of all the software available for micros and PCs is a monumental task because

- new products come out every day;
- products and vendors become obsolete and perish;
- new releases of existing products appear;
- new hardware arrives and products for it appear.

Simply keeping track of products in the marketplace is a considerable job. Some specialized companies provide a listing of manufacturers' summaries for products. Such compilations have to be kept up to date. This useful service is on a subscription basis because of perishability. You should refer only to the most recent edition of such a guide. For each application package the guide shows the computers and the operating systems under which each works. A yearly subscription to this type of manual costs several hundred dollars.

A more comprehensive guide not only lists items but evaluates them. This takes time and a variety of available computers. Companies produce compendiums of this nature but they are more expensive, in the four hundred to five hundred dollar range. They describe the important packages, indicating their functions, characteristics and how well they perform.

Appendix I is a listing of services that you can use to help you evaluate packages.

Magazine Reviews

A number of magazines feature articles about software products. *Info-World, Byte, PC Magazine, Interface Age* and others rate products on a scale of poor to excellent. For instance, *InfoWorld* provides a review and a report card which rates a product on the following criteria:

382 APPLICATION SOFTWARE

- performance;
- documentation;
- ease of use;
- error handling.

Keep in mind when you read a review that the product vendor may advertise in the magazine. It is difficult to conceive of a completely negative review for a constant advertiser. When you do find a negative review, it is likely a true reflection of a poor product.

Several of these magazines from time to time publish special editions summarizing the features of products—hardware and software—which have been issued thus far in various categories.

Trial Packages

It should be apparent that the best way to evaluate a package is to sit down and try it out. But a complex package may take several hours to gain even the simplest familiarity with the basic functions. What can you do to get some exposure?

The Dealer

If you expect to get an adequate demonstration of a package from a dealer, forget it. Dealers work on a minimum markup and use all their demonstration machines to convince prospective customers to buy hardware. All you can expect from a dealer is verification that the package you buy is the one you ordered.

Purchasing a Demo

Some vendors sell a **demo** which incorporates a few basic features and gives you a chance to try them out on your own machine at your leisure. Demos sell for as little as $10 to $25, but don't expect a comparative evaluation. Your database demo, for instance, may contain 25 or 30 records. You can experiment with adding new records to the file, altering records changing fields, and so forth. But you can get no idea how easy it is to retrieve a particular record from a file of 2000. Still, a demo is better than nothing.

Rentals

There are a few software companies (see the popular computer magazines for their ads) that specialize in *renting* products of many vendors with an option to buy. To minimize their risk, you *purchase* the item with the condition that, if you return it intact in a specified number of days, you money will be returned except for the rental fee. You can get several products on this basis; choose the one that's best for you and return the others. This is an excellent way to evaluate a product with very little risk and at relatively little extra cost.

Friends

Perhaps the best source for experience with a product is a friend who has one or a school or other institution where one is installed and available. In this way, you get practice with the product without being rushed and without having to make an investment. This approach works even if the product is installed on a different computer under a different operating system. Thus experience with WordStar can help you get familiar with the product regardless of whether you use it on a S-100 Bus computer or an IBM PC.

10.5 PROGRAMMING

In certain instances programming is in order when

1. Writing simple programs from scratch;
2. Modifying packages;
3. Constructing a complete system.

When programming becomes necessary, who should do it?

A. For a small simple program, you or an associate may be able to do it.
B. A programmer from your staff may be advisable when there are enough people who need programming done.
C. Subcontracting consists of having a person or group come in from outside the firm to analyze your needs and write a program for you.
D. For a small business which is setting up a complete system, it is frequently advisable to have an outside firm supply a complete hardware and software system and all the programming required to make that system work within the business.

Writing Small Programs

There are several good reasons why even as a manager you should have some experience in writing a program:

1. Most important, you should know the train of events from the concept through analysis and logic to formal programming.

2. Most young professionals have been exposed academically to some kind of programming or else they should have been. Programming a micro is much easier than programming a mainframe or mini (the probable college experience up to the present) because the languages used on micros are easier to understand, more friendly, and often work interactively (for instance, BASIC) so that you can correct mistakes immediately. Knowing some programming for micros will aid you in working with your staff to develop or implement small computer applications.
3. Programming a small application such as a tickler file or a repetitive calculation is best done by the one who will use it. The user is aware of all the alternatives and errors which may arise and can make allowances for recovery in the program.
4. If programmers will be doing work for you, it is good to understand what they do and how they put their thoughts together. This way, you can supervise them and advise them in a way which does not irritate them.

There are more reasons but these should suffice for starters.

Modifying Modules

This is an involved and often a frustrating business. When you find that your package does not do exactly what you want, you look for some way to correct it. There are many levels at which modification can be done. The highest is the source level—using the language in which the program was written. The lowest level is the machine code module itself.

Source Code

None of the packages described in this book are supplied as source code. That is, an AP may be written in Pascal, C, PL/1, or a variety of other languages. Many business applications are written in CBASIC. However, they are supplied in intermediate or machine language form. Sometimes, if you pay a premium price you can obtain the original source code to make modifications in it.

Assembly Language

Few programs other than operating systems and specially designed programs are written in assembly language. Even when they are, you can rarely get your hands on them. The exception is public domain software. However, there are utilities called **disassemblers** that convert a package into assembly language. The result is almost incomprehensible; thus this method can be used only by a truly expert programmer.

Small Patches

Sometimes experts have examined existing packages to determine what has to be done to make them perform in a certain way. When this is documented, as in some magazines containing advanced applications, it is not difficult to alter your module.

You can use DDT, a utility for CP/M, to alter a module. It is invoked with the name of the module to be added. The module is loaded into the transient area (100H), where it is available to be modified. DDT commands let you examine and alter the program in memory. When you are satisfied, you can save the altered copy as a disk file (preferably with a new name so that if you have made a bad mistake you can go back to the original copy and try again).

Here are two examples to show why you might want to use this facility. The first is the PeachText, a word processing program. All files that you create with PeachText are automatically given the extension doc. Thus if you write a report and call it report1, the file containing it is actually called report1.doc. When you want to edit the file, you simply ask for it by the original name report1. But PeachText looks for the file with the extension doc. A text file created on another word processor with no extension (a coworker's report you wish to edit on your machine and WP for your own use, for instance) will not be recognized by PeachText, even if the file is totally compatible otherwise. There is a **patch,** a correction to the machine language program, which lets you specify a file as, for instance, report1, and PeachText will look for it with no extension.

WordStar has two extra emphasis commands which let the user specify emphasis but specific within WordStar. New dot matrix printers provide italics but unmodified WordStar does not use them. A small patch relates the commands to the control codes for your dot matrix printer. Then these commands do create italics emphasis on the printer.

Contract Programming

For **contract programming,** you hire a programmer on a job or an hourly basis to write a program which does the functions you need. The emphasis here is on *contract,* which should state precisely what is to be done. An acceptance test should be arranged whereby the program is put through its paces to demonstrate that it does what it is supposed to do. All this is difficult to set up; perhaps a consultant should be brought in. It is important that the consultant and the programmer are in no way related so that one acts as a check to the other.

Turnkey Systems

A **turnkey system** is a complete system—hardware, operating system and software—which works with your firm and the way it does business. An OEM (original equipment manufacturer) will put together hardware and software and even write programs to your specifications to provide a turnkey system, under contract to you. This alternative is expanded upon in Chapter 16.

11
Word Processing

11.1 INTRODUCTION

Importance

Word Processing **(WP)** is the most important personal computer application for the micro: more WP program packages are sold than any other type; only the electronic spread sheet runs a close second. Of course, the WP software package, *the program,* turns your personal computer into a word processor. Perhaps WP is so popular because, at little extra cost, it gives you much more than a typewriter.

Need

The WP is like a typewriter because the terminal has essentially the same keyboard arrangement. It would be nice if we could somehow get information directly from the written or printed page into the computer. There are machines that do this, called optical character recognition page readers. They cost much more than an office word processor and are only of use in very large offices and for typesetting applications for reasons beyond the scope of this discussion.

You enter a document into the WP by typing it on the keyboard. Then you can print it with the computer's printer to get **hard copy,** the paper document. Up to this point there is little difference between how you use the WP and the typewriter.

Which of us can enter a perfect document the first time around? It must be edited, refined, reformatted and improved upon. Here is the beauty of the WP. Imagine a document with just one character wrong. With the typewriter, you have to retype the entire page to correct a single character, unless you are an expert at whiteout and type-in. The WP allows you to call up a document, change one or many characters and print it out again—all in a couple of minutes.

Requirements

What you need to get a word processor up and running is the following:

1. A microcomputer;
2. A video display terminal (VDT);
3. A printer;
4. A WP program which runs your hardware configuration.

The Computer

Most computers that cost $1,000 or more can serve as word processors. WP programs use at least 48K of memory; some require 56K, 64K or even more. For 16 bit computers, some word processors need 128K or more. Much of the text you are working on is in memory as you work on it. More memory can hold larger documents and it is easier to edit and revise.

The Terminal

Most WPs work with most but not all terminals, you should check if yours is on the list when you buy your WP program. Office WPs have specially designed terminals with keys dedicated to word processing functions, which makes them easier to use. For micros, function keys facilitate WP use.

Printer

The printer may be the most expensive component. If type quality is important, use a fast daisy wheel printer in the $2,000 to $3,000 range or a slow daisy wheel in the $400 to $1,000 class. With carbon ribbon, the impression is equal to or better than that from most typewriters.

A dot matrix printer at $600 or less easily produces draft printing. For a little more some dot matrix printers with dual functions can approach correspondence quality; they suffice for personal letters and rough manuscripts.

The Program

The WP program turns your computer into a word processor and costs from $100 to $600. Sometimes a quality program is sold at a lower price because there is considerable demand for it and profit is made on quantity. WP features which you get are present only because the program furnishes them.

11.2 GENERAL FUNCTIONS

The WP performs these six functions:

1. Create a new document;
2. Edit an existing document;
3. Establish the format;
4. Print a document;
5. Manipulate text and files with utilities;
6. Produce form letters and merge and assemble documents with advanced functions.

Subsequent sections examine these in detail. This section discusses the purpose of each and the way that you invoke it.

Function Selection

There are several ways for you to select a function depending on your particular WP:

- Each function is a separate program invoked from the operating system.
- You give a command from the main WP program.
- You choose from a menu presented by the WP program.
- A combination.

From the Operating System

The WP consists of a number of programs, each with a name. The operating system prompts and you reply by giving the name assigned to the function that you need. For instance, to edit a document called MYDOC using Magic Wand (now called PeachText):

   A>edit mydoc   (11.2.1)

When the WP function is finished, you *end* the (edit) program which returns to the operating system.

By Menu

A **menu** is a display listing choices from which you may select one. Each choice shows as a line of text, preceded by a letter or number. Choose one by hitting the corresponding key. A typical menu appears in Figure 11.2.1.

```
SELECT: Create
Edit Delete View List Name Print
Spell Teach Merg Help Quit Run


   Create    -   to CREATE a new document
   Edit      -   to EDIT or change a document
   Delete    -   to DELETE a document
   View      -   to get a scrolling VIEW of a document
   List      -   to LIST all the documents in your directory
   Name      -   to assign a new NAME to a document

   Print     -   to PRINT a document
   Spell     -   to check your SPELLING

   Teach     -   to TEACH you to use SELECT
   Merge     -   to MERGE a document with a mailing list
   Help      -   to HELP explain the commands
   Quit      -   to QUIT your SELECT work session

   Run       -   to RUN a program outside SELECT
   Alter     -   to place SELECT into program development mode
```

Figure 11.2.1. A main menu.

Some menus require you to hit return after you choose, to give you time to verify your choice and retract it. But an extra keystroke is required; as you become expert at using the program, this becomes relatively time consuming.

After you choose a function, the main WP program brings the selected subprogram into memory and starts it running. When you say you are finished, that subprogram returns control to the main program and the menu is presented again. One choice is to *quit* the WP program and return to the operating system.

Combination

Another alternative invokes one function while another is in progress, a nice feature on the advanced WP. For example, while editing one document with WordStar, you can print some *other* document. Call for printing directly from the editing program by entering a command (for WordStar, with ^KP). Another WP might take you to the function menu from which you choose the print option.

Creation

Some WPs (and people) consider creating and editing as different functions, while others don't. I consider them different and talk about them in that way in sections that follow. **Creating** enters text at the keyboard to become an **electronic document (ED).** EDs have distinctive names by which you request to edit or print them. A *directory* helps you determine which documents are which and what versions of each are available.

For most WPs, documents are files no different from any other file as far as the operating system is concerned. Text documents under CP/M have names of one to eight characters. Some WPs require a specific extension. While WordStar does not require *any* extension, PeachText requires the extension .DOC: any name followed by .DOC is a document file which may be used with PeachText.

Text files created with a word processor can be accessed via operating system utilities: erase (destroy), copy (to another disk), rename, etc.

Once you have named a file and entered text, you have begun to create an ED. Key text continuously into the file until you are done. As you do, you may discover mistakes, which you correct; or you may decide to insert or delete text here and there. In this case, you are actually *editing* as you create the file. No matter; we discuss the two functions separately.

Editing

To edit, supply the ED's name; the WP finds it and puts its first part on the the screen. The directory distinguishes old versions of a document from new ones. Editing itself consists of these actions:

- locate text where action is to take place;
- insert characters, words, phrases, etc.;
- delete characters, words, phrases, etc.;
- get the WP to find a particular set of characters to make a change;
- get the WP to make repeated changes;
- set up blocks of text to be deleted, copied or moved.

Format

Editing and creating provide the content of your document; **formatting** determines how the document looks on paper. For a draft, formatting is less important. For the final document, text "packaging" affects impact on the reader and merits consideration. Here are some aspects of formatting:

- margins—top, bottom, left, right;
- line spacing—single, double, intermediate;
- tabular work, which includes columns of numbers or of text;
- headings and footings—material included at the top and bottom of *every* page;
- justification—whether there are uniform or jagged margins;
- emphasis—underline and boldface.

Printing

The time has not yet arrived when you have to deal directly with electronic documents (sent over telephone lines or passed about as floppy disks). You expect a letter or report *printed* on a piece of paper.

Printing can occur at several stages of document preparation. Depending on the word processor, it may be possible to

A. Print a specific page from an altered document to verify it.
B. Print the entire document from beginning to end, entering page numbers if desired.
C. Print a portion of the document starting with a given page number and ending with a particular page.
D. Print on a preprinted form.
E. Print a page directly from the keyboard.
F. Merge documents together and print form letters.

Advanced Features

Under the heading of advanced features are document merge and multiple form letters. Other things covered in Sections 11.7 and 11.8 are spelling, error detection and correction, hyphenation and help in the preparation of complex documents.

Utilities

Manipulating text files as a whole requires utilities. These can copy files, delete them, provide backup or combine a number of small files into a single file.

11.3 CREATING

Startup

To use a micro WP, you have to install it first.

Install

The WP is shipped on one or more floppy disks. A large guide is furnished, usually a loose leaf binder, and may consist of up to three parts:

1. A tutorial on how to use the WP;
2. An instruction manual;
3. A reference manual

One of these contains instructions on how to **install** the system, fit it to your hardware, when necessary.

Regardless of what the instructions say, *make copies of all the disks.* Some vendors ask you to tailor the original disks to your computer. This alters the disks and then they may not be usable on another similar system.

Installing tailors the WP's drivers to run your terminal and printer. This tells the WP what control codes move the cursor on your terminal to specified coordinates, delete text from the terminal's memory, insert a character at a given position, etc. It gives the codes for head and paper motion for the printer.

Now the WP is tailored to your hardware on its disk and the original copy is put away safely. Next, write a copy of the OS on *this* disk so that the disk is self-sufficient. With CP/M, use **SYSGEN**; with PC-DOS, use **SYS**.

Invoke

With the new WP system disk in the A drive, issue a command to load the WP program software with perhaps, **WP**. After the sign-on message, the WP presents a menu or an action prompt. You direct it to create a new file, either from the menu or by a command. Furnish a name for the file. The WP checks that it does not exist. A blank screen appears with perhaps a **status display:** one or two lines at the top or bottom of the screen which describe the status of text you are entering:

- the name of the document you are creating;
- the position in the document where you are typing—page, line and column number;

- the function in progress—insertion, deletion, and so on;
- the current format—line spacing, margins, and so forth.

You can start typing to the blank screen. Characters appear as you type. We now consider

1. Backspace correction;
2. Wordwrap;
3. Automatic scroll.

Backspace Correction

As you type along, you may become conscious of hitting the wrong key. Studies reveal that most typists know exactly when they make a mistake. The WP makes correcting easy: simply back up and correct the error. This is in lieu of what you might do with a rough draft on a typewriter, "x-"ing out the mistake and then typing on; but that's too sloppy for most purposes. Overtyping for the WP eliminates the old, unwanted characters, *replacing* them with correct copy.

Typewriter Correction

On the less expensive common typewriter, to make a proper correction you must move the paper up, take out your error with an eraser, correction tape or opaquing fluid, reposition the paper, then go back and enter the correct character or characters. For the correcting typewriter, the correcting key backspaces over the letters, overtyping them with white material so that they disappear. You have to remember which characters you have just hit, or examine them on the paper and then type the same keys in the correcting mode; then type in the correct copy. With the memory typewriter, all the characters on this line are already in memory and, as you backspace-correct, the proper keys are struck automatically to overwrite each position with white material. Then type in the wanted characters, which also overwrite the previous characters in memory.

Rub

All word processors provide **backspace correction.** This makes correcting recent mistakes simplicity itself. All you do is press rub or delete as many times as you need to move backwards along the text line on the screen. Each touch erases one character. When you erase the last bad one, enter the new characters to replace the deleted ones. This is illustrated in Figure 11.3.1.

Let's see why it is so easy to correct mistakes on a word processor. As you key text into the keyboard, the codes for the characters received by the WP program are placed in a *text* area in memory. More and more characters pile up in memory. But the WP program keeps an accurate count of exactly where they go in this work area. When you hit rub, its code is picked up by the WP. The WP checks every code it receives from the keyboard to distinguish *text* from *commands*. It reacts to rub as a command. It simply moves back the pointer to the memory text area by one character position. It's as though you had not typed the last letter. Hit rub several times and the WP moves back the pointer that many positions.

Wraparound

For the simple typewriter, *you* have to keep track of how much you put on each line. As you come near the end of the line, the bell rings to inform you that only a few more positions are left. You can add a short word and hit return or hyphenate a long word. But if you type too many letters, you hit the **margin stop,** which prevents the carriage from moving further. To add characters *beyond* the margin, you press the **margin release** and continue to type. It is better practice to stop before you come to the margin and press return to bring the carriage to the beginning of the *next* line.

No Line Return

For the WP, you can forget about the end of the line entirely! Just keep typing continuously past the end of the line. The WP provides **wordwrap** or **wraparound.** It monitors where you are typing. As you approach the end

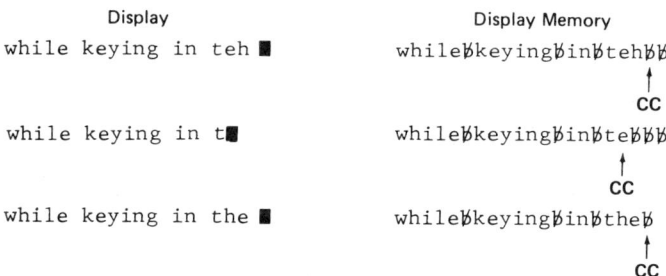

Figure 11.3.1. Backspace correction.

of the line, it is alert. When the word you are typing exceeds the line length, the WP automatically removes it from the current line, puts it at the beginning of the next line, fills up this line with blanks and puts further characters you type after the moved word. Figure 11.3.2 shows how this works. You type without thinking about whether the line is full, or looking up to see. The only time you use return is at the end of a paragraph to tell the WP to start a new line even though the present line is not full.

Return causes the WP to start a new line. If you want to indent that line, hit tab, which moves the first word to the first tab position. For some WPs, you can specify by the number of spaces by which all paragraphs are *automatically* indented.

Automatic Scroll

As you type, you fill up one line after another. As each line completes, the cursor moves to the start of the blank line below. Eventually, the screen fills up completely. What happens then?

When you finish (or get wordwrap for) the last line, the text on the screen moves up by one line, called **automatic scroll.** It happens within the terminal; the WP program does not have to monitor it.

Recall from Section 3.5 that the terminal has a display memory which holds the screen image. The usual capacity is 24 lines of 80 characters. But when it is full, the terminal merely reuses one line's worth of memory. It discards the top line and resets pointers so that the second line moves to the top, the third line replaces the second line, and so on.

Hence the botton line is unused. The terminal clears it and puts the cursor at the left. The next character keyed goes there. That's why, with a long document, you are usually typing at the bottom of the screen. You should adjust the physical position of the CRT to get the best visibility for the screen bottom.

At the bottom of the screen, you see both wordwrap and automatic scroll

```
This is the start of the text lrqw
Mastron osllewtry slet ohn danw sesu
rotom rtoucy octeges nmutua noy
rahen tnipe tserverhan emit rilibtani
ofopam rof robht toymo bleuodos se
always entered at the end. This pos ▇
```

```
This is the start of the text lrqw
Mastron osllewtry slet ohn danw sesu
rotom rtoucy octeges nmutua noy
rahen tnipe tserverhan emit rilibtani
ofopam rof robht toymo bleuodos se
always entered at the end. This
posi ▇
```

Figure 11.3.2. Wordwrap. Display just before wordwrap (left). Display just after wordwrap.

simultaneously. When the WP notes that the last letter fills the bottom line, it retransmits the last few letters of the line as *blanks*. This finishes that line; then the WP sends the beginning of the word as the start of the next line, which induces automatic scroll.

Other Corrections

If you are composing as you type, you may remember something that you forgot to enter earlier. You may make this or any other kind of correction, much more easily with the WP than with the typewriter, of course! This is *editing,* discussed next.

11.4 EDITING

Editing is corrections in existing text, whether created at this sitting or earlier at some other sitting. I have outlined some of the functions performed during editing. Before we attack those topics, we examine how to get to a particular place in the text.

Mode

There are two WP design philosophies. The problem that they solve is how to distinguish text from commands. In Chapter 2, I discuss special codes generated with the control key. This is one way to tell the WP what to do.

Another alternative is to say to the WP, "OK, whatever I say from now on is a command and not text." But you have to tell the WP this is the case. A special key is used for this purpose. The escape key, esc, is one choice for changing mode from **text mode,** where you enter text, to **control mode,** where you enter commands. The IBM PC has many function keys, one or two of which the WP can designate to change modes.

For a WP that uses two modes, like Benchmark, here is how you work:

1. Enter the control mode by pressing the proper key (esc).
2. Hit a key which gives a direction to the word processor, such as I for insert or D for delete.
3. Do the action: insert or delete.
4. Go back to the text mode when finished, perhaps with esc again.

Positioning within the text

Before you request an action, you have to find the place in the text where the action is to take place. Then you may delete, insert or alter text there.

Call this place the **target character**; it only shows when the text containing it is displaying, the **target screen.** You designate the target character by putting the **cursor,** a distinguishing mark on the screen (see Chapter 2), where you want something to happen. There are two ways to find the target character. Do it yourself or get the WP to help. The latter is called *search,* discussed at the end of this section. If the place you want is on the screen, use the *arrow* keys to get there. Otherwise, you must look for it in text which is not now showing.

Most personal computers CRTs show 24 lines of text (or less). Your manuscript may consist of many **screenfuls** of information. To alter text, you must first find the target screen, *then* move the cursor to the target character.

Scroll

To **scroll** is to move from one screen of the text to the next. From central text, to go forward to the *next* or go back to the *previous* screen is to **scroll forward** or to **scroll backward** respectively. Scrolling is **exclusive** when none of the current screen shows on the screen next displayed. There is a loss of context. There is no continuity between the two screens. Therefore WPs provide **screen overlap:** as you scroll forward, one or two lines from *this* screen appears at the top of the next screen; scroll backward and the top one or two lines of this screen appears as the bottom line(s) as the previous screen is presented.

Some WPs provide **continuous scroll** where text on the screen moves as though you were looking through a train window. For forward scroll, text moves up the screen, with the top line disappearing as a new line appears at the bottom. For backward scroll, the text moves off the bottom of the screen as new lines from earlier text move in at the top. A few WPs let you set the scroll rate (fast or slow).

Forward line scroll moves *one* line off the top as a new line appears at the bottom; **reverse line scroll** moves a new line in at the top. Figure 11.4.1 illustrates line scroll. Here the frame BS shows before scrolling; F frames the content after forward line scroll; B frames the content after backward line scroll.

Moving the Cursor

At the target screen, it is necessary to move the cursor to the target character. For most WPs, <u>arrow</u> keys move the cursor in the prescribed direc-

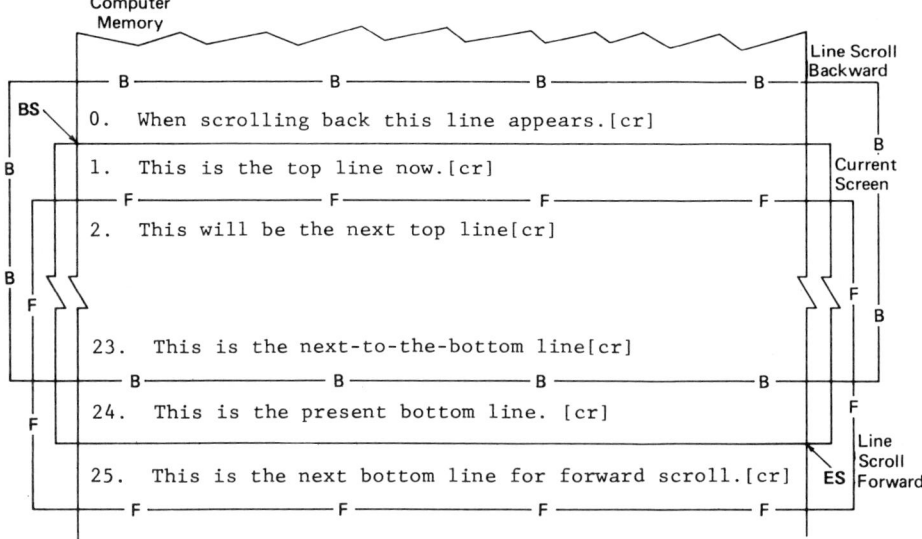

Figure 11.4.1. Scroll.

tion. The trouble is that sometimes these keys don't return a *standard* code from an off-beat terminal. To get around this, some WPs require control codes for cursor movement, since they *are* standard.

When you press arrow, the keyboard sends a code which tells the WP which way to move the cursor. Holding down the arrow key causes **repeat action** after a second, and sends codes at the rate of 10 per second for fast positioning. Some WPs use **express keys** (such as *home*), control codes or function keys to send the cursor immediately to a particular place on the screen, such as the upper left hand corner, the lower right hand corner or to the beginning of the line.

Context positioning moves to the next grammatical entity. If the WP permits, you can position by word, sentence, paragraph or page. You may be able to position either forward or backward by context. This turns out to be faster to get to the next word or the third word ahead or the previous sentence, and so on.

Some WPs furnish **content positioning.** In this mode, when you press a "printing" key, the cursor moves to the next occurrence of this letter or symbol. For instance, hit D, space or period to move the cursor to the next D, the space before the next word or to the end of the sentence. This is found in only a few WPs for micros.

Delete

Delete removes unwanted sequences of characters from the text. Several ways to do this are described.

Immediate

When positioned where you wish to delete, **immediate deletion** removes one character for each request made with a function key, an alpha key, if this is a *delete mode* or a control code. In the latter case, ^D, for instance, might delete the character where the cursor sits. After the character(s) is removed, the text is compacted from the right; characters move over to replace the deleted one, sometimes pulling back a whole word from the next line.

Most WPs provide immediate deletion, which erases the character *at* the cursor, while rub erases the character *preceding* the cursor.

To delete a number of characters at one place, repeated single character deletion consumes time. **Context deletion** eliminates text in terms of a sentence, paragraph or page units: to delete a word for Magic Wand, press control Y; for WordStar, press control T.

Geometrical deletion eliminates text by the line or page: for PeachText, press control N twice to eliminate a line; for WordStar press control Y.

By Content

Several WPs (Select and Benchmark) let you choose a **string**, a sequence of characters to be deleted, by content. After you have entered *delete* mode, type any character to define a string from the present cursor position to the first occurrence of the character. For instance, press space to mark to the next word. Press space several times to call for the deletion of several words. Press period to mark text up to the next period, the remainder of this sentence. Request several sentences by pressing period several times.

It's important to *see* the string scheduled for deletion. You may forget where the cursor was originally. WPs which provide content deletion **highlight** the string: they make the string stand out by

- higher or lower intensity.
- reverse video.
- underline.

With a string highlighted, *affirm* the choice to delete this string. To rescind your request, *cancel* the delete action; do this if you highlight too much. Control codes or function keys *affirm* or *cancel* the delete request.

In summary, for content deletion the steps are:

1. Go into *delete* mode;
2. Highlight the string to be deleted;
3. Confirm or cancel the delete request.

Figure 11.4.2 shows a string highlighted for deletion and the text closed up with the string removed after you affirm the request.

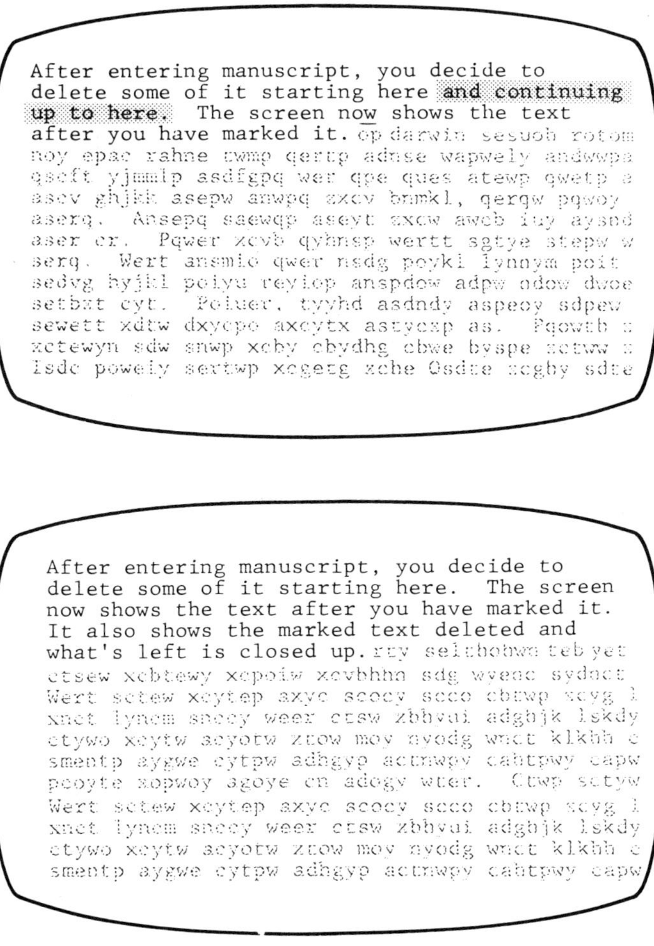

Figure 11.4.2. Block mark and deletion.

Recall

For most WPs, what you delete is gone for good. However, FinalWord provides **undelete** to bring back what was just deleted. That text is moved to a buffer when you delete it; if you press a control sequence, it is restored to its original position.

Insertion

Insert enters new text anywhere in the manuscript. There are three chief methods.

Pushaside

For **pushaside insertion,** key in the new material at the cursor. As you hit a key, the character enters at the cursor and the line is pushed to the right one position. The cursor moves right one position, too. When the line is full, the last word *wraps* to the *next* line. This may wrap a word from the next line, too, and so on, like falling dominoes. Figure 11.4.3 shows the action.

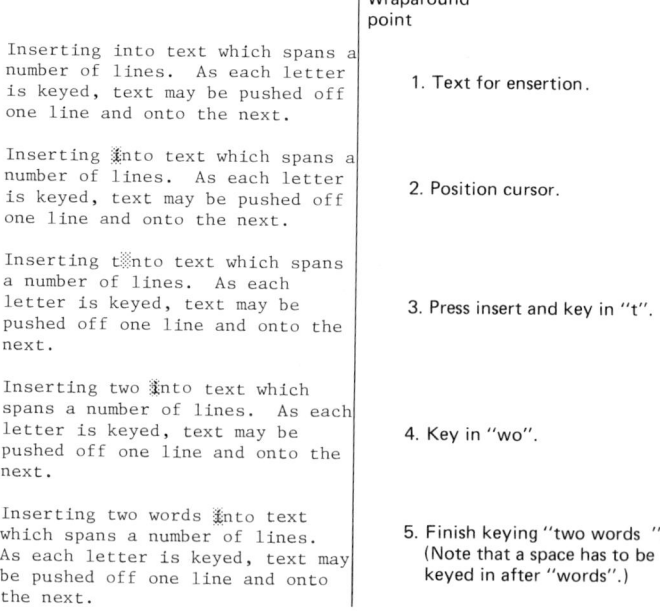

Figure 11.4.3. Pushaside insertion.

Open Up

Open up insertion parts the text at the cursor so you can write there. When done, it closes up the text, which resumes its appearance with the insert in place.

For PeachText, move the cursor to where you want to insert and tell the program with <u>control O</u>. The text opens at the cursor; the right hand part of this line and the remainder of the line directly following the cursor, with perhaps another line or two, are put at the bottom of the screen so that you can see the context of what you enter. Thus you have a number of blank lines on the screen to enter the addition and you know what appears *after* the new piece you put in.

Now key in new text. The characters appear at the cursor, which moves to the left as you key in. Should you fill up this line, wraparound occurs and the next word goes to the next screen line. When finished, notify the WP and the remaining text (at the bottom of the screen) is pasted on at the current cursor position. Tell the WP you are done for PeachText by hitting <u>control O</u> again. Figure 11.4.4 illustrates this.

```
Let's add to this line.  OK?           1. Line to add to

Let's add ▌o this line.  OK?           2. Position cursor

Let's add ▌                            3. Press open
     to this line.  OK?

Let's add something ▌                  4. Key in "something".
     to this line.  OK?

Let's add something to this            5. Press close or halt.
line.  OK?
```

Figure 11.4.4. Open up insertion.

Overtype

For **overtype,** or **exchange,** key *over* text to replace it, exchanging characters at the cursor with ones that you type. Unlike on the typewriter, new characters totally replace old ones. Overtyping is useful when the string that you replace is the same size as the one being replaced; it is easy to replace "one" with "two." If the strings are of different sizes, you have to delete extra characters in the old words or insert extra characters for the new string. Figure 11.4.5 shows insertion by overtype of "this" with "that."

```
Products of th█s nature.        Read to replace
Products of tha█ nature.        Replace i with a
Products of that█nature.        Replace s with t
```

Figure 11.4.5. Overtype insertion.

Command Mode

Some WPs (Select and Benchmark), have a **command mode** to scroll or move the cursor around the screen. Enter another mode such as *delete* or *insert* at your destination. In the *insert* mode, the cursor keys become inoperative.

WordStar and PeachText do not have a *command* mode. In PeachText, arrow keys can take you anyplace on the screen. You arrive in *overtype* mode. If you want to *insert,* press ^V and you are in pushaside insert. To stop insertion, use the cursor keys to take you someplace else.

For WordStar, ^V is like a **toggle:** when you start up the program, you are automatically in *insert* mode. Wherever you are, characters are entered by *pushaside insertion.* Hit ^V once and you are in *overtype* mode. Alternate back and forth between one mode and the other by successively pressing ^V; hence the term **toggle.**

Reformat

When you add or delete, this lengthens or shortens the line. Some WPs automatically reformat the screen. The WP observes a change in line length and **reforms** the line as though it were written with wordwrap and keeps the screen looking neat.

But when you are working with a hand-edited WP-output manuscript, it is preferable *not* to reform; altering a line does not affect the format and content of other lines on the screen. This line may be very short or long or *partially* wrapped so as not to disturb the content below. Now if you have to fix the third word in the tenth line, it is still in that position even though you have made considerable alterations above it. With automatic reformatting, a word you may look for appears elsewhere on the screen and thus is more difficult to find.

With **manual reformatting,** you end up with some short and some extra-long (beyond the right margin) lines. But when you are satisfied with the content, *that* is the time to make a *reformat* request. For WordStar, put the cursor at the top of the paragraph and hit ^B; the screen reforms a you watch. This command also lets you hyphenate, as described in Section 11.8.

Search

When you have a short document, arrow keys are satisfactory for finding a place to start editing. For longer documents with heavy corrections, again it is easy to sequence from one site to the next, since the place the correction goes is on this screen or the next. For a long document with sparse corrections, it is often difficult to find where editing is required. This is especially so when the format of the paper document is different from that on the screen.

For the **search** function, you specify a string of characters, the **search string**. The WP examines the electronic document in memory, even text not on the screen, to find the first occurrence of the search string. There are several variations to the *search* request which we now examine.

Exact Match

The first form of search is **exact match.** If you ask the WP to find "can" for instance, it finds the first occurrence of these letters in this order and would stop at "candle", "cantor", "decant", and "cannon". It does *not* find "CAN", nor "Can". The WP puts the cursor on the first character in the text where a copy of the designated string appears. (WordStar put it on the *last* character of the string.) If the string is farther ahead and not showing, the WP scrolls and displays a screen containing the string.

Whole Word

Some WPs let you specify the **whole word** option. An occurrence of "can" is found only if it is *not* part of another word. To do this if you *don't* have this option in the WP, put a space before and after the word you seek thus: " can ".

Ignore Case

For an exact match, the found string is identified with the search string. The code for an upper case C is different from the code for lower case C. If you want the search for "can" to turn up "Can" or "CAN" also, use the **ignore case** option.

Reverse Search

Search normally begins at the cursor and moves forward through the text in memory. A **reverse search** looks backwards in the text for an occurrence of the string. Of course, the string must appear in the sequence you enter it, not reversed; look for "can" not "nac".

Wild Cards

Sometimes you don't remember exactly how a phrase is written; you may have put "day time" in one place and "day-time" in another. You *could* do the search twice, once for each. Instead specify the string as "day?time" where the WP views ? as a **wild card.** That is, whatever appears between "day" and "time" is not compared by the WP during the search. It finds "dayXtime" too.

Repeat

After you have found the first occurrence of a string, most WPs let you direct a **repeat search** with a single key or control code to find that same string again. This saves the time of reentering the search request and string.

Extent of the Search

For most WPs, a string is sought from the cursor through text *currently* in memory. What happens for a very long document, twenty or thirty pages, all of which is *not* in memory? Text not in memory is usually not examined. You should find out if your WP has this restriction (most micro WPs do). Bring in the other piece(s) of text and search again if you want to find *all* occurrences.

Search and Replace

The WP can find any given string; wouldn't it be nice if it could also replace one string with another that you specify? Replace "Mrs." and "Miss" with "Ms." This is called **search and replace.** As with *search,* there are a number of alternatives to examine.

The Command

All options provided for *search* are also available for *search and replace.* You are prompted successively for

1. A search string;
2. The replace string;
3. Options.

To elucidate:

- the string sought is called the *search string;*
- a string that is found is the **target string;**
- a target string is replaced with the **replace string.**

The search string and the replace string need *not* be the same size. Most WPs reform after replacing.

Case

For the *exact match,* the case (upper or lower) of the *search* and *target string* must be the same for it to be replaced by the *replace string.* **Ignore case,** furnished in some WPs, does not require an exact match. Format is maintained between the two strings. Thus "this" is replaced by "that"; "THIS" is replaced with "THAT"; "This" is replaced with "That".

Multiple

While *search* is useful only if *you* take action as each string is found, *search and replace* can go on automatically. You request **multiple** actions as follows:

- **by number,** supplying the *number* of target strings to be replaced;
- **globally,** where *all* instances found are replaced.

For both cases search may be

- forward from here.
- backward from here.
- forward from the beginning.

Remember

At the end of the search, the cursor is not where you started. For a long text, you may have to search back to find your place. Some WPs keep track of the departure point to return there by command.

Discretionary

For **discretionary** *search and replace,* once a *target string* is found, it displays in context for you to decide whether replacement actually takes place.

Reply "Yes" or "No" to the prompt. FinalWord will even make the substitution so you can see if you like it. If you decide against it, the search string is returned to place.

Repeat

For some WPs, after you make a *search and replace* request, a different control code does it again from your current position in the text.

Cut and Paste

Cut and paste is a writer's technique, to *cut* up a manuscript and then *paste* it back together in an improved form. With your WP, cut and paste is done electronically with little fuss and bother. *Cut* is done by creating a **block**; *paste* is several action choices discussed below for using the block.

The Block

A **block** is a *piece* of text that *you* define. Most WPs handle only one block at a time. To define a block, you mark its beginning and end. Each WP has a distinctive method for doing this. Here are a few examples.

For Magic Wand, put the cursor at one end of the block and hit control U; do the same at the other end. The screen displays the string with underline marks bracketing it. If there are other underlines in the text, it is sometimes difficult to distinguish which marks a block and which applies to underlining. For WordStar, place the cursor at the beginning of the block and hit control K B. A mark, <KB>, appears to show that you still need an end to the block. Now go to the end of the block and press control K K. You can mark the end first with ^KK: then <KK> appears there. When both beginning and end are marked, the block is highlighted.

For Benchmark, you mark a block in the same way as you mark text for deletion. Place the cursor at the beginning of the block; hit M to mark the block, then hit (printing) keys to move through the text by content. The block is highlighted to show the block's beginning and end as the cursor moves to the right.

For Select, move the cursor to one end of the block. From the menu, select to mark the cursor position and press a numeric key. You put a different marker at the other end of the block. Then the block is defined by markers 1 and 2, for instance.

Action

You can do several things with the block. How you ask for each depends on the WP. You can

1. **Delete** the block.
2. **Move** the block. You usually do this by placing the cursor at a position in the text where you want the block Then you direct the WP to move the block. It is *removed* from its current position and placed at the cursor.
3. **Copy** the block. Place the cursor where you want a copy of the block. The original block remains intact; a copy is inserted at the cursor.
4. **Write** out the block. In this case, the block remains in the text and is duplicated as a named file on a disk. From there, it is may be inserted in this or another text file anytime you want.

11.5 FORMAT

How text appears on paper is important. But you should not have to worry about this detail the first time you get on the WP. The WP package supplies **default** values for format parameters. Margins, page length, etc., are built into the package so that you can start creating and editing text immediately. The result appears later on the printout in the predefined format.

Default Format

With default format parameters built into the package, you can sit down at your WP as soon as you get it, bring up the program, start typing onto the blank screen and create a document. Then when you ask the WP to print the document, it appears in some sensible format on the paper.

Typical format parameters and their common default values are listed below and illustrated in Figure 11.5.1.

- Page size—width and length of the paper: $8^1/_2 \times 11$ inches.
- Margin, white space on each side of the paper: 1 inch on top, bottom, right and left.
- Character width: 10 characters per inch (cpi).
- Lines per running inch: 6 lines per inch (1pi).
- Line spacing: single space.
- Tab setup: one every 5 or 8 characters.
- Justification: ragged right margin.
- Page numbering: none.

Setting Format

Default format quickly gets you on the word processor and productive. Once you have learned to deal with the WP, *you* want to control format completely. **Long term format** is set at the beginning of the ED (electronic

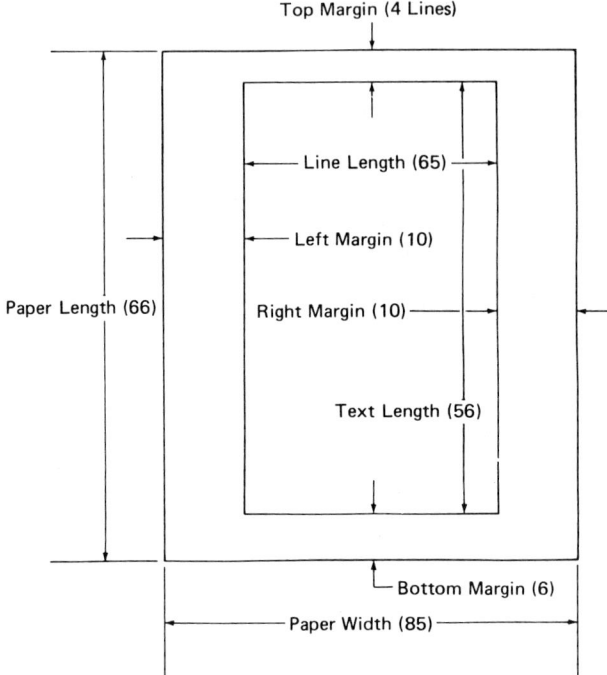

Figure 11.5.1. Format parameters.

document) and remains in force until the end, unless you decide to change it along the way. **Short term format,** such as underline and boldface, applies to one or two words and then is turned off. However, any format change is possible any place in the text.

For some configurations, the screen can display most, if not all format; this is called a **responsive display,** which we examine at the end of this section. Now let us see how to instruct the WP about format.

Format Menus

A favorite tool for setting format is the format menu. With a control code or function key, you go into **format mode.** This brings a summary to the screen, as in Figure 11.5.2, which gives the format values now in force. With arrow keys you can move to any parameter and type over it with a new value.

After you set parameters to suit your needs, return to editing. A format display such as shown in Figure 11.5.3 appears within the text to indicate

11.5 FORMAT

```
FORMAT> Enter command, then value, then (RET); (ESC) to exit


Top Margin                     6    Bottom Margin                  8
Left Margin                   10    Right Margin                  75
      Indent Margin                 10

Paper Length                  66    Spacing of Lines               1
Characters per inch                 Vertical lines per
   [10 or 12]                 10      inch [6 or 8]                6

       Number Pages                 1

         Justify [left or Center or Right or None]        L
         End current page [Yes]                           N

Automatic Return             Yes    Display Status Line          Yes
Mark Pointer                 Yes    On Screen Justification      Yes
```

Figure 11.5.2. Format menu.

where you have made a format change. This format is in force until the next one: you invoke the format menu again and make another change. Benchmark is one of the few micros WPs which provide this facility.

Embedded Commands

An **embedded command** is a set of characters *included* in the electronic document. The sequence begins and ends with a special character to convey

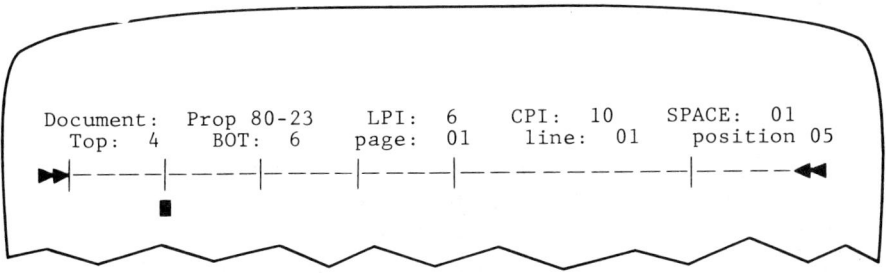

Figure 11.5.3. Tab line display.

(to you and the print program) that these are format instructions and not text so that the WP does not print them.

The embedded command is recognized by the print program as a directive. It responds by adjusting format instead of printing the characters. Therefore, it is important that the format command appear in a special way.

One way is to bracket a format command with a printing character (which shows on the screen) that is infrequently used. For Magic Wand, PeachText and Select the special character is the backslash \, a slash at 135 degrees instead of 45 degrees. For Select, all format commands are proceeded and followed by return. For Magic Wand backslashes bracket the format command.

WordStar uses a period at the left margin. This is necessarily proceeded and followed by return.

After the prefix character (backslash or period), two characters convey your request. These are called a **mnemonic** because the letters to should remind you of the format function. The mnemonic is sometimes followed by a value. For instance, this WordStar dot command asks for a left margin of 15 positions:

.lm 15 (11.5.1)

Table 11.5.1 is a summary of dot commands for WordStar.

Embedded commands differ considerably between WPs, both in the bracketing characters and the mnemonics they use. This is the most important reason text from one WP cannot be used directly by another WP without considerable editing. Still, format commands are *similar* in function and in some of the mnemonics they use.

Long Term Format

These factors are set usually for the duration of the document. Sometimes you make occasional changes along the way.

Paper Setup

Figure 11.5.1 illustrates settings which tend to remain static for the document. Although most paper in the office environment is $8^1/_2 \times 11$ inches, you may occasionally use legal size stock 14 inches long. Wide stock is convenient for table and journal printouts and may be 11, 14 or even 17 inches wide when your printer accommodates it.

Most printers provide two or more character widths. Standard size (pica)

TABLE 11.5.1 Summary of Dot Commands

COMMAND	FUNCITON	UNITS	DEFAULT
.LH	Line Height	1/48 inch	8 = 6 lines to the inch
.PL	Paper Length	lines	66 default lines = 11 inches
.MT	Margin at Top	lines	3 default lines = 1/2 inch
.MB	Margin at Bottom	lines	8 default lines = 1 1/3 inch
.HM	Heading Margin	lines	2 default lines = 1/3 inch
.FM	Footing Margin (page # margin)	lines	2 default lines = 1/3 inch
.PC	Page # Column	columns	1/2 default right margin
.PO	Page Offset	columns	8 default columns = 4/5 inch
.PA	New Page		
.CP	Conditional Page	lines	
.HE	Heading		blank
.FO	Footing		page number at .PC column
.OP	Omit Page #'s		
.PN	Page Number		1
.CW	Character Width	1/120 inch	12 for standard pitch, 10 for alternate pitch
.SR	Subscript Roll	1/48 inch	3
.UJ	Microjustify	OFF(0) ON(1)	ON (1)
.BP	Bidirect.Print	OFF(0) ON(!)	ON (1)
.IG	Comment (also..)		

is 10 characters per inch; 12 (elite), 15 and 17.5 cpi are also common. When you alter character width for the daisy wheel printer, you reset the WP and change the print wheel; the same print wheel does not print two different basic widths of type. Some dot matrix printers have width switches on the front panel; others are controlled by the program. Many WPs *cannot* switch widths on the dot matrix.

Figure 11.5.1 shows margins at the top, bottom, left and right. These can always be altered with the appropriate embedded command or from the format menu. Table 11.5.1 lists typical embedded commands.

Lines per inch (lpi) refers to the paper advance in the printer, the height of each line. It is associated with specific character width:

- 6 lpi for 10 cpi (pica).
- 8 lpi for 12 cpi (elite).

These settings must be made in *both* the WP and on the printer. The default is pica, the most popular setting. To change to elite, you have to

- change to 12 cpi (.cw 10);
- change to 8 lpi (.lh 6);
- make similar settings on the daisy wheel printer.

The dot commands required by WordStar are in parentheses.

Lpi is different from **line spacing,** the number of lines advanced for each line printed. It is common to provide single, double and even triple spacing (1, 2 or 3 lines spaced for each one printed). It is also useful to have 1½ line spacing. Some WPs do not furnish this option. Although WordStar does not, you can get 1½ line spacing for pica by changing the lpi from 6 (.lh 8) to 4 (.lh 12).

Headings and Footings

A **head (header, heading)** is text which goes in the top margin of every page; a **foot (footing, footer)** is text in the bottom margin of each page. They are important when you deal with multipage documents. At the very least, you should number each page in case then should get out of order. It is also a good idea to have the title of a manuscript or proposal at the top of each page.

It is nice to have a choice; some people prefer titles in the head (top margin) while others use the foot (bottom margin). Most WPs for micros (WordStar) restrict the size of the head or foot to one line. I prefer several lines (as provided by PeachText and Benchmark). That way, I can show a chapter, section name, page number, book name and revision date in the header.

Setup

You provide the head and foot for most WPs with a format command: the dot command in WordStar (.he and .fo) and the backslash command in Magic Wand. For Benchmark, the *head* command takes you to the format menu to set up or alter both the header and footer.

Page Numbers

It is convenient for the head or foot to contain a page number. A special symbol in the header, such as #, tells the WP where the page number goes; the WP increments this number by 1 for each new page. A WordStar header looks like this:

.he   Chapter 1   Page #   (11.5.2)

WordStar provides default footer page numbering; unless it is told otherwise, every page has a centered number at its bottom. This is convenient for first time use. However, if you are writing a one page letter, you must remember to turn off default page numbering (with .op, omit page numbers) or else you get "1" at the bottom.

Altering

At any point in the text, you may issue another *head* command. The new header you create replaces the old one for text which follows, starting with the first new page. This feature is useful, for instance, when the document is a chaper of a book. I issue a new *head* command as I go from one section to the next. I could repeat all the header information which remains constant and just change the section description.

Magic Wand has a nice feature which lets me selectively change just the section title.

Emphasis

We use inflection and other devices which alter our voice to convey emphasis. The only similar feature for the typewriter is underlining: you have to backup and overprint with the underline key. The printer provides the same facility automatically when run by the WP. For the daisy wheel, the same character positions are typed twice, the second time with the underscore; for the dot matrix printer, an underline can be printed simultaneously with any character.

Bold printing is also available with the WP; here **emboldened** characters show up darker than the rest. This is achieved by moving the carriage a fraction of an inch and printing the same character again. Some WPs provide several kinds of boldface:

- **simple boldface,** as described above;
- **shadow printing,** where the same character is struck twice *without* the carriage moving;
- **multistrike boldface,** where the character is struck and the carriage moves, this being repeated several times for each character.

The WP provides double emphasis by using underlining <u>and</u> boldface together.

Still another kind of emphasis is available. For the daisy wheel printer, it is possible to change the print wheel during printing and put in one with a different type face. Information written in this second type face, italics for instance, will stand out from the rest of the text. This means, however, that printing must stop and directions given to the operator to change the print wheel. That topic is discussed in Section 11.6.

Dot matrix printers produce expanded and compressed type, as described in Chapter 3. They also have italics and some have additional fonts. Few WPs provide for specifying italics, compressed characters or additional fonts.

Requesting Emphasis

You direct the WP to emphasize a string by one of two methods: little-used characters and control sequences, or function keys.

Printing Characters. The most popular method uses **special printing characters.** Typical choices are the "at" sign (@), the caret (^) and the underline character. There are keys for the printing symbols on the keyboard. If the WP uses these characters to show emphasis, then it does not print them but "obeys" them where found in the electronic document. (There are ways to get them to print.)

Emphasis characters should appear in pairs; they bracket emphasized text. When I have inadvertently disobeyed this rule, the results are surprising and disappointing. For some WPs, you may get a whole page underlined or in boldface. The first occurrence of the emphasis character turns on the emphasis; the second occurrence turns it off.

Control Sequence. The second method uses a control sequence to direct the WP where emphasis is needed. For instance, with WordStar you ask for underlining by hitting control PS (^PS) and for boldface with control PB (^PB). The screen shows which characters are emphasized. WordStar displays one or more characters to tell you that the following (or preceding) characters are slated for a particular kind of printing. Characters for underlining are preceded and followed by ^S; those for boldface by ^B.

The function key reduces keystrokes, by originating the proper sequence with a single stroke.

Character Count

The screen shows *extra* characters where emphasis is requested. The line seems to have more characters than actually print. If your screen has a status display, the column number for the cursor position is maintained accurately. If you have entered ^SABC^S for WordStar to print ABC, then

^, S and A register in the status display as the same column. Still the line on the screen shows longer than it actually prints. For WPs which use control sequences, there may be an easy way to handle it. With WordStar you can **hide** the emphasis marks with ^OD, lines of text display just as they print, but you can't tell which words are emphasized. This is important when you are concerned with page format. A responsive display, discussed later, is more common today, especially for the IBM PC, with bit map graphics.

Tab

Tabs help with tables and tabular material. The tab key on the typewriter moves the carriage to a particular position called the **tab stop**. For each column (one letter-width) there is a piece of metal on the typewriter frame: **tab set** moves it to an *on* position; **tab clear** moves it back to *off*. When you press tab, the carriage moves to the next tab position. Tab clear removes tabs from set positions; tab set enters new settings.

The WP has the same facility and more. Tab settings are held electronically in the WP program instead. WPs furnish a wide variety of tabs:

- The **standard** or **left tab** takes you to a designated column, where characters keyed enter from left to right as in normal typing.
- The **right flush tab** takes you to a column where keyed characters move leftward, so that the last one hit is aligned at the tab stop.
- Hit the **center tab** and the keyed characters are centered about this position.
- The **decimal tab** is especially useful for entering numbers. Keyed digits move the tab stop leftward until you hit the decimal point. Then typed characters appear to the right of the decimal point. Hence the number is aligned at its decimal point.
- The **indent tab** is especially useful for entering indented copy and for outline form. Text you key is entered normally from left to right. However, word wrap begins the new line at the indent tab stop instead of the left margin.

Setup

A control sequence or function key clears tab positions or sets a tab stop. You should also know how the tabs are presently set. A fine way to do both is the **tab line**, or **status line**, presented in Figure 11.5.3. Observe that

- the current setting of the left and right margin and the line width are shown by the extreme left and right positions of the status line and its length;
- a dot displays to indicate that no tab stop is set at this position;
- tab stops are represented by letters which also convey their type: T for normal, R for Right flush, I for Indent and D for Decimal.

There are many variations of the status line from one WP to the next: dashes instead of dots, different letters for kinds of stops, and so forth.

WPs let you set a new tab line with a control sequence or by returning to the menu. Once in **tab set mode,** you customarily overtype the current settings of the status line with what you want:

- To *reset* a tab, type a period over the existing character.
- To *set* a tab, type a letter to replace that position.

When the tab line looks right, exit *tab set* mode.

Use

The tab key produces a standard nonprinting ASCII code. When the WP edit program receives this code, it responds by putting enough spaces in the text to move to the next tab position. Once there, characters you type enter according to the kind of tab stop registered for that position.

Justification

Justification refers to how the line appears on the paper and, in some cases, on your screen.

The common mode called **unjustified, normal, ragged right** or **left justified,** is how text appears when typed on a manual typewriter. Lines are aligned at the left margin. Since each has a different length, a ragged margin results at the right. Most WPs also provide word wrap in this mode so that you never have to worry when the line ends; you only press return to end a paragraph.

Right justified (or simply **justified**) text has even margins on both sides. Text looks more like the printed page. This clearly cannot be achieved with the standard manual typewriter, but some memory typewriters can justify. Hence a justified printout is from either a word processor or a memory typewriter. Some people do not use justification because it seems mechanical and impersonal. Personally, I like justified copy because it really looks neat.

The WP program uses the computer to make calculations to justify text. The WP finds out how much space is left at the end of the line. Then it divides this space into equal parts and distributes them within the line so that the line ends at the right margin.

There are actually two ways to do this. Usually, additional space is put *between words* so that there is a little more space between them after justification. However, some WPs also provide **microjustification,** where the additional space is spread out between *all* the letters and the spaces on the line. It is a matter of opinion which is preferable.

In **center mode,** what you enter is centered within the line independent of the tab settings. Use it for centered titles.

In **right flush mode,** text is aligned at the right margin and has a jagged *left* margin. Some WPs do not furnish this. It is useful for pretty title pages where some information is centered, some left flush and others right flush. It is also good for secondary titles in long text.

Responsive Display

A **responsive display** shows exactly what prints on the paper: "What you see is what you get." No micro really provides a *totally* responsive display simply because its CRT screen is limited to 24 lines of text. Standard paper size ($8^1/_2$" $\times$ 11") allows 66 lines of text of normal (pica) type written solidly from top to bottom of the page. Allowing for top and bottom margins, 60 lines would do. Commercial word processors provide screens which can display 66 lines of text.

Pages

With a normal micro screen, you cannot see an entire document page on the screen. The best you can expect is a **page break,** a line of dashes, dots or stars put where the WP decides that a page ends. You see how each page begins and ends because part of a new page almost always appears when the end of the current page shows.

You may find a section title at the bottom of a page, or the end of a paragraph at the top of a new page. If this seems unattractive, you can *move* the page break back a line or two (but *not* forward) by setting a **manual page break.** This shortens one page; the WP recalculates page breaks for succeeding pages.

A few WPs automatically eliminate **orphans,** first paragraph line(s) at page bottoms; and **widows,** last paragraph line(s) at page tops, if you request.

Some WPs (Magic Wand and PeachText are examples) do not display page breaks because page makeup is done by the print program after editing. Hence, for a long document you have no idea where one page ends and the next begins. I find that I can live with that deficiency; with Magic Wand. I can alter a page break by editing it in, if a draft's breaks do not suit me.

Margins

Since you do not see an entire page, there is no need to show the top and bottom margins. It is not important to see the left margin; this can be adjusted by the print program or the paper can be offset. It is important to convey *line length*. If the screen and document line length are not the same, then it is difficult to edit an ED from a printout. The WP lets you set either the two margins or the screen line width; if the margins are set, then the WP calculates line width from them.

Sometimes you change a margin intentionally to get emphasis, for instance, to set off a quotation with a larger left and right margin. The tab line serves two needs: it shows the line length, margins and tabs; and it lets you change these factors. Thus you get a feeling for the page makeup.

Justification

It is pleasant, if nothing else, to see a document justified on the screen; however this is not a necessity. It is sufficient that the printout is justified.

Proportional Spacing

Until recently there was no good way to display proportional spacing (see Section 4.8), since most terminals display all characters the same width. With bit mapped video, such as provided on the IBM PC, it is now possible. This capability increases the WP program size, and the time to create and alter the display has little impact on the user. A few office word processors and the Lisa and Macintosh also perform this feat. If you need proportional spacing, be sure that the word processor you purchase can drive your printer to print proportionally. WordStar does not but MagicBind from computer EdiType Systems will print a WordStar ED proportionally on most daisy wheel printers which have a proper print wheel installed.

Emphasis

More and more terminals provide techniques for showing emphasis, including color (IBM PC), which helps distinguish one kind of emphasis from another. Hence WPs are beginning to implement a good display of this feature. Older WPs bracket emphasized material with special characters, or they highlight the string (which is preferable), but neither technique distinguishes one type of emphasis from another.

The trouble with bracketing emphasized strings is that the bracket characters take up room on the line and distort line length. Some WPs (WordStar) can hide emphasis characters, remove them, so that the line length shows properly.

11.6 PRINTING

When

You might expect that the WP would let you print a document anytime. That's not so. Most WPs have restrictions. Often the edit and print programs are large and separate. To print while editing, you need four things in memory:

1. The operating system;
2. The edit program;
3. The print program;
4. The text to be printed.

And suppose the entire document can't fit into memory because it is large.

Restrictions

The most restrictive WPs require that only a completed ED on disk can be printed and that no editing can go on during printing, as with Magic Wand. The versatility of some WPs makes up for this restriction. For WordStar, you may print an existing document file *while* you edit another document. The least restrictive WP allows you to print out portions of a document as you edit other portions of the *same* document (Benchmark).

How Much?

All WPs can print a complete document. But suppose you have edited some portion of text and you only want a copy of the edited material. Many WPs let you specify a page number to start printing and a page number to stop printing. Thus you can print any contiguous set of pages from a document file by giving the start and stop page numbers.

WPs let you abort the printing process. Thus, as you watch what's coming out of the printer and you have enough or see mistakes, you can key a request to stop printing. Even when your WP doesn't allow this, you can remove the disk and power down; this definitely stops printing. There is no risk in this since you are only interrupting the *reading* of a file.

It is often desirable to print a portion of your document as you edit to check what you have done, especially where a format change is involved.

Long documents can be printed, but practically no WPs let you combine EDs *as* you print them. This missing capability could become important when the WP (SuperWriter, for example) limits how long *any* ED may be (the size of available memory for SuperWriter).

Format Change

We have seen how to set format into a document (in Section 11.4). The print program observes embedded format requests and carries them out. For most WPs, if you want to change format you alter one or more format commands in the original electronic document. A few WPs have print programs which give you a chance to reset the initial format settings for *this copy only.*

At Print Time

Suppose you do not need to edit a document but simply want to make a change in the format of the copy printed now. For instance, I may have a single-spaced document from a few weeks ago that I would like to edit. It is difficult to edit single-spaced hard copy and I want a double-spaced printout. But that is the only real format change I want to make and should not have to take the extra work and time to go back and edit the ED for this.

You can ask the PeachText print program to display the format parameters after a print request. The print program makes a table of the format parameters in the start of the text. After it displays them, you can alter them—print a double-spaced copy with only a few key strokes.

During Printing

With PeachText as you watch the printout you may see a simple change in the format you would like to try out. Press any key at the keyboard. This causes the printer to stop and puts a backslash on the screen. Now enter any format command, then press return; printing resumes, using the augmented format.

When the print program encounters an incorrect embedded format command in the electronic document it is printing, it stops with a message such as "Unrecognizable format statement." If you see what that statement *should* be, issue the proper format command, followed by return, which the print program then obeys. Otherwise press return and the print program resumes, ignoring the statement which it could not interpret.

Suppress Formatting

Although many WPs do not provide dynamic formatting during printing, most let you **suppress formatting** entirely. You request this from the print menu. Embedded format requests usually consist entirely of printable characters (dots and backslashes). If you suppress formatting, the text prints as it appears on the screen *with the format statements* to keep a record of them.

Paper Setup

There are two kinds of paper you might use in the printer. For *single sheets* a page is ejected after it is printed. You need time to center and align the next blank sheet. The WP print program must pause to let this happen. Tell it to pause at print time by requesting **single sheet mode.** This mode requires your attendance while a document of several pages is printed.

Continuous forms come in a box in a **fan fold.** A perforation divides one sheet from the next; the sheets stay together yet are folded neatly in the box. After printing, the sheets rip apart easily at the perforations. Each edge of the paper has sprocket holes by which the tractor feed moves it through the printer. You can easily tear off the margins with the holes, aided by vertical perforations. You process the paper after printing by **bursting** it, tearing the paper at the perforations on all four sides.

Continuous forms are advisable when dealing with a large document, since you do not have to be present during printing. They are also useful for preparing reports on wider stock where correspondence quality is not necessary.

Setting Up the Printer

Switches on the printer should be set to correspond with the format in the ED to be printed. They control characters per inch and lines per inch to correspond to the print wheel in use (if a daisy wheel) *and* the embedded format in the document. The line advance signal from the computer causes the printer to advance as set by the *lpi* switch in some cases.

When the WP print program has finished sending all the characters on a page to the printer, it may send a form feed signal. The printer responds by positioning the form to the beginning of the next page. You should make two adjustments when you turn on your printer:

1. Set the printer for the proper number of lines per page so that it advances the form by the remaining number of lines to bring the form to the beginning of the next page.
2. Tell the printer where the beginning of the page is. When you turn it on, the printer assumes that the paper is adjusted to the beginning of a new page. If not, turn the platen so that the carriage is set to print on the first line after the perforation. Then press the *top of form* button.

11.7 PORTIONS OF DOCUMENTS

Pieces of any electronic document can be manipulated by the WP at your request. We discuss three kinds of document subdivision:

Blocks are designated by you on the screen and in memory.
Phrases you designate are extracted from text you are editing and set aside in memory or on storage. You may call up a phrase with a single key to enter into this or *any other* electronic document at will.
Subdocuments are portions of text on external storage which you can insert into any document as needed or put together in various ways as discussed later.

Blocks

Section 11.5 discusses how to define and use a block.

Phrase Storage

Some WPs, such as Benchmark, provide **phrase storage** to record a **phrase**, a set of words stored in a **phrase library** on disk. You can *recall* a phrase to enter it anyplace in text. Phrases are frequently used combinations such as salutations for letters, titles or names of personnel, company or department names or a name of a project.

Let's see how to define and use phrases with Benchmark. You can designate up to 52, one for each upper and lower case alphabetic key. We need to know how to:

1. Define it;
2. Put it away;
3. Call it up and use it.

Define It

The phrase to be stored may be in the text you are editing; if not, then you create it in *insert* mode. Press execute to go into command mode (cancel and execute are keys or command sequences specific to your terminal). Move the cursor to the start of the phrase. Press L (for *library* of phrases) and a prompt asks you to define it. Content addressing highlights the phrase in your text—for a sentence, press period—and text is highlighted up to the first period (see *deleting by content,* page 400.) Correct an error in highlighting with cancel.

Store It

When the phrase is highlighted, to store it press execute; a prompt asks which key to assign to it. Suppose you hit K; if K is already assigned, a prompt message asks you to choose another key or reassign K to this phrase, which is then stored on the disk.

Use It

When you need this phrase in the edit mode, press *cancel.* The alternate insert menu appears. Press K. The phrase is brought into the text at the cursor, which moves to the end of the phrase.

Subdocuments

A piece of a document or a complete ED on disk is a **subdocument.** The WP lets you define a subdocument, name it, put it on disk, save it indefinitely and later call it back from the disk library to any document you are editing. Each time you find a portion of text which may be of use later, you may save it, giving it a name you will remember. (It's a good idea to record the list somewhere.)

When you create a new document, you may realize that a subdocument saved earlier is of use here. Call it forth by hitting append and giving the name of the subdocument at the prompt. The subdocument is inserted at the cursor position without otherwise affecting text in memory. Once the subdocument is part of your document, you may edit it, modify it, move it or throw it away.

Any ED may be viewed a subdocument if you so choose. Simply insert it in your text as above and edit out unwanted material. The difference between phrases and subdocuments is that phrases are limited in size and recalled with a single key.

Automatic Assembly

The WP can help you assemble documents from subdocuments on a library disk. This assistance is invaluable in reducing the amount of time required to prepare repetitious documents. The three activities we now examine involve automatic document assembly.

Form Letters

The WP provides extensive help in sending the same letter to a number of people with only certain information changed. Three electronic documents are involved:

1. The **stencil** is a *copy* of the letter or document, with a special symbol where a substitution is made to create each tailored letter;
2. The **variable list** consists of sets of values to be filled into each position in the stencil;
3. The **output document** is a copy of the letter with one set of values filled in.

Stencil

The stencil looks like the letter except that a variable name or a switch code appears where a substitution should be made. A **switch code** is a special symbol, often a graphic, which displays on the screen but does not print. It tells the print program that something is missing here. Most micro WPs use **variable names;** each starts with a special symbol such as an ampersand and continues with a label which identifies the variable to substitute at this point.

After you prepare the stencil, you may print it to show the variable names for reference. Later, when you make or add to a variable list, this tells you or another person what goes in each spot. Store the stencil on disk as a named ED or **electronic stencil,** which usually includes the name of the value list and the variable names to replace as a cross reference.

Variable Value List

The variable list has the information to be substituted into each form letter to create the output document. The *set* of values for one output document is a **record.** It is divided into **fields,** one value for each variable to substitute into the form letter.

To prepare for a mailing, collect all the values for each letter and put them in the right order in one record of the variable list, a named ED you create on the WP. You are usually required to put fields in the record in the order they are listed in the stencil; records are separated by <u>return</u>. This variable list is usually on the same disk as the stencil.

Output Document

Some WPs create one electronic document for each output document. However, this step is often unnecessary.

In most micro WPs, as an output document is assembled it is sent directly to the printer. The print program reads in the stencil, formats it and sends text to the printer continuously until it finds a variable name. Then the program looks at the variable list and finds the value in the associated field of the current record, substituting this value for the variable name. Then it switches back to the stencil, formatting more text for the printer. It stops at each variable name to reference the variable list. The same variable may appear several times in the stencil but need appear only once in the variable list. If you omit *one field value,* the whole operation may get out of step and messed up!

After each document is printed, the print program checks to see if there are more records in the variable list. If so, it advances to the next record and a new document is prepared. The stencil is reviewed again from the beginning and text is merged with values in the current record to print in the next output document.

Printing

Most micro WP vendors sell an additional package for document merge costing $100 to $200. MicroPro sells MailMerge for WordStar. Ask for MailMerge from WordStar's main menu and, when prompted, give the name of the stencil for the document to print. The stencil contains the name of the variable value list; the list is automatically found and the values entered into the letters being prepared. MagicBind combines merging and proportional spacing for WordStar EDs as well as other EDs.

Considerations

The *merge* package rules must be observed for letters to print properly. For instance, you don't want a new letter to start on the same page as the previous letter. Hence it is important to insert a hard (manual) page break at the end of the stencil.

The program exercises considerable "intelligence" in inserting variable values, especially since they usually differ in length. If the output document is justified, it is formatted with the wordwrap; adding a long value keeps this format, even if an extra line is required.

How do you send out a mailing in batches, adding to the variable list from time to time? You don't want to type up a complete set of letters each time a few new names are added. Simply put records for new names at the top of the variable list, making sure you know how many you add. A print request brings forth a prompt which lets you ask for partial printing: request as many records as you have added.

Envelopes

I prefer to get around the envelope problem by using letterhead **window envelopes.** I fold the letter so that the name and address at the top of the letter show through the window and I don't have to type an envelope.

The alternative is to have the WP prepare the envelopes at the same time. For a one page letter, prepare a stencil with a *second* page (hard page break) which has the name and address information centered for the envelope. (Define a sendee block from the letter and *copy* it to the second page.) Then as you print the letter, insert one letterhead sheet for each addressee. After the letter is printed, put in an envelope; this is printed as the second page of the stencil. The same variable value record serves for both the envelope and for the letter which precedes it.

Document Assembly

The WP is indispensable when much of the work in the office consists of putting together documents which resemble each other in many respects, yet are different. Documents are composed of standard subdocuments drawn from a library, together with text entered directly for particular documents. The WP document assembly feature performs this assembly function in a fraction of the time required to type the entire document.

For **document assembly,** the following are associated:

1. A **library** of standard subdocuments.
2. A set of **assembly instructions,** which you create as a new ED.
3. The output document itself.

Library

The library of standard subdocuments may be fabricated during normal document processing. When you see a paragraph that may be useful in the future, mark it as a block, give it a name and write the block to the library disk.

11.7 PORTIONS OF DOCUMENTS

Assembly Instructions

A hard copy printout of the standard paragraphs together with their names should be kept on hand for the executive to examine. A lawyer making up a will looks at the section of the directory which applies to wills. Once the paragraphs needed are found, they are listed in sequence in the assembly instructions ED which names the required subdocuments and the output document. Additional text (not in the library) may also be included.

Output

The WP is activated (often from the main menu) and you choose *assembly* or *merge*. This routine goes to the library, finds the subdocuments and copies them in sequence. It pastes them together with any text in the assembly ED to form the output ED from which to print the final hard copy.

Inserting Variables

Each section in the library ED is a complete set of text but may require variable information, like a copy of a form letter. It may be a stencil where you plug in values.

When the operator makes the assembly instructions, values are included for sections that need them. For example, sections for a will include the names of the beneficiaries, the bequestor, the attorney, dates and addresses. The operator puts these values into the assembly instructions after each such section or subdocument names is called. The WP prints the will by assembling the sections *and* inserting the variables into each.

Preprinted Forms

Offices abound with forms: petty cash, travel vouchers, travel requests, passes and so forth. These forms are annoying to handle even with the best typewriter because they require constant alignment of the form in the typewriter. The operator must move the carriage to the right position to enter each field so that the type lines up on the form.

Form Stencil

You can prepare a duplicate of the form at the WP and keep it as an electronic document on disk. Whenever you need to fill in a printed form, simply find the disk with the ED form. Then insert the printed form into the printer.

Now bring the electronic form to the screen. Position to the start of a field on the form. Overtype it with the field value. (That is, overtype *Address* with 108 Eighth Avenue). Make sure to overtype *all* of the field and *every absent* field with *blanks* (or part of the field name will print). When you're finished filling in the electronic form, direct it to be printed.

11.8 EDITING ASSISTANCE

The WP may provide invaluable assistance in creating a document by helping you to format, hyphenate, spell and do other things described below.

Reformatting

Reformatting reorganizes and displays the text after editing so that it conforms to the format that you have specified. Some WPs provide **automatic reformatting,** which might seem more desirable: as you add words to a line, characters at the right move to the right and words are pushed over to lines which follow using the principle of word wrap. Your editing is immediately reflected on the screen.

When you make corrections from a marked up document *and* the document and the screen correspond almost exactly, it is preferable *not* to have automatic reformatting. Thus if lines on the marked copy have the same beginning as the lines on the screen, it is very easy to find a line that needs correction. If you add to or delete from a line near the top of a paragraph and automatic formatting is provided, all the paragraph's line beginnings from there on are altered; it is then more difficult to correlate further changes in the paragraph with the places they should be made on the screen.

For this reason, some WPs (such as WordStar) let you edit without reformatting. When you remove words, the line stays short—words do not wrap back. When you add words, the line is extended far past the right margin. When you have edited the entire paragraph, you can go back to its beginning and ask the word processor (WordStar) to reform it (with ^B).

Some aspects of reformatting are not visible unless you have a responsive display that shows a margin change or paragraph indentations. It would be nice to see the effect of the changes on an electronic document which uses space emphasis. For instance, a paragraph indented on both sides stands out but seems too narrow when printed. Maybe it would look better if you made the margin settings a little wider. With a responsive display that shows reformatting, you can *see* the effect of changing the margins on the screen.

Hyphenation

Wordwrap assures that lines only contain whole words: a word which does not fit is wrapped to the next line, which contributes to ragged lines. Some

WPs (WordStar and Benchmark) provide on screen justification *after* word-wrap: when a line is complete, it is justified to full line width.

Even through justification provides even margins, short lines have large spaces between the words. When your copy is fully edited and polished—the final document—both appearance and readability are improved if lines are about equally packed with characters, with uniform spaces between words. Hyphenation helps to do this.

Automatic

Some office WPs, such as CPT, provide **automatic hyphenation.** As you type, before a large word is wrapped, it is examined and rules applied to where to put the hyphen. The hyphen is inserted automatically and the word is split before it is wrapped. Most such programs are only 80% accurate and mishyphenation often results.

Computer Assisted

Computer assisted hyphenation helps you, but you must do some of the work. This routine is run against your text when you are satisfied that it is almost perfect. The program accepts all lines of a reasonable length. When a line is particularly short, the word which was wrapped is left on the line instead, and the program stops. It presents the line with the large word extending into the margin and the cursor positioned for optimum separation.

It is unlikely that the cursor is at a position for *correct* hyphenation. You may move the cursor (backwards only) to the appropriate position and press hyphen. A **soft hyphen** is inserted where you designate. Then the word is separated with the second part (without the hyphen) wrapped to the next line. If you decline to hyphenate, the whole word is wrapped again.

A soft hypen is so-called because it prints only when the hyphen comes at the end of the line. A **hard hyphen** such as in "mother-in-law" always prints. If you print the text as displayed just after running the hyphenation program, the soft hyphen prints at the end of the line. However, you may edit the text further and the hyphenated word moves so that the hyphen does not come at the end of the line. Even if the soft hyphen shows, it *does not print*.

Some WPs, such as WordStar, provide a combined reformatting and hyphenation command (^B). When you have edited a paragraph, move the cursor to its beginning. Then hit ^B. Each line is readjusted. The WP stops for lines where a large word would be wrapped to the next line. It presents the word for you to hyphenate as described.

Spelling

Spelling programs effectively cope with misspelled words. They ferret out misspellings and some even provide choices for correction. Large dictionaries are built into them to verify a wide range of words.

Spelling programs themselves may make two kinds of mistakes: they may erroneously flag properly spelled words; they may accept words which are incorrectly spelled. The second class of error is intolerable. A speller that misses bad words is really not very helpful. But the first kind of mistake is only natural. So many disciplines which have their own **jargon**—words which are unique to that discipline and do not usually come up in normal conversation. We could not expect a spelling program of reasonable size to cope with all disciplines.

A good spelling program adds any word that you flag (such as jargon) to a supplementary dictionary. When the program examines the next document you can ask it to refer to this **supplementary dictionary** and it no longer calls these words incorrect.

Complete Run

It is not important to us how the spelling program determines if a word is correct; how easy is it to make a correction after the program has flagged a word? One type of spelling program detects and marks the words without stopping. It scans the electronic document; and marks a possible error with a distinctive character. The program takes several minutes to scan the text, depending on length, but it can operate unattended. The result is another copy of the text marked with special symbols.

Next you review the document, checking the words where the special symbol appears; use *search* to find each flagged word in context. Then *repeat search* moves the cursor from one flagged word to the next with a single keystroke (^L for WordStar) without having to review the intervening text. This is how SpellStar (provided by MicroPro for WordStar) operates. You determine whether each word should be altered, replaced or kept and change it (if they are jargon not listed in the dictionary, main or supplementary).

Interactive Correction

I prefer interactive spelling error detection and correction. Here is how you use two of these programs.

Aspen Software provides a program called ProofReader, which includes an electronic copy of the *Random House Dictionary*. The program works in either the **mark** (as above) or **interactive** mode; here we examine only the latter. You start the program from the operating system, naming the document to be checked. First the program scans that document to list all the *different* words it finds there. A 3000 word document may use 400 or 500 different words. The program presents this *number* to you for your edification after the run.

The list of words is next compared against a main and a supplementary dictionary and absent words are noted. The list of missing words is sorted. Then the program reviews your text again, this time creating a new copy as it goes along. When it reaches a questionable word on the list, it stops to show the word in a line of context containing it.

You are now presented with a number of alternatives:

C—Correct
D—Dictionary
L—Learn
A—Accept
I—Ignore
Q—Quit
E—End

Hit C if you know that the word is wrong and how to correct it; the program prompts for the new spelling.

Hit D because the word is probably wrong but you are not sure how to spell it. The program goes back to the dictionary to produce a list of all words spelled similarly. You now have another opportunity to enter the alteration.

For the next three alternatives the word is jargon not listed in the dictionary. For L, the word is copied into the auxiliary dictionary (which thus "learns" the word) and accepted for the rest of the session; for future documents, ProofReader will continue to use the auxiliary dictionary to find words not in its standard dictionary. Accept a word *only* for the rest of the session by pressing A. Hit I for the third alternative, to ignore the word this time but not to inhibit the program from displaying another occurrence of the word.

When finished, you get on a disk corrected copy of your text and the original with the extension **BAK**. ProofReader displays a list of the number of errors, changes and so forth, which may be helpful.

MicroSpell

MicroSpell, by Trigram Systems, has a somewhat better way to help you decide the spelling of a word. Give it a file name and a supplementary dictionary. It scans the text four times, each time with one quarter of the dictionary in memory. The first time, it looks up words beginning with A through F, and so forth. The dictionary for MicroSpell contains roots, prefixes and suffixes. Hence the dictionary is smaller. As MicroSpell scans text without stopping, it displays how the prefixes, suffixes and roots are combined to make words in the text.

It stops at a questionable word and displays a line of context containing the word and, below it, a number of guesses to correct the word. Choose one of these guesses by pressing a couple of keys, such as $\underline{C1}$ or $\underline{C2}$ for the first and second choice. This word is substituted for the $\overline{\text{displayed}}$ word; the new word also follows the original for capitalization. Occasionally no choice is presented because no sense can be made of the "word". Letters in the prompt let you put the word into the supplementary dictionary and pass it from here on, or flag it as OK for this sitting only, as with ProofReader.

Grammar and Proper Form

Aspen Software produces Grammatik, a particularly useful program for improving your manuscript. It detects poor writing in your text: wordy phrases, trite words and sexists terms. It, too, is interactive but not totally.

Grammatik reviews your text, stopping where it finds a possible error. It presents the line in context and tells you why it has stopped at this point. You may choose to ignore Grammatik's flag and carry on or mark the place in the revised copy of the manuscript Grammatik produces. You may select the kinds of errors that Grammatik looks for or ignores. For instance, you may suppress a check of punctuation but leave in a check for wordy phrases.

When Grammatik is finished, go back to the WP and do a global search for the special symbol by which Grammatik marks the error. The only complaint I have with this program is that the mark appears *after* the error. Thus, when you find the special mark, you must back up one or more words to make the correction; you must also *remove the marks* or else they remain in the final text.

Outline Form

Some WPs have **automatic outline form** which helps you set up and maintain an outline, even during heavy editing. These programs are useful in some situations and almost indispensable in others, such as preparing a proposal for the military where each paragraph is numbered and indented according to rules.

No micro WP really provides a complete outline form. Benchmark includes an *indent tab* described earlier. If you set it up for each level of your outline, it is simple to create an indented outline. WordStar's ^OG lets each tab setting be an indent setting for outline creation in force until you hit return.

The problem arises when inserting or deleting topics alters the indents for other topics. Actually, there are only two office WPs (NBI and Dictaphone) that actually do this well.

Tables and Charts

Business reports often include charts and tables. Sometimes this results in a wide (or turned) page, an oversize document. Some WPs (WordStar) manipulate columns as well as rows in tables; move, delete, alter and interchange columns.

A wide document's entire width does not show on the screen (80 characters per line). With **horizontal scrolling** you move the screen contents to the left or the right to display "invisible" portions of a wide document.

Some WPs provide an arithmetical capability as an option. The WP can put totals and subtotals in tables and do all kinds of arithmetic useful in reducing the operator's time for checking existing totals.

As more vendors become aware of the need to have several programs work on a document, three solutions are possible:

1. A uniform exchange format.
2. A combined product (1-2-3 and MBA).
3. A total operating environment (Lisa, DesQ, VisiOn).

The simplest solution is (1) and many WPs and spread sheets can interchange data. Later (2) is described in Chapter 14 and (3) in Chapter 16.

Footnotes

Footnotes are important, especially in the law offices and in writing where many references are made to articles in the literature. Few micro WPs have footnote programs which enable you to edit your text without adversely affecting the footnotes. (For instance, you can leave them on the wrong page when editing moves the text reference point to a different page.) Footnotes should be kept with the page on which they are cited, regardless of what editing occurs in the text.

12
Data Base

12.1 INTRODUCTION

What Is It?

Data base is the most abused term; it means so many different things. Here are a few properties of a data base:

- It is a collection of data.
- It is organized for quick retrieval of a particular piece of information.
- It is accessible by direct inquiry.

Let's see how people in different segments of the industry use data base.

For the Mainframe

In the large corporation, the data base is part of an **information management system.** All the company's files, with a few exceptions, are entered into this data base. Any change or **transaction** which alters information in one file used by that application is available to the entire system immediately. Files for all aspects of an application are integrated.

Just consider how many application programs are run against the accounts receivable file. It may be necessary to access it when

- an order is received;
- the order is released to shipping;
- a shipping statement is issued;
- the account is billed;
- a back order is shipped;
- a partial payment is received;
- a bank statement comes in.

12.1 INTRODUCTION

A **data base management system (DBMS)** in the large firm keeps track of all such activities and makes information about them immediately available to management.

This large DBMS requires an initial outlay of several hundreds of thousands of dollars for the program alone. Many people write application programs to run under the DBMS to service this company's system. Clerical personnel are involved in entering raw data into the system.

The Tiny System

You can buy a so-called "data base file manager" for your Apple or TRS80 for as low as $30. It keeps track of personal mailing lists, index files or phonograph record collection. This is nothing more than a file manager designed to retrieve data quickly.

For the Small Business

There are some decent **data base managers (DBMS)** available for small computer systems in the price range from $500 to $2000. They have been used to design individualized accounting systems which work very well. They store all kinds of data from which you need answers. They can be the basis for integrating your accounting procedures. Even if you are not ready for it now, you should have some idea of the resources they provide.

Components

The remainder of this section sketches out the components which comprise an adequate data base manager (DBM) system for micros. Sections which follow examine each component and its use.

Data Definition

The information to be managed consists of units called **records,** each of which describes an **individual** in the real world, for example, a person, part, account or business transaction. Each value which describes *one characteristic* of an individual is kept in its own **field** (see Chapter 9 for units of data). The **data definition component** of the DBM accepts your definition of each field of a record and its format. Data entered are checked against this.

Data Entry

There are no free rides in the computer business. Data does not get into the computer unless entered by human hands. There is no other way to computerize your files than to enter the data at the keyboard (unless you go through elaborate measures, such as optical character recognition, which rarely pay off).

Unfortunately, humans err more frequently than does the computer. Measures to insure the validity and correctness of the data should be taken at almost any cost. The **data entry component** checks all incoming data against the definition and asks you to reenter data it finds to be invalid.

Record Update

To repeat, each record in the data base represents an individual of interest. Each characteristic of an individual is recorded in a field. The value in each field corresponds to one attribute of that individual.

Most individuals of interest in the commercial world are constantly changing. For instance, a record, be it for accounts receivable, accounts payable or an employee, varies according to the company's dealings with the individual it represents. The better the data base, the more accurately it reflects the *present* state of the individual. This is achieved by frequent data entry, giving changes in the individual's characteristics (like how much an account owes us) to keep the record up to date.

Record update alters fields of an individual's record to correspond to the current status. The DBM should be able to locate an individual's record quickly so that the operator does not have to wait to alter fields.

File Update

The **population,** the collection of individuals of interest to us, may change at a slow or rapid rate. The **file** is a collection of records, one for each individual in our population. As new individuals (accounts) enter the population or (are put on the books) as others expire, records should be added or deleted from the file; this is the **file update.** The DBMS should facilitate this operation to make it as easy as original data entry.

Query

The tremendous power of the DBM is to furnish structured information on request. You **query** the system, ask it questions about its contents. Here are examples of queries you might make:

1. For accounts receivable, which clients with credit rating D are in arrears for more than 60 days in an amount which exceeds $100?
2. From the sales file, list all salespersons and show their purchase orders for last month in Massachusetts over $200 for our household product line.
3. From the personnel file, find all people assigned to project 714, which is now expiring, who have been with the firm two years or more and who have some accounting background.

Reports

A **query facility** looks at the data base and pulls out records for individuals which meet criteria that a manager supplies. These may be presented on the screen and judgments or actions taken immediately.

Sometimes it is preferable to direct the DBMS to assemble the information and print it in a format you describe to produce an attractive report for management. It is then useful at a meeting to make a point and to convince others.

A **report facility** not only lets you collect the information but also prints it with suitable titles and with the data positioned as you choose on the printed page. Headings and footings, as discussed in Chapter 11 on word processing, make a presentable professional report.

Sort and Index

The DBM has facilities for acquiring information as described above. How well these facilities are actually used is determined by their speed. This in turn depends on the file organization. One feature of importance is the order in which records appear in the file. This order can be changed by **sorting** the file. A sort utility provided with the DBMS puts the file in key order. The power and speed of the sort is also important.

An **index** for a database file is an extra file, much like an index for a book. It enables us to look up features of interest and then move directly to records with these features. Instead going through the entire book (file), examining it a page (record) at a time for particular features, the index gets us there directly.

Utilities

A **utility** provides services such as to

1. Copy a file from one disk to another.
2. Reformat a file to be handled by a word processor.

3. Append a batch of records to a file.
4. Create another file with partial information from an existing file.

Programming

The DBM provides many features described above. However, their use requires a first level of sophistication. That is, you must be able to invoke the operating system, give commands and format your entries properly to communicate with the DBM.

Personnel assigned for simple activities, such as data entry, should not have to know *anything* about the DBM. It should be easy for them to coordinate hard copy documents to enter data at the keyboard. This is best done with application oriented menus and prompts from the screen.

Some DBMs provide "a programming language" to get the system to present menus or prompts to an untrained operator. Often this is a special language developed just for the DBM to facilitate user activities.

The System

Sections which follow describe the components summarized above. To make the discussion meaningful, examples come from a widely used DBM called dBase II®, a product of Ashton-Tate™. The $30 index card system does not have needed features and is useless for good examples. A complete system for micros, such as the Micro Data Base System (MDBS), a relational data base, costs $1000 to $3000 and has all you need and more, but takes a full fledged programmer to set up to do useful things in the business environment.

Our compromise, dBase II, is the most popular system for micros; it works on all S-100 CP/M computers, the Apple, TRS-80, the IBM personal computer and its clones. A new version called dBase III™ became available in 1984; it works only on IBM PCs and clones. However, it is upward compatible with dBase II. Hence hereafter we refer to this AP simply as dBase™.

12.2 DATA ENTRY

Specifying the Function

The software package designer chooses either menus or prompts as the dominant means of user communication. The pros and cons are discussed elsewhere. We now review a few of these approaches.

Menus

The **menu** presents a group of alternatives to the operator. A phrase describes each and indicates a key to hit to initiate action. The operator touches the designated key and the chosen routine is given control. If the action has options, one or more further menus may be presented.

This method is good for the beginner and the occasional user, if the alternatives are described with sufficient clarity. There is no need to memorize command letters to invoke a routine.

Mnemonics

A **mnemonic** is one or more letters which conveys an action alternative keyed in response to a prompt. The dBase, prompt is a period and arises when the last request has been fulfilled; it asks for a mnemonic, which is how you make your next request.

This technique works better for the intermediate or expert user, especially where options or suboptions are involved. The user can key options as fast as physically possible and the system picks them up immediately.

Help

You can forget a mnemonic though by definition it is supposed to be a memory aid. Then you have to go to the reference manual and look it up.

A useful alternative is the **help panel**. It is a directory which presents mnemonics and the commands they represent. A well designed system displays a help panel on request at any point in the session. Often it is invoked by hitting the question mark key (?) at the terminal as with dBase provides one.

Requirements for Creation

One DBM function creates a new file or data base if you furnish its name to the data base manager (hereafter designated **DBM**). If omitted, the DBM requests the name with a prompt.

We should distinguish two kinds of prompts.

- An **action prompt** asks for a command mnemonic for a new action because the DBM has finished its last request.
- A **data prompt** is a question asking for a name or value.

Answer an *action prompt* with a *mnemonic;* supply information for the *data prompt.*

Fields

Once you supply a file name, you define the record structure by describing each of its fields with the following:

1. Field name.
2. Its length in characters.
3. The type of data contained there.
4. Options which further describe the data type.

Establishing the DBase File

We use dBase for examples in the rest of this chapter. DBase is invoked by answering the *system* action prompt thus,

    A >dbase   (12.2.1)

Answer in upper or lower case. In the displays of this chapter, *your* responses are in *lower case* and prompts appear in *upper case.*

The OS brings in the dBase program, which presents various announcements on the screen, including a request for the date, which you may furnish or bypass. The date is entered into files that you create or alter. If you omit the date, there is no **date stamp,** a useful function. When you list dBase file names, each shows its most recent date of alteration, as shown in Figure 12.2.1.

Eventually the dBase prompt appears, the period. To define a new file, reply,

    .create   (12.2.2)

The dBase creation routine wants the file name. To create a name and address file called people, reply to the data prompt,

    ENTER FILE NAME: people   (12.2.3)

Now dBase checks and, if the file does not exist, it accepts your definition. (If the file exists, an error message displays.) Then this data prompt appears,

    ENTER RECORD STRUCTURE AS FOLLOWS
    FIELD   NAME,TYPE,WIDTH,DECIMAL PLACES
    001   [ ]   (12.2.4)

```
A > dbase
. list files

DATABASE  FILES    # RCDS    LAST UPDATE
ADD/S     DBF      00127     12/01/84
ADD       DBF      00127     12/01/84
NEWADDS   DBF      00083     00/00/00
REPRINT   DBF      01867     00/00/00
TAPE      DBF      00340     04/23/83
TAPEC     DBF      00340     04/23/83
TAPER     DBF      00343     00/00/00
TAPERS    DBF      00303     00/00/00
CODES     DBF      00129     09/22/84
XREPRINT  DBF      00061     06/10/84
NAME      DBF      00005     02/13/84
SALES     DBF      00040     00/00/00
```

Figure 12.2.1. LISTing the files.

where [ ] is the cursor. The first line instructs you; the second has column labels to show where information should be entered. On the third line, the first column is the field number. You fill in the field description under NAME. It consists of a field name, type, length and, for a number, its decimal places. Your entries should be separated by commas with no spaces intervening.

People is a simple file which lists last names, first names, addresses, a city, state and zip code. In (12.2.4), the cursor is in the first position of the second column, under N. Type in the first field name; since it holds the last name, it is called lname, a character field of length 12. For nonnumeric fields, (all fields of people) no decimal places are supplied.

Describe the field, hit return and the next field number, 002, appears and you continue. The results are

FIELD   NAME,TYPE,WIDTH,DECIMAL PLACES
001   lname,c,12
002   fname,c,12
003   address,c,25
004   city,c,20
005   state,c,2
006   zip,c,5
007   return   (12.2.5)

There are six fields in this record, but the DBM does not know how many to expect. It keeps presenting field numbers until you say there are no more by hitting return.

The DBM now establishes PEOPLE.DBF on the default floppy (unless you specify otherwise). The extension DBF is for *data base files.*

The DBM next offers you the option to enter records into the new file. Should you reply "no," you receive an action prompt. To terminate the session, reply quit thus,

 .quit   (12.2.6)

Example File

Throughout this chapter, some of the concepts are further illustrated by operations on a file which describes my open-reel tape recordings. Its format is shown in Figure 12.2.2; here is the meaning of the fields:

1. **Tape** is the 3 digit number on the reel box.
2. **Side** is F or R for forward or reverse.
3. **Number** is the numerical portion of the selection on the side.
4. **Composer** is usually the composer but is sometimes the performer for jazz and rock.
5. **Piece** is the name of the composition.
6. **Code** is J for jazz, C for classical, Z for ethnic, etc.
7. **Performer** is usually the artist and group but is often missing.

Entering Data

Getting the File

After you create the file you can put records in it at once. Put records into people during a different session thus,

 A >dbase
  .use people
  .append   (12.2.7)

```
. use tape
. disp stru
STRUCTURE FOR FILE:   A:TAPE     .DBF
NUMBER OF RECORDS:    00340
DATE OF LAST UPDATE:  04/23/83
PRIMARY USE DATABASE
FLD       NAME        TYPE  WIDTH   DEC
001       TAPE         C     003
002       SIDE         C     001
003       NUMBER       C     001
004       COMPOSER     C     018
005       PIECE        C     036
006       CODE         C     001
007       PERFORMER    C     018
** TOTAL **                  00079
```

Figure 12.2.2. DISPLAY STRUCTURE for the tape file.

12.2 DATA ENTRY

Answer the system prompt by requesting dBase. After the product announcement, and supplying the date answer the dBase prompt by putting people into use then ask to *append* records. It you omit USE, dBase prompts with NO FILE IN USE.

Supply Values

Immediately after (12.2.7) is issued, a data entry panel appears as in Figure 12.2.3. At the top is the number of the new record (1 more than the number of the last record in the file since you are adding to the file). Along the left are field names, each followed by a data area bracketed by colons. The cursor appears at the left of the first data area. You may mix numbers and upper and lower case letters for each field value. Each field is the fixed size defined (12.2.5) and starts in column 12. As you key characters, they appear in the space provided and the cursor moves to the right. Should you make a mistake, *backspace correct* by hitting rub.

After entering a field value, hit return and the cursor moves to the beginning of the next field. Should the value fill the field completely, the terminal bell rings. Characters hit thereafter go into the next field. This is obviously wrong. When it arises because the operator forgets to hit return, it is easily fixed with *edit* commands, examined later.

If the value is acutally longer (more bytes) than the field length, the design is wrong; with proper design, this difficulty should never arise. When it does, you must shorten the field value somehow. Modifying the record design is examined near the end of this chapter.

Continue to enter fields thus. Where a field value is blank or unavailable, to be supplied at a later date, hit return when the cursor enters that field.

Finishing

After keying the last field, hit return and the DBM stores the record and displays a new empty form; the record number is increased by 1.

When you have entered the last record for this session, inform the DBM. Suppose that the last record is number 63. After this record is put away, a

```
RECORD 00006
LNAME    :[  ]         :
FNAME    :'            :
ADDRESS  :                      :
CITY     :             :
STATE    : :
ZIP      :    :
```

Figure 12.2.3. The data entry panel for APPEND.

form for record 64 appears. Simply hit return. You get the dBase prompt, the period. If you are finished using dBase, type .quit (12.2.6).

Editing

Editing a record alters its contents by changing values of one or more of its fields or enters values for blank fields.

Need

You may find that information has been entered incorrectly after listing the contents of the data base (see Section 12.3. Or you may want to supply omitted values for certain records. Editing should be distinguished from posting (Section 12.6).

The Edit Command

DBase has a powerful and versatile *edit* command. The first way to use it is to go directly to a particular record, if you know its number (which is on the display when you create the record and also prints in a listing of the file).

Name the file to edit; then give the number of the record to be altered,

```
.use people
.edit 25
```
(12.2.8)

Record number 25 displays in the same form as created.

Now employ control codes displayed in Table 12.2.1. The first set of commands moves the cursor in one of four directions by one character. Keys involved in cursor movement form a cross on the keyboard as shown in Figure 12.2.4. Delete the character at the cursor with ^G or the character

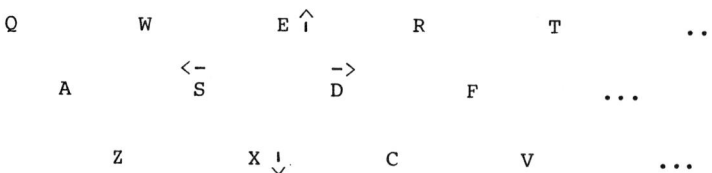

Figure 12.2.4. The diamond keyboard entry pattern, cursor control.

Table 12.2.1 Edit Codes

CODE	FUNCTION	TYPE
^E	Up	Character
^X	Down	Character
^D	Right	Character
^S	Left	Character
^G	Delete and close up	Character
rub	Delete left	Character
^F	Up	Field
^A	Down	Field
^R	Previous	Record
^C	Next	Record
^V	Insert/Overtype	Toggle
^U	Delete Record	Toggle
^W	Quit	With corrections
^Q	Quit	W/O corrections
^B	Scroll right	Browse
^Z	Scroll left	Browse

to the left of the cursor with rub. To insert control v (^V) toggles between overwrite and insert mode (See Section 11.4).

Once you edit *this* record, you can continue to an adjacent record: press control C to display the next higher numbered record; press control R to display the previous record. When finished, control W writes edited records back to the file. If you don't want to store a corrected record, quit editing mode with control Q, which ignores corrections.

Deleting a Record

To delete a record, press control U when the record displays and **DELETED** appears in the upper right hand corner of the screen. To restore this record, press control U again and **DELETED** disappears.

Deleted records remain in the data base. They display as you pass through the data base (with **DELETED** in the corner) and they list if you print them out. They may also be acquired during selective retrieval discussed in the next couple of sections. However, a deleted record appears with an asterisk at its beginning to indicate that it is scheduled for deletion.

PACK for a file in use gets rid of deleted records. The file is rewritten without the records scheduled for deletion. The holes in the file are closed up with **PACK**.

Multiple Nonadjacent Corrections

Edit without a number (12.2.8) works as described with one improvement. *Edit* assumes you want to continue editing and prompts,

EDIT RECORD NUMBER: (12.2.9)

Enter a record number and dBase displays the record. Use the same commands to alter fields in the record. When you are done, press ^W again and you get the prompt (12.2.9). To stop editing, hit <u>return</u> at the prompt.

12.3 SIMPLE RETRIEVAL

Introduction

Perhaps the most important use for the micro data base is to retrieve information quickly and simply. However, if all you need is simple information retrieval, some file structures (as supplied with BASIC, for instance) work as well. **Simple retrieval** looks for information in the order it was created and placed in the file; it is *serial*.

A data base is most useful if it provides **selective retrieval:** information acquired and displayed according to *several* selection criteria. For **people,** the name and address file, you might want to find those

- who reside in a range of zip codes;
- whose names begin with G;
- who combine both criteria—whose names begin with G and live in the Western part of the country.

If you do lots of selective retrieval, a DBM makes the job easier. Sorting and an index or directory which facilitates further are examined in Sections 12.4 and 12.5. Now we discuss **serial retrieval.**

Simple Display

After invoking the dBase, name the data, file to use

.use people (12.3.1)

To make a record of what you do, issue <u>control P</u> at any time to turn printing on or off (toggle),

.^P (12.3.2)

Three dBase commands display information (or print after you issue ^P): LIST, DISPLAY and BROWSE. DBase commands have several options. Each may be truncated or shortened to a minimum of four characters: instead of DISPLAY, issue DISP. LIST and DISPLAY are only slightly different, but we examine both of them.

LIST

This command takes the form,

$$\text{LIST [scope][OFF][criteria][range]} \tag{12.3.3}$$

where, in this general form of the command, you may include or omit the options shown in brackets here (and in the rest of the chapter). After putting a file into use with (12.3.1), you display it continuously thus,

$$.\text{list} \tag{12.3.4}$$

Each record displays completely, with the record number at the left. If it's a long record, it continues on the next line(s). OFF with LIST turns off record numbers (although they are useful for editing).

Fields are spread out along a line (not one field per line as when created). A record more than 80 characters long occupies two or more screen lines. Records display continuously. After the screen fills up, new records continue to display, scrolling upwards. They pass by so quickly that you can't really read them. You can halt display by hitting <u>control S</u>, a toggle: the display stops when you enter ^S and starts again when you next hit ^S. To stop display entirely, hit <u>escape</u> and you get a prompt. When display stops, you can toggle on the <u>printer</u> (with ^P) to get output (provided that you turn on the printer power, make sure the cover is closed and there is paper).

Figure 12.3.1 LISTs with ^P the first few records of **tape**; note that room is left for all fields, even empty ones. That accounts for blank lines. When printed with some (dot matrix) printers, the line wraps so that the record takes up two lines (top); others (daisy wheel) with a large carriage assume that there is paper on the left and just keep printing.

```
. list
00001  048 F 1 IVES              SONATA - VIOLIN & PIANO          M DRUIAN & SIM
00002  048 R 1 DONAVAN           WOOD NOTES                       M
00003  048 R 2 KORN              CONCERTINO                       M
00004  048 R 3 KAY               PIETA FPR ENGLISH HORN & STRINGS M
00005  049 F 1 COPELAND          FANTASY FOR PIANO                M
00006  049 R 1 WAXMAN, DONALD
```

Figure 12.3.1. LIST displays all fields of records.

Scope

Scope in (12.3.3) restricts the records examined with four alternatives:

- if absent, DISPLAY applies only to the current record;
- ALL examines all records of the file in sequence;
- *n* examines only the record numbered *n*;
- NEXT *n* examines *this* record *and* the *n*-1 records which follow.

In all cases, selected records in the file display continuously. But at most 15 records may appear on the screen at once and they stay there until you hit some key as directed by the prompt. Anytime you have seen enough, hit escape.

The pp Pointer

A pointer is maintained to the record just found or used by a dBase command. This is the **present position (pp)** setting. The NEXT option displays this record and several more given by the number, the total given by *n*. Then,

.list next 3   (12.3.5)

displays the pp record and the next two more, and changes the pp. Thus with the pp at 100, (12.3.5) displays 100, 101 and 102 and leaves the pp at 102. Figure 12.3.2 is another example.

Setting the Pointer

Two commands alter only the present position. GOTO resets the pp to a number you supply and can be shortened to GO or shortened further by just supplying the number. You can use TOP or BOTTOM to reset the pp to the *beginning* or *end* of the data base. Here are examples,

.goto top; .go bottom; .go 8; .17   (12.3.6)

```
. 4
. list next 4
00004   048 R 3 KAY              PIETA FPR ENGLISH HORN & STRINGS       M
00005   049 F 1 COPELAND         FANTASY FOR PIANO                      M
00006   049 R 1 WAXMAN, DONALD   SUITE FOR PIANO                        M
00007   065 F 1 BACH             SONATAS FOR HARPSICHORD & VIOLA (3)    C MARLOWE&GREE
.
```

Figure 12.3.2. LIST with *scope* restricts the records displayed.

The first and second commands position to the beginning and end of the data base. The third command sets the pp to record number 8; the fourth to record 17.

These commands position the pp absolutely; SKIP lets you move backwards or forward *relative* to the current pp setting and is issued thus,

.SKIP $+n$ (or .SKIP $-n$) (12.3.7)

Here plus (+) or minus (−) moves the pp forward or backward respectively; n is the number of records to move. Use SKIP without a number to advance to the next record. Figure 12.3.3 shows examples of positioning the pp, along with the use of *range*, discussed next.

```
. goto top
. list next 4 tape composer piece off
048    IVES               SONATA - VIOLIN & PIANO
048    DONAVAN            WOOD NOTES
048    KORN               CONCERTINO
048    KAY                PIETA FPR ENGLISH HORN & STRINGS
. 1
. list tape composer piece
00001  048 IVES            SONATA - VIOLIN & PIANO
00002  048 DONAVAN         WOOD NOTES
00003  048 KORN            CONCERTINO
00004  048 KAY             PIETA FPR ENGLISH HORN & STRINGS
00005  049 COPELAND        FANTASY FOR PIANO
00006  049 WAXMAN, DONALD  SUITE FOR PIANO
00007  065 BACH            SONATAS FOR HARPSICHORD & VIOLA (3)
00008  065 PUYANA          HARPSICHORD
00009  066 BEETHOVEN       QUARTET #14
00010  066 BEETHOVEN       QUARTET #13
0001
. 44
. list next 2 tp_ape composer piece
00044  077 YARDOUMIAN      SYMPHONY #1
00045  078 MAHLER          SYMPHONY #4
. skip -4
RECORD: 00041
. list next 4 tape composer piece
00041  076 MAHLER          SYMPHONY #3
00042  077 SOLER           SIX CONCERTOS FOR 2 ORGANS
00043  077 YARDOUMIAN      VIOLIN CONC
00044  077 YARDOUMIAN      SYMPHONY #1
. go bottom
. list next 3 composer piece
00340  MCLAUGHLIN, JOHN    MISC
. 80
. skip 10
RECORD: 00090
.
```

Figure 12.3.3. LIST with *range* restricts the fileds displayed.

452 DATA BASE

Restricted Display

Range displays only the selected fields of records. If omitted, all fields display; otherwise, only those fields specified display. Thus to display last names and zips in the **people** file, use

    .list lname zip   (12.3.8)

More examples appear in Figure 12.3.3.

Selective display is achieved by including *criteria*. *Criteria* selects records from the file and *range* selects the fields from those records to display. Selection using *criteria* is examined in Section 12.4.

Other Uses

LIST can show the structure of a file thus,

    LIST STRUCTURE   (12.3.9)

which display approximately like (12.2.5), the way you created the file. An example in Figure 12.3.1 shows the structure of the **tape** data base.

LIST shows files on a floppy (like DIR for CP/M). This is useful while running dBase if you have forgotten the exact name you gave a file. Use

    LIST FILES [drive]   (12.3.10)

where *drive* can view file names on a nondefault drive (such as **b:**). Only files associated with dBase display with this form. (See Figure 12.2.1). To get other files to show, use this form,

    LIST FILES LIKE stencil   (12.3.11)

where *stencil* is an ambiguous file name. For instance, to see command file with extension CMD, use

    .list files like *.cmd   (12.3.12)

To list *all* files on the disk, use

    .list files like *.*   (12.3.13)

DISPLAY

The DISPLAY command has this format.

    DISPLAY [scope] [OFF] [criteria] [range]   (12.3.14)

Selecting

DBase gives you three kinds of selection:

Scope selects a group of records by position in the file;
Criteria selects records from this group according to the characteristics of the value in specified fields;
Range selects those fields which display.

To display one file record pointed to by the pp, use

    .display   (12.3.15)

This does not move the pp. To display only two fields from the current record use

    .display fname lname   (12.3.16)

Show these fields for the next ten records, starting with this one,

    .display next 10 fname lname   (12.3.17)

As (12.3.17), but omit the record number,

    .display next 10 off fname lname   (12.3.18)

BROWSE

BROWSE is a later addition to dBase. It lets you view many records in position and simultaneously in a convenient format. Further, while viewing the records, you can go to any record, alter it and save the alterations. It takes this form,

    BROWSE [fields range]   (12.3.19)

454   DATA BASE

Activation

Here is a typical activation,

   .use people
   .27
   .browse   (12.3.20)

Use specifies a file. Then 27 moves the pp and BROWSE displays a group of twenty records starting with number 27.

Display

A record displays along a single line. Each field is allocated as many characters as defined. Part of a large record does not show. Horizontal scrolling lets you see the remaining fields. Move right with ^B; left with ^Z.

At the top of the screen, above each column, a label names a field. If the field name is longer than the field, it is shortened to fit above the column. For instance you may see only S above the column for SEX; the name has been shortened (truncated) to the size of the field.

DBase uses the properties of your terminal to make the displays effective. For BROWSE, if your screen can display two intensities (which most can), then the entire screen displays in low intensity except for the line containing the cursor, which displays in high intensity.

Editing

While showing many records at once, BROWSE lets you edit any. Table 12.2.1 displays the command codes used for normal editing (Section 12.2); these also apply to BROWSE. Control codes move you to the next or previous record (^C,^R), move the cursor by field left (^A) or right (^F) or by character, left (^S) or right (^D). To correct a field, use delete character (^G or rub): there is an insert toggle (^V); you may delete a record by toggle, also (^U). You may type a value into an empty field.

Scrolling

Unfortunately there is no way to go rapidly through a group of records. ^C moves the cursor down one line to the next record, but this takes about a second. If you continue to press ^C, the cursor moves to the bottom of the screen and, after a few seconds, displays a new group of records. If you hold down the down arrow, it produces codes faster than they are acted on; you may be surprised to see the cursor continue moving down for several seconds after you lift your finger. This also applies to moving backward by record (^R), which invokes vertical scrolling at the top of the screen.

Table 12.2.1 shows the two commands for scrolling right and left (to see the hidden part of records). There is no **automatic horizontal scroll:** moving the cursor to the extreme right (left) does *not* cause the display to scroll left (right).

Although BROWSE could stand some improvement, it is excellent for reviewing and editing information.

12.4 SELECTIVE RETRIEVAL

Selective retrieval finds only records selected according to *criteria* supplied in a command. **Simple selective retrieval** is based on one criterion conveyed by a **simple expression.** Multiple criteria are conveyed by a **compound expression.**

Expressions

Perhaps the greatest advantage that the DBM provides over a file manager is the ability to select records according to criteria. The simple expression is defined thus,

simple expression :: fieldname relation value   (12.4.1)

Here

- the double colon means "is defined as";
- *fieldname* names a field of a record for the file in USE;
- *value* is a quantity which dBase compares to the value contained in *fieldname*;
- *relation* is the way in which the field value must be related to *value* for a record to be accepted.

One of six relations is used in a simple expression,

$$
\begin{array}{ll}
< & \text{less than} \\
<= & \text{less or equal} \\
= & \text{equal} \\
> & \text{greater than} \\
>= & \text{greater or equal} \\
<> & \text{not equal}
\end{array}
\qquad (12.4.2)
$$

An example expression is

lname = 'Smith' (12.4.3)

where **lname** is a field, = is a relation and **Smith** is a value sought (alpha values must be supplied within quotes). The expression is true for records where the field, **lname**, has a value which begins with **Smith**.

Criteria

An expression supplies criteria for selecting records from the group preselected by the *scope* of **DISPLAY, LIST** or other such commands. *Criteria,* found in (12.3.8) and in other places, hereafter takes this form,

criteria :: FOR expression (12.4.4)

Clearly *expression* is the driving force. When a limitation is applied to the people file by using (12.4.3) as the *criteria* of **DISPLAY**, dBase finds and displays those names in the file for which the last name begins with "Smith." The expression of (12.4.3) is combined into **DISPLAY** as follows,

.display all for lname='Smith' (12.4.5)

Notice that for a *character field,* a value *must be* supplied between single (or double) quotes. We have encountered this rule before, in formal languages such as BASIC (see Chapter 8). DBase goes to the top of the file and examines *all* records. Only if one has Smith in its last name field does it display the record. The file need not be ordered.

Figure 12.4.1 shows two queries for works by particular composers. For the first composer only one record is found, which displays selectively as requested. **BERG** has several compositions in the file which display.

```
. display all for composer="KAY"  composer piece tape
00004   KAY              PIETA FPR ENGLISH HORN & STRINGS      048
.
. disp all for composer="BERG" piece tape off
CONCERTINO                       103
QUARTET   OPUS 3                 105
LYRIC SUITE                      112
CHAMBER MUSIC FOR 13             114
3 PIECES FOR 2 PIANOS            114
```

Figure 12.4.1. Simple retrieval with *criteria.*

Partial Values

Character values are entered into fields from left to right. If you specify only a portion of the character value field than the rest of the field is ignored. Thus you could request all last names that begin with C thus,

.display all for lname = 'C'   (12.4.6)

and those which begin with A or B with

.display all for lname < 'C'   (12.4.7)

and those which begin with A, B or C with

.display all for lname < = 'C'   (12.4.8))

Figure 12.4.2 requests records where the composer's name is BAR, which is interpreted as a partial value. This returns a number of records. The file is *not* in sequence by composer.

You can demand an exact match for any query with SET EXACT ON (see Table 12.7.1).

Collating Sequence

It is clear that A comes before (is less than or <) B which precedes C and so forth. But it is not clear that lower case letters *follow* upper case letters. It is the character set code which determines whether a number, letter, punctuation mark or control code comes early or late in the alphabet. All micros and PCs use ASCII, so that simplifies matters. The value of the ASCII

```
. disp all for composer="BAR" composer piece tape off
BARTOK            PIANO CONCERTO #2              069
BARTOK            DIVERTMENTO FOR STRINGS        073
BARBER            SYMPH #1                       079
BARATI            CHAMBER CONC                   083
BARTOK            V & P SONATA #1                100
BARTOK            V & P SONATA #2                100
BARTOK            CONC #3                        103
BARTOK            CONC #1                        103
BARTOK            PIANO CONC # 1                 103
BARTOK            PIANO CONC # 1                 103
BARTOK            CONC 2 PIANOS & PERCUSSION     111
BARTOK            MUSIC STRING PERC & CEL        111
BARBER            QUARTET                        113
```

Figure 12.4.2. Partial simple retrieval with *criteria* and *range*.

code when viewed as a binary number determines this. For instance, from Table 9.2.1 we see that, in hex,

- —the code for esc is 1B
- —the code for $ is 24
- —the code for 4 is 34
- —the code for M is 4D
- —the code for W is 57
- —the code for m is 6D
- —the code for p is 70
- —the code for rub is 7F

This leads to the relation,

$$\text{esc} < \$ < 4 < M < W < m < p < \text{rub} \qquad (12.4.9)$$

The sequence of the symbols within the alphabet, as determined by the numeric value of a symbol's code is called the **collating sequence.** It can be derived from Table 9.2.1, the ASCII code set. The first symbol is found in the upper left hand corner of the table and the delete symbol is the last one in the lower right hand corner. The sequence of the codes might also be displayed thus,

$$\text{control codes} < \text{punctuation} < 0..9 < A..Z < a..z \qquad (12.4.10)$$

Control codes appear first, then some punctuation symbols. Following them are numbers, capital letters and the lower case letters with a few punctuation symbols interspersed. This collating sequence determines the meaning of *less than* ($<$) and *greater than* ($>$).

Figure 12.4.3 shows a request for records about composers whose names start with W or higher. If you use rub while answering the prompt, your answer is corrected. But, for ^P the wrong letters are printed already; hence an underline prints for each rub as shown in the figure. Since the file is in tape order, records are not displayed in composer order. Note also WAITING, which gives you a chance to view what is now on the screen or to stop entirely (esc). Finally, note my mistake at the top, "composser," which I caught and fixed.

Numeric Fields

Numeric fields are viewed from right to left, whereas character fields are viewed from left to right. When numeric field values appear in expressions, they are not surrounded by quotes.

```
. disp al_ for composser___er>="W" composer piece tape off
WAXMAN, DONALD    SUITE FOR PIANO                          049
YARDOUMIAN        VIOLIN CONC                              077
YARDOUMIAN        SYMPHONY #1                              077
WALTON            FACADE SUITE                             102
WALTON            SYMPH #2                                 103
WEBERN            5 PIECES                                 112
WEBERN            5 PIECES                                 112
WEBERN            6 BAGATELLES                             112
WEBERN            6 BAGATELLES                             112
WEINBERG          QUARTET #3                               122
XENAKIS           ORIENT OCCIDENT                          125
XENAKIS           METASTATIS                               127
XENAKIS           PITHOPRAKTIA                             127
XENAKIS           EONTA                                    127
XENAKIS           CONC P-H II, DIAMORPHOSES II             138
WAITING
XENAKIS           ORIENT-OCCIDENT III                      138
WUORONIN          CONC FOR AMPL VIOLIN & ORCH              138
WEATHER REPORT    MISC                                     164
```

Figure 12.4.3. Here *criteria* uses the file order.

Strings

We have encountered the concept of **string** before, a group of contiguous characters. DBase provides powerful ways to deal with strings to facilitate retrieval.

Logical Operator

A useful facility finds strings which contain a given substring anywhere. It has this form

'substring'$string   (12.4.11)

where *substring* is a specified string which may be embedded within the named *string*. Usually *string* is the name of a field; if it is actually a string, the answer is trivial. To request last names which contain "son" anywhere, use,

'son'$lname   (12.4.12)

It finds Wilson, Hanson and Johnsonville, but not "Sons and Lovers" or "Abbot and Sons," since here the capital "S" does not provide an exact match.

Upper Case

The exclamation point (!) is the upper case operator. It converts a string to upper case. If you are not sure in what case (upper or lower) the string appears, use,

 'SON'$!lname   (12.4.13)

This converts the string at lname to upper case before matching it with 'SON'. Hence (12.4.13) would turn up records where lname is Johnson, Wilson, Sontag, Albert and Sons, and HANSONVILLE, but (12.4.12) would miss the last three.

Extraction

To withdraw a substring from a named string, the *extract* operator, $, is employed,

 $(string,start,length)   (12.4.14)

where *length* characters beginning at *start* are extracted from *string*. If the date is stored in an eight character field with two digits each for month, day and year in that order separated by a slash (such as 12/31/83), then

 $(date,7,2)   (12.4.15)

extracts the year (83). We ask to display the account number and date selectively for all records where the year in date is (19)77 with

 .display all acctnum date for '77'=$(date,7,2)   (12.4.16)

Concaternation

Pasting strings together is necessary in reports and displays. This is done with + or −, but the latter removes trailing blanks. Thus,

 lname + ',' + fname   (12.4.17)

pastes the first and last names together, putting a comma between them but leaving all the blanks at the end of the last name. But

 lname−', '+fname   (12.4.18)

removes terminal blanks before adding the comma, the space and the first name. Thus with (12.4.17), a name shows as

    James   ,Harry   (12.4.19)

while with (12.4.18), it shows as

    James, Harry   (12.4.20)

Compound Selection

Compound selection makes use of a **compound expression** which combines two or more simple expressions for a number of criteria. A compound expression is formed by one of the following:

- **denying** a simple expression;
- connecting two simple expressions together;
- both of the above;
- combining compound and simple expressions with the help of parentheses.

Three reserved words make possible the construction of compound expression:

    .NOT. is the denial. A compound expression is true only when the simple expression .NOT. modifies (precedes) is false.
    .AND. is placed between two expressions; the compound expression is true only when *both* the simple expressions are true.
    .OR. is placed between two expressions so that the compound expression is true when *either* the first *or* the second (or both) is true.

We now examine them, giving examples.

Denial

Consider the data base called **people** and suppose that it includes phone numbers in a field called **phone**. Suppose also that we have omitted some phone numbers because we didn't know them or because our friend doesn't have a phone. We could display the records for all people for whom phone numbers are not listed, with

    .display all for phone=' '   (12.4.21)

Let's suppose we wanted to find only those people who *do* have phone numbers listed. Use

.display all for .not. phone=' ' (12.4.22)

As another example, all the zips for New York City begin with 100. To find all those outside of New York City, use

.display all for .not. zip='100' (12.4.23)

Notice that zip is a *character* field, so 100 is placed in single quotes. Note further that information always appears aligned at the left and we ask for zip codes which begin with 100 (or, as in this case, which do not begin with 100).

Disjunction

Disjunction combines simple expressions so that if any one or more of the conditions is true it selects a record. The connective is *or* in common language but must begin and end with a period for dBase (.OR.).

Sometimes conditions (simple expressions) have nothing to do with each other and could not possibly exist at the same time; they are called **mutually exclusive** or **disjoint**. For example, consider an expression to include names from the people list that come from two states thus,

state='CT' .or. state='NJ' (12.4.24)

Notice that *an expression* is on both sides of .or. In spoken language we leave out part of the statement to simplify the vocalization. We might say "the state is Connecticut or New Jersey." This gives rise to an improper compound statement,

THIS IS WRONG: state='CT' .or. 'NJ' (12.4.25)

because a state name, *not* an expression, should be found at the right of .or. Figure 12.4.4 shows a proper example for the tape file.

It is possible to combine more than two conditions; remember that an expression *must* come both before and after .or. For example,

state='CT' .or. state='NJ' .or. state='MA' (12.4.26)

selects a record from any of three states

```
. disp all for composer="A" .or. composer="WA" composer piece tape off
WAXMAN, DONALD    SUITE FOR PIANO                         049
ADASKIN           SERANADE CONCERTANTE                    084
WALTON            FACADE SUITE                            102
WALTON            SYMPH #2                                103
ARROW             STRING QUARTET                          120
ARROW             UNDERWORLD                              120
AMRAN             TRIPLE CONC                             156
```

Figure 12.4.4. Disjunction within *criteria* using .OR. .

Not Disjoint

All of the above conditions are mutually exclusive. If a person has an address in one state, that person is not also listed in a second state (unless the file were more complicated). However, consider this compound expression:

state = 'CT' .or. title = 'DR.' (12.4.27)

Here a person could live in Connecticut or have the title of Doctor, or perhaps both conditions apply. DBase will display a doctor from Connecticut only once for this selection. The denial can be combined with disjunction. When it appears after a dot, it is preferable to include the simple expression within parentheses thus,

.not. (title = 'Mr' .or. title = 'Dr.') (12.4.28)

This should be equivalent to

title = 'Ms' .or. title = 'Miss' .or. title = 'Mrs.' (12.4.29)

Both these compound expressions will find all the women in the files except those with the title "Dr."

Conjunction

For **conjunction,** a compound expression, both conditions specified by the simple expressions surrounding .AND. must be true. Again, simple expressions must appear on either side of).and. Thus we capture all doctors from Connecticut with

title = 'Dr.' .and. state = 'CT' (12.4.30)

For a sales report to find those in the sales file who have sold over $10,000 this month and work in area 201, use this compound expression:

sales > 10000 .and. area = '201' (12.4.31)

Notice here that the sales figure is numeric. The value is not bounded by quotes; although the area field is specified by a number, it is in a character field and hence is in quotes.

Figure 12.4.5 shows conjunction. It's a long query and I left out the dots before and after "and" so dBase gave me a chance to correct it. Often it's easier to retype the line, so I just hit <u>return</u>. Here I ask to change and to .and., which is accepted by dBase. <u>M</u> is the code for modern music.

```
. disp all for composer<="C" and code="M" composer tape piece off
*** SYNTAX ERROR ***
                                 ?
disp all for composer<="C" and code="M" composer tape piece off
CORRECT AND RETRY (Y/N)? Y
CHANGE FROM :and
CHANGE TO   :.and.
disp all for composer<="C" .and. code="M" composer tape piece off
MORE CORRECTIONS (Y/N)? N
COPELAND          049 FANTASY FOR PIANO
COWELL            073 STRING QUARTET #5
BARBER            079 SYMPH #1
BARATI            083 CHAMBER CONC
COLLECTION        083 MODERN HARPSICHORD
ADASKIN           084 SERANADE CONCERTANTE
COPELAND          088 VITEBSK
CAGE, JOHN        092 MISC
CARTER            092 SUITE FOR PERC HARP & PIANO
BERG              103 CONCERTINO
BERG              105 QUARTET  OPUS 3
BERGER            114 CHAMBER MUSIC FOR 13
BERGER            114 3 PIECES FOR 2 PIANOS
ARROW             120 STRING QUARTET
ARROW             120 UNDERWORLD
WAITING
CASTIGLIONO       122 GYMEL
BERIO             125 MOMENTI
CARTER            133 CONC FOR ORCH
COWELL            140 SYMP #5
CROFT             140 CONC FOR PERCUSSION
BROSHI, GEO.      140 SYMPHONY
CARTER            145 8 ETUDES
CARTER            145 QUINTET
BLACKER           151 CONCERTENITE
COPLAND           152 SYMPHONY #3
AMRAN             156 TRIPLE CONC
COWELL            156 SYMPH #16 (ICELANDIC)
BERIO             157 GIRDES
COWELL            163 SONATA
CRUMB             168 STAR CHILD
```

Figure 12.4.5. Conjunction within *criteria* using .AND. .

12.5 FACILITATION

Sorting

There are several reasons to have a sorted file. You can disregard how you enter records into an unsorted file because *sorting* them later puts them in the desired order. They are then in a convenient sequence when printed out.

If you request frequent retrieval on a particular key field but not the one originally used for ordering the file, then it is sometimes desirable to create another sorted file. This makes it quicker to find a group of records with the other key.

Invoking

The command to sort a dBase file now in use is

SORT ON field TO file [DESCENDING] (12.5.1)

where *field* is the field to sort on and *file* receives the sorted output. The option chooses descending order instead of ascending (the default). It is possible to sort a file in position, where *file* of (12.5.1) is the one in use, but this is dangerous. If there is an electrical problem while the sort is in progress, you may lose both the sorted output and the file being sorted. Hence it is advisable to sort to a temporary file with a different name, and check it after the sort. Only when you are sure that everything is proper, DELETE the original file and RENAME the new file to the old name. Here is an example of how to do this:

```
.use people
.sort on lname to temp
100 RECORDS SORTED
138 RECORDS SORTED
.use temp
.list
.delete file people
.rename temp to people                    (12.5.2)
```

The first line puts the file to sort, called **people**, into use. It is sorted on last name, **lname**, to a new file called **temp**.

Sorting may take several minutes. As each hundred records is sorted, a message appears, **100 RECORDS SORTED**, to tell you something is really happening. A final message indicates how many records have been sorted (and this should correspond to the original number provided). After the sorted file has been put in use, the sixth line of (12.5.2), list, shows the file on the screen. Check that it resembles the original file closely. It is preferable to get a printout to compare with the original (^P). Next delete the old file and finally rename temp to people.

Figure 12.5.1 lists part of tapec, the result of sorting tape on composer. The records are now ordered by composer, not by tape.

More Commands

DELETE

The DELETE command deletes either a record or a file. Hence it has two forms,

> DELETE [scope] [criteria]
> DELETE FILE filename   (12.5.3)

The first form deletes a record or several records. You delete the record at the present position with

> .delete   (12.5.4)

You can delete the next three records with

> .delete next 3   (12.5.5)

Delete all records for which *criteria* holds by supplying a FOR expression. For instance, we might delete all records which have no last name with

> .delete for lname=' '   (12.5.6)

```
. use tapec
. list next 10 composer piece tape code
00001    ADASKIN      SERANADE CONCERTANTE                      004 M
00002    AMRAN        TRIPLE CONC                               156 M
00003    ARROW        STRING QUARTET                            120 M
00004    ARROW        UNDERWORLD                                120 M
00005    BACH         2 PART INVENT IN A/A SHEEPMAY SAFELY      142 E
00006    BACH         BRANDENBURG #5                            142 C
00007    BACH         MAGDELAINE SUITE                          142 C
00008    BACH         MAGNIFICAT                                118 C
00009    BACH         SONATAS FOR HARPSICHORD & VIOLA (3)       065 C
00010    BACH         SWITCHED ON BACH SUITE #2                 142 E
```

Figure 12.5.1. DISPLAY for a sorted file.

To delete an entire file, use the second form of 12.5.3) and supply *filename*.

RENAME

RENAME gives a new name to an existing file as in (12.5.2) after sorting people to temp. RENAME takes this form,

    RENAME thisname TO thatname   (12.5.7)

Multiple Sort Fields

Sometimes a file is most useful when it is ordered according to *two or more* fields. A printout of a sales file is best reviewed when listed by salesman, then by date, sales and order number. Another valuable listing is by account number, and within an account, by sales date. Here account number is the **primary sort key;** sales date is the **secondary sort key.** Sorting may involve several **levels** of keys.

The dBase sort only handles one sort key at a time. Do multiple key sorts by performing sorts in this order: *primary key sort* last; the other sorts in reverse order of their importance.

For the people file, arrange it by last name, then by first name, thus,

    .use people
    .sort on fname to temp1
    .use temp1
    .sort on lname to temp2   (12.5.8)

After this, the resulting file is checked, the old files deleted and the result file, temp2 is renamed.

DBPlus

Humansoft produces DBPlus, a set of several utility programs among which is a sort. This sort has three clear advantages over that found in dBase II:

- it is several times faster;
- it is totally menu driven;
- you can request a single sort on multiple fields in whatever priority required, using either ascending or descending order.

The Index

An **index** is a separate auxiliary file constructed using one or more fields. It helps you find records quickly. An indexed file acts just like a sorted file. An index made with a single field contains each field value in collating sequence order and the relative location (record number) of records with that value in the parent file. Usually (but not always) the index file is shorter, more compact and easier to use than the parent file.

Issue FIND to find a record or set of records when an index is created and in use. DBase looks in the index for the first entry which contains the value furnished, to find the first record in the main file with that value. DBase now keeps track of records through the index; the pp (present position) points to the current *indexed* record.

You can then supply additional criteria not associated with the index when asking for records with DISPLAY. Then dBase uses the index to find candidate records which it then screens against the criteria found in the DISPLAY command. The system response time for an indexed search is shorter than for a serial search.

Use

There are several steps in setting up and using an index. These are

1. Create the index with INDEX;
2. Connect the index and the file with USE;
3. Locate a record which has specific field values, with FIND;
4. Examine records with LIST, BROWSE or DISPLAY.

Figure 12.5.2 illustrates the four steps above. After tape is put into USE, an index is requested with INDEX. DBase displays the progress of the sort, which in this case takes about 2½ minutes. Next, the works of a composer are sought; note that the name need not be surrounded by quotes, but it must be entered as all capitals to agree with the entry in the file. DISPLAY is for more items than are listed for BACH, so the next composer is found. The remainder of the figure constrasts the use of DISPLAY with tapec, which takes longer because the tape must be examined to the end.

We now examine these activities more closely in the order of the listing above.

Creating

Use INDEX to create an auxiliary index file for a main file *now in use* thus,

INDEX ON field1 [+ field2,...] TO ndxname   (12.5.9)

12.5 FACILITATION   469

```
. use tape
. index on composer to cndx
00100 RECORDS INDEXED
00200 RECORDS INDEXED
00300 RECORDS INDEXED
00340 RECORDS INDEXED
. find BACH
. disp next 7 composer piece tape
00007   BACH              SONATAS FOR HARPSICHORD & VIOLA (3)   065
00170   BACH              MAGNIFICAT                             118
00251   BACH              SWITCHED ON BACH SUITE #2              142
00252   BACH              2 PART INVENT IN A/A SHEEPMAY SAFELY   142
00253   BACH              MAGDELAINE SUITE                       142
00254   BACH              BRANDENBURG #5                         142
00092   BAEZ,JOAN         VOLUME 5                               095
. use tapec
. disp all composer piece tape
. disp all for composer="BA" composer piece tape
00005   BACH              2 PART INVENT IN A/A SHEEPMAY SAFELY   142
00006   BACH              BRANDENBURG #5                         142
00007   BACH              MAGDELAINE SUITE                       142
00008   BACH              MAGNIFICAT                             118
00009   BACH              SONATAS FOR HARPSICHORD & VIOLA (3)    065
00010   BACH              SWITCHED ON BACH SUITE #2              142
00011   BAEZ,JOAN         VOLUME 5                               095
00012   BARATI            CHAMBER CONC                           083
00013   BARBER            QUARTET                                113
00014   BARBER            SYMPH #1                               079
00015   BARTOK            CONC #1                                103
00016   BARTOK            CONC #3                                103
00017   BARTOK            CONC 2 PIANOS & PERCUSSION             111
00018   BARTOK            DIVERTMENTO FOR STRINGS                073
00019   BARTOK            MUSIC STRING PERC & CEL                111
WAITING
.
```

Figure 12.5.2. Indexing tape on composer with cndx; using FIND.

Here *field1* is the field on which the index is created; the index file is the name you provide, *ndxname,* with the extension NDX. When several fields are used (*field2*, etc.), field names are connected by + in the command.

To create a last name index for the people file, use,

.use people
.index on lname to pndx1   (12.5.10)

The action may take several minutes. A message appears for each 100 records examined. A completion message summarizes the action and the dot prompt appears. The index just created is automatically connected now to the primary file. To give some idea of time, it takes about 2½ minutes to prepare an auxiliary index file on the composer field for the tape file consisting of 340 records.

Request an index on both last name and first name for the people file with

.index on lname+fname to pndx2   (12.5.11)

Connecting the Index

You connect an index to a primary file with USE thus,

   .USE file INDEX index   (12.5.12)

Here *file* is the primary file name and *index* is the name of an index file created earlier. Connect the first index file to people with

   .use people index pndx1   (12.5.13)

You may create several index files with different (simple or multiple) keys. But *only one index may be in use at any time.* USE both disconnects the present index file and connects another index file. To switch to pndx2,

   .use people index pndx2   (12.5.14)

Effect

Creating *and* connecting an index to a file changes the *effective* order of the file; the file *seems* to be in the order provided by the index key. This is evident when you use LIST or DISPLAY. After (12.5.13), issue

   .list   (12.5.15)

and the people file displays in order of last name.

    GO TOP and GO BOTTOM is with respect to the *index file*. For (12.5.13), TOP and BOTTOM find the alphabetically lowest and highest last name record in people respectively. Only GO *num* is unaffected.

    NEXT requests more records *according to their order in the indexed file.* Use *scope* with indexed DISPLAY, for example,

   .display next 3 lname fname phone   (12.5.16)

Updating

An index is established with the particular set of records currently stored in the file. When you add or delete records, the index becomes incorrect, unless it too is updated. Updating records of a file *with an index connected* also updates that index. This is very convenient.

    But what happens if you have created several different indexes? With USE, (12.5.13), only one index is connected to the file for query. You may connect *all the indexes* to be simultaneously updated by any of these commands:

- APPEND
- EDIT
- REPLACE
- PACK
- CHANGE

To make indexes available during alteration, use,

SET INDEX TO index1 [index2] ... [indexn] (12.5.17)

FIND

FIND locates records by indexed key field(s) and can only be used with an index attached. It takes this form,

FIND value(s) (12.5.18)

For the simple index (one established for a single key field), the request is terse. Since the field name and type are associated with the index, neither is repeated in the command. Hence character variables *need not* be surrounded by quotes. To find Smith in the people file, make this request,

.use people index pndx1
.find Smith (12.5.19)

A partial value request is also honored. Find those with last names starting with "Sm" thus,

.find Sm (12.5.20)

FIND sets the present position (pp) when it finds the first matching key in the index and then produces a new action prompt.

Multiple Fields

For an index created on several fields, you may specify values for them in FIND, each separated by a blank. For example,

.use people ndxp2
.find Smith John   (12.5.21)

You may still use **FIND** with a value for only the first field. Thus **find Smith** works fine in (12.5.21). But you *cannot* supply a value for the second field alone—**find John** does not work. Hence the rule is: You may supply fewer values than the maximum for the index with **FIND**, as long as they start with the first field the file was indexed on and are consecutive.

FIND may turn up a record for which the indexed fields have the value(s) or partial values you supply. Then it sets the pp accordingly. It may turn up none, in which case it displays the message,

NO FIND   (12.5.22)

To see a record found with **FIND**, use **DISPLAY**. The entire record displays with

.display   (12.5.23)

To see selected fields, name them thus,

.display title fname lname   (12.5.24)

More than one record displays using **NEXT** command thus,

.display next 5   (12.5.25)

The next five records determined by the index display in index order. If there are less than five with that field value, only these display. You can use *scope* and *range* with **DISPLAY** thus,

.display next 5 title fname lname   (12.5.26)

The title, first and last name only display for the next five records found. If less than five records remain, an end of file message appears.

Example.

Figure 12.5.2 shows examples **INDEX**, **FIND**, and **DISPLAY**. Recall that **tape** is ordered by tape number, not by composer. **INDEX** creates an index; **FIND** and **DISPLAY** then function on the composer field. The remainder of the figure displays a similar result with the sorted file, **tapec**, using **LOCATE**.

LOCATE

LOCATE works like FIND *but uses no index.* LOCATE reviews a file sequentially to find records which meet specific criteria. It takes this form.

    LOCATE [scope] criteria   (12.5.27)

Criteria always appears to supply the characteristics of the records sought. When *scope* is omitted (explained shortly), LOCATE examines the file from the beginning. It stops at the first record which meets the criteria, sets the pp and presents the record number. You can now display the record or selected fields.

For example, search for the first record with the title Dr., with

    locate for title = 'Dr.'   (12.5.28)

When found, its number displays thus,

    RECORD 00029   (12.5.29)

Since the pp is at 29, you can display its fields selectively with

    .display title fname lname   (12.5.30)

Since LOCATE does not use an index, (12.5.25) shows all the fields of the located record and the four immediately after, regardless of whether *they* meet the criteria.

There may be more records in the file which fulfill *criteria*. To point the pp to the next of these, use

    CONTINUE   (12.5.31)

You might issue the truncated form thus,

    .cont   (12.5.32)

DBase finds the next record meeting the criteria of the preceding LOCATE and displays its record number. You may show the information in that record with DISPLAY as in (12.5.30). When no more records meet the criteria, then CONTINUE gives a message to that effect:

    END OF FILE ENCOUNTERED   (12.5.33)

Starting Point

Many commands set the present position pointer (such as GO). To find records which meet criteria but which lie after the current pp setting, supply *scope* with LOCATE. Indicate the number of records to examine against the *criteria*. *Scope* can exceed the number of remaining records without a problem; LOCATE produces a message when it hits the end of file. Here is an example of how to initiate a search from this pp setting for multiple criteria:

.locate next 100 for title='Dr.' .and. state='CT' (12.5.34)

Examples

Figure 12.5.3 shows some interesting things about FIND and LOCATE. Let's examine it from the beginning. The file called tape has been sorted on composer to make a new file, tapec. We could make a query about composer using DISPLAY or LIST. LOCATE takes us to any composer by name or partial name and from there we could display continously. However, now we have lost the ability to present things in order of tape number. To remedy this, we have created an index called tndx which sits on top of this file and reorganizes it in terms of tape number.

Mind you, we could have done the inverse action: we could take tape and provide an index on top of this, cndx, so that we could find any composer with FIND. Either action works, but tndx is smaller because it is created on a three character field, namely the tape number. Recall from Figure 12.2.2. that the composer field is 18 characters long.

Using a Memory Variable

During the rest of the example, I want to give a long display command. So instead of issuing it each time I need it, I store the command in a cell called R. That is the purpose of the second line. After dBase puts the string away in the memory variable, it repeats its contents on the third line for you to verify.

On the fourth line, I position to record number 140. Note that this is a *record* number, not a *tape* number. Now I give the command to display the next three records. The command itself in R does not print. I precede the command with an ampersand. If I simply key Rreturn, dBase would reject this, because it attaches no meaning to R alone. The ampersand indicates that I want to use the contents of the variable, R.

The next three records display below this command. Notice that the first of these has record number 140, just as I had expected. However the two

```
. use tapec index tndx
. store "display next 3 composer piece tape" to R
display next 3 composer piece tape
. 140
. &R
00140    INDONESIA              GAMELON                            067
00142    IVES                   3 PLACES IN NEW ENGLAND            068
00196    MIXED                  AMERICAN MUSIC FESTIVAL            068
. find 140
. &R
00050    BROSHI, GEO.           SYMPHONY                           140
00081    COWELL                 SYMP #5                            140
00083    CROFT                  CONC FOR PERCUSSION                140
. &R
00083    CROFT                  CONC FOR PERCUSSION                140
00129    HOVHANESS              MAGIC MOUNTAIN                     140
00304    STRAVINSKY             SYMP IN D                          140
. use tapec
. 140
. &R
00140    INDONESIA              GAMELON                            067
00141    IVES                   3 PAGE SONATA, SOUTH PAW PITCH     090
00142    IVES                   3 PLACES IN NEW ENGLAND            068
. locate for tape="100"
RECORD: 00023
. &R
00023    BARTOK                 V & P SONATA #1                    100
00024    BARTOK                 V & P SONATA #2                    100
00025    BEATLES                ABBEY ROAD                         124
. continue
RECORD: 00076
. &R
00076    CORRELLI               MISC                               100
00077    COUNTRY JOE            MISC                               126
00078    COUNTRY JOE & FISH     MISC                               121
. cont
END OF FILE ENCOUNTERED
.
```

Figure 12.5.3. Examples of retrieval using an index and FIND.

that follow are numbered 142 and 196. Next refers to the **ipp**, the **indexed present position**. From the top line, you see that the file is indexed with respect to tape number, which is in the right column; the selections are in tape number sequence.

Following, on the next line I issue FIND and refer to tape reel number 140. Note that the next three selections belong to reel 140 and are in alphabetical order.

Issuing DISPLAY again shows three more selections from tape 140. However the last of the previous group is the first of this group because the ipp is not advanced after use.

Without an Index

Let's disconnect the index with use tapec in Figure 12.5.3. We put the file into use again but do not specify an index. Again, let us specify record 140.

Recall that the record number is associated with a record regardless of the index in use. Therefore we would expect to position to the Gamalon selection. The display command shows the next three records, but since there is no index in use, the present position pointer is the reference marker and the next three successive records present. Tapec is in alphabetical order by composer whereas the tape number field skips about.

LOCATE

Next, issue LOCATE asking for the first item on reel 100. DBase tells us it has found record number 23. Now we ask it to display the next three records with the command &R. Items are in alphabetical order by composer and not in tape reel order (except one, accidentally).

CONTINUE asks dBase to find the next record which fulfills the LOCATE (the next item on reel 100). Now we display three successive records the first of which, has a tape number of 100. The next CONTINUE (here abbreviated cont) doesn't turn up any record, as evidenced by the message to that effect. There are no more selections on reel 100.

An Experiment

Each of the tape files described consists of 340 selections. There are exactly three selections on tape 100. I thought it would be interesting to find out how long it would take to find them using various techniques using dBase II with CP/M on a fast Z80 computer. Here are the results. First, let's try without an index using tape directly:

- locating the first record takes 14 seconds;
- displaying the three records and getting a prompt takes 1 second.

Now let us attach the index by tape numbers, tndx:

- FIND gets the first record almost instantaneously;
- LOCATE takes 42 seconds to find the first record;
- DISPLAY with a request to find all the records for which the tape number is 100 comes up with all three in 44 seconds. However, it takes 2 minutes and 21 seconds altogether to get the prompt back because dBase continues to look.

As you can see, LOCATE with or without an index is not nearly as fast as FIND with an index. The LOCATE and DISPLAY functions are slowed down by an index on the field sought.

12.6 FILE UPDATE AND MODIFICATION; UTILITIES

INSERT

INSERT puts a new record anyplace in the file. It takes this form.

INSERT [BEFORE] [BLANK] (12.6.1)

It operates at the present pp setting. To put a new record in the file, first find the record it belongs after; set the pp with GOTO or LOCATE, then give INSERT thus,

.insert (12.6.2)

The original input record form associated with the file appears on the screen with the cursor positioned at the first character of the first field. Type values for fields you want to enter now. Use *edit* commands to alter information when you make mistakes. After entering the last field, hit return and the record is put away.

The new record goes *after* the one to which the pp points, so dBase must rewrite the entire bottom portion of the file to make a place for the new record *after each* INSERT. For large files it takes considerable time to copy *all* the records past the pp. Hence Figure 12.6.1 shows a record INSERTed after #4; record 5 through 100 must be copied to become 6 through 101 to make room. APPEND is better to add a group of records, examined shortly.

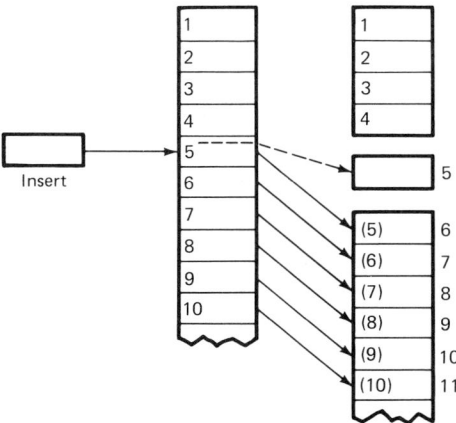

Figure 12.6.1. INSERT puts a new record in the file and recopies the bottom of the file.

To put the new record *before* the current pp, use

   .insert before   (12.6.3)

Perhaps you know where a new record should go but you don't want to fill it in now. Specify **BLANK** and a blank record goes after (or before) the pp (present position) and the file is reorganized; no record form is presented. An action prompt appears after the file has been rewritten. This is requested thus,

   .insert blank   (12.6.4)

To add records you might first print the file, showing record numbers. If a record should be inserted after record 36, call up a form to fill out thus,

   .36
   .insert   (12.6.5)

Suppose, from the listing, the *next* new record goes after record 123. Make sure that you position *to 124* instead; you have inserted a new record at position 37 and all record numbers have increased by one.

LOCATE also finds where a new record belongs. **LOCATE** for the key value of the record to be added comes up with **END OF FILE** because the record with that key is missing. Therefore **LOCATE** the record *right after* the one where this one goes. For instance, to insert a new record for Mr. Hanson in a sorted file, issue these:

   .locate for lname >'Hanson'
   .display
   .insert before   (12.6.6)

DISPLAY verifies that the record belongs here. Should you have Hanson in the file,

   .locate for lname> ='Hanson'   (12.6.7)

APPEND

APPEND adds records to the end of a file. We have seen how it is used with **CREATE** to enter records originally as in Figure 12.6.2A. It takes two other forms. Here are the prototypes,

12.6 FILE UPDATE AND MODIFICATION; UTILITIES

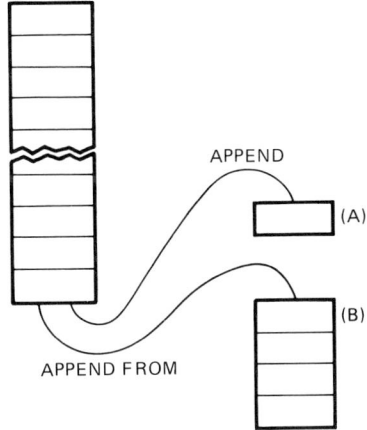

Figure 12.6.2. APPEND adds a new record or file to the end of the file in USE.

APPEND FROM file [criteria] [SDF]
APPEND BLANK
APPEND (12.6.8)

For the first form, set up another file with the same format (see COPY) but with a different name. Enter records there and then later APPEND that file to the original file as in Figure 12.6.2B. This is especially useful in a multiuser system where entering records would tie a file up, preventing access by other users. Instead, one or more files for appending (NAMES1, NAMES2, etc.) may be in use for adding new records while a user queries the original.

For example, an operator puts new names in a file called nupeople, while people is available for query. After nupeople is prepared, it is pasted to people with

.use people
.append from nupeople (12.6.9)

The resulting file may be reordered with SORT.

To APPEND only some new records, *criteria* in (12.6.8) describes which. Appended records should then be deleted from the transaction file to prevent later duplication:

.append from nupeople for .not. lname=' '
.use nupeople
.delete for .not. lname=' ' (12.6.10)

It is also possible to create the additional file on a word processor which uses the standard data format for ASCII text files. In that case, the option SDF is included with APPEND to have dBase alter them to its format. Then records are reformatted by dBase before they are appended to the existing file.

REPLACE

REPLACE enters values in one or more fields of records in a file in use,

    REPLACE scope field WITH value [more] [criteria] (12.6.11)

Scope specifies which records to consider and could be ALL or NEXT *n* or omitted (then REPLACE only applies to the record at the pp). *Field* is the name of the field where *value* is entered. The phrase *field* WITH *value* may occur more than once. That is, you can specify several fields and a value for each; these additional replacements require additional phrases represented by *more*. Finally, *criteria* selects records from those described by *scope*. Changes are made only in selected records. Examples follow to make this clear.

Scope

When *scope* is omitted, REPLACE applies to the current record given by the pp. If you find a record which is incorrect for one or more values of its fields (as seen with DISPLAY), then you can issue REPLACE immediately thus,

    .replace phone with '987-6543' (12.6.12)

If the next few records are incorrect in one field and should be changed to the same value, request with a single command like,

    .replace next 3 code with 'C' (12.6.13)

where the next three records have (C) entered into their code field. This is illustrated in Figure 12.6.3.

REPLACE is most powerful for the ALL option. Adjust the cost of all items in your inventory file by a designated factor with a single command thus,

    .replace all cost with 1.1*cost (12.6.14)

Values in the cost field of all records are increased by 10%.

12.6 FILE UPDATE AND MODIFICATION; UTILITIES

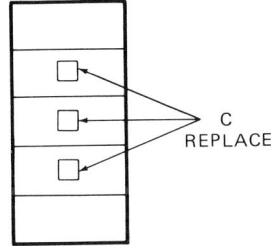

Figure 12.6.3. REPLACE alters the same field in several records.

As another example, enter the new values for **grosspay** in this week's payroll file which is based on new **hours** and the current **rate**. Then calculate pay with

.replace all grosspay with hours*rate (12.6.15)

Selective

To update selectively, supply *criteria*. For instance, those on vacation, **hours** is empty; assume 35. Suppose that vacation is specified by **status**. DBase does the calculations with

.replace all grosspay with 35*rate for status='V' (12.6.16)

Selection might be on the current value of the specified field. For instance, in the **tape** file some records I prepared had a blank in the field, **code**. This was an oversight. To replace all of them with the code letter **C** for "classical," use

.replace all code with 'C' for code=' ' (12.6.17)

CHANGE

CHANGE reviews selected file records of a file submitting them to you to replace existing values with those entered from the keyboard. It takes this form,

CHANGE scope FIELD list [criteria] (12.6.18)

Scope determines which records are examined. *List* is a set of field names whose values are offered to you for change. *Criteria* selects records.

Position dBase where changes are to be made. Then issue a command such as

.change next 10 field date   (12.6.19)

DBase offers the date field of the next ten records to be altered thus,

RECORD:00028
DATE: 08/19/81
CHANGE? 19
TO: 29

DATE: 08/29/81
CHANGE? return   (12.6.20)

DBase presents its record number and current date value, then it asks for a change. Reply by typing characters of the field. If they appear more than once, the first occurrence is used.

When dBase prompts TO:, enter replacement characters. In (12.6.20), type the correct day, 29. DBase skips a screen line and then shows the field name with its new content. You get another chance with the prompt CHANGE? If satisfied, hit return. Figure 12.6.4 shows that CHANGE

1. Extracts a record;
2. Lets you alter it;
3. Returns it to the file.

With CHANGE you don't see other information in the record. In the example above, you might want to change the dates of some transactions if you know their nature. Nevertheless, CHANGE is powerful when incorporated in a command program (see Section 12.7) which displays other information about the record and then provides a quick means for editing.

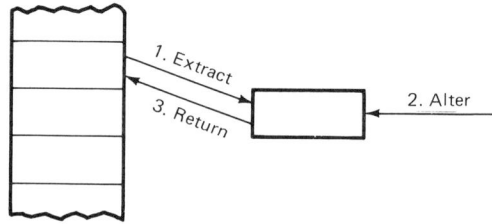

Figure 12.6.4. CHANGE presents selected field for several records for user to change.

12.6 FILE UPDATE AND MODIFICATION; UTILITIES   483

Another Example

My data base, tape has a field also called tape which contains a three digit tape number. For tapes with numbers below 100, I enter two digits such as 77. Since a character field is left justified, this is recorded as two 7's and a blank. It is recorded thus, "77 ".

Sorting tape by number puts 77 after 100, not what I would expect. I have to change 77 to 077. That was easy to do with CHANGE.

.change all field tape for ' ' $tape   (12.6.21)

Criteria asks for records with a tape field that contains a blank somewhere. Their tape number is presented for change. For '77'. ask that 7 be replaced by 07. This pushes the field over to contain 077 as required.

You can stop CHANGE any time by pressing escape.

UPDATE

An operator prepares a transaction file without reference to a master file. In multiuser systems, data entry should not interfere with other users of the data base. The information from the transaction file is passed to the master file in use with UPDATE invoked thus,

UPDATE FROM tfile ON key [ADD afields] [REPLACE rfields]
(12.6.22)

Tfile is the transaction file with new information. There are always two files associated with UPDATE. Records on the two files are matched on the *key* field. When a key match occurs, the contents of *afields* from the record on *tfile* are added to values in *afields* of the master record. Fields of the *tfile* record indicated by *rfields* replace those in the master record. Remaining master fields are unaffected. This is shown in Figure 12.6.5.

Both files *must be in key order*. Both must be sorted, except that the one in USE could have an index. This is the sequence:

1. A transaction record is read and its key extracted;
2. Master records are read in order until one is found which matches the transaction record;
3. The indicated fields are replaced or added to;
4. If a higher master record key is found first, the transaction record is discarded.

484 DATA BASE

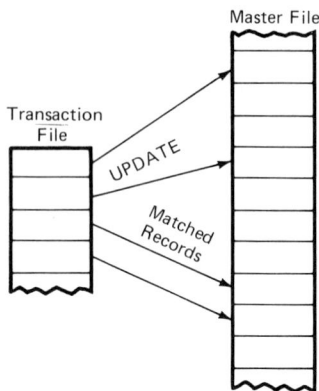

Figure 12.6.5. UPDATE changes master file records (in USE) according to records in a transaction file.

Thus records are ignored on both files if there is no record with a corresponding key in the other file.

This philosphy is all right for master records but creates a problem for transaction records which do not match. The key was probably entered incorrectly. However, when a record is ignored, there is no way of knowing that the information has been bypassed. To avoid this problem, UPDATE is best incorporated in a command program (Section 12.7).

Examples

Here is how update might be used with a simplified sales recording file:

```
.use master
.update from trans on id add cost tax netcost
   replace status date                            (12.6.23)
```

For matched records, the cost and the taxes for this purchase are added to the customer's record. The status and latest date of action are replaced.

Another example applies to an inventory file.

```
.update from invtrns on partnum add onhand
   replace date                                   (12.6.24)
```

It applies to both receipts and withdrawals. The onhand quantity for each transaction is added to the current onhand quantity for the master. For a withdrawal, onhand is negative in the transaction file record.

COPY

This utility copies files, providing additional facilities. COPY does the following:

1. Duplicates a file, giving the copy a different name;
2. Copies chosen fields in the order designated;
3. Reformats a file to be used for other purposes;
4. Copies only the file structure if requested.

Here is the format of the command:

    COPY TO newfile scope FIELD flist criteria [SDF] [STRUCTURE]
        [DELIMITED [WITH delim]]   (12.6.25)

where

    Newfile is the name of the new file created.
    Scope may restrict the records to be examined for copying to *newfile*.
    Flist lists fields in the order they are placed in *newfile*.
    Criteria is a FOR expression describing how to choose records.
    SDF puts the output file in standard data format;
    STRUCTURE requests an empty file with the structure of the original file;
    DELIMITED says that fields of the new file are separated by some character;
    WITH *delim* says that fields of the record are separated by the *delim* character.

Examples

First let's copy the file in use to a new file, *tape1*

    .copy to tape1   (12.6.26)

For the same file (illustrations use the file called **tape**) make a copy of records with a code of **C**,

    .copy to clastape for code = 'C'   (12.6.27)

Copy only composer, piece and tape number to **tapex**,

    .copy field composer piece tape to tapex   (12.6.28)

486　DATA BASE

Do the same but only for classical pieces,

    .copy field composer piece tape to tapexc for code = 'C'　(12.6.29)

Let's just copy the next ten items,

    .copy next 10 to btapes　(12.6.30)

We might copy the whole file, putting it in standard data format thus,

    .copy to tape.dat sdf　(12.6.31)

Finally, we might make a similar copy but this time delimit fields with a /,

    .copy to tapes.txt delimited with /　(12.6.32)

MODIFY

This command takes two forms. The first is

    MODIFY STRUCTURE　(12.6.33)

It gives an existing file a different structure: adds or deletes fields or changes field size. The second form, for constructing command programs, is examined in Section 12.7. MODIFY (12.6.33) flushes out all records from *an existing file*. If you apply it to a structure you have just created but you have put no records there, there is no danger.

With COPY

The following set of commands modifies **tape** without destroying the contents:

    .use tape
    .copy to work structure
    .use work
    .modify structure
       Use edit commands to modify work.
    .append from tape
    .browse
    .delete file tape
    .use
    .rename work to tape　(12.6.34)

Once the structure of tape is copied to work, MODIFY lets you modify work's structure:

1. Enter a new field definition;
2. Delete a field;
3. Shorten or lengthen a field.

When satisfied with the new structure of work, you can append the records from tape which dBase handles thus:

- data in deleted fields is ignored;
- in shortened fields, data is truncated—removed from the right;
- there is no data in the old file for a new field.

Verify that records have been properly copied *and* that the structure is correct with BROWSE. Then delete the old file and rename work to tape. The extra USE takes all files out of use so that RENAME can operate.

Editing the Structure

When you issue MODIFY, the file structure appears on the screen. Edit the structure as you would a record. The edit commands of Table 12.2.1 are applicable with the addition of two more:

- ^N inserts a blank line wherever the cursor is;
- ^T deletes the line that the cursor is on.

Transform

An easier way to transform files is to use dBPlus, sold by Humansoft. Transform is only one program of dBPlus, invoked and specified completely by menu. You define new fields, shorten or lengthen fields, or eliminate fields, all from the menu. Field position in the record is also under your control. Once you have defined the new structure, the utility creates a file with a new name and transfers all the records there.

12.7 COMMAND FILES

Introduction

Command files are programs written in **dBase language** with a text editor or with MODIFY COMMAND, requested after dBase is invoked. These files can be accessed only from dBase and do not execute on their own—

they are not machine language programs. They have the extension **CMD**, or **PRG** for later versions (not **COM**). From dBase you ask to execute a command file at the prompt thus,

    DO cname   (12.7.1)

where *cname* is the command file. You may also start a command file running as you bring up dBase with

    .dbase cname   (12.7.2)

Creation

Use **MODIFY** to create a command file in this form,

    MODIFY COMMAND cname   (12.7.3)

Key in the program as you would text. Each command occupies a line and terminates with return. The edit codes of Table 12.2.1 operate with **MODIFY** as a screen editor for creating command programs.

Commands

What kind of commands are there? They

1. Manipulate the screen, clear it and display messages and variables;
2. Establish variable to hold constants and information from the keyboard;
3. Create loops and call other command programs as subroutines;
4. May include any dBase command discussed earlier.

Power

DBase provides mnemonics to do many simple things. When used as primitives and built upon, many complex functions can be created. For example, although **REPORT** makes crude reports, you can design command programs which provide more flexibility.

Modifying the Screen

Commands construct menus and puts messages anyplace on the screen. Recall from Chapter 3 that cursor positioning and full or partial erase is activated by control code sequences unique to each vendor's terminal. Hence, to get the benefit from screen dBase commands, it is vital that proper control sequences are sent to *your* terminal. You (or your dealer) must customize the dBase terminal driver to suit your terminal with the INSTALL program provided

ERASE

When your DO program takes over, there may be junk showing. It's neat to erase the screen with

ERASE   (12.7.4)

which may also be given directly from dBase.

Display Something

Let's now look at two commands:

?[?] something   (12.7.5)

NOTE message   (12.7.6)

The single ? displays the value of *something* which can be

- the name of a data base field;
- a constant;
- an expression;
- a memory variable;
- a function.

Used directly, dBase puts the value on the next screen line. Here are examples,

```
.? 5+9
   14
```
(12.7.7)

```
.? lname
   Hanson
```
(12.7.8)

```
.? 'First Name:' fname
   First Name: Albert
```
(12.7.9)

```
.? #
   19
```
(12.7.10)

For (12.7.7), dBase calculates a quantity. For (12.7.8), dBase shows the contents of a field; (12.7.9) prints a message *and* the content of the field; (12.7.10) shows the number of the record to which the pp points. Above, ? interrogates dBase from its action prompt (.). ? may also be used in a command program, for which it produces no prompt, and then produce a new dot prompt on the line below.

For the double question mark (??), the question is answered on the same line; no line advance occurs as with (?). This may be used in a command program to write several items on the same line.

NOTE puts a message in the program, but has no effect on the display. Here is an example,

```
? 'This message displays.'
NOTE This does not
NOTE The next line is skipped on the display
?
? 'There is a blank line before this one'
```
(12.7.11)

Screen Position and Display

While the question mark displays answers on the next screen line, @ moves the cursor and displays a message thus,

@ coord [SAY message] (12.7.12)

Coord is where *message* starts and is given with

coord :: line,position (12.7.13)

Here *line* is the line number and *position* is the character number on the line where display begins. *Message* displays if provided after SAY and takes this form,

message::'string',variable (12.7.14)

A string of letters or characters is included at *string* within quotes or a variable or expression may be evaluated and presented. For example,

```
erase
@ 3,5 SAY 'Account Name:',Acct:Nam
@ 4,5 Say 'Account Number:',Acct:Num
```
(12.7.15)

displays messages and field values on lines 3 and 4 at position 5 of each. Thus SAY is like ? with cursor positioning.

You may also specify coordinates relatively, referring to the current line or position number by $. Thus (12.7.15) might be rewritten as

```
erase
@ 3,5 SAY 'Account Name:', Acct:Nam
@ $+1,5 SAY 'Account Number:', Acct:Num          (12.7.16)
```

Memory Variables

The dBase language provides for variables which you establish, as in BASIC, by naming them in a STORE statement, thus,

STORE expression TO name $\qquad$ (12.7.17)

The value described by *expression* is placed in the variable called *name*, the object of TO. The variable takes on the quality of the value stored there. If the variable was previously defined, the new value replaces the present content; otherwise a new memory location is established for *name*.

Here is how a string is stored in Coname:

.store "IBM Corp" to Coname $\qquad$ (12.7.18)

Then a numeric variable is established as Hours,

.store 53 to Hours $\qquad$ (12.7.19)

Next, a value described by an expression which refers to a defined variable is stored in a new variable,

.store Hours−40 to Otime $\qquad$ (12.7.20)

Display

There are two ways to display the contents of a memory variable. One is with ? thus,

```
.? Otime
13                                                (12.7.21)
```

for one or more named cells. All cells in use are displayed with

> DISPLAY MEMORY (12.7.22)

One or more memory cells can be destroyed and made available for future use thus,

> RELEASE name (12.7.23)

Data put in a memory variable during this session is in memory and disappears when the equivalent is turned off. To keep it for the next session, use SAVE,

> SAVE TO file [ALL LIKE form] (12.7.24)

where *file* is a disk file with extension .MEM. To save all memory variables to vfile use,

> save to vfile (12.7.25)

Form is a stencil with wild cards to let you store variables selectively, thus

> save to vfile all like M??? (12.7.26)

saves MAct, MNam, but not Money (five characters). When you start dBase, bring back variables with RESTORE:

> RESTORE FROM file [ADDITIVE] (12.7.27)

This fills variables from *file* but deletes existing variables unless ADDITIVE is specified.

INPUT

Input commands get information from the keyboard. Characters and variables input thus are the basis of decisions and direct the program.

WAIT

WAIT helps the operator select from a menu. It takes this form,

> WAIT [TO char] (12.7.28)

where *char* is the name of a single character variable for which the value is set from the keyboard when a key is hit (without return). Consider a program to examine tape selections. Issue a *prompt* (?) to the operator to select pieces according to type, implemented with WAIT thus,

> ? 'Hit letter for type of piece to display:'
> wait to Incode   (12.7.29)

Incode is the memory variable where the character entered is stored. (Memory variables are shown hereafter with an initial capital.)

WAIT without a destination lets the operator terminate a display. Thus a paragraph shows on the screen for the operator to read. It ends with a request to hit any key when ready. The key stroke reactivates the program but is not saved. The program can now display the next panel to the operator.

INPUT

INPUT displays a prompt *and* accepts a multiple keystroke input of any kind,

> INPUT['prompt'] TO variable   (12.7.30)

Below INPUT requests a composer name for which compositions are sought,

> input 'Enter the name of a composer' to Incomp   (12.7.31)

The operator must bracket the composer's name with quotes since it is a character string. The prompt may be omitted. This is handy when the screen is formatted previously by other commands such as with,

> erase
> @ 9,10 say 'Enter Composer's Name:"
> input to Incomp   (12.7.32)

The prompt appears on line 9 and the cursor goes to line 10 to echo the operator's response.

ACCEPT

ACCEPT makes it unnecessary to place character strings in quotes as with,

> ACCEPT ['prompt'] TO variable   (12.7.33)

and would be used thus,

> accept "What is the name of the piece?" to Inpiece   (12.7.34)

494 DATA BASE

Combining Screen Formatting with Input

GET and READ both format the screen and acquire variables keyed in. DBase moves the cursor to the screen position named in the command to display what the operator enters. GET is combined into an extended form of @ thus,

@ coord [SAY message] [GET variable] (12.7.35)

Message is presented on the screen at the *coord* position. If GET is included, *variable* refers to something previously defined with a STORE command (in the case of a memory variable). Otherwise *variable* may be a field of a record currently in use.

Separate SAY and GET

First we examine the case where SAY and GET are on different screen (and command) lines. SAY puts a message on one line; then the cursor positions to the line and position as directed by @ for GET. For instance, in (12.7.36) below, the first command gives the operator the name of the datum required; the second accepts what is keyed, displays it at line 3, and puts it in a memory location called Title.

@ 2,0 say 'Title'
@ 3,0 get Title (12.7.36)

A Sequence

A sequence of SAYs and GETs in a command program formats the screen to present all the prompts simultaneously. Following this sequence, READ places the cursor at the position designated by the first GET.

Now the operator keys in the value associated with this variable, followed by return. The cursor advances to the coordinates for the next GET. That variable is entered, and so on, until all GETs preceding the READ have been serviced. Then the command program goes to the next command after READ.

Example

To enter information for a name and address file, why not format the screen as below.

Title	Last Name	First Name	
[ ]			(12.7.37)

The header line describes the information collected on the line below. The cursor positions on the second line underneath the first field to be collected, Title. Enter the *title* and press return; the cursor moves under the second heading, Last Name. After entering it and pressing return, the cursor positions under the last heading. When it is entered and the operator presses return, the command program continues.

The original CREATE panel is presented in Figure 12.7.1. Below in the figure, the display program is printed by WordStar. First it establishes the three variables, Title, Fname, Lname and fills them with blanks. The screen is cleared. Now pairs of commands write the field description and then issue GETs against the field value.

GET positions the cursor under the first variable name. Entry occurs for the three values as described earlier. DISPLAY MEMORY in the program shows the memory variable values to the operator for verification. Figure 12.7.2 shows a more complete example, a printout of several entries.

Single Line

GET and SAY are commonly combined into a single line,

@ 10,4 say 'Title' get Title (12.7.38)

```
        create name
        ENTER RECORD STRUCTURE AS FOLLOWS:
        FIELD    NAME,TYPE,WIDTH,DECIMAL PLACES
        001      title,c,5
        002      lname,c,20
        003      fname,c,16
        004
        INPUT DATA NOW? N

   store "      " to Title
   store "                  " to Fname
   store "              " to Lname
   erase
   @ 2,0 say 'Title'
   @ 3,0 get Title
   @ 2,7 say 'Last Name'
   @ 3,7 get Lname
   @ 2,40 say 'First Name'
   @ 3,40 get Fname
   read
   display memory
   TITLE        (C)   Dr.
   FNAME        (C)   Ivan
   LNAME        (C)   Flores
   ** TOTAL **        03 VARIABLES USED   00044 BYTES USED
```

Figure 12.7.1. A command program to store values typed.

```
* Command program to add records to the NAME file.
use name
store ' ' to continu
do while continu <> 'S' .and. continu <> 's'
          append blank
          erase
          @ 2,0 say 'Title'
          @ 3,0 get Title
          @ 2,7 say 'First Name'
          @ 3,7 get Fname
          @ 2,40 say 'Last Name'
          @ 3,40 get Lname
          read
          accept "Hit S to stop" to continu
enddo
```

```
   .
     disp all
     00001  Dr.    Flores          Ivan
     00002  Dr.    Mendelsohn      Naomi
     00003  Mr.    Terry           Chris
     00004  Prof.  Rabinowitz      Mannus
   .
```

Figure 12.7.2. A command program to present a panel for entering new records into a file.

Messages are presented at the specified coordinates for a group of SAYs. When READ is encountered, the cursor is positioned after the first unsatisfied GET, directly after the colon following the SAY message. After entry, the cursor drops down to the colon after the next unsatisfied SAY, etc.

SAYs and GETs of Figure 12.7.2 are done in three lines instead of six in Figure 12.7.3.

Validating the Input

DBase checks data entered to verify that it conforms to a particular pattern. GET is followed by PICTURE thus,

    GET variable PICTURE 'format'   (12.7.39)

Format is a set of characters such as in the COBOL PICTURE which states whether numerals (9), letters (A) or specific characters should appear in each position keyed. For example consider,

    get ssnum picture '999-99-9999'   (12.7.40)

This requests a social security number consisting of exactly nine digits: three digits separated by a hyphen, two more and a hyphen and a final four. The

```
* ex3 Demonstrating say, get and picture
store "      " to Title
store "                  " to Fname
store "              " to Lname
store "          " to SSnum
erase
@ 2,5 say 'Title' get Title
@ 3,5 say 'Last Name' get Lname
@ 4,5 say 'First Name' get Fname
@ 5,5 say 'Social Security Number' get SSnum picture '999-99-9999'
read
display memory


        do ex3


        TITLE         (C)  Mr.
        FNAME         (C)  Morgan
        LNAME         (C)  Henry
        SSNUM         (C)  345-58-9878
        ** TOTAL **        04 VARIABLES USED   00056 BYTES USED
```

Figure 12.7.3. SAY GET can use PICTURE for data entry verification.

hyphens display and are automatically skipped over as the operator keys in the number. PICTURE is used in Figure 12.7.3. The data stored in variables by the program are displayed at the bottom of the figure.

Collecting Data

The program of Figure 12.7.1 collects data, but puts it in memory, not into the file. That's easy to do—just use field names instead of memory variables. A program to collect field values is shown in Figure 12.7.2. We examine its function a line at a time. Although we have not discussed WHILE, it works as with Pascal, Chapter 8, and gets attention soon.

1. A comment starts with *.
2. Put name in use.
3. Continu keeps track of whether the operator is done.
4. Continue WHILE the variable is not 'S'.
5. Append a blank record.
6. Erase the screen.
7-12. Set up for all the fields.
13. Read the operator's input into the record.
14. Ask if there are more records to enter.
15. Terminate the loop.

Unfortunately, there is no way to print out the screen contents during entry. As with the conventional format, if a field is not filled to its maximum, return advances to the next field.

The bottom of the figure shows DISPLAY used to verify the existence of the new (and only) record.

Decisions and Loops

Three powerful statements make decisions and provide loops: IF, CASE and DO WHILE.

Decisions

IF has this form,

IF criteria
    statement
    [statements]
[ELSE
    statements]
ENDIF   (12.7.41)

In its simple form, ELSE is omitted; IF and ENDIF bracket one or more statements, executed if *criteria* (12.7.41) proves true; if false, *none* of the statements is executed.

The inclusive form provides for both alternatives:

- If *criteria* is true, execute statements between IF and ELSE.
- If *criteria* proves false, then statements between ELSE and ENDIF are performed.

IF Example

As an example, consider a menu which allows the operator to choose the kind of query to make with reference to the tape file. A query can be initiated for a composer or for a particular piece of music. The menu asks the user to hit C to select a composer and P to choose a piece.

The choice initiates one or another command program, shocomp or shopiece. These have further menus (not shown) to name a composer or a piece. This command program chooses between two other command programs,

```
? 'Hit C to Select a Composer'
? 'Hit P to name a piece'
wait to Hit
if Hit = 'C'
     do shocomp
else
     do shopiece
endif                                                    (12.7.42)
```

The first two lines present messages. The next line stores the character entered in the memory variable Hit. IF checks whether C was struck and, if so, invokes shocomp. If some other key is struck then shopiece is entered.

IF statements may be **nested:** one of the statements after IF may be another IF. To demonstrate this, let's present three choices instead of two. This is to choose the type of composition (classical, folk, etc.). Here is a nested IF:

```
if Hit = 'C'
     do shocomp
else
     if Hit = 'P'
          do shopiece
     else
          do shotype
     endif
endif                                                    (12.7.43)
```

Note there must be one ENDIF for each IF.

Another form of decision, CASE, takes this form,

```
DO CASE
     CASE crit1
          statements
     CASE crit2
          statements
     . . . . . . . . . . . . . . . . . . . . . .
     [OTHERWISE
          statements]
ENDCASE                                                  (12.7.44)
```

Use as many CASE alternatives and statements as needed. OTHERWISE is a catch-all; if all criteria prove false, statements between it and END-CASE are done.

Now (12.7.43) is rewritten in a better form as

```
do case
   case Hit = 'C'
         do shocomp
   case Hit = 'P'
         do shopeice
   case Hit = 'T'
         do shotype
endcase
```
(12.7.45)

Loops

A **loop** is a set of statements which are repeated as long as a stated condition prevails. It takes this form,

```
DO WHILE criteria
   statements
ENDDO
```
(12.7.46)

Statements are repeated as sequence as long as *criteria* proves true. *Criteria* is checked before each repetition of the statements. Presumably one of the statements alters variables in the criteria.

As an example, refer to the **tape** file sorted on the composer field which is now in **USE**. The user chooses to display all pieces by a particular composer. The name of the composer is currently stored in the memory variable, Comp. Suppose that we have found the first instance of a selection by this composer with LOCATE. Here is a program segment to display all selections listed for this composer:

```
do while composer = Comp
   erase
   @ 5,10 say composer
   @ 5,60 say code
   @ 7,10 say piece
   ? 'Hit any key to continue'
   wait
   skip
enddo
```
(12.7.47)

Statements between do and enddo are repeated for each record as long as composer is the one chosen by the operator and stored at Comp. Since the first such record has been located, *criteria* proves true when DO WHILE is first encountered. The statements within the loop erase and format the screen to show the three fields of the first record in the chosen positions. One record appears and the operator has a chance to view it. No memory variable is associated with WAIT, so any key hit continues the program and the key's code is discarded.

The next command, SKIP, moves the pp to the next record in the file. That is the end of the loop. Only when the record skipped to has a composer field *different* from the one selected does the loop terminate.

Switches

DBase provides **switches** which record action alternatives. Those are listed in Table 12.7.1, along with their names, functions and default values. To set a *switch* to its alternate value, issue this command,

SET switch ON/OFF
SET switch TO data   (12.7.48)

Switches which can only be ON or OFF are set by the first line (12.7.48). The last three items in the table (20–22) use the second form of SET which supplies information at *data*.

Examples

The switch settings are explained in Table 12.7.1, but a few examples help clarify the overall intent.

As each command of a command file is executed, it also displays on the screen if ECHO is set ON.

TALK produces screen feedback when certain commands complete. For instance, when LOCATE turns up a record which meets *criteria*, the record number displays; if unsuccessful, an end of file message displays. This is helpful in the interactive mode. It is distracting when executing a command program, so a dBase program can SET TALK OFF.

BELL rings the terminal bell when a field is filled up during APPEND or EDIT; keys you hit thereafter put characters in the next field. The bell is helpful in some cases. But records with a lot of short fields keep the bell ringing. This becomes annoying, so why not

.set bell off   (12.7.49)

Table 12.7.1 SET Switches

	SWITCH	DEFAULT	MEANING
1.	ECHO	OFF	Commands from .CMD echo on screen.
2.	STEP	OFF	DBase halts after each command from .CMD file and waits for user to continue—for debugging command programs.
3.	TALK	ON	Command results display on screen
4.	PRINT	OFF	Display echoes to printer.
5.	CONSOLE	ON	Display goes to screen.
6.	ALTERNATE	OFF	Display goes to a disk file.
7.	SCREEN	ON	Full screen operations for EDIT, CREATE, etc.
8.	LINKAGE	OFF	Sequential commands apply to secondary file also.
9.	COLON	ON	GET is bounded by colons as with APPEND.
10.	BELL	ON	Bell sounds if data exceeds field length, etc.
11.	ESCAPE	ON	Esc aborts command file execution.
12.	EXACT	OFF	Matches for *criteria* must be exact.
13.	INTENSITY	ON	Dual intensity display for full screen operations.
14.	DEBUG	OFF	Output from ECHO and STEP sent to printer to check full screen commands with display clutter.
15.	CARRY	OFF	In APPEND, data from previously entered record is carried over to next record automatically.
16.	CONFIRM	OFF	No skip to next field in full screen w/o return.
17.	EJECT	ON	Report produces initial form feed automatically.
18.	RAW	OFF	A single space is placed between the fields of a record for DISPLAY and LIST.
19.	SCREEN	ON	Full screen editing provided for EDIT, APPEND, INSERT and CREATE.
20.	HEADING		TO *heading*. Sets up an additional heading only for this report.
21.	FORMAT		TO [SCREEN] [PRINT] *format file*. Determines whether @, GET and READ send information respectively to the screen, printer or to a disk file.
22.	DEFAULT		TO *drive*. DBase seeks all files from an alternate drive.

CARRY is useful when adding new records to the file, especially with **APPEND**. If **CARRY** is **ON** the field values entered for the previous record are *carried* into the fields for this record. Fields with duplicate values in most records appear automatically. Unique fields can be typed over. Thus if each record has a field for date of entry, it is the same for all of today's records. Entered for the first record, this field is then *carried* over to all the rest. Other fields which are not to be duplicated are typed over (the normal means for record entry).

EJECT causes a form feed whenever a report begins to print. Once you have set up the form, it is annoying to find that a sheet of paper is wasted because the printer advances to the next sheet. The initial form feed is deactivated with **SET EJECT OFF**.

HEADING is an example of a switch that does not have two settings; it provides a line of information which goes on every page of a report. For a report form you frequently use, **HEADING** lets you tailor the heading (to include today's date, for instance) each time you print a report.

12.8 REPORTS

A **report** is an important product of the data base manager; it is customarily hard copy output. The same data base may produce several different styles of report. Each user may have a different need, arrangement and requirement.

Just consider the *tape* file. I could probably request a report for this file organized in any of these ways:

- by tape number and contents.
- by composer.
- by the type of selection.
- by selection organized by composer for classical music.
- by country for ethnic selections.

DBase provides a rather simple **REPORT** facility which meets only bare needs. You can expand it to any depth with command files. We now examine this facility.

Report

The **REPORT** command has many options:

REPORT [SCOPE] [FORM fname] [criteria] [TO PRINT] [PLAIN]
$$(12.8.1))$$

REPORT is issued both to create and generate a report; the first time REPORT is used it designates how the printout is formatted. It sets up a **report form,** a file with the extension **FRM**.

Creating a Report Form

The simplest way to use REPORT is without options to create a report form to your specifications thus,

.report $\hspace{6em}$ (12.8.2)

Interaction

Now dBase works with you interactively. A typical exchange appears thus,

```
ENTER REPORT FORM NAME: rl
ENTER OPTIONS, U=LEFT MARGIN, L=LINES/PAGE,
   W=PAGE WIDTH
IN=10
PAGE HEADING (Y/N)Y
ENTER PAGE HEADING: First Report
DOUBLE SPACE REPORT? (Y/N)n
ARE TOTALS REQUIRED? (Y/N)y
SUBTOTALS IN REPORT? (Y/N)y
ENTER SUBTOTALS FIELD: cost
SUMMARY REPORT ONLY (Y/N)n
EJECT PAGE AFTER SUBTOTALS? (Y/N)n
ENTER SUBTOTAL HEADING: Cost
COL   WIDTH, CONTENTS
001   20,account
ENTER HEADING: Account
002   6,actnum
ENTER HEADING:
003 [ ]
```
(12.8.3)

Options are chosen here to make the most inclusive dialogue.

Information displayed by dBase appears in upper case letters as it does on the screen. The response appears in lower case or mixed type, although you may enter upper case names. The overall action is examined first and then some of the details.

Overall Action

When you make your request with (12.8.2), the first prompt (12.8.3) asks for a report name (here rl). Next you may format the report: set margins, page width, and lines per page. Now you may furnish a heading to appear on *every* page of the report at its top. You may specify double spacing and up to two kinds of totals; these are taken only on numerical fields which you specify in the case of a subtotal. For subtotals, a summary report can be produced which does not list details. This is handy when a simple report to management is required.

With these format details out of the way, you now determine what appears on each line (or set of lines) of the report, the bottom of (12.8.3).

Report Field

A **report field** is one of the fields in the report and it should be distinguished clearly from a **data field,** one of the fields defined for a record of the file *on which* the report is based. A report field is defined by the dialog of the REPORT command. After each field is specified, a prompt follows to ask what should be displaced at the head of the column. Here is how part of (12.8.3) will transpire:

```
COL   WIDTH,CONTENTS
001   20,account
ENTER HEADING:[ ]
```
(12.8.4)

The report field may contain record fields or literals in quotes. After you define a report field, dBase repeats the column titles, (12.8.4) advances the column number by 1 and puts the cursor under WIDTH. You may now define the next field. Thus the report field corresponds to one column of the report.

The distinction is important. A report field:

- is one or more data fields, constants or literals printed for every record;
- occupies one or more rows in the report;
- may contain an expression which uses constants or fields from the current record and may perform a calculation which present results in this column.

You define a report field by giving its width first (12.8.4). The content after the comma may fill up this width. If not, the field is padded with blanks. If the content *exceeds* the report field width, then the information wraps over to the next line (or lines). For example, if the report field width is 20 positions and the length defined by CONTENTS is 31 positions, then the field consists of two rows, the first of 20 characters.

You get the display (12.8.4) once more after defining all the report fields. Simply hit return and the definition is complete. DBase makes a file for the report form using fname (12.8.1) and the extension FRM.

Heading

A **report heading** appears at the top of each page to describe this use of REPORT. A **column head** defines the content of each report field, the column. It too may consist of one or more rows of information. If the heading is longer than the report field, it wraps after filling the first row. This may not be the ideal way to break the heading. Here are some of the alternatives for setting up headings:

- When the heading occupies more than one line, a semicolon tells dBase where to break it to make it into two lines. The semicolon does not appear in the printed heading.
- When the heading is shorter than the record field, it is centered within that field.
- A less than sign (<) preceding the heading places the heading flush left.
- A greater than sign (>) preceding the heading places it flush right.

Using a Report Form

Once you have created the report form, it is simple to produce a report display in the format defined with,

.report form rl (12.8.5)

Here rl is the name of the form and applies to the file currently in USE (with extension DBF). Besides displaying the report, you can print it simultaneously with

.report form rl to print (12.8.6)

The PLAIN option suppresses date and page information so that REPORT can be incorporated into a command file with text surrounding it.

Limiting the Records Reviewed

There are several ways to limit the records examined for the report. One uses *scope*. For instance, after positioning to record 100, you produce a report based on the next 50 records thus,

.100
.report next 50 form rl (12.8.7)

Criteria limits the records printed. To a report on only classical selections for *tape* issue,

.report form taprep for code='C' (12.8.8)

The two limitations are combined in this example,

.report next 100 form taprep for code = 'Z'   (12.8.9)

WHILE can also be used for *criteria* thus,

```
.use tapec
.locate for composer = 'BAR'
RECORD 00085
.report form taprep while composer = 'BAR'
```
    (12.8.10)

Totals and Subtotals

DBase can provide totals and subtotals for designated fields in a report. In this way, you can achieve a kind of control break, explained in Section 12.9 which also discusses how a command program can implement this feature.

Total

A **total** is the sum of all values occurring on each line of the report for a designated numeric field. It is printed in the same column at the end of the report. A total can be taken only for a numeric quantity. The word TOTAL appears in the left column, surrounded on each side by two asterisks. Beneath this, totals show in appropriate columns. When you set up the report form, you describe each column, its width and contents. DBase requires for a heading and nothing more if this is a character column; for a numeric column, it asks if a total is required. If you answer "Yes," the numeric column is totalled, but not otherwise.

Subtotals

Subtotals may be requested when creating a report and are based upon a designated **subtotal field** which may be alpha or numeric. Whenever its value changes, a control break occurs and **subtotals** are printed for requested fields, summing values between the last control break and this one.

The file should be ordered according to the subtotal field by sorting it or by creating an index.

Example

Let us examine the kind of reports that the report facility can prepare.

File

Begin with a simple file called sales which has the structure displayed in Figure 12.8.1. Add records to provide a base for creating reports; forty records give the general idea. Then print in out with DISPLAY as in Figure 12.8.2.

No Breaks

Prepare the first report with no breaks—a simple listing. Figure 12.8.3 sets up the report form called rsl which also provides a grand total for sales. Immediately upon completion of the form, the report is produced (displayed as Figure 12.8.4).

Once the report form has been created, one may call it up at any time to view the contents of sales. To print the report, simply say TO PRINT in (12.8.1).

Break by Salesperson

Now let us prepare a report by salesperson. As you see from Figure 12.8.2, the file is already sorted on this field. Specify the report, rs2 as shown in Figure 12.8.5. Here subtotals are requested; the subtotal field is given as sman.

Figure 12.8.6 is immediately produced on screen. Since the salesperson's name appears on each break line (after the *), it is clear that the name need not appear as a field directly underneath.

Break by Account

As a final example, let us see how to create a report by account name. We would get multiple breaks as the file is now arranged. Hence we should either sort the file or create an index for it. Figure 12.8.7 shows how to prepare an index.

Now let's set up the report form called rs3 as shown in the figure. Even though the file has not been sorted, the output of Figure 12.8.8 results. Here the account name has been dropped from each report line, since it would then be redundant.

```
. use sales
. disp stru
STRUCTURE FOR FILE:  A:SALES   .DBF
NUMBER OF RECORDS:   00040
DATE OF LAST UPDATE: 00/00/00
PRIMARY USE DATABASE
FLD       NAME       TYPE WIDTH   DEC
001       SMAN        C    005
002       ACCT        C    005
003       DATE        C    006
004       AMNT        N    007    002
** TOTAL **               00024
.
```

Figure 12.8.1. The structure of sales.

```
. list
00001   Abe    AAA    120183     34.23
00002   Abe    AAA    120683      1.01
00003   Abe    AAA    121083     12.37
00004   Abe    AAA    121583    244.08
00005   Abe    ABC    120183     21.10
00006   Abe    ABC    120283     66.00
00007   Abe    ABC    120583     22.33
00008   Bob    AAA    120183    101.83
00009   Bob    AAA    123083     23.70
00010   Bob    ABC    120183     23.45
00011   Bob    ABC    120683     17.08
00012   Bob    OXY    120383     22.45
00013   Bob    OXY    122183    234.70
00014   Bob    RIG    121183     44.50
00015   Bob    RIG    122783    199.00
00016   Chet   AAA    120383    220.00
00017   Chet   AAA    121483    400.00
00018   Chet   RIG    121583   1020.00
00019   Chet   RIG    122583     45.00
00020   Chet   ZIP    120783     10.00
00021   Chet   ZIP    120783     25.00
00022   Chet   ZIP    121783     35.00
00023   Chet   ZIP    121883     22.00
00024   Chet   ZIP    123083    185.05
00025   Daisy  ABC    120383    200.00
00026   Daisy  MEOW   120283    503.00
00027   Daisy  MEOW   122383    175.00
00028   Daisy  MEOW   122883    660.50
00029   Daisy  MEOW   120483    389.00
00030   Daisy  PAN    123083    903.00
00031   Daisy  PAN    123083     17.00
00032   Daisy  RUBR   121283    101.00
00033   Daisy  RUBR   121483     53.00
00034   Daisy  RUBR   122183     72.00
00035   Ellen  ABC    120183     55.80
00036   Ellen  ABC    120583     21.00
00037   Ellen  ABC    121883    488.00
00038   Ellen  RUBR   121283    225.00
00039   Ellen  RUBR   122683    401.00
00040   Fred   FRDJR  121183     66.35
.
```

Figure 12.8.2. A listing of sales.

```
. report
ENTER REPORT FORM NAME: rsl
ENTER OPTIONS, M=LEFT MARGIN, L=LINES/PAGE, W=PAGE WIDTH
PAGE HEADING? (Y/N) y
ENTER PAGE HEADING: sales
DOUBLE SPACE REPORT? (Y/N) n
ARE TOTALS REQUIRED? (Y/N) y
SUBTOTALS IN REPORT? (Y/N) n
COL     WIDTH,CONTENTS
001        15,sman
ENTER HEADING: Salesms__man
002        10,acct
ENTER HEADING: Account
003        10,date
ENTER HEADING: Date
004        10,amnt
ENTER HEADING: Amount
ARE TOTALS REQUIRED? (Y/N) y
005
```

Figure 12.8.3. Report form rsl to list and total sales.

```
                                     sales
       Salesman       Account      Date      Amount
       Abe            AAA          120183       34.23
       Abe            AAA          120683        1.01
       Abe            AAA          121083       12.37
       Abe            AAA          121583      244.08
       Abe            ABC          120183       21.10
       Abe            ABC          120283       66.00
       Abe            ABC          120583       22.33
       Bob            AAA          120183      101.83
       Bob            AAA          123083       23.70
       Bob            ABC          120183       23.45
       Bob            ABC          120683       17.08
       Bob            OXY          120383       22.45
       Bob            OXY          122183      234.70
       Bob            RIG          121183       44.50
       Bob            RIG          122783      199.00
       Chet           AAA          120383      220.00
       Chet           AAA          121483      400.00
       Chet           RIG          121583     1020.00
       Chet           RIG          122583       45.00
       Chet           ZIP          120783       10.00
       Chet           ZIP          120783       25.00
       Chet           ZIP          121783       35.00
       Chet           ZIP          121883       22.00
       Chet           ZIP          123083      185.05
       Daisy          ABC          120383      200.00
       Daisy          MEOW         120283      503.00
       Daisy          MEOW         122383      175.00
       Daisy          MEOW         122883      660.50
       Daisy          MEOW         120483      389.00
       Daisy          PAN          123083      903.00
       Daisy          PAN          123083       17.00
       Daisy          RUBR         121283      101.00
       Daisy          RUBR         121483       53.00
       Daisy          RUBR         122183       72.00
       Ellen          ABC          120183       55.80
       Ellen          ABC          120583       21.00
       Ellen          ABC          121883      488.00
       Ellen          RUBR         121283      225.00
       Ellen          RUBR         122683      401.00
       Fred           FRDJR        121183       66.35
       ** TOTAL **
                                              7360.53
```

Figure 12.8.4. Using rsl for sales.

```
. report
ENTER REPORT FORM NAME: rs2
ENTER OPTIONS, M=LEFT MARGIN, L=LINES/PAGE, W=PAGE WIDTH
PAGE HEADING? (Y/N) y
ENTER PAGE HEADING: Sales by Salesman
DOUBLE SPACE REPORT? (Y/N) n
ARE TOTALS REQUIRED? (Y/N) y
SUBTOTALS IN REPORT? (Y/N) y
ENTER SUBTOTALS FIELD: sman
SUMMARY REPORT ONLY? (Y/N) n
EJECT PAGE AFTER SUBTOTALS? (Y/N) n
ENTER SUBTOTAL HEADING: Salesperson
COL     WIDTH,CONTENTS
001     15,sman
ENTER HEADING: Sap_lespoer___erson
002     1:_0, 7__acct
ENTER HEADING: Account
003     8,date
ENTER HEADING: Date
004     10,amnt
ENTER HEADING: Amou t__nt
ARE TOTALS REQUIRED? (Y/N) y
005
```

Figure 12.8.5. Report form rs2 to subtotal sales by salesperson.

```
                            Sales by Salesman
     Salesperson    Account    Date      Amount
    * Salesperson Abe
    Abe            AAA       120183      34.23
    Abe            AAA       120683       1.01
    Abe            AAA       121083      12.37
    Abe            AAA       121583     244.08
    Abe            ABC       120183      21.10
    Abe            ABC       120283      66.00
    Abe            ABC       120583      22.33
    ** SUBTOTAL **
                                         401.12

    * Salesperson Bob
    Bob            AAA       120183     101.83
    Bob            AAA       123083      23.70
    Bob            ABC       120183      23.45
    Bob            ABC       120683      17.08
    Bob            OXY       120383      22.45
    Bob            OXY       122183     234.70
    Bob            RIG       121183      44.50
    Bob            RIG       122783     199.00
    ** SUBTOTAL **
                                         666.71

    * Salesperson Chet
    Chet           AAA       120383     220.00
    Chet           AAA       121483     400.00
    Chet           RIG       121583    1020.00
    Chet           RIG       122583      45.00
    Chet           ZIP       120783      10.00
    Chet           ZIP       120783      25.00
    Chet           ZIP       121783      35.00
    Chet           ZIP       121883      22.00
    Chet           ZIP       123083     185.05
    ** SUBTOTAL **
                                        1962.05
```

Figure 12.8.6. Using rs2 on sales.

```
                        Sales by Salesman
    Salesperson      Account    Date      Amount

    * Salesperson Daisy
    Daisy            ABC        120383      200.00
    Daisy            MEOW       120283      503.00
    Daisy            MEOW       122383      175.00
    Daisy            MEOW       122883      660.50
    Daisy            MEOW       120483      389.00
    Daisy            PAN        123083      903.00
    Daisy            PAN        123083       17.00
    Daisy            RUBR       121283      101.00
    Daisy            RUBR       121483       53.00
    Daisy            RUBR       122183       72.00
    ** SUBTOTAL **
                                           3073.50

    * Salesperson Ellen
    Ellen            ABC        120183       55.80
    Ellen            ABC        120583       21.00
    Ellen            ABC        121883      488.00
    Ellen            RUBR       121283      225.00
    Ellen            RUBR       122683      401.00
    ** SUBTOTAL **
                                           1190.80

    * Salesperson Fred
    Fred             FRDJR      121183       66.35
    ** SUBTOTAL **
                                             66.35

    ** TOTAL **
                                           7360.53
```

```
.
.
.
. id_ndex on acct to andx
00040 RECORDS INDEXED
. report
ENTER REPORT FORM NAME: rs3
ENTER OPTIONS, M=LEFT MARGIN, L=LINES/PAGE, W=PAGE WIDTH
PAGE HEADING? (Y/N) y
ENTER PAGE HEADING: Sales by Account
DOUBLE SPACE REPORT? (Y/N) n
ARE TOTALS REQUIRED? (Y/N) y
SUBTOTALS IN REPORT? (Y/N) y
ENTER SUBTOTALS FIELD: acct
SUMMARY REPORT ONLY? (Y/N) n
EJECT PAGE AFTER SUBTOTALS? (Y/N) n
ENTER SUBTOTAL HEADING: ACCOUNT
COL     WIDTH,CONTENTS
001     15,sman
ENTER HEADING: Salesperson
002     10,dz_ate
ENTER HEADING: Date
003     10,amnt
ENTER HEADING: Amount
ARE TOTALS REQUIRED? (Y/N) y
004
```

Figure 12.8.7. Indexing sales by acct to andx; then making report form rs3 with subtotals by account.

12.8 REPORTS

```
                          Sales by Account
    Salesperson      Date        Amount
    * ACCOUNT AAA
    Abe              120183       34.23
    Abe              120683        1.01
    Abe              121083       12.37
    Abe              121583      244.08
    Bob              120183      101.83
    Bob              123083       23.70
    Chet             120383      220.00
    Chet             121483      400.00
    ** SUBTOTAL **
                                1037.22


    * ACCOUNT ABC
    Abe              120183       21.10
    Abe              120283       66.00
    Abe              120583       22.33
    Bob              120183       23.45
    Bob              120683       17.08
    Daisy            120383      200.00
    Ellen            120183       55.80
    Ellen            120583       21.00
    Ellen            121883      488.00
    ** SUBTOTAL **
                                 914.76


    * ACCOUNT FRDJR
    Fred             121183       66.35
    ** SUBTOTAL **
                                  66.35


    * ACCOUNT MEOW
    Daisy            120283      503.00
    Daisy            122383      175.00
    Daisy            122883      660.50
    Daisy            120483      389.00
    ** SUBTOTAL **
                                1727.50


    * ACCOUNT OXY
    Bob              120383       22.45
    Bob              122183      234.70
    ** SUBTOTAL **
                                 257.15


    * ACCOUNT PAN
    Daisy            123083      903.00
    Daisy            123083       17.00
    ** SUBTOTAL **
                                 920.00
```

Figure 12.8.8. Report by account of sales using rs3 (part 1).

```
                                    Sales by Account
           Salesperson      Date      Amount
        * ACCOUNT RIG
          Bob             121183         44.50
          Bob             122783        199.00
          Chet            121583       1020.00
          Chet            122583         45.00
        ** SUBTOTAL **
                                       1308.50

        * ACCOUNT RUBR
          Daisy           121283        101.00
          Daisy           121483         53.00
          Daisy           122183         72.00
          Ellen           121283        225.00
          Ellen           122683        401.00
        ** SUBTOTAL **
                                        852.00

        * ACCOUNT ZIP
          Chet            120783         10.00
          Chet            120783         25.00
          Chet            121783         35.00
          Chet            121883         22.00
          Chet            123083        185.05
        ** SUBTOTAL **
                                        277.05

        ** TOTAL **
                                       7360.53
```

Figure 12.8.8. Report by account of sales using rs3 (part 2).

12.9 REPORT COMMAND PROGRAMS

This section combines features examined in the last two sections. The report facility described in Section 12.8 is useful for the novice who can enter a simple report specification to get a report immediately. If satisfactory, the report form can be used again and again as the file changes.

With experience, one always wants more. The REPORT command always prints in a particular way:

- no control break is possible without subtotals;
- these is single spacing between control breaks;
- the total always is preceded by a printout saying TOTAL,
- and so forth.

It would be wasteful to incorporate all possible alternatives into a report generating program. It would take too long for the operator to specify, even though reports might come out quickly. Still, there is an ideal medium to describe a complex report—the command language.

Control Break

The **control break** is an important feature which divides a report into smaller ones, each with its own heading. With multilevel control breaks, these small reports can be divided into minireports, and so forth. Two and three level control breaks are discussed at the end of this section.

A **single level control break** is specified with respect to one field. Uniform print action continues as long as the value for this field remains constant from one record to the next. When the value of the specified field changes, this marks a control break. To make the most effective use of the feature, the file should be sorted according to control break fields. If we want to report on the salesperson, then every change of that field value causes a control break. But if the file is not sorted, subreports may be produced at different places in the report for the same salesperson.

One Level Control Break Loop

The **DO WHILE** loop is an ideal way to enforce a control break facility. A prototype of this, with numbers keyed to the description, is shown in Figure 12.9.1. The first line sets the limits for the loop; the single level break applies to the entire file. The field on which to break is called **bfield**. Keep track of the value of this field for the previous record in a variable called **Obfield** (5). When the two are unequal (2), a control break is signaled: print the new value of **bfield** (3), together with the column titles (4) for the report. This check is made with an **IF** statement: when true, the statements following are performed; it is terminated by **ENDIF**.

Hence for each record examined, the present and last settings of **bfield** are compared and, if different, titles are printed. This works even for the first record, as long as the quantity stored in the variable in the beginning of the program (not shown) is a set of blanks or something like it.

```
1.     do while .not. eof
2.        if bfield <> OBfield
3.           ? "     ***      ",bfield,"     ***"
4.           ? "Title1     Title2     Title3"
5.           store bfield to Obfield
6.        endif
7.        ?field1,field2,field3
8.        skip
9.     enddo
```

Figure 12.9.1. The control break prototype in command language.

516 DATA BASE

Next the values of the fields of the report are printed out along one or more lines (7). Now the current value of the break field becomes its old value and we skip on to the following record(8).

Partial Report

Let us see how to use a command program called comp to produce a partial report without a control break, Figure 12.9.2. The function of each statement is given by line number below:

1. The first line is a remark which prints the name of the program.
2. The tape file sorted by composer is put into use.
3. A variable called More is set to M to display the report in different forms more than once.
4. Responses, normally returned from some commands, are suppressed.
5. This DO loop is repeated as long as More contains either an upper or lower case M.
6. ERASE clears the screen.
7. The program prompts for the composer's name or its first few letters, which are stored in Comp.
8. LOCATE finds a composer name, if any, which begins with these letters.
9. An internal DO loop prints information for all records which list this composer. If we omit .AND. .NOT. EOF and the last record in the file is chosen, this record continues to display innumerable times.
10. The composer, the piece and the tape number are displayed for this record.
11. We move to the next record.

```
 1: * comp to show composer's works
 2: use tapec
 3: store "M" to More
 4: set talk off
 5: do while !(More)='M'
 6:      erase
 7:      accept 'Give name or first letter for composer' to Comp
 8:      locate for composer="&Comp"
 9:      do while Comp$composer .and. .not. eof
10:          ? composer+piece+tape
11:          skip
12:      enddo
13:      ? "hit M for More"
14:      wait to More
15: enddo M
16: return
```

Figure 12.9.2. Command program, comp, to display compositions by composers selectively.

12. If the composer's name has changed and it does not begin with the letters supplied, we pop out of the loop. ENDDO officially ends the inner loop.
13. The operator has a chance to ask for another report.
14. DBase waits for a key to be hit which is recorded in More.
15. The outer loop ends if M or m is not hit.
16. RETURN ends the command program. In this way comp can be called from another DO program.

This command program only displays; to make it print, simply add SET PRINT ON somewhere in one of the early commands, as at (2) or (3).

Printout

Examples are shown using comp in Figure 12.9.3. Notice that when you ask for composer by giving the complete surname, BACH, that name prints on every line, which is really unnecessary. But if you ask for composer by a partial name, like BA, compositions by several composers may print; only then do you need to associate a composer with each composition.

Partial Report with a Control Break

It is not difficult to change this program so that the composer's name prints only once on a separate line preceding all of his or her compositions, as in Figure 12.9.4. The operator specifies a full or partial composer name at the prompt message. Each unique composer name prints on its own line followed by all the pieces and their tape numbers, one to a line.

For an ambiguous name, the first few letters for which there are several composers, then the composer's name prints on a separate line and his or her compositions follow on lines beneath. Figure 12.9.4 shows the printout from comp2 which is oriented for screen display. Hit ^P before use and the prompts also print. To adapt this program for printouts you would suppress the printing of requests to the operator and perhaps put additional empty lines between composers (? for each extra line).

Command Program

Figure 12.9.5 is the command program for the printout. The central loop continues as long as the variable More contains M or m (6). The screen is cleared (7) and a prompt given to enter all or part of a composer's name (8).

LOCATE the first record requested (9). The inner loop (10) is executed as long as a composer's name contains the desired first letters, but not after

```
. do comp
M
Give name or first letter for composer:BACH
BACH           2 PART INVENT IN A/A SHEEPMAY SAFELY142
BACH           BRANDENBURG #5                        142
BACH           MAGDELAINE SUITE                      142
BACH           MAGNIFICAT                            118
BACH           SONATAS FOR HARPSICHORD & VIOLA (3)   065
BACH           SWITCHED ON BACH SUITE #2             142
hit M for More
WAITING M
Give name or first letter for composer:BER
BERG           CONCERTINO                            103
BERG           LYRIC SUITE                           112
BERG           QUARTET  OPUS 3                       105
BERGER         3 PIECES FOR 2 PIANOS                 114
BERGER         CHAMBER MUSIC FOR 13                  114
BERIO          GIRDES                                157
BERIO          IMAGIO A JOYCE                        125
BERIO          MOMENTI                               125
hit M for More
WAITING M
Give name or first letter for composer:BA
BACH           2 PART INVENT IN A/A SHEEPMAY SAFELY142
BACH           BRANDENBURG #5                        142
BACH           MAGDELAINE SUITE                      142
BACH           MAGNIFICAT                            118
BACH           SONATAS FOR HARPSICHORD & VIOLA (3)   065
BACH           SWITCHED ON BACH SUITE #2             142
BAEZ,JOAN      VOLUME 5                              095
BARATI         CHAMBER CONC                          083
BARBER         QUARTET                               113
BARBER         SYMPH #1                              079
BARTOK         CONC #1                               103
BARTOK         CONC #3                               103
BARTOK         CONC 2 PIANOS & PERCUSSION            111
BARTOK         DIVERTMENTO FOR STRINGS               073
BARTOK         MUSIC STRING PERC & CEL               111
BARTOK         PIANO CONC # 1                        103
BARTOK         PIANO CONC # 1                        103
BARTOK         PIANO CONCERTO #2                     069
BARTOK         V & P SONATA #1                       100
BARTOK         V & P SONATA #2                       100
hit M for More
WAITING S
.
```

Figure 12.9.3. Using the comp program of Fig. 12.9.2.

the end of file. This last requirement is necessary or else the final record in the file will repeat endlessly if chosen for the printout.

The Break

A control break occurs when the new record contains a composer name different from that in the previous record as long as it begins with the letters

```
• DO comp2
Give name or first letter for composer:BER
        BERG
CONCERTINO                              103
LYRIC SUITE                             112
QUARTET  OPUS 3                         105
        BERGER
3 PIECES FOR 2 PIANOS                   114
CHAMBER MUSIC FOR 13                    114
        BERIO
GIRDES                                  157
IMAGIO A JOYCE                          125
MOMENTI                                 125
Hit M for More
WAITING M
Give name or first letter for composer:BA
        BACH
2 PART INVENT IN A/A SHEEPMAY SAFELY142
BRANDENBURG #5                          142
MAGDELAINE SUITE                        142
MAGNIFICAT                              118
SONATAS FOR HARPSICHORD & VIOLA (3) 065
SWITCHED ON BACH SUITE #2               142
        BAEZ,JOAN
VOLUME 5                                095
        BARATI
CHAMBER CONC                            083
        BARBER
QUARTET                                 113
SYMPH #1                                079
        BARTOK
CONC #1                                 103
CONC #3                                 103
CONC 2 PIANOS & PERCUSSION              111
DIVERTMENTO FOR STRINGS                 073
MUSIC STRING PERC & CEL                 111
PIANO CONC # 1                          103
PIANO CONC # 1                          103
PIANO CONCERTO #2                       069
V & P SONATA #1                         100
V & P SONATA #2                         100
Hit M for More
WAITING S
```

Figure 12.9.4. An improvement on Fig. 12.9.3 providing control breaks by composer using the command program comp2.

specified earlier and stored in Comp. To detect this after processing a record, the composer's name found there is put into a memory variable called Ncomp (15) before advancing to the next record (16). When we start the loop again (10), the next record's composer name can be compared to the name stored in Ncomp (11).

The control break is detected and acted upon by the IF sequence (11-13): print the composer's name, offset on the page so that it is centered (12) only when a new one is encountered (11). The composition and tape iden-

```
 1: * comp2  to show composer's works
 2: use tapec
 3: store "M" to More
 4: store "          " to NComp
 5: set talk off
 6: do while !(More)='M'
 7:      erase
 8:      accept 'Give name or first letter for composer' to Comp
 9:      locate for composer="&Comp"
10:      do while Comp$composer .and. .not. eof
11:           if composer <> NComp
12:                ? "             "+composer
13:           endif
14:           ? piece+tape
15:           store composer to NComp
16:           skip
17:      enddo
18:      ? "Hit M for More"
19:      wait to More
20: enddo M
21: return
```

Figure 12.9.5. Program, comp2, for control breaks for Fig. 12.9.4.

tifications are printed for *all* composers at or after the control break (14). Note that the first time the loop is performed, the variable Ncomp has blanks in it (4) and hence the first composer located is always printed (11).

Print Output Only

Comp2 of Figure 12.9.5 is for display only. Hitting ^P before saying DO makes both output *and* prompts print. Add SET PRINT ON at the beginning (3 or 4) to do the same thing. SET should be issued only when printing is to begin; SET PRINT OFF should be put in the programs before prompts appear. Figure 12.9.6 shows comp3, a modified version of comp2, where prompts display and results print; a printed sample is seen in Figure 12.9.7.

Multiple Breaks

The best way to see how to construct a command program is to walk through an example. We start by examining the data.

The Data

For tutorial purposes we select a simple example. The sales management data base called sales has the structure shown in Figure 12.8.1. Each sale for each salesperson forms a record containing the salesperson's name, the account name, the date of the sale and the amount of the sale. An actual

```
 1: * comp3 to show composer's works
 2: use tapec
 3: store "M" to More
 4: store "        " to NComp
 5: set talk off
 6: do while !(More)='M'
 7:     erase
 8:     accept 'Give name or first letter for composer' to Comp
 9:     locate for composer="&Comp"
10:     set print on
11:     do while Comp$composer .and. .not. eof
12:         if composer <> NComp
13:             ? "        "+composer
14:         endif
15:         ? piece+tape
16:         store composer to NComp
17:         skip
18:     enddo
19:     set print off
20:     ? "Hit M for More"
21:     wait to More
22: enddo M
23: return
```

Figure 12.9.6. This improvement on comp2, the command program called comp3, prints the report but not prompts to the user nor the replies.

```
              MAGUZAMI
    PRELUDE                          135
              MAHAVISHNU
    MISC                             163
              MAHLER
    SYM #10 CON'T                    070
    SYMPH #3                         167
    SYMPH #9                         080
    SYMPHONY #10 - PART              070
    SYMPHONY #3                      076
    SYMPHONY #4                      078
    SYMPHONY #6                      141
              MAKEBA
    MISC                             106
              MALIPIERO
    OBOE CONCIERTO                   154
              MARTRIANO
    L'S GA                           122
```

Figure 12.9.7. Printout of a request to comp3 for all composers with names beginning with "M."

data base would include much more information, such as the invoice number and the parts purchase in each sale.

Forty records now in sales are listed by record number in Figure 12.8.2. Normally they are not entered in the proper order for processing; a SORT command does this.

The Report

For such a small file, it's easy to extract information directly from the printout except for totals. For demonstration, we print a report using two control breaks: one is for salesperson and the other for account. We give subtotals by salesperson and provide a grand total for the period covered. We could easily provide subtotals by account by salesperson to give a third level of detail. The report is displayed in Figure 12.9.8.

```
. do sales
                        ***  Abe  ***
   Account:  AAA
      120183                                              34.23
      120683                                               1.01
      121083                                              12.37
      121583                                             244.08
   Account:  ABC
      120183                                              21.10
      120283                                              66.00
      120583                                              22.33
                                                       ==========
                                                         401.12
                        ***  Bob  ***
   Account:  AAA
      120183                                             101.83
      123083                                              23.70
   Account:  ABC
      120183                                              23.45
      120683                                              17.08
   Account:  OXY
      120383                                              22.45
      122183                                             234.70
   Account:  RIG
      121183                                              44.50
      122783                                             199.00
                                                       ==========
                                                         666.71
                        ***  Chet  ***
   Account:  AAA
      120383                                             220.00
      121483                                             400.00
   Account:  RIG
      121583                                            1020.00
      122583                                              45.00
   Account:  ZIP
      120783                                              10.00
      120783                                              25.00
      121783                                              35.00
      121883                                              22.00
      123083                                             185.05
                                                       ==========
                                                        1962.05
```

Figure 12.9.8. Multiple control break printout of sales by both salesperson and account (part 1).

```
                    ***  Daisy  ***
Account:  ABC
   120383                                          200.00
Account:  MEOW
   120283                                          503.00
   122383                                          175.00
   122883                                          660.50
   120483                                          389.00
Account:  PAN
   123083                                          903.00
   123083                                           17.00
Account:  RUBR
   121283                                          101.00
   121483                                           53.00
   122183                                           72.00
                                                ===========
                                                   3073.50


                    ***  Ellen  ***
Account:  ABC
   120183                                           55.80
   120583                                           21.00
   121883                                          488.00
Account:  RUBR
   121283                                          225.00
   122683                                          401.00
                                                ===========
                                                   1190.80


                    ***  Fred  ***
Account:  FRDJR
   121183                                           66.35
                                                ===========
                                                     66.35


         GRAND TOTAL                                7360.53
```

Figure 12.9.8. Multiple control break printout of sales by salesperson and account (part 2).

Command Program, Major Break

The command program is presented in Figure 12.9.9. Line numbers are not permitted in command programs, so you may wonder how they got here. The CP/M utility called PIP prints the command program file thus,

PIP

    *lst:=sales.cmd[N]   (12.9.1)

Here, LST: directs PIP to copy the file to the printer instead of to a disk file and [N] asks that each line be numbered and indented as shown.

The first few steps initialize (1–6); the outer loop reviews the file (7–30).

524 DATA BASE

```
 1: * sales - to print sales data with several control breaks
 2: set talk off
 3: use sales
 4: store "      " to Osman
 5: store 0 to Sum
 6: store 0 to Grndtot
 7: do while .not. eof
 8:    if sman<>Osman
 9:       ? "                              *** ",sman," ***"
10:       store acct to OAcct
11:       store sman to Osman
12:       ? "Account: ",acct
13:       ? "  ",date,"                                       ",amnt
14:       store sum+amnt to sum
15:       skip
16:    endif
17:    do while sman=Osman .and. .not. eof
18:       if acct<>OAcct
19:          ? "Account: ",acct
20:       endif
21:       ? "  ",date,"                                       ",amnt
22:       store acct to OAcct
23:       store sum + amnt to sum
24:       skip
25:    enddo
26:    ? "                                             ==========="
27:    ? "                                             ",sum
28:    store Sum + Grndtot to Grndtot
29:    store 0 to sum
30: enddo
31: ?
32: ?
33: ?     "        GRAND TOTAL                         ",Grndtot
34:
```

Figure 12.9.9. Command program, sales, for printout of Fig. 12.9.8.

The major control break is the first statement of the outer loop (8). The name of the salesperson in the current record, sman, is compared with that in the previous record, Osman. Should the two differ, all statements up to ENDIF (9-15) are executed. They print the salesperson's name (9), store the account number and salesperson's name (10,11), print the minor break, the account name (12), and the date for the control break record (13), accumulate a subtotal (14) and move on to the next record (15). Note that a major break always implies a minor break.

Minor Control Break

The inner loop (17-25) detects and processes the first and all subsequent minor break records within this major break and all the remaining major break records. It remains in force for records associated with the current salesperson (17). IF detects a minor break, a change in account name (18), and prints the new account name (19). The date and amount for all the salesperson's sales except the first (13) are printed here (21).

The account number is stored to a memory variable OAcct, for the next minor control break (22). The salesperson's sum is accumulated (23) for later printout. Finally, advancing to the new record (24) ends the loop (25) but only when a new name is encountered (17).

The Subtotal

Dropping out of the loop (25) signals a major control break. A total line and the sum accumulated for this salesperson is then printed (26,27)—the subtotal. To accumulate a grand total, the sum is added to a variable collecting this information, Grndtot (28). Then Sum is cleared to start accumulating the next subtotal (29).

After completing the outer loop (30), we have examined all the file as signalled by EOF (7) and can print out the grand total (31-33).

Extension

To accumulate minor totals by salesperson *and* by account, establish one more counter. It prints at the minor break and is then cleared for the next account listing for the salesperson (18-20).

Further Levels

Once you understand how to establish major and minor control breaks, it is simple to extend the principle to as many levels as required by your application. The dBase command language is an ideal vehicle for tailoring reports to your needs.

13
Graphics

13.1 INTRODUCTION

Graphics, as used here, is the creation of visual images with the aid of the computer. Your actions at the terminal or tablet make images in black and white or color on the display. They are volatile, but there are ways to save or print them for later use and enjoyment.

Some systems provide screen images but no permanent output while others provide output but no screen images. Each restricted system has its use.

Not all computers do graphics; less expensive entertainment computers do graphics but not much else. On the other hand, some business computers designed to help the manager and owner of a small business do not provide any graphics capability because additional equipment is required. If this were not so, all the more expensive computers would have graphics. The Apple II has made graphics more common; the IBM PC with some additional hardware, has moved it from entertainment to an office tool.

What and Why?

Information in pictorial form consists of lines, textures and colors. Often meaning is clear without words. The International road sign symbols alert you to conditions without language. The symbol conveys what to expect without words.

Text appearance and configuration do not convey its meaning; they are understood only by reading. Graphics informs immediately. Pictorial forms on the page often convey their part of their message without text.

Most graphic systems provide text to supplement the visual forms. A pie chart or bar graph conveys quantitative relations about several variables. But, without labels, there is no way to identify which variables are which.

Hence you expect to find labels. Since the main information content is in the picture, only supplemented by the text, it is more quickly grasped by the observer.

Quick communication is the aim of graphics in the business environment. The board meeting or executive briefing is a concentration of managers, each of whose time is worth a small fortune. It is essential to pass information back and forth as quickly as possible. But how can a manager concentrate on a lengthy text document and still listen to the meeting and converse with peers? A picture with a short verbal explanation and printed labels communicates information in a fraction of the time.

State of the Art

Advanced graphics help you do many marvelous things from designing a microprocessor chip to developing a movie sequence as in TRON. These terminals cost tens of thousands of dollars and often hook into a large commercial computer.

Technology is moving so fast that computer power improves by an order of magnitude every two or three years while cost actually drops. Capability which is now prohibitive will be available to small business in a few years. We may not be prepared to use graphics: you can't put technology to work until you understand what it has to offer. This chapter reviews the state of the art and looks at equipment which will be economically available soon.

This Chapter

This section describes what graphics does today. The rest of the chapter continues as follows:

2. The second section describes alternatives for hardware which comprises the system.
3. How is the image displayed? What actions cause its parts to appear on the screen?
4. What is the screen like?
5. How is an image constructed?
6. What input devices facilitate image creation?
7. How do menus expedite image construction?
8. What forms of output are there?
9. Facilities available for the IBM PC.

528 GRAPHICS

Following is a brief overview, divided into three parts aimed at low, medium and high resolution graphics. Higher resolution shows more detail in the picture.

Games and Amusements

The biggest application of **low resolution** graphics is for arcade and television games. Many months of design on a personal computer create the presentation and program. Once perfected, further effort is invested to put the program on a chip, a ROM (read only memory). Mass produced ROM chips cost only a few dollars.

The chip *is* the program which runs a small, single purpose display computer. This is part of the game set you buy, such as made by Atari or Coleco. The computer contains RAM to hold data given to and altered by the players. The background graphics and the action program are on the chip in a cartridge plugged into the game box. Data are collected from the input buttons and the joy stick during play.

Entertainment personal computers provide low resolution graphics as part of the software package. These use a monitor terminal or tie into television sets.

At the next level of cost, personal computers provide a language interpreter, usually an additional set of BASIC commands. These plot points, draw lines and curves and fill in figures. To write a BASIC program to project a graphic image on the screen is a challenge. Adding animation can also be fun.

Software suppliers (such as Stoneware) provide packages for micros (such as the Apple) to let you *draw* crude images. You can even attach a joy stick or tablet.

Business

Business applications are best done with **medium resolution** graphics. Nobody wants to look at a chart where the lines look like a flight of steps. Software helps create bar and pie charts as in Figure 13.1.1. Displaying them or incorporating them in hard output is even more valuable. Graphics software does the following:

1. Creates pictorial forms, bars or sectors of circles;
2. Tailors each quantitatively;
3. Determines the size of the chart;
4. Positions it on the display and printout area;
5. Colors parts to distinguish them;
6. Enters text for labels.

13.1 INTRODUCTION

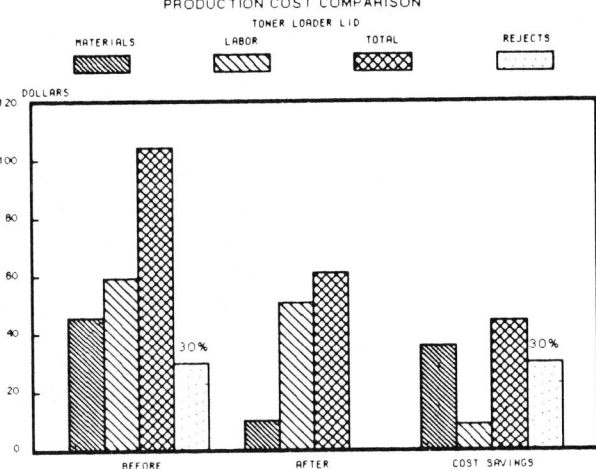

Figure 13.1.1. Bar chart.

Graphs

Graph software accepts pairs of points, plots and scales them and displays them as shown on the screen in Figure 13.1.2. Some handle multiple superimposed graphs. If an appropriate display and peripheral device are available, these may be colored.

Figure 13.1.2. Graphs.

530 GRAPHICS

Advanced Business Applications

Graphics has a real place in business beyond graphs and charts. Here is a bare outline:

1. Office layout. Today's office is in constant flux. People move constantly. Partitions and furniture are pushed about to accommodate them. The careful office manager makes a new office layout at frequent intervals to suit growth and attrition. Computer graphics can create an empty floor plan and a top view of all furniture. From the terminal, you can position the furniture freely on the office floor plan with a mouse to see how different arrangements look, as in Figure 13.1.3. Alternative plans can be printed for reference and quick modification.
2. Flow charts and PERT charts are aids to plan and run complex projects. Figure 13.1.4 shows an example.
3. Illustrations for reports and texts help explain the latter and aid the busy executive. Illustrations are sketched at a graphics terminal and printed

Figure 13.1.3. Office layout.

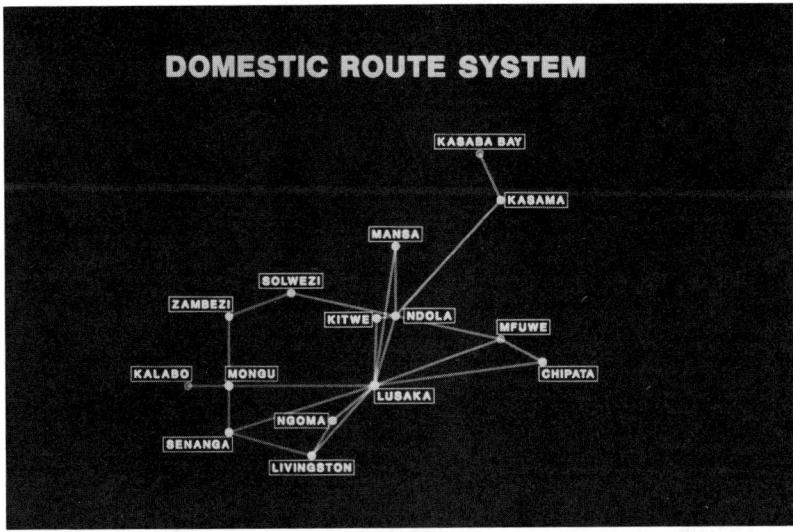

Figure 13.1.4. PERT chart.

on a dot matrix printer integrated with the report or plotted separately. A typical illustration embedded in a manual is shown in Figure 13.1.5.

> The Toner Loader Lid (See Figure 4-2) was previously produced using a vendor casting process plus an in-house machining and painting procedure. A recent production change order changed the process to a 100% numerically controlled vendor machined part. Details of the machined part are shown in drawing D-2682-20182-1.

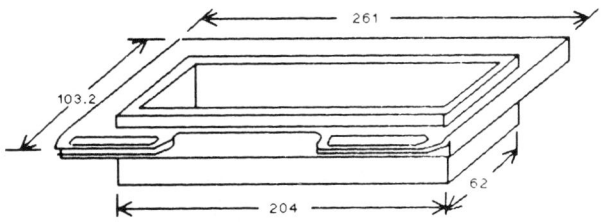

Figure 13.1.5. Sketch for report.

4. Data available in machine readable form is growing exponentially. It is hard to find and digest. If we could apply graphical methods for data base integration, things might be a lot easier.
5. The Fingraph system provides a graphical presentation showing the complete status of the company's finances: assets, return an investment, leverage, etc. (see Irwin M. Jarrett, *Computer Graphics and Reporting Financial Data,* John Wiley & Sons, 1983) It is incorporated into a service available to a micro. The bar graphs communicate far more efficiently than the accountant's summary reports.

High Resolution

Architecture and Engineering

Engineering and architectural plans require detailed mechanical drawings. Draftspeople still spend many boring hours drawing lines and hand lettering text on drawings such as in Figure 13.1.6. Now this tedium has almost become a thing of the past in large manufacturing facilities. It is simple to make a drawing, no matter how complicated, on a CRT screen with zoom and pan capability (Section 13.5).

Parallel and perpendicular lines common in mechanical drawings require an accurate T-square and drafting skill. A square grid may be superimposed on the screen; rough lines drawn are repositioned and aligned automatically.

The final output, an inked, scale drawing, is produced on a plotting board costing from $700 to several thousand dollars. The board's cost is more than made up for by the tedium it eliminates.

Medicine

We are just beginning to scratch the surface. Medical illustrators do not appreciate graphics as yet. It is just coming into use in images for sketches and plots of experimental results and patient monitoring. Laboratories are applying image analysis to diagnoses.

Education

Computer aided instruction (CAI) has been around for several decades. PLATO is one such teaching system. Teaching programs involve words and language. However, illustrating principles of physics, mathematics, biology and so forth is aided considerably with graphics. The instructor sets up a

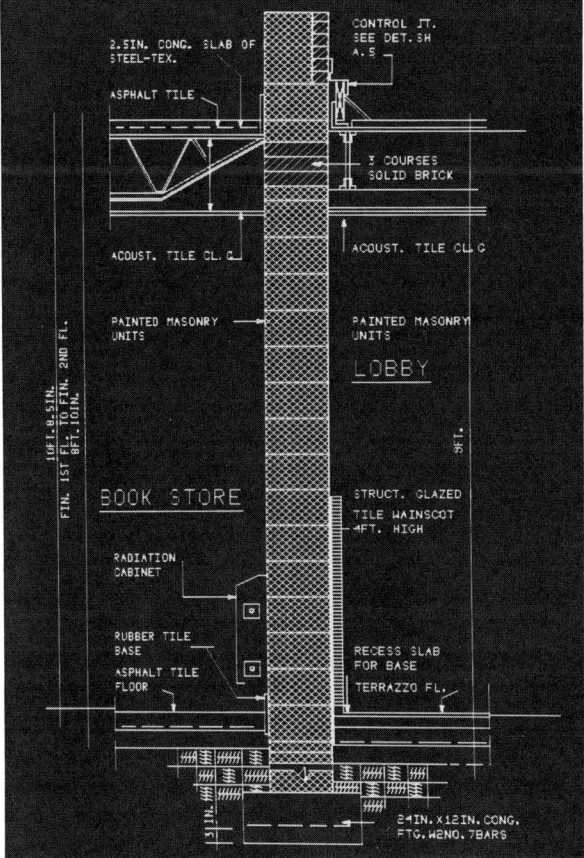

Figure 13.1.6. Architectural drawing.

lesson with illustrations created on the screen, which may include animation, and students work with graphics at individual terminals both to stimulate and reinforce learning.

Publishing

Scientific and technical books include a host of illustrations, all hand tailored to the author's sketches. Now an artist can create illustrations, including labels and captions, at the CRT. Then a plotter produces them accurately and quickly.

Graphics is also applied to typography for the creation of new type faces.

Cartography

A large map can be stored on a floppy. To make changes (new roads or buildings) you simply bring it to the screen, alter it, print a copy with a color plotter and store the "electronic map" back to disk. A topological map can be constructed at the terminal and printed on a plotting board to show the vertical projection in three dimensions as in Figure 13.1.7, where an area of interest is localized and magnified.

Statistics

Programs plot one or more graphs and superimpose them. A more complicated program for multiple variables displays a three dimensional solid comprehensible to the less technical person. Statistical qualities of collected data can be extracted and displayed visually in a penetrating manner.

Visual Arts

Computer animation is a part of our lives. Yet we hardly recognize it as such. Many television programs now use computer animation for logos and advertisements. Most news broadcasts begin with a computer animated display. Computer animation is the principal medium for cinema sci-fi (*TRON*, *Star Wars*).

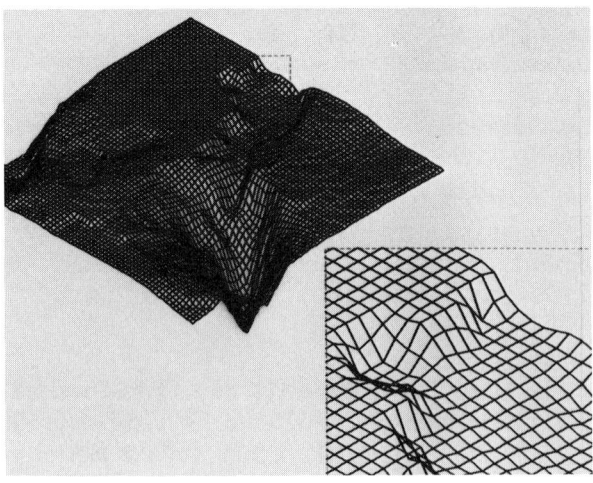

Figure 13.1.7. Cartography.

Serious artists use graphics as a medium for pictures and three dimensional sculpture models.

CAD/CAM

Computer aided design (CAD) and **computer aided manufacture (CAM)** have come a long way due to computer graphics. The entire design process can be performed on the terminal. Programs take a design and convert it into other programs to run milling machines, boring machines, multiple hole drillers, robots and so forth—a portion of an assembly line.

13.2 THE GRAPHIC SYSTEM

A complete graphic system lets you:

- enter graphics commands;
- create and view graphic images;
- enter text labels;
- manipulate images in complex ways to augment them;
- produce graphic output on paper, film and other media;
- record images in machine readable medium form to recreate later.

Few systems provide *all* these facilities.

The Overall System

Figure 13.2.1 is a block diagram of a graphic system which always includes a digital computer; left of the dashed line is part of the basic computer: additional devices, right, make this a graphic system. The dividing line between the computer and the graphic system is rarely clear in practice. We discuss alternative system configurations later.

Additions for Graphics

The most important additional hardware for graphics is the display. The graphic display terminal includes a screen comparable to a television set in technology and size but of higher quality and resolution. Most terminals associated with micros, personal computers and mainframes are *not* satisfactory for graphics.

Next, we require an image memory made from RAM components as used in computer memory; smaller systems assign a part of main memory for this. The format of graphic information stored there is different. Image

536 GRAPHICS

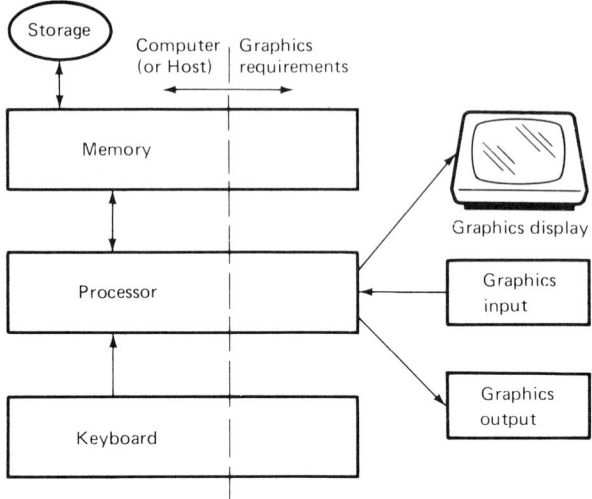

Figure 13.2.1. The graphics system.

memory and the display must coordinate so that pictorial information appears properly.

Optional graphic input devices convey pictorial information to the system. A terminal keyboard intended for text entry suffices, but is inconvenient for pictorial input.

The screen displays the picture you create, which disappears when you turn off the equipment. The screen picture is rarely the end result. Most of us are not satisfied unless it is captured on paper or some intransigent medium. Most computer output devices do not handle graphics. An exception is the dot matrix printer. Equipment to produce the image as a drawing or a set of dots (hard output) may be expensive; price varies with the amount of detail you need and whether color is included.

External storage may store graphics programs and data, for instance on the floppy, represented by the elipse in Figure 13.2.1. Graphic images or command sequences stored there can produce images created earlier, dot for dot or line for line.

Levels of Systems

Graphics systems are graded according to capability and price:

- The **home** or **hobby system,** available for a few hundred dollars uses a television set for display.

- The **managerial system** costs a few thousand to $10,000 and includes a monitor.
- The **professional terminal** for $10,000 to $25,000 consists of a keyboard monitor and an internal computer for image generation in a single terminal. Although capable of creating some images on its own, it usually depends upon a host computer.

The Hobby System

Figure 13.2.2 shows a typical hobby system (Atari or Commodore), in a small box a couple of inches high and about 9″ × 12″. On the top surface, a keyboard enters data and commands. In the box is a processing chip on a printed circuit board and RAM (random access memory) ranging from 16K to 64K. Read-only memory (ROM) may also be present.

Part of RAM stores the image, since this is low resolution (little detail). A television screen shows either a black and white or a three or four color image (sometimes sixteen or more). The colors displayed are fixed, usually red, blue and green.

The computer contains a digital to analog convertor (D/A) which changes the computer's output to suit the television set. Although this is complex, a large investment by semiconductor manufacturers has put all the circuitry required on a single chip. This has made possible inexpensive television and video "arcade" games.

The output signal feeds the antenna input of a television set, usually through a switch which chooses among the roof antenna, cable television,

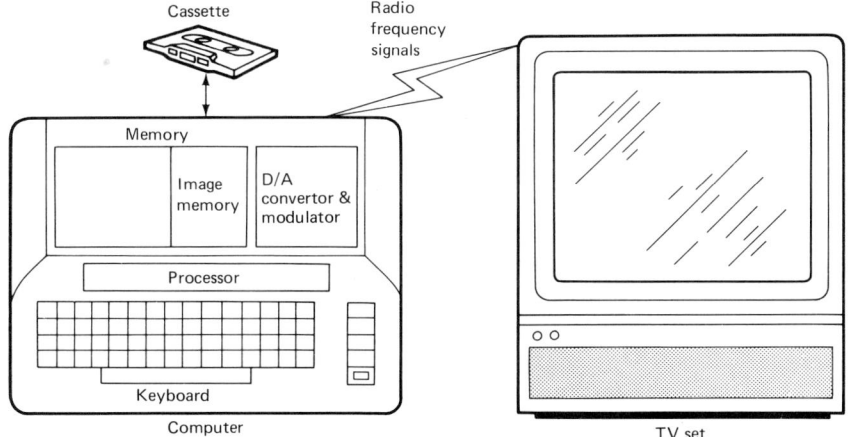

Figure 13.2.2. Low cost graphics system.

538 GRAPHICS

a game or the computer. Usually cassette input brings in different games or programs.

No other output device is shown in Figure 13.2.2. A dot matrix printer costs more than the entire computer. The system is for entertainment, so what appears on the screen need not be saved.

The Management Work Station

This system is intended for the serious but occasional user. Data processing services may be supplemented by graphics features available (and sometimes go unused).

The configuration shown in Figure 13.2.3 might be a typical micro or personal computer. Two floppy disks provide program and data. The printer *should* have graphics capability. A terminal CRT might show black and white or color images. A graphics board may be required to drive it (as with the IBM PC). A conventional keyboard with additional function keys helps request graphic functions.

Image Display

Part of RAM holds the image, which may display in two ways. One method keeps the image in digital form in main memory. Each refresh cycle of the monitor examines RAM and recreates the image many times per second on the screen as described in Section 13.4—as for Apple graphics and the IBM PC.

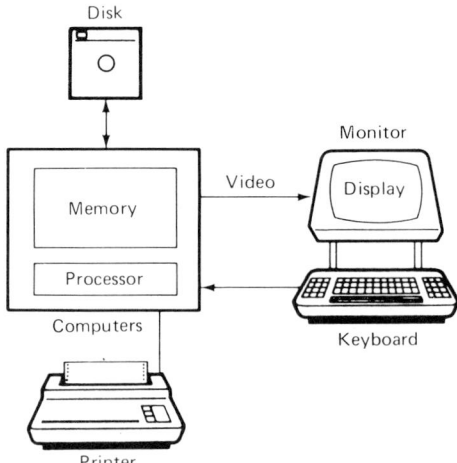

Figure 13.2.3. Manager's PC graphics.

For the other method, the monitor has its own memory which can be in either *graphics* or *character mode*. Data sent to the monitor in graphics mode is stored there and interpreted by the monitor as an *image*, not *text*, and vice versa.

Professional Graphics Work Terminal

The professional terminal, Figure 13.2.4, is almost self-sufficient. Images created at the keyboard or through graphic input devices display immediately on the monitor. Their purpose is related to problems in the real world, such as PC design or office layout. Therefore, hard copy output and a medium for storage during the creation cycle, which may cover several sessions, are needed. The work station is connected to a host micro, mini or mainframe for additional image processing. A large host supports several work terminals.

The terminal contains a large image memory (100K bytes or more) and its own processor; programs which run the terminal processor are in ROM or RAM or both. A monitor is often built into the terminal cabinet but may be separate. Circuitry in the terminal displays the stored memory image on the monitor.

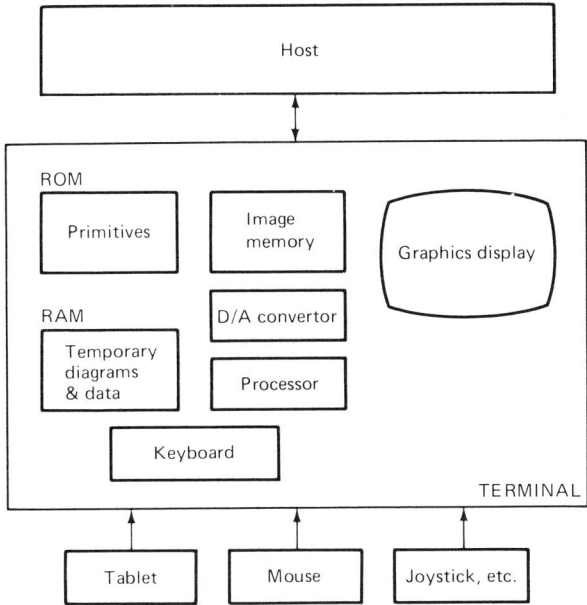

Figure 13.2.4. Graphics work station.

The graphics work station is designed to create complex images with speed and efficiency. Its keyboard can be used to enter data and commands into most conventional computers or micros when not used for graphics.

Application

The hobby system is intended for entertainment regardless of the ads. However, many educators are working on programs to help youngsters to think, learn and develop visual concepts. Programs such as LOGO are expanding students' horizons.

The personal computer can provide useful graphic output depending on the amount of graphic facility incorporated in the overall system. Tables, figures, bar and pie charts and even a certain amount of drawing can be done with some equipment. Apple's Lisa computer is meant to help the manager in office planning; its display is a black and white screen of medium resolution. The LisaDraw program enables the manager to draw simple objects and move them around as described later in this chapter. This $4,000 to $8,000 computer is made specifically as a management work station.

The professional graphics work station is intended for complex applications. However, the price for some have dropped to $10,000. Makers combine this type of terminal with a complete computer run by a 68000 microprocessor to make a system with extensive capabilities selling in the $15,000 to $20,000 range. The Apollo computer contains a complete high resolution graphics facility of the type discussed; the low end of the line sells for $10,000.

New and more powerful processor chips are constantly emerging. Memory prices are plummetting. Some high quality graphics will soon be available to all who want it.

13.3 THE IMAGE AND ITS DISPLAY

Graphics equipment produces pictorial images and text. The equipment helps the operator to create and manipulate images which may be edited many times over. This section describes how the image is created, stored and displayed. Later sections describe how to load, modify and save a copy on external media.

Strokes

The first way to create the picture is called the **vector**, or **stroke**, method. It works like the artist who makes strokes with a pen or brush to paint a picture as black (or colored) lines on white paper.

13.3 THE IMAGE AND ITS DISPLAY

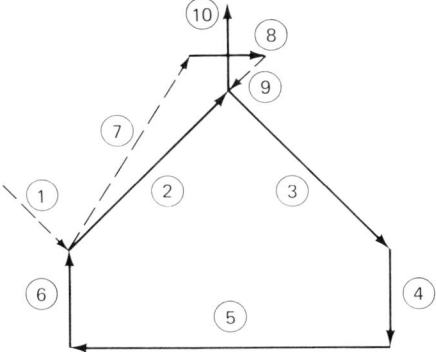

Figure 13.3.1. Image of church created by strokes.

This method, illustrated in Figure 13.3.1 displays the church, a figure of five lines with a cross on the top. An electronic beam traces out the **closed figure** on the CRT screen a line at a time; the end of one stroke is the beginning of the next (1-6).

To create the cross at the top of the church, after tracing out the building, the beam is moved to the beginning of one edge of the cross with the beam off (7), draw the line (8), move to the end of the other line with the beam off (9) and draw it (10).

Computer generated images have replaced mechanical drawings throughout industry. The stroke method of image generation is especially applicable here. It mates well with the plotting board (Section 13.8).

Although the stroke method is effective and many systems based on this concept are in use, its share of the market is decreasing steadily. The newest technology is based on the raster scan because color is difficult and expensive to include with the stroke method. Hence the rest of this chapter is based on that technology. Table 13.3 contrasts their characteristics.

Table 13.3.1 Contrast of CRT Display Characteristics

CHARACTERISTIC	STROKE	RASTER
Resolution	Very high	Low to high
Drawing speed	Slow	Fast
Brightness	Low	High
Ease of correction	Poor	Great
Color	Monochrome	Full
Flicker	Low	Moderate
Availability	Expensive	Reasonable

Raster Scan

The raster scan display is the most popular because television sets and monitors for text, programming and word processing use this technology. The monitor CRT is affordable. For **raster scan,** the CRT beam sweeps out the entire screen in a rectangular pattern or raster, writing the image as it goes along. This sweep pattern is shown in Figure 13.3.2. (The actual pattern uses several hundred lines per screen.)

The beam sweeps across one horizontal line of the picture at a time, a **scan line.** The beam writes in only one direction—from left to right, turned on for white and off otherwise. It is *always off* on the downward trip from right to left, dashed in the figure. Figure 13.3.3 shows how the church with the cross is produced by raster scan. Dots appear in places where the beam is on.

When the beam has traced out one scan line, it moves down by a small amount and over to the left side. It is off on the way back, called **retrace,** and moves much faster. After retrace, the beam is ready to scan the next lower line.

There are places along the line called **resolution elements,** or **rels,** where the beam is either turned on or off to make a **dot** or **undot** (no spot). The number of rels along the scan line is predetermined. The screen is a **grid,** or **raster,** a number of horizontal and vertical lines, and at their intersection is a *rel* for a *dot* or an *undot*. The more rels there are, the higher the resolution.

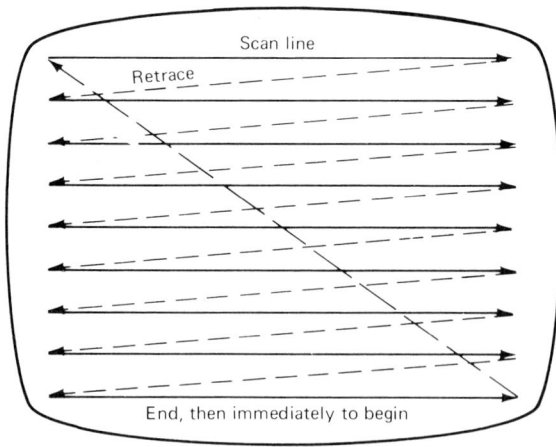

Figure 13.3.2. Raster scan.

13.3 THE IMAGE AND ITS DISPLAY

Figure 13.3.3. Raster scan of church.

Resolution

Resolution is the amount of detail, the **definition** which the screen displays. The raster defines the screen as a number of lines or rows and a number of columns. The home television set provides 512 lines of about 300 rels. Anything with greater definition is **high resolution graphics**.

Recording the Image

The stored image is composed of dots and undots. The ideal situation provides memory of one or more bits for each rel. For high resolution, this amounts to millions of bits. The image is kept in **image memory**.

The Pixel

Pixel is a contraction of *picture element*; its use varies from one author to another and could mean two things:

1. A single rel on the screen;
2. A single element in the image memory.

We have defined the **rel** as (1); we reserve **pixel** for an element in image memory. The distinction makes it clear that a pixel *may* represent a *number* of rels, which is the case for low resolution graphics as illustrated in Figure 13.3.4.

The *pixel* represents an image area of one or more rels and does not overlap other pixels; all the pixels taken together cover the screen. Figure

544 GRAPHICS

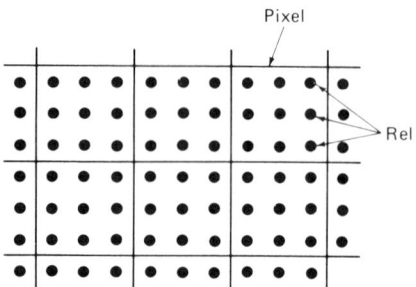

Figure 13.3.4. A pixel represents several sites.

13.3.4 shows a pixel representing a 3 × 3 square of rels. An image is composed of a number of such squares. For **monochrome** (black and white), one bit per pixel suffices. Hence fewer bits store an image at low resolution.

The size and shape of a pixel (not necessarily square) may be under the control of the host computer. The Atari 400 and 800 have several graphic modes which define differently shaped pixels.

Creating the Image

Methods for producing an image include planes of **LEDS** (light emitting diodes) and storage tubes. The most important uses the **cathode ray tube (CRT)**.

The CRT

The CRT consists essentially of two parts: a gun and a rectangular screen. The inside tube face is coated with material which **flouresces,** emits light when hit by a stream of electrons. A **gun** creates an extremely narrow beam of electrons, focused to hit the screen at a *rel*.

The Gun

A gun to create the electron beam and direct it to a particular spot is shown in Figure 13.3.5. At its bottom the **filament** heats the **cathode** to emit large quantities of electrons.

Vacuum

The CRT is evacuated to make it ideal for electrons to traverse. There is *nothing* for them to hit as they are guided by an accelerator and focussing

13.3 THE IMAGE AND ITS DISPLAY   545

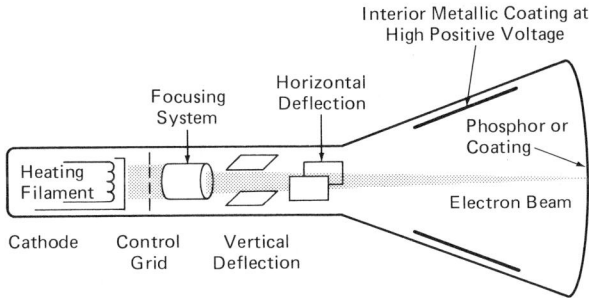

Figure 13.3.5. Gun for cathode ray tube. (Adapted from J. D. Foley and A. Van Dam, *Fundamentals of Interactive Computer Graphics*. Copyright © 1982 by Addison-Wesley Publishing Company, Reading, Massachusetts. Fig. 3.14. Reprinted by permission of the publisher.)

plates to the screen. Bundled together by a magnetic focusing system shown as the cylinder in the figure, electrons leave as a thin beam aimed at the screen's center.

Positioning

The beam is moved by **deflecting** it either magnetically or electrostatically. The electrostatic method, developed first, is easiest to understand. For magnetic deflection, a magnetic yoke surrounds the neck of the tube; this method has replaced the electrostatic method almost completely.

For electrostatic deflection, voltages are applied to two pairs of plates:

- **vertical deflection plates** move the spot up or down;
- **horizontal deflection plates** move it left or right.

The spot can be positioned anywhere on the screen by varying voltage on the deflection plates.

A **control grid** varies the intensity of the beam to get gradations of black and white when the beam hits the screen. Its extremes turn the beam on or off, producing dots or undots.

Linearity

To create a picture accurately, even a line drawing, it is important to eliminate image distortion. All its causes are well known to CRT design engineers. Many forms of compensation are incorporated in the CRT electronics so that the picture is accurately reproduced. Realism in the home television set attests to this.

13.4 THE SCREEN

This section discusses properties of the screen and color formation. **Persistence** is how long a spot emits light after the electron beam is turned off. CRT screens for raster scan have a persistence of only a fraction of a second and therefore they must be **refreshed**—the image recreated many times per second, or it disappears. **Refresh memory** is another name for image memory, the bits which store the image in pixel form.

To create the image, a **refresh register** is filled with a number of pixels from image memory as shown in Figure 13.4.1. Each scan is synchronized with access to this register. As a line sweeps out, the bits in the register activate the grid to turn the beam on or off. For low resolution, because a pixel spans several lines the refresh register is used on several scans. Figure 13.4.1 shows how refresh memory, the screen, the refresh register and the scan beam are synchronized. Here the pixel is a 3 × 3 square; the small triangle shows the current scan position with reference to the screen, refresh register and the image memory.

Phosphors

When a **phosphor** which coats the inside of the screen is hit by the beam, it produces light. A single phosphor produces a single wave length, a spectral color, pure light.

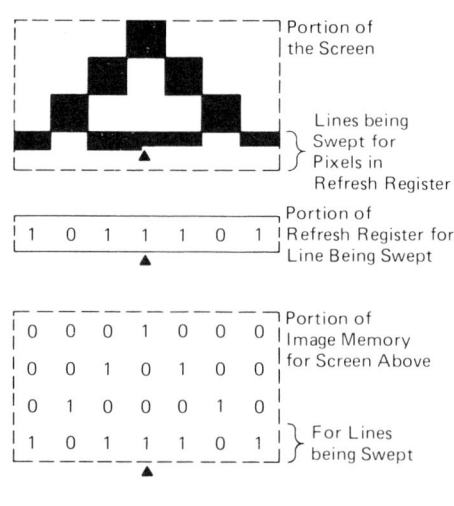

Figure 13.4.1. Display synchronization.

Mixed Phosphors

A **monochrome screen** emits a single color: usually white, green or amber. The color should be pleasing and comfortable to the operator. Most monochromatic phosphors, including white, are mixtures to get pleasing colors and a flickerless image.

Intensity

The grid turns the beam on and off, creating dots and undots, black and white in the screen image. A photograph or pictorial image contains **gradations**—grays. A picture is produced on black and white television by varying the grid voltage between the two extremes to create grays.

To store or present a pictorial image with gradations of gray, it is first **digitized**. Each pixel records a level between 0 (black) and a maximum (white); grays are intermediate. The accuracy of the image depends on the number of levels.

Image Memory

A digitized image is stored as pixels in image memory. Usually a pixel represents a square area. For black and white, a pixel is a single bit. For **gray scale**, a pixel is a *set* of as many bits required to give the number of *levels* used. The pixel determines the voltage applied on the grid when scanning the rel it represents. Sixteen levels, or 4 bits per rel, provide good reproduction of most photos.

Color

Colors are combinations of spectral colors. A nonspectral color such as aquamarine is a combination of light of several wave lengths. "Can we find a *set* of spectral color components, which when added in the proper proportion, can make any conceivable color?" If so, "Can we find phosphors to produce them?"

Phosphors are available which, in combination, produce *almost* all conceivable colors. The minimum components required are three: the most popular set is **red**, **green** and **blue**, abbreviated **RGB**. Before we examine the technology, we look into the properties of color.

Color Qualities

The three qualities of color perception are hue, saturation and brightness. **Hue** or **chroma** distinguishes one color from the next. **Brightness** is the intensity of the color; a spot of color emits light in proportion to its brightness.

A color is **saturated** if it includes no white. When white is mixed in, this reduces the amount of color relative to the overall light; this is a **tint** and is less saturated.

The Color CRT

The Tube Itself

The color CRT is more expensive than the black and white CRT because of extra technology. A front view of the screen, Figure 13.4.2, shows that each rel consists of a **color triad:** three tiny light emitting red, green and blue spots arranged in a triangle. The center of each triad is at the center of the rel.

Behind the screen is a **color mask,** a metal plate with holes precisely centered above each rel. An electron beam aimed at the hole hits the center of the triad. Actually there are three guns, each aligned so that its beam hits the proper color in the triad: the beam from the "red" gun hits the red dot, etc.

Producing Color

Each gun has a separate grid to control beam intensity. The deflection yoke aims all guns at the same hole as shown in Figure 13.4.3. The three beams enter at different angles. During the scan, the guns are simultaneously aimed at successive holes along a scan line. Each gun grid is activated to send a different intensity beam to its spot in the triad, which contributes a different quantity of its color to the color mixture produced at the dot.

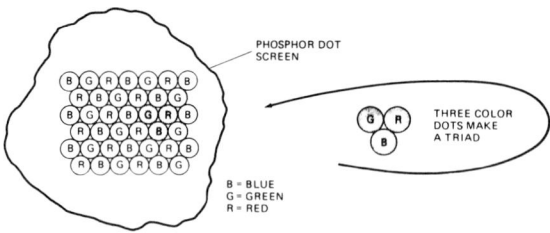

Figure 13.4.2. Color screen with triads.

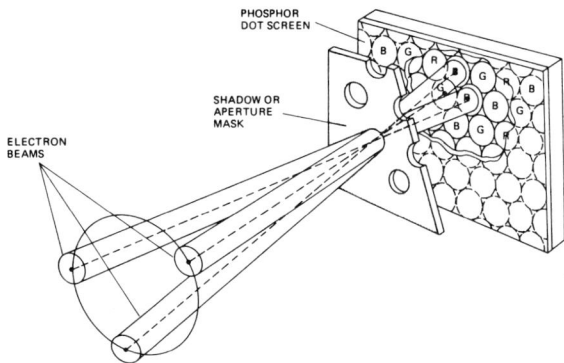

Figure 13.4.3. Each beam hits the right triad.

Controlling the Color

What determines the three qualities of a color at a rel—its hue, saturation and brightness? These are controlled by the voltages on the grid of the three guns:

1. Hue is determined by the intensities of the R, G, and B beam *relative to each other* with no white light present.
2. Saturation is determined by the ratio of the color, with no white light added, to the total light present.
3. Brightness is the overall light intensity.

Storing the Image

Pixels Again

An image is stored by a code for the color of each pixel. The number of pixels and their size (in bits) determine the amount of image memory required. Low resolution for the Apple or Atari uses a few hundred pixels of two bits. High resolution graphics can use 1024 × 1280 pixels of 8 bits.

A **color packet (CP)** stores each pixel. Its size determines how many colors can display simultaneously, the **palette size.** With a byte size CP (8bits), the palette shows 256 colors. A high resolution display with this palette size requires 1M byte of image memory, an impressive figure.

550 GRAPHICS

The Bit Plane

One way to set up the CP uses several bit planes. A **bit plane** has one bit of each pixel; several form a **bit plane array**. The logic addresses all bit planes simultaneously to find the CP for that pixel. Palette size depends on CP size. Eight bits, 256 colors, are sufficient for most applications.

Color Tables

The CP does *not* specify hue, saturation and brightness. A **color table** such as Table 13.4 contains one entry for each CP combination. The entry has four parts: a CP and a color value for each gun.

Granularity is the number of levels of control for each gun. With one byte or 256 settings for *each* of the three guns, the number of colors available is 256 cubed, or about 16 million colors. For image memory with one byte per pixel, as the scan proceeds,

1. Image memory is accessed for the CP for this pixel;
2. It designates an entry in the color table;
3. Those three bytes are applied to digital to analog converters;
4. The D/A converter produces three voltages;
5. They are sent to the RBG guns;
6. The guns generate the color spot for this pixel.

Summary

To set up a palate, one color is assigned to each CP combination. This creates one entry in the color table.

An image created with one palette (one particular color table) can be "recolored" by resetting the color table. One way to animate an image is

Table 13.4.1 A Color Table

ENTRY NUMBER	RED	BLUE	GREEN
0	0A	00	00
1	0A	04	04
2	0A	08	08
253	CA	D0	D0
254	D0	D0	D0
255	D8	D8	D8

to reset the color table at frequent intervals. Section 13.7 tells how to do this.

13.5 MAKING THE PICTURE

There are several ways to enter an image:

1. point by point (not very efficient);
2. by primitive commands;
3. with complicated software programs which manipulate existing images by simple requests;
4. from host programs which give you high level choices;
5. with facilitating hardware (Section 13.6).

The Software

You give directions to create an image, either at the terminal keyboard or with an input device. Commands are interpreted by the terminal software and hardware to place bits into image memory, the basis for the screen image which is generated. This software or firmware is included in the higher priced terminal. **Firmware** programs are permanently built into a terminal's ROM. Otherwise, a graphics software package is brought from disk storage to the host's memory. It sets up the image you create and puts it in image memory to drive the display. Wherever the software resides, only the principles of *image generation* are important.

Pixel by Pixel Image Generation

To write a point on the screen you need commands to

1. *Move* the **cursor,** a visible screen marker;
2. *Set* color and intensity.
3. *Enter* the point.

Usually a cursor is available—for graphics, a **cross-hair,** a pair of lines intersecting at a right angle, a quarter or half inch in length. It spotlights one pixel called the **current access position (CAP).**

Motion

To change the CAP, move the cursor. A direct command referencing an imaginary superimposed grid moves the cursor quickly and precisely. The coordinates of a pixel, its row and column number, are determined by **pixel resolution**. **Absolute positioning** identifies each pixel by an *X-Y* coordinate (row and column number).

A **normalized scale** makes reference independent of the terminal's resolution: X and Y coordinates use a scale of 0 to 1. If H is the number of pixels per row and V is the number of rows, then divide absolute position (X, Y) by pixel resolution (H, V) to get the normalized coordinates (x, y). For V=512 and H=400, we have

$$X = 375, \; Y = 217; \quad x = 0.732, \; y = 0.543 \tag{13.5.1}$$

Relative positioning requests movement by number of pixels from the CAP along the *X and Y* axes in either direction. **Normalized relative positioning** expresses increments on a scale of 0 to 1 from the CAP.

Setting Color and Position

Request color by reference to the palette, perhaps by number: setcolor, for 16 entries, specifies a color by a number from 0 to 15, the **current color (CC)**. Set a point into the display with a simple mnemonic like setpoint. This marks and displays the current color at the CAP into image memory.

Primitives

With 10,000 or more pixels, it could be tedious to enter an image point by point. Professonal graphics terminals implement **primitives.** There are several "standard" primitive sets but none universally accepted. Brief descriptions of some follow.

Draw a Line

Line connects two points by a line in the current color or **texture** (dotted, dashed, solid, and so on). With the CAP at the starting position, *line* includes a terminal point. It sets to 1 the points closest to the imaginary line between the two points.

Linerel gives the relative *X-Y displacement*: how many pixels to move to reach the terminal point.

Smoothing

The **line drawing routine** does geometry and smoothing, setting points closest to the actual line between the points, which might intersect few, if

13.5 MAKING THE PICTURE

any, pixels. An unsophisticated routine produces sick looking lines. This illness is called the **jaggies** because lines look jagged like the blade of a saw.

The cure for the jaggies is **antialiasing**. Higher priced displays include this feature, which sets rels so that the line does not have rough edges. An example of the disease appears in Figure 13.5.1. One cure, as shown in the figure (right), uses gray level averaging (for monochrome) for points close to the line or edge. Points of lower intensity do this for colored lines. Of course, higher resolution also helps.

Circles

Circle draws a circle with a specified radius in the current color pattern with the center at the CAP. Arc includes an angular position to start and stop, making a rounded corner at intersecting lines. If there is no arc primitive, you can simulate it by drawing a complete circle tangent to the lines, connecting the ends of the desired arc by a chord, and painting the unwanted sector black; only the tangent arc remains visible.

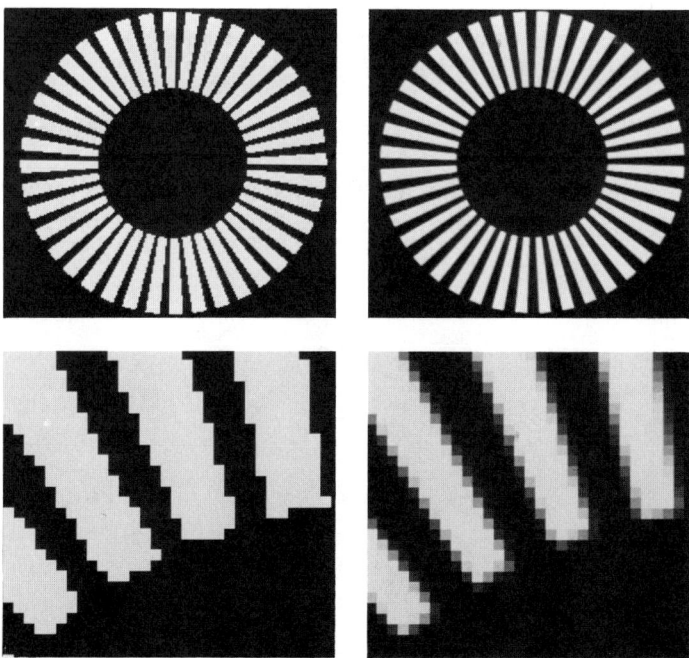

Figure 13.5.1. Jaggies (left) and antialiasing (right). (Diagrams produced by Paul S. Strauss and James K. Rinzler at Brown University)

Polygonal Fill

Polygonal fill colors or shades the areas of a *closed* figure. Fill finds two boundary points at a particular level at each side of the figure and draws a line (in color) between them within the figure. To color a closed figure, position the cursor and mark a spot within it. The current color fills this area, setting all the internal points to the current color as shown in Figure 13.5.2. Monochrome displays fill with a pattern, such as diagonals, cross-hatching, and so forth.

Fill searches for the top point in the closed area, finds the left boundary and draws a colored horizontal line to the right boundary. It steps down a line and continues thus to the bottom of the area.

Partial Displays and Windows

Zoom, pan and scroll magnify an area you describe and move a window about within your "field of vision." The terminal either

A. Provides a memory plane with dimensions (in pixels) larger than the display raster size, or
B. Provides less definition in the magnification mode—a portion of the screen is enlarged, but lacks detail.

Using the Memory Plane

The number of pixels is usually less than the number of rels for low resolution graphics. Now consider the reverse situation with more pixels than

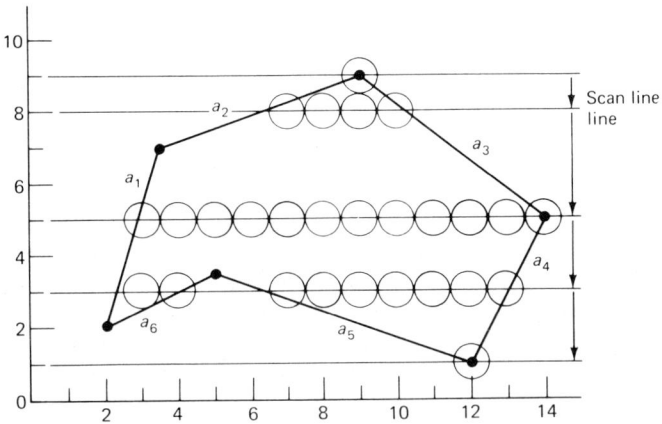

Figure 13.5.2. Polygonal fill.

rels. The memory plane(s) describes an object or scene with greater detail than can be displayed, several pixels per rel. **Zoom in** to look at detail in a particular area of the scene, reducing the number of pixels per rel, perhaps even reversing the ratio. This magnifies a particular image area. Figure 13.5.3 shows an image before and after zoom.

Zoom out to view a *larger* portion of the image by increasing the number of pixels per rel. The routine chooses the number of pixels and area to display. For either, tell the routine the magnification factor and the origin for the (magnified) **window**. Specify an integer multiple (1-to-16, say) to

Figure 13.5.3. Zoom.

556 GRAPHICS

give greater detail, and the magnified view jumps to the screen. However the difference between ×1 and ×2 is considerable while between ×15 and ×16 is hardly noticeable. A more sophisticated scaling is logarithmic, where each change might be ×1.1 of the previous one.

Once zoomed in, you can move to a different area keeping the magnification: **scroll** moves the window by jumps to a new position in the scene; **pan** is *continuous scrolling* in a designated direction, as shown in Figure 13.5.4.

Host Routines

Routines for elaborate manipulations are in the host. A sampler of these follows.

Object Definition

We have described how to draw a set of lines, create a polygon and fill a closed figure with color. you may define an object **absolutely** (at a particular spot on the screen) or **relatively** (starting anywhere by giving drawing commands relatively). *Commands* (or actions with input devices, Section 13.6) define the object. (This is comparable to defining a processing *procedure* in a higher level language or a *macro* in assembly language.)

Operations to produce a relatively defined object may be stored in memory and/or incorporated into a graphics library (from which they may be

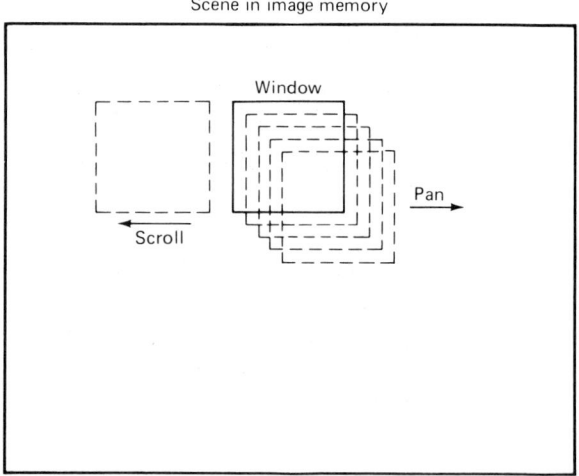

Figure 13.5.4. Scroll and pan.

recalled). Move the cursor anywhere and request a copy. The operations are executed relative to this CAP to produce a copy, as shown in Figure 13.5.5. To destroy an object, start at its origin and draw it again (with these operations) in *black*.

Rotation

Define an object an mark a center of rotation. *Rotate* rotates it through a designated angle. Alternatively it rotates the object slowly but continuously until directed to stop. The routine:

1. Calculates start and end of *each* line segment;
2. Erases the old object by writing it in black;
3. Creates a new object by drawing lines between the vertices it has just calculated;
4. Stores these directions relatively.

It does this once or repeatedly. Figure 13.5.6 shows a scene, an object copied there and then rotated.

Three Dimensional Objects

Programs to handle three dimensional objects are complex and consume considerable computer time. They may require the assistance of a main-

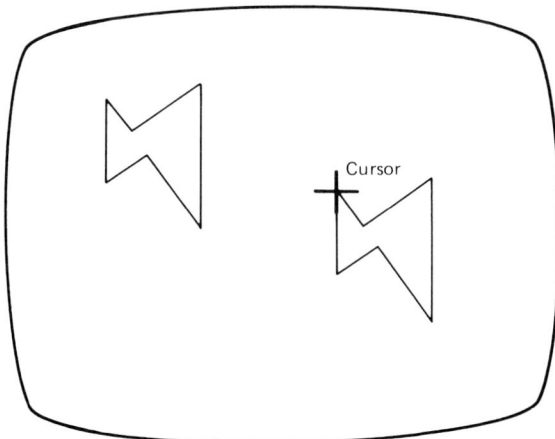

Figure 13.5.5. Copy an object.

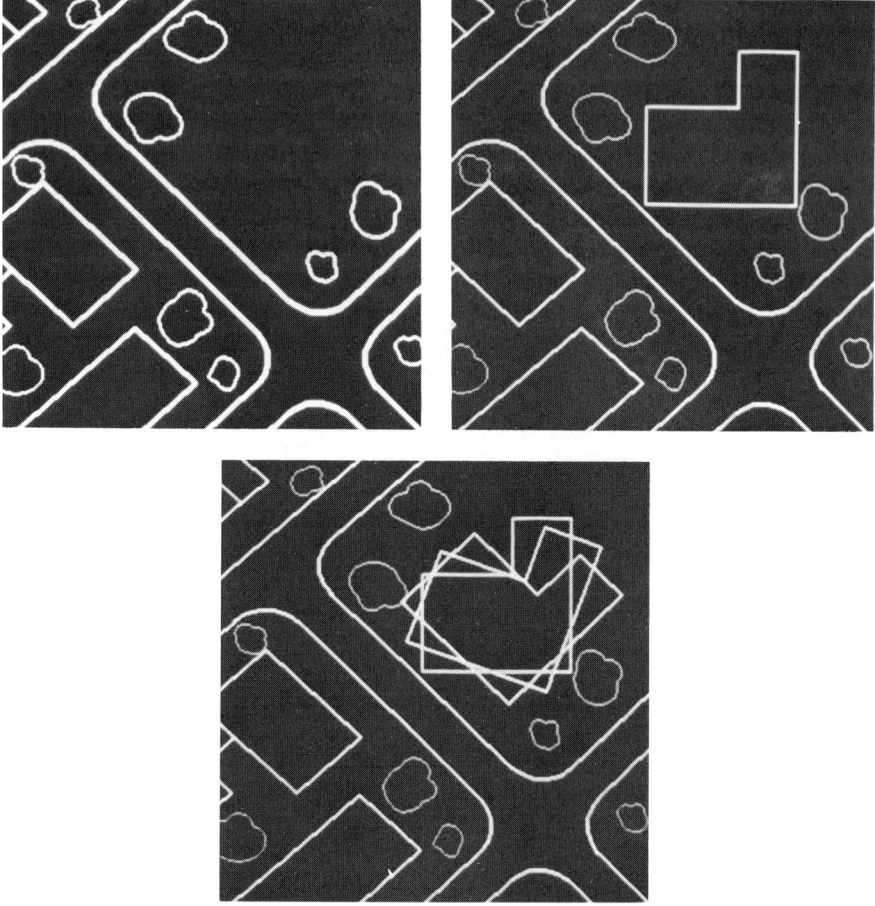

Figure 13.5.6. Copy and rotate an object.

frame or minicomputer but powerful micros are coming into their own. To deal with three dimensional objects:

1. Specify the object in three dimensions.
2. Show it viewed from a particular direction.
3. Rotate it about an axis and show its appearance after rotation.
4. Keep track of all hidden lines.
5. Hide portions of lines which should not display.

Entering the detailed dimensions of the object is formidable. A wire mesh figure as shown in Figure 13.5.7 gives the planar cross section dimensions in many successive planes, each at a different depth from the "eye".

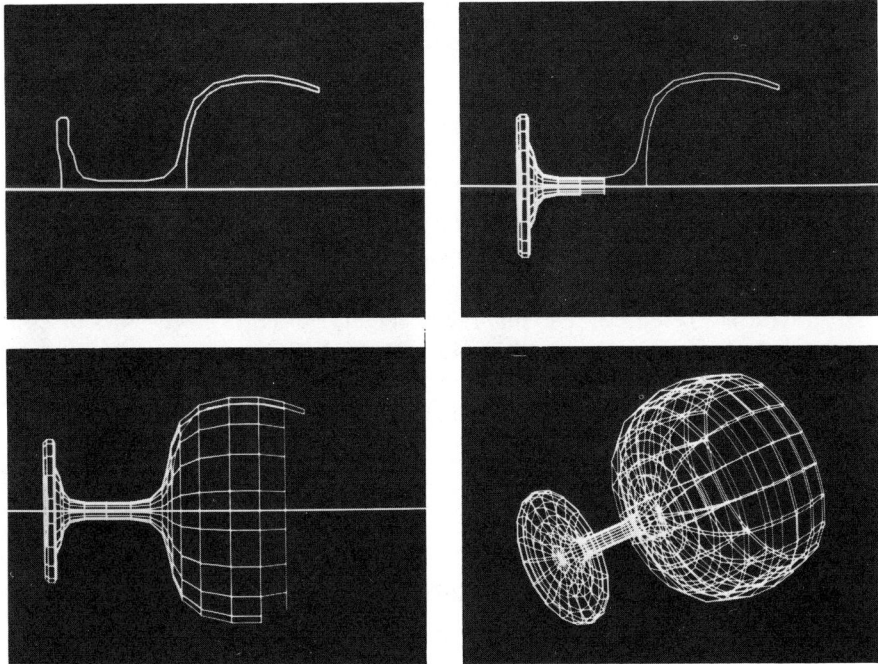

Figure 13.5.7. A mesh figure development.

A mesh figure is easy to rotate because no line is ever hidden. You see wire mesh automobiles on television rotated and zoomed rapidly on screen sometimes shown with multiple images overlayed.

Calculations for the next view of the rotated figure may take seconds on a high speed computer. A new image is a sequence of commands to generate each line for the new position. This command sequence can be stored and the image regenerated in a fraction of a second. It is one "photo" of the rotating object. "Photos" can be calculated and stored as a command sequence. Then the sequence shows the rotating figure much more rapidly since the calculation time is eliminated. What you see on television is speeded up hundreds of times.

To show a *solid* three dimensional car, visible surfaces are colored and hidden lines and surfaces eliminated. This takes additional time. To make an object appear realistic, each surface is colored differently.

Shading

Additional complexity is added for shading and lighting each surface. A sophisticated program calculates shading for curved surfaces. The object is tinted as though light from a point source were hitting it. This produced realistic interpretations of *imaginary* objects.

13.6 INPUT DEVICES

Need

The keyboard may control the display: arrow moves the cursor; other keys (in command mode) initiate activity. You can create a complex image in this way. However, there is a discrepancy between how the image is entered and how it is presented. The display is visual, but entry is verbally or conceptually oriented (*move* thus, *make* a line). Why not make construction similar to presentation?

With input devices, you simply and naturally control the display by moving a cursor or a stylus on a tablet or your finger on the screen itself. This gives both tactile and visual feedback.

Classifying

Let's classify input methods according to the ease with which they interact with the display:

1. **Direct**—move a stylus on the screen or touch it with a finger;
2. **Indirect**—draw on a model of the screen;
3. **Conceptual**—perform actions which affect the screen but are tactically and kinesthetically different, as with the keyboard.

Other Topics

Input is discussed without regard to whether signals go to the terminal or the host computer. An elaborate terminal which provides primitives in firmware, acts on the screen and sends a "note" to the host computer. A subsection is devoted to that topic.

Direct and indirect input make possible *graphic* menu selection, which is indeed powerful. You choose from alternatives on the screen by *picking* "visually."

This section examines conceptual, indirect and direct input devices in that order. Within each category, devices are discussed in order of complexity.

Conceptual Input (Indirect Entry)

For **conceptual input,** actions to *create* a set of lines are in the operator's mind as an idea or *concept*. But instead of drawing, the operator hits a key sequence, turns knobs, etc.

Commands

A **mnemonic** commands the cursor to move by a set of letters. For instance, MOV 35,45 moves the cursor to the column 35, row 45. Relative commands in the form MVR 3, −8 move the cursor 3 pixels right and 8 pixels up from the CAP.

Cursor Key

Arrow moves the cursor by a fixed increment (which is often uder your control) in the indicated direction. Four more keys with arrows pointing in diagonal directions are *sometimes* combined with another command code key, such as home, to position quickly to screen limits.

Knobs

Turning a **knob,** such as one of those shown in Figure 13.6.1, varies the output of a potentiometer. A **digitizer** converts this and sends it to the software to move the cursor. The rotation of two knobs determines the horizontal and vertical position of the cursor. A **vernier** on each knob helps.

Figure 13.6.1. Keyboard with knobs and joystick.

Joy Stick

The **joy stick**, also shown in Figure 13.6.1, is popular for television and arcade games. It has two degrees of freedom: left or right and up or down. For the **positional joy stick**, one combination of rotation and tilt corresponds to one position on the screen. The cursor moves quickly but *positioning accurately* is difficult. Only a slight stick motion causes the cursor to jump about considerably.

The **incremental joy stick** is an improvement. The *direction* of tilt determines the *direction* of cursor motion. The *amount* of tilt determines the *rate* of cursor motion:

1. There is a vertical dead spot (with the joy stick upright), where the cursor is not moving.
2. Tilting the joy stick makes the cursor move in that direction.
3. The rate of cursor motion is determined by the amount of tilt.

Tilting the joy stick steeply to the right moves the cross-hair quickly rightward. As it approaches the destination, ease up and the cursor slows down. At the objective, put the joy stick on dead center and motion stops.

Roller Ball

A **roller ball**, about the size of a golf ball, is seated in a square container as shown in Figure 13.6.2. Slapping it rotates it rapidly. Rotation is digitized for direction and speed. When the cursor arrives, you stop the ball.

The Mouse

The **mouse**, as in Figure 13.6.3, is a small handheld device with a rolling ball underneath. Place it on the table and move it in some direction; digitized signals transmit each new position. This device is inexpensive yet effective, provides feedback and is found with and without a tablet. It is becoming very popular. The crosshair of the mouse in the figure lets you trace out a drawing affixed to the tablet.

Position Entry

Once the cursor is at the site of a new activity, a button on the joy stick or on the top of the mouse reports this position as the new CAP.

13.6 INPUT DEVICES   563

Figure 13.6.2. Roller ball.

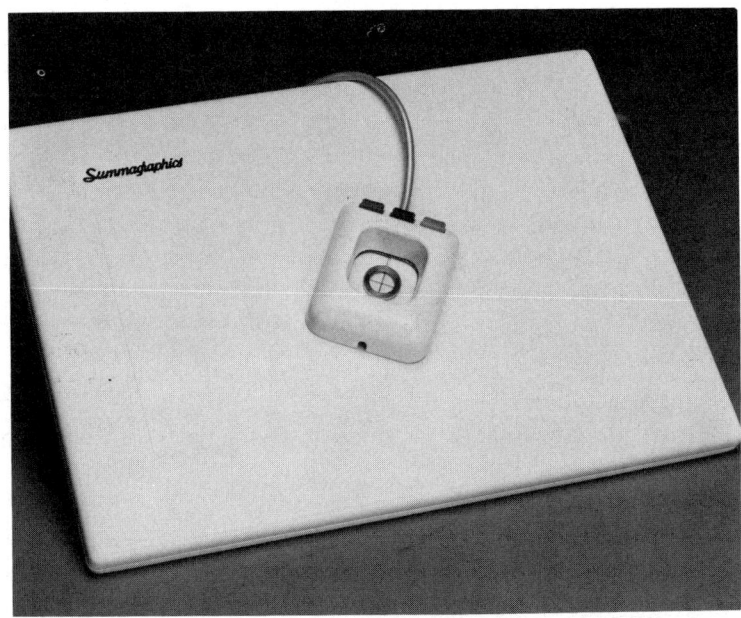

Figure 13.6.3. Mouse and tablet.

The Tablet

The **tablet,** a square or rectangle about the size of the screen, as shown in Figure 13.6.4, is indirect input. A **stylus** or multibutton mouse (as in Figure 13.6.3) matches the tablet design. Built into the tablet is a **coordinate grid** to sense stylus position and convert it into digital coordinates. The resulting signal goes to the terminal.

Alternative methods for detecting stylus position on tablets include

- an electrical grid.
- a capacitive effect.
- a sound source and several microphone pickups.

Positioning

The stylus position on the tablet shows immediately on the screen. As you move it, the tablet reports each new position to the program, which moves the cursor. Tactile/visual feedback tells you how to move the stylus. Keep your eye on the screen, adjust the direction of stylus motion and the cursor goes where it's supposed to. Press the stylus button to set position; the software confirms by displaying a marker.

Figure 13.6.4. Stylus and tablet.

Continuous Mode

This mode is particularly effective for entering sketches, maps and line drawings attached to the tablet. Rear illumination through translucent glass helps you trace a sketch.

Continuous mode scans the stylus at a fixed rate, as you move it, to report points along the way. The program then makes lines between pairs of points which show on the screen as a continuous curve. The rate of line segment generation is adjustable. Turn continuous mode on or off with a button on the stylus or mouse, from the menu (Section 13.7) or with a function key.

To end a curve, press the button. Now further stylus movement does not produce lines. Move to another position, press the button and begin drawing again. Erasing mistakes and reentering corrected lines is easy. The mouse works the same way, but you move it along the table to draw with it.

Light Pen

The light pen is true **direct entry.** Put the stylus on the CRT screen; its position is scanned and reported to software in either the terminal or the host with both visual and tactile feedback. The stylus CAP is reported anywhere on the screen that is lit.

Stylus

The stylus is called a **light pen,** but this is a misnomer; it does not *emit* light; a photosensitive detector at its tip *detects* light. A button on top reports an action. A light pen in use is shown in Figure 13.6.5.

The light pen is coupled to software synchronized with raster generation. The pen's position on the screen emits light during only a fraction of each raster scan, which the photocell detects, emitting a signal. The software notes when the signal arrives relative to the raster scan and determines the pen's coordinates. When the stylus is in motion, its position is reported once on each raster scan. Raster scan rates, either 30 or 60 per second, are fast enough for most purposes. Reporting fails if the photocell is in a dark area. You cannot pick up light from a black screen.

Positioning with a Grid

A superimposed grid overcomes this difficulty. An additional (ninth) memory image plane produces grid of horizontal and vertical lines on the screen. Any point on the grid can be reported.

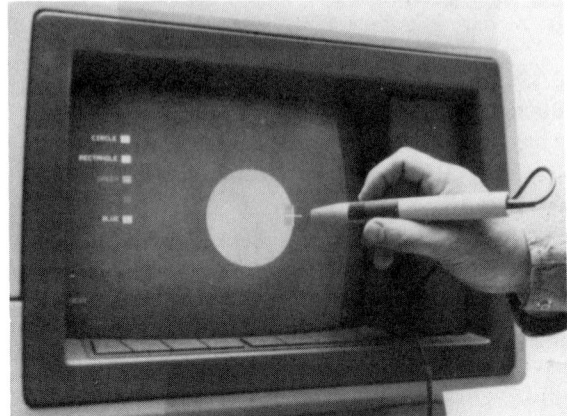

Figure 13.6.5. Light pen.

Cursor Feedback Loop

A cursor stylus feedback lets you move the cursor through a dark area on the screen: the stylus picks up light in an *area* rather than from a point. The photocell covers a number of rels on the screen.

It appears as though the stylus drags the cursor across the screen. Actually, the software picks up a new position as long as the stylus overlaps *part* of the cursor. The next raster scan presents the cursor at its last previous detected position. The cross hair pursues the pen!

Figure 13.6.6 makes this clear. At the left, the crosshair shows as a vertical and horizontal line of dots. The stylus intersects most of them. While in motion, the circular photocell picks up light from only some of the dots in the cross-hair but enough for an accurate fix as shown at the right of the figure.

The software receives signals from the stylus during several different parts

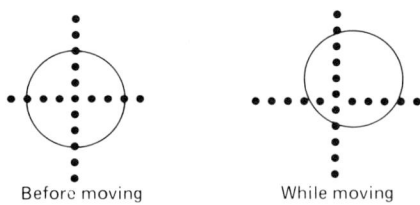

Before moving   While moving

Figure 13.6.6. Cursor feedback.

of the raster scan. The feedback module averages out the signals and calculates the position of the stylus for *this* raster, which displays as a crosshair on the *next* raster.

This works well as long as you don't move the stylus too fast: if the stylus moves out of range, the cursor detects *no* light and there is no way to figure out its position. One solution is to **flood the screen**. When the cursor is lost, ask for *flood* and *all* the screen is lit for an instant; the software finds the photo cell and the cursor reappears.

Text

Few visual images communicate without text. Most require labels, names, scaling and dimensions. For business, bar and pie charts make no sense unless each bar or sector is labeled. Mechanical and architectural drawings need text, too.

Creating

One or more character generators is included in the terminal with one or more ROMs. Other character sets can be **downloaded,** transmitted by the host to the terminal.

A simple command to the terminal software puts it in text mode. Keystrokes are now recognized as characters instead of commands. Control sequences still convey certain requests, such as changing the character set, its size or switching to menu control. One command sequence restores graphics mode. Commands in the text mode enable you to select the

- typeface;
- size of the characters;
- characteristics of the characters used—italic, bold, underline, etc.;
- orientation - horizontal, vertical or rotated;
- color of the text.

An Extra Plane

Sometimes an *extra* image plane is available just for text. Characters keyed at the cursor are placed in this plane and appear as an overlay, generally in white.

The beauty of an additional plane is that when its color is set to black the text disappears; you can alter an image without distraction; restore it to white when done. It also allows you to alternate between text and menus, a much easier way to give commands which we now examine.

13.7 MENU DRIVEN GRAPHICS

A **menu** for the word processor and application program presents a set of text alternatives. This expedites response because you need not remember a command mnemonic nor key sequence. Choose by hitting a key named in the menu.

An interactive entry device is often available for graphics. Choose by **pointing** at a square in a **graphics menu:** move the cursor to a labeled square and press the button.

General Description

Let's examine how menu driven graphics works in the middle of a session to alter a complicated color image on the screen. The menu is an overlay which does not detract from the image. In Figure 13.7.1, a menu and picture share the screen. Figure 13.7.2 shows a menu system in use.

There are so many things to do in the graphics environment; it is im-

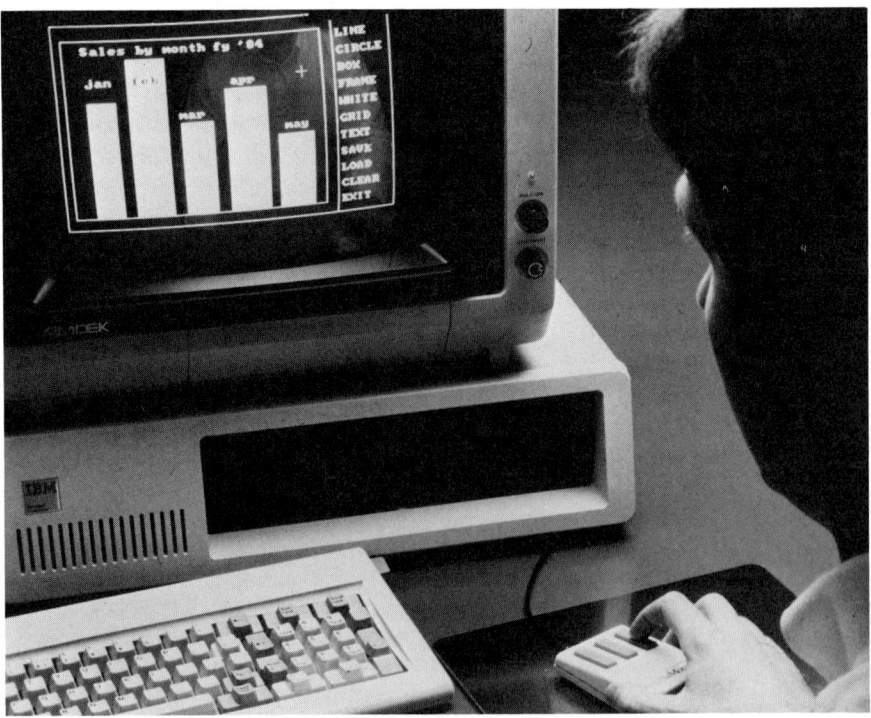

Figure 13.7.1. Menu at the right of the image.

13.7 MENU DRIVEN GRAPHICS

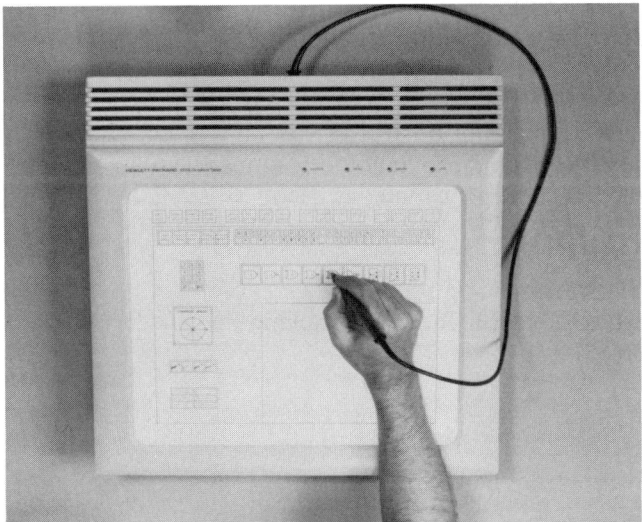

Figure 13.7.2. Menu activated from tablet overlay.

possible to put all of them on a single menu. Instead, a number of **submenus** often list actions of one type and name other submenus.

You get to a submenu from the **main menu** or another submenu. Here is a sample of typical submenus:

- construction by line segments and circles;
- sketching with continuous lines;

570 GRAPHICS

- color table definition and fill;
- object naming, definition and manipulation;
- zoom, pan and scroll.

Even these *simple* activities may not be available in all systems. Constructing three dimensional objects, and moving and rotating them are complex actions which may require multiple submenus each.

Action

The operator **points** at a submenu choice by moving the cursor to its box and pressing the stylus button.

Scenarios

A few scenarios show how simple this is.

Straight Line Figures

For **polygon** generation, move the cursor to its first point and press the button. A symbol called an **icon** or a dot appears. Move the cursor to the next point and press the button. A line segment joins it to the first point; the icon moves to the cursor position. Continue thus until finished. Move the cursor to a box in the menu for a new mode or submenu and press the button to exit.

Color Fill

The color terminal provides a palette (of 4 to 256 or more colors). The palette is chosen from a larger range of colors, sometimes as many as one million. The system may provide a **default palette,** a preselected set of colors, to let you get started. For some color micros   e is a fixed set of colors.

Try to describe a color; nothing is as effective as seeing it. To make color choice simple, the palette is reproduced within the color submenu. Let us see how to fill a closed area with a chosen color:

1. Select the *color fill* option from the color submenu;
2. Put the stylus someplace in a closed figure and press the button;
3. A cross hair appears within the figure;
4. Put the stylus on one of the variegated color bars of the palette to select a color;

5. Press the button;
6. The area is filled with the chosen color;
7. Turn off the fill feature to do something else.

Changing the Palette

To add new colors to the palette, select an empty color bar. You might set up a larger square on the main display to see the color better. Three squares containing the primary colors (red, blue and green) are also on the palette submenu to mix into the square.

Select a color, choose to *add* color to the square and indicate an increment rate by picking boxes on the menu. Color fills the square at a low intensity, becoming more intense at the rate you set. Hit the stylus button to stop. Mix in a second and third spectral colors, watching the result. If too much of one color is present, choose to *subtract* that color.

You increase or decrease the *brightness* of the color when it is the right hue by *proportionately* increasing the amount of each primary color. Pick the *bright* or *dull* menu square and press the stylus button both to start and stop the change.

This is probably a *saturated* color. To get a tint, add white: place the stylus on the *tint* square and press the button to add increments of white. Should the color become too pale, point to *untint* to reduce the tint by *decrementing* white. Thus by touching boxes on the menu you adjust the color of a bar on the palette to the hue, intensity and saturation you desire.

A palette change alters an existing image which is colored by a changed color bar. Any palette color is changed as described. Areas in the image change simultaneously as the palette is altered. (A change takes effect on the next scan.)

Menu Requirements

The graphics menu is *not* built into the terminal. It is run by a program in the host.

Communication

The operator talks *to the menu program* via input devices and the stylus. The keyboard is mostly inoperable. Imagine that the input device is a tablet and stylus with entry buttons and that an image and the menu now display. Move the stylus on the tablet to move the cursor. Talk to the terminal only via the tablet. The terminal picks up the stylus coordinates and alters image memory to display the cursor in a corresponding position. The host is not involved yet.

If the cursor is in a square of the menu or a point on the image and you press the stylus button, the terminal returns the present stylus (and cursor) position to the program. It interprets the stylus position and directs the terminal by issuing one or more graphic primitives.

The program then resets the terminal to

- respond to tablet input internally by moving the cursor;
- transmit the next position *only* when the operator hits the entry button.

Implementation for a Submenu

Examine a typical submenu program in block form invoked from a menu, shown as Figure 13.7.3. If a submenu program is not in memory, an executive program brings it from the system disk.

Submenu Image

First the submenu image is projected on the screen. The submenu file is a set of commands which the program issues to the terminal to create the menu in the ninth image plane (superimposing it on the margin). The com-

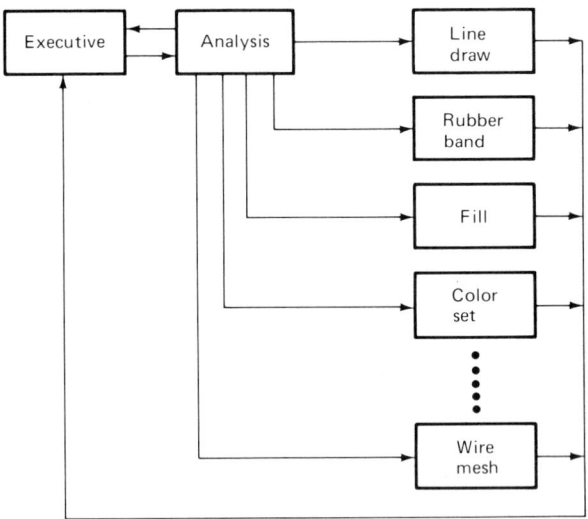

Figure 13.7.3. Interrelation of menu routines.

mands erase the previous submenu and *create* the new one: they make boxes, write text on the screen and enter colors in boxes where appropriate.

Executive Routine

An **executive routine** accepts and interprets your choice. It activates the stylus and awaits input. Choose a box, put the sylus there and press the button. This transmits a coordinate pair through the terminal to the executive routine.

An **analysis routine** examines the coordinate pair, comparing it to several ranges of coordinates. It

- finds which range the pair belongs to, if any;
- calls a routine to fulfill the function;
- displays an error message if the stylus is not in a choice box and returns to the executive routine.

Line Segment Routine

The **line segment** routine (LS) receives stylus positions and moves the cursor accordingly. When you mark a coordinate by pressing the button, and LS sends an icon to the terminal and reactivates the tablet. For the second (or other successive) point, the LS routine sends a line command to the terminal and enables cursor display again.

Any screen pixel in the image area is a proper terminal point for a *line* command, but pixels on the menu are out of bounds. Thus you have a way to stop drawing lines and do something else. The analysis routine screens out messages for a function change from its directions. A function request gives control to the executive.

Sketching Aids

The "graphics processor" helps sketch figures on the screen. A few instances show how.

Rubber Band

Figure 13.7.4 illustrates **rubber band** aid for creating line segments. A diagram hardly does justice to how simple it is to position a straight line anyplace on the screen—you have to experience it.

In rubber band mode, place the cursor at the initial point and press the stylus button; an icon appears. Now moving the cursor pulls a line away

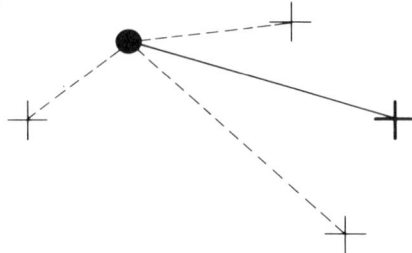

Figure 13.7.4. Rubber band.

from that point, like pulling out taffy. The line follows the cursor like a rubber band, except that the line is guaranteed to remain straight: stretch it way out or bring it back; it follows. Press the button to *set* the line.

The rubber band routine uses line to create and erase lines. It *continuously* monitors signals from the stylus, comparing each coordinate pair with the last CAP received. Should the two differ, the rubber band routine changes the current color to black and issues a line command to erase the old line; then it resets *X* and *Y* and issues line to write in the previous color.

Rubber Circle

You continuously change the radius of a **rubber circle.** Enter this mode through the menu; establish the center of the circle by *pointing*. Move the cursor outward from the center and a circle appears with its circumference passing through the cursor, as in Figure 13.7.5. As you move the cursor towards or away from the center, the circle's radius changes.

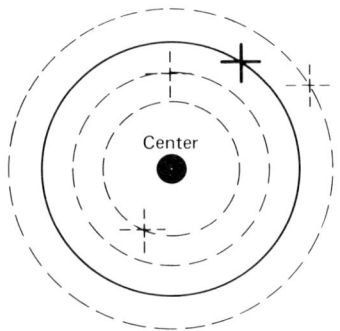

Figure 13.7.5. Rubber circle.

Rubber Rectangle

Establish an origin and move the cursor. The routine draws a rectangle with sides parallel to the *X* and *Y* axes (as shown in Figure 13.7.6) defined by a *diagonal* from the origin to the CAP. Moving the cursor erases the rubber rectangle and constructs another in the new position.

Rotated Rubber Rectangle

You establish an origin (*start*) *and* an axis for this extension of the rubber rectangle as shown in Figure 13.7.7. Move the cursor to define a diagonal between the origin and the CAP. The rectangle has two sides parallel and two perpendicular to the axis.

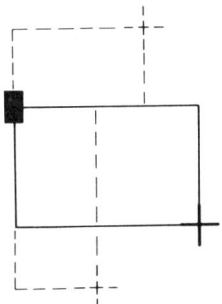

Figure 13.7.6. Rubber rectangle.

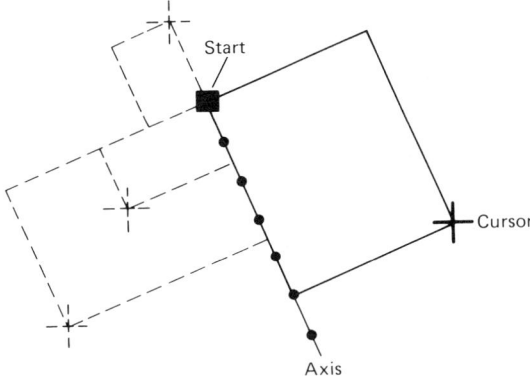

Figure 13.7.7. Rotated rubber rectangle.

Grow

The **grow** (or scaling) routine changes the size of an object defined relatively. Choose a *grow* factor: greater than 1 to enlarge it, less than 1 to reduce it. Make the object grow, continuously; or in single steps of the factor by pressing the button as in Figure 13.7.8.

The routine reworks all lines by progressively determining the vertices of the enlarged object. To find the *next* vertex, it finds the angle and length of this line segment, and increases its length by the factor.

Drag

After creating an object relatively, you can move it with **drag**. With the cursor on its origin, as shown in Figure 13.7.9, move the stylus and the object is *dragged* across the screen.

This works like *rubber band*. As the CAP changes, the routine erases the old copy of the object (by writing it in black) and draws a new copy at the CAP.

Figure 13.7.8. Making an object grow.

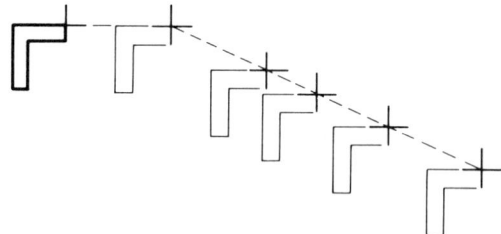

Figure 13.7.9. Dragging an object.

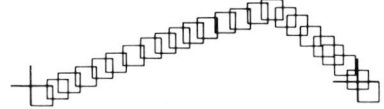

Figure 13.7.10. Multiple image draw action.

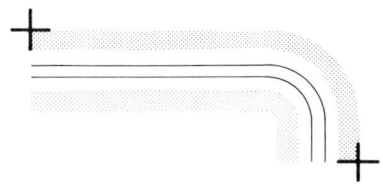

Figure 13.7.11. Brush stroke.

Multiple Images

Alter the procedure for *drag;* instead of erasing each image, let it stay on the screen. Now, as you drag an object across the screen, multiple images are produced as shown in Figure 13.7.10. You set the image production rate thus if you move the stylus faster, fewer copies of the object appear.

Brush Stroke

Instead of using a thin line to sketch with, define a **brush,** which is a short line segment. As you *drag* the line segment across the screen, it produces a brush stroke of the predefined color and width. Create irregularities in the brush by making it dashed, dotted or irregular to produce a brush stroke like that shown in Figure 13.7.11. You can even make the brush an object.

13.8 OUTPUT

Introduction

A visual image is transient; turn off the computer and it disappears. It is no longer in the image plane memory on powering up. It can be preserved as

- a digitally recorded image on disk;
- hard copy by printing or by photography.

Digital Storage

An image in progress is held as bits in the image planes. It can be dumped on disk and later returned to image memory. If done bit by bit, its storage may take up a whole floppy disk for a single high resolution color image and also take considerable time—several minutes. **Compression,** discussed below, reduces the space required.

An alternative procedure records the *commands* that produced the image. When reissued, they create a new image in exactly the same sequence before your eyes.

Hard Copy

Hard copy for graphics includes photographs, and plots and printouts on on vellum, Mylar or paper.

Digital Storage

Bit by Bit

After a session of creating and revising, the image is in two forms:

- on the screen;
- stored in the image plane.

On request, a computer program transmits a byte at a time from the image memory to a named file. The time required to store or retrieve the image depends upon the number of pixels.

Data Compression

A monochrome line drawing displays as a black screen with just a few white areas. Image memory contains mostly 0s and very few 1s. Instead of recording all the bits, why not *compress* the data? For **run length encoding,** a routine writes the current bit value (1 or 0), followed by a *number* for the quantity of successive bits which has this value. An area which contains a thousands 0s can thus be encoded in a few bytes. For line drawings, the data reduction factor may be a factor of 10 or more. Compression applies also to recording color.

Storing Commands

By issuing keyboard commands or through routines, primitives create an image. If reissued, starting with a clear screen, the drawing sequence produces the same result, only speeded up many times.

During image creation, as the graphics package sends commands to the terminal, another routine can assemble an edited primitive list. When you finish, you may elect to write this list to disk. The space required to store primitives may be smaller than that needed for compressed image bits.

Culling

An intelligent recording routine can cull out unnecessary commands of several classes ranging from obvious to subtle:

1. Communication commands turn on and off stylus control and accept information passed back and forth.
2. Intermediate commands, as for rubber banding or form movement, produce a form and then erase it until it is *set* into the picture.

The executive routine may make a command file omitting directives about transmission (1). A set of commands to destroy or move an existing object (2) corresponds to a previous set which created the object and appears earlier in the command file. The executive routine searches the command file to see whether an *erase* command set has an equivalent *create* command set. These erase commands are forwarded to the display. But instead of being entered into the command file, the comparable creation commands are removed.

Effect

Compressing the command file reduces both storage and the time to recreate the drawing. An image created from a command file looks like a drawing produced by an invisible hand, an especially dramatic effect if slowed down with a programmed time delay. For a small drawing, the entire command file is read back and executed so quickly that the image jumps onto the screen without a production sequence being shown.

Sometimes the host has a command file collection program built into the graphics package. It provides automatic backup: at frequent intervals the memory copy of the command history file is rewritten to disk. This is an important safeguard. After a full day's work on an important drawing, such as a microchip design, a power failure can wipe you out. Automatic backup keeps a very recent image.

Photographic Images

The CRT is a source of light, but its face reflects light which the camera captures. Hence the CRT and camera combination must be shielded, or room lights made very dim.

An attactive alternative, a self-contained unit attaches by cable like an external supplementary monitor. It consists of a miniature high intensity color CRT built around a camera holder and costs less than $3000.

When the screen image is satisfactory, you would activate this unit and snap the picture. Use Polaroid, color negative, monochrome or slide film; the latter is by far the most popular. After developing, slides of bar charts, pie charts and so forth, with captions formatted attractively, are immediately available for an executive briefing.

Hard Copy

Graphics hard copy is produced by printing or plotting with ink on paper, Mylar or vellum. Three difficulties arise in creating a faithful image:

1. Pigment and light do not obey the same rules for mixing.
2. Raster presentation may need to be adapted to stroke drawing, or stroke generation to dot matrix printing
3. Large areas of intense color may not reproduce well.

Hard copy is never quite as good as photography for full color fidelity.

Mixing Colors

The CRT produces most colors *additively*: light produced by the three spots in the triad is added and smoothed by the eyes.

A *pigment* is **subtractive:** it absorbs all light *except* those frequencies which produce its characteristic color; red pigment absorbs all except red light. A red dress appears almost black in blue light because the red pigment absorbs all the blue light and there is little left to reflect to the viewer's eyes.

Almost everyone has played with paint, watercolor, crayon or coloring pencils. Mixing rules for pigments are not the same as for light: if you want violet, mix red and blue paint; red and blue *light* mixed in equal proportions produce magenta.

Metering Pigments

Assume that there are rules to generate *pigment* mixtures for each color on the palette. How do we actually mix the pigments in the proper proportions while printing? Methods described below can reproduce only a few screen colors accurately.

Image Generation Technique

The methods examined shortly create an image as either

- a sequence of dots;
- a line drawn by a pen.

These correspond respectively to raster scan and vector stroke image production. A raster scan image is easy to convert into a sequence of dots, but requires a program for strokes to control a pen type output. Similarly, a vector stroke method easily produces pen output, but requires a program to convert to a dot sequence.

Solid Colors

A broad expanse of color on the screen is impressive. Produced on paper as a sequence of dots or horizontal and vertcal lines, it is often dull and insipid.

Dot Matrix Printer

The dot matrix printer produces a line of text by scanning across the paper from left to right. The print head has a number of print needles, activated individually to print dots, part of a vertical line segment (for a typical grid, see Figure 4.3.1). Print needles lay down a pattern of dots for each letter, hitting a black ribbon to leave an impression of a character on the paper.

This printer readily prints graphics: each needle prints successive dots on *one* line of the raster. The top 10 lines of a graphics display print in one pass for a print head of ten needles. The paper is advanced (by 10 scan lines) and the next pass prints the next 10 lines.

The head prints in either direction and many printers can automatically invert the order of dots in the print buffer. Matrix printers have reached a high stage of development, are inexpensive ($400–$1000) and are ideal for monochrome business graphics. Since solid black areas do not print as well, it is preferable to fill boxes or sectors with patterns. A page should print in a few minutes.

Color matrix printers use multicolor bonded ribbon. Many machines print each color of each dot separately. This increases print time considerably. A page may take up to an hour to print.

Color matrix printout cannot produce an accurate rendition of screen colors. If hue, saturation and tint are important, this method leaves much to be desired. If color only distinguishes one kind of box from another, as with bar charts and pie charts, then color rendition is less important and the matrix printer serves well.

Ink Jet Printer

The ink jet printer is similar to the dot matrix printer, but jets of ink substitute for print needles. Via multiple reservoirs, jets of two or three inks provide color output. Quality tends to be better, because the ink is fluid and distributes itself evenly to produce better-formed lines. Metering colors is still a problem, except when only two or three colors display on the copy.

Plotter

These important devices come in a wide range, from the size of a pad of paper to twelve feet long. Figure 13.8.1 shows a small business plotter; they cost from $600 to $2000. Figure 13.8.2, p. 584, shows drafting print beds.

A flat plate or a cylinder holds a sheet of paper firmly as the drawing is made. An arm holds a pen. Commands from the computer lower or raise the pen. Other commands position the pen or draw straight and curved lines. The pen is raised, repositioned and lowered to start a new line.

To change colors, the device returns the pen to its holder and chooses another. A variety of colors, perhaps a dozen or more, may be available according to plotter design and cost. A long line of any color is drawn in a fraction of a second.

It is easy to see that this method of producing the image is not compatible with the raster. A program to produce a drawing on the screen must be converted to line drawing primitives. Any curved line is produced with a number of short straight line segments. Text characters are actually drawn thus.

Multiple pens provide a range of colors. Superimposing lines or areas

Figure 13.8.1. Pen plotter for business applications.

makes different hues. An area of solid color is produced by a series of lines with wide nibs with overlapping strokes.

13.9 IBM PC/XT GRAPHICS

Introduction

Section 13.2 contrasts three types of graphic systems, from hobby graphics through management systems to the professional terminal. The intermediate management system has limitations in resolution and lacks some fine points but is suitable for many business applications.

IBM has taken the memory mapped technique for its graphics and embellished it to provide medium quality, medium resolution graphics in a small, moderately priced system.

584 GRAPHICS

Figure 13.8.2. Drafting quality plotters.

Memory Mapped Video

Figure 13.9.1 shows memory mapped video. One memory (in the center) stores the graphic image in bit form. The program constructs the image pixel by pixel. The program can no longer give a simple command to the terminal, line, and then let you continue to create the image by selecting new commands as necessary.

At the left in Figure 13.9.1 is the microprocessor and the program to create the image. At the right is the display circuitry to review image memory many times per second and create and refresh the image on the display.

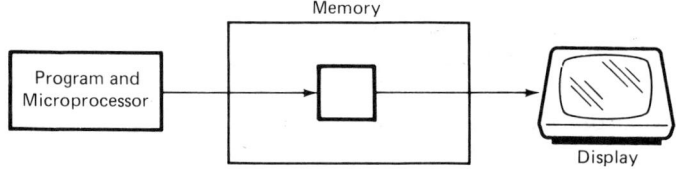

Figure 13.9.1. Simple form of memory mapped video.

Figure 13.9.2 shows this in pictorial form, oriented to the IBM PC chassis. At the bottom, the microprocessor chip runs a program which creates bits to place in image memory. It sends these bits to the graphics PC board plugged into a slot on the PC. (Note that *PC* has two meanings: *printed circuit* and *personal computer*.) The PC display board has the memory which holds the image. It is connected directly to the display circuitry, which projects the image.

Problems and Solutions

Limited Memory

Memory mapped video has two problems, obvious in the small hobby computers when creating images for games and learning programs. The first is the amount of memory available for the image. The hobby computer usually has a total maximum memory of 64K. If more memory is used for

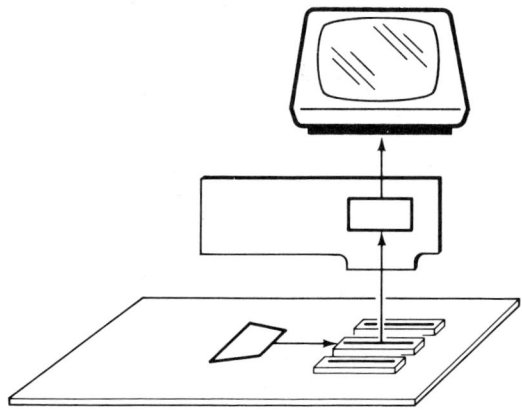

Figure 13.9.2. Pictorial view of PC chassis with video board.

image storage, then image definition is higher. But less memory is left for the program which creates the image.

The PC solution is simple: it addresses up to 1MB. The 16K image memory makes hardly a dent in the memory left for program purposes.

Program/Display Conflict

The second problem is the conflict arising when two agencies need to use the same area of memory:

- the computer puts part of the image into refresh memory;
- the display accesses image memory constantly to refresh the screen 60 times a second.

The solution is **two port memory;** two paths to memory are shown in Figure 13.9.3. The path for writing does not interfere with that for reading, except when the same exact byte is addressed; then the display gets it, holding up the processor for only one cycle. Thus the computer program can create an image while the display simultaneously presents it on the screen.

Graphic Boards

There are several kinds of so-called **graphic (PC) boards.** IBM provides a monochrome and a color graphics board; competitors also produce boards

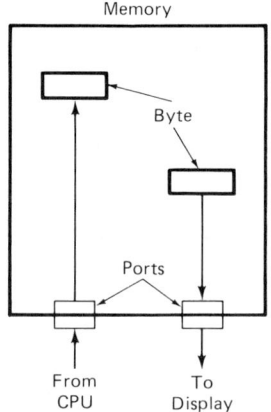

Figure 13.9.3. Two port memory.

with multiple options, such as expansion memory and communication as well as a real time clock.

All boards plug into an expansion slot on the system board (see Figure 6.6.4) and contain at least these items:

- RAM chips for graphic image memory;
- dual ports to RAM;
- interfacing to the system board bus;
- timing and scan circuitry to examine image memory;
- generation circuitry to create the signals to drive the monitor;
- circuits to interface with the monitor.

Memory

The PC has considerable addressing space (1MB), all of which is usable, regardless of physical position. Referring to the memory map from Section 6.6 displayed here as Figure 13.9.4, we see that

- minimum memory (64K) is addressed staring at the bottom of the addressing space, paragraph 0;

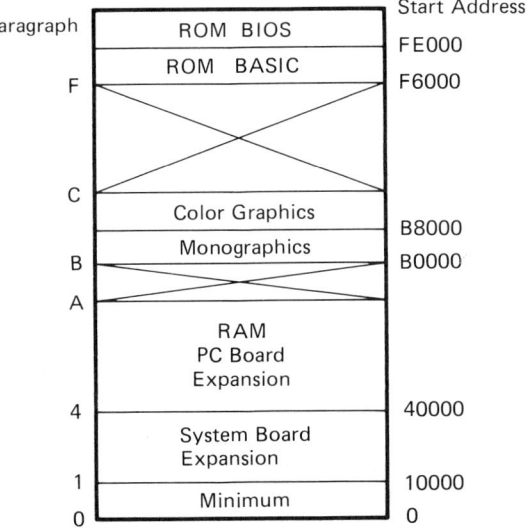

Figure 13.9.4 IBM PC memory assignments.

- chips added to the system board are addressed just above this at the bottom of the space, paragraphs 1 to 3;
- the ROM on the system board is at the top of memory, paragraph F;
- expansion memory on PC board may occupy paragraphs 4 through 9;
- graphic memory occupies parts of paragraph B.

A complete 64K segment is allocated for graphics (64K) starting at B0000. Half of this, beginning at segment B0000, is for the monochrome display; the other half, at location B8000, is for color graphics.

Commonality of Memory

All memory is immediately accessible to the microprocessor. According to the address value, the system board RAM or ROM or memory on any other board is activated. All memory looks identical to the microprocessor.

Memory Mapping

Image memory stores the information to be displayed on the screen in digital form.

Character Storage

Although 32K is set aside for character memory, only 4K is actually used and incorporated on the graphic board. The monitor displays 25 lines of either 40 or 80 characters. Most screens display 80 character lines so that a total of 2000 characters is displayable. Two bytes describe each character to display (4K required to display 2000 characters). The first byte is its ASCII code; the second, or **attribute byte** says how it displays: brightness, underline, blink, color of both foreground and background where applicable, and direct or reverse video.

Image Display

The IBM graphics card provides two kinds of image display:

- High resolution consists of 200 lines of 640 pixels each.
- Medium resolution consists of 200 lines of 320 pixels each.

High resolution graphics produces good definition but no color; medium resolution graphics produces color at less definition.

Interlace

The standard television set produces an **interlaced image** to reduce flicker which would otherwise be annoying at a scan rate of 30 frames per second. Lines of the image are even or odd according to their number, as shown in Figure 13.9.5. The scan for each frame is broken into two parts.

First, even lines are generated, starting at the top and ending with the last even line at the bottom. Then the second half of the scan returns the beam to the top and produces odd numbered lines in order. As even numbered lines fade away, odd numbered lines light up, thus reducing flicker in the image.

Two Part Memory

At the bottom of Figure 13.9.5, we see that image memory consists of two parts: an even line block for even lines and an odd line block.

High Resolution

The high resolution display uses 1 bit pixels, 640 pixels per line, to convey on-off for monochrome packed into 80 bytes per line. This corresponds to the text information line, which is also 80 bytes. Storing the image takes 16K: 200 lines of 80 bytes.

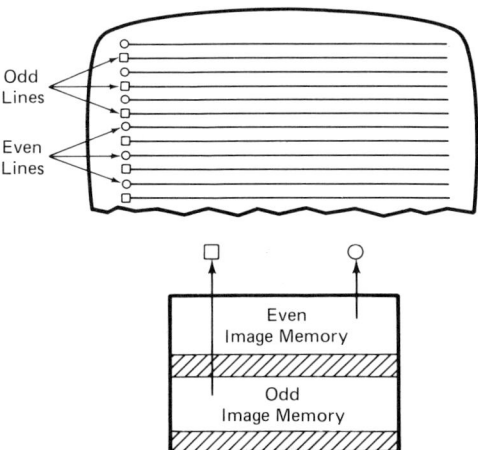

Figure 13.9.5. The interlaced image.

Medium Resolution

Medium resolution uses 2 bit pixels and 320 pixels per line, or 80 bytes. Again, 16K of image memory is needed.

Two bit pixels convey only four alternatives. Yet the monitor displays 16 standard colors. How is this managed? The program sets up a **palette** of 4 out of 16 colors with a command which sets a register on the graphic board. This is a tiny color table, where the two bits are decoded into one of the four colors, each described by 4 bits of another 16 bit register.

Text Mode for Graphics

The color graphics board operates in **text mode** on command. Then ASCII character codes are stored in memory. A character generator in the graphic board's ROM is referenced, using this code to determine the pixels which govern each REL. When the color graphics board is used to display text, image memory stores character codes, not pixels.

But image memory is 16K, which is four times larger that than required for a full 80 by 25 character display. Why let all this memory go to waste? Instead, divide the 16K into four 4K pages. Then each page can store one screen of text. (This works for 25 lines of 40 characters also, now providing eight pages of 2K each.)

The multipage text memory feature is ignored by many application programs because they have to be compatible with the monochrome display, but you can readily see its advantage. The program can prepare a new page for display while the old page is in view of the operator. When the new page is composed, the program switches to it and the operator sees a new display at once.

This requires these hardware features on the graphics board under program control:

1. Both ports are used;
2. Writing to and reading from a page to the display are switched by computer;
3. Reading and writing are independent.

The 8088 processor does not have specific commands for switching pages. This is actually an I/O request. Service requests to the BIOS in ROM make graphic paging simpler for the application programmer. Graphic features in BIOS are explained shortly.

Character Graphics

There are a number of special characters in ROM for character graphics: solid squares, half squares, quarter squares and so forth. They are called up by special ASCII codes. You can form images on the screen by combining these characters in different ways. True, these are crude pictures, but this technique is ideal for creating bar charts. The sample music program on the system disk (provided by IBM when you purchase the PC) shows a piano keyboard created with character graphics.

A savvy user can create an additional set of graphics in RAM which is then available through BIOS, as explained below.

Text Colors

Text for color graphics, as noted on page 588, uses two bytes per character. The first is the character code and the second is the attribute byte. Text displays with a foreground and a background color. One nibble of the attribute byte indicates foreground color and the other background color. Many different color combinations for text result. Further, a few attribute combinations are reserved to distinguish special characters, like the cursor.

Video Services In BIOS

Section 7.8 discusses how application programs request special services from the operating system. In brief review, the application program puts a number into a processor register showing the service it requires. Then it issues INT (a command), a program initiated interrupt. Control goes through the interrupt vector to a set of commands in ROM at the top of the addressing space.

INT activates a routine in the operating system in system ROM. The OS determines the service required from the number passed in the register and passes control to that routine. These services are called BIOS, Basic Input Output Serivces. A group of these services is devoted entirely to the graphics boards. For simplicity, let me coin the phrase VIOS for Video I/O Service.

VIOS has created problems for IBM's competitors. The code in ROM is copyrighted. Look-alike manufacturers have copied VIOS in their ROM. Several were sued by IBM but settled out of court and agreed to desist. Other companies manufacturing compatible systems have had difficulty in making legal substitutions for the VIOS functions by putting them in RAM. That is why IBM PC look-alikes rarely have comparable graphic functions and hence many graphic programs which run so well on the PC and XT do not perform as well or at all on the look-alikes.

Functions

Here is a sample of functions performed by VIOS:

A. Switch between the various text and image modes;
B. Set cursor size;
C. Move the cursor to a specified position;
D. Read cursor position and size for the AP;
E. Read the light pen position;
F. Switch pages for the display;
G. Scroll graphics (see below);
H. Set character attributes;
I. Set the color palette;
J. Set or read the pixel color;
K. Enter a character and move the cursor;
L. Backspace.

Window Scrolling

Window scrolling is an example of a powerful VIOS feature. A program can move a portion of the screen currently recorded in image memory either up or down by a specific number of lines, entering new information at the bottom (or top). A command transmits the position of the window by naming its upper left and lower right hand corner.

Programs have come out recently to take advantage of this feature to provide a programming environment (see Chapter 15) which lets the user access two or more programs simultaneously. The screen shows a "window" into each program, which is manipulated independently.

14
Spread Sheets

14.1 INTRODUCTION

This chapter is a detailed discussion of typical electronic spread sheet programs and applications. VisiCalc was the first and the most widely used **electronic spread sheet, ES program** or simply **SS**. Introductory examples are drawn from SuperCalc but the material presented applies to most SSs, including CalcStar, Perfect Calc, ProCalc, MicroPlan, MiniModel, Plan 80 and VisiCalc. SuperCalc, Multiplan and Lotus 1-2-3 are described in detail.

SS software has had an enormous impact. VisiCalc sold desktop computing to the business community more than any other software product.

Popularity

Millions of copies of ES programs are used on all popular computers, including the IBM PC and its clones; the TRS 80 III; Apple II and Apple III. Here are some reasons why ES programs are so popular:

1. They are **user friendly.** They are easy to operate and can be learned quickly, especially by those with an accounting background or who have experience working with columns of numbers.
2. You have **instantaneous feedback** when developing a spread sheet. If you change a single number, the SS automatically recomputes all affected items.
3. **Complex formulas** are written and tested rapidly. The SS has a cell oriented editor for rapid entry of formulas and data.

Effectiveness

The effectiveness of SS software products lies in their design and the incorporation of principles which guarantee the immediate acceptance of their functionality.

1. *Common frame of reference.* Almost everyone has worked out problems on paper by setting up rows and columns, filling in the blanks and making calculations to arrive at an answer.
2. *Easy to apply.* The spread sheet is a generic format; it is not specific to any application. With little experience you become aware of just how many things can be set up using it.
3. *Easy to use.* Only a few commands are required to start using a spread sheet; it is not necessary to know programming. The spread sheet program provides a number of screen reinforcements—mode indicators, alternative command or menu choices, even help menus which facilitate your progress.
4. *Instant feedback.* Changes are immediately reflected on the screen, giving you a feeling of control and enhancing the idea that you are using a tool. You are hardly aware that you are working with a computer.

Description

The electronic spread sheet program provides a columnar pad which displays entries directly on the screen exactly as entered from the keyboard. Just peek ahead at some of the figures in this chapter if you have never seen a spread sheet (**SS**) display.

The Pad

The SS program can store a sizeable pad, larger than can display on the screen at one time. The portion showing has labels for the columns and rows, and brackets the cell you are working on. A **cell**, the intersection of a column and row, contains information entered from the keyboard; the cell can be altered or its contents removed by directions from the keyboard.

In addition to the ability to enter and display a spread sheet, the SS program can

- store the SS on disk for future use;
- load an SS into memory from disk for update on call;
- print out the current SS in memory;
- modify individual entries or cells in the SS;
- incorporate all or part of a disk spread sheet into one that is already in memory.

Cells

A cell is generally given a default size of nine positions on a particular line. This is, a **row** is assigned *one line* in the spread sheet screen, and a **column** is initially nine positions wide. All spread sheets consistently maintain this row size, a single line, but let you vary the column width, either throughout the spread sheet or for columns you select.

A cell contains one of three kinds of information:

1. *Numbers* can include a decimal point and, in some spread sheets, additional characters such as commas, dollar signs and asterisks, or parentheses (for debits).
2. *Text* for *labels* appears above columns and at the left of rows. Text may also appear in the spread sheet to list part numbers, vendor names and so forth.
3. *Formulas* describe calculations made to provide answers displayed in the cell.

The SS records these two things for a formula:

1. The formula itself is hidden except when you work on that particular cell.
2. The result of applying the formula is displayed on the spread sheet at other times.

Entry

It is so easy to get information into the SS. First, position to the desired cell; then key in directly from the keyboard. This is simple even if you are a poor typist because you have backspace correction (see Chapter 11, Word Processing) and you can edit an existing entry. Further, you can erase an entry and start over if you wish. Even when the column is limited to nine positions, long formulas can be stored in a cell because only the *result* of applying the formula usually displays, not the formula itself.

Ways to Use

There are principally four ways to use the SS facility, itemized here and then discussed. Detailed descriptions and examples of each mode are given in other sections of this chapter. The four modes are:

1. Rows are text entries and no calculations are involved.
2. Each row is a text entry but a small amount of calculation is required.
3. Cells mainly contain numbers and formulas for calculation.
4. Models for decision making are easy to set up with an ES.

Without Calculation

This is the simplest type of application. An example is a telephone list. Each row describes one telephone extension: the extension number, department number, the person's name and other important information. Keeping this on a spread sheet makes it easy to delete an entry (by removing an entire row) or to add an entry by inserting a blank row any place and putting in the new information. For a SS which provides it, the list can be sorted by extension number or by its owner's name.

With Modest Calculations

Think of a checking balance as an example of this application. The top line shows the new balance for this period. Each row represents a transaction, a check written against your account or a deposit. At the right is the new balance, the preceding balance plus this transaction. As long as checks and deposits are entered dutifully, this is an excellent way of keeping a checkbook. It provides the current status of your account at a glance and you can get a printout any time.

When you get your statement at the end of the month, just call up the checking account SS. Then reconcile the account and the statement right on the machine. Even if you have made a mistake, it is simple to get a corrected balance sheet by removing the checks returned and replacing the starting balance with the statement balance. The SS program recalculates all the totals for you.

Predominantly Calculation

There are many tables of useful calculations you might create for your business: mortgage payment schedules, amortization, depreciation and so forth. Set up the first column with initial values and the second column with the formula. If you tell the SS how, using the *replicate* command, it alters the formulas accordingly and puts them in each cell of the columns and fills in the table before your eyes.

Models for Decision Making

The SS excels at helping with projections. There is hardly a budgeting department in a large firm that doesn't use the SS for this; applications are so varied that a complete section in this chapter is devoted to its ramifications.

Calculations

SS programs are used for business, scientific and engineering applications that you would typically solve using a pencil, an accounting pad with rows and columns and a calculator. The SS easily does these things among many others:

- sums columns of numbers;
- takes differences between columns;
- multiplies and divides cells across columns and rows;
- solves formulas.

Most SSs do complex financial calculations with a *single statement,* such as computing the present value of a stream of receipts and disbursements. SS programs also provide mathematical functions to compute

- averages, standard deviations, etc.;
- the maximum or minimum or a row or column of numbers;
- calendar arithmetic for time dependent calculations such as investment yields;
- trigonometric and exponential functions.

Perhaps the most popular use of the SS is in "What if?" financial planning and budgeting. These applications involve an iterative review process. A single spread sheet is recalculated many times with different input assumptions.

14.2 BASICS

The Virtual Spread Sheet

What Is It?

The spread sheet (**SS**) consists of a set of cells or boxes, each containing an item of information (or a blank). Cells are arranged in a rectangle as in Figure 14.2.1. Each cell has a *height* and *width,* Figure 14.2.2, which limits what may display. A cell is always one character high and nine (or ten) wide when you first get the spread sheet, its default size. You may alter width.

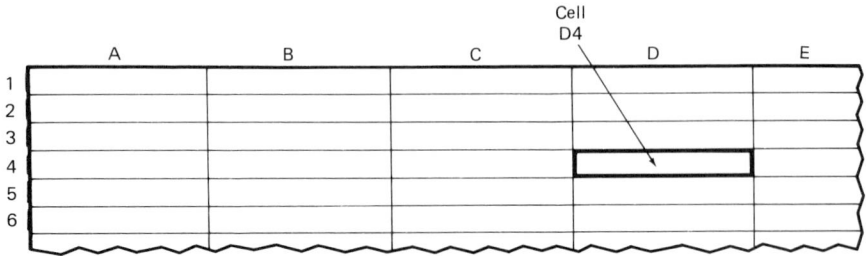

Figure 14.2.1. Cell makeup of the spread sheet.

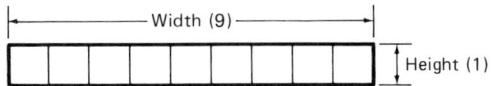

Figure 14.2.2. A typical cell.

Size

Your spread sheet is stored in memory where the amount of room available for it depends on:

- the size of hardware memory;
- the size of the operating system;
- the size of the spread sheet program.

Memory left after bringing in the OS and the SS program and available for the SS is called the **virtual spread sheet (VS).** Earlier spread sheets such as VisiCalc for the Apple and SuperCalc for Z80 computers were limited by a hardware memory of 64K. There, the maximum VS is 63 columns and 254 rows as displayed in Figure 14.2.3. A spread sheet you construct cannot exceed this maximum.

The IBM PC and its look-alikes and systems with the expanded S-100 bus architecture can accommodate 512K bytes of memory or more. The SS program has taken advantage of this: the program itself has grown in size and also provides a larger VS. Lotus 1-2-3, for instance, provides up to 2048 rows and 256 columns.

During creation, the VS space is hardly ever used up. The space in use at any moment is the **actual spread sheet size (AS),** displayed in Figure 14.2.3. This is determined by the right-most column and the bottom-most row which have entries, shown in the figure by the sectioned cells (shaded).

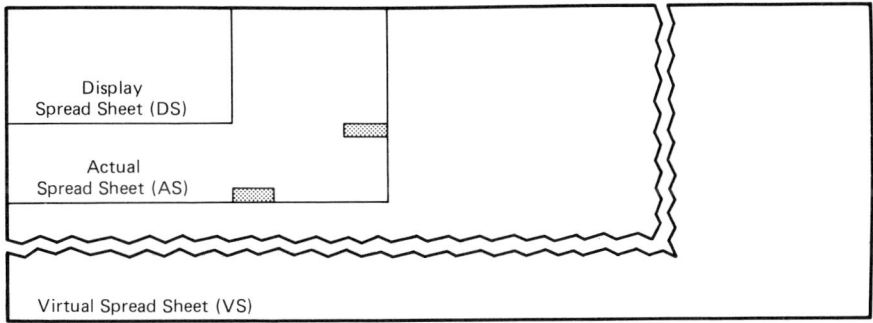

Figure 14.2.3. The display spread sheet (DS), actual SS (AS) and virtual SS (VS).

Referencing

Each row, column and cell has an identifier. The system developed by VisiCalc is perpetuated in *all* other spread sheets (except Multiplan) is:

- a letter (or two letters) identifies each column;
- a number identifies each row;
- a letter and number combination identifies a cell.

This is shown in Figure 14.2.1. Columns are assigned letters starting at the left with A and proceeding alphabetically. Rows are numbered starting at the top with 1 and increasing by 1 as you go downward.

You never run out of numbers for rows: when you run out of single letters, use pairs. SuperCalc uses letters in this order: A...Z, AA, AB, AC...AZ, BA, BB...BK. A cell is named by column letter(s) then row number; cell D4 is emphasized in Figure 14.2.1.

The Screen

Figure 14.2.4 shows the screen content, the *part of the AS that shows,* referred to in Figure 14.2.3 as the **display spread sheet (DS).** In this figure, we see how the VS, AS and DS relate to each other:

- the VS is the largest any SS can be;
- the AS is the area occupied by *this* SS;
- the DS is the portion of the AS now showing on the screen.

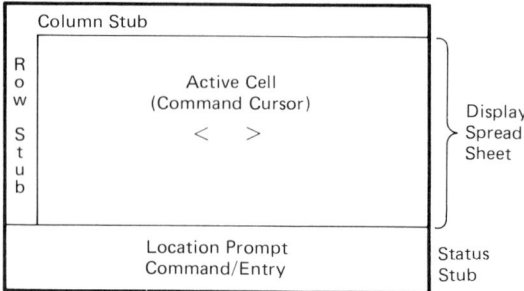

Figure 14.2.4. How the SS screen is used.

Now let us see what shows on the screen--what the DS consists of. The screen in Figure 14.2.4 shows five areas:

- most of the display is taken up by the DSS, a rectangular portion derived from the actual spread sheet;
- the **column stub,** just above, identifies columns;
- the **row stub,** at the left, identifies rows;
- the **status stub** gives you information about the display;
- the **active cell** is the one emphasized by highlighting or brackets and named in the status stub.

The status stub usually requires three lines depending on the SS and may be found at the screen top or bottom: VisiCalc and 1-2-3 place it at the top; SuperCalc and Multiplan, at the bottom.

Initiation

Start the SS running by answering the OS prompt with the name of the program (SC for SuperCalc). Usually the SS gives you a sign-on message. Eventually you get a start-up display with cell A1, at the upper left. Each cell has the default size, generally one by nine characters. The column stub uses one row and the status stub uses three rows, leaving 20 rows for the DS (80 × 24 screen required). With three characters for the row stub, eight columns, A through H, of nine positions each are presented. The result is a DSS 20 rows by 8 columns.

We start with an emply spread sheet and an empty DS. We work at the **active cell,** which is either highlighted or bracketed with a special symbol. VisiCalc uses highlighting while SuperCalc employs the *less than* and *greater than* signs (< >) for brackets. Either is called the **cursor** (for the SS). At startup, the cursor is in cell A1; the status stub indicates this by displaying A1.

The Command Cursor

The cursor pinpoints the active cell, so let's call it the **cell cursor.** The status stub provides a command line shown in Figure 14.2.4, which contains a **command cursor.** When you hit a key, that character appears on the command line and the command cursor moves right. In this way, you formulate a command or assemble data for a cell. Data are not put in the cell until you hit return.

Positioning The Cursor

The *cell cursor* is where the action is; there are two ways to move it, using

- arrow keys;
- the cell number.

Arrow Keys

Modern keyboards have four arrow keys, each producing a code unique to that keyboard. SS programs can be tailored to accept these codes. Press right, left, up or down to move the cell cursor one cell in that direction. As the cursor moves to a column or row not currently displaying, **automatic scrolling** brings that column or row into view. Since the screen is being rewritten, this takes a second or so. Otherwise, cell cursor repositioning is instantaneous.

Many second generation SS programs provide page scroll as with word processors, a useful feature which lets you move by the screenful instead of a row or column at a time.

Status Stub

The **status stub** describes the current cell and command. The stub for SuperCalc consists of three lines. The first line begins with a symbol showing the direction in which the cell cursor was moved last and will continue to move when you hit return. Following is the address of the command cursor, a letter and number such as D17. The second line contains the column width, the number of kilobytes of memory left and the extent of the AS (actual spread sheet area) given by the address of its lower left cell. It also displays options as you enter a command. The third line displays the command or datum as you construct it.

Direct Cursor Movement

Direct cursor movement moves the cell cursor to any place in the VS. You do this with a command: enter an equal sign (=) for SuperCalc or a greater-than sign (>) for VisiCalc, followed by a cell address. The SS program repaints the screen so that the DS has the named cell at the upper left corner and the cell cursor positioned there.

Figure 14.2.5 illustrates this. With the DS at A1, issue the command

$$=T41 \qquad (14.2.1)$$

and cell T41 appears at the upper left hand corner of the display, even if the screen includes parts outside of the AS, as shown in the figure.

Cell Entry

There are three things that you can put in the **active cell (CC)** where the cursor is sitting:

- numbers.
- text.
- formulas.

These may *not* be mixed. Text is alphanumeric and may contain numerals. But these numerals are inseparable from the text; the SS program cannot do arithmetic on them.

The display in the status stub shows the cell address and its current con-

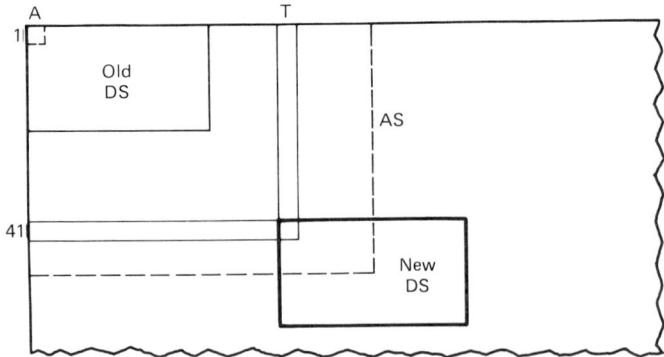

Figure 14.2.5. How the DS may be moved.

tent, if any. What you now key in appears on the entry line. Regardless of its current contents, the entry line goes into the cell when you hit return.

Numbers

Key in digits and, for decimal fractions, use the period for the decimal point; end with return. If the number entered has more digits than can display in the cell, it is still accurately recorded internally. The display is restructured to show scientific notation using the exponent to the base 10. For instance, if you enter 2500000000, too large to display properly, 2.5E9 appears in the cell. Similarly, when the result of a calculation is too large to display properly, it is converted into scientific notation. Numbers display **right justified**: the last digit appears at the right of the cell and the number is preceded at the left by blanks.

Text

To enter *text* for SuperCalc, you must start with a double quote("), a requirement that I often forget (this is easy to correct: see below). The text string may be all letters, mixed letters and numbers or only numbers, positioned with the first character at the left, **left justified.** This holds for numeric data entered as text.

Correction

Anything you key can be corrected before you hit return. The entry line is one dimensional and right and left move the cursor in those directions without affecting information on the line. But up and down are of no other use, so they have these functions: up introduces a blank between the cursor and the letter on its left each time hit; down deletes the character at the cursor. This is all you need to correct your line.

For instance, if you forget the initial double quote for text, move the command cursor to the beginning of the entry by hitting left repeatedly; hit up to insert a blank; then hit the double quote (") at the beginning. Now, regardless of where the command cursor is, hit return: the entry goes to the designated cell. To correct something in another cell, first move the *cell cursor*; then proceed as above.

Formulas

Formulas, from simple to complex, specify actions that use the contents of various SS cells, but the result appears in that cell, not the formula. We address this later in the chapter. To get the flavor, suppose, with the active cell C3, you enter this command:

C3: C1 + C2   (14.2.2)

Because the entry does *not* begin with a double quote, the SS program knows it is a *formula*. Immediately the SS calculates the sum (if there are numbers in both C1 and C2) and displays it in C3.

Commands

Commands begin with a slash (/). As soon as you hit /, alternatives appear on the prompt line indicating further letters that you might hit. These are insensitive to case (may be entered as lower or upper case).

Most commands have options selected by hitting additional letters. Options may have suboptions; these alternatives appear on the prompt line.

Cancel

To cancel a command or data entry and start all over, hit control Z (^Z).

Simple Commands

An **SS command** directs the SS program to perform a particular function and is a set of keystrokes. The Visicalc standard prefixes all commands with the slash (/). Most other SS programs have followed this lead, including SuperCalc, Lotus 1-2-3 and MBA. CalcStar and ProCalc use a semicolon (;); Multiplan uses no prefix.

Entry

As you enter a command, it appears on the entry line while options or a message shows on the prompt line (for SuperCalc). This may be

- a choice for the next key that you may hit;
- a prompt for you to enter specific information such as a file name.

This becomes clear shortly. When you hit /, permissible letters to hit next appear on the prompt line. You *do* have to know what each leter is calling for.

Now we shall discuss simple commands.

Quitting

You invoke the SS program from the operating system by keying its name (SC for SuperCalc, for instance). You may create several spread sheets at this session. When done, go back to the operating system with the quit command, /Q. A prompt line asks you to confirm. The dialogue looks like this,

/Q
EXIT SuperCalc Y(es)? N(o)?
Y   (14.2.3)

You may have spent considerable time creating a spread sheet, but when you quit, what is in memory is destroyed. The message is a reminder to be sure that you have *saved* a spread sheet you wish to use again.

Save and Load

/S saves the spread sheet which is now in memory, that is, it places the AS in a file. The prompt line asks for the file name. Press return to get a directory (so that the name you choose does not conflict with names of existing files). Supply a file name and the extension .CAL is appended.

When you enter a file name, SuperCalc searches the directory, and if the file already exists, it issues this prompt,

File already exists: C(hange name), B(ackup) or O(verwrite)?
                                                                     (14.2.4)

If you hit

- C, you can provide a new name for your spread sheet file.
- B, the extension for the existing file is changed to .BAK.
- O, the existing file is overwritten with the current spread sheet and is thus destroyed.

After making a choice, you are prompted thus,

A(ll), V(alues) or P(art)   (14.2.5)

Here

- A saves the entire spread sheet including formulas and values currently in each cell;

V writes back only the values and does not save the formulas, which makes the file smaller.

P saves only part of the file.

For P you choose whether all or just the values are saved.

Following this, another prompt asks for the range of values discussed below. For example,

/SCHECKreturnA (14.2.6)

It saves all of the spread sheet called CHECK.

Load

The load command, /L, has the opposite effect; it brings in a spread sheet from a file on disk. /L prompts for the file name. Again <u>return</u> brings forth the disk directory. Here is a request to load all of CHECK

/LCHECK<u>return</u>A (14.2.7)

If SuperCalc finds the file, it asks whether you want all or part (A or P). For P, you must know the specifications of the incoming spread sheet file and name the cell in the upper left hand and lower right hand corner of the block to be loaded. You position it in the current spread sheet by specifying the cell where the block is put. The upper left hand corner of the block coming in goes there. There are also other options, beyond our scope, for formula adjustments.

ZAP

To work on more than one spread sheet during a session, put the first spread sheet away using /S. But saving it leaves a copy in memory. The screen displays as before the command. To load another spread sheet or start one from scratch, clear out memory with *zap*, /Z. It prompts

Entire worksheet Y(es) to clear everything, else N(o). (14.2.8)

This lets you recover if you give the command by mistake. Answer N, the command line clears and you can continue. Otherwise the screen goes blank, except for the column, row and status stubs.

14.3 SIMPLE APPLICATIONS

Now we examine some simple spread sheets which require either no calculations or simple ones. In so doing we learn some additional commands and see how to build applications.

Time Sheet

As our first assignment, we create a manual time sheet, a form for an employee to fill out each day. I need just such a form, Figure 14.3.1, for my part-time secretary. It looks as if this would require a lot of work to do on a SS program, but that's not so.

Setting Up Actions

To describe what happens, we use a common presentation format. Texts about spread sheets use this method. One line both names a cell and what you key there. A letter, number and colon names the active cell. Move the cursor there with <u>arrow</u> (or the = command); key what follows.

```
                    TIME SHEET

Name    _____

Date_____ Task_____ Start_____ End_____  Total_____
               Task_____ Start_____ End_____  Total_____
               Task_____ Start_____ End_____  Total_____
               Task_____ Start_____ End_____  Total_____
Date_____ Task_____ Start_____ End_____  Total_____
               Task_____ Start_____ End_____  Total_____
               Task_____ Start_____ End_____  Total_____
               Task_____ Start_____ End_____  Total_____
Date_____ Task_____ Start_____ End_____  Total_____
               Task_____ Start_____ End_____  Total_____
               Task_____ Start_____ End_____  Total_____
               Task_____ Start_____ End_____  Total_____
Date_____ Task_____ Start_____ End_____  Total_____
               Task_____ Start_____ End_____  Total_____
               Task_____ Start_____ End_____  Total_____
               Task_____ Start_____ End_____  Total_____

                                          Hours_____
                                          Rate_____
                                          Total_____
```

Figure 14.3.1. The manual time sheet.

The partial time sheet shown in Figure 14.3.2 is developed a step at at time. First set up the top line with

    D1:"TIME SHEET   (14.3.1)

The quote (") in (14.3.1) indicates to the SS that text which follows should be stored into cell D1. Text is ten characters long, counting the blank, but the standard column width is only nine. SuperCalc has an excellent feature missing in VisiCalc: if you enter text larger than the cell size, it carries over to the next cell in the row, providing it is empty (the case here). This creates the title **TIME SHEET**.

Now skip a line; move the cursor to A3 (using arrow). Enter the *name* label,

    A3:"Name   (14.3.2)

which enters **Name** into cell A3. To make the line, enter,

    B3:'_   (14.3.3)

That is, move the cell cursor to B3 and enter a single underline (_) preceded by a *single* quote ('). For a string preceded by a single quote, SuperCalc repeats that string interminably until it reaches an occupied cell. Since there

```
      |    A    ||   B   ||   C   ||    D    ||   E    ||   F   ||   G    |
 1|                                  TIME  SHEET
 2|
 3|Name    _____
 4|
 5|Date_____Task_____Start_____End_____Total_____
 6|                        Task_____Start_____End_____Total_____
 7|                        Task_____Start_____End_____Total_____
 8|                        Task_____Start_____End_____Total_____
 9|Date_____Task_____Start_____End_____Total_____
10|                        Task_____Start_____End_____Total_____
11|                        Task_____Start_____End_____Total_____
12|                        Task_____Start_____End_____Total_____
13|Date_____Task_____Start_____End_____Total_____
14|                        Task_____Start_____End_____Total_____
15|                        Task_____Start_____End_____Total_____
16|                        Task_____Start_____End_____Total_____
17|Date_____Task_____Start_____End_____Total_____
18|                        Task_____Start_____End_____Total_____
19|                        Task_____Start_____End_____Total_____
20|                        Task_____Start_____End_____Total_____
21|
```

Figure 14.3.2. The printed time sheet has row and column stubs.

is no occupied cell in this row, it makes a set of dashes the length of the AS.

Now move down to the first group of the form, which begins at A5, and enter the date information,

$$A5:\text{"Date} \underline{\hspace{2cm}} \tag{14.3.4}$$

This fills up the two cells, A5 and B5. With the cursor at C5, enter the remaining information for this line thus,

$$C5:\text{"Task} \underline{\hspace{1cm}} \text{Start} \underline{\hspace{1cm}} \text{End} \underline{\hspace{1cm}} \text{Total} \underline{\hspace{1cm}} \tag{14.3.5}$$

This is most of the text needed in the form.

Copy Command

Copy, initiated with /C, copies a range of cells from one place in the spread sheet to another. A range may be a single cell. This is used the first time we issue the *copy* command, displayed thus,

$$/CC5\underline{\text{return}}C6\underline{\text{return}} \tag{14.3.6}$$

which accurately gives the key strokes necessary to issue the command. However we omit the final <u>return</u> in future displays without confusion. Also, a presentation convention which we adopt replaces internal <u>returns</u> with commas. Thus (14.3.6) becomes

$$/CC5,C6 \tag{14.3.7}$$

requesting that C5 be duplicated to cell C6. C5 holds most of row 5 entered with (14.3.5); (14.3.7) copies it to row 6.

Copy duplicates a range of cells. A **range** is specified (for a block as shown in Figure 14.3.3) by giving the upper right hand corner of the block (B4) followed by a colon and the lower left hand corner cell (J9) (thus B4:J9).

Copy the right hand portion of rows 5 *and* 6 directly below (to rows 7 and 8), making the request thus,

$$/CC5:C6,C7 \tag{14.3.8}$$

We have now prepared one group of Figure 14.3.2, rows 5 through 8. Copy this group below with

$$/CA5:C8,A9 \tag{14.3.9}$$

610 SPREAD SHEETS

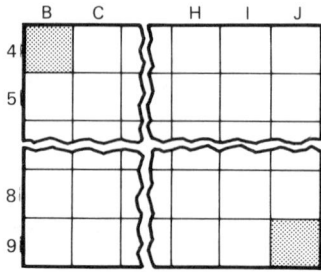

Figure 14.3.3. Cells on a block's diagonal determine a range.

Finally we get four groupings (through row 20) with

/CA5:C12,A13   (14.3.10)

Put the summary information in the lower left hand corner of Figure 14.3.1, in cell G22, thus

G22: Hours _____   (14.3.11)

and so forth.

Borders

If you print the spread sheet now, the output, Figure 14.3.2, has column and row stubs. Certainly the format of Figure 14.3.1 with the stubs removed is preferable. The *global* command, /G, removes borders and performs other functions. After you key in /G, a set of options appears:

B turns on and off the border, the row and colum stub;
F turns on and off formula display;
N turns on and off the *next* option;
T turns on and off the tab option which causes the cursor to automatically skip over protected and empty cells;
M is for manual recalculation, requiring you to hit an exclamation point to recalculate the spread sheet.
A causes automatic recalculation of the spread sheet whenever a new datum is entered;
R does recalculation a row at a time;
C does recalculation a column at a time.

Most of these are **toggles**; the first time you enter the command, SuperCalc turns the feature on and the next time it turns the feature off. B turns off the border thus,

/GB   (14.3.12)

The other options are self-explanatory with the exception of a couple. The formula option is valuable and is missing from VisiCalc (available with Advanced Version). It displays cell formulas instead of calculated values. This helps in debugging spread sheet calculations. The *next* option automatically moves the cell cursor to the next cell, after the entry is completed for this cell (via return). The direction that the cursor moves is how it moved most recently: if you position to this cell by moving from left to right, then after you enter data and hit return the cursor moves right.

Printing

With borders removed, SuperCalc prints the SS with the output command issued thus,

/ODrangeP   (14.3.13)

/O requests output and you are asked if you want the display or the values. Hit D, enter the *range* to print and the next prompt asks for the form of output (Disk or Print); hit P to print.

Boiler Plate

The next project uses the spread sheet for a check register. The result should appear as in Figure 14.3.4. Notice that the top has a title, the name and address of the company. If you use a title on a lot of our spread sheets, why not prepare it separately and insert it on new spread sheets as needed?

The chapter on word processing discusses **boiler plate,** a chunk of information used on many documents. The title block is boiler plate for our spread sheet. After creating it, save it as a separate file called TITLE. Then, to begin a spread sheet, load TITLE from the disk thus,

/LTITLE,A   (14.3.14)

As usual, SuperCalc prompts after each field of the *load* command. But a *friendly* feature lets you type ahead without waiting for prompts. If you do, the SS program does not bother to display prompts but goes ahead to

```
                              Flores Associates
                              108 Eighth Avenue
                              Brooklyn NY 11215


                 CHECK REGISTER                         July 1983
================================================================
 Number      Date      Payee             Check    Deposit   Balance
                       Old balance                          636.71
 976         722       Cecelia           253.31             383.40
 977         722       Prisma Graphics   400.00             -16.60
             722       From savings               750.00    733.40
 978         725       Dr. Sekular        65.00             668.40
 979         804       Stereo Review       4.99             663.41
 980         804       Glenn             200.00             463.41
```

Figure 14.3.4. A check register.

execute the command as with (14.3.14). To create the check register SS displayed in Figure 14.3.4, first load in TITLE to the top three lines as discussed above—enter the headings, the date, the line separator (with ' =) and column titles.

Changing Column Width and Format

The third column, (C) in Figure 14.3.4, is actually 18 characters wide. The *format* command adjusts this.

Format Command

The format command, /F, has four options,

G for global, affecting the whole spread sheet;
C for column;
R for row;
E for entry or cell.

For the last three options, key in respectively the column (letter), row (number) or cell (letter and number) when prompted, followed by return.
To set column width, either for a single column or globally, key in a number, anything from 0 (to hide something) to 127 (a *very* wide column).

To make the payee column width 18, use

/FCC,18 (14.3.15)

where F is for format, C is for column, and C is for Column C.

Normally text is left justified and numbers are right justified. Since the date and payee column are next to each other in Figure 14.3.4, a digit from date and a character from payee are always adjacent to each other, making reading difficult. However, the format command can cause text or numbers to be justified differently. Let us *left justify* columns A and B. The secondary option letter, when present, requests,

I, all numbers as integers, rounding the cell's content when required;
E, all numbers in exponential form;
G, numbers in the general format discussed earlier;
$, all numbers to two decimal places;
R, numbers right justified;
L, numbers left justified;
TR, right justified text;
TL, left justified text;
*, bar graph form, a series of asterisks.

To set column B left justified, use

/FCB,L (14.3.16)

Formulas

Figures 14.3.4 and 14.3.5 show that the old balance, F8, is entered from the statement by you; no calculation is required. The balance in cell F9 is

```
        ||  D     ||  E      ||  F         ||  G   |
     7| Check     Deposit    Balance
     8|
     9|                      F8+E9-D9
    10|                      F9+E10-D10
    11|                      F10+E11-D11
    12|                      F11+E12-D12
    13|                      F12+E13-D13
    14|                      F13+E14-D14
    15|                      F14+E15-D15
    16|                      F15+E16-D16
    17|                      F16+E17-D17
```

Figure 14.3.5. Formulas for calculating the next balance.

calculated by adding a deposit to and subtracting a check amount from the old balance with the formula,

F9: F8 + E9 − D9 (14.3.17)

The calculation for F10 is almost identical:

F10: F9 + E10 − D10 (14.3.18)

All formulas in column F look similar. It is easy to derive the formula for any cell from that in F9.

Replicate

Any SS program can create *all* the formulas in column F with one command. For SuperCalc (and VisiCalc) this is the replicate command, /R. It prompts first for a source range which may be a cell, row, column or block; then it asks for a destination range. You have three options:

N for no adjustment;
A for SuperCalc to ask whether to adjust or not;
V for values only.

If you hit return SuperCalc adjusts *all* variables: as it progresses down (up) a column, SuperCalc adds (substracts) 1 to all row references in cell numbers; moving across rows adjusts column references similarly.

For this application with the formula (14.3.17) in cell F9, issue *replicate* thus,

/RF9,F10:F35 (14.3.19)

This places formulas into cells F10 through F35, each properly adjusted as shown in Figure 14.3.5; 1 is added to each successive row reference.

You may wonder how the display of Figure 14.3.5 was made. After creating the form but before putting in the values, issue this command,

/GF (14.3.20)

which causes formulas to display for cells that contain them.

14.4 MORE FUNCTIONS AND EXAMPLES

Electronic Time Sheet

In Section 14.3, we created a manual time sheet form. This form can be duplicated and used by employees to enter time and work assignments. Then wages can be determined from their entries on the form.

But manual entry seems wasteful: the calculating capability of the SS is unused. Why not create an *electronic* time sheet filled in at the keyboard?

The Electronic Form

Figure 14.4.1 shows the top of the electronic time sheet. Only the first four columns are filled in after an assignment is completed or at the end of the day. The SS program does the rest. A typical result appears as Figure 14.4.2.

Setting Up The Formulas

The formulas in the time sheet are shown in Figure 14.4.3, produced by issuing the global formula command, /GF.

```
    |   A    ||   B    ||   C    ||   D    ||   E    ||   F    ||   G    ||   H    ||   I    |
1|                         ELECTRONIC TIME SHEET
2|NAME:
3|
4|Date              Task     Start    Stop     Hours    Rate     Total    Cum Total
5|                                                       0        6         0        0
```

Figure 14.4.1. Top of the electronic time sheet (ETS).

```
                        ELECTRONIC TIME SHEET
NAME:      Ricki

Date       Task      Start    Stop     Hours    Rate     Total    Cum Total
9/20/83    CHQ                 1.1      2.2      1.1      6        6.6        6.6
           SBC14               2.2      4.5      2.3      6       13.8       20.4
           SB8                 4.5      5.2       .7      6        4.2       24.6
9/21       SB8                 1        2.1      1.1      6        6.6       31.2
           SB14                2.1      4.4      2.3      6       13.8       45
                                                 0        6        0         45
                                                 0        6        0         45
                                                 0        6        0         45
                                                 0        6        0         45
```

Figure 14.4.2. ETS with entries.

616 SPREAD SHEETS

```
    |  A    ||   B    ||   C   ||   D  ||    E    ||   F   ||   G     ||    H     |
 1|             ELECTRONIC TIME SHEET
 2|NAME:
 3|
 4|Date      Task     Start     Stop     Hours      Rate     Total      Cum Total
 5|9/20/83   CHQ       1.1      2.2      D5-C5      6.00     E5*F5      G5
 6|          SBC14     2.2      4.5      D6-C6      6.00     E6*F6      G6+H5
 7|                                      D7-C7      6.00     E7*F7
 8|                                      D8-C8      6.00     E8*F8
 9|                                      D9-C9      6.00     E9*F9
10|                                      D10-C10    6.00     E10*F10
```

Figure 14.4.3. Formulas embedded in the ETS.

The powerful replicate command creates most of the formulas; only three are entered directly. The first formula (E5) is the difference between the time stopped and the time started. The second, the pay for that period at G5, is the product of pay rate and hours. This is also put in H5 to be accumulated down column H. Thus H6, the sum of H5 and the new total, G6, is the third formula entered manually.

Now replicate these three formulas down their columns. For instance, to fill column E, use

/RE5,E6:E20   (14.4.1)

which asks to replicate (R) the formula in E5 into cells E6 through E20. To fill column H, use

/RH6,H7:H20   (14.4.2)

Inconveniences

This electronic time sheet has three inconveniences:

- time must be entered in tenths of an hour instead of hours and minutes;
- you must use a 24 hour clock so that the hours before and after noon do not cause problems;
- the date and task are entered as text and must always be preceded by double quotes.

Improved Electronic Time Sheet

Let us cope with the first objection by setting up the time sheet to accept minutes and hours. The second objection is minor and the third is inherent in SuperCalc.

14.4 MORE FUNCTIONS AND EXAMPLES

A redesigned time sheet, Figure 14.4.4, expects entries in hours and minures. Some columns are made narrow to fit a modest size page. Also the rate is in a single cell, J2, at the beginning of the time sheet.

Formulas

Formulas for each column are printed in Figure 14.4.5. The column widths of Figure 14.4.4 were altered for this printout only, so the formulas print properly.

Calculate task time in *minutes* in G5. Convert stopping time into minutes from the beginning of the day; E5*60+F5. Convert the starting time to minutes similarly: C5*60+D5. Then subtract start time from stop time to get task time in minutesG5.

Wage, H5 is the time in minutes, G5, multiplied by the rate, J2 divided by 60 (since J2 is in dollars per *hour*). The first cumulative total, I5, is H5. Each of the other totals is the sum of the preceding total and task wage.

```
     |   A    ||   B    ||C||D||E||F||  G  ||   H   ||   I   ||   J    ||  K
  1|                                          ELECTRONIC TIME SHEET
  2|NAME_____Rate:          6.00
  3|Date       Task       Start Stop  Time Wage    Total
  4|                      H   M  H  M
  5|9/20/83    CHQ        1   5  2 15   70  7.00    7.00
  6|           SBC14      2  15  4 30  135 13.50   20.50
  7|           SB8        4  30  5 10   40  4.00   24.50
  8|9/21       SB8        1   0  2  8   68  6.80   31.30
  9|           SBB14      2   8  4 25  137 13.70   45.00
 10|                                     0   .00   45.00
 11|                                     0   .00   45.00
 12|                                     0   .00   45.00
```

Figure 14.4.4. Improved ETS with entries.

```
     |C||D||E||F||          G              ||      H      ||    I    |
  1|                                          ELECTRONIC TIME SHE
  2|_____Rate:
  3|Start Stop  Time                          Wage           Total
  4|H   M  H  M
  5| 1   5  2 15  E5*60+F5-(C5*60+D5)         G5*J2/60        H5
  6| 2  15  4 30  E6*60+F6-(C6*60+D6)         G6*J2/60        I5+H6
  7| 4  30  5 10  E7*60+F7-(C7*60+D7)         G7*J2/60        I6+H7
  8| 1   0  2  8  E8*60+F8-(C8*60+D8)         G8*J2/60        I7+H8
  9| 2   8  4 25  E9*60+F9-(C9*60+D9)         G9*J2/60        I8+H9
 10|              E10*60+F10-(C10*60+D1       G10*J2/60       I9+H10
 11|              E11*60+F11-(C11*60+D1       G11*J2/60       I10+H1
 12|              E12*60+F12-(C12*60+D1       G12*J2/60       I11+H1
 13|              E13*60+F13-(C13*60+D1       G13*J2/60       I12+H1
 14|              E14*60+F14-(C14*60+D1       G14*J2/60       I13+H1
 15|              E15*60+F15-(C15*60+D1       G15*J2/60       I14+H1
```

Figure 14.4.5. Formulas for the improved ETS.

It is simple to replicate the formulas in the three columns, G, H and I. Note one important difference in the use of the replicate command. The calculation for wages in column H uses the time calculation from the G column of that row. But the rate should *always* come from J2. Hence we do *not* want **automatic adjustment**: instead, the formula row number is changed to the object row number as the formula is copied down a column (examine columns E and G of Figure 14.4.3 to see an example of this). Request replication thus,

/RH5,H6:H20,A (14.4.3)

where A is for Ask. Before the formulas are copied, a prompt shows G5 and asks if each variable it contains is to be adjusted. Since the formula for H6 uses G6, found by adjusting G5, answer Y for yes. The prompt for J2 asks if it should be adjusted by the answer is N, for no, because J2 itself should appear in the formula in cell H6 and the others below.

Check Reconcilliation

The Problem

In Section 14.3, we set up the check register displayed as Figure 14.3.4. What happens when the first statement comes in? It records all checks cashed and returned by the payee's bank, which usually does not clean out the current check register because of checks

- issued after the statement date;
- issued but not returned.

Therefore the current check register should be broken into two parts:

- Returned checks become a history file.
- Outstanding checks form the new check register for this month, but each should be posted against the balance from the statement.

Solution

The outline of the solution is presented in Figure 14.4.6 with numbers keyed to the text below:

1. A new section at the bottom of the SS is created for unreturned checks.
2. Unreturned checks in the check register not on the statement are transferred there.

14.4 MORE FUNCTIONS AND EXAMPLES

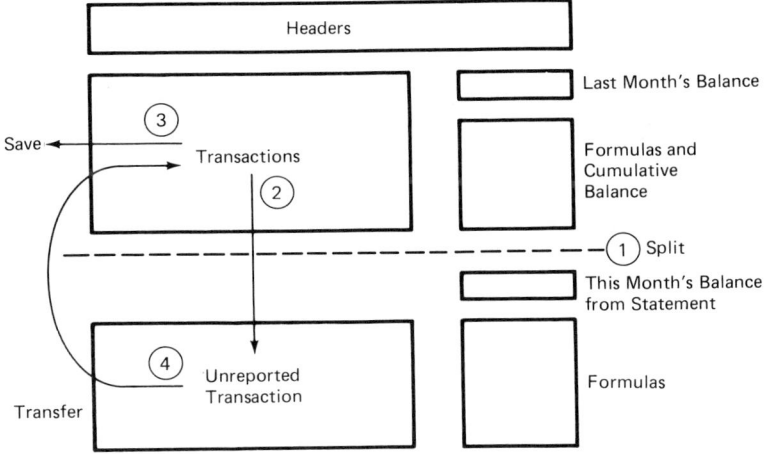

Figure 14.4.6. Requirements for check reconciliation.

3. The returned checks for last month are verified. The result may be saved as a separate spread sheet file.
4. The top portion is removed and replaced with the bottom portion, which now becomes *this month's* check register.

Set Up

Set up consists of creating a two part check register, as shown in Figure 14.4.7. Actions to do this are:

1. Copy column titles from row 7 to row 37.
2. Enter a balance formula in F39.
3. Replicate it down column F.

The figure shows the formulas in both the top and bottom portions; some checks have been transferred from the top to the bottom. Before we do this, let us look at two other ES facilities: title locks and windows.

Title Locks

We see the column and row stub displayed respectively at the top and the left of Figure 14.4.8. Most spread sheets also have column heads, labelled **horizontal title** in the figure; they also may have names for the rows along the left, labelled **vertical title** in the figure.

Titles for large spread sheets get lost when you scroll away from them.

620 SPREAD SHEETS

```
         |   A   ||   B   ||      C         ||    D     ||    E     ||    F      ||  G
   1|
   2|                                          FLORES ASSOCIATES
   3|                                          108 Eighth Avenue
   4|                                          Brooklyn NY 11215
   5|                          CHECK REGISTER                            July 1983
   6|============================================================================
   7|Number    Date      Payee                 Check       Deposit     Balance
   8|                    Old balance                                   636.71
   9|                                                                  F8+E9-D9
  10|  977     722       Prisma Graphics       400                     F9+E10-D10
  11|          722       From savings                      750         F10+E11-D11
  12|  978     725       Dr. Sekular           65                      F11+E12-D12
  13|  979     804       Stereo Review         4.99                    F12+E13-D13
  14|  980     804       Glenn                 200                     F13+E14-D14
  15|                                                                  F14+E15-D15
  16|                                                                  F15+E16-D16
  17|                                                                  F16+E17-D17
  18|                                                                  F17+E18-D18
  19|                                                                  F18+E19-D19
  20|                                                                  F19+E20-D20
  21|                                                                  F20+E21-D21
  22|                                                                  F21+E22-D22
  23|                                                                  F22+E23-D23
  24|                                                                  F23+E24-D24
  25|                                                                  F24+E25-D25
  26|                                                                  F25+E26-D26
  27|                                                                  F26+E27-D27
  28|                                                                  F27+E28-D28
  29|                                                                  F28+E29-D29
  30|                                                                  F29+E30-D30
  31|                                                                  F30+E31-D31
  32|                                                                  F31+E32-D32
  33|                                                                  F32+E33-D33
  34|                                                                  F33+E34-D34
  35|                                                                  F34+E35-D35
  36|
  37|Number    Date      Payee                 Check       Deposit     Balance
  38|                                                                  716.72
  39|  976     722       Cecelia               253.31                  F38+E39-D39
  40|  981     804       Fishman               120                     F39+E40-D40
  41|  982     805       Nevins                25                      F40+E41-D41
  42|                                                                  F41+E42-D42
  43|                                                                  F42+E43-D43
```

Figure 14.4.7. Two part check register.

For instance, for our check register, when you scroll to rows 21 and below, the titles at the top scroll off the screen. Without the column titles you may forget which column is which.

Horizontal

A **horizontal title lock** keep the column stub and horizontal title stationary when the display scrolls vertically. To set the lock, position the cursor in the bottom row of the title and issue the *title lock* command,

/Toption   (14.4.4)

Specify horizontal lock with H for *option* and all the rows above and including the cursor remain fixed as you scroll vertically.

14.4 MORE FUNCTIONS AND EXAMPLES 621

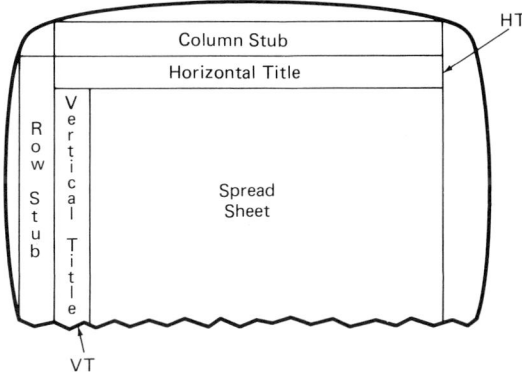

Figure 14.4.8. Stubs and titles on the SS display.

Figure 14.4.9 illustrates this for a narrow spread sheet. The sectioned area at the top, rows 1 through 7, is the locked horizontal title. You have scrolled down the screen to view a lower portion of the spread sheet. The figure shows the actual spread sheet area (AS) in memory: the locked top area and a second lower area to which you have scrolled displays. Rows 20 through 32 in the figure make up this lower area. The top and bottom (rows 1-7 and rows 20-32) are the **display spread sheet (DS)**. The area in between with 'X' in it does not display.

A better way to lock the **CHECK REGISTER** is to scroll rows 1 through 6 off the screen first. Then only row 7, the column titles, remains; now issue the lock command. This leaves 19 rows of the AS visible, that is, *any* set of 19 rows reached by scrolling.

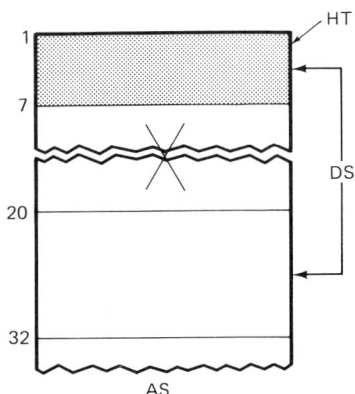

Figure 14.4.9. Composing the DS with horizontal title lock.

Options

The title lock command has four options:

H for horizontal, as described above.
V for vertical, locking the vertical title.
B for locking both vertical and horizontal titles.
C which clears any lock now in effect.

Figure 14.4.10 demonstrates **vertical title lock,** which is useful for a short, wide spread sheet as for a financial plan which extends for many months or years. The vertical title displays the meaning of each row while the AS is scrolled horizontally to different columns. In Figure 14.4.10, the titles in column A are locked while columns H through L make up the rest of the DS. The arc marked 'X' does not display.

Both

For very large spread sheets, both horizontal and vertical title locks are advisable, initiated by B. As illustrated in Figure 14.4.11, the following areas make up the DS:

- column A, rows 1 through 3 (corner);
- columns H through L, rows 1 through 3 (top title);
- column A, rows 20 through 36 (side title);
- columns H through L, rows 20 through 36 (SS content).

These areas are pushed together to fill the screen.

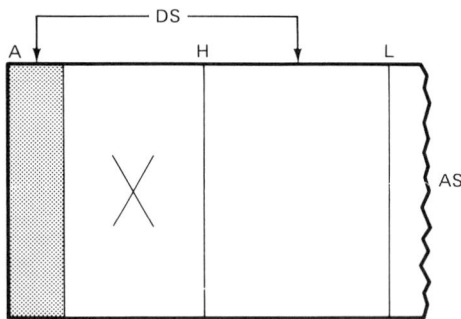

Figure 14.4.10. The DS with a vertical title lock.

14.4 MORE FUNCTIONS AND EXAMPLES   623

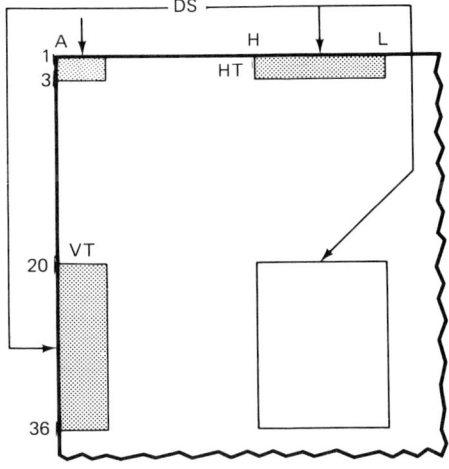

Figure 14.4.11. The DS with double title lock.

Windows

You only see one data area even with the lock feature. In the reconciliation problem, we would like to work with data in both the top and the bottom of the SS. But how can we see both at once? The **window** is the solution. You see two (or more) areas of the AS.

Window Options

The window command has five options:

H splits the screen horizontally.
V splits the screen vertically.
C clears the split and shows only one contiguous area.
S synchronizes scrolling in both portions.
U for unsynchronize, scrolls windows independently.

The horizontal split occurs at the cursor as displayed in Figure 14.4.12. After /WH, four stubs display: a horizontal top and bottom stub (THS and BHS) and a vertical top and bottom stub (TVS and BVS). The cursor appears in the bottom half. The display at this point looks like Figure 14.4.13.

As you move the cursor within the **bottom window (BW),** it induces scrolling at the window limits. The top rows disappear from the bottom

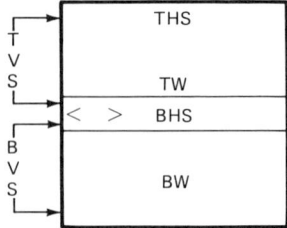

Figure 14.4.12. Setting a horizontal window.

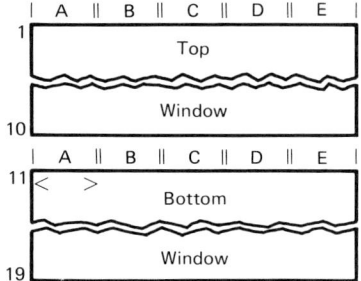

Figure 14.4.13. Display after setting a window.

screen and other rows take their place if you keep moving the cursor down. At some point, the display might look like Figure 14.4.14.

Figure 14.4.15 shows the actual spread sheet area, how it is broken in two parts (the top and bottom windows, TW and BW) which form the display spread sheet, DS.

You switch from one window to the other by hitting the semicolon (;). Arrow or = causes the cursor to move within the selected window.

Synchronism

When you reach the limit of an active display window on either side, further motion of the cursor causes scrolling within that window. In the **unsynchronized** (default) mode, scrolling occurs only for the active window. If the information in the two windows is related, you would like scrolling to be **synchronized** between them, requested with the S option. Then scrolling in one window causes scrolling at the same rate in the other windows. To turn synchronism off, specify U with /WU.

To shut off the windows, issue the window clear request, /WC; this re-

14.4 MORE FUNCTIONS AND EXAMPLES

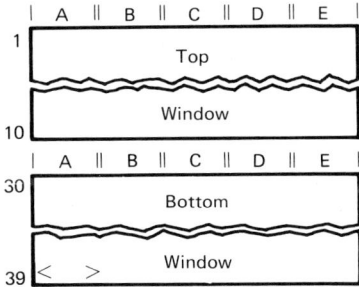

Figure 14.4.14. Screen with horizontal window after scrolling.

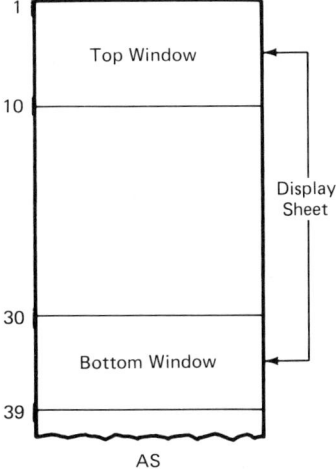

Figure 14.4.15. DS for Fig. 14.4.14.

moves the bottom (left) window for the horizontal (vertical) mode. The window is replaced by the remainder of the spread sheet.

Vertical

A **vertical window** works as displayed in Figure 14.4.16. The DS consists of two parts, a left and right window, WL and WR. Scrolling within windows can be synchronized or independent; switch between them with semicolon (;). The figure shows that neither window need be positioned at the beginning of the AS.

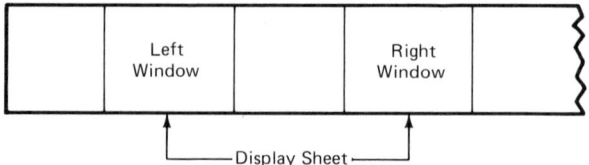

Figure 14.4.16. DS for vertical window.

Windows and Title Locks

You can lock titles and have windows, shown for a long thin spread sheet in Figure 14.4.17. The DS consists of three parts:

HT, the locked horizontal title;
TW, the top window;
BW, the bottom window.

Switch between windows with ; and move or scroll in either. They may be synchronized.

A wide but short spread sheet with vertical windows and locked titles is shown in Figure 14.4.18. The display consists of three parts:

VT, the vertical title at the left;
LW, the left window;
RW, the right window.

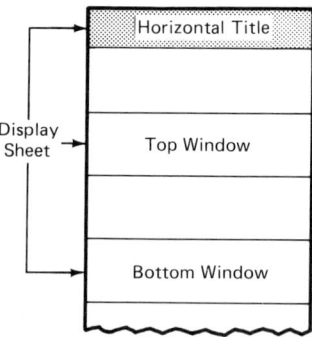

Figure 14.4.17. DS for horizontal window and title lock.

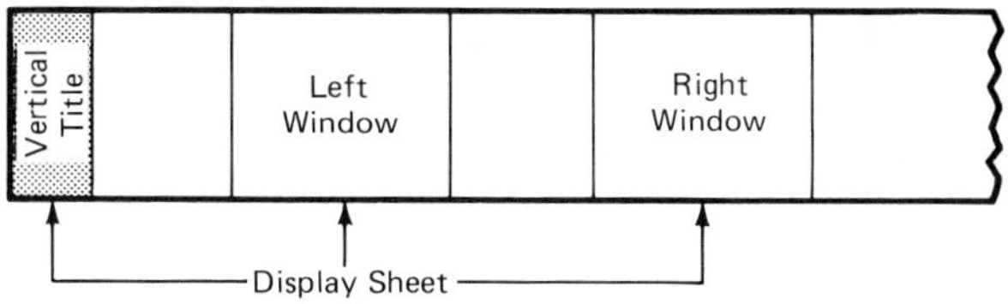

Figure 14.4.18. DS for vertical window and title lock.

Reconciling Continued

To reconcile a statement against a check register, set up the spread sheet in Figure 14.4.7 with these steps:

1. Reset the spread sheet so that the column names are on the top line (=A7);
2. Set the horizontal title lock on (/TH);
3. Move the cursor half way down the page (with down);
4. Create a window (/WH).

Now take the closing balance from the statement and make it the opening balance in the *second* part of the spread sheet, F38 of Figure 14.4.7. Next examine the statement. An item in the check register which is absent from the statement is moved to the lower check register.

For instance, check #976 is not on the statement. Copy columns A through E for that check to the lower half of the sheet with,

/CA9:E9,A39 (14.4.5)

This duplicates the *data* in row 9 (A9:E9) to row 39. The calculation is automatically made in the lower register to update the balance. The figure shows the item moved.

Blanking

But the information remains in line 9. The delete command, /D, can delete either a row or a column. /D is *not* used here because it would invalidate the formula in E10. That formula refers to F9, which is removed if you delete row 9. If you actually delete the row, much of column F fills up with ERROR. Instead, to remove data, blank it out with *blank,* /B.

Continue to remove checks not on the statement by copying them into the lower part of the spread sheet and then blanking them out in the upper section. Often, later transactions are missing from the statement and form a block. A group of checks is copied with a single command. For instance, checks 981 through 984 in rows 15 through 18 are copied with

/CA15:E18,A40 (14.4.6)

The area is blanked with

/BA15:E18 (14.4.7)

Finishing Up

When done, the top register has blank lines for checks on the statement moved to the bottom register. The top register should be complete and accurate and correspond to the statement. Correct it if there are discrepancies. If empty rows offend you, the register may be compressed with *copy* or *move*.

Now you may print the top register with a *partial print* command or keep it in machine readable form by *saving* the top part with the /S command to a history file such as **CR783** (for the check register of July 1983).

To update the check register (CR) requires four actions:

- blank out the data in the upper register;
- transfer the data from the lower register;
- blank out the lower register;
- save the updated check register in CR.

These commands do this:

/SACR783
/GB
/ODA1:F14,P
/BA9:E36
/CE38,E8
/CA39:E60,A9
/BA39:E60 (14.4.8)

14.5 "WHAT IF?"

Predictions

The SS program is effective in saving time and work. It does the best job at creating models to make predictions. Most managers plan and budget their resources, not only money but time and people. If the people resource is underestimated, for instance, it takes a long time to requisition, advertise for, evaluate and hire new personnel.

Predictions are based on judgment and intuition. Psychologists are not clear on exactly how the decision process works. Certainly having more tools to make decisions can speed it up.

Decisions are made from predictions which in turn are based on trends and assumptions. Analysis of trends and assumptions can often be wrong. Sometimes the best policy is to hedge bets; then if something goes wrong, losses will not be so great. This may reduce chances for maximum gain, but isn't that what insurance is all about?

Model

Predictions are best made by establishing a quantitative model which produces estimated values for specific variables concerned on a periodic basis. A model is simple at first. It immediately brings to light difficulties and deficiencies. Successive adjustments are made to compensate for them, which increase the complexity of the model. These in turn may bring forth further problems, improved upon by still further adjustments. Let us now examine a particular example which shows how useful the spread sheet is.

Early Cash Flow Model

Figure 14.5.1 shows a spread sheet established to start a cash flow analysis. Row 1 contains the title, put in cell A1 so that it displays with the file name when the directory is brought up. (This is a convenient feature of SuperCalc.)

Row 2 names the months for the period examined. The figures cover eight months, but this period can be extended easily. The third row shows the sales for these months from the historical data. Sales peak in September because ours is a seasonal industry.

Collections

Sales unfortunately are not income; revenue has to be collected, (A5). Collection rates vary (according to business type). A review of our operations shows the approximate distribution in column C: 20% (0.2) of the month's sales are collected during the month, 70% one month later and the rest during the third month.

Because of collection lag, the analysis is not current for two months, until final collections on all accounts. Since the SS starts with sales in May, it

	A	B	C	D	E	F	G	H	I	J	K
1	CASH FLOW										
2				May	June	July	Aug	Sept	Oct	Nov	Dec
3	Sales			10000	10000	20000	30000	40000	20000	20000	10000
4											
5	Collections										
6	1'st month	.2		2000	2000	4000	6000	8000	4000	4000	2000
7	2'nd month	.7			7000	7000	14000	21000	28000	14000	14000
8	3'rd month	.1				1000	1000	2000	3000	4000	2000
9											
10	Total					12000	21000	31000	35000	22000	18000
11											
12	Purch (% next mo)	.7		7000	14000	21000	28000	14000	14000	7000	0
13	Payment (1 mo lag)				7000	14000	21000	28000	14000	14000	7000
14											
15	Disbursements										
16	Purchase				7000	14000	21000	28000	14000	14000	7000
17	Wages				1000	1000	2000	3000	4000	2000	2000
18	Rent				500	500	500	500	500	500	500
19	Others				100	200	300	400	200	200	100
20	Taxes						8000				
21	Pay on Machines							10000			
22											
23	Total				8600	15700	31800	41900	18700	16700	9600
24	Net Gain					-3700	-10800	-10900	16300	5300	8400
25	Beg Cash Bal					6000	2300	-8500	-19400	-3100	2200
26											
27	End Cash Bal					2300	-8500	-19400	-3100	2200	10600

Figure 14.5.1. Cash flow analysis SS (CFA SS).

takes until July to catch up. The collection formula is set up in the first applicable cell of the row:

$$\text{D6: C6} * \text{D3}; \quad \text{E7: C7} * \text{D3}; \quad \text{F8: E8} * \text{D3} \qquad (14.5.1)$$

Each formula is replicated across its row, requesting adjustment so that during copying the sales figures migrate across row 3.

Row 10 contains the total collections for each month and is empty until July. Thereafter row 10 contains the sum of the collections in row 6, 7 and 8, written thus,

$$\text{F10: F6} + \text{F7} + \text{F8} \qquad (14.5.2)$$

The formula is replicated across the rest of row 10.

Functions

The sum provided in (14.5.2) is simple to write and not too long. However, if many items were to be totalled the formula would be tedious to write. There is a simpler way to do this, called a **function.** Some SS programs begin functions with @ so that they are easy to distinguish from text

(VisiCalc and Lotus 1-2-3); for others, no prefix is required (SuperCalc and Multiplan).

The function which takes a total is called SUM. Write it in a cell, enclosing a range in parentheses thus,

$$\text{F10: SUM(F6:F8)} \tag{14.5.3}$$

Functions may be replicated; for F10 this provides the remaining entries.

Purchases

A review of our records shows that, as sales come in, purchase orders go out for material to fill them. The material is prepared by the vendor, shipped to us and then we are billed.

Customer orders do not appear in this spread sheet. An order is recorded as a sale only when we ship the merchandise to the customer. Raw materials purchased to make items to fill orders are based on *next* month's sales, hence are recorded *before* the corresponding sales are recorded.

Purchases are a fixed proportion (D12) of next month's sales. Also, there is a lag between purchase time and payment time. These are reflected in the following formulas,

$$\text{D12: C12} * \text{E3; \quad E13: D12} \tag{14.5.4}$$

The purchase amount (D12) is estimated at 70% (C12) of this month's sales (E3); it is paid next month. Both these formulas are replicated across their rows.

Disbursements

The next few rows show the costs for running the business. Most are periodic. Purchase costs are copied from line 13. Wages are a proportion of last month's sales. Rent and some other expenses are fixed. Miscellaneous expenses vary.

Two major outlays in line 20 and 21 are nonrecurring on this spread sheet. The total of all our expenses appears on line 23 and is calculated with the SUM function.

Cash Flow

The meat of the analysis starts on line 24. First calculate the net gain thus,

$$\text{F24: F10} - \text{F23} \tag{14.5.5}$$

632 SPREAD SHEETS

Start with a cash balance, here $6,000. The ending cash balance is this starting cash balance plus the net gain,

F27: F24 + F25 (14.5.6)

The ending cash balance for one month is the beginning cash balance for the next, replicated across the sheet.

G25: F27 (14.5.7)

Negative Cash

A glance at Figure 14.5.1 shows that the ending cash balance in many cases is negative. This is theoretically acceptable; it would be nice if you could run a business that way. We know better. Assuming that the business is solvent, it is not difficult to take out a loan on receivables, but then we *pay* interest on it.

Why not crank this into the picture? When the opening cash balance is negative, we have an additional cost for interest on the amount borrowed to cover the cash deficit. Let us put the interest rate per month in C26 of Figure 14.5.2. Then calculate the interest on the beginning cash balance (row 26) and add it in (row 28). An empty row 26 is inserted with the *insert row* command, /IR26. A positive cash balance *earns* interest. A negative cash balance *costs* interest at the same rate. That's okay for this time around. The formula is then

F26: C26*F25;   F28: SUM(F24:F26) (14.5.8)

These are replicated across the sheet, adjusting the beginning balance cell (F25) but not the interest cell (C26) so the formula is always correct. The value set into C26 is 9% interest (=.09) divided by 12 to get the monthly rate, .0075.

Recalculation

The spread sheet is displayed properly in Figure 14.5.2. However, after entering the interest rate, the SS program calculates the new results, which do not look right. The ending cash balance for July at F28 is correct but the beginning cash balance for August (G25) is not! How could that be?

Part but not all of the sheet seems to be recalculated correctly. Figure 14.5.3 shows this effect when the interest rate for the SS in Figure 14.5.2

```
     !  A  !!  B  !!  C  !!  D  !!  E  !!  F  !!  G  !!  H  !!  I  !!  J  !!  K  !
 1!CASH FLOW
 2!                              May    June   July    Aug   Sept    Oct    Nov    Dec
 3!Sales                        10000  10000  20000  30000  40000  20000  20000  10000
 4!
 5!Collections
 6!  1'st month          .2      2000   2000   4000   6000   8000   4000   4000   2000
 7!  2'nd month          .7              7000   7000  14000  21000  28000  14000  14000
 8!  3'rd month          .1                    1000   1000   2000   3000   4000   2000
 9!
10!  Total                                    12000  21000  31000  35000  22000  18000
11!
12!Purch (% next mo)     .7      7000  14000  21000  28000  14000  14000   7000      0
13!Payment(1 mo lag)                    7000  14000  21000  28000  14000  14000   7000
14!
15!Disbursements
16!  Purchase                           7000  14000  21000  28000  14000  14000   7000
17!  Wages                               1000   1000   2000   3000   4000   2000   2000
18!  Rent                                 500    500    500    500    500    500    500
19!  Others                               100    200    300    400    200    200    100
20!  Taxes                                            8000
21!  Pay on Machines                                        10000
22!
23!  Total                               8600  15700  31800  41900  18700  16700   9600
24!Net Gain                              -3700 -10800 -10900  16300   5300   8400
25!Beg Cash Bal                           6000   2345  -8437 -19401  -3246   2029
26!Int on Cash         .0075                45     18    -63   -146    -24     15
27!
28!End Cash Bal                           2345  -8437 -19401  -3246   2029  10445
```

Figure 14.5.2. CFA SS with interest due for negative balance.

is changed to .008. The first column is calculated correctly, but the ending cash balance is not carried forward. That is, G25 should be the same as F28.

Press the exclamation point (!) to request further recalculations. Then you see column G recalculated, but column H is still incorrect. You have to do this many times to get the full spread sheet calculated properly.

The problem is the *sequence* of recalculations. Unless you request otherwise, recalculation is done along rows first, then down columns. Thus the beginning cash balance for August (G25) is copied from F28 before the new interest (F26) and new cash balance (F28) are recalculated; H25 is copied from G28, etc. When SuperCalc has finished recalculating the spread sheet, F28 is correct, but is not what was copied into G25.

Fortunately, it is possible to specify the order of calculation. If we go down *columns* sequentially instead of across rows to do the recalculation, everything works alright. A single SuperCalc command,

/GC   (14.5.9)

requests recalculation **G**lobally by **C**olumn instead of row.

SPREAD SHEETS

	A	B	C	D	E	F	G	H	I	J	K
1	CASH FLOW										
2				May	June	July	Aug	Sept	Oct	Nov	Dec
3	Sales			10000	10000	20000	30000	40000	20000	20000	10000
4											
5	Collections										
6	1'st month		.2	2000	2000	4000	6000	8000	4000	4000	2000
7	2'nd month		.7		7000	7000	14000	21000	28000	14000	14000
8	3'rd month		.1			1000	1000	2000	3000	4000	2000
9											
10	Total					12000	21000	31000	35000	22000	18000
11											
12	Purch (% next mo)		.7	7000	14000	21000	28000	14000	14000	7000	0
13	Payment(1 mo lag)				7000	14000	21000	28000	14000	14000	7000
14											
15	Disbursements										
16	Purchase				7000	14000	21000	28000	14000	14000	7000
17	Wages				1000	1000	2000	3000	4000	2000	2000
18	Rent				500	500	500	500	500	500	500
19	Others				100	200	300	400	200	200	100
20	Taxes						8000				
21	Pay on Machines							10000			
22											
23	Total				8600	15700	31800	41900	18700	16700	9600
24	Net Gain					-3700	-10800	-10900	16300	5300	8400
25	Beg Cash Bal					6000	2345	-8437	-19401	-3246	2029
26	Int on Cash		.008			48	19	-67	-155	-26	16
27											
28	End Cash Bal					2348	-8436	-19405	-3256	2028	10446

Figure 14.5.3. Changing the interest rate in the SS of Fig. 14.5.2 causes only partial recalculation.

Some second and third generation SSs automatically determine the best way to recalculate, find the most important cells and fill them first. You do not have to specify the order of recalculation.

Differing Interest Rates

The idealized method for calculating interest uses the same rate regardless of whether we borrow or lend, an impractical view. We know it costs more to borrow than to lend money. It's simple to fix this with the conditional function, IF, which takes this form

$$\text{IF(cond, formula1, formula2)} \qquad (14.5.10)$$

This function chooses a formula depending upon the prevailing condition, *cond*. Apply a different interest rate according to whether cash on hand is positive or negative. IF chooses *formula1* if *cond* is true and *formula2* if false.

Let us establish two interest rates. First, insert a row after row 26 with /IR. For a positive balance, use the interest rate now in C26; to borrow money, use a higher interest rate in C27. Then IF in F26 calculates interest for that cell thus,

F26: IF(F25>0,C26*F25,C27*F25)   (14.5.11)

The interest for other months (G26:K26) uses the same formula, where F25 is adjusted while C26 and C27 are not. Replicating over the range G26:K26 produces the result shown in Figure 14.5.4.

Cash Reserve

Taking into account interest charged for loans to make the cash balance positive and interest earned on cash for a positive amount on hand is not close enough to practice. We need a **cash reserve,** a minimum amount of cash on hand. When we dip into this reserve, we then borrow money. The reserve collects no interest because it is *cash* in a safe. Determine how big the cash reserve should be, then alter the formula in F26, Figure 14.5.4, to reflect this.

	A	B	C	D	E	F	G	H	I	J	K
1	CASH FLOW										
2					May	June	July	Aug	Sept	Oct	Nov	Dec
3	Sales				10000	10000	20000	30000	40000	20000	20000	10000
4											
5	Collections										
6	1'st month		.2		2000	2000	4000	6000	8000	4000	4000	2000
7	2'nd month		.7			7000	7000	14000	21000	28000	14000	14000
8	3'rd month		.1				1000	1000	2000	3000	4000	2000
9					===						
10	Total						12000	21000	31000	35000	22000	18000
11											
12	Purch (% next mo)		.7		7000	14000	21000	28000	14000	14000	7000	0
13	Payment(1 mo lag)					7000	14000	21000	28000	14000	14000	7000
14											
15	Disbursements										
16	Purchase					7000	14000	21000	28000	14000	14000	7000
17	Wages					1000	1000	2000	3000	4000	2000	2000
18	Rent					500	500	500	500	500	500	500
19	Others					100	200	300	400	200	200	100
20	Taxes							8000				
21	Pay on Machines								10000			
22					===						
23	Total					8600	15700	31800	41900	18700	16700	9600
24	Net Gain						-3700	-10800	-10900	6300	5300	8400
25	Beg Cash Bal						6000	2338	-8452	-19447	-3351	1905
26	Int on Cash +		.0075				38	10	-95	-204	-44	7
27	Int on Cash -		.01									
28											
29	End Cash Bal						2338	-8452	-19447	-3351	1905	10312

Figure 14.5.4. CFA SS with separate rates for + and − balance.

We might put the cash reserve amount into a cell so that it is accesssible to be altered; then the whole spread sheet is subject to quick automatic recalculation. Assume a minimum cash reserve of $1,000. Then the new quantity for cell F26 is

F26: IF(F25>1000,C26*(F25−1000),C27*(F25−1000)) (14.5.12)

Here is the meaning of this formula: as long as the cash on hand is greater than $1,000, the dividend we *receive* is the interest rate (C26) times all but $1,000. When the cash on hand goes below $1,000, we *pay* interest on a negative cash balance or any amount less than $1,000. After entry and replication, the result appears as Figure 14.5.5.

Testing Some Other Assumptions

The main effort in generating the spread sheet is establishing the model and entering the initial data. Great value is realized with little additional effort. Let's test a few more hypotheses now, noting how easy this is to do.

```
     !   A   !!  B   !!  C   !!  D  !!  E  !!  F  !!  G  !!  H  !!  I  !!  J  !!  K  !
 1!CASH FLOW
 2!                               May   June   July   Aug   Sept   Oct    Nov    Dec
 3!Sales                         10000  10000  20000  30000  40000  20000  20000  10000
 4!
 5!Collections
 6!  1'st month          .2       2000   2000   4000   6000   8000   4000   4000   2000
 7!  2'nd month          .7              7000  14000  21000  28000  14000  14000  14000
 8!  3'rd month          .1                    1000   1000   2000   3000   4000   2000
 9!                                     =========================================
10! Total                                12000  21000  31000  35000  22000  18000
11!
12!Purch (% next mo)    .7       7000  14000  21000  28000  14000  14000   7000      0
13!Payment(1 mo lag)                    7000  14000  21000  28000  14000  14000   7000
14!
15!Disbursements
16!  Purchase                           7000  14000  21000  28000  14000  14000   7000
17!  Wages                              1000   1000   2000   3000   4000   2000   2000
18!  Rent                                500    500    500    500    500    500    500
19!  Others                              100    200    300    400    200    200    100
20!  Taxes                                            8000
21!  Pay on Machines                                         10000
22!                                     =========================================
23! Total                                8600  15700  31800  41900  18700  16700   9600
24!Net Gain                                   -3700 -10800 -10900  16300   5300   8400
25!Beg Cash Bal                               6000   2345  -8437 -19422  -3316   1951
26!Int on Cash        .0075                     45     18    -84   -194    -33     15
27!                    .01
28!End Cash Bal                                2345  -8437 -19422  -3316   1951  10365
```

Figure 14.5.5. CFA SS with a cash reserve.

14.5 "WHAT IF?"

Less Seasonality

Figure 14.5.1 shows a seasonal balance sheet. The company could put an effort into making sales more uniform over the year. But first ask, "Would this really increase the end cash balance, at least for the current set of figures?"

To test the assumption that a uniform income would improve our profit situation, examine the overall sales for the eight months from May to December. Total sales are $160,000, an average $20,000 per month for eight months. Let's make the sales for each of the eight months $20,000. Enter 20000 in D3 and copy D3 to E3:K3.

The resulting spread sheet shown in Figure 14.5.6 has an ending cash balance for December $2,000 less than for seasonal sales. This seems to show that uniform sales are disadvantageous.

Improving Collections

Perhaps cash flow would look better if we could bring accounts receivable in earlier. Let's offer a discount for early payment: 10% for payment within

	A	B	C	D	E	F	G	H	I	J	K
1	CASH FLOW										
2				May	June	July	Aug	Sept	Oct	Nov	Dec
3	Sales			20000	20000	20000	20000	20000	20000	20000	20000
4											
5	Collections										
6	1'st month	.2		4000	4000	4000	4000	4000	4000	4000	4000
7	2'nd month	.7			14000	14000	14000	14000	14000	14000	14000
8	3'rd month	.1				2000	2000	2000	2000	2000	2000
9				======	======	======	======	======	======	======	======
10	Total				20000	20000	20000	20000	20000	20000	20000
11											
12	Purch (% next mo)	.7	14000	14000	14000	14000	14000	14000	14000	14000	0
13	Payment (1 mo lag)			14000	14000	14000	14000	14000	14000	14000	14000
14											
15	Disbursements										
16	Purchase			14000	14000	14000	14000	14000	14000	14000	14000
17	Wages			2000	2000	2000	2000	2000	2000	2000	2000
18	Rent			500	500	500	500	500	500	500	500
19	Others			200	200	200	200	200	200	200	200
20	Taxes						8000				
21	Pay on Machines							10000			
22				======	======	======	======	======	======	======	======
23	Total			16700	16700	24700	26700	16700	16700	16700	
24	Net Gain				3300	-4700	-6700	3300	3300	3300	3300
25	Beg Cash Bal				6000	9338	4700	-1972	1298	4600	
26	Int on Cash +	.0075			38	63	28	-30	2	27	
27	Int on Cash -	.01									
28											
29	End Cash Bal				9338	4700	-1972	1298	4600	7927	

Figure 14.5.6. CFA SS with uniform sales.

30 days and 5% for payment within 60 days. Let's change the quantity in C6. Assume that we collect 25% of A/R in the first month after sales, but the amount is reduced by 10%, the discount we offer. Hence the fraction of current sales price received is .225. For 65% of A/R in the second month, less the 5% discount, the fraction of the previous month's sales received is .6175. Now change the original assumption that all outstanding sales are acutally collected in the third month. Assume that only 70% of the still due 10% are ever collected, this fraction being .07.

Changing these three numbers produces the printout of Figure 14.5.7. The cash situation has worsened considerably.

Uncollectible A/R

Could all this be due to uncollected bills? Restore the third month collectibles to 10% and the result is in Figure 14.5.8. Back in the black, let's compare this with the information in Figure 14.5.5. We learn two things from this contrast:

```
     ! A  !!  B  !! C  !! D !! E  !! F  !! G  !! H  !! I  !! J  !! K  !
 1!CASH FLOW
 2!                                Mav   June   July   Auo   Seot   Oct    Nov    Dec
 3!Sales                          10000  10000  20000  30000  40000  20000  20000  10000
 4!
 5!Collections
 6!  1 st month           .225     2250   2250   4500   6750   9000   4500   4500   2250
 7!  2'nd month           .623            6230   6230  12460  18690  24920  12460  12460
 8!  3'rd month           .07                     700    700   1400   2100   2800   1400
 9!                                      ===========================================
10!  Total                               11430  19910  29090  31520  19760  16110
11!
12!Purch (% next mo)      .7      7000   14000  21000  28000  14000  14000   7000      0
13!Pavment(1 mo lao)                     7000   14000  21000  28000  14000  14000   7000
14!
15!Disbursements
16!  Purchase                             7000  14000  21000  28000  14000  14000   7000
17!  Waoes                                1000   1000   2000   3000   4000   2000   2000
18!  Rent                                  500    500    500    500    500    500    500
19!  Others                                100    200    300    400    200    200    100
20!  Taxes                                                     8000
21!  Pav on Machines                                                 10000
22!                                      ===========================================
23!  Total                                8600  15700  31800  41900  18700  16700   9600
24!Net Gain                                     -4270 -11890 -12810  12820   3060   6510
25!Beo Cash Bal                                  6000   1768 -10117 -23038 -10458  -7513
26!Int on Cash +         .0075                    38      6   -111   -240   -115    -85
27!Int on Cash -          .01
28!
29!End Cash Bal                                  1768 -10117 -23038 -10458  -7513  -1088
```

Figure 14.5.7. CFA SS with early payment incentive.

14.5 "WHAT IF?"

```
      !  A   !!  B   !!  C  !!  D   !!  E   !!  F   !!  G   !!  H   !!  I   !!  J   !!  K   !
 1!CASH FLOW
 2!                                    May     June    July    Aug     Sept    Oct     Nov     Dec
 3!Sales                                10000   10000   20000   30000   40000   20000   20000   10000
 4!
 5!Collections
 6!  1'st month           .225   2250   2250    4500    6750    9000    4500    4500    2250
 7!  2'nd month           .623          6230    6230    12460   18690   24920   12460   12460
 8!  3'rd month           .1                    1000    1000    2000    3000    4000    2000
 9!                                             =================================================
10!  Total                                      11730   20210   29690   32420   20960   16710
11!
12!Purch (% next mo)      .7    7000    14000   21000   28000   14000   14000   7000    0
13!Payment(1 mo lag)                    7000    14000   21000   28000   14000   14000   7000
14!
15!Disbursements
16!  Purchase                             7000    14000   21000   28000   14000   14000   7000
17!  Wages                                1000    1000    2000    3000    4000    2000    2000
18!  Rent                                 500     500     500     500     500     500     500
19!  Others                               100     200     300     400     200     200     100
20!  Taxes                                                        8000
21!  Pay on Machines                                      10000
22!                                              =================================================
23!  Total                                8600    15700   31800   41900   18700   16700   9600
24!Net Gain                                      -3970   -11590  -12210  13720   4260    7110
25!Beg Cash Bal                                  6000    2068    -9514   -21830  -8338   -4171
26!Int on Cash +          .0075                  38      8       -105    -228    -93     -52
27!Int on Cash -          .01
28!
29!End Cash Bal                                  2068    -9514   -21830  -8338   -4171   2887
```

Figure 14.5.8. CFA SS as in Fig. 14.5.7 but with no bad sales.

- uncollected sales tend to ruin profit and loss;
- trying to collect earlier by offering a discount is a bad policy for these figures.

Other Hypotheses

The SS program can test innumerable policies. They also help you reach a reasonable model. The illustrated model could be improved considerably perhaps if we took a more realistic approach to labor costs. Row 17 shows wages are proportional to sales. But some wages are there regardless of sales, like clerical and managerial overhead. It is also often hard to vary the number of manufacturing employees, especially in a union establishment. Improving these assumptions might make for a better model.

Functions

Functions add great power to the SS program. They perform actions on one or more values or on a range of values. Each function has a name to call it forth in a formula; within the parentheses that follow are variables that are acted on. Functions fall into several classes according to use. Names below are typical but not universal.

Range

We have already used SUM to add a set of values in a range of cells. Similar functions, named and described below supply a range within parentheses:

SUM adds numbers and puts the total in the cell;
COUNT finds the *number* of nonblank entries;
MAX finds the largest number;
MIN finds the smallest number;
AVERAGE takes the average;
STDEV calculates the standard deviation;
VAR calculates the variance.

Mathematical

Here a value is returned for a single variable within the parentheses. These are examples:

ROUND rounds up or down to the nearest integer;
INT returns the integer portion of a number, disposing of the fraction;
LOG returns the logarithm to the base 10;
ROOT takes the square root;
ABS returns the absolute value.

Other functions find the power, the natural logarithm, the exponential and so forth.

A whole group of trigonometric functions are usually available, but of little use for business applications.

Financial

Financial functions calculate important accounting measures such as

- net present value;
- future value;
- internal rate of return;
- modified internal rate of return;
- annuity;
- depreciation;
- interest and principal payment.

Logical

Logical functions handle logical values and include AND, OR, NOT, TRUE and FALSE. If is particularly useful as seen earlier.

Table Lookup

CHOOSE handles small tables it is not nearly as important as LOOKUP. Some SSs have only two column LOOKUP. Multiple column table search, such as furnished by Multiplan, is more useful and takes this form,

LOOKUP (value,range) (14.5.13)

Here *value* is a value or a cell designation and *range* is a range which defines the table. (Both *value* and *range* can be named for Multiplan, as described in Section 14.6.) For a table that consists of more rows than columns, here is how LOOKUP works. *Value* is searched for in the first column of the table until a value is found there which exceeds it. Then the preceding row is used; the entry is extracted from the last cell in this row.

This is more complicated to explain than to visualize. Look up a salary $4000 in Table 14.5.1 to find what rate applies. Salary is in column C1. The third row is entered because 4000 exceeds 3400 but does not exceed 4400. The rate in column 3, row 3, is 16%.

Let's see how Table 14.5.1 calculates income tax. This is like tables in the IRS 1040 form. The first column contains salary groupings; the second column contains a base tax rate while the third column is a percentage to apply to the amount that exceeds the group amount.

Table 14.5.1 Income Tax

	C1	C2	C3
R50	0	0	0%
R51	2300	0	14%
R52	3400	154	16%
R53	4400	314	18%
R54	6500	692	19%
R55	8500	1072	21%

Group: C1
Base: C1–C2
Rate: C1–C3

Only one table is needed for making the tax calculations. To simplify matters, let's give things names. Use Sal for the salary on which we are calculating the tax. Then let's name the table: the first column alone is called Group, the first and second columns together are called Base; and the entire table is called Rate. This formula calculates any tax within the extremes of the table:

$$\text{LOOKUP (Sal, Base)} + \text{LOOKUP (Sal, Rate)} * [\text{Sal} - \text{LOOKUP (Sal, Group)}] \quad (14.5.14)$$

The first term looks up the salary and finds the base entry from column 2. The second term calculates the tax on the remaining amount. Thus first look up the group salary and subtract it from the actual salary; then multiply this by the rate.

14.6 MULTIPLAN AND THE SECOND GENERATION

Classification

We have seen the potential of SS products by examining spread sheets constructed using SuperCalc. Actually spread sheet products fall into three categories:

- **first generation products** such as VisiCalc and SuperCalc;
- **second generation products** with many improvements in basic SS functions;
- **combination products** with improved SS functions and other features such as graphics, word processing and communications;
- **fourth generation products** further extend capabilities.

This section defines the differences among these products. Then it takes a closer look at the second generation product, Multiplan. Third and fourth generation products are examined in Sections 14.7 and 14.8.

The First Generation

VisiCalc, the first spread sheet program, has sold over 400,000 copies. It was originally designed to work on the Apple. Its application base did not broaden until the IBM PC came along. Then another version was created to run under MS-DOS.

Microplan, developed by Chang Laboratories, was the first SS product to work with CP/M. It was written in CBASIC. Therefore the user had to

14.6 MULTIPLAN AND THE SECOND GENERATION 643

have a copy of the CBASIC interpreter (a mixed mode interpreter examined in Chapter 8). This reduced efficiency and slowed up the program considerably. Microplan was difficult to use and was not readily accepted.

SuperCalc, developed by Sorcim Corporation in 1980, is written in assembly language. It is well designed and has sold over 250,000 copies. It runs under CP/M but has been adapted for a large number of other personal computers and OSs. The rights to this product were sold to Peachtree Software, which now markets it as part of PeachText. In return, Sorcim received the rights to the MagicWand word processor, which it altered somewhat to become SuperWriter.

Other software houses jumped on the bandwagon to produce many products, such as CalcStar and PerfectCalc, which do not differ much from the original concept developed by Software Arts as VisiCalc (and distributed by VisiCorp).

Second Generation

It quickly became apparent that spread sheets are a fantastic product responsible for selling thousands of computers. One way to capture a share of the market is to make a better spread sheet. Microsoft set out to do this and came up with Multiplan, which soon sold in the hundreds of thousands. It has many attractive features, described in this section. VisiCalc's creators saw that they could not keep their lead without improving their product considerably, and released a new version, called VisiCalc Advanced Version, in 1982. Sorcim, too, saw the writing on the wall and made improvements in their product by issuing further releases. Early in 1983, they released SuperCalc 2 with important improvements, and later that year, SuperCalc 3, designed to compete with Lotus 1-2-3. At the end of 1983, VisiCorp produced VisiCalc IV, which includes sorting, graphs and keysaver commands. Other new products entered the fray but are less important.

Combinations

Products with multiple capabilities are limited by the memory available. When IBM came out with the PC and then the XT, much more memory became available. Not limited to 64K as are 8 bit systems, versions of these computers provide 512K or more. They accommodate much larger spread sheets, and multiple programs available at a moment's notice. Two companies immediately saw their benefits and made products which combined several resources, restricting them to computers which had enough memory to run them. Both MBA (by Context Management System) and Lotus 1-2-3 run on the IBM PC or XT. Although similar in features offered, 1-2-3 is faster and friendlier; Section 14.7 is devoted to it. VisiOn, a new product by the makers of VisiCalc, combines a number of functions.

Lisa is a computer and software product produced by Apple, combining five major programs in a state-of-the-art computer released in the beginning of 1983 for a price of $10,000. It did not sell well initially and has gone through at least two price reductions. The concept is excellent and is based on **icons,** which represent objects and actions. A mouse points to an icon and initiates an action or opens a window to display data. The computer uses a 68000 chip, has 512K of memory or more and includes a hard disk to hold all the programs. It has an excellent graphics package which, among other functions, lets the user make office layouts, and include illustrations in textual material.

Lisa has encountered problems of this sort:

- the system is slow to start and occupies most of the soft disk;
- there is little room left to hold user's files;
- functions are good but are not the best available so that the word processor and spread sheet programs, for instance, are outdistanced by other products;
- the response of the programs is slower than expected;
- since Lisa has its own operating system, it does not currently work with software products designed for other systems so that the user has a relatively narrow choice of applications, though Apple is working to ameliorate this handicap.

Lisa does seem, though, to be the wave of the future and many of its concepts have been adapted in Apple's Macintosh.

Multiplan

Multiplan is just one of a group of second generation SS programs which includes VisiCalc IV and SuperCalc 2. All have additional features and departures from the first generation format. However, Multiplan's features make it an excellent bridge to composite systems.

Cell Selection

Cell Address

Multiplan numbers *both* rows and columns. First the row, then the column number are named. R5C8 designates the fifth row, eighth column. Numbers display in row and column stubs.

14.6 MULTIPLAN AND THE SECOND GENERATION

It would thus seem that address entry requires more keystrokes than for the other systems. However the VisiCalc system uses a separator between the column letter and row number because some columns may be designated by double letters, such as AB or BC. The separator is return: You designate cell F7 by keying Freturn7. To enter a Multiplan address, use the tab key: row 5 column 8 is keyed with 5tab8. Thus on both systems you perform this function with three keystrokes.

Direct Positioning

To position to a cell so that it appears in the upper left corner of the display, use the *goto* command, G. Enter command letters directly (without a prefix). Thus to position to row 5 column 8, issue

G5tab8   (14.6.1)

or four strokes. The screen command line precedes the row and column number with R and C to remind you which you should enter first.

Two Cursors

One problem encountered with other SS programs while entering a command is that you may forget the target cell address. Since the arrow keys are for editing the command line, they do not move the active cell cursor to scroll or manipulate the spread sheet.

This is remedied in Multiplan by providing two sets of cursor controls. The keys used to activate the two cursors depend on the terminal. Arrow keys work for both functions on the PC and compatibles. For my Soroc IQ 120, arrow controls the command cursor and control combinations manipulate the active cell cursor. These are the ones used by WordStar and form a diamond on the left side of the keyboard:

up = ^E; left = ^S; down = ^X; right = ^D   (14.6.2)

As you issue commands which refer to cell addresses, the SS program enters the present address of the active cell on the screen command line. You have three choices of getting a cell address into the command:

- Use the active cursor address supplied by default.
- Key in the row and column number.
- Move the cursor with control keys to a cell and hit tab or return.

Multiplan expedites motion within large spread sheets in several ways. One is **page scrolling,** making jumps by units of a screenful, done by a multiplier code, ^R. Used with the codes in (14.6.2), the display shows the next screen in the requested direction: ^R^D moves to the next right screen; ^R^X moves down one screen. (These are *case insensitive*: ^r^x works too).

You can go to the top of the AS with ^Q (to R1C1) or to the bottom of the active area with ^Z.

Entry

Once positioned at a cell, enter a command, information or a formula. *All* SS programs require a prefix for *some* of the modes of entry. Table 14.6.1 illustrates this.

Numbers

All SS programs enter numbers directly into any active cell.

Text

For VisiCalc, enter text into an active cell without a prefix. For SuperCalc, text begins with a double quote. For Multiplan, hit A for the *alphanumeric* first. (You can use return instead of A.).

Multiplan has a neat feature for filling a number of title boxes. If you enter an *active cell cursor positioning* control code instead of hitting return, Multiplan puts the string entered so far into the active cell and moves the cell cursor in the direction requested, awaiting entry of *similar* data. For the PC, after entering text, you can enter more text in the next cell to the right by hitting right.

Multiplan also provides for long titles much like SuperCalc, but requires a little more effort. You must preformat the cell where you enter the long title *and* its right hand neighbor(s) as *continuing* text cells. Titles can span two or more such formatted cells.

Table 14.6.1 Prefixes for Entry

	VISICALC	SUPERCALC	MULTIPLAN
Text		"	A(lpha)
Numbers			V(alue)
Formulas			V(alue)
Command	/	/	
Function	@		

Formulas

For SuperCalc, a formula is entered directly without a prefix. For VisiCalc, a formula must always begin with a plus or a minus sign. For Multiplan hit V, the *value* command, first. If you move the active cell cursor at the end of formula entry, then you are prepared to enter a formula into the next cell you go to.

The Name Command

The **name command** (Multiplan) lets you name a cell, row, column or block. Then this entity can be referred to in any other command or calculation. This is not only a powerful simplification but also helps in figuring out what formulas mean.

To use *name*, hit N. The prompt asks for a name. Any alphabetic label you enter, up to 31 characters (which may include dashes and underscores but no blanks), applies to the entry that you define. Then hit tab and the prompt shows that the name now applies to the active cell. You can change this by

- entering a row and column number to replace this; or
- moving the active cell cursor to another cell, the address in the command changing as you do—if you then hit return, the name applies to that cell.

To name a range of cells, adjust the name of the starting cell as described above, then hit colon (:). This tells Multiplan to expect another cell address to complete the range. You supply this address by moving the cursor or by keying an address (or name). When you hit return, the name is defined and the cursor returns to its original position on the display so as not to inconvenience you.

What If The Name Exists?

Suppose the name you enter already exists. Multiplan responds by displaying the address(es) of cell(s) assigned to this name. To reassign the name, edit the reference address displayed, which then becomes the new definition for the name. (The previous definition is destroyed.)

You may forget names you have already assigned. After starting a *name* command, the direction keys (arrow) let you step through the current set of names and their assignments. When you have seen them all, you may enter a name and a reference.

Commands

Multiplan provides many commands, each with one or more options. Multiplan is rich in both its number of options and the means for selecting among them. Although command entry is different than for other spread sheets, the experienced user requires little time to accommodate to it. In the long run, it turns out to be fast and easy to use.

Selection

Command selection begins after you

- enter a command and Multiplan executes it, or
- enter information for Multiplan to place in a cell

Immediately two prompt lines show all possible commands. A square bracket positions around **A** for Alpha. You select a command by

- typing the first letter of the command, or
- positioning the bracket to another displayed command and hitting return.

Position the brackets by moving them left to the next command with space.

Help

When you first use Multiplan, you do not know what every command does. Position the brackets to a command and hit the question mark (?) to bring forth a help panel for that command. Often a command has several help panels. Sequence through the set of panels by hitting **N** (for next) or **P** (for previous) or terminate the help function with return.

Options

Most commands have options. Selecting the command brings an option list to the prompt line. Select an option as before, with one addition:

- move about the options with direction keys or space and then hit return;
- type a character which designates your selection;
- type in an entry, such as the name of a file or the address of a cell or range, and hit return.

When the number of options is limited and know to you, selection can be rapid. For instance, to print a spread sheet using the default option, hit **P** to select the print command and hit P again to start the printer. Just two keystrokes are sufficient; even return is unnecessary.

Example: Window Command

Another example is the window command, W. It sets up windows, of which as many as eight may be active at once; it also locks titles. Here is how you might step through the options. To select the window command, hit W. This option message then displays:

> WINDOW: Split Border Close Link (14.6.3)

Select the *split* option to divide the screen or set up a new window by hitting S or return to get this display.

> WINDOW SPLIT: Horizontal Vertical Titles (14.6.4)

The *title* option freezes titles. The other two create a horizontal or vertical window as described for SuperCalc. If you choose the horizontal option you get this display,

> WINDOW SPLIT HORIZONTAL at row: 17 linked: Yes No (14.6.5)

which says that Multiplan assumes you want to split the screen at line 17 because the cursor is sitting there, and that the windows are synchorized. You can change this or press return.

Multiplan provides a **proposed response** based on the active cell. Alter it by overtyping or by moving the active cell cursor to where you want the split. Then hit tab to select whether the windows are synchronized; answer Y or N.

Prompts Eliminated

Experience can eliminate prompts entirely. If the active cell cursor is where you want the split, simply type WSH return.

Formulas

A formula in a cell causes the SS to make a calculation based on it. The value calculated then appears in the cell. The formula consists of

- **operators,** which may be +, −, etc.;
- **operands,** which refer to another cell or group of cells;
- a **value,** which may be text or a number.

Reference

Values are keyed in an expression where needed. Thus to add 3 to an expression entered so far, type +3. Cells and groups of cells are referenced in three ways: absolutely, relatively and by name.

Absolute references are illustrated by these examples:

- a cell by row and column number, R3C5;
- a row or column by its number, R3 or C5;
- part of a row or column by range, R3:7 or C5:8;
- a block by a double range, such as R3:7C5:8 or by the upper left hand and lower right hand corner, such as R3C5:R7C8.

A **relative reference** describes a cell (or block) by its position relative to the active cell. It displays as a number in square brackets, how many rows (columns) to go to the right (down). The opposite direction, left or up, is indicated by a minus sign. Brackets are omitted to designate the current row (column). Three examples are:

R[−3]C points three rows up in this column;
RC[4] points four cells right in this row;
R[−3]C[−4] points three rows up and four left.

Designate a relative row, column or block similarly, as explained in the Multiplan manual.

To **reference by name,** enter a name set up previously for a cell, column, row or block with the N command. A formula for a value that goes in a cell is different from an equation. It would be nice to say PAY = RATE × TIME, where each name applies to a column for instance, but this is not permitted. The name for a column or a column segment in an expression applies to the intersection cell of that column with the active row in the formula. Even so, referencing by name is very useful.

Entering

Relative addressing provides a real simplification. As implemented for Multiplan, you need key in little. You use **pointing,** moving the cell cursor to a cell whose value should be entered into the formula. Here is how it works.

To enter a formula in the *active cell,* either hit V or =. Immediately VALUE appears on both the prompt and command line. How do you enter the time formula for the electronic time sheet example in Section 14.4? A block of these formulas developed for Multiplan appears in Figure 14.6.1.

14.6 MULTIPLAN AND THE SECOND GENERATION 651

```
                 7                            8              9
 5  "Time"                                  "Wage"         "Total"
 6
 7  60*RC[-2]+RC[-1]-(60*RC[-4]+RC[-3])     R3C7*RC[-1]/60  RC[-1]
 8  60*RC[-2]+RC[-1]-(60*RC[-4]+RC[-3])     R3C7*RC[-1]/60  RC[-1]+R[-1]C
 9  60*RC[-2]+RC[-1]-(60*RC[-4]+RC[-3])     R3C7*RC[-1]/60  RC[-1]+R[-1]C
10  60*RC[-2]+RC[-1]-(60*RC[-4]+RC[-3])     R3C7*RC[-1]/60  RC[-1]+R[-1]C
11  60*RC[-2]+RC[-1]-(60*RC[-4]+RC[-3])     R3C7*RC[-1]/60  RC[-1]+R[-1]C
12  60*RC[-2]+RC[-1]-(60*RC[-4]+RC[-3])     R3C7*RC[-1]/60  RC[-1]+R[-1]C
```

Figure 14.6.1. Copy down duplicates formula without replication.

Let us see how to create the formula for *time worked,* row 7 column 7 of the figure.

Stopping time in minutes is the product of time in hours and 60, plus the minutes. Stopping time in hours is two columns left; the additional minutes are one column left. Begin the formula by typing 60 and then the asterisk. Move the active cell cursor two columns left, and the relative position of the active cell appears on the command line like magic as RC[−2]. Type + and the cursor returns to the active cell. Now move it left one cell and you find RC[−1] on the command line. This establishes the stopping time in minutes, so hit the minus sign.

Continue to enter the formula thus: move the cell cursor to the cell you want to use, then hit the key for the next operator. When the formula is complete, hit return and it enters the cell.

The formula for wages in row 7 column 8 has an absolute reference. You can type this in directly from its position on the screen. Otherwise, move the cursor to the cell, in this case the one for pay rate. The command line displays its *relative* position, not what you want. The absolute location is required (we see why shortly). Hit @ and the reference in the command changes from relative to absolute.

Replicate

The commands available in Multiplan include no *replicate* command. How can that be? This is one of the great powers of VisiCalc. But remember what the replicate command does: it duplicates formulas to other positions on the spread sheet, offsetting references in the expression as required for this particular cell.

Relative references make this unnecessary. *Copying* formulas with relative references is equivalent to *replicating* them. Figure 14.6.1 shows all the formulas in column 7 as identical. Although in different cells, each correctly refers to the same *relative* column for the target cells which are all in the same row. Formulas in column 8 have been copied correctly: rate is an absolute reference; time is the next cell to the left. Most of the totals in column A are the sum of the cell on the left and the cell above.

Adjustment for the replicate command lets *you* decide whether to use absolute or relative references for cell address in an expression. For Multiplan, this determination is made when you create the formula.

Copy

Copy formulas (or values or text) with the *copy* command, C. It has three options: right, down, and from. *Right* copies a cell or a column into a group of cells or columns on the right; *down* copies a cell or a row segment downward cells to rows below. *From* copies a cell (or block of cells) into a block starting at a specified cell.

Let's look at *copy down* for copying the formulas in both the time and wage column of Figure 14.6.1. To start, hit CD and this prompt appears,

COPY DOWN number of cells: 1 starting at: R7C7 (14.6.6)

Type in the number of copies of the formulas you want. For 10, you get the original and nine more in rows below. Then hit tab. The active cell R7C7 is the default cells entered automatically. To ask for both R7C7 and R7C8, append :8 so that (14.6.6) shows R7C7:8, and hit return. As Multiplan goes to work, results appear in the cells to which the formulas are copied. Where no values are available, 0's appear instead.

Combining Spread Sheets

First generation spread sheets can be broken up into smaller spread sheets and then recombined later. This is a necessity as users plan larger and larger spread sheets. With 63 columns and 255 rows, you wouldn't expect to run out of space very soon. But the virtual spread sheet (VS) size is not the limitation; it is the *available memory*. The actual spread sheet (AS) size is limited by hardware memory.

The technique breaks out parts of the model. Consider a profit and loss statement. The first round of modelling shows that the model works. Let us break out three kinds of costs: material, labor and overhead. You can make separate spread sheets for each. Actually an overall model might well be small enough to hold all the submodels simultaneously within the boundaries of VisiCalc or SuperCalc, but it serves as a convenient example.

Consolidation

Even with older SS programs, it is possible to run experiments on the cost spread sheet and then to return its totals to the profit and loss statement. This is how to go about it with SuperCalc.

First, create the P+L model. Then create the cost submodel. Play with it until you are satisfied. Save it, blank the screen and bring back the profit and loss statement using these SuperCalc commands,

/SDP+LCostA   /ZY   /LAP+L   (14.6.7)

where the **submodel** is P+LCost. We have that

- the first command saves all of P+LCost;
- the second zaps the screen;
- the last loads P+L.

Now let's incorporate the labor costs from the submodel into row 7 of P+L which contains formulas to calculate labor costs from sales costs. You would not want to load the results from the submodel into the formula area. Therefore blank out the formulas in row 7 starting with column G (command not shown). Load in the labor total from the submodel with

/LP P+LCost,D9:09,G7   (14.6.8)

This is a SuperCalc *partial load* (/LP) from P+LCost specifying the source range for labor cost (D9:09). The corner of the destination block on P+L, G7, is then named. (You may bring in a single value, row, column or block.)

Thus information from several submodels can be incorporated in a single model. However,

1. You must know the location of the required block of information in each source submodel.
2. You must supply the destination cell for each load action.
3. You may extract more than one block from a submodel, but need a separate command for each.
4. Every time you update a submodel, you must bring in the model and issue *load* commands.

Multiplan Linked WorkSheets

Automatic Linkage

An attractive feature of Multiplan (and others like it) is that, once consolidation is designated, it may be done automatically thereafter. Set up **links** in the model—connections between it and the submodel. Whenever you load the model, blocks from the specified submodels come in automatically. Further, you can establish a **multilevel** system where submodels depend on lower level submodels. We examine this shortly.

Storing Worksheets

The Multiplan model is stored under the name of P+L for profit and loss with

TSP+L (14.6.9)

for transfer store P+L. For the submodel P+LCost, each important row, column or block is named with N. Suppose this submodel has three rows of totals, OCost, LCost, and MCost, for overhead, labor and material cost respectively.

Load and Link

To establish links, first load the model with

TLP+L (14.6.10)

Next find the submodel and link it to the model with the external command, X, which has three options:

- C for *copy*: copies a portion of the submodel and establishes a link, if desired.
- L for *list*: lists models, submodels on which they depend and those which depend on the model.
- U for *use*: permits substitutions for submodels.

The copy option, XC, calls forth this prompt,

XC
EXTERNAL COPY from sheet: name: to:R7C7
linked (Yes)No (14.6.11)

14.6 MULTIPLAN AND THE SECOND GENERATION

This requests four entries:

- the name of the submodel;
- the name of the block in the submodel to be copied;
- the cell on this SS where the block goes;
- whether a permanent link is established.

Example Of External Copy

Any area to be copied into must be blanked the first time, since values might collide with formulas or values there. Therefore the material, labor and overhead row segments in the P+L model are blanked with the B command before XC is issued. When the prompt appears, the name of the submodel is furnished first, P+LCost. After hitting return, you would enter MCost, the first field. This is to be transferred to row 5 column 2. Since a link is desired, hit return twice. This completes the command; the field is found and incorporated into the model, P+L.

The same action is repeated for the other two named fields called OCost and LCost; as each row segment arrives, calculations in the model are performed where requried.

In this example, all the fields come from the same submodel, but a different submodel might be supplied for each field.

Automatic Loading

If XC specifies a link, then, whenever the model (P+L) is loaded, the associated submodel (P+LCost) is found, the fields located and transferred. When several submodels are required as displayed in Figure 14.6.2, each is activated in turn. Here details come from MC, OC and LC.

A link is destroyed by issuing XC for the same source file, field name and link, but with an *empty* destination.

Multiple Dependencies

Figure 14.6.3 shows a model dependency graph where model F depends on other models which in turn depend on still other models. Alteration of submodels and their loading must be done in the proper order to produce a proper final model. For instance, in this figure models A and D should be altered first. Then the second level models, B and C, can be loaded, updated from A and D automatically and altered. Subsequently the third level model E and finally the fourth level model F are loaded, updated, altered and used. As each higher level model is loaded, results from the preceding

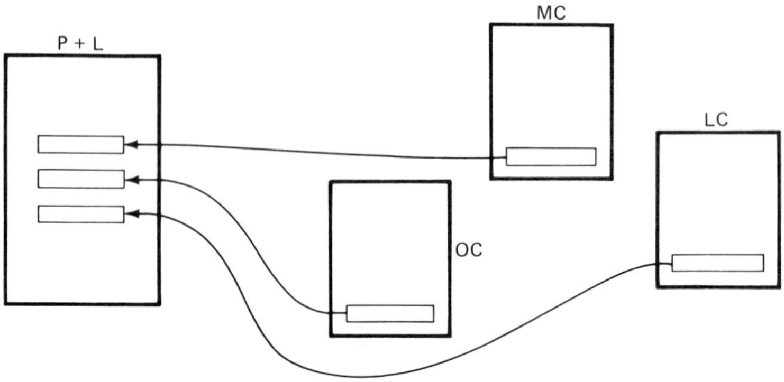

Figure 14.6.2. External copy (X) does automatic linking.

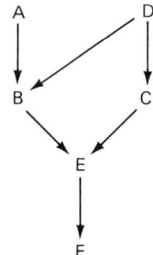

Figure 14.6.3. Model dependency graph.

models are entered automatically, calculations made and results prepared and displayed.

Models may depend on *each other*. This is circular, but proper, as displayed in Figure 14.6.4. Here the profit and loss model, P+L, depends on both sales and costs; costs in P+LCost, in turn, depend on sales from P+L. The way to use this pair is first to alter sales in the P+L. But the

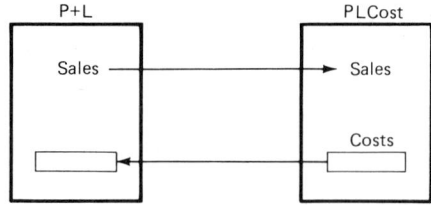

Figure 14.6.4. A circular model dependency graph.

14.6 MULTIPLAN AND THE SECOND GENERATION

labor costs are also in the submodel. So save model P+L and load PLCost along with the new sales figures, since the two are linked. Then save PLCost and bring in P+L again. Since the labor costs are linked forward into the profit and loss statement, they are automatically transferred.

List

The *list* option of X displays all direct dependencies of other spread sheets on the active spread sheet. **Direct dependencies** are those which automatically call up this spread sheet or are called up by this spread sheet. For example, in Figure 14.6.3 the direct dependencies of E are F, B and C. Thus although E depends on A and D also, this information is relayed through spread sheet B and is an indirect dependency.

The XL command with E the active SS displays,

    Sheets supporting E
              B
              C
    Sheets depending on E
              F   (14.6.12)

Use Option

Suppose you have created a complicated model which includes several submodels, one of which is Budget82. You would like to substitute a new submodel called Budget83 (different values and/or formulas).

You could disconnect existing links between the model and Budget82 with one or more XC commands and connect it to the new submodel, Budget83, by issuing an equal number of XC commands. A similar action is necessary to reverse the process.

The *use* option, specified with XU, lets you support an active spread sheet with a different submodel with just *one* command. This assumes that the substituted supporting submodel uses the same names and number of fields as the original submodel and that substitutions are made at the same places in the active spread sheet. The XU command prompts thus,

    EXTERNAL USE file name: instead of: Budget82
    Enter file name: (14.6.13)

To specify the substitution, enter Budget83 now.

If you substitute submodels frequently, you can set up a dummy submodel, one which does not exist. Then tie in submodels with XU. For instance, call the dummy submodel BUDGET. To link to a submodel, issue XU to replace BUDGET with Budget83, regardless of what currently replaces BUDGET.

Sorting

Sort, S, reorganizes the rows of a spread sheet. The key (Section 12.5) for the sort can be any single column. To initiate the command, after hitting S, indicate a *range* of rows to sort and the column which contains the sort key (for which Multiplan proposes the active column). Then Multiplan rearranges the rows in ascending (or descending) sequence by collating the sequence of the key, the sequence of the characters in the ASCII code (See p. 53.)

When done, if Multiplan is in automatic recalculate mode, results are recalculated. This is often undesirable, and mode should be set to *manual*. A sorted spread sheet which involves formulas should not be saved to disk, since recalculation would be done as that spread sheet is loaded from disk, but in perhaps the wrong sequence.

Use

There are many times one might like to sort information in the spread sheet. Let us examine one such time.

I create a roster of my students in alphabetical order by last name with a Multiplan SS. It contains formulas for calculating grades during a term and for determining the final grade. However, at the end of the term it is improper to post grades by student name. It is OK to use social security numbers. The names can be blanked out for printout, but students can tell other students' names by their position in the list. However if the list is sorted by social security number, no such guesses can easily be made.

14.7 LOTUS® AND THE THIRD GENERATION SS*

Introduction

Third generation SSs which take advantage of the greater resources provided in the IBM PC and compatibles include Lotus 1-2-3®, SuperCalc 3 and Context MBA. They provide

- larger virtual spread sheets;
- data base capabilities;
- ability to plot, display, and print business graphs in several formats.

---

*Lotus and 1-2-3 are registered trademarks of Lotus Development Corporation.

Context MBA claims to provide three additional functions: communication, word processing, forms generation. It includes a communication program which works with most modems. However, the word processing and forms generation are less than one might expect.

Advantages

1-2-3 is faster than most SS programs. And although it costs more, it provides more. Coordinating graphics with the spread sheet is advantageous to the manager. Value changes in the model take immediate effect because of the high speed of the SS program. When the results display in graphical form, their impact is heightened many times. They convey the possible direction of further changes to reach an objective and hence to close in on it more rapidly.

Requirements

Third generation SSs require at least 128K of memory and work better with more. Graphs display in color or in black and white, but on the IBM PC and most look-alikes a graphic PC board must be used; on the other hand, a color display, available with the graphics board, is more spectacular. Color in the spread sheet provides highlighting; negative entries may be distinctly colored. This entails two expenses: the color graphics board and a color monitor.

Spread Sheet Characteristics

The 1-2-3 SS program is not much different from SuperCalc or VisiCalc except that it has

- a much larger virtual spread sheet;
- quicker response time;
- expanded commands and capabilities.

Cell Addresses

1-2-3 provides a virtual spread sheet with 254 rows and 2048 columns. Rows are numbered; columns use single (A–Z) and then double letters starting with AA. The VS could conceivably provide 50,000 cell but is considerably smaller because of memory and disk restrictions.

Commands

All commands begin with a slash (/). There are few commands but each has many options, which effectively multiplies the number of available alternatives. The prompt line lists commands with the first letter capitalized. Ready 1-2-3 by hitting /; the command letter changes the prompt line to display the first option. Each time you choose an option, the prompt line displays the next set of choices.

Cell Entry

The first character keyed determines the kind of entry. After completing the previous action, 1-2-3 enters the *ready* mode (the status line shows this) and

- a slash begins a command;
- a letter starts a label or text entry;
- a number begins a value;
- a number, operator or left parenthesis begins a formula.

A large number of formats are available, set up with the format command (/F); one can format a large nonrectangular array of cells.

Text is justified right, left or centered according to the prefix hit first, respectively the apostrophe ('), quote (") or caret (^). Long text continues over several columns if adjacent columns are empty (without formatting them). You can set up an area three rows by four columns, say, where keyed text is justified.

Keys

Lotus 1-2-3 takes advantage of the large number of keys on the IBM PC keyboard, including ten function keys, and sets them to perform specific actions. 1-2-3 is designed for the PC or XT and its terminal, keyboard and operating system match properly: arrow works without an install routine; so do page up and page down as well as a host of others.

Ranges

Recall that a *range* may be a single cell, row or column segment or rectangular block. It is specified by two opposite corners along a diagonal of the rectangle. Instead of the colon as a separator, a single dot or a series of dots is used, such as A5..C12. Regardless of how many dots *you* enter, the two range cells appear on the command and prompt line separated by exactly two dots. A range designation is insensitive to which corner is mentioned first: C12..A5 or A12..C5 is exactly equivalent to A5..C12.

Pointing

1-2-3, like Multiplan, names a range by **pointing**. As you fill in a formula or command where a range is required, name the starting cell by accepting the proposed response (with enter), by moving the cursor or by keying it. To continue a range definition, type one or more dots. This **anchors** the first cell as the starting point for the range definition. Now arrow moves the terminal point any place on (or off) the screen. As you move, the range defined is highlighted and the opposite corner address appears on the command line.

Anchor

After you set the terminal point, you may find that the initial point is incorrect. To change it, **move the anchor** thus: hitting the period moves the anchor clockwise around the vertices of the defined rectangular area and changes the vertices which define the range on the prompt line; they still define the same range though. After resetting the anchor, arrow moves the diagonally opposite unanchored point to redefine the beginning of the range.

Figure 14.7.1 shows how this works. The anchor point is now B6 and the free point is G10, indicated in two places: the cell cursor, a blinking underline appears in cell G10; the command line shows the range as B6..G10. To alter the range to include a segment on row 5 requires changing the anchor to G10.

First, hit the period key (1). This moves the blinking cursor for the **free point** to B10 and the anchor G6; the range is now reported as G6..B10. Hit the period key again (2). This moves the anchor to G10 and the free point

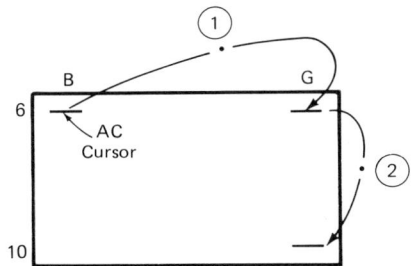

Figure 14.7.1. Moving the anchor of the range.

to B6; the range is reported as G10..B6. Press up once, the cursor moves up and the range is reported as G10..B5.

Naming Areas

The range name create command (/RNC) labels a range or a group of ranges. Then you can use this name in commands or formulas as with Multiplan.

Replicate

Taking the lead from Multiplan with relative addressing (p. 650), 1-2-3 has no replicate command. They have improved on the copy concept. Multiplan addresses are either absolute or relative. But 1-2-3 adds **mixed references:** you can fix a row and make the column reference relative or fix a column and make row reference relative. With this facility, you can enter a single formula in one corner of a rectangular array and copy and adjust it for every cell of the array.

Example

An example, a table showing return from both a changing investment amount and interest rate, shows the usefulness of mixed references. In Figure 14.7.2, columns of row 5 have the interest rate; rows of a column B have the investment amount. The table, kept short for the purpose of illustration, covers the range C6:E8. With absolute addresses as required for VisiCalc, each cell contains a different product as shown.

To create this table with the replicate command, put the first formula in C6. Then replicate across row 6, providing adjustment for the first factor

	A	B	C	D	E
			INVESTMENT TABLE		
4			********* RATE	**********	
5		Amount	.08	.09	.10
6		$1000	C5*B6	D5*B6	E5*B6
7		$2000	C5*B7	D5*B7	E5*B7
8		$3000	C5*B8	D5*B8	E5*B8

Figure 14.7.2. Investment return (IR), absolute addresses.

but not the second. This fills in the formulas along row 6. Now replicate row 6 over the rest of the range; this time keep the first factor constant and adjust the second factor. (These formulas could also be created by starting with column C and replicating over the other columns of the range.)

Absolute and relative addressing do not improve matters as illustrated in Figure 14.7.3. Again, set up the formulas for the first row of the table. Address the investment relatively as RC[−1] and address the interest rate absolutely in the first cell as R3C5. It should be clear how the other formulas in row 6 are formed. But there is no way to make these formulas automatically. They must be repeated for each cell of row 6. Then the contents of row 6 (R6C3:5) can be copied to row 6 and 7.

Another way to set up the table is to enter the formula in row 6 column 3 and copy it into the other cells of the row; then edit the revised formulas into the other cells of row 6. Once row 6 is set up, simply copy that row segment into the rest of the table, since these are identical.

With mixed mode, illustrated in Figure 14.7.4, one formula is entered in C6, C$5*$B6. Only one *copy* command copies it into the entire table using **automatic adjustment.** Of course, it may take a little while to figure out *what should be* in C6 so that automatic adjustment works properly.

	1	2	3	4	5
6			RC[-1]*R5C3	RC[-2]*R5C4	RC[-3]*R5C5
7			RC[-1]*R5C3	RC[-2]*R5C4	RC[-3]*R5C5
8			RC[-1]*R5C3	RC[-2]*R5C4	RC[-3]*R5C5

Figure 14.7.3. IR with relative addresses.

	A	B	C	D	E
6			C$5 * $B6	D$5 * $B6	E$5 * $B6
7			C$5 * $B7	D$5 * $B7	E$5 * $B7
8			C$5 * $B8	D$5 * $B8	E$5 * $B8

Figure 14.7.4. IR with mixed addresses.

Adjustment

Let's see how adjustment works. The first term in C6, C$5 (Figure 14.7.4) specifies that C as relative and subject to adjustment as the formula is copied to other columns. But $5 is absolute and is always the same regardless of what row it is copied to. This first term is the interest rate. As it is copied across the row, the column letter changes from C to D to E and so forth to say which column to find it in. But the absolute row number always records that the interest rate is in the *fifth* row.

The second factor, $B5, refers to the investment amount. The column is always B because of the preceding dollar sign. The row number is adjusted when copied into other rows. During copy across a row the investment amount remains the same; but moving down the column to a different row, the row number changes.

To summarize, when you set up a formula, you say you want no adjustment by preceding the row or column designator by a dollar sign. If both have dollar signs, neither is adjusted (absolute addressing). If either lacks a dollar sign, it is adjusted according to whether it applies to a row or column.

Keystroke Programming

Keystroke programming creates a string of keystrokes to enter labels, formulas or move information about; it assigns the string to one key. Assemble a sequence of keystrokes in one or more cells on the spread sheet. Since some of them might move you out of the cell, such as up, use a *name* for that keystroke: substitute {up} for up. Names for keys are put in braces. Assign a key to represent the keystrokes. The *range name* command, /RN, does this, but the details are unimportant.

To call up the keystroke sequence, hit the key assigned earlier, pressing alt at the same time. Thus a single combination of keystrokes calls forth the series of keystrokes anywhere on the spread sheet. This facility is sometimes called a **macro.**

The keystroke facility is available in other advanced spread sheets such as VisiCalc IV and in the form of the *execute* command for SuperCalc.

Graphs

The most exciting feature of 1-2-3 is graphs. It makes them to your specifications based on spread sheet contents. They appear on the color monitor. With two monitors, you can view the spread sheet on one and see a color-graph representation of part of the spread sheet on the other.

14.7 LOTUS AND THE THIRD GENERATION SS

1-2-3 makes five kinds of charts: bar, stacked bar, pie, line, X-Y. 1-2-3 superimposes several sets of data on a single chart of a particular type. You can label the axes, put titles at the top and enter legends at the bottom. 1-2-3 automatically finds the best scaling for the graph, but you can override it.

Once you have established the form and labels for a chart, you can save them in a disk file. What is truly spectacular is dynamic graphing capability. After setting up a chart and perhaps saving it, you can go out of graph mode to make "What if?" speculations on the spread sheet. When you press the *graph view* key, F10, newly calculated data based on these speculations immediately display in the requested graph format.

The Graph Command

You enter graph mode by hitting /G which displays the main graph menu thus,

Type X A B C D E F Reset View Save Option Name Quit
(14.7.1)

Each menu option starts with a different letter. Invoke an option by hitting a letter or moving the cursor and hitting return. Since a graph setup requires a number of parameters, you remain in graph mode (to select parameters) until hitting Q.

Type

T chooses one graph type from the five discussed below.

The Bar Chart

The height of a bar in the bar chart, Figure 14.7.5, conveys the relative size of a value in a cell of the SS. Up to six bars may be displayed.

1-2-3 can display six ranges of data simultaneously. Each range has a distinctive bar type, provided by color or shading for monochrome. Bars for the first value of *each* range are clustered together as shown in Figure 14.7.6. The same goes for the second, third, etc. An alternative for showing multiple ranges is the **stacked bar chart** of Figure 14.7.7.

Figure 14.7.8 shows a spread sheet, a caption range (X-range) and four data ranges (A range..D range) for the graphs of Figures 14.7.6 and 14.7.7.

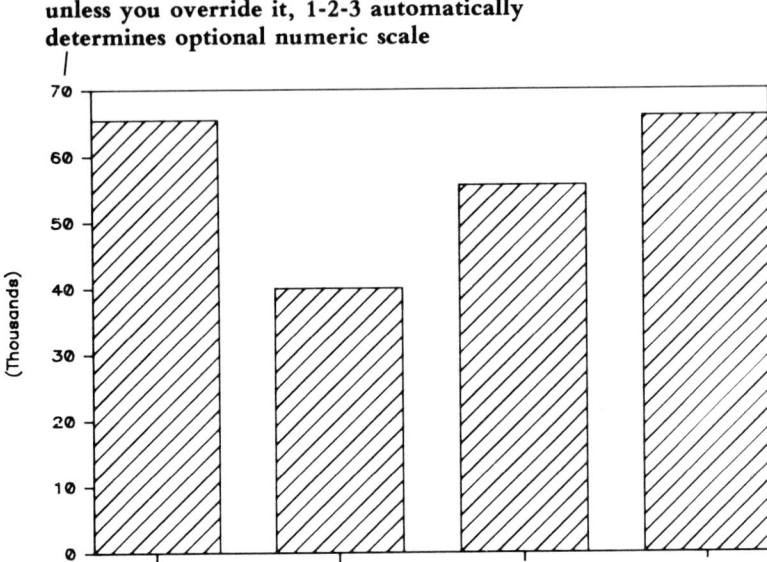

Figure 14.7.5. Bar chart.

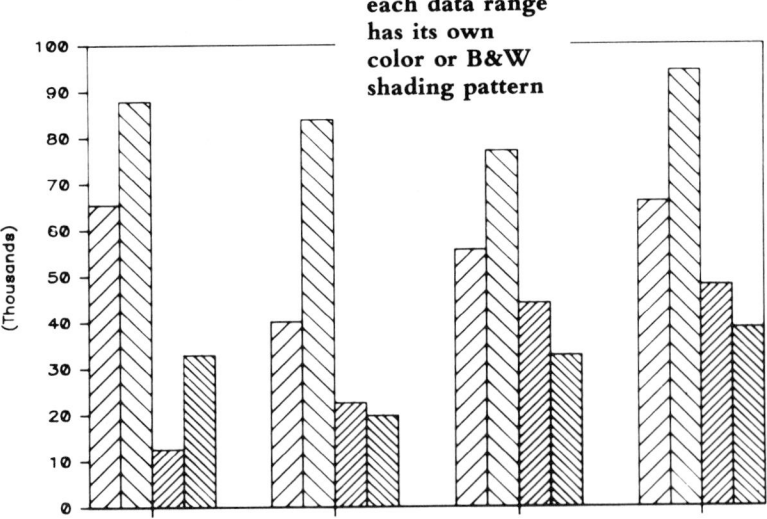

Figure 14.7.6. Bar chart with four data ranges.

1-2-3 automatically rescales Y-axis

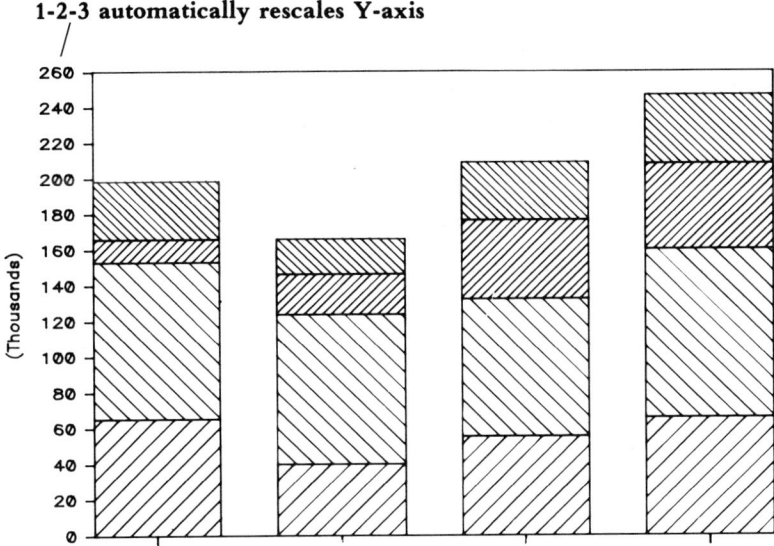

Figure 14.7.7. Stacked bar chart.

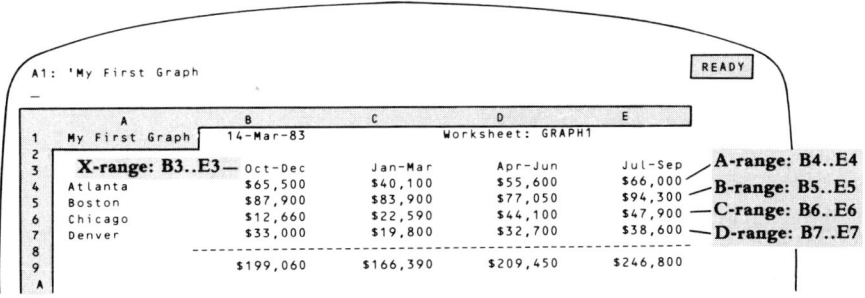

Figure 14.7.8. Four ranges in the SS for the graphs of Figs. 14.7.6 and 14.7.7.

Pie Chart

This is a familiar type of display, exemplified by Figure 14.7.9.

Line Graphs

A line graph, Figure 14.7.10, deals with quantitative versus qualitative data: the X axis distinguishes one quality from another; the Y axis is quantitative.

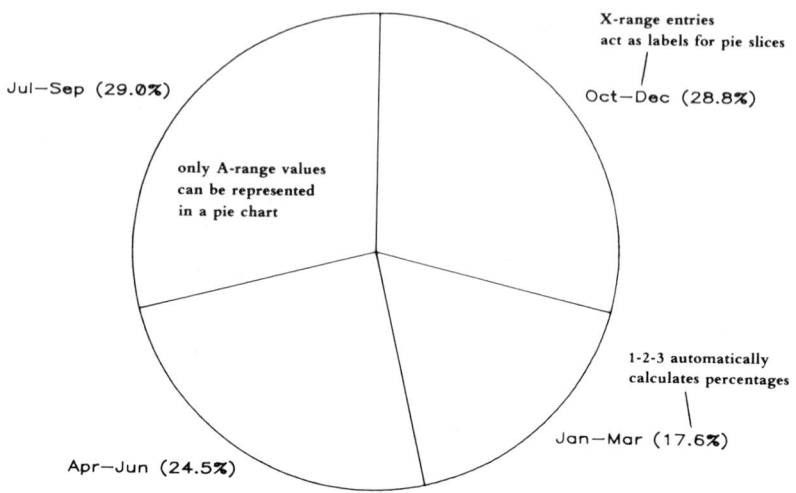

Figure 14.7.9. A pie chart.

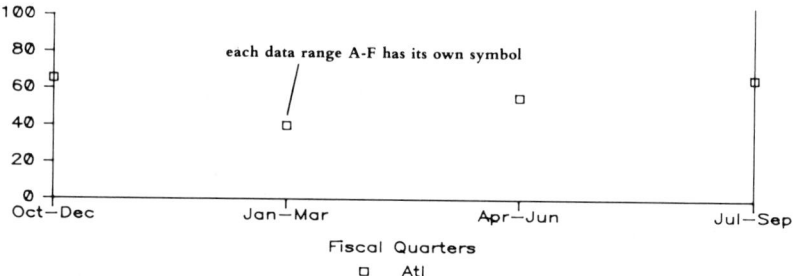

Figure 14.7.10. A line graph.

The line chart plots points, with the vertical (*Y*) axis conveying quantity. You may connect the points with lines, or not, as shown in Figure 14.7.11.

The X-Y Graph

For this graph type, Figure 14.7.12, *both* the *X* and *Y* axes display quantities. That is, each point represents a pair of values of the same type. When several graphs are superimposed, different icons, such as triangles and circles, display points from different ranges.

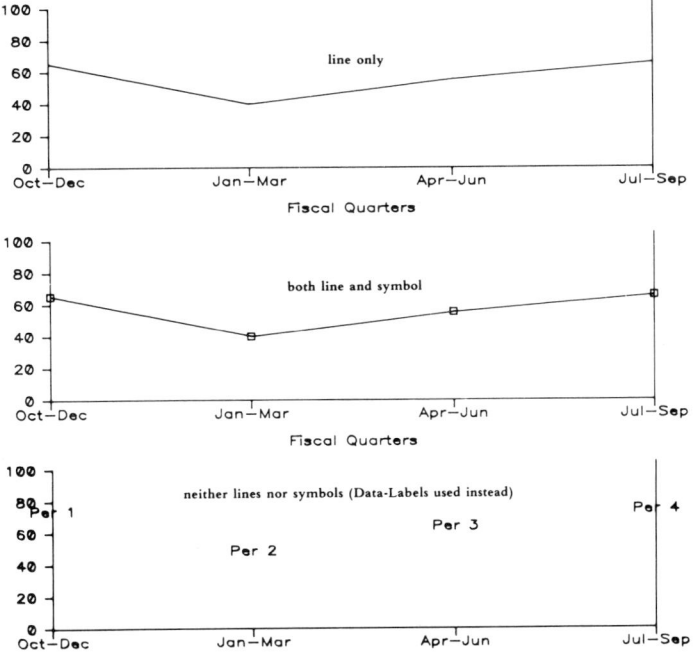

Figure 14.7.11. Other formats for the line graph.

Ranges

The graphic menu presents six letters, A through F, ranges for data to be plotted and superimposed. Each range is defined separately. Thus /GA *sets up* the A range of values. It prompts for a range stated by any one of these means:

- point to it by moving the cursor to extremes of the range;
- type in the extremes of the range;
- type in a name assigned currently to a range;
- press F3, the name key, which displays the currently defined names and their ranges—then point to one of them.

Figure 14.7.12 shows range definitions at the top related to the graph plotted at the bottom. Each of the six ranges must be set up with a separate command (such as /GB).

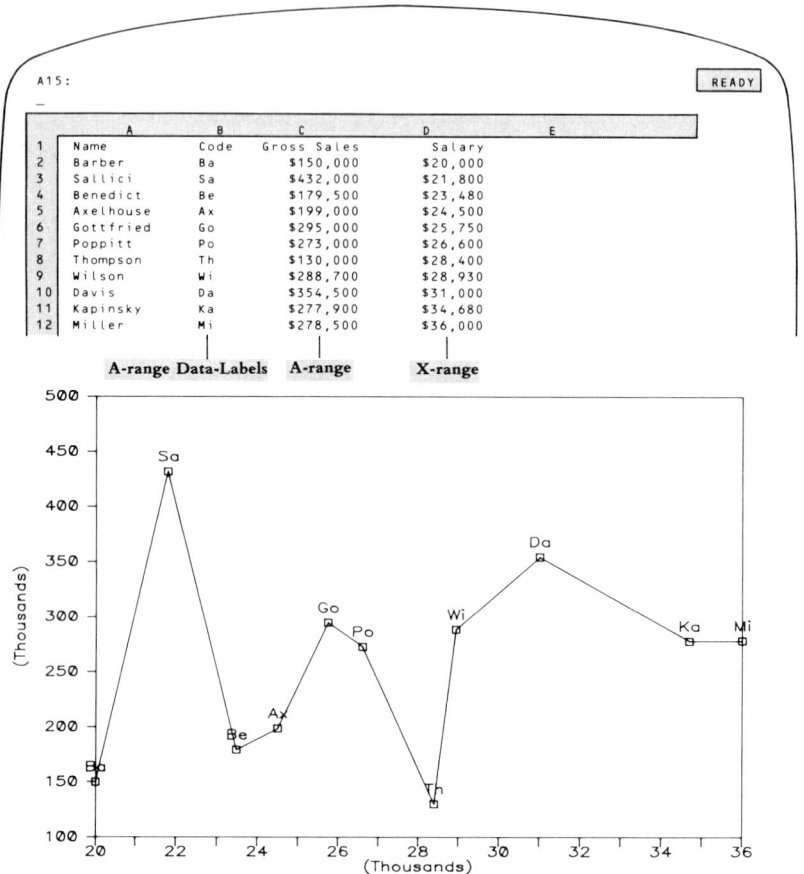

Figure 14.7.12. Range definitions on an *X-Y* graph.

Written Information

There are many places on the graph where written information provides explanation. 1-2-3 provides many alternatives. Let us look at some of them.

A **title** which names a group can be placed in several positions, conveyed with the graph options titles command, **/GOT** with options listed below. Choose one and key in a title on the command line:

  F to enter the first line of a graph title;
  S to enter the second of the graph title;
  X to put a title under the horizontal axis;
  Y to put a title along the vertical axis.

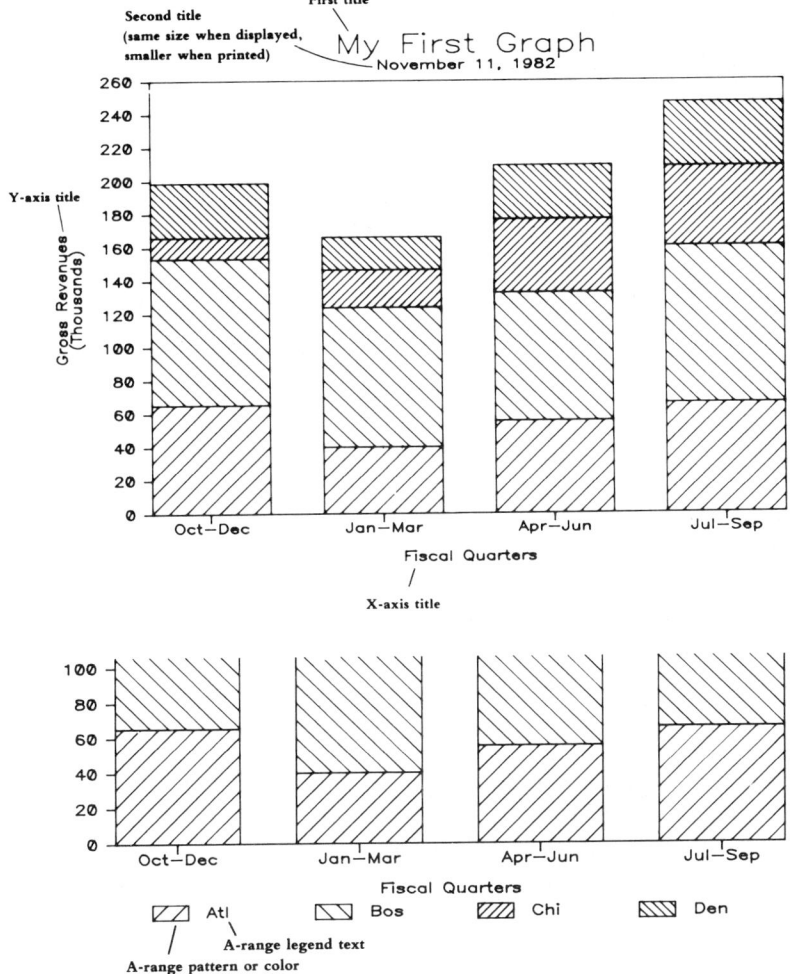

Figure 14.7.13. Four types of titles and range pattern (bottom).

All four types appear in Figure 14.7.13.

Labels to be placed horizontally along the bottom of the graph, called **X labels**, are requested with **/GX** and apply to each vertical set of bars. **/GX** prompts for a range of cells; each contains a label placed in order along the X axis. The number of labels should be the same as the number of cells in the A–F range. The **X labels** illustrated in Figure 14.7.13 are "Oct–Dec," Jan–Mar" etc.

Points in each range, when superimposed, may also be given labels, requested with the data option, /GOD. Here one range of cells is required for each range of values, A through F.

Symbols to mark points are set with the graph options format command, /GOF.

Other graph options commands determine whether scaling is automatic or manual, whether a grid is superimposed, how numbers display and whether color or black and white is used.

Naming Graphs

After you set up a graph or group of graphs, you may give the description a name and set it aside. Then a new set of graph descriptions may be worked on and similarly named. An assortment is then available for use with the work sheet. Only one set of graphs may be in use at a time, selected with the *graph name use* command, /GNU. When a group of graphs is no longer of use, it may be deleted with /GND.

All the named groups of graphs are associated with the work sheet. The SS is put away with *file save,* FS, and the graph specifications go along. When the work sheet is loaded with the *file retrieve* command, /FR, all graph specifications return.

Viewing and Calculating

As you create groups of graphs, you can look at them with the *graph view* command, /GV. Return to the spread sheeet with *quit graph mode,* /GQ. Changes you make in the work sheet may produce recalculations. To see graphically the result of recalculations, press F10: the SS disappears to be replaced by the graph(s). If you have two monitors, graphs appear on the color monitor and the SS on the monochrome.

Printing

Screen graphs are transient and disappear when the power is turned off. You can take pictures of the screen, but this is difficult to do successfully. 1-2-3 interfaces with dot matrix printers, which may use color, or with pen plotters.

To produce a hard copy, first save the graph with *graph save,* /GS, in a picture file with a name you furnish and the extension PIC. A special program converts a PIC file to printed output.

Data Base

A 1-2-3 spread sheet can store a visible data base, as much as the display window can present: a few records or parts of large records. The format of the SS when used as a data base is shown in Figure 14.7.14. Each record is assigned to a row, each field to a column or a row. The top row contains field names to describe the field (column). The limitation in 1-2-3 when used for a data base is the number of rows and columns in the virtual spread sheet (VS) and the size of memory in your computer. For 1-2-3, the VS is much wider than deep, perhaps to accommodate the financial SS better. But this limits the number of records that may be stored to 254. A record may contain a couple of thousand fields, hardly likely. So the scheme is usable for a small data base.

While ordinary manipulation of rows as records is available in other SS programs, 1-2-3 is novel. A number of commands formulate and satisfy complicated queries.

Sorting

Sorting, rearranging a data base, SS or even a graph according to some characteristic, is of growing importance as the VS becomes large. It is requested with the *data sort* command, /DS, and arranges a set of rows on

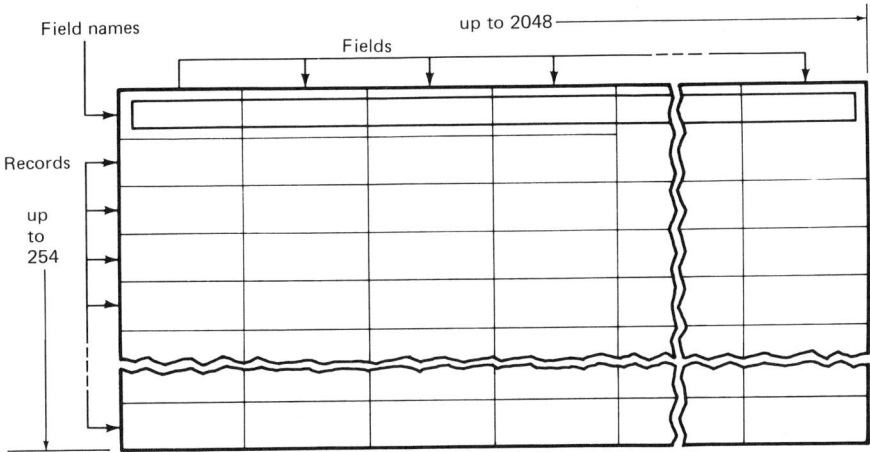

Figure 14.7.14. Format of the SS when used as a data base.

a single (primary) key and may refer to a second (secondary) key. The sort option menu is

Data-Range   Primary-Key   Reset   Go   Quit: (14.7.2)

When associated with a bar graph, a sort changes its appearance, as shown in Figure 14.7.15.

Simple Actions

Here is a summary of the simple activities available for setting up and maintaining a small data base:

Edit, alter a field by going directly to the row and column, fixing it;
Posting, done in the same way;
Insert a record by putting it at the end or by inserting a blank row and entering the fields there;
Delete a record with the *row delete* command;

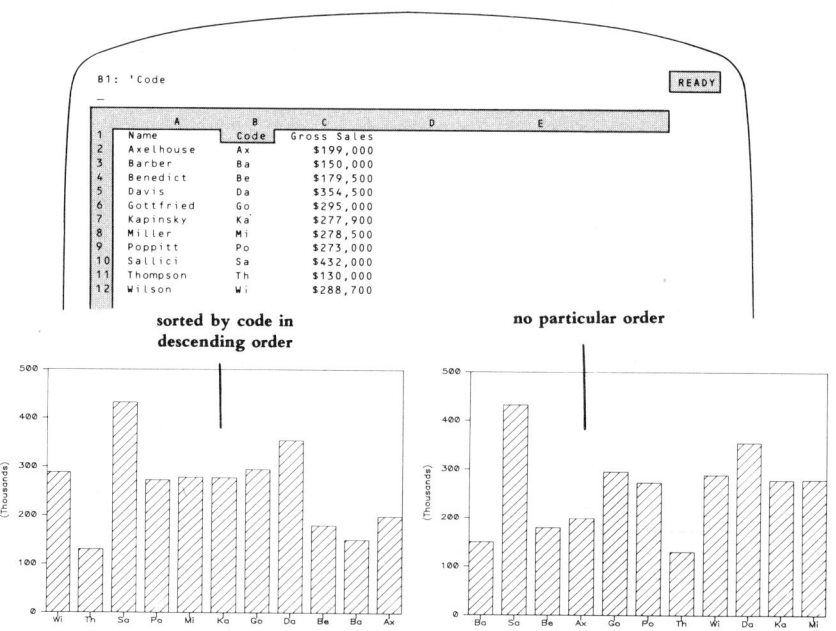

Figure 14.7.15. Sorting the data effects the graphs.

Record expansion, add columns for new fields;
Change field sizes by altering the column format.

Other ways to alter the file structure are obvious.

Data Query Command

Data base commands take two forms: *data query,* **/DQ,** is the most powerful and lets you ask complicated questions about the data base; *data functions,* described later, extract statistical information.

Three Ranges

Up to three ranges, illustrated in Figure 14.7.16, may be required for the options of the **/DQ** command:

Input range bounds the original data base or a contiguous part of it and must include the first row, which has the labels—the field names.
Criterion range is an area on the spread sheet which contains selection information.

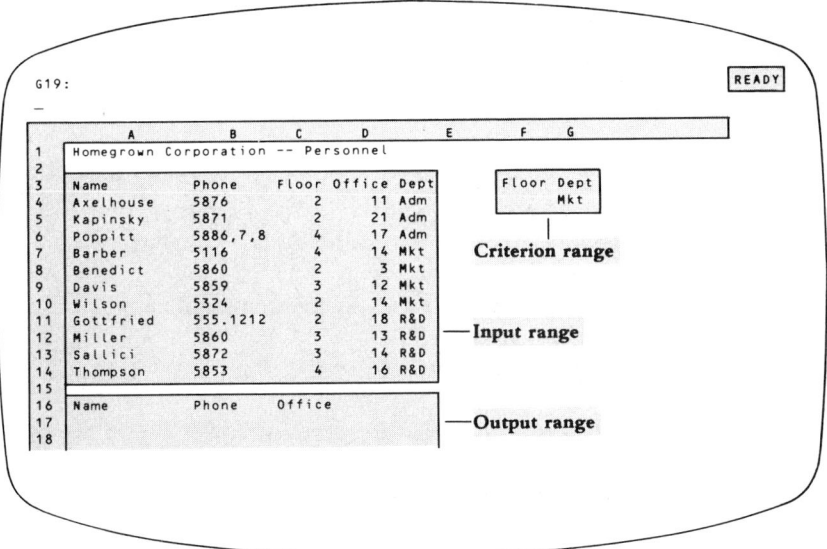

Figure 14.7.16. Three ranges for the data query command, /DQ.

Output range is a place to deposit records extracted from the file for some of the /DQ options. The first row of this range contains field names. Only some of these are present for partial output. Output range should provide enough rows for selected records. It may be left open ended by giving only the first row containing the field names. However, everything else below the first row in these columns is erased and overwritten with selected records, so use this alternative with care.

Options

/DQ options appear on the prompt line thus,

 Find Extract Unique Delete Reset Quit Input Criterion Output

(14.7.3)

Selecting an option displays the current range settings on the prompt line. If they are satisfactory for this request, hit enter and action begins. When terminated, the option line reappears and you can make further /DQ requests.

Here is what the options do:

Find locates records which meet the criteria, highlights them, but beeps should none be found. Down or up moves the highlight to the *next* selected record; left or right moves the cursor along fields within the record, Home moves the highlight to the top of the list, while end moves to the last record in the list regardless of whether it was selected. Enter or escape returns to the /DQ menu.

Extract finds records in the input range and copies their fields to the output range only where titles appear in the first row of the output range. If there is not enough room in the output range for all the records found, the keyboard beeps. Figure 14.7.16 shows an example.

Unique does the same job as extract, except that duplicate rows in the output range are eliminated.

Delete removes the selected records from the input range and closes up the ranks.

Reset clears specifications for all three ranges for resetting when the option menu appears.

Quit leaves data command mode and enters *ready* mode.

Input, Criterion and **Output** let you enter ranges which tell 1–2–3 where areas are found.

Criteria

Put criteria for selection in the **criterion range**. Its top row names fields which are the basis for selection. The second row as shown in Figure 14.7.17 contains a **compound criterion** (1). Other rows contain similar criteria.

Criterion (1) is a combination of statements, one about each selection field with the name over it and assumes that these statements are connected with AND. An empty statement is disregarded.

A single criterion statement is based on a relation between a field value for a record and a value furnished such as $Pay < 30000$.

A criterion row may contain a single statement about one field: look for all people who earn less than $30,000. Empty boxes in a criterion row are disregarded. All the statements in a criterion row must prove true (AND) for a record to be selected.

When more than one row is furnished, if a record is not selected by the first criterion row, then it is checked against the second row and so forth. In other words, *rows* in the criterion range are combined by OR. Figure 14.7.17 shows two *criteria* combined to select for (Floor=2 AND Dept=Adm) OR (Floor=4 AND Dept=Adm).

Issuing the Command

The three ranges are set up before /DQ is issued. Its results become available, but you are still in *data query* mode. Choosing Q for *quit* returns to *ready* to work on the spread sheet, such as to print results of the command from the output range.

You may prepare new selection criteria in the criterion range and hit F7 instead of /DQ. This reissues the previous *data query* command. But, since the criteria are reset, it has a different effect. Then when the command is done, it returns to *ready* mode for you to work again with the worksheet.

Name	Floor	Dept	Field Names
	2	Adm	Condition (1)
	4	Adm	Condition (2)

Figure 14.7.17. The criterion range.

Data Functions

Several data functions are particularly effective. They are used like other functions (Section 14.5). All the 1-2-3 data functions take this form,

function(input range,offset,criterion range)   (14.7.3)

Here *function* is a function name, always beginning with D and preceded with @. *Input range* describes the data base area; *criterion range* gives the criteria for selecting records for the function; *offset* gives the number of the column counting from the left on which to base the calculation. This becomes clearer below.

Here are the functions:

DSUM takes the sum of values in the designated field for records selected.
DAVG averages items.
DVAR finds the variance for the items.
DSTD takes their standard deviation.
DMAX finds the maximum of values examined.
DMIN finds the minimum.
DCOUNT counts the number of items which meet the criterion.

Now look at the example in Figure 14.7.18. It prepares a summary report for salespeople in the DB. THe input range is a list of sales indicating date of sale, salesperson's name and sale amount. The summary lists total sales, number of sales, and the largest sale for a specified salesperson extracted by the three data functions in the figure.

The criterion range is two cells at the top of column G. G1 lists the name of the field to be searched, name, corresponding to salesperson's name. G2 has the name of the salesperson for this summary report. When you hit enter calculations begin as 1-2-3 scans through the data base. The first calculation asks for the sum of sales for Wilson. Sales are in column C; this corresponds to an offset of 2 (the offset is 0 for the first column, 1 for the second column, and so forth). 1-2-3 scans down the requested column looking for Wilson. For each of Wilson's sales, it adds in the amount in column C until it reaches the bottom of the list. This sum goes into G7. The number of items for Wilson is placed in G8. The sales figure are monitored; the maximum is found and put in G9.

Now this section of the spread sheet may be printed by naming the print range (D2..G9). Other summaries are created in a like manner. To find the sales for Benedict, put her name in G2. As soon as you hit enter, the calculations are made and the summary presented.

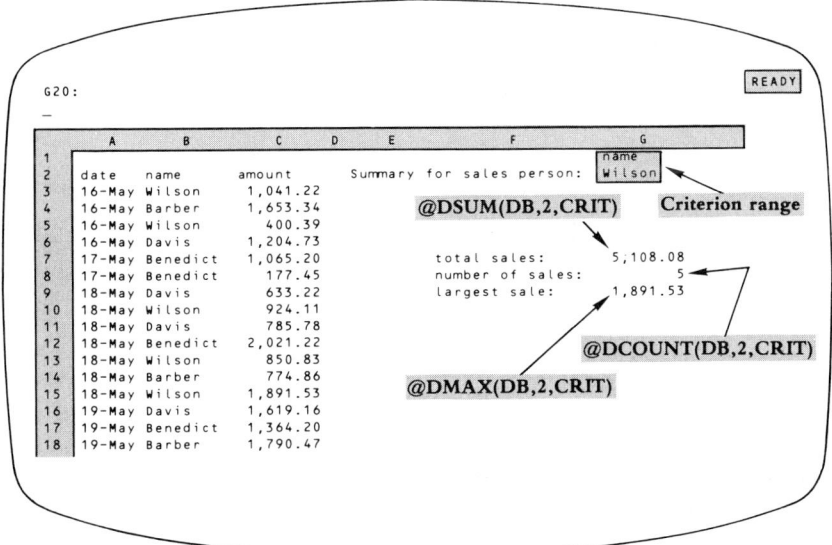

Figure 14.7.18. A summary report can be made using data functions.

Summary

Lotus provides three complete functions, two of them integrated with the third, the SS program. Graphics are especially effective in seeing the results of "What if?" speculations quickly and precisely. The data base functions manipulate the spread sheet and summarize its contents quite effectively. However, one cannot expect a full blown data base program such as dBase which can do complete accounting functions.

15
Fourth Generation Spread Sheets

15.1 INTRODUCTION

Software fabricators at the time of this writing seem to believe that the more features they can pack into a package, the more likely it is to be purchased. One approach takes an existing program with several functions and adds new functions; thus Symphony was created by Lotus from 1-2-3. A second approach starts from scratch and combines a number of services under a unifying theme. This is the approach of Jack 2 and Framework. The many forms of integrated application are described in Section 16.3.

Because of the importance of this approach, this chapter was added after the chapter on spread sheets while the book was in production to provide an up-to-date overview.

Candidates

The integrated application package is a popular approach, expected to sell. A large variety of such packages have emerged from both small and large companies. Most are destined to failure because of cutthroat market competition. Even a firm with considerable financial background and a good product can fall on its face. For instance, Jack 2 is a good product, but the cost of advertising required to market it was more than the company could afford and has since perished. Even though copies may still be available through some vendors, it is disregarded here because of lack of support.

The Chosen Ones

It would be foolhardy to try to cover more than two such products. Framework is described rather thoroughly because of its fresh approach. Symphony is summarized briefly in Section 15.5, since 1-2-3 has been extensively covered. While Symphony is rooted in the SS, Framework is founded on text and outlines. The two packages are assessed in the final section.

The marketplace is so competitive that no vendor has sufficient time to prepare its product adequately. Both Framework and Symphony were rushed to market to arrive before the other. As a consequence, they both have flaws which may be remedied in future releases. However, some difficulties that the user encounters are inherent in the product. Both the advantages and disadvantages of each are described below, although minute details are omitted.

Windows

The **window** is an important concept for second and third generation spread sheets. The feature is expanded in these two packages. Chapter 16 examines special softward which lets you work with completely different packages from different vendors, providing windows for portions of each.

15.2 INTRODUCTION TO FRAMEWORK

Framework™, by Ashton-Tate, is an integrated package; its theme is the outline. It assumes that most work at the computer is in one of five areas: word processing, spread sheet, graphics, data base, or communications. The package seeks to provide good services in each of these task areas.

The second assumption is that you will often integrate two or more of these tasks. Figure 15.2.1 shows how several tasks display with Framework. Eventually you will produce a report which incorporates several of the tasks into a single printed unit. Framework allows you to print such a document.

Finally, Framework is most attractive to people who prefer the outline form. It helps to chop up the work into chunks. These chunks may be further separated into pieces to be expanded so that you can work on each more easily. The outline is a good device for making this division. Figure 15.2.2 shows a Framework outline on screen. The division of an outline is the frame and contains any kind of data mentioned above, but only one kind. Thus tools are provided specific to each kind of frame.

At any point, a few key strokes can print any selected group of frames in their present order.

When all the frames are at a stage for review, all, or only the desired ones, can be moved to a container for printout. The final document may include all of the frames printed in their original sequence in the outline or in some other order that you put them in the container.

Framework integration is good, except that communication is a separate task and not accessible from Framework proper.

682 FOURTH GENERATION SPREAD SHEETS

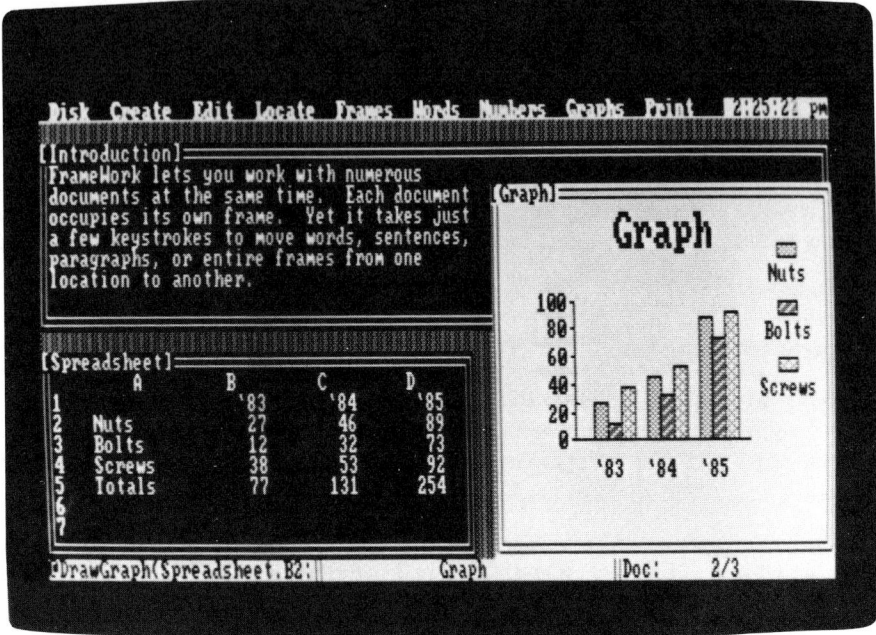

Figure 15.2.1. Display combines types of documents.

Requirements

Framework was designed for the IBM PC and its 100% compatibles. It will barely operate in 256K of memory, *if* you suppress the communications option. With that option, 384K of RAM is required. However, the more memory you have, the better the system works; 512K or 640K are recommended.

The Frame

Since the concept of the frame is central, we now examine it. A job or activity is divided into several different areas, each called a **frame**. What is in a frame? It may

- be empty;
- contain other frames;
- contain text;
- be a graph;
- be a spread sheet;

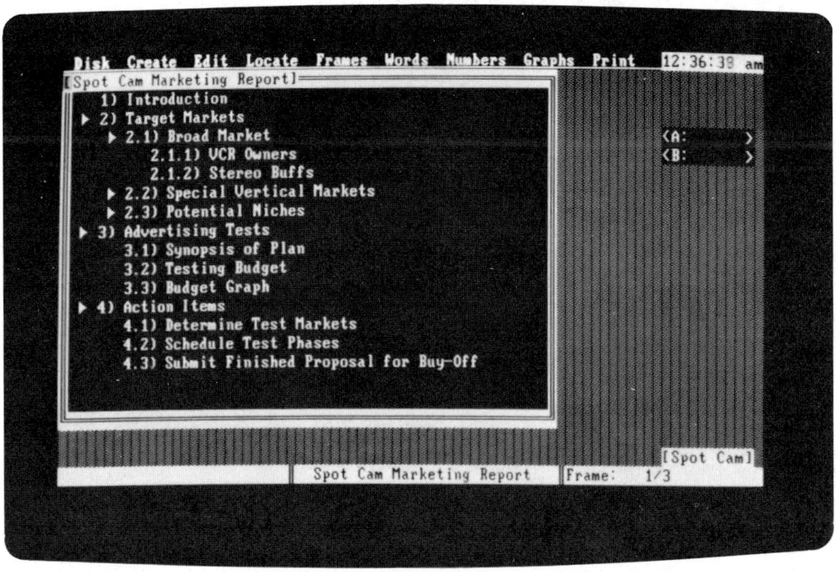

15.2 INTRODUCTION TO FRAMEWORK   683

Figure 15.2.2. Typical Framework outline.

- be used as an entry to the operating system and hence to another program to run without leaving Framework.

One important rule to observe without question: you cannot put two kinds of information directly into one frame, such as text and a graph. But each may be in its own frame, and these put inside an outer frame.

The Outline

Many, but not all people, think or work in outline form. They begin with the general outline. Then they build upon each topic, adding further and further detail as subtopics in the outline. Other people, especially those with an accounting background, tend to think in terms of columnar paper; Symphony is better oriented for their purposes, but we leave this for later.

When you start Framework on a new job, you can request an outline frame* containing three empty frames, each containing in turn three empty

---

*This is the default number of empty frames and subframes. This default, as well as all others, can be reset easily to whatever values you choose.

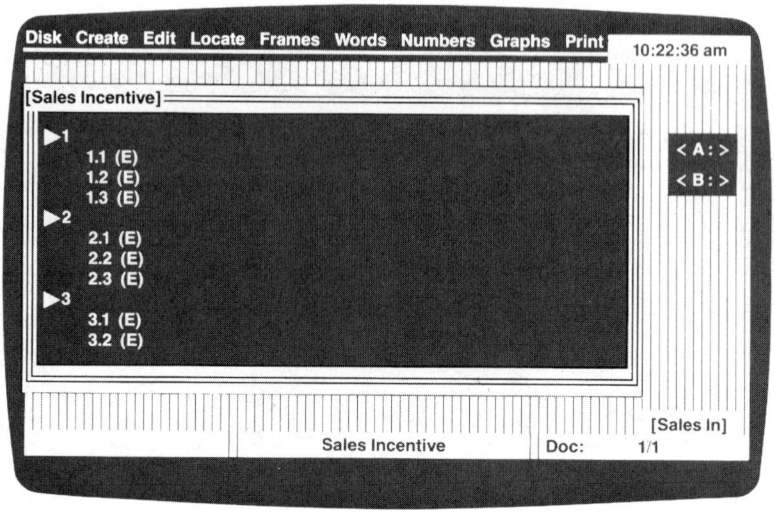

Figure 15.2.3. A fresh empty outline form.

subframes, as shown in Figure 15.2.3. You can put titles, as shown in Figure 15.2.2, into the outer frame and into the outline from the keyboard. When ready for the next level of detail, you can create a frame of the proper type to replace any empty frame, named or unnamed. This is described shortly.

Expansion

You can expand an outline to any depth. Thus you can pick a topic, assign a frame for each subtopic. Then within a subtopic frame you may create new frames to assign for subsubtopics. There is practically no limit to this process, except that imposed by the amount of computer memory.

Operation Selection

The system comes up with one of the disk drive icons highlighted. Hit ins (Instruct key) and a **menu bar** appears at the top of the screen, as in Figure 15.2.2, showing operations that you can perform. Going from left to right, we see *Disk, Create, Edit, Locate, Frames, Words, Numbers, Graphs, Print*. At the extreme right is the highlighted time of day. When ins is hit the very very first time, the menu bar displays with the *Create* operation highlighted and a pattern on the screen. There are now two ways to choose an operation:

- Move the cursor (the highlight) along the menu bar in either direction with right or left.
- Hit control, together with the first letter of the menu function (such as ^W for *Words*).

Either alternative brings forth an option menu discussed shortly. There is still another way to get to this option menu; if you are performing an operation or function, hit ins, the menu bar and the last used option menu appears. From there, you can choose an option or use either method given above to choose a different operation.

Options

As soon as you choose an operation, the option menu appears right below it, as with Lisa or Mac (see Chapter 16), but without the need to pull it down with a mouse. The option menu immediately appears. To choose an option, either

- move the highlight with up or down in the option menu and hit return to call forth the option; or
- hit the first letter of an option menu choice.

Screen Content

We have seen how to select an operation from the menu bar; an option menu appears at once. Let us now see what else normally displays on the screen as illustrated in Figure 15.2.4 (refer also to Figure 15.2.2):

1. The *menu bar* is always present, highlighting the current operation, but an option frame appears only as an operation choice is made.
2. The highlighted line at the bottom of the screen (Figure 15.2.2), the **status bar,** is divided into three parts. At its left is the **formula panel,** often empty, described later. In the middle is the **frame path** showing the current frame name and its predecessor(s), if there is room for them. Path names are truncated at the left so that the most significant part of the name displays. At the right is the **level display** showing the active disk or the ordinal number of the active frame with reference to other frames on this same level. Here 3/5, for instance, means the third frame of the five at this level.
3. When an action is initiated by a function key (as described later), a **prompt line** on the display's twenty-fifth line describes what action is requested and how you should react.

686 FOURTH GENERATION SPREAD SHEETS

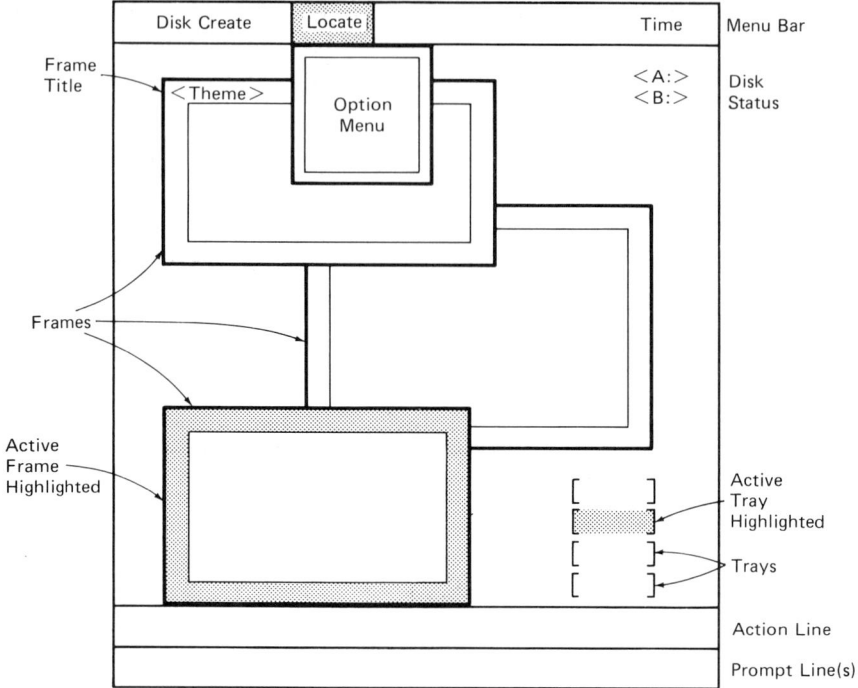

Figure 15.2.4. Kinds of items the screen displays.

4. The upper right portion of the screen shows one box for each disk drive on your system with its drive letter. The last drive used is highlighted after you hit scroll lock.
5. A number of **trays** in the lower right corner of the screen represents frames which are now in memory. The **active frame,** the one you are working on, is highlighted.
6. A number of frames may display in all or part of the dynamic area of the screen. Each frame appears in its own window. When the active frame shows, it has a highlighted border.

Function Keys

The IBM PC's ten function keys are put to good use. They are applied uniformly across all the main menu functions. Figure 15.2.5 shows their layout. Here are the functions that they perform:

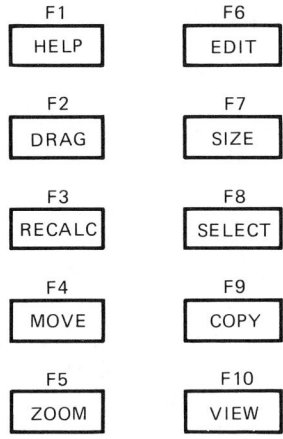

Figure 15.2.5. Function key assignments.

F1, HELP, to bring forth a help screen for the current function.
F2, EDIT, to alter a frame label, enter a print command or enter a formula into an SS or DB cell.
F3, DRAG, to move the active frame with arrow.
F4, SIZE, to alter the bottom, top, or size boundary of the active frame with arrow.
F5, RECALCULATE, to recalculate all cells in SS or execute a Framework macro program.
F6, EXTENDED SELECT, to highlight text to *move, copy* or *delete*.
F7, MOVE, to put a highlighted area (from F6) in another frame or elsewhere in this frame.
F8, COPY, to make a copy of the highlighted block or frame.
F9, ZOOM, to toggle the active frame between full screen size and its current size setting.
F10, VIEW, to toggle between the current active frame and the overall outline.

Hereafter they are referenced by function (VIEW), not number (F10).

Navigation

As you can see from the description of the screen and Figure 15.2.4, there are many places that you could be working at any given time. How do you move around in an area and how do you move from one area to another? Here is the general policy:

- *within an area* use arrow to go in the direction inscribed on the key;
- make the disk display active or inactive with scroll lock, which acts as a toggle;
- go to the *menu bar* with ins and back to the current active frame with esc;
- go to the *outline* and from the outline to the active frame, both with VIEW which is a toggle;
- *within the outline* (which changes the active frame) with up or down;
- *into a frame* from a position on the outline or in the tray with + and back out with −. Use only the + and − on the numeric keypad.

Many of these keys and their use are shown in Figure 15.2.6.

Frame Status

A frame can have one of three statuses:

- *Active* means that the frame is in use or selected and you may operate with it.
- *Open* means that the frame is showing on the desk top even if only part of it is visible.

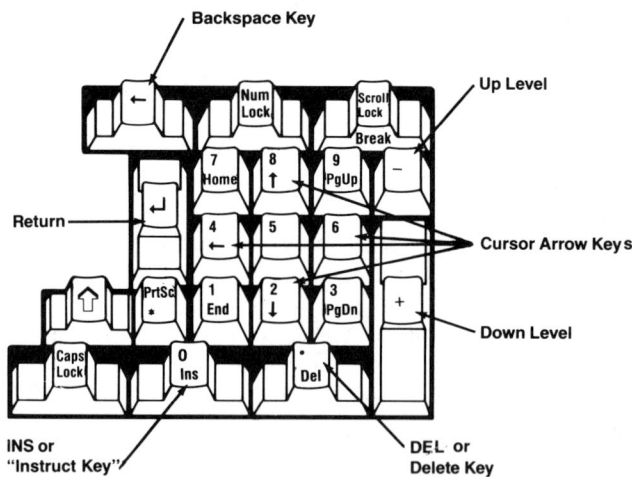

Figure 15.2.6 Keys on numeric keypad move the cursor.

- *Closed* where it is not showing on the desk top but is available in one of the trays showing in the lower righthand corner.

To make a frame active, you retreat from the current frame with either VIEW or by hitting −. This returns you to the outline. Now you can move within the outline with up or down. When you move to a frame thus, its border is highlighted and it becomes active. Hit + to enter that frame and work with its contents.

Whenever you create a frame, it becomes both open and active. A frame becomes open but inactive if it is displaying and you switch to another cell, making the target cell active.

If you retreat from a frame to the outline and move to another frame which is displaying, you can close it by hitting return. The frame disappears from the display and seems to flow into the tray on the desktop.

Disk Transfers

Save

You can save all the frames which are part of the same outline or containing frame: their image is in memory and can be stored on the disk from the *Disk* menu. If you use the *save and continue* option, their memory image is put on the disk, but remains in memory in whatever status it had. Another way to do this directly from the frame border is to hit ^return. However, if you use the *put away* option from the *Disk* menu, not only is the frame saved on the disk, it is cleared from memory and becomes unavailable. In all these cases, the file is saved under the name of the outermost frame.

To save an inner frame and its subframes or contents, first select the frame by highlighting its label. Then use COPY or MOVE. A copy is made on the default drive. COPY leaves the frame in memory while MOVE removes it to disk and closes the file.

Drives

To get from any frame to a drive directory, hit scroll-lock. This highlights a drive icon at the right. Move to a different drive with up or down. Make this the default drive with ^return. The **default drive** is where files are saved and printing is spooled, unless you indicate otherwise.

To bring forth a directory, hit +. Move the highlight among the file names with up or down. A hard disk has multiple directories. To enter a lower level directory, find its name in the current directory and hit +. Move to a higher level directory with —. Make this the default directory with ^return.

Load

When a file is highlighted in the directory, return brings it into a frame of its own, bearing the same title as the file name. Or you can go to the disk menu with ^D, select *get file by name,* type in the file name, preceded by the drive letter if it is not on the default drive, and hit return.

To bring a file into an outline, first select it by moving the cursor to the outline frame. Then find its name in the directory. Next hit COPY or MOVE. Now go to the outline frame and hit return.

15.3 FRAMEWORK MENU CHOICES

The menu bar at the top of the screen starts major operations. When you have finished an operation in the active frame, you need the menu bar to start an operation in this or another frame. Hit ins to bring forth the last used menu and its options along with the menu bar. Chose another operation in one of two ways described earlier: (1) hit control and the first letter of the operation; or (2) step through the menu bar with space or arrow and hit return to make a choice.

Options

When you move the cursor to a menu bar choice, the alternatives are grouped together functionally in the option menu. Options which don't properly apply are displayed in a different typeface, usually italics. For instance, if you have just started a project and have not yet created any frame, the option *save a frame* would not be applicable—you have nothing to save.

Disk

Disk options, shown in Figure 15.3.1, combine a number of functions, many involving access to the disk. *Disk* also includes executing other external programs and access to the DOS.

One *Disk* operation *saves* frames you are not working on (in the trays) to disk to free memory. Another *loads* data from disk to establish a file as a frame or outline in memory. Then there are some totally internal operations which have to do with the screen and the set of trays. These are useful and are neatly executed by Framework.

For instance, suppose you have four frames showing but, for the mo-

15.3 FRAMEWORK MENU CHOICES

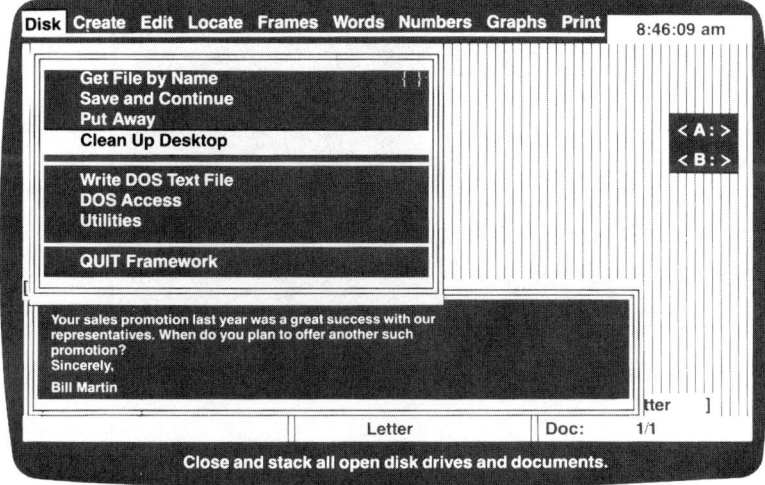

Figure 15.3.1. *Disk* options.

ment, you don't need to work with one or two of them. You don't want to go through the time-consuming procedure of putting them away on disk and bringing them back again later. Instead, simply **close a frame.** That is, put it back into its tray in the stack on the desktop. When you close a frame, it shrinks down to nothing and pushes into its tray in the stack. Now you have more room on the screen. To revive a frame, that is, to **open** it, go into outline form. Move within the form to the desired frame; hit + to open the frame. Then use SIZE and DRAG (see Section 15.4) to set the frame's size and position.

Another group of options lets you access DOS utilities, Framework utilities and separate programs, which, when finished, return control to Framework.

Finally, the *Disk* menu contains an option to *quit* Framework, the only way to leave the program except to remove the disk and turn off the power.

Create

When you enter Framework, you have no frames in memory. You face an empty screen with only the menu line at the top and the disk activity list at the upper right. To start, call *Create* from the menu bar. Its option menu, Figure 15.3.2 lets you choose the kind of frame to create. A logical way to start is with an outline frame, though this is not the only alternative.

Create

Outline	
Empty/Word Frame	
Spreadsheet	
Database	
Width (# Cols/Fields)	{14}
Height (# Rows/Records)	{14}
Columns/Fields: Add	{1}
Rows/Records: Add	{1}

Figure 15.3.2. *Create* options.

Outline

You can select an outline frame which contains three headings each containing three subheadings as shown in Figure 15.2.2. Each heading and subheading in the outline represents an empty frame marked E and with no label (Figure 15.2.3). You can write a title or label next to the outline number of any heading or subheading.

Three levels and three sublevels may not suffice. With main topics 1, 2 and 3 established, it's simple to add 4, 5, 6 and so forth. Further, when working at 3.1 you can create another depth of level, such as 3.1.1, 3.1.2 and so forth. Simply hit ^ + once for each frame required.

Once you are at an inner outline frame—one which does not contain other frames—you can start working on that fame or call up the *Frame* menu. For instance, to put text into a frame, hit + to enter the frame and type in text. When you return to the main outline, this heading is marked W for word processing.

Independent Frame

You may create a frame outside the outline form from the *Create* menu to request the fame of the type desired. When it appears, you can enter a name in the title bar and start working with it. When you return to your outline, you will find the name of this frame at the bottom at the highest outline level, but with no number. You can MOVE a named but unnumbered frame anywhere in an outline and number it by turning off and on the *number frames* option of the *Frames* menu.

Edit

Edit options are a mixture, Figure 15.3.3. One set of three items is applicable to spread sheets and data base. You can delete a column or a field, a row or a record and lock titles at the top or the side of a spread sheet.

Choices following these provide for protecting and unprotecting cells in a spread sheet. Next is a typeover choice which toggles between insertion and overtype during word processing. The last item displays hidden characters, paragraph marks embedded in your text.

Undo

The *undo* item at the top of the *Edit* menu, highlighted in Figure 15.3.3, is very useful. It reverses an action just taken but which was in error. It can return material you have deleted, providing another action does not intervene.

Actions which you may *undo*, but only *directly after* they are done, include

- deleting a frame or set of frames;
- deleting a block of text;
- deleting a column or row of SS data;
- moves and sorts;
- label and formula replacements.

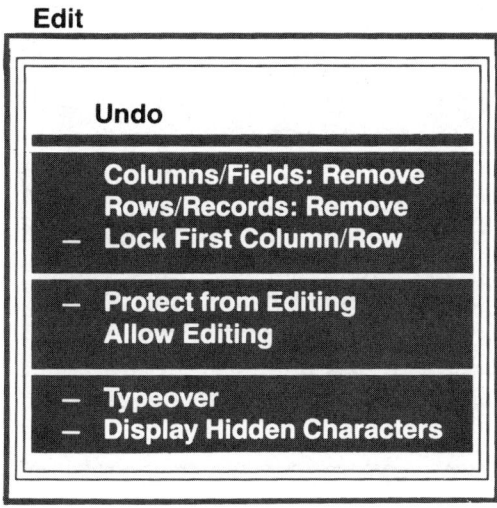

Figure 15.3.3. *Edit* options.

Locate

The *Locate* menu, Figure 15.3.4, is for both sorting and locating.

Sort

Sorting is applicable to frames in an outline, cells in a spread sheet and records *or* fields in a data base. Before you start a sort, SELECT the pertinent area:

- For an outline, SELECT either the general outline or a frame containing subframes.
- For a spread sheet, SELECT a column containing key items for which the corresponding rows are to be sorted.
- For data base records, SELECT one key field for sorting them.
- For fields in a record, SELECT the record.

Then move within the option menu to choose ascending or decending sequence. For the sort to ignore capitalization, mark that option. Recall that the ASCII sort sequence places lower case letters *after* upper case.

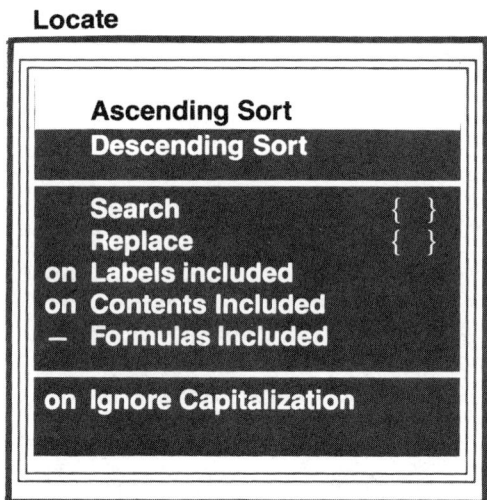

Figure 15.3.4. *Locate* options.

Search

SELECT determines the extent of a search. If you select an outer frame, all inner frames are searched. The option menu determines the part of each frame searched. It may include any combination of labels, contents or formulas which you set on the menu. The capitalization option applies here too. The wild cards, the asterisk (*) and the question mark (?) let you search for partial strings as explained in the chapter on word processing. Up and down permit you to institute another search, either backwards or forwards, providing no other key is hit (which terminates the search.) That is, after making a search, if you make a correction, you have to go back to the search menu to request a new search, reenterring the search string.

Search and Replace

Search and replace, instituted from the option menu, requires that you enter both a search and a replace string. When an instance of the search string is found, you have several alternatives:

Return replaces the destinatin string with the replace string and inititates a new search;
Down skips replacement and starts a new search;
Home causes the replacement but stops the search;
End causes all occurrences of the search string to be found and replaced;
Esc exits the search and replace operation.

Frames

The *Frame* operation has a number of options, Figure 15.3.5, which affect the current frame(s) and all frames included within it (them). The *blank* option clears the *selected* frame(s) and all frames within it (them). This option leaves frame labels and protected information intact. *Close* and *open* affect all selected frames.

The next two options affect the position of internal frames. The *column* option rearranges the internal frames in a column within the enclosing frame. The *drag* option permits frames to be moved about within the enclosing frame.

The next options pertain to frame style:

- display the labels in the outline;
- display the number for the outline level;

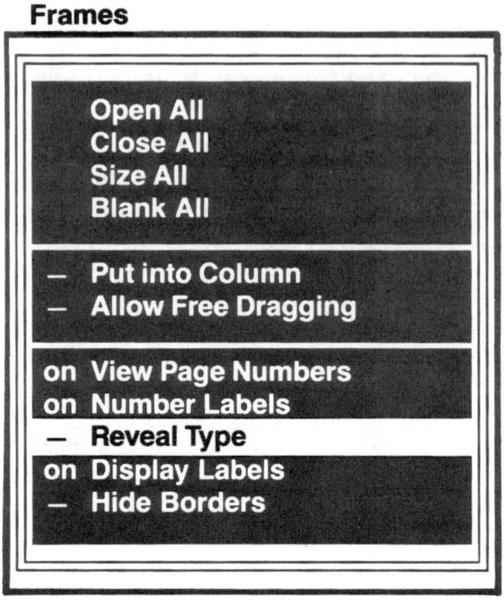

Frames

```
Open All
Close All
Size All
Blank All

— Put into Column
— Allow Free Dragging

on View Page Numbers
on Number Labels
—  Reveal Type
on Display Labels
—  Hide Borders
```

Figure 15.3.5. *Frames* options.

- show the type—D for database, etc.;
- hide or alter frame borders.

Words

Emphasis

Word operations, Figure 15.3.6, apply mostly to word processing. The exception is *type style,* which can be set in any kind of document except graphs. The top four items let you SELECT words to be in normal type, italics, underline or bold, alone or in combination.

Alignment

The next four items apply to WP text and determine whether a line is aligned at the left, flush right, centered or justified.

Format

The bottom set of options determine the left and right margin, paragraph indent and tab size. These are dynamic format requests; they may be altered at any moment; they require a numerical value.

Words

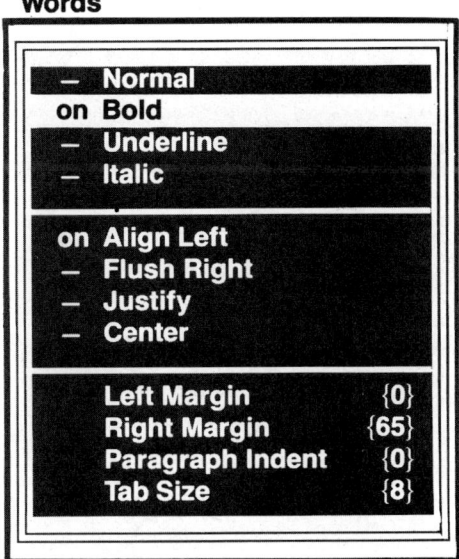

Figure 15.3.6. *Words* options.

Numbers

Display

The *Number* operation, Figure 15.3.7, affects number format in the SS and DB. The alternatives are integer, fixed decimal, currency, business, percent, scientific and default; all have the standard meaning and are mutually exclusive. Additionally, the number of decimal places can be set. Other alternatives determine how numbers and text appear within a field or cell.

Recalculation

The final alternative deals with recalculation and only applies to the spread sheet. When you select this option a suboption menu appears with the following choices:

- *Automatic* recalculates values throughout the spread sheet whenever you enter or edit a formula or number; this is the default setting.
- *Natural* sets recalculation order according to the relationships between the numbers as predetermined in the package.
- *By row* recalculates the spread sheet a row at a time, from top to bottom.
- *Manual* recalculates the spread sheet only when you press RECALC.

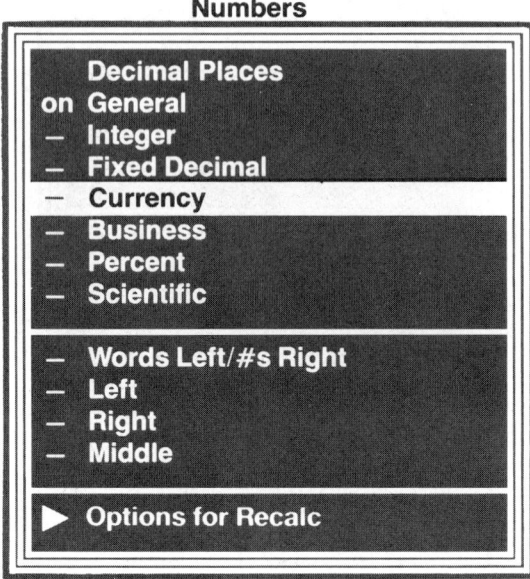

Figure 15.3.7. *Numbers* options.

Graphs

Data

To draw a graph, SELECT a group of contiguous cells in either a column or row within an SS or a group of continguous field values in a DB. You SELECT the data cells before you enter the *Graph* menu to elicit its option menu, Figure 15.3.8.

Graph Type

From the menu you choose different kinds of graphs. There is also an entry here to select the labels from either the column or the row of the spread sheet or data base.

Start Graph

After you select a type of graph, ask Framework to draw a new graph in a frame created for it, by selecting *draw a new graph*. An unlabeled frame appears on the screen with a graph in the selected format. You can change its size or drag it around as suits you. Enter the frame border to name the

Graphs

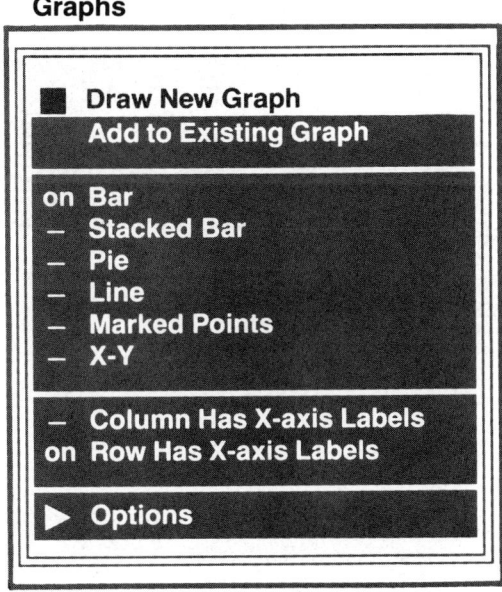

Figure 15.3.8. *Graph* options.

frame, which also puts a label in the graph. ZOOM from within the frame to expand the graph to fill the screen and display it in color (if you have a color monitor). Hitting ZOOM again diminishes it to its previous size.

Repeat

You can select a second series of points and request that they be plotted on the same graph. After hitting RECALC, both display within the same frame.

Print

Print options, Figure 15.3.9, are fairly simple. *Begin* and *stop* effects those actions. The next two options let you *pause* or causes the printer to *wait* after each page is printed for single sheets. You can restart the printer with *begin*.

Suboptions

Two suboption menus brought forth from the final two options. The first, Figure 15.3.10, routes output to one of two printers, a plotter or a disk file. The second displays output *options* (described later), Figure 15.3.9.

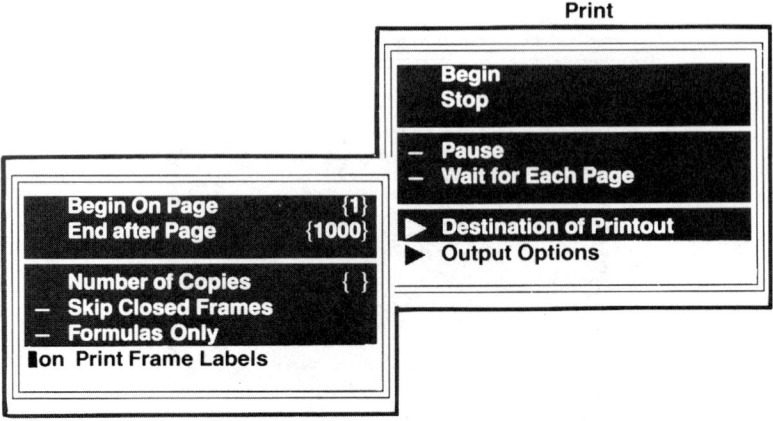

Figure 15.3.9. *Print* options, output suboptions.

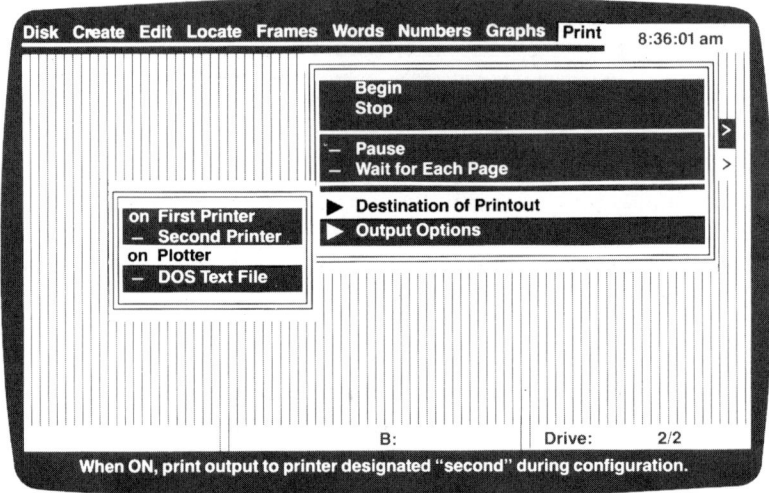

Figure 15.3.10. *Print* options, destination suboptions.

15.4 TASKS

Framework can do a number of complete tasks: outlines, WP, SS, DB and graphs, integrating the operations and functions into a whole. A separate communications program called MITE is furnished, but it is not integrated with the other aspects of Framework. You must exit Framework to call up MITE or call it from an empty frame like any other "foreign" program.

We now discuss the five main tasks.

The Outline

The unifying theme of Framework is the outline. Consequently the designers have furnished features to help you organize and reorganize your outline. Other features help unify the remaining tasks as described below.

You start a **dynamic outline** from the *Create* option menu by choosing to create an outline frame. An outline is *dynamic* because, as you alter it, Framework can automatically renumber it and reset levels as required. After creation, Framework leaves the cursor in the empty title of the main outline frame. If you type a title into the main frame border, it also enters the file box in the lower right screen corner.

Moving

Up and down moves the highlight from one outline frame to another. At any level in the outline you can enter a title, a descriptive name for this level.

Frame Types and Names

Remember that an *outline* frame can only contain other frames; it cannot contain other data of any type. But it may have a title. An *empty* frame presently contains nothing. Put a title in an empty frame border to name that frame. You may convert any empty frame (E) to a data frame (see Figure 15.2.3); it may be a word processing frame (W) a spread sheet frame (S) or a data base frame (D); when you put an empty frame to use, E, which had displayed with its name, if any, becomes a descriptor for the data type it is assigned to. Table 15.4.1 shows how to navigate around an outline as well as in other documents.

Expansion

Framework lets you add new levels and new sublevels from the *Create* menu. Further, as you develop an outline, you may decide that a topic in one position should be moved or copied to another position. To move (or copy) an outline frame from one position to another, put the cursor or highlight on the topic and press SELECT. You may move the cursor to other frame borders with up or down to select multiple frames. Then put the cursor at the position below which the frame (or frames) should appear, and press MOVE (or COPY). Not only is the frame moved (or copied), the entire outline is renumbered to suit the new structure if *number labels* in the *Frames* menu is on. There are clear rules about how you make the frame a topic at the same level or at a higher or lower level.

702 FOURTH GENERATION SPREAD SHEETS

Table 15.4.1 Cursor Movement Commands

KEY	OUTLINE	FUNCTION	WORD PROCESSING	SPREAD SHEET	DATA BASE
Down	Down Item	Down Frame	Down Line	Down Row	Down Record
^Down	Down Level		Down Sentence		
Up	Up Item	Up Frame	Up Line	Up Row	Up Record
^Up	Up Level		Up Sentence		
Right	Down Item	Down Frame	Right Character	Right Col.	Right Field
^Right			Right Word		
Left	Up Item	Up Frame	Left Character	Left Col.	Left Field
^Left			Left Word		
Home	Top of Level	Top Frame of Level	Start of Line	Beg. of Row	First Field
^Home	Top Level		Start of Doc.	Top of AS	First Record
End	Bot. of Level	Last Frame of Level	End of Line	End of Row	Last Field
^End	Bottom Level		End of Doc.	Bot. of AS	Last Record
PGUP	Prev. Screen	Previous Frame	Top of Scrn./scrl.	Prev. Scrn.	Prev. Screen.
^PGUP			Up by Paragraph		
PGDN	Next Screen	Next Frame	Bot. of Scrn./Scrl.	Next Scrn.	Next Screen.
^PGDN			Down by Paragraph		
+	Down from the border into the frame				
–	Up from the frame into the border				

15.4 TASKS 703

Entering Data

An outline is most useful when you embed data in it. Position to any topic or subtopic. To put text into the frame, simply press + to move down into the frame where, after hitting ZOOM, you can begin writing using the WP. To make an empty SS or DB frame, decide where you want it in the outline. Then move to the frame which the new frame should follow. Next, go to the *Create* menu and set the parameters for the SS or DB and hit return. The outline form returns with a new numbered topic stuck in, with no title but with the letter S (or D) showing it is an SS (or DB) frame. Add a title if you wish. After doing so, press ZOOM to enter the frame and start working with the SS or DB. When done, either temporarily or permanently, press ZOOM again to pop out to the outline.

The procedure for creating a graph and putting it into an outline frame is different and is discussed below under the topic Graphs.

Word Processing

There are two ways to acquire a word processing frame. If you are working with an outline, go to an empty frame, enter a title if you wish, then press +, then ZOOM; the cursor enters the frame. If you are not using an outline, create a WP frame from the *Create* menu.

Start Up

When a WP frame is active, simply hit ZOOM to zoom the frame to full size. There are several ways to bring in a disk file. Use the disk icon reached with *scroll lock* from any frame, bring up the directory, use up or down to choose a file and then hit return for Framework to bring in the file with the highlighted name. The *Disk* option, *get file by name,* lets you specify a file by name for a frame.

Editing

Once inside a WP frame, you have a friendly, powerful WP program to create and edit text. Automatic wordwrap and backspace or rub deletion aid text entry.

Margins, alignment and emphasis, as well as tabs, are specified from the *Words* option menu. Thus you have text and frame formatting available within a couple of keystrokes.

The default setting for editing is the insert mode. Move any place within the WP frame and start to type in insert mode. To change this go to the

Edit menu (with ins) and switch to *overtype* mode. This setting is a toggle which can be reset to *insert* mode.

You have great freedom for navigating within the word frame with cursor and control keys as displayed in the WP column of Table 15.4.1.

SELECT is used extensively to highlight a section of text for many WP operations. Here is how. Move the cursor to where you want to start selection. Then press SELECT. Now use the cursor movement commands (Table 15.4.1) to highlight text as a block. When satisfied, hit return. (If you highlight too much, if you err, press esc to escape.)

The marked block is now eligible for various actions. Use emphasis from the *Edit* menu: choose bold, underline or italics. Otherwise, you may delete (with del), MOVE or COPY the block. *Search and replace* and *search* are both available from the *Words* menu.

Long term format, such as margins, page length, line length, headers, footers, page markers and so forth, is established by embedded format commands. All these commands begin with "at" (@). You put them as a formula into the text frame border or you may reserve this action until you are ready to print the document. A list of these commands appears as Table 15.4.2.

Table 15.4.2 Format Commands

COMMAND	DESCRIPTION	EXAMPLE
Margins:		
@tm	Top margin: use to set the number of lines in the top margin. Default is 6 lines.	@**tm**(6)
@bm	Bottom margin: use to set the number of lines in the bottom margin. Default is 6 lines.	@**bm**(6)
@po	Page offset: use to set the number of blank spaces between the left edge of the paper and the first character printed at the left margin. Default is 10 spaces.	@**po**(10)
Page Format:		
@pl	Page length: use to set the total number of lines on a page. Default is 66 (standard for 8½ × 11 inch paper).	@**pl**(66)

Table 15.4.2 Format Commands (cont.)

COMMAND	DESCRIPTION	EXAMPLE
Page Format (cont.)		
@ll	Line length: use to set the number of characters that print on a line. Default is 65 characters past the page offset.	@ll(65)
@sp	Line spacing: use to set whether a frame is single, double, or wider spaced. Default is single spacing.	@sp(1)
Pagination:		
@np	New page: use to specify that a frame's contents should start on a new page.	@np
	You can also use @np(n), where the "n" in the parenthesis is a number. Use @np(n) to specify that a frame's contents should start on a new page and the new page should be numbered what you've entered in the parenthesis. For example, to start a frame's contents on a new page numbered 33, center @np(33).	
@kp	Keep: use to tell Framework to keep the contents of a frame all on one page.	@kp
@sk	Skip: use to skip the specified number of blank lines before printing the contents of frame.	@sk(3)
Headers:		
@hl	Header left: prints a header lined up at the page offset.	@hl("Chapter 5")
@hc	Header center: prints a header centered between the page offset and line length.	@hc("TOYCO, INC.")
@hr	Header right: prints a header flush with the line length.	@hr("Chapter5")
@hp	Header position: use to indicate on what line you want the header printed. Default is **3**.	@hp(6)

(continued)

Table 15.4.2 Format Commands (cont.)

COMMAND	DESCRIPTION	EXAMPLE
Headers (cont.)	For example, to put the header on the sixth line from the top of the page, enter @**hp(6)**.	
@**hf**	Header/footer start: use to indicate on what physical page to start printing headers and footers. Default is **1**.	@**hf(3)**.
	For example, to start printing headers and footers three pages later, enter @**hf(3)**.	
Footers:		
@**fl**	Footer left: prints a footer lined up at the page offset.	@**fl("9-20-84")**
@**fc**	Footer center: prints a footer centered between the page offset and line length.	@**fc("9-20-84")**
@**fr**	Footer right: prints a footer flush with the line length.	@**fr("9-20-84")**
@**fp**	Footer position: use to indicate on what line you want the footer printed. Default is **3**.	@**fp(6)**
	For example, to put a footer on the sixth line from the bottom of page, enter @**fp(6)**.	
@**pn**	Page number: use to have Framework automatically number the pages of a document. You can use @**pn** in either a header or footer.	@**pn**
	For example, to number the pages in a centered footer, enter @**fc(@pn)**.	
@**hf**	Header/footer start: use to indicate on what page to start printing headers and footers. Default is **3**.	@**hf(3)**
	For example, to start printing headers and footers on the third page, enter @**hf(3)**.	

Source: Framework Tutorial Manual

Spread Sheets

You set up an SS frame from the *Create* menu, specifying the number of rows and columns you want. The empty SS frame, with rows and columns labeled as in Figure 15.4.1, then appears on the desk. You can move about the frame with the cursor keys listed in Table 15.4.1.

The Framework SS has most of the features described in Chapter 14 for Multiplan and Lotus. Letters specify columns and numbers specify rows. To put a formula in a cell, position to the cell and hit EDIT. Then type the formula. As with 1-2-3, cells and ranges can be specified by pointing, moving the cursor and hitting return. Further, mixed references are available. When you point to a referenced cell, if you hit $, Framework steps through the four mixed mode reference types; when you come to the one you want, hit return.

Names

Framework does not let you name a region. However, if you have put titles in columns and rows, you can reference a cell by title. For instance, for a row named TOTAL and a column named JUNE, the cell at their intersection as referenced as JUNE.TOTAL. This is extended to name a range with a starting and ending cell and colons between then. Use this method

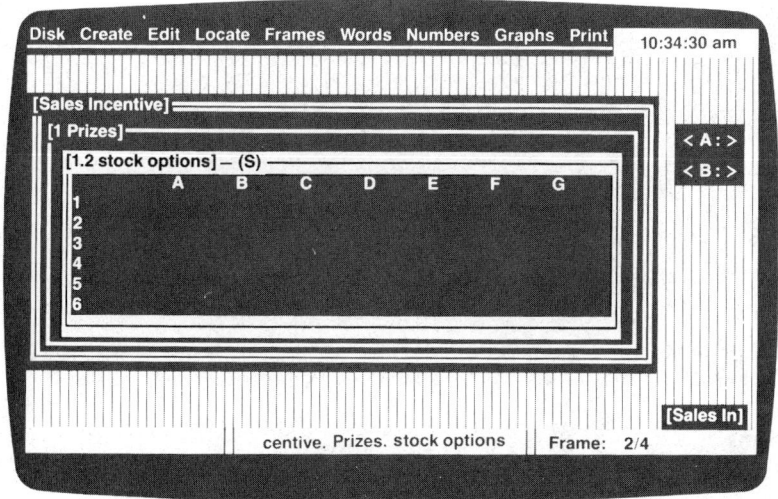

Figure 15.4.1. Empty SS frame.

to specify a column, a row or a block of cells, such as JAN.TOTAL: MAY.TOTAL. Columns in Figure 15.4.2 have names '83, '84 and '85; rows are Nuts, Bolts, Screws, and Totals.

Formulas

You create a formula in a cell as with other spread sheets, using arithmetic signs for connecting terms and creating products in the expression. Framework has a large number of functions available, all of them beginning with the "at" sign (@). It has two useful and powerful table functions.

Windows

A missing feature in the SS is windows. Although title locks are provided, there is no means for splitting an SS frame into parts, a powerful and important SS function. It is suprising that Framework lacks it, since frames come so naturally. Actually, you can simulate this function by creating another SS frame, copying a portion of the first SS into it and linking values

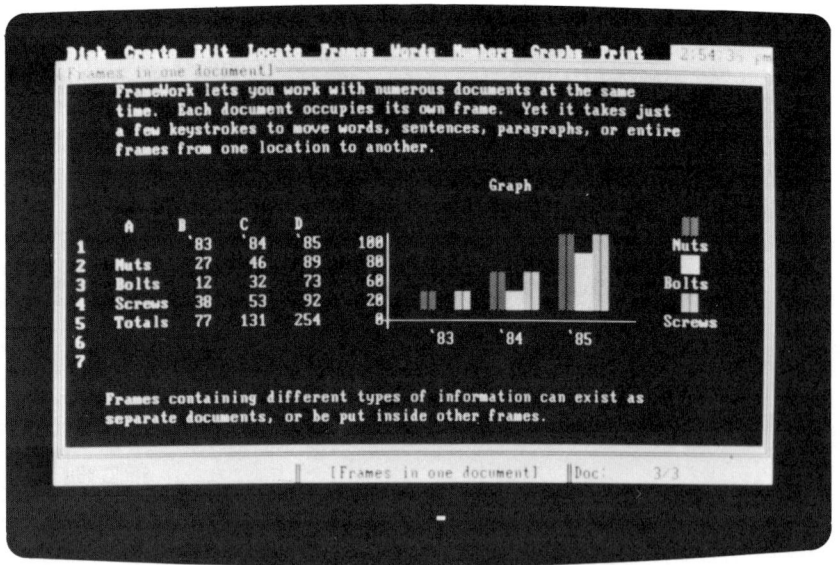

Figure 15.4.2. Container frame with SS and graph.

in the new frame to summary values in the original frame. This alternative is especially important for coping with the large SS. Break it into several modales, each in a frame.

Data Base

Size

Create options let you specify width (the number of fields per record) and height (the number of records in the database). If you do not specify either, you get a data base with fourteen records, each with fourteen fields. It is preferable, if you can, to determine the size and number of records beforehand; in that way, space is reserved in memory and you know you have enough room. At any time you can add fields, remove fields, and add or remove records.

Setup

Framework formats the screen with a double line near the top. You enter field names by putting labels in the dummy record above this line. Simply type in a field title and tab to the next field. To adjust field width, put the cursor in a field and hit SIZE, then hit right to move the cursor right, increasing the size of the field as you go (or hit left to narrow it). When the width suits you, hit return.

Data Entry

Once field labels are entered, it's simple to position within the data base to enter data. Cusor movement commands let you position to any field in any record as shown in Table 15.4.1. Enter data as with spread sheets. Numerical data and text starting with an alphabetical character can be enterred directly into a field. However, text which begins with a numeral should be preceded by a blank to show that arithmetic cannot be performed on this data.

Any field can be a function of other fields in the record. Type a formula into the field. Use pointing as with the SS.

You can enter data in any sequence. The data base can be sorted from the *Locate* menu, but only on one field at a time (as with dBase). You can sort on multiple fields by using the least important field first. Figure 15.4.3 shows the "sales" DB with field names and four records entered.

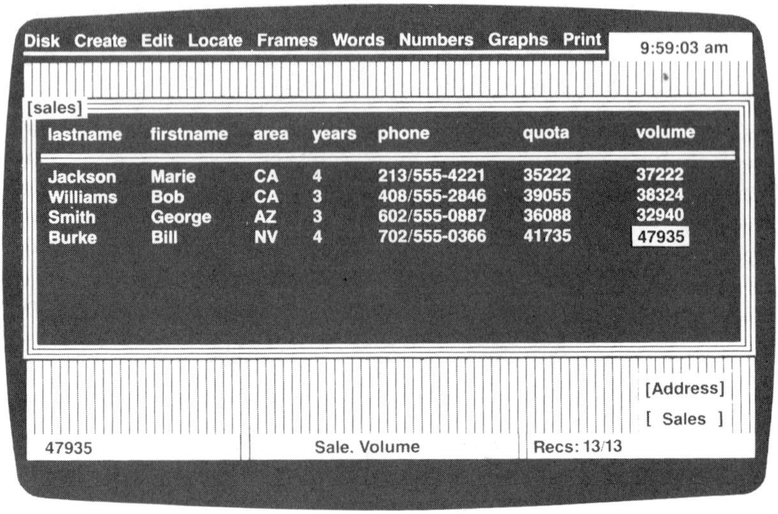

| Disk | Create | Edit | Locate | Frames | Words | Numbers | Graphs | Print | 9:59:03 am |

[sales]

lastname	firstname	area	years	phone	quota	volume
Jackson	Marie	CA	4	213/555-4221	35222	37222
Williams	Bob	CA	3	408/555-2846	39055	38324
Smith	George	AZ	3	602/555-0887	36088	32940
Burke	Bill	NV	4	702/555-0366	41735	47935

[Address]
[Sales]

47935　　　　　　　Sale. Volume　　　　　Recs: 13/13

Figure 15.4.3. A DB frame with field name showing above the double line and four records.

Altering

To add records to the data base or fields to a record, go to the *Create* menu and exercise either option. To delete records or fields, SELECT them and remove them using the *Edit* menu. You may not *undo* this.

Search and *search and replace* work within a DB frame as global requests. That is, they are not specific to a particular record or field within all the records.

Queries

Framework has a query facility for selecting records by criteria you furnish. Formulas state a query, phrased similarly to requests used in dBase's LOCATE and FIND, but must start with "at" (@). The formula's action is called **filtering.** To set up a filter, move the cursor into the frame label and press EDIT. Then type the selection formula and press return. Framework hides all records which do not meet the criterion. After processing the DB, Framework displays the altered frame, showing only those records which meet the requirements. The DB has been filtered.

The selected records become the new content of the DB. You can perform *further* selection by entering another formula, as described above. This formula applies to records now showing in the frame. In other words, further filtering is done on what's showing.

There are two ways to restore the data base, unhiding the records which have disappeared. For the first, go back to the frame label, use the *Frame* menu and *open all frames*. The old formula remains in the frame label and the same filtering can be done again by pressing RECALC. For the second method, erase the filter formula from the frame and press RECALC. For both methods, records will not be in the original order after filtering; they must be sorted to recover that order.

Selecting Fields

Selecting records, as described above, retains *all* fields within selected records. What if you want only certain fields of certain records? This is done easily, if you keep a copy of the DB on disk. Choose fields to eliminate from the frame with the *delete rows* command on the *Edit* menu. Then select records by entering a filter formula into the frame. Filtering may be repeated until the final selection results.

To make another query, delete the data base from memory and bring a new copy of the same data base from the disk.

Title Lock

Title lock is possible with DBs, as with spread sheets; that is, to keep the field names at the top of the screen by choosing *lock first row* from the *Edit* menu.

Normally the data base displays much like a spread sheet. A record occupies a row. For a large record, some of it may not display, since the screen is not large enough to accomodate its width. To see that portion of the record which is not displaying, move the cursor to the right. As it reaches the edge more of the record becomes visible (horizontal scrolling). This display type is called **table view**.

Forms View

The large record will not print as one line from the table form, but requires several lines. To print, all first lines of records are put on the first page(s); the second lines go on the next page(s), and so on. This is sometimes inconvenient and hard to read. But another more convenient view of the record called the **forms view,** is possible.

To initiate the forms view, press VIEW. It works differently for a data base than for other documents. Each field occupies a separate frame with the field name at the top. Figure 15.4.4 shows an example of a DB frame in forms view. Forms view allows you to design printed forms as well as

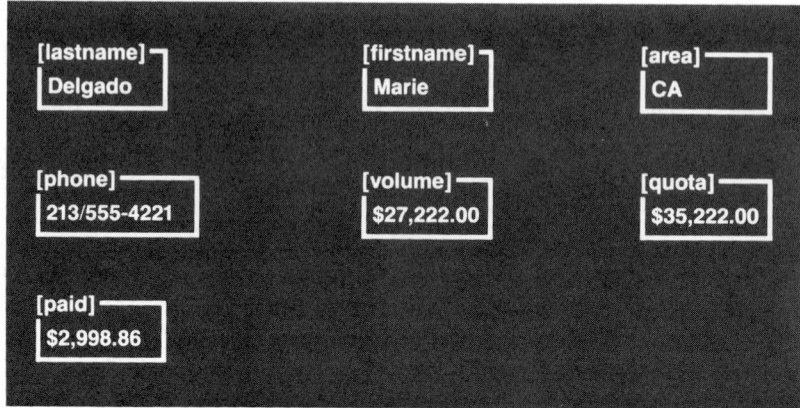

Figure 15.4.4. A frame view of a DB.

screen displays for entering data. You can alter the display with DRAG and SIZE. Position the cursor on a field frame title. Then hit SIZE and left or right to expand or contract this frame. Hit DRAG and use arrow to reposition the frame within the larger DB frame.

From the *Frame* menu, you can select one of three options for presenting each field frame: highlighted, outlined or absent. This is useful both for display and printing records.

You may enter data in forms view, also. Find a record and a field within the record to start entering data, using cursor commands shown in Table 15.4.1. Go to *forms* view with VIEW. Move the cursor to appear on the frame of the field in question. Press + and the cursor moves into the frame. Enter a datum there and hit tab. This moves the cursor into the next field frame for entering the next datum. Continue thus to the end of the record; then tab brings you into the first field of the next record.

File Size

To be used, a DB file must reside in memory. The size of your computer memory determines the maximum file size which Framework can handle. However, you may use Framework as an adjunct to dBase. If the dBase file is small enough to fit into memory, it can be brought in automatically by Framework, which views and filters the dBase file so that it is available for use. If the dBase file is too large to fit into memory, handle it in sections by requesting a range of record numbers.

Graphs

The steps to create a graph are these:

1. Move the cursor to the spread sheet or data base containing the data to be plotted;
2. Open the SS or DB and SELECT one or more columns or one or more rows;
3. Go to the *Graph* menu with <u>ins</u> and <u>arrow</u> or with ^G;
4. Select the type of graph from the six showing on the *Graph* menu;
5. Specify which dimension of the spread sheet (columns or rows) is the horizontal axis;
6. Select the *draw a new graph* option and press *return*;
7. A graph appears in black and white in a frame created for it;
8. Label the graph frame (the label will appear as the title of the graph);
9. Press ZOOM and the graph fills the screen, displaying in color on a color monitor.

Types

The choices for graph display (item 4 above) is similar to those discused for 1-2-3. Choose your favorite from the *Graph* menu, Figure 15.3.8. Once a graph frame appears, it can be expanded or contracted with SIZE or it can be dragged around the screen after DRAG.

Replot

A graph frame has a formula associated with it. You can see this formula by putting the cursor in the graph label and pressing EDIT. The formula associates the graph with the spread sheet or data base which contains the data. Thus any change you make in the data can be reflected in a new plot of the graph. After making a change, go back to the graph frame and press RECALC to replot the data.

You can make the replot take place automatically for the SS. Choose an empty cell and put the "at" sign followed by the name of the associated graph frame. Now, whenever you change the data, the graph immediately changes. You can hide the link cell in the spread sheet by shrinking its width to 0.

The graph is listed at the end of an outline, with title if any. It may be MOVEd into position and renumbered, if desired.

Printing

There are many ways to print frames, depending upon the kind of frames and the current view. Printing is always initiated from the *Print* menu. After options are selected, move the cursor to *begin* and press <u>return</u>.

Spooling

Printing is usually done by **spooling.** That is, Framework writes a temporary text file to the currently logged drive and subdirectory. When the file is complete, a Framework print routine picks it up and passes it to the printer, leaving Framework free to process your further requests. The exception occurs when the default drive is write protected or full. Then Framework gives you the option to print directly from memory.

You can spool several documents. Print requests are kept in a queue. After printing, a request is eliminated and the disk space for the temporary file is released. Another way to schedule multiple documents to print is to use SELECT to chose a number of frames and send them to print.

Printing Single Frames

A frame which contains a primary document—text, SS, DB, G,—can contain nothing more. Only an outline or containing frame can contain multiple frames. How do single frames print?

Content prints only in frame view. So select a content frame, toggle with VIEW to frame view and make the request from the *Print* menu, Figure 15.3.10.

The frame label should contain format commands, regardless of the type of frame, or else the default format is used. Format commands convey line and page length, margin offset, and so on. For the text frame, additional information can be entered there, such as headers and footers, page numbering, top and bottom margins and so forth. A wide SS and DB prints as two or more groups of lines, where the second and later groups are placed at the page offset following after the first group. After printing, you can cut the page into horizontal pieces and paste them together to make a wide page.

Data Base

A data base in table view is formatted similarly: if all the fields fit on the line, one line per record is printed. Otherwise, multiple groups of lines result.

If you put the data base itself in *forms view,* you are free to arrange field frames within the DB frame as you wish. As you do so, only one record shows. But the arrangement applies to the entire data base. You can DRAG the field frames around. You should enlarge each field frame with SIZE, so that all of the field value displays. You may print fields selectively by highlighting the ones you desire and closing the others. Choosen fields automatically print in their entirety. You can filter records that you don't need to print.

The Outline

The central theme of Framework is the outline. In fact, it is the "framework" for receiving, setting up, expanding and broadening your document. Therefore it is not surprising that Framework provides extensive facilities for manipulating the outline: the ability to move, copy, renumber and print parts or all of an outline.

Zoom and View

The Framework outline facility shows various aspects of the outline with ZOOM (F9) and VIEW (F10). VIEW toggles between frame view and outline view. Recall that the outline view shows only topic and subtopic numbers, titles and types. Topic number and type may be surpressed from the *Forms* menu. **Containing frames,** those without content, but which have other frames inside, have a triangle pointing to them (►) to indicate their function, as shown on Figure 15.2.2.

The frame view shows each topic as a frame—a rectangular box with number, title and type at the upper left (if not surpressed), along with one or more lines of content. An outer frame or a containing frame contains inner frames nested in boxes inside of its box. You may move between frames in frame view with the cursor keys as for the outline view (see Table 15.4.2). Move to a frame and it becomes active and its border is highlighted.

In outline form, move to any topic or subtopic and hit VIEW; you enter frame view with the chosen frame as the outer frame of the display. Hit VIEW again and return to the outline view with the same frame active. VIEW works both from the frame border and when you are inside.

In Frame View

For a frame at the lowest level which contains content, ZOOM expands that frame to fill the screen so that you can work on it directly. This is called **full screen form.** If the frame is closed—put aside in one of the trays—

it is also opened. Use ZOOM as a toggle between full screen and either frame or outline form.

While in outline form, ZOOM to a containing frame and it expands to frame form, showing only the contents of that frame, not the frame border or title. Labels for *containing frames* show, while the label and a small part of a *bottom level* frame display. The first frame of the sublevel is highlighted.

Again, if the highlighted frame is a content frame, hit ZOOM to expand it to full screen. Otherwise, if it is a containing frame, hit ZOOM to get a context view of frames at the inner levels.

Printing

To print an outline, go to outline form by toggling ZOOM and VIEW so that only the outline results. Get into the outer frame and then call up the *Print* menu. Issue *begin* from within its options. Detail can be supressed by closing nested frames prior to printing.

To print a portion of an outline, move the cursor to the desired containing frame before beginning to print. Then only the topic titles within the containing frame whose label is highlighted prints. From the *Frame* menu, you can turn on and off outline type and numbers. From the frame label you can enter print format instructions to set margins, headers and so forth.

Printing the Document

To print an entire document, highlight the outer frame. Enter frame view with VIEW. From the *Frames* menu, open all frames. You may also suppress outline numbers and type. Then only low level frame content prints. Format is controlled globally from the formula in the label in the outer frame. Individual content frame labels may have a print formula which takes over for that frame. Thus print format is controlled through formulas in labels. Page numbering is controlled from the print option menu.

Partial Document

You may print part of the content of your document in outline sequence. You go to frame view and select one or more outline frames within which appear the segments of your document. Proceed as above.

The Container

The procedures described above constrain printing to documents in the sequence in which they appear in the outline. Although portions of the output can be rearranged horizontally, they cannot be altered vertically and still remain in outline sequence. Therefore a useful alternative is a container.

The **container** is an outer frame where you can place content frames in any order or position. Create this container frame, as any other, from the *Create* menu. Then put frames to be printed in any sequence within the container.

Memory is a problem here. If you COPY frames into the container, additional memory is consumed. You may run out of memory before you have the right arrangement. You may MOVE content frames from the outline into the container, but then the original document gets messed up. A safe method is to *save* the complete original document on disk. Then MOVE frames into the container to print. Now you can mess up the memory document because you have a copy on disk.

The container gives you real freedom in arranging frames on the printed page. Once in a container frame, content frames can be moved around and altered in size and shape with DRAG and SIZE. Text, data base and spread sheet information can be placed side by side on the page. Care must be exercised to adjust margins and line widths of frames put side by side so that they do not conflict. Be sure to select *allow free dragging* from the *Frame* menu.

A graph may be positioned by breaking up text horizontally and putting the graph frame between them. However, it is not practical to put a graph and text side by side because the dot matrix printer would then have to operate in different modes on different sides of the page, which is not feasible. Graphs should have no horizontal interference.

15.5 SYMPHONY

Symphony™, a product of Lotus Development Corporation, came out in mid-1984*. Its overall purpose is to extend the facilities of 1-2-3.

Requirements

Symphony is intended for the IBM PC and 100% compatibles. It requires 320K of RAM, a graphics card and either two floppies or a floppy and a hard disk. It works best with two monitors so that you can see changes in spread sheets in graphical form at the same time you make the changes. However, the same capability is possible with a single monitor and windows provided by the package.

---

*Symphony is a trademark of Lotus Development Corporation.

Goals

Symphony extends 1-2-3's capabilities by adding word processing and communication. Lotus had suggestions from many of its users on how to improve functions and simplify procedures. They put these suggestions to work in Symphony.

A vendor cannot expect to sell an identical product to the same customer base. With a new, improved and compatible product, one might expect a large proportion of the customer base to pay a relatively small fee to get an improved product which would also entice first time users. The Lotus strategy offered Symphony to 1-2-3 owners for only $200 and sold it as a new product at a list price of $695.

Worksheet

The central concept of Symphony is the worksheet. That is, memory left over after the program is loaded is configured like a spread sheet. All five functions of Symphony may have areas within this worksheet assigned to them. Memory allocation is handled here as described in Chapter 14, using the virtual spread sheet concept (VS). Symphony provides a VS consisting of 256 columns and 8192 rows, or over 2 million cells (of 9 bytes), obviously more than available in any existing micro. **Worksheet (WS)** is another word for spread sheet.

Work Environment

Corresponding to Framework's concept of the frame, Symphony has the concept of a **work environment.** This is a restricted range on the worksheet, operating under one of Symphony's five tasks:

SHEET—the spread sheet;
DOC—word processing;
FORM—data base;
GRAPH—graphics;
COMM—data communication.

The user requests a work environment **(WE)** be established as needed. None, one or several WEs may be currently assigned to areas of the WS.

The user sets up a **range** of cells on the WS for each WE, which restricts the area available for the WE. Thus the WE is like the actual spread sheet area (AS) of Chapter 14, except that its boundary is fixed in advance. When a WE is established, a window is provided automatically for it. You may give it a title. By command, additional windows may be assigned to the same WE.

Windows

The window concept is secondary only to the worksheet concept for Symphony. Four parameters are associated with a window. These are

1. Its type, whether DOC, SHEET, and so forth;
2. Its range, the worksheet area assigned to it;
3. Its size, the area it occupies on the screen in lines and line width;
4. A title, if you chose.

With the *Window Create* command, you can get additional windows. You set screen size and position at the active windows with arrow; scroll lock toggles the effect of arrow between window size and position. With a function key, you can select, hide, expose or bring a window to the top of the window stack on the screen. When you turn on a window with a function key, it pops into a particular area on the screen. As with Framework, you can zoom any window to fill the screen.

Note the difference between range and size: *range* describes an WE with respect to the WS, the position of the AS within the VS. A range is described by the cells it occupies, such as A1:H256. *Size* is the area and location of the window on the screen.

Mobility

You have great control over the window. You can change any of its aspects: type, title, range or size; you can create and eliminate windows at will; and you can save their contents and load them from disk.

Control

Symphony provides four ways to control actions in the WS.
These are

1. The functions keys, F1-F10.
2. Menus, one for each WE type.
3. A service menu for general services.
4. Setting sheets, which hold parameters for each WE.

Function Keys

Function key requests are extended by combining the activation with the alternate key, alt. Thus 20 functions can be entered directly by pressing a function key, with or without alt. Services include selecting windows, activating the service menu, zooming in and out and so forth.

Menu

You bring forth the menu for the WE you are using by pressing F10. Its menu bar appears at the top of the screen. Step through the menu with *space* or hit the character which begins a request displayed on the menu bar.

As with 1-2-3, this brings forth a list of options on the prompt line. You make an option choice in the same way which may, in turn, elicit a suboption menu.

Note this difference with 1-2-3, however. You *do not prefix* a command with the slash. Instead, you use F10. This inconsistency makes macros created for 1-2-3 unusable with Symphony. Still, you can type your directive as a key sequence, without waiting for the menus and options to display. This expedites entering a command.

Services

These functions are common to all Symphony environments: Window, File, Print, Configuration, Application, Settings, New, Exit.

By hitting F9, you initiate the service menu to bring forth its menu bar. A choice again elicits an option prompt.

Settings Sheets

The **settings sheet** holds a group of parameters. It may be associated with a working environment or some other aspect of the WS, such as printing parameters, configuration parameters and so forth. When you start Symphony, all the setting sheets needed are brought into memory along with the program. Each sheet contains suitable parameters, the *default parameters,* which may not be the ones you prefer.

You can change any settings sheet from the service menu. You enter the *Change Settings sheet* command and the type of settings sheet. The settings sheet displays its current values. You can move the cursor to any value and change it; change as many as you wish. When done, the information entered goes into the settings sheet, which is put back into its slot in memory.

It would be inefficient to have to enter this information every time you bring up or create a WS. Therefore you may name the settings sheet and store it on disk. Then, the next time you need it, use the *Setting sheet Load* command from the current WE (work environment) to load it by name from disk into its slot in memory.

The Task

Let us now examine the tasks or WEs and their fulfillment in Symphony.

Spread Sheet

As you might expect, Symphony is still an exceptionally powerful spread sheet, since it is based on 1-2-3. However, it requires over 300K for its multiple programs. Those who recalculate very large spread sheets frequently will find that 1-2-3 has more space for the SS and recalculates faster.

Using Symphony "feels" about the same as 1-2-3 since the familiar commands are in the same format. Cell format and other static parameters are now stored in a setting sheet and you can alter several of them in a single shot. Formulas have been expanded form 49 to 70, most of the additions being for string functions.

Macro capability has been improved by providing many additional command key words, mostly for the advanced spread sheet user. Symphony facilitates production of macros with a new Learn function which records keystrokes as you enter them.

Data Base and Graphs

Data Base activities and use remain similar to 1-2-3. Graphics sits on top of the spread sheet and data base. Methods for employing the graphs have not changed much. A few additions have been made, such as high-low charts and exploded pie charts. Printing a graph still cannot be done from the worksheet environment. You must leave Symphony and bring in the print program; you cannot combine text and graphs in the same printed document.

Word Processing

The DOC WE has minimum WP facilities. It provides for the document format on a setting sheet, which is overridden by entering individual format lines in the text. A format line can be named and duplicated anyplace in text.

You can move pieces from other windows into a DOC window, but you cannot keep the DOC insert linked to its original source. Of course, there is no way to get graphs into the text.

A number of eccentricities exist which may mess you up until you get used to them. For instance, since del is right next to down, you may inadvertantly delete something you cannot restore, since there is no *undo* function.

Communication

COMM works very well. You can make a setting sheet for any kind of communication terminal or modem, name it and store it on disk. Call it up when necessary with a few keystrokes, to send material from the WS to a receiving station.

COMM also allows for the capture of data being received and its routing to a spread sheet, printer or disk file. Thus you can reformat data for any WE.

Worksheet Mapping

Everything described so far, except for the program itself, occupies part of the worksheet. It's clear enough initially that you need worksheet space for all window environments. Settings sheets and macros also require space.

Symphony manages space only for setting sheets; it does not manage any worksheet space. You determine where to put each WE, macro library and format line. Since some of these change dynamically as you work with them, you must be sure that their space does not overlap or interfere with other WEs. You may move them later when one bumps into another. But this is not salubrious.

15.6 ASSESSMENT

We may consider assessment in many different ways. Most reviewers who describe packages in micro magazines examine packages in terms of how well they meet their specifications, how well they perform and ease of use. It is hard to assess the worth of a package to *you*. This section examines some considerations which seem to get lost in the shuffle.

Complexity

Many aspects of these packages convey their complexity. For example, their sheer size might put you in awe. Each uses over 300K; many mainframe applications are smaller than this. From the size of each program you can imagine how many different things it can do. And all of them are integrated.

Now you can go to Hertz or Avis, pick up a car, get the keys, sit behind the wheel and drive right out of the lot. Sometimes you have to grope around to find where the shift is. Later, instead of turning on the lights as you intended, you may find the windshield wiper going. But in a few minutes you are a master of the situation.

High tech products that you buy for your household such as refrigerators, hifi stereo recorders, cameras, and VCRs can be put to use within at least a few minutes.

Here is where the problem develops. A single feature, simple to use, inexpensive program such as VisiCalc or Bank Street Writer can be mastered in a few hours. Single function programs have gotten large and hard to master. Second generation programs take a day or so. Most can be cranked up to get useful work done, still in a matter of hours. But then you lose sight of the innovations and important features. A day may suffice to learn Multiplan.

The advanced package, such as Samna Word III, an excellent single-function package, takes days to learn thoroughly.

Now consider the multifunction package. It took me over a week to get acquainted with the features present in Framework. A first time user of either Framework or Symphony will find it difficult to do any useful work the first day. If you are not ready for this type of product and do not have the time to invest in it, you will get irritable and impatient.

Tutorial

A **tutorial,** as described in Chapter 10, interactively teaches you how to use a package. Both Symphony and Framework have tutorials, but they pose problems. Let us examine why.

A tutorial is a kind of programmed learning. When you start the tutorial, it presents information to read on the screen, introducing the product and how to use it. With large products, there is a lot of material to cover. Hence the tutorial is broken down to a number of topics.

Then the tutorial demonstrates how different facets of each function works and asks questions. If you have learned a topic, the tutorial goes on to the next. If not, it returns to an earlier place for review.

Locked In

Both tutorials are **locked-in** programmed learning. Framework uses Fred, the FRamework EDitor, to present and animate the tutorial. Your only interaction is pressing keys or requesting the next frame. I need a *live* tutorial to find out just what to do. The locked-in lesson teaches how to drag and size a frame. Then I press a key and watch a frame move across the screen and change in size. This is not practical enough.

After learning how to drag and size a frame, I want to have immediate experience with that function, which is monitored by the tutorial to see that I am doing it right. Neither package provides this hands-on type of tutorial.

Capabilities

Let us examine the capabilities that these products provide.

Symphony

Symphony contains the same high quality SS program as 1-2-3. It has added more functions and gathered a number of parameters into the setting sheet, making them easier to change. Although the commands and their options have been altered slightly, they are easy to master for one with experience with 1-2-3. SS data developed on 1-2-3 is compible with Symphony, and vice versa.

Macros which work with 1-2-3 are *not* compatible with Symphony where commands are initiated with a function key. Lotus has remedied the situation by providing a macro translator.

The new communication program is excellent and can be invoked from Symphony. It supports many terminal configurations and can bring data directly into Symphony, reformatting as it goes.

The graphics package presents excellent graphs and has been enhanced to provide additional graph types.

The data base manager is mediocre but sufficient for small managerial type files. Though a little difficult to use, if you are acquainted with 1-2-3, you will have no trouble with its implementation.

The WP may suffice for small notes or letters but slows down considerably after accepting a few thousand words of manuscript.

Framework

Framework has two new features which make it valuable to some users. First is the ability not only to create and manipulate outlines but also to use them effectively to cope with the other frames of data that Framework manages. Second, Framework combines all its forms into a single printed document.

Framework does all its tasks well, including word processing, spread sheet analysis, data base management and graphics. Although not as good as the best single packages, these functions are well above average.

The communication function can only be reached by exiting Framework proper. This function is mediocre, so that if it is required, it would better be replaced by a full-function communication package.

Recommendations

Chapter 16 discusses many alternatives to the multifunction package. Should you still want one, here are some considerations.

If you are a first time user, oriented towards text but with a desire to incorporate other functions, then Framework is your best bet, especially if you think in outline form. Further, if you have experience with dBase and need to manipulate one or more data bases, again Framework is your choice.

Symphony includes the best spread sheet on the market. If that is your main activity, Symphony is your choice. The only exception occurs when you use very large spread sheets and recalculate them frequently; then 1-2-3 may be a better bet.

V
Putting It All Together

16
Systems

16.1 THE COMPUTER SYSTEM

Scope

This chapter examines the **computer system,** which consists of the hardware, the operating system and application programs. The computer system is part of a larger overall system including people and procedures. Of particular consequence in the *business* environment.

Purpose

This book examines computer systems intended for **professional** use related to work or personal economics. "Professional" describes the system's *capability,* not its *employment:* if you want to play games on it or bring it out of the closet once a month, you are still assured that it does a professional job, characterized thus:

1. It can support professional application programs;
2. It can operate continuously over long periods of time;
3. It is ruggedly constructed;
4. As a consequence, the cost for such a system is greater than that of a hobby system.

As of 1984, the cutoff price for such a system is at least $1,000.

Exclusions

We exclude hobby computers, such as the Commodore 64 and the Coleco Adam. Although Apples appeared in the office environment several years ago, they were usually bought professionally only to take advantage of spread sheet programs, particularly VisiCalc. Since the third generation of SS programs is upon us, only micros which support them should be considered. Presently no model in the old Apple line supports these SSs. Apple's newer products, which include Lisa and Macintosh, are discussed in this chapter.

While the IBM PC certainly qualifies as a professional computer, the PCjr is a borderline case. Although it can be used as an input terminal with computing capability to a network system and perhaps to a mainframe, it still does not quality as a stand-alone professional micro.

Minicomputers are also excluded. A system based on Digital Equipment's PDP-11/23, for instance, may well be a competitor to more expensive micro systems. However, the market for them is limited.

Topics

Let's see what's in the sections of this chapter and why the topics are covered:

16.2. The IBM PC has been covered in several sections in this book. However, there are many competitive systems which represent themselves as being compatible with the IBM PC and XT. This section discusses compatibility.

16.3. The operating environment is a feature which lets you work with several APs simultaneously. What is it and how does it work? Should it be a part of your system?

16.4. Lisa and Macintosh are emerging systems which have received considerable publicity. Are they suitable for your applications? This section describes them and discusses their advantages and limitations.

16.5. A computer system for business may need to accommodate several users at the same time. What kind of systems are available to do this? What are their pros and cons? How do they work?

16.6. The graphics system is gaining importance and will certainly impinge on the business environment soon. Alternatives are examined here.

16.7. Selecting a system, especially one the involves custom programming, requires professional assistance. The system house has long been a resource for this and is examined here.

16.2 THE IBM PC AND ITS CLONES

The IBM microcomputer has taken the industry by storm. Two factors have contributed to its success: IBM's reputation and its marketing strategy. The PC combines a number of features which make a capable computer. Among these are bit map graphics, multiple function keys and an integrated design. Other hardware choices for the PC, such as the 8088 chip and the bus design, leave something to be desired.

IBM's marketing policy worked up considerable interest among software vendors, who created many APs for the machine before it was released. Hence there are a host of products on the market intended just for the IBM PC and XT.

When it became clear that IBM had indeed cornered a considerable portion of the PC marketplace, hardware vendors wanted to jump on the bandwagon. Could they entice buyers away from IBM? If so, what could they offer to make their product more attractive? Here are three alternatives:

- a lower price tag.
- faster performance.
- better graphics.

All these features can be realized at the hardware level. But the purchaser wants to be assured that software which vendors produce for the PC and XT will run on it. How can the hardware vendor who provides any of the above advantages guarantee that APs which the user purchases will function properly on the **clone**, the IBM look-alike? Are the competitive systems **compatible?**

Levels of Compatibility

There are three levels of compatibility to examine and understand:

1. Hardware compatibility;
2. Operating system compatibility;
3. Application program compatibility.

What does each form of compatibility mean?

Hardware Compatibility

A clone is **hardward compatible** when it can execute the same machine language programs as its "parent." This is easy to achieve. It simply means that the target computer uses an upward compatible chip from the same family. Machine language code which runs on the 8088 also runs on the 8086, 80186 and the 80286. The latter are faster and better chips, the 80286 with the larger instruction set.

Operating System Compatibility

Operating system compatibility means that the combination of hardware and an operating system designed to mate with the hardware provides the same overall functions as the target computer. This is not total compatibility because the functions may not cause the computer to respond in exactly the same way. Thus a machine with OS compatibility may show graphics, but not exactly as the IBM PC.

AP Compatibility

For **AP compatibility,** an application program works on the clone exactly as on its parent. This is **total compatibility,** what the hardware vendor would like for all application programs on the market for the parent.

Achieving Compatibility

Hardware compatibility is almost automatic; choose the right microprocessor chip and there it is.

OS

OS compatibility is harder to achieve. When the OS is not tied into the hardware, there is little if any problem. For instance, a program that operates under CP/M-86 and works on the IBM PC in that mode will also work on any other hardware compatible computer which uses a compatible version of CP/M-86.

IBM put part of its operating system, PC-DOS, into ROM, which created a problem that worked to its advantage. They got a copyright for this portion of the OS. All the graphics routines (which I call VIOS) are stored there. No company has yet decided to tangle with IBM about the copyright. A couple of companies did copy the ROM; but when IBM threatened litigation, they withdrew the ROM portion of their OS.

The alternative is to determine all *functions* that are supplied in ROM. Then put them into code stored in RAM using assembly language (AL) variations. The AL code in ROM differs from the new RAM AL version in minor ways, such as the sequence of steps or the use of equivalent commands; they are not identical. Yet they act the same. This is legal and has been adopted by many vendors and works up to a point.

Achieving AP Compatibility

Some vendors of APs for the PC not only use the services of PC-DOS but also make direct jumps into it to speed up execution. For the clone, this requires hardware and OS compatibility. It is not sufficient that the two OSs are functionally identical; they must also be physically identical or else the jump does not take the AP to the proper physical position in memory, whether ROM or RAM. Such APs do not work properly even when the systems are OS compatible; they need total compatibility.

When the hardware vendor provides a machine with OS compatibility but the AP does not work, there is only one viable solution. If the machine has been on the market and achieved consumer acceptance, it has a customer base which the AP vendor cannot ignore. The AP vendor makes a version the AP which works identically on the vendor's machine (but now does not work on the IBM PC). The compatibility issue has been avoided. The consumer has a product for this configuration which works perfectly on it.

Of course, a clone owner can no longer borrow and copy an AP from a friend who has a PC. That version of the AP does not work on the clone and vice versa. While this might distress the owner, if certainly provides the AP vendor with more protection then he might ordinarily have.

The prospective buyer of an IBM compatible system would like to know its kind of compatibility. This seems like a reasonable question. However, things change from month to month and a list of this sort would be obsolete by the time the book came out. Also you cannot simply rely on a vendor's statement; a system must be checked against existing APs. Since at least two vendors have been forced to change their approach by the threat of litigation, you cannot be entirely sure, even after testing a number of products, whether the information applies to particular serial numbers of these products.

16.3 THE OPERATING ENVIRONMENT

The Problem

The problem, if that's what to call it, is to make the best use of the myriad functions that the micro can provide. Preceding chapters describe the four most important APs: word processing, spread sheet, data base and graphics. Since sorting is such an important adjunct to several of these functions, APs often include that capability.

A report is most effective when it is not simply text; charts, tables and other kinds of illustrations make a much better communication. Even the fact that a document is not simply an array of letters printed on paper makes it less boring and easier to read.

So one need is to combine multiple compound functions within a single multimedia AP. The second and less difficult requirement is to apply the same AP function to multiple documents; to apply a data base program to several data bases simultaneously; for WP, to combine two documents. Often an application program provides this capability internally.

Data Compatibility

I stress the importance of compatibility, especially with respect to the overall system: between the operating system and the hardware; between the application program and both the operating system and the hardware. There is a further demand for compatibility of the external media. It is not possible to use a disk from an IBM PC on an Apple, even though the disks are the same size and both fit into the drive. We know that the disk format is different; one drive cannot read another's disk.

There is never a problem of self-consistency unless a program is damaged. That is, the program should be able to read data it produces. If this were not so, we would be in big trouble!

A problem may arise on one computer system when applying different APs on the same electronic document (ED). Can we always expect the output of one program to be intelligible to another program? The answer is "No." Programs which use standard ASCII format have little, if any, problem passing output to other ASCII format APs. When ASCII format is not used, conversion may be possible. Some APs include routines to reformat output to the ASCII standard; SuperCalc and dBase II, for instance, can create a standard ASCII file, although they use a different internal data format to write data to disk for their own use.

Another way to handle multiple data formats on your disk is a **conversion program**. It takes output produced by one AP and changes it into the format required for a second AP. (Conversion for disk formats for other micros is not the problem here.)

Multiple Functions

There are a number of ways to apply different functions to a single electronic document. These are arranged below from the simplest to the most complicated, combined approach which requires specific hardware. Here is the list:

1. Apply multiple compatible APs which have an *identical data format* sequentially to the ED.
2. Same as (1), but use *internal reformatting* or an *external conversion program* where the APs have incompatible data formats.
3. One vendor may sell separate APs which form an *application family*. These have a consistent data format so they can be applied sequentially to the same ED without problems. Examples are families from MicroPro (WordStar, DataStar, InfoStar and so forth), from the Perfect Group, from PFS, and from Peachtree. Some packages, such as Peach Text provide a menu to select an AP to work on any ED.
4. The *multifunction AP* includes several built-in functions which may be applied to the same ED, as for instance Lotus 1-2-3 Context MBA FrameWork and Symphony described in Chapters 14 and 15.
5. An *operating environment family* such as Visi On lets you use several of *its* specially designed APs concurrently, displaying an active data area for each in a separate window. You may jump from one window to another and thus from one AP to another and can pass data between APs.
6. Other specialized operating environments, such as Quarterdeck's Desq and Microsoft's Windows, supposedly allow you to work as with Visi On but while running unmodified or barely modified commercial APs.
7. *Complete systems* such as Apple's Lisa and Macintosh and Xerox's Star let you work concurrently with multiple application programs, designed for these particular computers and OSs.

Classification

The methods of applying a number of functions to a single electronic document fall into three categories for which we now examine the properties.

The first four solutions (1-4) use simple programs commonly available. As you purchase additional APs, a little planning lets the APs you purchase coordinate with each other. Now that micros have been around for a few years, it is not difficult to plan to purchase a compatible family of APs, if that's the best way to go.

The second set of solutions (5-6) lets you work on the same ED or different EDs simultaneously with different APs perhaps from different vendors. While this has immediate appeal, there are difficulties and costs to consider. Therefore much of this section is devoted to discussing this approach, the **operating environment,** or **OE**.

The last solution (7) requires a completely integrated system: hardware, operating system and APs. This is an attractive alternative and it is examined in Section 16.4.

The Operating Environment

The operating environment is characterized by **windows,** each showing one of several views of data from the same file or data from different files. Data viewed in a window may be altered and, in some cases, copied to another window. One window is associated with each AP, although more than one window may belong to the same AP.

The window first appeared as a way of looking at different parts of the same spread sheet, discussed exhaustively in Chapter 14. Although business word processors do have windows, few micro WPs provide this feature, the notable exception being the FinalWord. Windows for word processors show two portions of one document or, better still, portions of two or more different EDs. Text can be transferred between windows with ease. It is simple for most WPs to move text as a block within an ED. Without windows it is necessary to put the block in a new file, close the current source ED, open the destination ED, then insert the temporary text file.

For the OE, windows not only make parts of several files available, they also require several available APs. Therefore the OE must have a technique for going back and forth between APs. It should be emphasized that the different APs are in memory, so that switching among them does not also require loading programs into memory. Thus the OE requires a host computer with a large enough memory for the OE itself and all active APs.

Actions

The best way to understand the OE is to go through a scenario. Suppose you want to prepare a composite ED. Here are the steps you might use:

1. First, call up the OE.
2. Talk to the OE and tell it which AP you need first.
3. Once the AP is running, name a file for it to access and specify a target area, a window.
4. Tell the OE where to place the window on the screen and how much space to give it.
5. Scroll through the data file to find an area of interest.
6. Work there as long as possible.
7. Give a command to return to the OE.
8. Repeat steps (2-7) for each AP that you need hereafter.

9. You work with an AP's original commands to direct it within the OE. Additional commands talk to the OE to control the size, shape and position of windows or to switch control between resident APs.
10. You terminate each AP separately to be sure a revised ED is stored where necessary.

Block Diagram

An operating environment, in general, makes two initial requirements on the system. First, an OE needs a huge amount of RAM to support multiple application programs. Since the facility takes a toll in time because of additional support software, it would be prohibitive if all of the application program were not resident and immediately available when the operator switches to.

A facilitating requirement is *bit mapped video* to make it easier to chop up the screen into windows and change window sizes. Vendors are aiming for the largest market; since the biggest fraction of this user base has either an IBM Personal Computer or one of its clones, they have enough memory *and* bit map video.

The Components

Figure 16.3.1 is a block diagram of the related OE software components, each shown by a hexagon. At the bottom is the operating system with which we are familiar. At the top are several application programs. Each AP is resident in memory so that the OE can switch to it almost instantaneously. The center hexagon, entitled OE, represents the operating environment. The OS has an obvious role in bringing in the OE and each AP and also in retiring APs. It also has a role during the operating phase of the OE which we now examine.

Input

We have seen how the operating system supports a running application program by providing a keyboard driver which accepts codes for characters as you key in data. In the single AP environment, the keyboard driver in the OS simply provides a service by forwarding codes from the keyboard to the AP. The OS does the same thing in the OE; but the codes first go to the OE. Why would this be if you are talking to one particular application program, say AP1 in the figure? If you are connected directly to an AP, how else could you leave that program and talk to either the operating environment or some other AP?

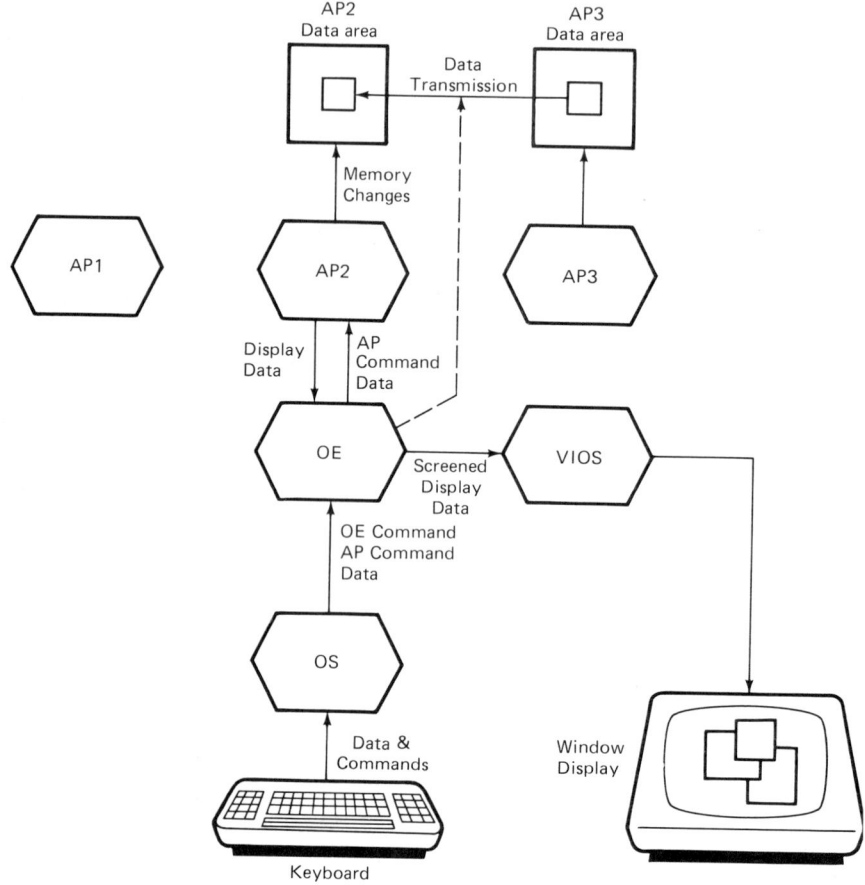

Figure 16.3.1. The operating environment.

In truth, all input to an AP is screened by the OE. Unique codes distinguish commands intended for the OE from those for an AP. Thus there are three kinds of information with different meanings passing from the keyboard:

- data for the AP;
- commands to the AP;
- commands to the OE.

The OE reacts to its commands and passes along the other two. The AP distinguishes between commands and data. Clearly all three types of information must be unique and distinguishable.

Output

APs for micros operate interactively, constantly producing data to display on the screen. In a solitary environment, an AP sends data directly via its own driver, the OS display driver or VIOS for the IBM PC. The AP controls the display and determines data placement in its own internal windows, if any.

But the OE must intercept data for display to put it in the window assigned to this AP. VIOS commands provided by PC DOS greatly facilitate the control of specific rectangular areas in the bit map display (see Section 13.9).

Still, an AP "believes" that it has a full screen to which it sends data; it is up to the OE to make the proper allowances and corrections so that data display properly in the window assigned to the AP.

Intercourse

The third function of the OE provides intercourse between resident APs. In this way you can request information in one window to be passed to another AP for insertion in its window. Normally input and output are directed by and from the AP. Now you have to designate one AP for transmission and another for reception. This cannot be done instantaneously since we have to switch from one AP to the other. Therefore the OE must act as an intermediately. After setting up for the transmission, the actual command must be given by the OE so that both transmission and reception start simultaneously and are synchronized: when the source AP starts transmitting, the receiving AP is waiting and ready to receive the message.

Pros and Cons

The immediate appeal of the operating environment is the opportunity to view two or more documents and interchange information between them at will. There is no free lunch in the computer marketplace. This facility costs a lot and the question is whether it is worth the luncheon bill.

Cost

The obvious cost seen by examining the block diagram, Figure 16.3.1, is overhead. Every character keyed is fielded by three different programs: OS, OE and AP. When typing at full speed into a WP in an OE, you may find that the WP is not as responsive as it used to be. You can type ahead, but it may take a few moments for the WP to catch up; nothing ever gets lost.

This is the simplest of actions. Imagine what happens during scrolling and other functions because the OE gets involved.

The second price is expected from the outset. Instead of one screen display, there are always two: the OE displays directions to tell you how to operate it, should you forget. So the working screen is diminished considerably, especially when you consider that each AP has status displays.

A supposed advantage of the OE system is spontaneity; you can make changes that come to mind by reference to different EDs in their windows. However, for the reasons discussed, this is not as easy as it appears and is further slowed by the reaction time of the multiple programs involved.

Results

One aim of the OE is to produce a document not otherwise available under earlier alternatives—a single printed document containing text, tables and illustrations. That sounds like a great idea, but requires a dot matrix printer, which can switch between graphics and text mode and produce a combination document. This, however, may serve your needs.

There are some who would like to step into the kitchen, press a button and have a cooked meal delivered quickly without having to touch the stove or refrigerator. Technology makes this possible *today* if you are willing to accept a frozen dinner heated in a microwave oven.

I prefer text from a daisy wheel printer and a sketch from a pen plotter rather than both produced on the dot matrix printer. It's worth the effort to cut and paste to get a near-perfect looking document. Then I can work on each on different APs at top speed and, with only a little effort later, get a document I am proud of.

16.4 LISA, MACINTOSH, LISA 2 AND THEIR ILK

The Managerial Work Station

Computer professionals, including specialists from the private and public sectors as well as higher education, have been trying to develop an ideal management work station since the late 1970s. Can they make an attractive computer input device so that managers will capitalize on the computer resources available now and on the horizon? There has always been considerable resistance by managers to go near a computer. What has discouraged them so?

The Theory

It seems as though the manager is more visually than mechanically oriented; in fact, many are mechanically inept. They do not like to type, nor will they

16.4 LISA, MACINTOSH, LISA 2 AND THEIR ILK

go near a typewriter, with few exceptions. Although managers are verbal, it is impossible to get the computer to comprehend human speech within the cost and size limitations of a desk top package at this time and probably through the next decade.

Can the computer work station take advantage of a conceptual and visual orientation to attract the manager to use them?

Method

The first approach used **icons,** visual constructs of items that appear in the office setting, to stand for data or EDs handled by the computer. The office abounds with documents. These are classified and put away for safe keeping. Documents about a particular topic are put into a labeled folder. The folder then goes into a drawer, part of a cabinet, one of many in the office. The manager needs a way to get to a document immediately; perhaps he or she is used to having an executive secretary find it. Maybe the computer can take the place of the secretary, make the computer system simulate the office by imposing a similar hierarchical structure.

Names are now supplemental, with visual symbols representing cabinets, drawers, folders and so forth. The manager choses among named icons, sketches of cabinets, drawers, folders.

The next principle is to move away from the keyboard. Furnish the manager with a mouse or pointing device to move a screen pointer to an icon; press the button on the mouse to make a choice without using the keyboard.

Another principle is to make the screen appear like the manager's work place. Show an IN and an OUT box and several "named" folders to work on. After documents are perused and no longer needed, they can be discarded in a wastebasket. Files and work areas are also represented by icons. The manager takes an action by moving a document icon to an area icon with the mouse. Thus one can select a document from a pile, read it and, use the mouse to *drag* it to a file to be stored or to the wastebasket to be destroyed.

Implementations

Early work lead to the development of a language for programming such a system called Smalltalk. It was designed to be used with large computers. Prototype systems were developed, but no commercial product.

Eventually Xerox marketed the Star work terminal, designed specifically for managers and discussed shortly. This terminal was never much of a success.

Apple espoused the idea of the manger's workplace and put a lot of money into incorporating it into the Lisa computer. Lisa did not prove to be an immediate success and another group at Apple started work on Macintosh. Although Lisa got a lot of attention and approval from many sources, it was too expensive. Macintosh does not have that problem and orders are flowing in. We examine Macintosh at the end of this section.

Fallacies

While the approach to the management work station is not without merit, there are several fallacies which I would like to point out.

First, consider the manager's aversion to keyboards. Is it the professional's clumsiness that keeps him or her away, or are there other reasons? One way to circumvent the keyboard is to use a different input device. In retrospect, we see the importance of psychological and social factors in overcoming resistance to the keyboard: create an urgent need. When spread sheets arrived on the scene, managers had no compunction about sitting at the keyboard to use them; they knew they could get work done in a fraction of the time compared with the old pencil and paper method.

The second fallacy concerns concepts. Man is the most adept of creatures in dealing with them. Again, if there is a need, one can deal easily with new terms and concepts.

The third fallacy concerns making a computer space appear like a work space for the manager to become immersed in. Managers are notorious for not being at their desks, especially when telephone calls come in. They are out there talking to employees and peers. When they are at their desks, its only for a few minutes at a time to get information or make phone calls. The manager has no time to create an environment before the information arrives. Top managers don't dial telephone numbers; somebody does it for them.

The Xerox Star

When Xerox came out with Star in the late 1970s, they called it a management work station. Instead, it was actually a very good word processor. The operator could see *exactly* what the output would look like. It had many different type faces from which to choose and you could mix faces and alter their size with the result showing right on the screen.

But there were several problems. First, it was not a *management* work station. No manager worth his salt would sit down at such a terminal, compose a document, choose typefaces and format it. This is too time consuming for a manager; someone would have to do it for him or her.

These features appeal to technical writers, so we might expect Star to sell to them like hotcakes. Not so! The price of the terminal with the capability described is about $16,000. This alone is not prohibitive, but what printer can produce the output as you see it on the screen? There was only one answer—a laser printer from Xerox selling for about $30,000. But wait a minute, we're not through yet; we have no storage medium at the station. We need a File Server and a Central Executive. Put it all together and you have something like $70,000 for a word processor. That's why the Star didn't sell well.

Lisa

Apple's product line, Apple II and III, seemed limited, for the most part, to home computer users since it had not cornered the spread sheet market via VisiCalc. In fact, other computers such as the IBM PC could run better spread sheets with better graphics and better presentations. Then how could Apple stay in the corporate world?

Some of the principles of Star seemed attractive. They might make a marketable product if Apple could

- produce a complete system at an affordable price;
- make the system self-contained with a small footprint to fit on a manager's desk;
- provide additional functions that a manager really needs;
- make it possible to switch from one program to another without delay;
- make parts of several documents available simultaneously on the screen and pass information between them.

The result, Lisa, came into the marketplace at the end of 1982, mostly meeting the requirements above, but it had a price tag of $10,000. It was a milestone; but milestones don't sell machines!

The Hardware

When design on Lisa began, the Motorola 68000 chip was available, a powerful, fast and inexpensive microprocessor with a large addressing space. But there was little software on the market for it. Memory had gotten cheap, so it was no problem to furnish one megabyte at a reasonable cost. This is enough for several programs to be resident; you could switch between them in no time at all.

Apple's experiments with bit map displays indicated their feasibility; this and large internal memory made possible high resolution monochrome graphics.

Considerable storage is required for large programs and data; Lisa has two 5¼ inch floppy disks each with a 860K of storage; there is a 5 megabyte hard disk, called Profile, which sits on top of the cabinet so as to maintain its small footprint.

Interaction is by means of the mouse, specially designed by Apple with a single button so as not to confuse the user.

Two optional printers are available: the dot matrix printer produces graphics and draft quality or text; the daisy wheel printer produces high quality text.

Software

Lisa's bundled software certainly makes an attractive system:

1. A desk top for manipulating documents by icons;
2. Many helpful utilities;
3. A spread sheet program, called LisaCalc;
4. A graphics program, LisaGraph, activated by data supplied by LisaCalc;
5. A drawing program, LisaDraw;
6. A project management program, LisaProject;
7. A word processor, LisaWrite;
8. A data base program, LisaList.

Pascal and COBOL compilers and the BASIC-Plus interpreter are optional.

Desktop

Lisa has not carried the desktop principle to the extreme proposed by Xerox, with a presentation exactly like the top of your desk. Folders are shown as in Figure 16.4.1, each labeled, with additional empty folders available. At the bottom of the screen, icons show tasks to chose from, many independent of existing documents. Figure 16.4.2 shows a typical Profile display as it appears on Mac.

Task selection for Lisa is unique and a valuable advance over the keyboard method. With most computers you choose a program and then a file for it to work on; for Lisa each electronic document has a particular kind of program associated. Therefore, selecting a document automatically calls up its AP.

The great power of the mouse is how it selects. As you move the mouse along the table, an arrow moves along the screen in the same direction. Bring it to a named icon for the document to process or a task to do and press the mouse button. The folder or activity is highlighted by reverse video to verify your choice. Press the button again and action starts. A menu for the program appears on the top line of the screen.

16.4 LISA, MACINTOSH, LISA 2 AND THEIR ILK 745

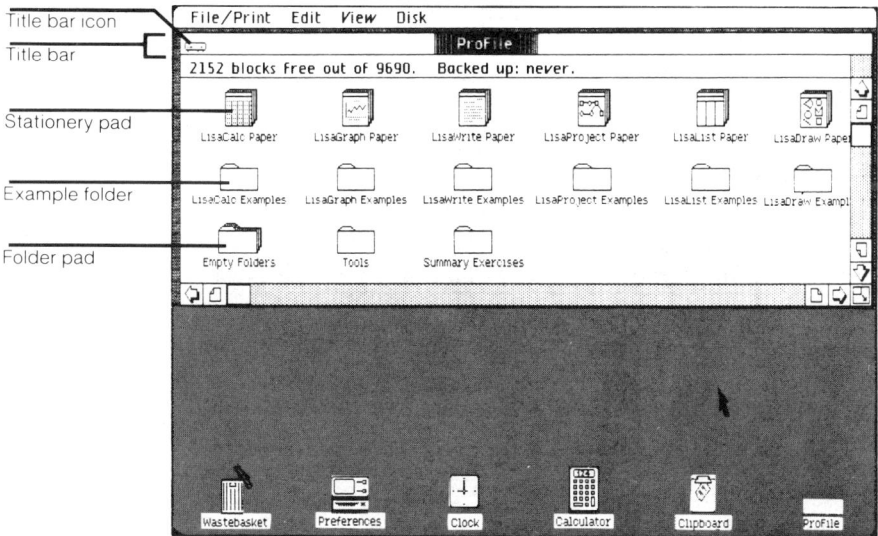

Figure 16.4.1. The Profile window shown diagramatically.

Figure 16.4.2. Photograph of Mac showing Profile window.

The Folder

Documents on the disk are organized into **folders.** When you start using the Profile, its contents appear on the screen as icons. The available folders display as in Figure 16.4.1. You choose a folder by pointing the mouse at it and clicking the button. The folder appears in the Profile window as a shadow, a much fainter icon as in Figure 16.4.3. The folder's contents then appear as another window superimposed upon the current window, as illustrated at the top of the figure. The window is the entity you work with; it is important to understand the function of every aspect of the window.

Around the active window in Figure 16.4.3 is a **frame** containing a **pane** where the content of the ED shows. (Note a different use of *frame* from that in Chapter 15 on Framework.) The top bar of the frame has an icon at the left indicating the type of folder; its name appears in the center of the bar. The title of the active frame is more intense to show that it is active. Bars at the top, right and bottom of the frame have icons to use to control actions taken on the EDs in the folder and are discussed shortly.

When you "open" a **folder,** a group of documents for selection, a number of labeled icons appear on the screen. An icon's shape indicates the kind of document it represents. For instance, the ED on the left, lower half of Figure 16.4.3 showing many wiggly lines conveys that it is text; the grid

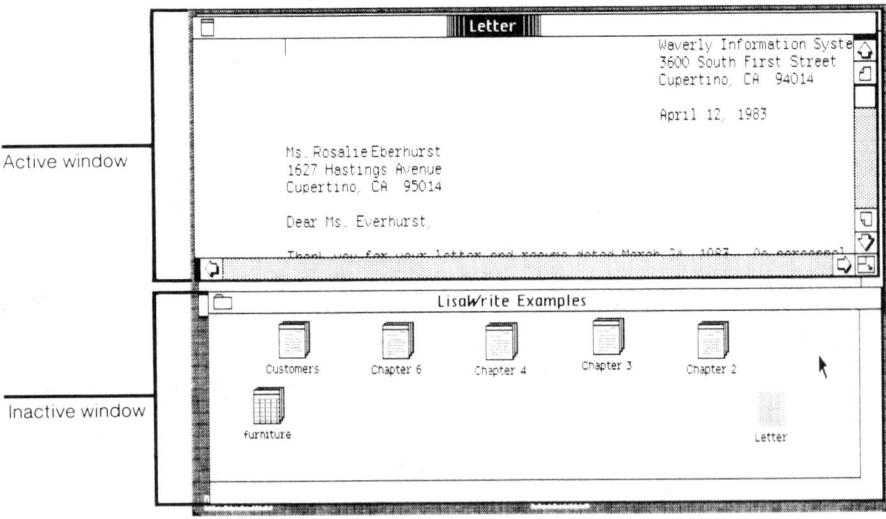

Figure 16.4.3. The active window (top) contains a text document called *Letter;* at the bottom are the contents of a folder called *LisaWrite Examples* which contains *Letter,* which, in turn, is active, hence shown in shadow.

on the rectangle at the left is for a spread sheet. Icons for graphs, drawings, project control and lists may be present. To activate a document, point with the mouse by moving the screen arrow to it and click. The icon then shows in reverse video to verify that it has been picked; another click opens the document and puts it in its own window. As a short cut, point and double click.

Positioning Commands

You position the window itself on the screen with the **title bar,** the upper horizontal bar of the frame. The window remains the same size as you move it. To move a folder or document, put the arrow *in* the title bar and hold the button down as you move the mouse; the entire window moves with the mouse. For example, in Figure 16.4.4, *Regional Sales* is the active document, shown with its title in **heavy print**. Put the arrow in the title bar, press the mouse button, move the mouse and the frame moves correspondingly. Release the button when the window is where you want it. You can have up to twenty windows on the screen. They may overlap and and cover one another partially or totally as in the figures. The active window is al-

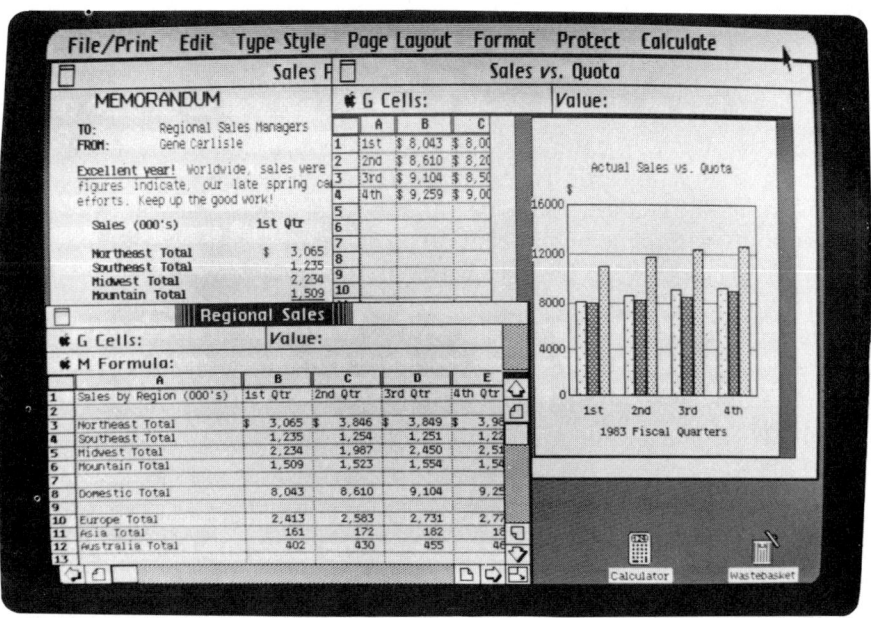

Figure 16.4.4. A Lisa 2 screen with the active document, *Regional Sales*.

ways on top. Bring a different window, showing in part, to the top of the stack by pointing to its title bar and clicking.

The icon in the lower right hand corner controls screen size. Put the arrow there, click the button and move the mouse: pulling the mouse diagonally to the right bottom makes the window larger; pushing it up left makes a narrower window; pulling straight down makes a longer window of the same width, and so forth.

Within the Pane

The left and bottom bar of a window frame have icons to position the ED within the pane of the window.

Three kinds of icons on the window frame are for positioning the ED in the pane:

- the arrow is for row or column scrolling—up, down, right, left;
- the notched rectangle is for screen scrolling (with some overlap);
- the box is for relative positioning within the document.

These are now explained.

Line scrolling for text, or incremental scrolling for other documents, is done with the large arrow. Put the indicator arrow in the arrow box, which points in the direction you want to move the document using the mouse. For each click of the mouse button, the document moves by one increment within the pane.

Screen scroll with the notched rectangle. The direction of the notch helps identify the direction of scroll; but the rectangle is also next to an arrow which points in the direction of scroll and helps to remind you. Move the mouse pointer to the icon and click; the ED scrolls one page in the desired direction for each click. Overlap between screens is provided as described for scrolling in Section 11.4.

The rectangle lets you position relatively within a document. Move the mouse pointer to it, click and hold it down. Now move the box along the window frame to an approximate position you want to view the document. When you release the button, that portion of the document should appear in the pane.

The Clipboard

There are a number of icons outside the windows at the bottom of the screen. Their function is clear from the icon shape and their label. A most interesting item is the clipboard seen at the bottom of Figure 16.4.1.

16.4 LISA, MACINTOSH, LISA 2 AND THEIR ILK 749

The **Clipboard** is used to transfer data from one window to another, to move it from one document to another. Work with one document using the appropriate program: Lisawrite for text, Lisadraw for pictures, and so forth. That program has a method for selecting a portion of the ED: a block of text; an object in your drawing; and so forth. Once selected, move the item to the Clipboard by grabbing it with the mouse pointer and dragging it there. Click the button and the clipboard is highlighted.

The Clipboard holds only *one* item at a time. You can transfer it from the Clipboard to another position in this or any other ED. If you move another item to the Clipboard, the current item there is destroyed.

But there is another alternative when you want to deal with multiple items. Simply move them to the **Scrapbook.** They are actually written on a disk file and can be sent via the mouse from the Scrapbook file to any other ED or another part of this ED.

Applications

All applications work approximately the same way. For Lisa you select a "pad of paper" of the proper kind: drawing paper for LisaDraw, writing paper for LisaWrite, etc. **Pads** are provided in the Profile window, Figure 16.4.1. This is how you tell Lisa which AP to use to create the new electronic document. Select a "sheet" from the Pad by clicking the mouse at it, which brings in the AP and starts it working. You can give the ED a title at any time, which then appears centered in the top window frame. Above the window frame appear classes of functions you can perform on your ED. This is illustrated in Figure 16.4.4 for the LisaCalc spread sheet program.

Select a class of commands by moving the mouse pointer to the applicable word and clicking. The command class name is highlighted. A panel of commands opens up like a window as you pull down the command word in the title bar with the mouse as in Figure 16.4.5; the panel displays commands for editing. Action is highlighted by reverse video. The figure shows **pasting,** moving a block, here an illustration created with MacDraw.

Select the desired format by moving the mouse pointer to the cell in the format menu and clicking. As you move the mouse up and down, the selection with the arrow in it on the menu is highlighted. When you click, that item is checked. Thus, where multiple items apply, you know the ones selected so far. The figure shows that you have selected a dollar sign presentation without commas.

You select active areas on the spread sheet in a natural manner. To select a cell, move the mouse pointer there and click. To select a column, move the cursor to its letter in the column stub; to select a row, move to its num-

Figure 16.4.5. The Lisa 2 computer.

ber in the row stub and click. If you click at the intersection of the row and column stub, you select global action. In all cases, a selected area is highlighted.

To alter an item in a cell, select the cell and type in its new content at the keyboard. Edit an item in a cell by first pointing to a cell and then to the character and clicking. Now any key you hit replaces the current position, which is highlighted.

Evaluation

The Lisa configuration is especially easy for the novice. With no experience with computers, you do not have to worry about hardware and software compatibility, programming and so forth. A tutorial, which relies heavily on the mouse and tactile visual feedback guides you through the system. If this is your first experience with a computer, it is easy to start with this concept. It takes retraining for those who have used APs on other machines.

Lisa 2

When Lisa first came out, its price, almost $10,000, frightened a lot of people away. Lisa's price was reduced to $8,000.

At the beginning of 1984, Apple's strategy was to unbundle everything: sell all the APs, software, hardware and printer separately. Lisa 1 is no longer for sale; Lisa 2/5 and Lisa 2/10 respectively have a 5 megabyte and 10 megabyte hard disk as well as a soft disk. Lisa 2/5 is functionally equivalent to the original Lisa, and, when everything is included, the cost is about the same. However, the larger hard disk is more serviceable, and the system operates more efficiently. Figure 14.6.5 shows Lisa 2.

Software

Very little software appeared for Lisa other than the packages originally delivered with it. Prospective vendors had little to work with, since its ToolKit—software for writing APs—had not been provided. The ToolKit was made available the end of 1983 along with another item called QuickPort. This is a Lisa program which sets up a window for a vendor's application program. With QuickPort you can cut and paste using the Clipboard or Scrapbook to any other Lisa AP.

Vendors have announced programs to become available throughout 1984, including dBase and a combination package from Sorcim, as well as some accounting packages.

Unfortunately, although the overall approach is similar, the operating systems for Lisa and Lisa 2 are different from that for the Macintosh, which we examine shortly. APs for Mac do not work directly on Lisa or Lisa 2. There is a Mac emulation disk which you can purchase for Lisa 2 to run any Mac AP in a Mac environment on Lisa 2. But it does not run those APs in the Lisa desk environment. Therefore there is no way to interchange data between a Mac AP and a Lisa AP, nor to run Lisa programs on a Mac.

Macintosh

The Macintosh (or simply **Mac** hereafter) was announced early in 1983 and finally released for sale in January 1984. It comes in a small cabinet with an optional carrying case to make it portable. It's 13½ inches high by 10 inches wide and 11 inches deep, a small footprint. The cabinet includes a 9 inch black-on-white bit mapped display screen, a single sided 400K Sony 3½ inch disk drive and two fixed circuit boards, one of which holds the

68000 processor, 128K, of RAM and 64K of ROM for the screen manager and operating system. There are a disk controller and I/O interfaces. The cabinet weighs 16 pounds and has a built-in handle at the top. By late 1984, the "Fat Mac" became available with 512K of memory, a reasonable figure; an expansion kit for existing Mac's was also released.

The screen display area is 7 by 5 inches with a resolution of 512 by 342 pixels, or about 72 pixels per inch. With MacWrite, the screen displays a 6 inch line within the pane. Scroll bars in the surrounding frame are for moving within a document.

The soft disk drives for Mac and Lisa 2 are the same Sony unit, holding 400K. Only one drive is provided with Mac, which makes operating procedures difficult. A second soft drive, available for about $500, is housed in a separate box, which detracts from simplicity and compactness. Hard disk external drives are also available.

The keyboard is essentially the same as for Lisa, except that the numeric keypad is omitted (obtainable as a separate option). There are no expansion slots in Mac. Several cabinet jacks, labeled with icons, connect to the mouse, the printer, a modem, an external disk drive and headphones.

Imagewriter is a reasonably conventional matrix printer with resolution of 80 dots per inch, capable of good graphics and fair text.

Operating

Mac is a paired down and cored Apple Lisa which works in approximately the same manner but with fewer resources. When you start the system, it takes about 24 seconds to read in the disk and load the desktop display. A pleasant humming sound and a clock appearing on the screen tells you that something is happening if you only wait.

Mac provides windows that work essentially as decribed for Lisa and illustrated previously in this section. Mac's windows are smaller but work the same as with Lisa. You can pile several on top of each other and move any to the top of the pile. You can even show more than one window at once. But the screen is so small; you can't really see what's happening with two windows showing.

There is no question that the combination of mouse and window makes it easy for the totally inexperienced person to start using Mac.

Software

Mac comes with only two programs: MacWrite and MacPaint. There is a long list of vendors who are preparing software for Mac.

MacWrite is the word processor for Mac. we find

- it is quite easy to use;
- it shows the text extremely well, distinguishing among type sizes and showing emphasis;
- it reacts very fast, indeed faster than MicroSoft Word;
- pagination functions are unsatisfactory for most applications;
- page sizes are restricted;
- only ten pages of text can be accommodated;
- no 10 point type faces are provided.

MacWrite is satisfactory for users who have an occasional call for word processing, but are not use-intensive.

MacPaint, the drawing program, is a lot of fun to play with. The printer does a fine job of producing hard copy. You can combine text, graphics and pattern fill into a neat presentation. A version of Multiplan released for Mac is easy to use and provides all the features of the original AP.

Evaluation

There are still relatively few programs available as of late 1984. The Mac combined with the Imagewriter can produce documents with both text and graphics and a wide variety of type faces, sizes, and styles, but has a weak word processor. The screen is small and requires constant scrolling when using spread sheets. It takes 20 seconds or so to both close and open an AP. This means a minimum 40 second wait to terminate one AP and start another, unsatisfactory for the office.

Lay people who first use the Mac are very enthusiastic about how simple it is and how quickly they grasp its principles. It is certainly much easier to use for the first time user than the IBM PC or a clone. The screen provides better resolution.

The biggest initial problem was the limitation in external storage and memory, now largely solved by the availability of a 512K Mac, and a second soft or hard drive; early systems can be upgraded as well. The fact that there are two different operating systems for Mac and Lisa doesn't help matters, however.

16.5 MULTIUSER SYSTEMS

Introduction

Most micros and PCs out there are single user systems: only one person at a time. The only way to share information is by passing disks between users or by sending data and programs by modem over telephone lines to another PC using a telecommunications program.

Need

Setting up a spread sheet or typing a document is a solitary activity; single user operation is appropriate and satisfactory. The need for multiuser operation arises only in specific situations:

A. multiple terminals, where users are doing jobs which require very little computer capacity and where the cost of the system is of primary importance;
B. a computerized business system, where several users must share a data base or group of files.

Examples of (A) are found in the school setting: students developing programs, learning to do word processing, studying about micros or doing assignments aided by the computer. An example of (B) is a word processing shop, where operators type letters and documents which require little computer attention. Documents are kept on hard disk and the printer is shared serially.

Alternatives

A multiuser system can reduce overall system cost while increasing efficiency. There seem to be three alternatives. The first (multitasking) is actually only an elaborate version of the single user system, examined here to put the alternatives in perspective. They are

1. **Multitasking** does several jobs at the same time for one user.
2. **Multiprogramming** lets several users each run a program on one computer, accessing it by many terminals.
3. **Multiprocessing** provides the same facilities as (2), with the advantage that each user has an independent slave not affected by other users.

These are now examined.

Multitasking

Description

Multitasking lets one user do several tasks, run several programs at the same time: the programs run **concurrently.** An advantage derives from this when one of the programs is not interactive (for example, printing or sorting) and

16.5 MULTIUSER SYSTEMS

runs without operator intervention, except for emergencies. Printing can go on without help from the operator, unless paper, ribbon or some mechanical part on the printer needs service. Similarly, sorting is usually disk-limited but needs no operator attention. Information is sent back and forth between memory and the disk until it is in order.

The other task is often interactive, such as data entry or word processing. There are many pauses while the operator thinks or keys data. Pause time becomes available for the first task, which then keeps the computer busy until the user begins to enter data or makes a request of the interactive program.

Figure 16.5.1 is a block diagram of the multitasking OS **(MTOS)** components. Two application programs are shown resident in memory. The MTOS takes charge. It notes when the interactive program becomes free and uses this time for the **background** (noninteractive) program. Conversely, when the interactive program has input, MTOS takes control away from the background program so that the operator gets immediate response.

The MTOS must respond to emergency situations which an AP senses. If a disk runs out of space or the ribbon in a printer expires, the background AP cannot continue. The operator must be informed. This means ringing a bell and probably putting a message on the screen to let the operator know what has happened.

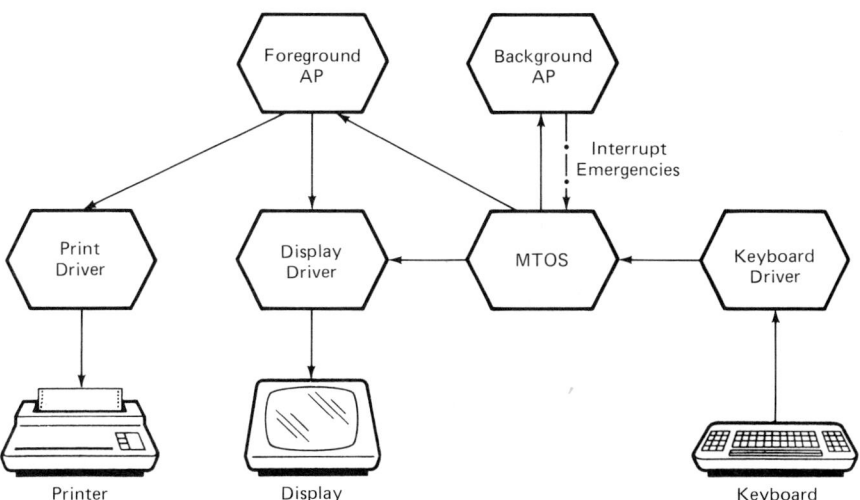

Figure 16.5.1. Multitasking block diagram.

Requirements

Multitasking requires a specially designed operating system, considerable memory and when running in this mode, at least two APs. One AP must be relocatable because two APs cannot run at the same fixed position in the transient area. One nonrelocatable program file has the extension COM and runs at the bottom of the transient area. However, the second and additional APs must be relocatable, with the extension EXE. The MTOS intercepts device commands which signal a service request for the AP. This causes AP2 to relinquish control when AP1 needs the computer.

Examples

Concurrent CP/M, a version of CP/M, works on the 8086, 8088, 80186 and 80286 processors and provides multitasking. A forthcoming version of MS DOS may also provide multitasking.

Pros and Cons

While multitasking permits two programs to run concurrently, it doesn't seem to be worth the time and trouble. It is like moving from 12 inch black and white TV to a 19 inch black and white TV set. Why not go all the way?

Multiprogramming

Multiprogramming truly provides multiuser access with an multiprogramming operating system **(MPOS)**.

Hardware

Most microcomputer families can support an MPOS. Each user must have specific hardware for entry and display; the system has as many terminals as there are users to be supported. Further, each terminal needs a hardware interface. For the bus computer, one or more multiport PC interface boards provides interfacing for one to four (sometimes eight) users, connecting by cable to terminals.

Drivers

Every device in the system needs a driver; each terminal has a pair of drivers, one for the keyboard and one for the screen.

16.5 MULTIUSER SYSTEMS

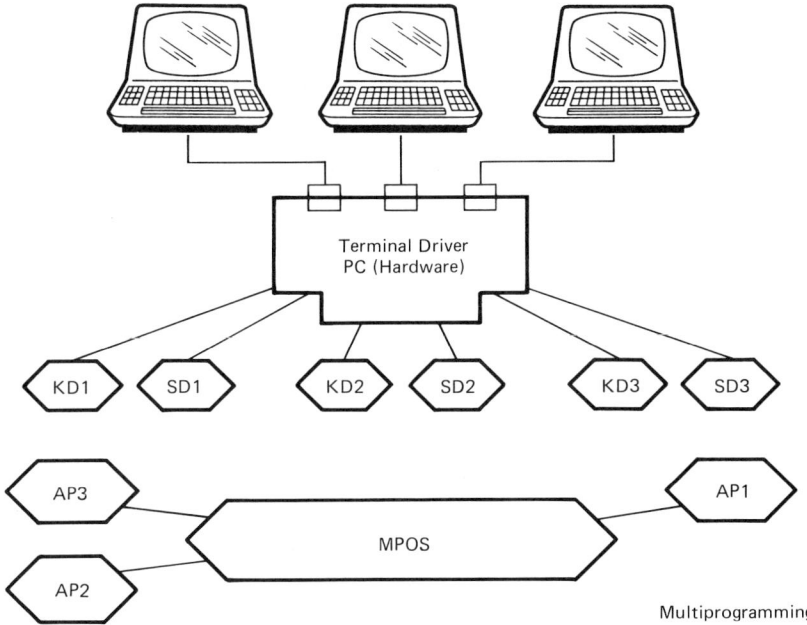

Figure 16.5.2. Multiprogramming block diagram.

Spooling

Programs generally produce output. The MPOS file manager handles the disk files, necessitating only one disk driver for all users. One large hard disk accommodates many users.

When several programs produce output simultaneously, obviously they cannot all run the printer. Output would get garbled. **Spooling** redirects a program's print output to a temporary disk file. A record is kept of this by a control block placed in a **spool queue,** a list of jobs waiting to get output printed. A separate **despooling task** takes a temporary disk print file for a terminated AP and directs it to the printer to produce hard copy. Thus several programs share important resources which include the hard disk and printer.

Operation

A user goes to an available terminal and logs-on. This causes an interrupt, intercepted by the MPOS. Most systems have a protection scheme enforced by a **log-on procedure.** A message is sent to the terminal before it is usable, asking the operator to enter a password which is checked against a file of valid passwords. If the entered password is improper, the user is denied the facility. Protection is not only provided for the overall facility but also for the use of certain programs and files. Such precautions are necessary when users of different categories operate a shared facility.

After the user has been awarded the terminal, entering a command brings up a program. It seems as though the computer belongs only to the user. The only difference might be a degradation in response time.

Behind The Scenes

There is only one computer in the multiprogramming system. It supports the MPOS, many APs, device drivers and a spooling routine. All these items share the computer as well as the other hardware facilities. Considerable memory must be available to hold all the APs, drivers and the MPOS. Otherwise, considerable time would be wasted getting a disk copy of a program every time it is needed.

Sharing the computer is made possible by the hardware interrupt and a hierarchy of priorities. The latter determines which competing program actually is awarded the computer. Interrupts notify the MPOS which APs need the computer at any given moment.

Requirements

Here are some of the requirements for an MPOS:

- tailored to the number of users and the hardware;
- a large amount of memory to support all competing routines;
- a terminal and a set of drivers for *each* possible user;
- a priority and software scheme as well as a competent executive to switch between competing requestors.

Pros and Cons

A multiprogramming system certainly makes better use of the computer resource. When the number of users is small—two, three or four—the system runs fairly efficiently. For more than four users, response degrades so much that users become dissatisfied and may not tolerate the delay. The alternative, multiprocessing, discussed next, costs a little more but provides more effective service.

Examples

The oldest system, produced by Digital Research, called MP/M, for MultiProgramming Microcomputer OS, is quite reliable. Others produced by Ithaca Computer Systems, CompuPro and Morrow Designs are variations on this theme, having improvements that make them somewhat more efficient. There is no multiprogramming for the IBM PC or its clones except a system provided by NorthStar which does not include compatible IBM graphics.

The Multiprocessing System

Description

Figure 16.5.3 shows the components of a typical multiprocessor multiuser microcomputer system. The double line down the center is the bus. Each

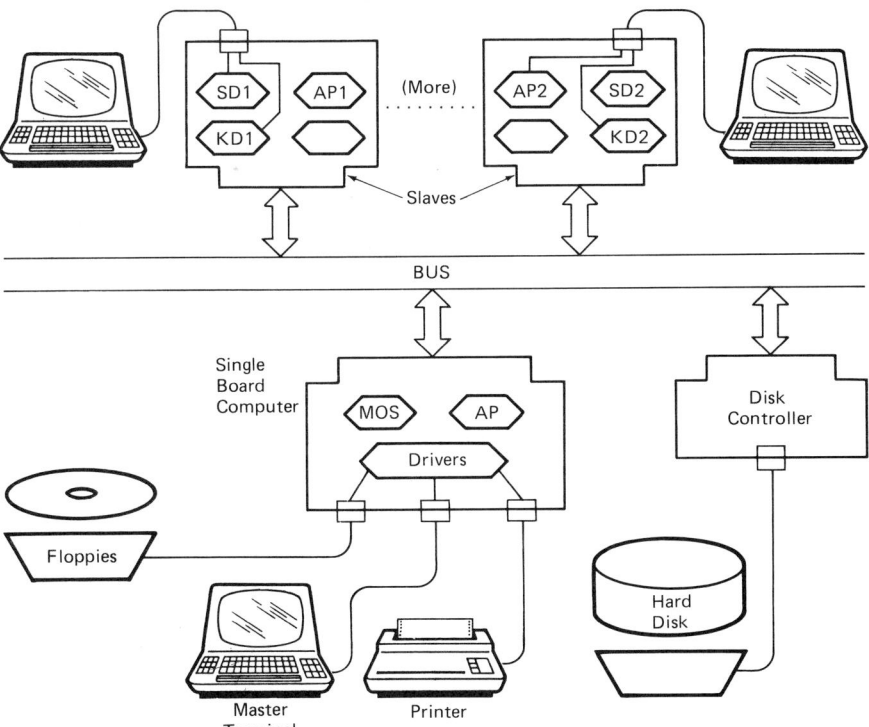

Figure 16.5.3. Multiprocessing block diagram.

major hardware component is shown as a PC card. Each user has a slave PC (see Chapter 6) which plugs into the bus. It contains a microprocessor and a complete memory, 64K or 128K and circuitry to drive a terminal. There is adequate room in slave memory for a complete application program and a slave operating system. Early in 1984, PC boards came on the market with *two* complete slave computers and connectors for two separate terminals.

The master board in the center of the figure also plugs into the bus and contains a complete computer and hardware drivers for a terminal, printer and disk drives. This **master PC board** controls all resources not *directly* available from a user's slave AP.

Operation

Let us examine the operation of the multiuser system using the Turbodos operating system **(TOS)** of Software 2000 as the example. I have such a system with a master and two slaves. The system disk contains both CP/M and Turbodos. I bring up CP/M and ask the Turbodos loader to bring in TOS, a command file on the system disk. TOS is put in memory on the master board. When loaded, it takes over and sends copies of the slave operating system (SOS) to memories of all the slaves. The SOS is also a file on the system disk, accessible to the TOS. Once slaves have their SOSs loaded, they become available to users.

The user terminal presents a sign-on message and a prompt like that used by CP/M (programs which work under CP/M also work with Turbodos). The user signs on by giving a password (if you include this protection measure).

The operator requests an AP and files as with CP/M. However no disk is directly accessible to the user. The request is sent to the TOS which arranges for the transfer.

It may seem time comsuming that information coming from the disk has to be arranged for by the master. The saving grace is that the slave takes over total use of the bus. With a DMA controller, information from (or to) the disk goes directly onto the bus for the slave without intervention by the master. There is no degradation in loading a program into a slave with TOS as compared with a CP/M system.

Requirements

The hardware requirements are a terminal and one (or at least a half) PC board which includes interfacing hardware for the terminal for each user and one master PC board for the system. A multicomputer operating system, such as Turbodos, controls the entire operation. Expense for the hardware is compensated for by constantly dropping costs. A single user slave board may cost only $700 including memory and interfacing.

Spooling

As with any multiuser system, users cannot *simultaneously* share the printer. Turbodos has spooling: as an AP prepares print output, it is diverted to a temporary spool file. A despooler prints spool files, a queue of which is established by TOS.

Only closed spool files are noted on the waiting list. Printing is by FIFO from this list. When done, the spool file is automatically deleted.

In addition, with Turbodos any one user can be locally attached to the printer so that output is printed directly from the AP. Other users' output go to a spool file and must await completion of the locally attached user. Thereafter, their output is printed by FIFO.

Role of the Master

The master computer runs the master operating system (TOS) which supervises access to resources for the SOS and their APs. Other portions of memory are buffers to hold information as it is spooled to temporary files or to keep track of resource allocation.

Still, there may be enough space in master memory to run a small program such as a print formatter. The executive functions of the master take precedence and requests from slaves interrupt the master's AP for priority attention. If the master runs APs, it needs a console.

A slave can issue a command to take control of a master and set a program running there. However, the slave terminal must remain attached to the master as long as that AP runs, to report errors, request data or recover input. Hence the best solution is to have one terminal for each user and one more for the master.

Pros and Cons

The multiprocessor system is by far the fastest multiuser configuration obtainable. The slave is completely autonomous until it needs a system resource. It passes requests to the master and transmission occurs directly from or to the desired resource.

For some idea of efficiency, consider an application in which an operator does considerable word processing of large documents. After the operator enters changes to a document, its author would like to see a printout, make corrections on it and return it to the operator, now working on another document. A multitasking system takes several minutes to format the document to a spool file; this file may then be printed with the despooler while work proceeds on the second document, perhaps more slowly. This is the only recourse in a multitasking system. The operating system must share time with both the despooler and the application program, both of which are slowed down.

With Turbodos, as soon as the first document is edited, work starts on the second. Another user brings up another terminal and start the print formatter AP in local mode to print out the first document directly. Both activities require little attention of TOS. Even when both files are on the same diskette, there is no degradation in either printing or word processing speed. It's like having two computers. In fact, *that is the case*—the slave augmented by its master.

16.6 GRAPHIC SYSTEM

Purpose

A high resolution graphics system answers all your drawing needs: illustrations for manuscripts and reports, slides for presentations and mechanical drawings, properly dimensioned for all kinds of technical purposes. While a high resolution color graphics capability increases the cost of the system, perhaps doubling it, this important function is well worth it. And technology is bringing down the price of such equipment tremendously.

Components

High resolution color graphics requires an appropriate screen capable of displaying a minimum of 512 lines; 1200 lines is feasible these days. A hardware unit which goes between the host computer and the display should be capable of generating a number of graphic primitives and contain a large memory array for holding an image. Often the screen, primitive generating hardware and image memory is incorporated in a single terminal costing anywhere from $5,000 to $30,000. The specific system described here includes the Vectrix 384A hardware unit which attaches by cables to the host computer and to the Electrochrome display.

I/O

Input and output hardware are also required. A digitizing pad with a mouse, stylus or a light pen lets you interact with the image. Color output provided by a dot matrix printer is usually satisfactory for a few primary colors, but is slow. A pen plotter is excellent for black and white; a camera produces excellent slides. Satisfactory slides can be made by taking pictures of the screen in the dark. But a better arrangement, if you can afford $2,500 or so, is a combination unit, described in Chapter 13, which includes a small camera and its own CRT, coupled to the main color display. When the screen displays a satisfactory image, manually trip the shutter.

Both the tablet and the plotter have to *interface* with the computer. Both hardware and software are required to make input and output devices operable. Let us only consider the input problems; output has much the same requirements.

Tablet

We confine our attention to the digitizing tablet. It has a mouse, cursor or stylus which reports its position to the hardware and software. Most tablets, such as my Houston Instruments HiPad digitizer, are capable of operating in several modes, such as

- **point mode,** in which only a single datum is transmitted when the button is pushed;
- **stream mode,** in which data are constantly transmitted;
- **switch stream mode,** in which data are transmitted in stream mode while the button is pressed by not when the button is released.

Each datum consists of a number of bytes comprised of several fields:

- a **flag** indicates which button is pressed.
- X and Y coordinates give the cursor position on the tablet;
- terminal characters indicate that transmission is complete.

Interface Board

The interface board has several functions. As the name implies, it goes between the device and the processor. Its functions consist mainly of timing, accumulation of information and shaping and interchange of signals with the computer.

Each device needs a port for entry or egress of data passing between the computer and the device. An additional PC card, which takes up a slot provides one or more ports and associated circuitry for each. Many Z80, CP/M computers and the IBM PC and XT have additional slots for just such a purpose. It is essential to determine whether a serial or parallel port is necessary for hardware and software support.

Of paramount importance is the lack of complete standards, even where a standard *seems* to exist, such as the RS-232C cable standard for connecting a device to the computer: It is totally inadequate. The RS-232C standard simply describes the number of pins on the connectors found at the back of the computer and on the cable which mates devices to the computer. It does not make precise signal assignments to wires nor does it give voltage requirements for signals. Device vendors set up their own specifications, including number of wires used, which wires are used for what signals and what voltages are expected. Even signal timing is set in different ways. The byte from the device may consist of from 8 to 11 bits and have odd, even or no parity.

Once a datum is processed by the interface board, it produces a standard byte which is applied to the bus. But there is still a weak link in communication between the computer and the interface board: this is the lack of standardization for status and command signals which determine when a datum is available and what the interface board should do next.

Software

The graphics system *can* be activated by a BASIC, PL/I or Pascal program which you design yourself. This is hardly the way that most users would go. Here are two programs providing ready-made facilities:

1. AutoCAD, from Autodesk, Inc., lets you design all kinds of mechanical drawings and straight line illustrations.
2. PAINT, from Vectrix, helps you draw pictures in color.

The first is available for most types of computers. The second is available only for the IBM PC at this writing, but by the time this book is in print, it should also be availabe for CP/M.

AutoCAD

The AutoCAD system allows you to make professional drawings using a tablet and stylus, with output via a pen plotter. The plotter, a Houston HiPlot in this case, not only draws lines but also creates text as required, for instance, to dimension and label various types of graphs, and organizational and flow charts. The block diagram of a typical AutoCAD system appears as Figure 16.6.1. The figure itself was constructed and drawn by the AutoCAD system; another example is Figure 5.1.1.

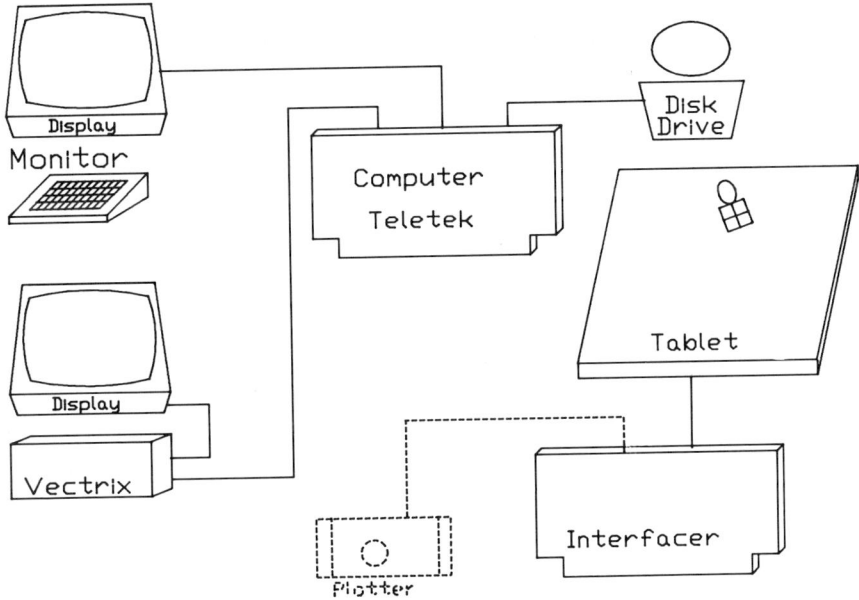

Figure 16.6.1. Block diagram of a complete high resolution creative graphic system, itself created on S-100 computer using the Vectrix graphics display, the Houston HiPad digitizer and Plotter and the AutoCAD software.

In principle, AutoCAD works a little like LisaDraw or MacPaint. Use the tablet and sketch on it with the mouse. If you create a grid, you move points to grid points. In orthogonal mode, lines you draw are made parallel to X and Y screen axes. Smooth shapes can be created, copied; they look as if drawn by a draftsperson. You can zoom in and out, enlarging details for easier working, then reducing them again. All the functions described in Chapter 13 for monochrome mode also apply here.

When used with the Vectrix Color Display color coding helps you create multiple layer drawings, such as for printed circuit board layout and performs various other helpful functions for you.

PAINT

PAINT, currently available for the IBM PC and available perhaps in the near future for CP/M-80 machines, provides many of the capabilities discussed in Chapter 13. With the tablet, you can draw freehand and fill in closed objects with color. You can do rubber banding, create objects, move them and zoom in and out. You choose a palette of 512 colors from 16 million. You can alter the qualities of these colors on the palette dynamically to meet your needs. Many different kinds of "brushes" are available: circular, chiseled and so forth. There is also an air brush facility which lets you shade in areas.

16.7 THE SYSTEM HOUSE

What Is It?

A **system house** supplies a complete system according to your needs and with full support:

- the computer hardware, including all peripheral devices;
- an operating system mated to the hardware, with drivers tailored to the devices supplied;
- all application programs for your installation, altered to suit your needs and matching the operating system and computer;
- services to obtain the items necessary, install them, get them going and keep them going.

Particularly important are the services provided by the system house to supplement the products you purchase. Services can be extensive or limited. Let us see what they might be.

Services

The number of services, their range and extent, depends on the particular system house and your requirements. The list below applies to the largest and most competent of them:

1. Review the business operation to determine what aspects can be automated by computer. During this phase the system house works closely with management. They make a **charter,** a plan which indicates which areas of the operation they examine and which are excluded. However, this charter is constantly under review and you can expand or contract its scope.
2. The second phase determines the general types of programs to be installed.
3. The third phase selects compatible APs which fulfill system objectives. Some might require tailoring to conform with accounting procedures. Programs matching your business methods not found as off-the-shelf packages might better be created by programming them in a suitable language.

4. Once programs have been selected, this phase determines the hardware, including all micros required for a multicomputer system, the peripheral devices and additional PC cards.
5. Off-the-shelf APs are purchased and installed.
6. Special programs are designed and debugged.
7. The programs are put into the system environment and checked out there.
8. Operators and users are trained.
9. A maintenance procedure is derived for periodic checkouts and preventive maintenance to keep system downtime low.
10. A system upgrade procedure is established so that system needs can be reviewed periodically and new equipment and programs acquired as necessary.

System House Alternatives

There is a wide range of organizations that perform system house activities. At the low end is the one-person "garage operation," so-called since the person operates from a dwelling, basement or garage. At the high end, the accounting houses are now into system activities. They include the "Big 8" firms such as Arthur Andersen and Peat Marwick.

It always surprises small businesses that the cost of services and the needs review may be greater than the combined cost of equipment and software. However, consider that many small to medium sized businesses have faced bankruptcy because of poor decisions about computer acquisition. Instead of employing an independent consultant to determine their computing needs, including hardware and software, they took the advice of manufacturers' representatives. They felt confident because they were protected by contracts which guaranteed that the equipment and software would perform according to written specifications. When their needs were *not* met satisfactorily, their accounting procedures were stymied because of the ineffectiveness of the computer system. After the manufacturers' failure to remedy such problems, these users sought redress through litigation, only to find that court battles cost considerable money and time; during that time, business continued to go downhill. All major mini and mainframe companies have been involved in litigation of this nature.

Micros

You don't see the manufacturers of micros and PCs involved in such suits because they do not install systems and rarely manufacture software. Micro software is so inexpensive (less than ($1,000) it doesn't pay to make a fuss about it.

A properly working small business computer system is really a worthwhile investment. It can save thousands of dollars and provide sources of information which the company never had before. However, small business managers persist in seeing the total cost as the hardware and software but not the installation. This is a mistake! Considerable labor is required to design and install a good system. Part of it may be done by the managers themselves, but rarely do they have the competence or the time to acquire it. Therefore, the additional cost for "know-how" must be invested to guarantee that system design includes these badly needed services.

The Operation

System houses are well aware of the attitude of the small business. They want to reduce the apparent labor charges and know that you are usually willing to spend a little more for equipment. A system house is sometimes called an **original equipment manufacturer,** or **OEM.** Hardware and software vendors furnish equipment and supplies directly to the OEM and give it a quantity discount, anywhere from 20% to 40% of list price. The OEM generally charges list price. The small additional profit is included in *its* estimate for the services it supplies.

As described in other parts of this book, you can buy equipment and software through mail order distributors, sometimes below OEM cost. That is because the mail order houses make carload purchases at a larger discount than OEMs and work on a very small markup, since all they do is repackage and ship the products. Your mail purchase may be guaranteed by the original manufacturer but not the seller. If you need service, you must seek it directly from the manufacturer, not the distributor. Purchases from the system house are usually backed by their service group; your complaints are remedied directly by the OEM. This is an important factor to consider.

Selection

A list of resources for finding system houses is provided in Appendix I. Locating OEMs is not difficult; evaluating them is the chore. A one person operation may give you a low price which may work out satisfactorily if your needs are modest. The top-of-the-line accounting firm is all but unaffordable, except for the largest small business operation, for whom it is an absolute necessity.

Once you have found one or more OEMs, it is up to you to exercise the care necessary for purchasing any kind of service or product. Without exception, legal instruments should be in writing and supervised by a good lawyer. We must agree with the late film mogul Samuel Goldwyn that "Verbal promises are not worth the paper they are written on." The enforceability of an instrument should also be determined; Dun and Bradstreet is good for checking firms with whom you do business. The point is, remember that a legal instrument, though a necessity, is only of use during litigation and you want to steer clear of that recourse.

APPENDICES

A. Abbreviations
B. Glossary
C. BASIC Commands by Type
D. BASICA Commands and Their Meaning
E. Word Processing Packages
F. DBase Commands and Their Action
G. Spread Sheet Characteristics
H. Bibliography
I. Resources

Appendix A
Abbreviations

A/D—analog to digital.
AL—assembly language.
ALU—arithmetic and logic unit.
APA—all points addressable.
AP—application program.
AS—actual spread sheet.
ASCII—American Standard Code for Information Interchange.
BDOS—basic disk operating system.
BIOS—basic input output system.
BISYNC—bisychronous.
BSC—bisychronous.
CAP—current access position.
CC—current color.
CCP—console command program.
CFA—cash flow analysis.
COM—command; extension for ML program file.
CP—color packet.
CP/M—Control Program for Micros.
CPU—central processing unit.
CRC—cyclic redundancy check.
CRT—cathode ray tube.
D/A—digital to analog.
DAA—data access arrangement.
DB—data base.
DBMS—data base management system.
DD—double density.
DIP—dual online package.
DS—display spread sheet.
ECDIC—Extended Binary Coded Decimal Interchange Code.
ED—electronic document.
EOF—end of file.
ETS—electronic time sheet.
FCB—file control block.
FD—file directory.
FM—File Manager.
Hz—hertz.
HLL—high level language.
I/O—input-output.
IR—investment return.
KB—keyboard.
KB—kilobyte.
LAN—local area network.
LCD—liquid crystal display.
LED—light emitting diode.
LSI—large scale integration.
MB—megabyte.
MHz—megahertz.
ML—machine language.
MOS—master operating system.
MPOS—multiprogramming operating system.
ms—microsecond.
ms—millisecond.
MS-DOS—Microsoft Disk Operating System.
MTOS—multitasking operating system.
ns—nanosecond.
OE—operating environment.
OEM—original equipment manufacturer.
OS—operating system.

PC—personal computer.
PC—printed circuit.
PC-DOS—PC disk operating system for IBM PC.
POL—procedure oriented language.
RAM—random access memory.
RGB—red, green, blue.
ROM—read-only memory.
SDLC—synchronous data link control.
SOS—slave operating system.
SS—spread sheet.
TOS—Turbodos operating system.
TPA—transient program area.
UART—universal asynchronous receiver/transmitter.
USART—universal synchronous/asynchronous receiver/transmitter
VDP—video display terminal.
VLSI—very large scale integration.
VS—virtual spread sheet.
WP—word processing or word processor.
WYSIWYG—what you see is what you get.

Appendix B
Glossary*

absolute number—The value part (without sign) of a signed number.
access time—Time required to get to a datum, either in memory or external storage
acoustic coupler—A device for coupling a computer to your telephone. Place the telephone headset in the cradle. The computer produces sounds gathered by the telephone microphone and receives digitized sounds from the telephone.
address—A symbol which designates a particular cell in memory, usually a decimal or hexadecimal number, but sometimes a symbol.
address, effective—Actual memory address accessed for a datum or instruction.
address, relative—The address of a datum or record relative to the beginning of a file.
addressability—The maximum amount of memory which the CPU instruction set can access.
adjustment—{SS} When a formula is copied from a cell or group of cells to a range of cells and cells named in the formula use relative or mixed referencing, the formula is rewritten in each cell, copying absolute row and or column addresses but altering relative addresses where appropriate. Done only in an SS where mixed mode references are possible.
algorithm—A sequence of actions performed either in hardware or in a program.
all points addressable—Another term for *graphics mode*.
alpha lock—See *lock, alpha*.
alphabet, computer—A set of symbols, one for each upper and lower case letter of the language alphabet, the numerals, punctuation marks and special symbols, as well as a number of nonprinting, special purpose symbols used in the computer for communication.

---

*The letter(s) in braces after a term to be defined in the Glossary indicates its area of application. These letters are used:

    H   —hardware.
    S   —software.
    GR —graphics.
    SS —spread sheets.
    WD—word processing.

alphanumeric(s)—All the letters, numbers and special printing symbols of the computer alphabet.

analog to digital (A/D)—See *converter.*

anchor—{SS} Cell in a range which is constant; you alter the range visually by moving the opposite end, the *free point.* For some SSs (Multiplan), the anchor remains fixed as you define a range. For others (Lotus), the anchor may be altered to redefine a range.

antialiasing—{GR} A process to cure the jaggies and make a straight line appear straight.

append—To add records to the end of a file.

application program (AP)—See *program, application.*

archive—The medium and the process for backing up volumes.

arithmetic and logic unit (ALU)—{H} See *processor.*

arm—Bar carrying one or more recording heads which moves horizontally along or above the disk surface(s) to position to one of many cylinders.

array—Set of values or variables arranged in a line, table or multidimensional rectangular configuration.

American Standard Code for Information Interchange (ASCII)—A code set. The most popular for micros is the 7 bit code set, ASCII-7.

assembler—Translator to convert from assembly to machine language.

assembly language (AL)—See *language, assembly.*

assembly, automatic—{WP} Bringing together a set of subdocuments to form a complete document.

asynchronous transmission—Data transmission does not depend on timing generated in the equipment; each byte transmitted begins and ends with timing bits. Also see *synchronous recording.*

attribute—Characteristic of an *individual,* which see.

attribute, value—The value of a given attribute for a particular individual, an item's cost, a client's balance and so forth.

attribute code—For the IBM PC and XT monochrome display printer adapter card, a byte which indicates how a character should display: reverse video, flashing and so forth.

attribute name—The name for an attribute of an individual such as height, balance, cost, etc.

autoboot—The process by which the OS can be altered to contain the name of a command file on the system disk so that, when you boot the system, this file is automatically found and the program begins to execute.

automatic assembly—{WP} See assembly, automatic.

backup, selective—Copying from a medium, such as a disk, only those files which have changed during the current operating period.

backup, total—Totally copying a volume to the backup medium.

background program—For multitasking or multiprogramming, a program which gets control only when there is no work for other programs.

backspace correction—{WP} Making a correction in text just typed by pressing rub or delete to backspace over incorrect characters.

backup—A second copy of a file preserved, preferably on a separate disk.

bank—A group of memory cells, usually 64K bytes.

bank number—A number by which a bank of memory is identified.

bank switching—Method for making available larger amounts of memory to a CPU which has memory addressability restrictions. Thus the Z80 computer, which as an 8 bit processor normally addresses a maximum of 64K RAM, can have available 128K or more of RAM by providing several banks of 64K and using bank switching.

BASIC—A POL which is simple, easy to learn and use and is popular for programming micros.

batch—A group of programs to be run successively in a particular order.

baud—Another name for bits per second.

belt—See *chain*.

bidirectional—Capable of conveying data in either direction, such as for reading or writing and for sending or receiving.

Binary Synchronous Communication Protocol (BSC or BISYNC)—A communication protocol in common use for micros.

birth—Adding a record to a file for a new individual entering the population.

bit—An electric signal, piece of data or number having exactly two states: on or off, 1 or 0, yes or no.

bit map—Table to control free space on a disk providing one bit for each track, block or other allocatable unit. A bit is set to 1 if the unit of space is allocated and to 0 if free.

bit plane—{GR} Part of image memory which stores one bit per pixel.

bit plane array—{GR} A color image memory using multiple bit planes, where one bit from each plane comprises the color packet.

blank—A character which, if writing with black on white, is entirely white. {SS} The SS command, *blank,* empties cells, columns, rows or blocks as requested.

blanking—Characters are written on the display along a line from left to right. When the beam returns from the right hand side of the screen to the left (retrace) it should produce no spots. *Blanking* turns off the beam during this period.

block—(1) Amount of information read from an input device, or written to an output device with a single computer command. For the disk, a block and a sector are the same size. Blocks are numbered consecutively, but the sectors which contain them may be interleaved on the disk because of skewing. (2) {WP} A piece of text that you define which can be manipulated by several action choices available in the WP. (3) Set of statements in a programming language which begin and end with reserved words and treated as a unit.

block mode—Transmittal of data stored in a terminal to the computer as a block.

block options—{WP} Possible actions on a selected block: delete it, move it, copy it, write it, read it back.

board, CPU—See *microprocessor board*.

bold face—{WP} Printing characters made heavier than normal by overprinting after moving the print carriage slightly.

boot—Bringing in the operating system and making the computer available. Generally booting occurs automatically when the computer is turned on with a system disk properly inserted in the default drive slot. The system is *rebooted* by pressing the reset button.

branch—A command for decision making which causes the computer to take instructions from another area of the program.

break—A key on most keyboards; the 200-millisecond spacing signal produced by that key when it is touched. The break signal tells the computer that the current telecommunication operation is to be aborted.

breakpoint—A command entered in a compiler or assembly language program to make the computer stop for the user to examine the content of registers and thus check program operation.

brightness—{GR} Quality which distinguishes colors of the same hue by intensity.

brush—{GR} Defining a brushstroke and using the graphics input device as though it were a brush.

buffer—{H} Memory included in a device which stores data as they pass between the device and the computer. An example is the print buffer which accumulates data. Printing begins as soon as output arrives. When the buffer is full, the computer is free to attend to other matters. {S} An area in memory where data is stored as it passes between the program and the device.

buffer, chain—Records the current position of each slug of the line printer.

bug—An error in a program which makes that program inoperable or unable to do its assignment.

bundle—To include software and APs in the price of a hardware computer system.

burst—To separate continuous printed output by testing it along horizontal perforations into single sheets and removing the perforated margins.

bus—A set of wires in the computer on which are soldered connectors called slots. Printed circuit boards fit into these slots to expand the functions of the computer.

bus, address—Wires in the bus which carry the address.

bus, control—Wires in the bus which carry control signals.

bus, data—Wires in the bus which carry data.

byte—A fixed number of bits, usually eight.

cabinet—A housing, usually plastic, which fits around the computer.

cable—A set of wires connecting an external device to the computer.

cable, Centronics—A parallel connection between the computer cabinet and a device. This standard specifies only the connector type, which is different from the RS-232. Most of the lines have standard requirements specified, but not all. Used with dot matrix printers such as Epson.

cable, RS-232C—A cable connection between the computer cabinet and a serial device. This standard specifies the mating male and female connector and some but not all wire assignments. It does not specify voltage requirements and tolerances. Connects a computer to terminals and daisy wheel printers.

call—Asking, with a single name, for the execution of a full subroutine or procedure at a point in a program where necessary.

capacity, line—The transmission rate a communication line can support. Usually rated in bauds.

carriage—Platform in the printer that holds the ribbon cartridge, print element and striking mechanism and moves horizontally for the print element to strike the paper at the proper position.

carriage advance—Movement of the carriage across the paper.

carriage advance increment—The smallest unit by which the carriage may advance. For daisy wheel printers this is generally $\frac{1}{120}$ inch. By varying the number of units by which the carriage advances, different typefaces and proportional spacing are accommodated.

carriage return—A key and a corresponding code which conveys the end of a line or a paragraph. Most APs react by returning the carriage (or cursor) to the left margin. Sometimes called *enter*.

case—Refers to the form in which a letter prints. A capital letter is referred to as upper case; a small letter is called lowercase.

catalog—A program to keep track of the files on one or more disks. Also the file containing this list.

cathode ray tube (CRT)—A tube which provides a display screen for presenting alphanumeric information and graphics.

cell—{H} A place in memory which holds a specific amount of information, a byte for 8 bit computers, a word for 16 bit computers. A cell has an address, a number which identifies it. {SS} A rectangular box one character high and usually 8 to 10 characters wide, with the width determined by a format command.

cell, active—{SS} The cell in the DS where the cursor is positioned.

cell entry—{SS} The contents of a spread sheet cell may be numerical, text or a formula. After the type of entry is established by the rules of the SS, the cell entry is keyed into the cell.

cell reference—{SS} The address by which you refer to a cell or group of cells. See *reference*.

centered—{WP} Within a document, a line (or lines) of text with equal spaces on its left and right so that it is approximately in the center of the page width.

central processing unit (CPU)—A combination of the two units called the control unit and the processor.

Centronics—see *cable, centronics*.

chain—A chain or, alternatively, a train or belt, is a circular arrangement of type slugs in a line printer.

change—To alter a record in fields which do not normally change during update.

character generator—An electronic device with a memory, usually ROM, which contains, in encoded form, one dot matrix for each character of the screen display alphabet.

character, target—See *target character*.

chassis—A flat piece of metal or plastic with holes to receive components.

check sum—Verifies transmission of data. An algorithm is performed on the data as they are sent, resulting in a number of check characters transmitted after the body of the message. The same algorithm is performed at the receiving end and should come up with the same check digits, verified by comparing with those at the end of the transmission. Since the algorithm often includes addition, the characters are called a check sum.

check, read after write—Checking the validity of data written to a medium instead of making a byte for byte test between the information recorded and that transmitted. Only the CRC is checked to make sure that what is written seems to be valid.

chip—Electronic circuits which perform a large number of functions are fabricated on a tiny chip of silicon about the size of a head of a pin. The chip is mounted in a plastic casing and soldered to projecting pins. It fits into a socket on a PC board.

chip family—A collection of CPU chips which are upward compatible so that the most competent one can execute all the instructions in the least competent one's instruction set.

chroma—See *hue*.

Clipboard—A place to store data as you transfer them from one Lisa or Macintosh program to another. Represented by an icon.

clock—A device which emits signals at a uniform rate.

close—Command to the File Manager issued by an AP when a file is no longer needed. The FM then writes the FCB to the disk file directory.

COBOL—A business programming language, primarily used on larger computers.

code—A specific combination of 0s and 1s, usually eight, which represents a symbol of the *computer alphabet,* which see. Sometimes used instead of *code set* when no confusion may arise.

code, control—A code, usually nonprinting, which may convey a command to an AP.

code, machine language—A translated program that can be called up and run directly without an interpreter or other intermediary.

code, nonprinting—A code of a code set for which there is no display or printing character.

code, object—The machine language output of a compiler.

code, source—Statements which comprise a program in a programming language.

code set—A set of codes, one for each symbol in the computer alphabet.

coil—See *core*.

color table—{GR} Translates a color packet into RBG signals. Thus each color packet represents a particular color of the palette but can be altered by changing the color table.

column—{SS} A group of contiguous cells arranged along the same vertical axis.

column stub—{SS} A row at the top of the screen which contains designators for each column of the display.

command—{S} Identical to instruction. {SS} A directive to perform an action such as to bring forth a copy of the spread sheet from disk, save the SS, reformat the screen.

command, embedded—{WP} A set of characters included in an ED which conveys a format request, generally prefixed by a (printing) format character such as a period or backslash.

command, name—{SS} Lets you name a cell, row, column or block of cells and use this name instead in a formula.

command, renumber—In a programming language where statements have numbers, this command reassigns numbers in equal increments.

command, tree—Command for searching the file directory, putting subdirectories into use, making new directories, defining paths and so forth.
command file—See *file, command*.
communication—Flow of information between the human and the computer, the computer and the human or between computers, whether micros or mainframes.
compact—Applied to a language, indicating that it requires few words to describe actions required.
compatible—Making one computer assume the characteristics of another.
compatible, AP—When a computer executes an AP in exactly the same fashion as its parent. Also called *total compatibility*.
compatible, hardware—When a computer can execute the same machine language program as its parent.
compatible, OS—When a computer and its OS operate in approximately the same manner as another computer but may not execute the same APs exactly.
compatible, upward—See *chip family*.
compiler—Program which translates a source program written in a POL or higher level language into a machine language.
compressed printing—Reducing the distance between verticals in a matrix printer so that characters print narrower, although of the same height, producing more characters per inch.
concaternation—Pasting together two strings to make a single string. Pasting together two files to make a single file.
concurrently—Where the computer executes commands from two or more programs serially, switching from one to another by means of the operating system. Because switching takes place so quickly, it seems as though the programs run simultaneously.
console command processor (CCP)—CP/M component which receives a character string from the keyboard, identifies it, validates it and executes it as a command.
content, positioning—See *positioning, content*.
context, positioning—See *positioning, context*.
continuous form—Roll or fanfold paper with holes punched on both sides. Pins in the platen or tractor pull it through the print mechanism evenly and positively. Horizontal perforations at page length intervals help to separate sheets.
control grid—Component in the CRT that varies the intensity of the beam, making a dot brighter or darker.
control key—See *key, control*.
control mode—{WP} When in control mode the WP accepts only commands and not text (until switched to text mode).
control program—Part of the OS which accepts and interprets the operator's request.
control sequence—A sequence of codes, usually beginning with a control code, which conveys control information to a device, such as a printer or terminal.
control system—Part of the computer which examines the program in memory, determines what to do next and delegates it to another unit.
controller—Hardware, often on a separate PC board on the bus, which controls one

or more devices of a particular kind. It mediates control signals from both the computer and the device and regulates the flow of data between computer memory and the device accordingly.

converter—Circuitry, often on a PC board, which converts between analog and digital signals. A/D and D/A distinguish between analog to digital and digital to analog respectively.

copy, hard—See *hard copy.*

core—Part of the recording head in a disk or tape drive, a soft iron bar, bent or fabricated so as to have a gap in it and a coil of wire wound about it.

correction, backspace—See *backspace correction.*

counter—An electronic device which stores a count; advanced by entering a pulse at its input .

counter, column—Records the column of the character presented on the screen.

counter, cursor—Maintains the current cursor position as a count.

counter, display—Keeps track of the position at which a character display is being created.

counter, instruction—See *instruction counter.*

counter, scan line—Records the number of the CRT line being scanned.

coupler, acoustic—See *acoustic coupler.*

Control Program for Microcomputers—A widely used operating system manufactured and sold by Digital Research, Inc.

CP/M system area—The disk area allocated to a copy of the operating system.

creation—{WP} Producing an ED with the WP from scratch (when none exists already).

crosshair—{GR} A pair of short lines intersecting at right angles, such as used in a periscope. Indicates the current position where action may take place.

cross-reference list—List of variables used in a program together with the memory locations which they occupy at execution time.

current access position (CAP)—{GR} Where the operator wants an action to begin, such as setting a point or beginning a line.

current color (CC)—{GR} The color to be used for the next action such as drawing a line or a circle.

cursor—Screen marker to show where keyed data will go. A character in reverse video or underlined, either static or blinking.

cursor movement, direct—{SS} Movement of the cell cursor by command to a designated cell.

cursor, cell—{SS} The highlighted area on the screen showing the active cell.

cursor, command—{SS} Highlighted position on the command line where a keyed character appears next.

cursor, graphics—See *cross-hair.*

cut and paste—See *block.*

cyclic redundancy check—An algorithm, set of operations, performed upon a bit stream being recorded on, or read from a sector of the disk producing two check bytes. During writing, those bytes are recorded at the end of a sector. When read back, the identical set of operations should create the same check bytes. If those created do not agree with those read, the data are invalid.

cylinder—For a disk drive with multiple surfaces, all the tracks under heads when the arm is in one of its many fixed positions comprise one cylinder.

daisy wheel—A print element consisting of a disk with spokes radiating from the center each with a type slug at the end.

data—Information in a form that can be manipulated by the computer.

data access arrangement (DAA)—Hardware to isolate a modem from the telephone lines but no longer required.

data set—A modem or acoustic coupler connecting a data terminal to a communication line.

death—Deleting a record for an individual that has left the population from a file.

debug—Removing defects from a program.

declaration—A statement of type for one or more variables in the program required for programming languages such as Pascal and PL/1.

decoder—Accepts a code consisting of 0s and 1s and activates exactly one of a number of output lines. Thus a 3-bit decoder accepts a set of three bits and activates one out of eight output lines.

dedicated—Totally available for a single user or a group of users or a single application or a group of applications.

default—When parameters are omitted by the operator, the package supplies them, thus making the package immediately usable to the novice.

default drive—The drive which the OS references for a file if a drive prefix is omitted when a file name is provided. Thus, if B is made the default drive by entering B: at the prompt; then when the command WS is given, the OS seeks the program file WS.COM on drive B.

deflection—Aiming the CRT beam to hit the proper rel.

delete—{WP} To remove one or more characters from text. See deletion.

deletion, content—{WP} To set up a string by content positioning and then asks if that the string should or should not be deleted.

deletion, context—{WP}To remove text by grammatical units such as words, sentences and so forth.

deletion, geometrical—{WP} To remove information as defined by screen geometry, for example, line, character or partial screen.

deletion, immediate—{WP} To remove information immediately by predefined units. Character deletion removes a character at a time; word deletion removes a word at a time; and so forth.

demo—A disk which including a partial program and data files, which you run to get the feel of how an AP works.

demodulation—Extraction of intelligence from a modulated carrier.

density—How close bits are packed on a medium, measured linearly in bits per inch or radially in tracks per inch.

descender—Portion of a letter which lies below the imaginary line it sits on, such as the tail of the letters j, g, p, etc.

deserializer—Accepts 8 serial bits as input and converts them into a parallel byte as output.

despooling—To print spool files.

device—Brings information from, or delivers output to the real world, for instance, a printer, keyboard, display, tablet and disk drive.

device, peripheral—Not an integral part of the computer, not in its cabinet, but connected by external cable.

dialect—A variation of a programming language suitable for a particular compiler or interpreter.

dictionary, supplementary—{WP} File which contains additional words, usually jargon, prepared while you use a spelling checking program. Supplements the main dictionary to prevent flagging jargon in the text.

digital to analog (D/A)—See *converter*.

DIP switch—See *switch, DIP*.

direct access—Positioning from one data area on the medium to another without passing through intervening areas.

direct memory access—Method of transmitting data between memory and a device. The controller takes over the bus and transmits (receives) information continuously without intervention by the CPU. The fastest data transmission method.

directory, default—For the directory tree, the current subdirectory in use.

directory, file—See *file directory*.

disassembler—A translator to convert from machine language to assembly language.

disk controller—Circuitry for controlling one or more disk drives, usually on a PC board which plugs into the bus. Some control eight or more drives, although few systems use more than four drives. Control signals from the CPU select and direct the disk drive. Status signals from the controller tell the CPU the progress of the activity.

diskette—A flexible removable plastic disk in its own paper envelope.

display—Where visual information from the computer appears, usually a CRT screen but may also be an LED display. May show text, graphics or both.

display memory—See *memory display*.

display, responsive—{WP} screen put up by a WP showing how a document would print. Sometimes known as "what you see is what you get," or WYSIWYG.

documentation—Manuals and printed material provided with an AP, instructing how to use it, providing tutorials or a reference source.

dot—{GR} An illuminated spot at a rel.

dot matrix—A rectangular grid defining the relative placement of visible dots on a display or printout, one grid for each symbol of the printing alphabet. Matrix size is defined by width and height in number of dots. Increasing matrix size (say, from 5 × 7 to 7 × 9 or 9 × 13) both increases the total number of dots in the character and decreases the space between dots so that the character shows more detail.

double density diskette—A diskette recorded with the new techniques to hold twice as much data as single density.

double sided diskette—Provides two surfaces where data may be written, doubling the amount of storage. Its drive must have two heads, selectable by the computer.

download—To send a program or data from one computer to another. Often applied to getting data from a mainframe data base through a transmission network to a micro.

drag—{GR} To move an object about the graphics display screen by seemingly pulling it with the input device.

drive, default—The disk drive whose volume is searched when a command is issued at the OS prompt. The response should be prefixed by the drive address when the file is on a different drive.

drive selection—Selecting which one of multiple disk drives attached to a computer is to transfer data.

driver—Program which interprets simple I/O commands from the AP and converts them into a series of machine commands to operate an input or output device. Usually part of the OS.

driver, hardware—Circuitry, often on a PC board, which converts control signals sent by the CPU into the form required by a device connected to it. A software driver is still required between the AP or OS and the hardware driver.

duplex—Permitting transmission in two directions.

duplex, full—Simultaneous communication in both directions.

duplex, half—Communication in both directions but not simultaneously.

echoplex—When codes from the keyboard sent to the computer are echoed directly to the screen.

edit—To alter an existing electronic document.

editor—A program which lets you enter and edit text.

editor, line oriented—Designed to edit text by line number where the programming language requires numbered lines (for example, BASIC).

editor, screen—Where all text on the screen is immediately accessible for editing by moving the cursor to it.

effective address—See *address, effective.*

electronic document (ED)—The copy of a document in the form of a memory image (in RAM) or on an external medium such as a floppy.

electronic spread sheet—See *spread sheet.*

embedded command—See *command, embedded.*

emphasis—{WP} A printing action which causes designated strings of letters to stand out in hard copy text.

encoder—A device with a number of input lines, only one of which may carry a signal. Produces signals on the output lines for the code corresponding to an input signal. An encoder in the keyboard converts a key closure to its output code.

end of file mark—A special character which tells the File Manager that this is the end of the file (EOF). For ASCII files, ^Z is used.

entry mode—The activity by which a source program is entered into a file for later translation.

error, syntax—An error in the source program due to violation of the program language rules.

error listing—Printout of all errors the compiler finds in the source program.

error recovery—Ability of an AP to recover and continue or to terminate properly when errors arise.

execute—Computer cycle which examines the contents of the instruction register and delegates the instruction to one of its units.

executive—Part of the interpreter which receives control after the execution of each statement. The executive scans the next statement and delegates it to a routine for execution.
expanded printing—Increasing spacing between verticals of a dot matrix printer so that characters print wider, fewer characters per inch, but each the same height as before.
express key—See *key, express.*
Extended Binary Coded Decimal Interchange Code—A code set used in large IBM mainframes and its compatibles and some competitors.
extent—A set of consecutive tracks or blocks within a file.
extension—Three characters entered after the period for CP/M and MS-DOS to identify the file type such as **COM** and **EXE** for program files, **BAS** for BASIC files, **DOC** for document files, and so on. See *file name.*
external storage—A device together with a medium to hold information. The device can write data to the medium and read them back later. For the micro, the medium is usually a diskette or hard disk.
family—See *chip family.*
fan fold—See *continuous form.*
fetch—Computer cycle which puts the next instruction from memory into the instruction register using the address in the instruction counter.
field—Part of a record corresponding to the attribute of an individual.
field name—The name for a field used in discussing it.
field value—Value assigned to a field in a record and describing a characteristic of the individual the record represents.
file—A collection of data, generally on a disk, which has a name by which it can be called forth. Space allocated to a file may be fixed or, depending on the OS, may be dynamic so as to grow or contract according to file use.
file, batch—A list of command files which should be executed in a particular sequence.
file, command—A file containing a machine language program and having the extension **COM** or **EXE**.
file, data—A collection of records, one for each individual of a population.
file, direct—Accessible directly. See *direct access.*
file, intermediate code—A file produced by a mixed mode interpreter after compilation.
file, random—Accessible by *direct access,* which see.
file, sequential—Where only sequential access is possible. See *sequential access.*
file, serial—See *file, sequential.*
file, source—Statements which constitute a program written in assembly, interpreter or compiler language.
file, streamed—See *file, sequential.*
file, submit—Created on an editor and listing APs to be executed in the same sequence.
file, text—A document, report or letter in the form of an ED, such as produced by a WP.

file, transaction—Collection of records for transactions which affect individuals in a given population.
file allocation table—A directory which lists files by name, together with the physical location of extents occupied by them. There are multiple entries in the table for large files with a flag in each entry indicating the order of extents in the file.
file control block (FCB)—Definition of a file acquired by the File Manager from the directory or created by a new file. It is kept in the system area below 100. It must be rewritten to the file directory when the file is closed.
file control block, default—An additional FCB also maintained in the system area. It may record the data file required by an AP.
file directory (FD)—See *file allocation table*.
File Manager (FM)—Keeps track of files, the records and unused space in each file on mounted disks. It is called the Basic Disk Operating System (BDOS) for CP/M and IBMDOS for PCDOS.
file name—A symbol, a combination of letters and numbers, which designates a file on a disk. A CP/M and PCDOS file name consists of up to 8 characters and an extension of up to 3 characters. The extension conveys the nature of a file and may be omitted in some cases in which only files of a particular nature may be used.
file name, ambiguous—Containing wild cards so that sometimes several different file names could fulfill a request.
file name, unambiguous—Passed in its entirety and thus unambiguous.
firmware—A program built into ROM such as part of an operating system or a permanent AP.
flood, screen—{GR} To light up an entire display and thus activate a light pen, should the cursor get lost.
floppy—A diskette, usually 8 inches in diameter. Also see *microfloppy, minifloppy*.
fluoresce—When the electron beam hits the terminal screen, causing its coating to emit light.
foot—{WP} Text in the bottom margin of each page. Also called a *footing* or *footer*.
footprint—Space a micro occupies on a desk, usually stated in square feet.
form, continuous—See *continuous form*.
form letter—{WP} One of a number of letters prepared with the same text but with portions personalized and inserted.
format—{WP} To determine how a document appears when printed on paper. {SS} To determine how numbers and text appear in a cell or group of cells in a spread sheet.
format, ASCII—In which fields are separated by commas, records are terminated with both <u>return</u> and <u>line</u> and files end with ^Z.
format, default—{WP} Format parameters assigned to a document if not stated otherwise.
format, long term—{WP} Format parameters which remain in effect for an entire document if not reset such as page size and top and bottom margins.
format, short term—{WP} Format parameters in effect for only a short portion of a document, such as emphasis.
format mode—{WP} Some WPs must be in this mode to change format parameters.

format program—See *program, format*.

formula—{SS} An expression inserted into a cell of a spread sheet; a combination of cell designators, constants and internally defined functions. The SS makes the calculation and replaces the formula by the result in the DS and its printout.

FORTRAN—A POL particularly useful for mathematical programs and associated with large computers.

frame—{GR} A complete scan of the screen from top to bottom which writes the contents of refresh memory.

free pointer—{SS} One point of range definition which changes as the display cursor is moved about the screen, thus changing the range definition in progress. Pressing a designated key fixes the free point and makes the range definition final.

frequency—With respect to files, how often batch processing is performed.

friendly—A programming language, AP or system which is easy to use and forgiving of operator errors.

function—{SS} A function in a cell formula combines variables from cells of a spread sheet as defined: SUM adds a number of cells; AVERAGE and STDEV take the average and standard deviation of a group of cells.

gap—See *core*.

generator, character—See *character generator*.

gigabyte—One billion bytes of information. (GB).

graphic—A nonstandard symbol produced on a terminal screen and/or on a printer when activated by an 8 bit ASCII code. Several symbols may be combined to create an image such as the piano keyboard provided by the IBM PC sample program.

graphics—Images of various kinds, as described in Chapter 13, produced by special harware and APs.

graphics, business—Generation of bar charts, pie charts and other kinds of charts which may be colored and have text but generally not including drawings.

graphics board—The monitor for the IBM PC has memory mapped video which requires two port memory incorporated in a graphics board plugged into a bus slot. One can purchase either a monochrome or color monitor, but usually each requires a different board.

grey scale—{GR} Black, white and tones of grey in between: the tonal range of a monochrome display.

grow—{GR} Causing a defined object to alter in size.

gun—The unit at the base of the CRT which creates a narrow beam of electrons to be positioned to a rel on the screen.

half duplex—See *duplex, half*.

hard copy—{WP} The printed document: a report, letter or manuscript as produced by a printer. {GR} Image output from a matrix printer or plotter, or a photograph of the screen.

hard disk drive—A disk drive with a permanently mounted medium consisting of rigid disks with several recording surfaces and heads. Sometimes the medium is removable.

hard sectored disk—A floppy disk which contains sector holes to generate signals photoelectrically for marking sectors.

hardware—The computer, its circuitry, peripheral devices and their PC boards which connect to devices and make them operable.

head—{WP} Text in the top margin of each page; sometimes called a *header* or *heading*. {H} A read/write head in a disk or tape drive.

head load—Heads are kept way from the disks during positioning, after which they are then either pressed against the floppy disk or released to ride on the air surface created by the rotation of the hard disk.

help screen—CRT display called up as a reminder of what command to give or how a command works. Often activated by hitting "?".

hexadecimal—Nibbles, sets of 4 bits, where binary values between 0 and 9 are represented by the numerals 0 through 9 and those between 10 and 15 are represented by A through F.

high level language (HLL)—See *language, high level*.

highlight—To make a string stand out for word processing or programming and sometimes for graphics by reverse video, low or high intensity display, etc.

hertz (Hz)—A frequency of repetition measured in times per second.

hole, index—See *index hole*.

home—(1) Known position on the CRT screen, such as the upper left corner. (2) For the disk drive, a signal indicating when the head is at the beginning of a track. (3) An arbitrary petal for the daisy wheel printer from which a character's petal position is measured.

host—In a multiple computer system, the one which is usually in control.

hotline—A vendor telephone number to call for direct support.

hue—{GR} Quality, or value, which distinguishes one color from another, so that blue, for instance, is perceived differently from green.

hyphen, hard—{WP} A hyphen which always prints, regardless of its position in the text.

hyphen, soft—{WP} If, after editing a document, a *soft* hyphen appears in a word internal to a line, the hyphen is removed and the word is printed as a unit.

hyphenation—{WP} Inserting a hyphen in the last word of a line to break the word in two, putting the second half on the succeeding line to space out the preceding line better.

hyphenation, automatic—{WP} Performed by the WP program without human intervention; rarely found in micro WPs.

hyphenation, computer assisted—{WP} The WP presents each line eligible for hyphenation and the operator decides if and where to place the hyphen.

icon—A pictorial symbol which appears in a display (as on Apple's Lisa or Mac) whose shape indicates its nature. An action or ED is requested by pointing at it with a graphics input device.

image, digitized—{GR} An image where the source is a picture that has been broken into square elements, each assigned to a pixel by a number representing its position on a grey scale.

image, interlaced—Creating alternate lines of an image during one period and the other set of lines during another. This allows a reduced scan rate to produce a good image with less flicker than otherwise possible.

image memory—{GR} A separate memory or a portion of main memory which contains an image in digital form. For monochrome, one bit per pixel suffices; for color, several bits are required to indicate the color at a pixel.

image plane—{GR} A portion of image memory which stores one bit of *each* pixel.

increment, printing—The length in fractions of an inch by which a print carriage can be controlled. A typical figure is $\frac{1}{120}$ inch.

index hole—Hole in a disk and its envelope, both at the same radius so that their alignment can be detected optically to produce an index pulse.

index pulse—Produced when the index hole in the disk and in the envelope are aligned.

individual—A person, part, account, vendor, customer or a similar entity. A member of a population.

input—Data brought into computer memory from the keyboard, a medium or an external source; or (verb) to bring data into memory.

input, conceptual—{GR} Commands, control keys and mnemonics entered at the keyboard to effect display output.

input, direct—{GR} To affect the graphics display with a light pen or by touching the screen.

input, indirect—{GR} To cause the cursor to move across the graphics display screen by drawing on a tablet with a stylus or by moving a mouse.

insert—{WP} To enter text somewhere in an ED. See *insertion, open-up* and *insertion, push aside*.

insertion, open up—{WP} The text at the cursor parts and one or two lines go to the bottom of the screen for context. The new material is entered at the cursor. When finished, a command restores and reformats the text.

insertion, push aside—{WP} During typing, characters are inserted at the cursor and text there is pushed aside. When a line overflows, wordwrap is invoked so that words are not split.

install—(1) {S} To use an installation program furnished by the vendor to alter an application program or operating system so that it mates with existing devices with which the computer interfaces. (2) The routine which alters the AP or OS.

instruction—Atomic element in a machine language program which tells the computer what to do; a basic action which the computer can perform.

instruction counter—A register which contains the address from which an instruction has been obtained.

instruction set—Collection of instructions or commands in the repertoire of a computer.

interface—Circuitry and/or software between two devices or between the CPU and an I/O device.

interpreter—A program which scans a source program written in a POL, determines the meaning of each statement and then executes a routine which does the processing to produce the results required by the statement.

interrupt—Hardware-initiated activity whereby a hardware or device condition takes control from the executing program and gives it to the operating system in such a way that the interrupted program can later regain control as though nothing had happened. Also see *I/O, interrupt driven*.
interrupt, nested—Interrupt during the processing of a previous interrupt.
interrupt, nonmaskable—An interrupt which cannot be prevented from occurring.
interrupt, vectored—Control going to one of several routines according to the hardware cause which initiated the interrupt.
interrupt mask—Register set by the OS to prevent temporarily the occurrence of one or more interrupts.
I/O addressing—How a computer command designates an I/O device.
I/O device—Device which performs input, output or both.
I/O driver—A routine in the OS or AP which gives directives to a device to perform the desired operations. It interprets the parameters sent by the program and creates signals to direct input and output.
I/O, interrupt driven—Device action takes place simultaneously with program execution. When finished, the device causes an interrupt which gives control to the operating system, taking it away from the executing program.
I/O, memory mapped—Addressing an I/O device as though it were a memory cell. This cell in real memory does not exist or can not be reached through a read or write command.
I/O, port—In an I/O command, a number which designates a port and not a memory address.
jaggies—{GR} At lower resolution some lines, especially those almost horizontal or vertical, appear like a series of steps.
justify—{WP} To print full lines in a document the same length from the left to the right margin. Also called *right justify*.
key—(1) A keyboard button, as on a typewriter, labeled with one or more symbols. When struck, the keyboard generates a set of signals, the code for the keytop character. Unless some other key is also pressed, the code generated generally corresponds to the bottom symbol or lower case letter. (2) Field used to organize or search a file.
key, arrow—Engraved with an arrow pointing left, right, up or down. Hitting this key generates a control code which an application program views as a request to move the cursor in the corresponding direction.
key, code—See *key, control*.
key, control—When held down while another key is struck, the keyboard emits a control code. An AP usually interprets this as a request to perform a specific action, such as halting a listing or rebooting the operating system.
key, cursor—See *cursor key*.
key, express—{WP} A key whose control code tells the WP to position the cursor immediately to some important position such as the screen's upper left hand corner. Example: *home*.
key, function—May be assigned a series of keystrokes or control codes.
key, partial—When only part of a search key is finished. See *key* (2).

key, repeat action—When a key is held down, it generates one code for the corresponding symbol; then, after a second or so, it produces duplicate codes at the rate of 10 per second.

key, shift—If held down while some other key is pressed, the code for the upper case letter or the upper symbol engraved on the key is produced.

key, special purpose—When hit, the keyboard creates a special code, usually nonprinting, and conveying a special function such as backspace, line feed or escape.

keyboard (KB)—A set of keys laid out in a rectangular pattern similar to the standard typewriters, consisting of 4 or 5 rows and perhaps 15 or 20 columns. Additional keys provide extra function codes required by the computer.

keypad, numeric—A duplicate set of numeric keys arranged on the keyboard in the pattern found on an adding machine.

kilobyte—Exactly 1024 or approximately 1000 bytes; abbreviated **KB**, or simply **K** when "bytes" are understood. Caution: A *memory* of 64K holds 64K *bytes;* A 64K memory *chip* has a capacity of 64K *bits*. Achieving a RAM of 64K, then requires *eight* 64K chips.

language, assembly (AL)—Low level language with mnemonics for machine language commands.

language, formal—With unforgiving rules and an exact meaning for each word (no synonyms). Typical for programming languages.

language, high level—A language which performs special functions not usually found in POLS. Such languages often incorporate a compiler language as a subset.

language, machine (ML)—The 1s and 0s found in memory and which comprise a command as interpreted by the computer hardware.

language, natural—Used by people in ordinary communication.

language, procedure oriented (POL)—A programming language in which it is easy to express procedures for performing the sequence of actions usually encountered in user applications. Also called a compiler language. Examples are BASIC, COBOL and FORTRAN.

language, programming—Used to write application programs, translated by assemblers, compilers and interpreters.

large scale integration (LSI)—Placing a large number of circuits—up to several thousand—on a chip the size of a pinhead. Also see *very large scale integration*.

latency—The average time to reach a desired sector once the disk head is positioned at the proper track.

leaf—A node from which no edges emanate. For the file directory tree a leaf always represents a file, not a subdirectory. See *node*.

level—For the tree, the distance of a node from the root, measured is the minimum number of nodes, including the beginning one, passed through to reach the root.

library—A collection of programs, routines or subroutines.

light emiting diode (LED)—Technology for presenting information on an almost flat screen.

light pen—{GR} A stylus to move on the display screen to position the cursor with one or more buttons to convey a command.

line, scan—See *scan line*.

line advance increment—Smallest distance paper may advance. For many daisy printers this is $\frac{1}{48}$ inch.

line feed—Advancing the paper (or cursor) to print the next line.

line printer—A printer with a drum, chain, train, band or belt rotating constantly at high speed. Printing occurs whenever some print slug arrives at the position at which it should be printed. A hammer strikes the slug to make an impression. Hence, different character positions of the line are printed almost randomly. Only when all the characters on the line have been printed does the paper advance.

line spacing—The number of lines advanced for each line printed. Single spacing advances one line; double spacing, two lines.

lines per inch (lpi)—Describes the print paper advance function. The pica setting, 6 lpi, requires a line advance of $\frac{1}{6}$ inch. Elite, 8 lpi, requires $\frac{1}{8}$ inch.

link—Program that takes an object module produced by a compiler and hooks it up to additional modules required to make a running program. Also called a *linkage editor*.

linkage—{SS} Establishing a relationship between two spread sheets when information in one depends on the other.

literal—A value provided directly in an assignment statement or command, rather than being calculated.

load module—A module of machine language code which is executable if loaded into memory.

loader (linking loader)—A program which takes one or more relocatable object modules and combines them into a load module which is now executable if loaded into memory starting at a specific location.

loading, automatic—{SS} For two linked spread sheets where automatic loading is specified; when the first is loaded, the relevant contents of the second are automatically entered into the first spread.

local area network—A special transmission line with devices and computers hooked into it. Such a line can support devices separated by thousands of feet.

local mode—Where data entered at the terminal keyboard is stored in terminal memory but not sent to the computer.

lock key—When pressed, the shift is maintained as though held down. See also *lock, alpha* and *lock, shift*.

lock, alpha—When pressed, letter keys produce upper case character codes. Numeric keys still produce codes for the numerals.

lock, shift—When set, causes the keyboard to produce the code for the upper symbol on the key pressed. For an alphabetic key, a capital letter is produced; for a numeric key the symbol above the numeral is produced.

log-on—Starting up a terminal of a multiuser system and identifying the user and priority for the system to validate.

logical device—A symbolic name which refers to a device of a particular class. You can address the device by this name rather than its physical port address (e.g., LPT: for the line printer).

loop—A set of statements which is executed a number of times. Most program languages provide a statement type for doing this, usually beginning with the word for.

M drive—See *semidisk*.

machine dependent—A machine language module or an interpreter which can run on only a particular machine for which it was designed.

machine independent—Most source language programs are machine independent because they can be compiled on any machine for which a compiler exists.

machine language (ML)—See *language, machine*.

macro—A series of assembly language statements defined in an assembly program and callable by name any place in the program for the assembler to substitute the statements there.

magnetic tape—Thin Mylar or plastic tape coated with a magnetizible material. Information is recorded and read from the tape as it passes beneath a read/write head on the tape drive.

main program—See *program, main*.

mainframe—A large computer, usually costing $100,000 or more.

maintain—To alter a file by adding or deleting records, regardless of whether update is taking place at the same time.

Manager, File—See *File Manager*.

mark—Another name for binary 1.

master—See *host*.

mating—Getting the parts of a computer system to fit together so that they work properly, including the operating system, hardware and APs.

matrix printer—An impact printer mechanism with a number of small, thin, flexible rods which make an impression on paper as a series of dots or undots.

medium—Physical material which stores data for access by an external storage device.

medium, sequential—A medium such as magnetic tape for which only sequential access is possible.

megabyte (MB)—A million bytes of information.

megahertz (Mhz)—A frequency of repetition of one million times per second.

memorize—To copy a datum from the CPU into memory.

memory—Part of the computer which stores data.

memory, display—Memory in the terminal which holds codes for characters to display on the screen.

memory, random access (RAM)—Read from or written into with the same access time regardless of the cell address.

memory, read-only (ROM)—Can be read from but not written into.

memory, refresh—Same as display memory. See *memory, display*.

memory, two port—Makes memory mapped video possible within time constraints, by enabling a computer and its terminal to access refresh memory simultaneously. Each has its own port to make this possible.

menu—A series of items presented on the screen for the operator to choose from by hitting a designated key. Often this key is the initial letter of the description, but it may also be a number.

menu, graphic—Screen menu activated by pointing with a graphics input device.

micro—See *microcomputer*.

microcomputer—Small, inexpensive computer which may not be portable but is not large and usually costs less than $10,000.

microfloppy—A small floppy, 3½ inches in diameter.

microprocessor board—PC board where the main component is a microprocessor chip. Other components generate timing signals, shape pulses and perform other functions necessary to run the microprocessor.

microprocessor chip—All the circuitry of the processor which does the calculating and executes the program. It is mounted in a socket of the microprocessor board.

microsecond (μs)—One millionth of a second.

millisecond (ms)—One thousandth of a second.

mini—Abbreviation for minicomputer, one between a micro and a mainframe in capability and cost.

minifloppy—A 5-¼ inch diskette.

mnemonic—A set of letters which represents and suggests an activity performed by a command or AP and which is easy to recall.

mode—One of alternative capabilities of hardware or software.

mode, answer—

mode, direct—In which an interpreter scans a statement the operator enters and immediately interprets and executes the statement to produce a result. Also known as *command mode*.

mode, format—See *format mode*.

mode, mixed—A program translation process where source code is first translated into an intermediate code file. This file is then acted upon by an interpreter instead of being directly executed by the computer.

modem—Contraction of *mo*dulator-*dem*odulator. Device for connecting a computer to telephone lines. An external device attached by cable or a PC card. It does not work unless supplied with a software driver to mate it to the OS and AP.

module—Part of a program.

module, load—A module in machine language form which is executable.

monitor—An external visual display unit; a screen. Connects to the computer by cable. Sometimes a television set is used with a low price micro.

monochrome—{GR} Showing only black and white, or black and one color (green, amber, etc.), on a display medium such as a screen.

motherboard—A plastic board on which circuits are printed and sockets are soldered to hold integrated circuits. It is attached to the chassis and usually supports a bus with expansion slots.

mount—To insert a floppy disk properly into a disk drive, or a disk pack, tape or tape cartridge on its device and putting that device online.

mouse—{GR} A small device that fits in your hand and has a roller ball underneath. As you move it around a table, the screen cursor moves in approximately in the same direction and distance. Use one or more buttons on its top to enter commands.

multiprocessing—Running programs for several users simultaneously.

multiprogramming—Running programs for several users concurrently.

multitasking—Running several programs for one user concurrently.

nanosecond (ns)—One billionth of a second.
network—A group of computers connected either directly or via telephone or other leased lines.
network, local area—A group of computers connected by a set of cables, not leased lines. (LAN).
nibble—Four bits, half a byte.
node—Point in a *tree* (which see), connected by lines, or edges, to other nodes.
nondestructive—Data read remaining intact at the source.
notch, write protect—See *write protect*.
nucleus—Resident portion of the operating system.
null code—The code for a blank.
numeric keypad—See *keypad, numeric*.
object code—See *code, object*.
object module—File containing machine language code produced by a compiler or assembler but which may not be in executable form.
online—A device and/or medium is online when a medium is mounted on a device, the device is connected to a computer and both are powered up and properly functioning so that information may be transmitted between the device/medium and the computer.
open—An AP request to make a file available. The File Manager creates an FCB from scratch or from the file directory for an existing file.
operand—A datum acted on during instruction execution.
operating environment (OE)—Functions which facilitate the interchange of data between APs.
operating system (OS)—Collection of programs designed to mate with the computer and which provides interfaces to the operator, devices and AP.
original equipment manufacturer (OEM)—Synonymous with *system house*.
originate mode—In full duplex communication by modem, establishes 1270 Hz for mark and 1070 Hz for space.
orphan—{WP} The first line of a paragraph when it appears alone at the bottom of a page.
output—Taking data from the computer memory and putting it onto an external medium or printing it. Also the data produced.
overlay—A portion of a very large program which may be brought in to replace part of the main program, thus making it possible to run that program in less RAM than the overall program size.
overtype—{WP} As you key text, it writes over existing text at the cursor.
package deal—A combination purchase consisting of hardware, an operating system and a number of APs.
packet, color—One set of bits for each pixel which conveys the pixel's color.
page break—{WP} A screen indication, usually a line of dashes, dots or stars, which shows where one page ends and the next begins.
page break, manual—{WP} Page break set by the operator to end a page, even if it can hold more text.
palette—{GR} The colors which can display at a particular moment. Some systems

have a fixed palette. Others have a choice from several fixed palettes. Still others let you choose from a universe of colors.

palette size—{GR} The number of colors available on the palette, determined by color packet size. For example, a 4 bit packet gives a choice of 16 colors. Not to be confused with the color universe, the colors from which to *choose* a palette. For expensive color graphics, a typical palette may have 516 colors chosen from 16 million.

pan—{GR} To move a display window across the memory image so that it seems as if you are moving it across a scene.

paper bail—A horizontal rod on a printer, with rollers to press the paper against the platen, move it up evenly and position it properly beneath the print element.

paragraph—{H} Same as *segment*.

parallel—Carrying a number of bits simultaneously via a set of wires. Parallel by character is implied: the 8 bits of a byte are transmitted all at once. Also see *serial*.

parameter—A datum passed to a called procedure or subroutine.

parameter, actual—When a procedure or subroutine is called, values passed to it and substituted for formal parameters which appear in the definition.

parameter, formal—A parameter used in the definition of a procedure or subroutine to indicate where in the procedure a passed value will be substituted.

parity—The code for each character contains an odd (even) number of 1s to provide for checking data transmission. For odd (even) parity a character is valid only if the number of 1s in the code received is odd (even).

parity bit—An additional bit appended to a character code so that the total number of 1s is odd (even). Thus any 7 bit code set can be made into an 8 bit code set with a parity bit for checking data transmission.

Pascal—A rigorous POL which provides its own documentation.

path— An alternate sequence of nodes in the directory tree by which the OS should search for files.

PC board—See *printed circuit board*.

PC card—See *printed circuit board*.

persistence—The amount of time that a dot written on the CRT screen continues to emit light.

personal computer—See *microcomputer*.

petal—A small projection on the print wheel of a daisy wheel printer, with a print character engraved on it.

petal register—Stores the petal number for the last character printed by a daisy wheel printer.

petal table—Stores a petal number with reference to home for each character on the daisy wheel printer.

phantom—Signal activated to disable part of memory.

phosphor—The chemical screen coating the inside of a CRT; produces light when hit by the electron beam.

phrase storage—{WP} Some WPs let you record a phrase and assign it to a key; hitting that key enters the phrase into a document at the cursor.

pin feed—On a printer, a set of projecting pins on both sides of the platen which fit into holes in continuous form stock of the proper width to advance it.

pitch—Characters per inch for each printer typeface.

pixel—{GR} One element in image memory. For high resolution graphics, a pixel represents a single rel; for lower definition, a pixel represents a group of rels, usually a square, but not always.

platen—A cylinder with a rough surface which holds the paper against the impact made by the print slug and whose friction moves the paper.

plotter—{GR} A hard copy output device with one or more pens. The AP controls pen position and contact with the drawing paper and selects a pen, if there is more than one, to draw lines on the paper. Areas can be filled in by using pens with wide nibs.

pointer—A field or link which gives the physical address of additional data.

pointing—{GR} Moving the cursor to a position on the screen, often within a graphics menu, and pressing the stylus or mouse button to request a command designated in the menu.

polled I/O—Where the AP or OS interrogates each device attached to a computer to see which, if any, requires service.

polygonal fill—{GR} Filling a closed figure with color.

population—A group of individuals of interest to a particular application. Basis of a data file.

port—A set of lines to an input or output device or a controller which carry data and control signals selected by a computer command.

position, absolute—{GR} Defining the CAP as coordinates given in terms of pixels in X and Y directions.

position, normalized—{GR} Using a scale of 0 to 1 for the X and Y coordinates, either relative or absolute, instead of absolute pixel numbers.

position, present—See *present position*.

position, relative—Giving the CAP by incremental pixel coordinates.

positioning, content—{WP} Moving the cursor to the next designated character symbol—to the next word by asking for the next blank; the next sentence by asking for the next period; etc.

positioning, context—{WP} Moving to the next grammatical entity such as the next word, sentence and so forth.

post—See *update*.

posting, interactive—Posting at a terminal by entering record changes in any order.

power supply—Computer component which converts line voltage where you plug in the computer at your office or home into the proper voltages required internally.

power supply, regulated—Power supply voltages kept closely within bounds, despite fluctuations in line voltage, noise and other disturbances in the commercial environment.

present position (PP)—{GR, WP} The position in text or image to which a command you issue is referenced.

primitive—{GR} A standard, but sometimes complex action, required in most high resolution graphics systems. Often implemented in firmware. Examples: drawing a line, smoothing, creating circles.

print buffer—A memory included in the printer which holds one or more lines as a sequence of character codes while printing takes place.

print element—The part of the printer which makes the inked impression on paper. For example, the spherical golf ball element or the wire matrix.

print wheel—A generic term for print elements such as the daisy wheel and thimble.

printed circuit board—A plastic board printed with wiring by a photochemical process. Sockets inserted in the board and soldered to the wiring receive integrated circuit chips.

printer—Prints information on paper, much like a typewriter, except that it is driven directly by the computer.

printer, dot matrix—A printer on which a set of nine or so vertically aligned thin wires comprises the print element. An individual hammer hits each wire to form a character out of little dots.

printer, impact—Printer where the character is formed on the paper by the impact of a hammer hitting a type slug or wires against an inked ribbon.

printer, ink jet—A nonimpact printer where multiple jets of ink are turned on and off to form a character as a matrix of dots.

printer, nonimpact—A printer which does *not* use impact to form a character on the paper. It uses heat, light or electric current or jets of ink.

printing, bidirectional—Printing while the carriage is moving either to the right or to the left. This speeds printing because it eliminates carriage return during which no printing takes place.

printing, multipass—Some matrix printers print the same line more than once. The second pass of the print mechanism is displaced vertically and is slightly different to produce greater character definition.

priority—The importance of one activity relative to another.

procedure—(1) A set of rules describing when and how a set of actions is done, in what sequence, by whom and which programs and computer activities take part. (2) A named set of statements defined in a program. When the name appears in the main program, the compiler replaces it with the statements.

procedure oriented language (POL)—See *language, procedure oriented*.

processor—{H} Part of the computer which does arithmetic, editing and logical operations. {S} The combination of a programming language and a compiler or interpreter.

program, application (AP)—A program or group of programs which solves a user's problem or set of problems. APs include such packages as word processing, spread sheets and data base managers.

program, communication—Allows an operator to talk to another micro or to a mainframe, if a modem and mating hardware are provided.

program, format—Called forth by the user to perform actions that make a virgin disk usable: checking out the entire disk to see if reading and writing are possible, and writing a directory, a bit map and sector information for soft sector disks.

program, keystroke—Assigns a string of keystrokes to one function key.

program, main—That part of the source program which contains only imperative commands. It does not include variable and procedure definitions.

program, source—Statements which comprise the program in a higher level or POL language.

programmable key—See *key, programmable*.

programmer—Person who writes a set of operations in a programming language, presumably to solve some useful problem.

prompt—A symbol on the screen to say that the OS or AP is ready to accept a new command or needs a line of text or a response.

prompt, action—Request from OS or AP for a command.

prompt, data—Request from an AP to enter data, such as the date, time, document number or file.

protocol—A set of codes that must be transmitted and received in the proper sequence to guarantee that the desired terminals are hooked together and can talk to each other.

RAM, dynamic—RAM which loses information stored there unless it is constantly refreshed many times per second.

RAM, static—RAM using semiconductors which stores its information indefinitely unless the power is turned off.

range—{SS} A contiguous array of cells: a partial column or row or a rectangular block of cells occupying parts of several columns and rows.

raster—A sequence of horizontal lines swept out, one below the other, by the beam of the CRT in creating a display. If the beam is turned on, the line is visible. If the beam is turned off, no visible line appears.

raster scan—{GR} A display method in which the CRT beam sweeps out the entire screen a line at a time in a rectangular pattern, writing the image as it goes along. The image is refreshed at rates between 30 and 60 frames per second.

read—(1) To bring information from an external storage medium and place it in memory. (2) To get information from a cell in memory for calculation within the computer.

read-only memory (ROM)—See *memory, read-only*.

readable—Applied to a language which is easy to read or understand.

recall—To copy a datum or instruction from memory to a computer register.

record—A collection of fields corresponding to the attributes of an individual which is of importance to an application.

record, fixed size—Describes a file in which all the records are the same length.

records, streamed—Written in a constant stream. The file containing the records is sequential and the format is ASCII.

record, transaction—Information about a record which is being changed.

record number, relative—See *relative record number*.

reference by name—{SS} Referring to a cell or group of cells by a name applied to it previously with a *name* command.

reference, absolute—{SS} Referring to a cell by its row and column designation; referring to a range of cells by naming the upper left hand corner and lower right hand corner.

reference, mixed—{SS} In which a cell's column address can be absolute and its row address can be relative or vice versa.

reference, relative—{SS} Referring to a cell or block by its position relative to the active cell. Displacement is positive or negative according to whether the cell is down (left) or up (right), respectively.

reform—{WP} See *reformat*.

reformat—{WP} To readjust line width with wordwrap after insertion or deletion. Some WPs have *automatic* reformatting after each edit action. For *manual* reformatting, the WP does not adjust lines until requested.

refresh—(1) Projecting a graphic image on the screen many times per second. (2) For dynamic RAM, rememorizing memory content periodically.

refresh memory—Same as *memory, display*.

refresh rate—Number of frames or refresh cycles per second. Common refresh rates are 30 and 60 cycles per second.

register—Place data is kept temporarily during program execution for fast access.

register, hammer—Stores bits which indicate which hammers should be activated next for the dot matrix printer.

register, instruction—Holds the instruction being executed.

register, program—Same as the *instruction counter*.

register, refresh—{GR} Contains a portion of image memory scanned during projecting.

register, segment—Holds high order address bits for the 8088 chip.

register, status—Records the state of the computer due to the effect of a recently executed instruction.

rel—{GR} See *resolution element*.

relation—A symbol (for example, =, >, <, AND) which indicates a relationship between two quantities in a POL statement. Different actions are taken according to whether the relation currently holds or not.

relative address—See *address, relative*.

relative record number—Ordinal number of the record within the file, determined by counting its position from the beginning of the file.

relocatable module—Machine language code not associated with a specific starting address, which is assigned by the loader before being executed.

repeat action—See *key, repeat action*.

replace string—{WP} A string to replace another (target) string.

replicate—{SS} To copy a cell or group of cells from one area of a SS to another, making adjustment by changing cell references in the formula as requested.

reserved word—In a programming language, a string of characters, a symbol, which is reserved and cannot be used as a variable name. Examples are if and end from Pascal.

resident—part of an OS kept in memory after the system is booted.

resolution—{GR} The amount of detail available in the screen image. Low resolution does not show much detail; higher resolution makes considerable detail available.

resolution element (rel)—{GR} The smallest point distinguishable on the raster scan screen. High resolution provides 500 rels or more in each direction. Where a dot or undot may appear.

response time—The time for an AP to react to a request or accept data.

responsive display—{WP} When the text on the screen is a duplicate of what prints. Different WPs offer different degrees of responsiveness.

retrace—{GR} For the raster scan, after a scan line is swept out, the beam returns to the left of the screen, moves down by a line space and begins another scan line. The beam is turned off during this period, only a fraction of the scan line time.

retrieve—To acquire information from a file about one or more individuals without altering the file.

return—Indication in a subroutine or procedure that control goes back to the caller, that the action of the subroutine or procedure is complete.

reusable—When it is easy to enter new information on a medium. Diskettes are reusable; punched paper tape and punchcards are not.

reverse video—To cause one or more characters on the screen to display in opposite video terms: dots which were white now appear black and vice versa.

ribbon, fabric—An inked cloth ribbon moved back and forth in both directions during use. It is reused many times until the impression gets too difficult to read.

ribbon, multistrike—A coated plastic ribbon on which successive characters strike at overlapping points. It is moved in one direction to its end and then must be discarded.

ribbon cartridge—A plastic case containing an inked ribbon on one spool and an empty spool on the other side. The cartridge may be installed on the carriage without the operator getting dirty hands.

richness—Ability to state a request in a programming language in more than one way.

right flush—{WP} A line with its right extremity aligned at the right hand margin while the positioning of its left end depends solely on its length.

rigid disk drive—See *hard disk drive.*

rollover—When two or more keyboard keys are pressed simultaneously, the first one released produces a code.

root—For a tree, the bottom point, or node, from which edges only emanate.

routine—Part of a source statement program which performs a particular function or set of functions.

routine, self check—Checks out the hardware, especially memory. For the IBM PC, AT and XT, it is in ROM.

row—The set of CRT scan lines required to make up one line of text, including spacing lines to separate characters on one row from those on the next. {SS} A group of contiguous cells on the same horizontal line.

row stub—{SS} At the left of the screen, a column which gives row numbers.

rubber band—{GR} A graphic sketching aid which lets you pull a line from a point and move it around the screen like a rubber band with a pointing device. When satisfied, push the command button. Similar facilities are rubber circles, rectangles and rotated rubber rectangles.

satellite—See *slave.*

saturation—(1){GR} Quality which indicates how much white a color includes. If unsaturated, the color includes no white; if tinted, the color is saturated and includes some white. (2) When a magnetic medium is magnetized to saturation, a stronger magnetic field cannot induce further magnetism.
scan line—{GR} Traced out by the raster display beam which passes horizontally from left to right.
screen—The visible portion of the CRT. Sometimes also the text or image displayed there.
screen capacity—For a textual display, the number of characters it shows. Rated in lines per screen times characters per line. A typical figure is 24 × 80.
screen, target—{WP} See *target screen*.
scroll—To cause another portion of an ED to appear on the display.
scroll, automatic—When creating an ED which takes up the entire screen, and typing continues on the bottom of the screen, automatic scroll causes text to move up by one line at workwrap time and text keyed now enters on a new empty bottom line.
scroll, continuous—{WP} The document appears to move continuously up the screen. A command stops the scroll.
scroll, exclusive—{WP} Next screen does not include text from the previous screen.
scroll, line—{WP} *Forward line scroll* advances screen contents by one line. *Reverse line scroll* moves a new line in at the top of the screen, pushing an old line out at the bottom.
scroll, overlapping—{WP} As you scroll in either direction, the next display contains some text from the previous screen, providing continuity.
scroll backward—{WP} To move backward in the document to a previous screen.
scroll forward—{WP} To move forward in the ED so that subsequent screens of information display.
search—{WP} To look for an occurrence of a search string within an ED.
search, repeat—{WP} Request for search using the same search string as the last.
search and replace—{WP} Search string is sought; if a target string is found, it is replaced by the replace string.
search and replace option—{WP} Options during search and replace, such as ignore case, do a specified number of replacements, search backward, etc.
search and replace, discretionary—{WP} Target string is presented in context. You decide if replacement takes place.
search option—{WP} Condition under which a search is performed, such as exact match, whole word, ignore case and reverse search.
search string—{WP} Set of consecutive characters sought.
sector—Portion of a track lying between two disk sector holes or as defined by the formatting process.
sector counter—Records number of sector being read.
sector hole—Holes in hard sectored disk at a fixed radius which generate sector pulses optically as they pass beneath the hole in the envelope.
sector pulse—Generated by the sector holes.
seek—Positioning the disk drive head to a track.

seek command—A request to move the heads in or out to a specified rack.
seek time—(1) Time to seek to an adjacent track. (2) Average time to seek from the inside to the outside of the disk.
segment—A 64K area of memory.
segment register—See *register, segment*.
semidisk—A large RAM, 256K to 1M or more and a software driver which makes it seem like a disk.
sequential access—Accessing a record of a file by scanning all the intermediate records from the starting position. An inherent property of media such as magnetic tape or punchcards.
serial—Signals representing data transmitted bit by bit sequentially in time.
serializer—Converts 8 parallel bits of a byte to 8 serial bits.
service, nonresident—See *utility*.
shift key—See *key, shift*.
shift lock—See *lock, shift*.
single precision—
skew—When consecutive blocks are not placed in consecutive sectors. Since time is required for OS functions between reading one block and the next, one or more sectors are skipped and the next block is assigned to a later-numbered sector.
skirt—The visible vertical edge of a key which may have an additional symbol engraved on it.
slave—A computer dedicated to a single user in a multiple computer system.
slot—Receptacle soldered to the bus to receive an expansion printed circuit board.
soft sectored—Disk format where an initialization and formatting program writes the track and sector identity at the beginning of each sector.
software—Any program which runs the computer, including the OS, AP, utilities, compilers and so forth.
source code—See *code, source*.
sort—To place information in order according to the collating sequence by a key field. If the data are records in a file, a separate AP—a sort program—does the job (for example, SuperSort). Some SSs have a sort built in: Multiplan and Lotus 1-2-3 sort rows of a designated range according to the content of one key column.
source file—See *file, source*.
source statement—See *statement, source*.
spacebar—Horizontal bar on the keyboard to produce the code for a blank.
spelling checking program—Reviews an ED to flag words which may be incorrectly spelled.
spool—To redirect print output to a temporary disk file.
spool queue—A list of temporary spool files yet to be printed.
spread sheet (SS)—A program to help with management planning and budgeting using a columnar pad approach. Examples are CalcStar, PerfectCalc, ProCalc, Multiplan, SuperCalc, Minimodel and Lotus 1-2-3.
spread sheet, actual (AS)—The rectangular range of cells size currently occupied by the spread sheet defined so far, determined by the highest numbered column and row use.
spread sheet, display (DS)—Portion of the spread sheet currently displaying.

spread sheet, virtual (VS)—Maximum spread sheet size specified by the vendor but available only if your computer provides enough memory.

stack, system—A list maintained by the OS which contains data and entry points into programs placed there by APs.

start bit—Sent to initiate asynchronous transmission of each character; always a space.

statement—A set of words and symbols which conforms to the syntax of a programming language. When the statement has a meaning which the compiler or interpreter can fathom, the statement is called *valid*.

statement, assignment—Source statement which assigns a value to a variable, either directly or by means of an expression.

statement, conditional—Where one of two alternative assignments or branch statements is chosen according to the evaluation of a condition.

statement, dimension—Declaring the size of an array so that the compiler or interpreter sets up enough room to store it.

statement, source—One statement in a compiler or interpreter language.

status display—Lines on the screen which give the current status of an AP such as a WP or SS.

status line—{WP} Line, usually in the status display but sometimes in the text, which shows the current left and right margin, tab stops and their type.

status register—See *register, status*.

status stub—{SS} Lines in the DS which describe the SS and shows what you are keying into the active cell.

stencil—{WP} A copy of a letter or document with special symbols where external information should be substituted.

storage, external—A means for storing data safely to be kept even when the computer is off and available when the computer is turned on again. It consists of a storage device and a medium, often removable.

string—A sequence of characters to be deleted or moved about in a document or a program.

stroke image generation—{GR} Image generation by creating sets of lines.

subdirectory—Portion of a directory. A subdirectory may list files and other subdirectories.

subdocument—{WP} Portion of a document stored on disk to be recalled and entered into another document.

subroutine—A portion of a program. See *routine*.

substrate—Thin plastic or metal coated with magnetic material.

support—Help from a vendor when difficulty arises in using an AP.

surface—All disks have two *physical* surfaces. One which can store data is a *recording* surface.

switch, DIP—A switch with dual in-line pins soldered to a PC board and which can be set manually to alter the parameters of the board such as baud rate, memory boundary, port number.

sync character—A unique code continuously retransmitted for synchronous transmission to coordinate the clock at the receiving end with that at transmitting end.

Synchronous Data Link Control (SDLC)—A communication protocol, mainly for large computers.
synchronous recording (or **transmission**)—Characters are recorded or transmitted at a continuous repetitive timed rate.
syntax—Rules governing how words in a formal language may be put together.
system, computer—The hardware, operating system and application programs which fit together and run properly.
system, computerized—The combination of people, procedures and a computer system.
system, graphics—A complete computer system including a high resolution screen, input devices and plotters for producing professional images.
system, integrated—A computer system and a set of programs, all of which talk to each other and interchange data properly.
system, operating—See *operating system*.
system, turnkey—Brings up the AP when you boot the system.
system board—The mother board containing circuitry and memory chips, the bus and slots for the IBM PC and XT.
system disk—A disk or diskette containing the nucleus and other required parts of the operating system and many of the utilities.
system house (DEM)—A vendor which not only supplies the hardware, operating system and APs but sets them up and provides extended service.
tab—{WP} (1) The marker set at one or more line positions. (2) A key which causes the cursor to move to the next tab stop.
tab, center—{WP} After tabbing, characters entered are centered on this position.
tab, decimal—{WP} Characters entered move left until you hit the decimal point; those hit thereafter move to the right.
tab, right—{WP} As you type, characters move leftward so that the last character that you hit is at the tab stop.
tab, standard—{WP} Characters typed enter from left to right. Also called *left tab*.
tab clear—{WP} Removing an existing tab.
tab line—See status line.
tab set—{WP} Setting the tab to a particular position(s).
table—A rectangular array of data arranged in columns and rows, the basis of the spread sheet.
tablet—{GR} Plastic rectangle about the size of a piece of paper. By moving a cursor with a cross-hair or a stylus around with the tablet you cause the screen cursor to move in a similar fashion. You can trace a drawing placed on the tablet to enter it into a graphics system.
tailor—To alter a package or OS to suit the computer hardware.
target character—{WP} The ED character where you want editing to start.
target screen—{WP} A screen which shows the target character.
telecommunication—Transmission of intelligence over a distance.
terminal—A combination display and keyboard in a single box.
text mode—{WP} Some WPs have to be in this mode before you can key in text.
thimble—A print element like the daisy wheel, but with all the spokes bent upward so that it looks like a thimble. Found on the NEC Spinwriter.

title lock—{SS} The SS on request can lock titles at the top and/or on the left of an AS. As you scroll, these titles remain fixed to show labels for rows and columns in distant parts of the AS.

toggle—A command which alternates an AP between two modes. For example, WordStar uses ^V to alternate between overtype and push-aside insertion.

track—Circular area swept out by the disk head when it occupies (seeks to) one of its fixed standard positions. Tracks are numbered from outside in, starting from 0 and going to the maximum applicable to the particular drive.

track register—{H} A register in the disk drive which records where the head is positioned.

tractor feed—On a printer, a mechanism with a grain of feed pins on each side to fit into holes in continuous paper stock. Line advance commands from the computer cause the paper to advance. Each train is horizontally movable so that the tractor accommodates forms of various widths.

train—See *chain*.

transaction record—See *record, transaction*.

transfer rate—Transfer rate from a disk or other peripheral device to memory or vice versa. Rated in kilo*bits* per second (Kb/s), not to the confused with kilo*bytes* per second (KB/s).

transient program—Program loaded and executed on command to the OS from a console prompt by entering its name. The OS finds the program on the disk, brings it into the transient area (TPA) and gives it control. When finished, the AP returns control to the OS.

transient program area (TPA)—An area in memory where transient programs are loaded and execute.

transmission, asynchronous—See *asynchronous transmission*.

transmission, synchronous—See *synchronous transmission*.

transparent—Characterizing an action which the operator or user is unaware.

transportable—When a program can be moved from one computer to another, especially if they are of different manufacturers or types.

trap—Another name for an interrupt, especially where a number of different interrupt types exist, each causing control to go to different areas in the OS.

tree—A graph structure containing points (nodes) and lines (edges) joining them. A structure for holding a large file directory.

triad, color—{GR} Three spots at a rel on the CRT screen, one each to emit red, green and blue light to produce a color image.

type—Category into which to place variables—for example, real (number), integer, character, string. Many programming languages have a number of types available to describe variables. The compiler thus determines what operations on the variables are legal and what kind of ML commands to use. Type appears in the variable declaration.

undelete—{WP} To bring back a string which has been deleted.

undot—{GR} A rel which is not illuminated.

universal asynchronous receiver/transmitter (UART)—An LSI chip which interfaces the computer with asynchronous devices. It converts the data with a serializer and a deserializer, adds start and stop bits, generates parity and clocks the data at the required rate. To receive, it recognizes and deletes the start and stop bits, checks parity, counts down an external clock to the data rate. It provides control signals to the computer and receives control signals from the computer.

universal synchronous and asynchronous receiver/transmitter (USART)—May be used for either synchronous or asynchronous transmission and reception as specified by the computer. In asynchronous mode, it operates like the UART. In synchronous mode, it examines incoming data to identify a sync character; thereafter, the bit stream is divided into groups of 8 bits passed in parallel to the computer.

unjustified—{WP} Text not justified: full lines have different lengths. Otherwise called normally justified, ragged right and aligned left.

update—To change one or more records in a file so that they show the current status of the associated individuals. This action does not alter the file's structure, since no records are added or deleted.

upward compatible—See *chip family*.

utility—A program, generally supplied with the OS, such as to copy files, format disks or give statistics about devices and volumes.

variable—A name or symbol in a program which represents a numeric value.

variable, string—A variable which represents an alphabetic value such as a person's name or department.

variable list—{WP} List of variables to be substituted in the stencil while a form letter is being created.

very large scale integration (VLSI)—Placing from tens of thousands to a million or more circuits on a pinhead-size chip. Also see *large scale integration*.

video display terminal (VDT)—a terminal with a CRT display screen for textual information and graphic displays.

video, memory mapped—Part of main memory shared by the computer and the terminal where characters are entered as dots and undots (rather than as a character code). Conversion from code to dot format is done by the OS or AP. Makes possible combining graphics and text.

volatile—Memory whose contents disappear when the computer is turned off.

volume—Quantity of medium mounted and available on an external storage device. Examples of volumes are cassettes, floppy disks and disk packs.

volume, permanent—Cannot be removed from the external storage device by the operator. Example is the volume for a hard disk or Winchester drive.

volume, removable—Can be removed from the external storage device and replaced by another, similar volume.

widow—{WP} The last line of a paragraph which appears alone at the top of a page.

wild card—{WP} Character(s) in a search indicating that this position should be ignored in the target string.

Winchester drive—See *hard disk drive*.

window—{SS} Lets you view different parts of a spread sheet simultaneously. Some SSs (Multiplan) provide up to eight. {OE} Show displays produced by separate APs.

window, synchronized—{SS} As you scroll this window, all others to which it is synchronized also scroll.

window, unsynchronized—{SS} Scrolling does not affect the display in any other window.

window envelope—{WP} Business envelope with a clear plastic insert so that a properly folded letter shows the addressee's name and address.

word—For the micro, 2 bytes, or 16 bits.

wordwrap—{WP} Senses the last word which fits on a line and automatically puts the next word on the succeeding line.

wraparound—See *wordwrap*.

write—(1) Placing data on an external storage medium. (2) Putting a datum into a cell in memory.

write protect—Each diskette has a notch in one of its corners, scanned optically in the drive. For the floppy (8 inch disk), this notch must be covered to write. For the minifloppy (5½-inch disk), a covered notch prevents writing.

WYSIWYG—What you see is what you get. See *display, responsive*.

zoom—{GR} To use the display like a zoom lense, thus making more or less of the image appear on the screen.

Appendix C
Basic Commands by Type

This appendix lists BASIC commands by type but with only a sketchy description. A full description is found in Appendix F.

DIRECTIVES TO THE INTERPRETER

COMMAND	ACTION
AUTO	Generates line numbers.
BLOAD	Loads a block of data into memory.
BSAVE	Saves a block of binary data.
CLEAR	Clears variables and memory.
CONT	Continuous program after STOP.
DELETE	Deletes specified program lines.
EDIT	Permits program lines to be changed.
FILES	Lists files.
KILL	Erases a file.
LIST	Lists lines of the program.
LLIST	Lists program lines on printer.
LOAD	Loads a program file.
MERGE	Merges a saved program with that in memory.
NAME	Renames a file.
NEW	Erases program memory and variables.
RENUM	Renumbers program lines.
RESET	Reinitializes disk.
RUN	Executes a program.
SAVE	Saves a program.
SYSTEM	Exits to OS.
TRON	Sets trace on.
TROFF	Turns trace off.

NONDEVICE PROGRAM COMMANDS

COMMAND	ACTION
CALL	Calls ML program.
CHAIN	Brings in and runs a program.

BASIC COMMANDS BY TYPE

COMMAND	ACTION
COMMON	Passes variables to chained program.
DATE	Sets the date.
DEF FN	Defines a function.
DEFtype	Defines variable names as specific types.
DEFSEG	Defines memory segment.
DEFUSR	Sets starting address of ML routine.
DIM	Defines array.
END	Terminates program.
ERASE	Eliminates an array.
ERROR	Simulates an error.
FOR TO STEP	Repeats program lines.
GOSUB	Calls a subroutine.
GOTO	Continues execution at line specified.
IF THEN ELSE	Conditional execution.
LET	Assigns variable value.
NEXT	Closes FOR loop.
ON ERROR GOTO	Defines error trap.
ON GOSUB	Multiple subroutine branch.
ON GOTO	Multiple branch.
OPTION BASE	Sets array subscripts.
PEEK	Reads byte from memory.
POKE	Puts byte into memory.
RANDOMIZE	Reseeds random number generator.
REM	Begins a documentation line.
RESTORE	Resets DATA pointer.
RESUME	Returns from error trap.
RETURN	Returns from subroutine.
STOP	Temporarily stops program.
SWAP	Exchanges values of two variables.
TIME	Sets the time.
WEND	Ends a WHILE loop.
WHILE	Begins a loop.

DEVICE DIRECTED COMMANDS

These commands are listed by device type.

COMMAND	ACTION
Audio	
BEEP	Beeps the speaker.
PLAY	Plays music.
SOUND	Generates a sound.
Communications	
COM	Sets trapping.
ON COM GOSUB	Enables trap routine.
OPEN "COM...	Opens file for communication.

COMMAND	ACTION
Files, Data and Printer	
CLOSE	Closes a file.
DATA	Creates data table.
FIELD	Defines buffer structure.
GET	Reads record from random file.
INPUT	Reads data from keyboard.
INPUT#	Reads data from a file.
LINE INPUT	Reads line from keyboard.
LINE INPUT#	Reads line from a file.
LPRINT	Prints data on the printer.
LPRINT USING	Formats and prints data.
LSET	Enters datum into buffer at left.
OPEN	Opens a file.
PRINT	Displays data.
PRINT USING	Formats and displays data.
PRINT#	Writes data to a file.
PRINT# USING	Formats and writes data to a file.
PUT#	Writes data to a random file.
READ	Gets data from DATA statement.
RSET	Enters datum into buffer at right.
WRITE	Outputs data to screen.
WRITE#	Outputs data to a file.
Graphics	
CIRCLE	Draws a circle.
COLOR	Sets colors.
DRAW	Draws a figure.
GET	Reads graphic information from screen.
LINE	Draws a line or box.
PAINT	Fills in an area with color.
PRESET,PSET	Draws a point.
PUT	Writes graphic information.
Joystick	
ON STRIG GOSUB	Traps joystick button.
STRIG	Sets function or trapping.
Keyboard	
KEY	Sets displays or enables keyboard.
ON KEY GOSUB	Trapping for a key.
Light Pen	
ON PEN GOSUB	Trapping for light pen.
Cassette Motor	
MOTOR	Turns motor on or off.

COMMAND	ACTION
Port	
IN	Brings in a byte from a selected port.
OUT	Sends a byte out to a port.
WAIT	Checks whether a port is free.
Screen	
CLS	Clears the screen.
LOCATE	Positions the cursor.
SCREEN	Sets screen characteristics.
WIDTH	Sets screen width.

NUMERIC FUNCTIONS

FUNCTION	RETURNS
Arithmetic	
ABS	Absolute value.
ATM	Arc tangent.
CDBL	Converts to double precision.
CINT	Converts to integer.
COS	Cosine.
CSNG	Converts to single precision.
EXP	A power of *e*.
FIX	Truncates to an integer.
INT	Rounds to an integer.
LOG	Natural logarithm.
RND	Random number.
SGN	Sign of number.
SIN	Sine of angle.
SQR	Square root.
TAN	Tangent of angle.
String Related	
ASC	ASCII code for first character.
CVI	Converts string to an integer.
CVS	Converts string to single precision.
CVD	Converts string to double precision.
INSTR	Position of substring within string.
LEN	Length of string.
VAL	Value for-first string character.
I/O and Miscellaneous	
CSRLIN	Vertical position of the cursor.
EOF	End of file.
ERL	Line number where error occurs.
ERR	Error code last found.

FUNCTION	RETURNS
I/O and Miscellaneous	
FRE	Amount of free space in memory.
LOC	Location of file.
LOF	Length of file.
LPOS	Carriage position of printer.
PEEK	Byte from memory.
POKE	Puts byte into memory.
PEN	Reads lightpen.
POINT	Returns color of point.
POS	Cursor column position.
SCREEN	Character or color at screen position.
STICK	Joystick coordinate.
STRIG	Joystick buttom command.
USR	Calls ML routine.
VARPTR	Address of variable in memory

STRING FUNCTIONS

FUNCTION	RETURNS
General	
CHR$	Character with ASCII code in.
LEFT$	Left hand substring.
MID$	Internal substring.
RIGHT$	Right hand substring.
SPACE$	String of spaces.
STRING$	With given ASCII value.
I/O and Miscellaneous	
DATE$	System date.
HEX$	Hexadecimal string equivalent.
INKEY$	Reads one keyboard character.
INPUT$	Reads several characters from a file.
MKI$	Converts an integer.
MKS$	Converts a single precision number.
MKD$	Converts a double precision number.
OCT$	Converts n to an octal string.
SPC	Prints spaces.
STR$	Converts an expression to a string.
TAB	Tabs to a position.
TIME$	System time.
VARPTR$	Variable type and addressing in memory.

Appendix D
BASICA Commands
and Their Meaning

$v = \text{ABS}(x)$ (1)
    Assigns the absolute value of the expression, x, to v.

$v = \text{ASC}(x\$)$ (3)
    Converts the first character of the string $x\$$ into the decimal equivalent of its ASCII code, assigning this to the numeric variable, v.

$v = \text{ANT}(x)$
    Uses x in radians for an angle and finds the arc tangent, assigning this to v.

AUTO [num][, inc] (4)
    When **AUTO** is requested without options, all commands in the program are renumbered, starting with 10 and with increments of 10. Line numbers which appear in **GOTO** statements are also altered so that the program should work properly. When options are included, the first line is assigned *num* and *inc* is the increment added to get the numbers for succeeding lines. Either the number or increment option may be used alone.

BEEP (5)
    Causes the terminal to issue a sound or beep.

BLOAD file [,offset] (6)
    The block load command brings in a machine language program segment usually programmed in assembly language, translated, and in a file called *file*. The position in memory where the incoming program segment is to be placed is determined by *offset* and is measured from the last defined segment declared by **DEF SEG**.

BSAVE file,offset,length (7)
    The block save command returns a block to *file* as defined by *offset* and having the length, *length*. This may be a machine language program, a pictorial image or any other data.

CALL sr[(var,[,var...])]   (8)
CALL gives control to a machine language routine supposedly somewhere in memory. Here *sr* is the name of the routine and variables may be sent along with it.

$V = $ CDBL(x) (9)
Converts an expression, after evaluating it, into a double precision format.

CHAIN [MERGE]file[,[line][,ALL][,DELETE range]]]   (10)
In its simplest form, CHAIN is a most useful command. It removes the current source program from memory, replaces it with *file* and starts interpreting it. In this way, you can break up your program into nonresident pieces and pass control back and forth among them. Normally, execution begins with the first command in *file;* if *line* is present, execution begins with that line number. When MERGE is present, the existing program is not removed but the incoming program is merged with it instead. ALL preserves variables in the issuing program so that they can be passed on to the incoming program. (Otherwise COMMON must be used to do this). When DELETE is present, a range of lines is deleted from the issuing program.

CHDIR path   (11)
A new directory, defined by *path,* is found and established as a default directory.

$v\$ = $ CHR$\$(n)$ (12)
Converts the decimal number, *n,* into its ASCII equivalent symbol and assigns it to the string $v\$$.

$v = $ CINT(x) (13)
Converts the expression to an integer by truncating the decimal portion.

CIRCLE$(x,y),r$[color[,start, end[aspect]]]   (14)
Creates circles and elipses as described in Equation (8.7.10), Chapter 8.

CLEAR [,[n][,m]]   (15)
Clears all variables from memory but leaves the program untouched. Clears up to *n* bytes if *n* is supplied and sets aside *m* bytes of stack space.

CLOSE [[#]file[,[#]file]...]   (16)
Closes one, several or all files, the latter when file numbers are omitted.

CLS   (17)
Clears the screen. Not available in MBASIC, since the control codes depend upon the terminal and a standard terminal is used for the IBM PC and hence BASICA.

COLOR [fore] [,[back][,border]]   (18)
In text mode only sets the color of the foreground, background and border as described in Section 8.7.

COLOR [back] [,[palette]] (19)
  For graphics, changes the color of the background and/or the palette.

COM(n) [ON] [OFF] [STOP] (20)
  Establishes communication to the particular adapter which may be of type 1 or 2 (for *n*). The three options turn communication on, off or stop it entirely.

COMMON vlist (21)
  Establishes an area where a number of variables are maintained to be exchanged when CHAIN is issued. The incoming program can then pick up the current values for these variables but not for others. Variable names appear in a list separated by commas, *vlist*.

CONT (22)
  Resumes execution of a program which is stopped because of STOP or END encountered in the program or because *control break* was hit.

$v = $ COS(x) (23)
  Finds the cosine.

$v = $ CSNG(x) (24)
  Converts to single precision.

$v = $ CSRLIN (25)
  Returns the vertical coordinate of the cursor.

$v = $ CVI(x$) (26)
$v = $ CVS(x$) (27)
$v = $ CVD(x$) (28)
  Used with random files where all data is in ASCII format. To convert into numerical format the string is supplied as *x$*. Then one of these commands converts it into an integer, single precision or double precision number respectively.

DATA dlist (29)
  This is a way to incorporate data in the program. *Dlist* is a list of constants which can be accessed with the READ command.

v = DATE$ (30)

DATE$ = $x$$ (31)
  Provides a constant which contains the current date and may be read into a variable.

DEF FNfunct(arglist) = exp (32)
  This function definition is the closest that we come to an open subroutine. Here *arglist* is a list of arguments which are used in the expression, *exp* at the right. This officially defines the function which may be used later in an assignment or other

kind of statement, at which time parameters are passed positionally and evaluated by the interpreter to give a value.

DEF SEG [= address] (33)
Defines a segment in memory to be used by one of the following commands: BLOAD, BSAVE, CALL, PEEK, POKE, USR. The address assigned to the segment follows at *address*. If omitted it applies to BASICA's data segment.

DEFINT [DEFSNG,DEFDBL,DEFSTR] [letters] (34)
Variable types are generally signaled by a suffix applied to the variable name (such as %, $, etc.). An easier way to handle such variables is to state that all of a particular type begin with a designated letter or letters. Then the suffix is not longer required. The statements of (34) let you establish beginning letters for variables of particular types, namely integer, single precision, double precision and string.

DEF USR[n] = offset (35)
Specifies the starting address of a machine language subroutine later called by the USR function.

DELETE [range] (36)
Deletes commands from the program as specified *byrang*e which is made up as specified with LIST, which see.

DIM var(subscripts) (37)
Establishes the dimension of a multidimensional array called *var*, either string or numerical.

DRAW string (38)
For graphics, moves the present position either relatively or absolutely according to *string* and does other fucntions described in Section 8.7.

EDIT line (39)
References *line* for editing so that you may alter it using the proper function keys or control sequences.

END (40)
When encountered, causes the program to terminate execution but not to relinquish control to the system.

v = EOF(num) (41)
This function checks the file with number *num* and when there is no data left in that file assigns -1 (false) to the variable. Used for checking termination of a file so as to suppress error messages.

ERASE vlist (42)
When variable space in the program runs short this command selectively erases selected variables, releasing the space they occupy.

BASICA COMMANDS AND THEIR MEANING   819

$v =$ ERL (43)
$v =$ ERR (44)

    Provides the line number (43) and the error code (44) for the last occurring error. These may be tested and used in an IF statement to determine when and why errors have occurred.

ERROR n (45)

    Simulates the occurrence of an error of type n.

$v =$ EXP(x) (46)

    Calculates the natural exponential function.

FIELD [#] file [width AS row...] (47)

    Chops up the buffer into fields, required for random files described in Chapter 9.

FILES [stencil] (48)

    Displays all the files on the default drive if no option is provided. Otherwise *stencil* is used as an ambiguous file name for displaying files.

$v =$ FIX(x) (49)

    Truncates the decimal portion of the number.

FOR $v = i$ TO j [STEP]
    statements
NEXT [v] (50)

    This is the looping statement. The variable v is initialized to i and is incremented by 1 after each iteration of the loop, unless the STEP statement is present, in which case k is used. The statements which appear between FOR and NEXT are executed at each iteration. Thereafter the variable is advanced by the increment and checked against j to determine if further iterations should be done. Iterations continue as long as i is less than j; otherwise they terminate. Since nesting may occur (loops within loops), the variable supplied with NEXT determines which loop the command applies to.

$v =$ FRE(x) (51)

    Determines the amount of free space for variables left in memory. Here x is a dummy variable and v will contain a number indicating the available space. House clearning is done when the command is issued, so that unused variable space is freed. This is always done automatically but takes less time if you include FRE periodically in your program.

GET [#] file num [,recnum] (52)

    Reads the requested *recnum* record from the designated file. If the record number is omitted, the next record relative to the previous request is accessed.

GET $(x1,y1)-(x2,y2)$ array (53)

    This graphics command reads all the points within the square defined by the diagonal of the command and places their value into *array*. Useful for storing graphic information.

GOSUB line (54)
The same as **GOTO** except that, after the subroutine is entered, execution continues up to the command **RETURN**. This causes control to go back to the command right after **GOSUB**.

GOTO line (55)
Causes the command at *line* to be executed next and continuation of execution of statements thereafter.

v$ = **HEX$**(num) (56)
Returns a string which represents the hexadecimal value of the decimal argument.

IF exp **THEN** clause [**ELSE** clause] (57)
IF exp **GOTO** line [**ELSE** clause] (58)
Evaluates the expression, *exp* and, if true, executes the series of statements in *clause* (57) or to *line* (58). If **ELSE** is present and the expression evaluates to false then the clause found there is executed. A clause is a single statement or a number of statements separated by colons.

v$ = **INKEY$** (59)
Reads a character from the keyboard.

v = **INP** (*n*) (60)
Returns the byte read from port *n*.

INPUT [;] ["prompt"] varlist (61)
After *prompt* is displayed, if present, the values keyed by the operator are assigned to the variables named in *varlist* in that order.

INPUT #file varlist (62)
Accesses the indicated file and obtains values for the variables provided in the list.

v$ = **INPUT$**(*n*[,[#]filenum]) (63)
Waits for *n* keys to be hit at the keyboard or entered from a file and assigns this string to the variable, *r*$. If no file number is present the keyboard is the source.

v = **INSTR**([*n*,]*x*$,*y*$) (64)
Searches for the first occurrence of the string *y*$ in the string *x*$ and returns to *v* the position at which the match is found. The optional offset, *n*, sets a character position for starting the search in *x*$. Returns 0 to *v* if the string is not found.

v = **INT**(*x*) (65)
Integer function which returns the largest integer less than or equal to *x*. In other words it truncates *x*.

BASICA COMMANDS AND THEIR MEANING

KEY [ON,OFF,LIST,n,x\$] (66)
Sets or displays the soft keys.

KEY(n) [ON,OFF,STOP] (67)
Activates and deactivates trapping of the specified key in the BASIC program.

KILL file (68)
Deletes a file from the default disk. *File* may be prefixed with a drive designation to delete a file from other than the default drive. Similar to the ERA command of CP/M.

v\$ = LEFT\$(x\$,n) (69)
Finds the leftmost n characters of x\$ and assigns them to v\$.

v = LEN(x\$) (70)
Returns the number of characters in the designated string, x\$.

[LET] $v = x$ (71)
Assigns the value of an expression to a variable. Obviously LET can be omitted.

LINE [($x1$,$y1$)]–$x2$,$y2$)[,[color][,B[F]][,style]] (72)
Draws a line or a box on the screen in the desired color and style. This may be completed to form a box and it may be filled if the options are specified.

LINE INPUT[;] ["prompt";]y\$ (73)
After issuing the prompt, if the *prompt* is present, this command reads all the keystrokes entered at the keyboard of up to 254 characters until *enter* or *return* is encountered. Assigns all symbols, including commas and so forth, to the string variable, v\$.

LINE INPUT#file,v\$ (74)
Reads an entire line, all the characters up to 254, not being influenced by the delimiters until *return line* is encountered. This is discarded and the next line input command begins where this one left off.

LIST [line] [–[line2]] [,file] (75)
Lists some or all of the program currently in memory, displaying it to the screen or sending it to a file described as an option.

LLIST [line1] [–[line2]] (76)
Lists all or part of the program currently in memory on the line printer.

LOAD file [,R] (77)
Loads the file designated into memory, replacing what is currently there, and runs that program if R is present.

v = LOC(file) (78)
Returns the current record number for both random and sequential files.

LOCATE [row][col][,[cursor][,[start][,stop]]] (79)
Positions the cursor on the active screen. Optional parameters turn the blinking cursor on and off and find the size of the blinking cursor.

$v =$ **LOF** (filenum) (80)
Returns the length of the file allocated to *file num*.

$v =$ **LOG**(x) (81)
Returns the natural logarithm of x.

$v =$ **LPOS**(n) (82)
Returns the current position of the print head within the print buffer of the line printer.

LPRINT [list][;] (83)
Sends data to the line printer. The list may include literals and variables. The terminal semicolon suppresses line feed.

LPRINT USING $v\$$; list[;] (84)
The variable statement, $v\$$, following **USING** specifies format for printing *list*.

LSET $v\$ = x\$$ (85)
Moves the datum $x\$$ into $v\$$ left justified, where $v\$$ has been declared in a field statement. This is preparatory to **PUT**.

MERGE file (86)
Merges lines from an ASCII basic program file into the program now in memory. If duplicate numbers appear in both files, incoming lines take precedence.

$v\$ =$ **MID$**($x\$,n,$[m]) (87)
$x\$$ is a string from which a substring is to be extracted, beginning at the nth character and continuing to the end of the string unless the m option is present. In that case, a substring of length m is extracted and placed in the variable $v\$$.

**MID$**($v\$,n,$[,m]) = $y\$$ (88)
The string $y\$$, is entered into the string $v\$$ at the nth position; if m is present, only that many characters are replaced.

MKDIR path (89)
Creates a directory or subdirectory on the specified disk.

$v\$ =$ **MKI$**(integer expression) (90)
$v\$ =$ **MKS$**(single expression) (91)
$v\$ =$ **MKD$**(double expression) (92)
Convert numeric values to string values.

BASICA COMMANDS AND THEIR MEANING

MOTOR {ON,OFF} (93)
Turns the cassette player on or off from the program.

NAME file1 **AS** file2 (94)
Renames *file1* as *file2*.

NEW (95)
Deletes the program in memory and clears all memory variables.

$v\$ = $ **OCT\$**(n) (96)
Takes the number n and converts it into an octal string.

ON COM(u) **GOSUB** line (97)
Sets up a line number in the BASIC program to execute should communication information on part u be available.

ON ERROR GOTO line (98)
When any error occurs, commands starting at *line* are executed.

ON exp **{GOTO,GOSUB}** linelist (99)
The expression should evaluate to an integer. At the end of the statement is a list of line numbers. The appropriate line is executed next according to the number provided by the expression. Thus if the expression yields the value 3, the third line number gets control next.

ON KEY(u) **GOSUB** line (100)
Sets up a line number for BASIC to jump to when the specified function key or cursor control key is pressed.

ON PEN GOSUB line (101)
Sets up a line number to which BASIC transfers control when the light pen is activated.

ON PLAY(n) **GOSUB** line (102)
Allows continuous background music to play during program execution.

ON STRIG (n) **GOSUB** line (103)
Sets up a line number for BASIC to jump to when one of the joystick buttons or triggers is pressed.

ON TIMER (n) **GOSUB** line (104)
Transfers control to given line number in BASIC program when defined period of time, n seconds, has elapsed.

OPEN {file,path} [FOR mode] AS [#]num [LEN = recl] (105)
A file must be opened before used, specified by name or, for the XT by a path to

the file. *Mode* indicates whether the file is for output, input or is a random file. The file is referred to in the program by *num*. For random files, the record length must be supplied as *recl*.

OPEN "COM... (107)
Opens a communication file. A modem must be part of the system. A large number of options must be specified, although omitted above.

OPTION BASE {0,1} (108)
Declares whether the lowest subscript for an array is 0 or 1.

OUT *n,m* (109)
Sends a byte described by the decimal number *m* representing the ASCII code for the character to output port *n*.

PAINT(*x,y*)[[paint][,bndry][background]] (110)
Fills in an area on the screen with the selected color in graphic mode.

v = PEEK(*n*) (111)
Goes to the byte in memory numbered *n* and finds its contents, placing this at *v*.

PEN {ON,OFF,STOP} (112)
Turns the light pen on so it may be used or turns it off. However, the **STOP** option lets information from the pen be received and remembered until the light pen is turned on again.

v = PEN(*n*) (113)
Reads the information supplied by the light pen. The argument *n* is a decimal digit which says which pen attribute is to be examined and transferred into *v*.

PLAY *v*$ (114)
Plays music as specified by the string, *v*$.

v = PLAY(*n*) (115)
Returns the number of notes currently in the music background buffer. Here *n* is a dummy argument and can have any value.

v = PMAP(*x,n*) (116)
Maps physical coordinates to world coordinates or world coordinates to physical coordinates for graphic use. Here *n* is a constant which indicates the kind of mapping desired.

v = POINT(*x,y*); *v* = POINT(*n*) (117)
For graphics, returns the color of the specified point on the screen or current graphics coordinate. In the second form, *n* determines what kind of value is returned.

BASICA COMMANDS AND THEIR MEANING   825

POKE *n,m* (118)
   Writes the byte determined by *m*, a decimal number between 0 and 255, placing it into memory between 0 and 64K. The exact memory location is determined by the DEF SEG statement issued earlier.

v = POS(*n*) (119)
   Returns the cursor column position.

{PRINT,?}list[;] (120)
   Displays data on the screen; evoked by either PRINT or ?.

PRINT USING *v*$ list [;] (121)
   Prints strings or numbers using the format specified by *v*$.

PRINT#filnum[USING *v*$;]list (122)
   Writes data sequentially to a file using the format *v*$, if specified. Data appear in the file exactly as they would display on the screen. If commas are used between variables or expressions, then the extra space that appears on the display is also put into the file.

{PSET,PRESET} (*x,y*) [,color] (123)
   Draws a point at the specified position on the screen in the color included. If no color is included, the background color is used for PRESET.

PUT [#]filenum [,num] (124)
   Writes record *num* from the buffer to a random file.

PUT(*x,y*), array[,action] (125)
   Writes colors into a specified area of the screen.

RANDOMIZE{,*n*,TIMER} (126)
   Seeds the random number generator so that it starts from scratch to create random numbers.

READ vlist (127)
   Reads values from DATA statements and assigns them to the variables in the order in which they appear in a READ statement. Values are read sequentially from all existing DATA statements until all have been read.

REM (128)
   Anything which follows this command up to the end of the line is ignored by the interpreter and is provided only as program documentation.

RENUM [new] [,[old] [inc]] (129)
   Renumbers all the command lines in the program. If options are omitted, the first

line number is 10 and the increment is 10. If supplied, *new* is used for the first line number and *inc* is the increment. If desired, renumbering can start with *old*.

RESET (130)
Closes all diskette files and clears the system buffer.

RESTORE [line] (131)
Allows **DATA** statements to be read from a specified line.

RESUME [{ ,0,NEXT,line]} (132)
Continues program execution after an error recovery is performed. The operand indicates whether execution resumes at the error statement (missing or 0), at the next statement (**NEXT**) or at a given line number (*line*).

RETURN line (133)
Last line in a subroutine (when you have reached this set of statements with **GOSUB**), which returns you to the next statement after **GOSUB** or to *line*.

$v\$ = $ **RIGHT\$**$(x\$,n)$ (134)
Extracts the rightmost n characters of $x\$$ for $v\$$.

RMDIR (135)
Removes a directory or subdirectory from the specified disk.

$v = $ **RND** [(x)] (136)
Returns a random number between 0 and 1.

RSET $v\$ = x\$$ (137)
Enters a variable $x\$$ into the buffer $v\$$ defined by **FIELD**, right justifying the information.

RUN {,line,file[,R]} (138)
Begins execution either from the beginning or from line number *line,* or by replacing the current program with one provided by *file*.

SAVE file {,A,P} (139)
Saves the program currently in memory in *file,* either in compressed format, ASCII format (A) or in encoded binary format (P).

$v = $ **SCREEN**(row,col[z]) (140)
Returns the ASCII code 0–255 for the character on the active screen at the specified row and column. The argument z is used to return the color.

SCREEN [mode] [,[boost][,[apage][,vpage]]] (141)
Sets the screen attributes for subsequent statements.

BASICA COMMANDS AND THEIR MEANING 827

$v = \text{SGN}(x)$ (142)
    Sets v according to the sign of x: 1 if positive, 0 if 0, and -1 if negative.

$v = \text{SIN}(x)$ (143)
    Calculates the sine of x in radians.

SOUND freq,duration (144)
    Generates a sound with given frequency and duration.

$v\$ = \text{SPACE}\$(n)$ (145)
    Assigns a string of n spaces to $v\$$.

PRINT SPC(n) (146)
    Skips n spaces.

$v = \text{SQR}(x)$ (147)
    Finds the square root of the number x assigned to v.

$v = \text{STICK}(n)$ (148)
    Returns the x or y coordinates of joystick. The coordinate and stick used is determined by n.

STOP (149)
    Terminates program execution and returns to the command level. You can resume execution by issuing CONT.

$v\$ = \text{STR}\$(n)$ (150)
    Converts the number x into a string $v\$$.

STRIG {ON,OFF} (151)
$v = \text{STRIG}(n)$ (152)
STRIG(n) {ON,OFF,STOP} (153)
    Sets the joystick buttons on or off or returns the status of the buttons.

$v\$ = \text{STRING}\$(n,m)$ (154)
$v\$ = \text{STRING}\$(n,x\$)$ (155)
    Returns a string of length n whose characters all have the ASCII code m (154) or the first character of $x\$$ (155).

SWAP $v1,v2$ (156)
    Interchanges values for the variables $v1$ and $v2$.

SYSTEM (157)
    Exits the interpreter and returns control to the operating system.

PRINT TAB(*n*) (158)
    Tabs to position *n*.

v = TAN(*x*) (159)
    Calculates the tangent of the value *x* in radians.

v$ = TIMES (160)
TIME$ = *x*$ (161)
    Sets or retrieves the time.

v = TIMER (162)
    Returns the number of seconds elapsed since midnight or since the system reset function.

TRON (163)
TROFF (164)
    Turns on and off the trace function. For TRON output sent to the display appears (included within a separate set of brackets) as well as the number of each and every statement satisfactory executed.

v = USR [*n*](arg) (165)
    Calls a machine language program that has been entered into memory by a previous command and identified as a user function *n*. Parameters may be passed at *arg*.

v = VAL(*x*$) (166)
    Strips blanks, letters and symbols from the string *x*$ and converts to a numeric assigned to *v*.

v = VARPTR({var,#file}) (167)
    Returns the absolute memory address of the variable or the file control block named.

VIEW [[SCREEN][(*x*1,*y*1)−(*x*2,*y*2)[,color][,[boundary]]]]] (168)
    Defines a subset of the viewing surface called a viewport onto which window contents are mapped for graphics only.

WAIT port,*n*[,*m*] (169)
    Suspends program execution while monitoring the status of the indicated port. When the byte arrives, it is exclusively ORed with *m* and then an AND function performed with *n*. Thus two masks determine whether data arrive at the port.

WHILE expression
    statements
WEND (170)
    Executes the series of statements as long as the *expression* evaluates to true.

BASICA COMMANDS AND THEIR MEANING 829

WIDTH {,file,device} , size (171)
Sets the width of the screen or the device associated with a file to a particular value, *size*.

WINDOW [[SCREEN]($x1$)–($x2,y2$) (172)
Redefines the coordinates of the screen.

WRITE list (173)
Outputs data to the screen. WRITE inserts commas between items as they are displayed and delimits strings with quotation marks while PRINT does neither.

WRITE #filenum,list (174)
Writes data to a sequential file. Inserts commas between items as they are written and delimits strings with quotation marks. Hence the user does not put explicit delimiters into the list. Puts a blank in front of positive numbers. *Return line* is inserted after the last item in the list.

Legend:

[]—option which may be omitted entirely.
{}—one of these options *must* be chosen.

Appendix E
Word Processing Packages

IBM PC WP Characteristics*

PROGRAM NAME:	EASYWRITER II	FINALWORD	LEADING EDGE
Company	Info Unlim.	Mark of Unicorn	Leading Edge
Price	$395	$300	$295
Memory required	96K	64K	256K
Default mode	Overstrike	Insert	Either
Orientation	Page	Document	Document
Multiple ruler lines	Yes	No	Yes
Decimal alignment	Yes	No	Yes
Background printing	Yes	Yes	Yes
Form letter merge	Yes	No	$55 Option
Widow/orphan control	No	No	Yes
Semi-auto hyphenation	No	No	No
Outline numbering	No	Yes	No
Split screen	No	2 H	8 H/V
Math	No	No	No
Spelling	Checker	No	No
Automatic footnotes	No	Yes	No
Index generation	No	Yes	No
Printer support	40	Many	All, by utility
Suggested users	Lawyers	Writers	Secretaries
Applications	{1}	{4}	{7}
Strengths	{2}	{5}	{8}
Weaknesses	{3}	{6}	{9}

1. Good for simple editing and for form letters. Poor for long documents frequently revised.
2. True WYSIWYG; pleasant interface; file folder document storage.
3. Slow; page-oriented.
4. Provides complex formatting (numbered outlines and sections).
5. Sectioning; files protected even if not stored on disk and power fails; menu bypass, outline numbering.
6. Complex interface; poor documentation; screen clutter.
7. Basic WP, not suited for form letters, multicolumn text, complex long documents.
8. Logical user interface; very forgiving.
9. Slow; documentation is tedious.

---

*Adapted from *The Seybold Report on Professional Computer,* Vol. 1, No. 2, March 7, 1983.

IBM PC WP Characteristics (cont.)

PROGRAM NAME:	MICROSOFT WORD	MULTIMATE	NBI
Company	Microsoft Corp.	MultiMate	NBI
Price	$375; 475 w/mouse	$495	$695
Memory required	128K	128K	128K
Default mode	Either	Overstrike	Either
Orientation	Document	Page	Document
Multiple ruler lines	Yes	Yes	Yes
Decimal alignment	Yes	Yes	Yes
Background printing	Yes	Yes	Yes
Form letter merge	No	Yes	Yes
Widow/orphan control	Yes	No	Yes
Semi-auto hyphenation	No	No	Yes
Outline numbering	No	No	Yes
Split screen	8 H/V	No	No
Math	No	Yes	No
Spelling	No	No	No
Automatic footnotes	Yes	No	No
Index generation	No	No	No
Printer support	Several	Many	Several
Suggested users	For complex format	Wang Secy.	Experienced
Applications	{10}	{13}	{16}
Strengths	{11}	{14}	{17}
Weaknesses	{12}	{15}	{18}

10. Complex formatting multiple fonts and attributes, varied paragraphs, spacing, indents, footnotes.
11. Multiple windows for cross-file referencing.
12. Odd command structure, difficult to learn.
13. Where keystroke programming helps.
14. Wang-like interface, selective file retrieval, broad functionality.
15. Slow; too many steps for most functions.
16. Outlining and mail merge.
17. Dedicated WP interface; excellent keyboard mapping.
18. Hardware modification required; must use NBI formatted diskettes.

IBM PC WP Characteristics (cont.)

PROGRAM NAME:	SAMNA WORD II	VISIWORD PLUS	VOLKSWRITER
Company	Samna Corp.	VisiCorp	Lifetree Sftw. Inc.
Price	$450	$375	$195
Memory required	192K	192K	128K
Default mode	Overstrike	Either	Overstrike
Orientation	Document	Document	Document
Multiple ruler lines	Yes	Yes	Yes
Decimal alignment	Yes	Yes	No
Background printing	Yes	Yes	No
Form letter merge	with sorting	No	No
Widow/orphan control	Yes	No	No
Semi-auto hyphenation	Yes	No	No
Outline numbering	No	No	No
Split screen	2H	2H	No
Math	No	No	No
Spelling	No	correction	No
Automatic footnotes	Yes	No	No
Index generation	No	No	No
Printer support	Several	Several	Several
Suggested users	Secys, mgrs.	Visicalc Exp.	Novice
Applications	{19}	{22}	{25}
Strengths	{20}	{23}	{26}
Weaknesses	{21}	{24}	{27}

19. For list processing, general editing.
20. Friendly; excellent help; mail merge with sorting; good documentation.
21. Cannot type in insert mode; system writes to disk too often and too slowly.
22. WP applications without merge or complex format.
23. Friendly interface; column manipulation.
24. Spelling corrector poor; incomplete help facility.
25. Good for straight input and editing of text.
26. Easy to master; good documentation.
27. Cannot easily enhance text; low functionality.

IBM PC WP Characteristics (cont.)

PROGRAM NAME:	WORD PERFECT	WORDSTAR	WORDVISION	XYWRITE II
Company	Satellite Intnl.	MicroPro Intnl.	Bruce James	XyQuest
Price	$395	$495	$79.95	$195
Memory required	128K	64K	96K	96K
Default mode	Either	Either	Insert	Either
Orientation	Document	Document	Document	Document
Multiple ruler lines	Yes	Yes	No	Yes
Decimal alignment	Yes	Yes	Yes	Yes
Background printing	Yes	Yes	No	Yes
Form letter merge	optnl sort pkg.	No No	No No	No No
Widow/orphan control	Yes	No	No	No
Semi-auto hyphenation	Yes	Yes	No	No
Outline numbering	No	No	No	No
Split screen	No	No	2	2 H/V
Math	Yes	No	No	Yes
Spelling	corrector	No	No	No
Automatic footnotes	Yes	No	No	Yes
Index generation	No	No	No	Yes
Printer support	Several	Several	Several	Most
Suggested users	Most	Secys	Mgrs/Writers	Writers mgrs
Applications	{28}	{31}	{34}	{37}
Strengths	{29}	{32}	{35}	{38}
Weaknesses	{30}	{33}	{36}	{39}

28. Where macro capabilities and column text are present.
29. Well designed features; macro capabilities.
30. Poor documentation.
31. For complex formatting.
32. Popular; extensive literature available.
33. Difficult to learn.
34. Unsuitable for secretarial use or for manuscripts; excellent quick and easy WP.
35. Speed; easy-to-learn interface.
36. Low-level functionality; tends to be "cute".
37. Jockeying between documents to customize features.
38. Speed; user-definable defaults; logical interface.
39. Poor documentation; unfamiliar interface.

Appendix F
DBase Commands
and Their Action

? expression   (1)
?? expression   (2)

The question mark at the dBase period prompt causes *expression,* which may include memory variables or field names for the record pointed to by the present position pointer, to be evaluated. If the variables cannot be found or the expression cannot be evaluated, another message is returned instead. The value prepared by dBase appears on the next line, followed by a new prompt.

When the question mark appears in a command program, the values determined by dBase display on the line containing the cursor. They are followed by *line return* so that the cursor moves down to the next line but, of course, no prompt appears. The double question mark also evaluates the expression and produces a value but does not provide *line return.* This is a way to get several items defined by different lines in the command program to appear on the same screen line.

@x,y [SAY 'prompt' [USING format]] [GET var[PICTURE pic]]   (3)

This command without the options causes the cursor to position to the coordinate, *x,y.*

The first option using **SAY**, displays a message furnished at *prompt* at the designated screen coordinate. The suboption, **USING**, describes how information entered should be formatted.

The next option, **GET**, asks dBase to acquire a value entered by the operator at the keyboard and to place it into the memory variable, *var.* The suboption, **PICTURE**, requires that the operator enter the value in a particular way which dBase verifies and rejects if unsatisfactory.

ACCEPT ["prompt"] TO mem   (4)

Causes a character variable supplied by the operator to be placed into the memory variable, *mem. Prompt,* included in double quotes, tells the operator the nature of the variable expected.

APPEND (5)
APPEND BLANK (6)
APPEND FROM file [criteria] [SDF] [DELIMITED] (7)
   APPEND alone adds new records to the end of the file in USE. A record display appears on the screen for the operator to fill in by sequencing from one field to the next. After the last field has been entered and terminated with *return,* a new empty record appears on the screen. If there are no more records to be entered, the operator hits *return* and the dBase prompt appears.
   For the second form (6), a blank record is appended at the end of a file and the dBase prompt reappears.
   With the last form (7), records are brought from another file named *file.* Records may be selected from *file* by providing *criteria.* Usually this is a different dBase file. However, appending can occur from a file produced with a word processor if that file is in Standard Data Format (SDF). For this format, the information is provided in fixed size fields with no separators, but is terminated by *line return.* Another alternative uses ASCII format; in this case, use the DELIMITED option.

BROWSE [FIELDS flist] (8)
   BROWSE lets you view twenty or so records on the screen simultaneously. Use horizontal scroll to view invisible parts of the record. Restrict the number of fields displaying with the FIELDS option and *name* them in *flist.*

CANCEL (9)
   CANCEL returns control from a command program to the dBase prompt.

CHANGE [scope] [range] [criteria] (10)
   Presents designated records for alteration as specified by *scope, range* and *criteria.*

CLEAR (11)
   If there are any pending GETS, these are removed and placed at the beginning of the command file.

CONTINUE (12)
   Used with LOCATE to find the next record which fulfills the requirements of the previous LOCATE.

COPY TO file [scope] [range] [criteria] [SDF] [DELIMITED [WITH delim]] (13)
COPY TO file STRUCTURE [range] (14)
   Copies selected records and selected fields for specified scope to *file.* The destination file may be an SDF or a delimited file, when specified.
   In the second form (14), only the file structure is copied, thus creating an empty file. When *range* is used, only designated fields are put into the structure of the destination file. When *file* already exists, COPY destroys it.

COUNT [scope] [criteria] [TO var] (15)
The COUNT function is used with appropriate options: (1) to count the number of records in a file; (2) to count records within the scope; (3) to find the number of records that satisfy the given *criteria;* (4) to store the count into a memory variable, *var.* DBase reviews the file sequentially and always comes up with a count statement before the prompt is issued unless you have SET TALK OFF.

CREATE [file1] [FROM file 2] (16)
Establishes a new file with the name *file1* if the first option is present. Otherwise the operator is prompted for a file name. The second option works like the COPY STRUCTURE command.

DELETE [scope] [criteria] (17)
DELETE FILE file (18)
With no options, the record pointed to by the *pp* is slated for deletion. When *scope* and/or *criteria* are provided, records thus designated are scheduled for deletion. The second form of DELETE (18) is like the CP/M erase command and destroys the designated file.

DISPLAY [scope] [criteria] [range] [OFF] (19)
DISPLAY STRUCTURE (20)
DISPLAY MEMORY (21)
DISPLAY FILES [ON drive] [LIKE form] (22)
DISPLAY STATUS (23)
In its various forms DISPLAY gives information. It shows selected fields of selected records within a given scope, with or without numbers (19). It shows the structure of the file now in USE (20). It can display the current contents of all the assigned memory (21). It can be used like DIR to show the files on a given drive (22). If the second option, LIKE, is omitted, only dBase files with extension DBF display. LIKE lets you ask ambiguously for files to display. Finally, (23) gives you information about the current files in use and their options.

DO file (24)
DO CASE
    CASE cond.
        statements
    [CASE cond.
        statements]
    [OTHERWISE
        statements]
END CASE (25)

DO WHILE condition
    statements
ENDDO (26)
The first form of DO (24) requests that a command file be executed. When execution is completed, control returns to dBase and the dot prompt appears.

The second form, DO CASE (25), is a bona fide case statement such as contained in PASCAL and some BASICs. There is one instance of CASE for each condition, stated as a relationship. If true, statements which follow up to the next CASE are executed. Should none of the conditions following any CASE statement be true, a catch-all, OTHERWISE, may be provided.
DO CASE must terminate with ENDCASE.
DO WHILE, much like the PASCAL equivalent, specifies a relation and is followed by a number of statements terminated with ENDDO (26). The statements are executed until *condition* proves false. Of course, one of the statements should alter a variable in *condition* so as to eventually terminate the loop.

EDIT [num] (27)
This command causes a full screen editor to be entered, the editor is activated by control codes as displayed in Table 12.2.1. The number, *num,* when specified, causes the corresponding record to be displayed in its entirety. The user sequences from one line of the record to the next by hitting *return*. When return is hit on the last line of the record, the next sequential record is brought up for editing. The user terminates this chain of events by hitting control W to write all edited records back to the file. Otherwise, escape causes a prompt for a new record number so that the user continue to edit.

EJECT (28)
When it appears in a command file after the printer has been set on, EJECT causes the printer to page-feed.

ERASE (29)
Causes the screen to clear, using the proper control codes for your terminal which have been furnished dBase with the *install* program.

FIND string [string...] (30)
Used with indexed files to set the pp to the first record for which the index field value corresponds to that furnished at *string*. More than one string may be furnished when indexing has been done on multiple fields.

GOTO RECORD *n* (31)
n (32)
GOTO TOP (33)
GOTO BOTTOM (34)
GOTO var (35)
The first two commands (31, 32) reset the *pp* to record number *n*. The remaining three variations respectively set the *pp* to 1, the last record in the file or a value found in the memory variable *var*.

HELP command (36)
HELP followed by a command name displays a help panel which describes what that command does.

838 APPENDIX F

IF condition
  commands
[ELSE commands]
ENDIF (37)
  The sequence of commands which follows is performed if *condition* is true. When *condition* is false, and if an ELSE clause is included, commands between ELSE and ENDIF are executed, ENDIF must always appear.

INDEX ON key [+ key...] TO ndxfile (38)
  Causes a file currently in use to be indexed on the key (or keys) supplied to create the index file *ndxfile*. Once prepared, it may be connected at any later time to the file with the USE statement.

INPUT ["prompt"] TO var (39)
  Displays *prompt,* if present, and then accepts a variable keyed by the operator, placing it in the named memory variable, *var*. Character information must be key within matched single or double quotes.

INSERT [BEFORE] [BLANK] (40)
  Without options, a new record is inserted after the one pointed to by the *pp*. Then the user is prompted to fill it in as with APPEND. For BEFORE, the new record goes before the one the *pp* points to. When BLANK appears, the user is not prompted to fill it in.

JOIN TO file FOR condition [FIELDS list] (41)
  Applies selected records from the file in USE to expand the record structure of *file*. Reviews the records of the file in use; when one is found for which *condition* is met, all the fields of the primary record which are missing from the secondary file record are added to it. When the FIELDS option is provided, only *list* fields are appended to selected records.

LIST [scope] [criteria] [OFF] [range] (42)
LIST [MEMORY] [FILES] [STRUCTURE] [STATUS] (43)
  LIST is the same as DISPLAY except that *scope* defaults to ALL and records display continuously instead of waiting after 15 are placed on the screen.

LOCATE [scope] criteria
  CONTINUE (44)
  Locates the first record within *scope* for which the criteria hold. When CONTINUE is issued, the next record which fulfills *criteria* within *scope* is located by setting the position pointer, or, if there is none, a message displays to that effect.

LOOP (45)
  Used within a DO loop to skip all statements between its occurrence and the end of the loop.

DBASE COMMANDS AND THEIR ACTION   839

MODIFY COMMAND file   (46)
Brings *file* .CMD to the screen where the user may apply screen editing commands to alter it.

MODIFY STRUCTURE   (47)
If the file in USE contains records, they are all destroyed but the file structure is maintained and presented on the screen. Then the user may alter the file structure using screen editing commands.

NOTE text   (48)
For command program documentation. *Text* in the command program after NOTE up to return is ignored during the command program excution. * can be used instead of NOTE.

PACK   (49)
Removes records marked for deletion from the file in USE. Where index files are associated, they may be attached and they will be updated at the same time.

QUIT [TO program]   (50)
Leaves dBase and, if the option is present, gives control to *program*.

READ   (51)
Brings in variables associated with preceding GETS which have not yet been satisfied. The cursor positions to the first variable outstanding. As the operator keys it in, the value appears on the screen until a field fills up or until *return* is hit. This action continues until all the variables have been supplied or at least passed through.

RECALL [scope] [criteria]   (52)
Removes the delete mark from records destined to be deleted which lie within *scope* and fulfill *criteria,* when specified.

REINDEX   (53)
Causes a new index to be created with the same name as the index now in USE for the file.

RELEASE [list] [ALL LIKE ambig] [ALL EXCEPT ambig]   (54)
Releases space occupied by listed current memory variable s. The default releases them all. Other options allow you to release just those listed, those which are structured like the template *ambig* of all *except* those structured like the template.

REMARK text   (55)
Displays *text* on the output device when the command is executed in the command file.

840 APPENDIX F

RENAME file TO name (56)
　　If *file* exists, it is given the new name, *name*.

REPLACE [scope] field WITH exp [field WITH exp...]
　　[criteria] (57)
　　For the specified scope and criteria replaces values at *field*(s) with the new value(s) specified by *exp*(s). Several such replacements can be made by the same statement.

REPORT [FORM fname][scope][TO PRINT][PLAIN][criteria] (58)
　　Causes a report to display or print. This may be from an existing report form, fname, from a particular *scope* in the file, to be printed, without page numbers or headings and when particular *criteria* are met.

RESET [drive] (59)
　　Used before removing and replacing a diskette in a drive and causes dBase to check whether any files are open. If any are open, a warning message is issued so that open files can be rewritten. When *drive* used, reset only applies to it.

RESTORE FROM file [ADDITIVE] (60)
　　Used with SAVE, which puts on disk memory variables defined during a session. These are brought back to memory locations with RESTORE. If ADDITIVE is omitted, current memory variables are destroyed and are replaced by the ones brought in from disk.

RETURN (61)
　　Gives control back to dBase when encountered in a command file.

SAVE TO file [ALL LIKE temp] (62)
　　Puts values of memory variables in *file*. If present, *temp* specifies the structure of the names of variables to be stored.

SELECT [{PRIMARY,SECONDARY}] (63)
　　After files have been designated primary and secondary, SELECT switches from one to the other.

SET [option] (64)
　　Has many toggles to turn various functions on or off or specify such things as headings, margins and default drives. Summarized in Table 12.7.

SKIP [+][−][num] (65)
　　Without any options, moves the *pp* to the very next record. *Num* is the number of records by which to move the pp forward (+) or backwards (−). For forward, + may be omitted.

DBASE COMMANDS AND THEIR ACTION   841

SORT ON field TO file [direction]   (66)
Sorts the entire file using the single field mentioned at *field* and creates a new file. If DESCENDING is specified for *direction,* then the resulting file should be in descending order.

STORE exp TO var   (67)
Here *exp* is an expression which includes file names or variable names which is first evaluated, then stored in *var,* a memory variable which is defined by this action.

SUM field [field...] [TO list] [scope] [criteria]   (68)
Used to sum up to five numeric fields. Applies to records defined by *scope* and *criteria.* If the *list* option is provided, the sums are also stored in memory variables, which are created if not previously defined.

TEXT copy ENDTEXT   (69)
In a command file, whatever text is found at *copy* between TEXT and ENDTEXT is sent to the display or printer, whichever has been selected with a SET command.

TOTAL ON key TO file [FIELD list] [criteria]   (70)
Makes a summary file from a detail file.

UPDATE FROM file ON key [ADD alist]
[RANDOM] [REPLACE[rlist]]
[FIELD WITH ffield]   (71)
Posts a transaction file to a master file, adding fields named at *alist* to their correspondents and replacing other fields with their correspondents in *rlist.*

USE file [INDEX ndxl [indx2...]]   (72)
Removes the current file in USE and puts *file* into USE. If the option is exercised, one or more indexes can be put into play. Only the first of these is referenced with respect to FIND. However, the others are updated when changes are made in *file.*

WAIT [TO var]   (73)
The command program pauses and waits for the operator to hit a single key. If TO is present, that keystroke is stored in *var.* Otherwise, hitting any key causes the program to continue.

Legend

Scope:
   if absent, applies only to the *pp* record;
   ALL causes all records in sequence from the beginning of the file to be affected;
   n causes only record *n* to be examines;
   NEXT *n* causes this record and the next *n*−1 to be examined.

Range fieldlist:
applies only to fields in *fieldlist*.
Criteria:
criteria :: = FOR expression;
simple expression :: = field relation value;
expression :: = simple expression connective expression.

Appendix G
Spread Sheet Characteristics

FUNCTION	CALCSTAR	PERFECTCALC	SUPERCALC2	VISICALC	PROCALC	MULTIPLAN	MBA	LOTUS 1-2-3
Number of rows	254	254	255	255	192	255	999	2048
Number of columns	127	52	63	63	132	63	95	256
Required memory, K	64	64	64		64	64	256	128
Maximum memory, K	256	64	544		128	256	544	544
FRIENDLINESS								
Tutorial on disk	y	y	y	n	y	y	y	y
On screen help	y	y	y	y	y	y	y	y
Cell Editing	n	y	y	y	y	y	y	y
Screen display								
Window number	n	y	n	y	n	y	n	n
Model name	y	y	y	y	y	y	n	y
Memory use	y	y	y	y	y	y	y	y
Command prompts	y	y	y	y	y	y	y	y
IBM function key use	5	5	5		4	8	5	9
FORMAT FUNCTIONS								
Windows	2	2	2	2	6	8	4	2
Models visible	1	2	1	1	4	1	1	1
Adjust col width	y	y	y	y	y	y	y	y
Minimum width	3	0	0	1	0	1	0	1
Form Input	y	y	y	y	y	y	y	y
Must display border	y	y	n	y	y	y	n	y
CELL FORMATTING								
User Defined	n	n	y	y	y	n	n	y
Floating $	n	n	y	y	y	y	y	y
Commas in numbers	n	y	y	y	y	y	y	y
Exponential	n	y	y	y	y	y	y	y
Percentage	y	n	y	y	y	y	y	y

844 APPENDIX G

FUNCTION	CALCSTAR	PERFECTCALC	SUPERCALC2	VISICALC	PROCALC	MULTIPLAN	MBA	LOTUS 1-2-3
CELL FORMATTING (cont.)								
Negatives in ()s	n	y	y	y	y	y	y	y
DR/CR notation	n	n	n	y	y	n	n	y
Bold/u'line	n	n	n	n	y	n	n	n
Integer	n	y	y	y	y	y	y	y
True integer	n	n	n	n	y	y	y	y
Fixed num decimals	y	n	y	y	y	y	y	y
Cell filler	n	n	n	y	y	n	n	n
Symbolic	y	y	y	y	y	y	n	y
Symbol used	*	*	*	*	*	*		*-+
Align right:	y	y	y	y	y	y	y	y
Align left:								
Text	y	y	y	y	y	y	y	y
Numbers	y	y	n	y	y	y	y	n
Align center:								
Text	y	y	y	y	y	y	y	y
Numbers	y	y	n	y	y	y	y	n
Formula display	y	y	y	y	y	y	y	n
Cell protection	n	y	y	y	y	y	y	n
Cell/range names	n	y	n	n	y	y	y	y
PRINT FORMATTING								
Headers	y	n	n	y	y	n	y	y
Footers	n	n	n	n	n	n	y	y
Flex margins:								
Top	n	n	n	y	n	y	y	y
Bottom	n	n	n	y	n	y	y	y
Left	n	n	n	y	n	y	y	y
Right	n	n	n	n	n	y	y	y
Page numbers	n	n	n	n	n	n	y	y
Page pause	n	n	y	y	n	y	y	y
Printer setup	n	y	y	y	y	y	y	y
Multiple printers	y	y	y	y	y	y	y	y
Print formulas	y	y	y	y	y	y	y	y
TEXT FUNCTIONS								
Justification	n	y	y	y	n	n	y	y
Lookup	n	n	y	y	y	y	n	n
in IF...THEN	n	n	y	y	y	y	n	n
Wide labels	n	y	y	n	y	y	y	y
Repeating labels	y	y	y	y	y	y	y	y

---

*Adapted from Henderson, Cobb and Cobb, *Spread Sheet Software* (see Bibliography [Appendix H] for Chapter 14).

Function	CalcStar	PerfectCalc	SuperCalc2	VisiCalc	ProCalc	Multiplan	MBA	Lotus 1-2-3
String functions:								
Substring	n	n	n	n	n	y	n	n
String length	n	n	n	n	n	y	n	n
Concatenation	n	n	n	y	n	y	n	n
RECALCULATION								
Manual	y	y	y	y	y	y	y	y
Automatic	y	y	y	y	y	y	y	y
Interactive	n	n	n	n	n	y	n	y
Natural	n	n	n	n	y	y	n	y
By row	y	y	y	y	y	y	y	y
By column	y	y	y	y	y	y	y	y
SAVE AND LOAD FILES								
Automatic recalc.	n	n	n	n	n	n	n	n
Partial load	n	n	y	y	y	n	y	y
Partial save	n	n	y	y	n	n	y	y
IMPORT FILES	n	y	n	DIF	n	y	n	y
Import text files	n	y	n	n	y	n	n	y
Save to text file	y	y	y	y	n	y		y
Format disks	n	n	n	n	y	n	y	n
Save format:								
DIF	n	n	n	y	n	n	n	y
SYLK	n	n	n	n	n	y	n	n
SDI	n	n	y	n	n	n	n	n
Sheet-to-sheet links:								
Data channels	n	7	n	n	4	8	n	n
Consolidation	y	y	y	n	y	n	y	y
Single-cell lnkg.	n	y	n	n	y	y	n	n
Multisheet links	n	y	n	n	y	y	n	n
Data base functions	n	n	n	n	n	n	y	y
Graphics functions	n	n	n	n	n	n	y	y
PROGRAMABILITY								
User Defined	n	n	y	y	n	n	n	y
IF THEN	—	—	n	n	—	—	—	y
GOTO	—	—	n	n	—	—	—	y
QUIT	—	—	n	n	—	—	—	y
User Menus	—	—	n	n	—	—	—	y
SPEED (in seconds) 1000 iterations of								
Simple addition	34	11	7		46	16	76	3
Multiplication	65	22	16		58	18	81	3

FUNCTION	CalcStar	PerfectCalc	SuperCalc2	VisiCalc	ProCalc	Multiplan	MBA	Lotus 1-2-3
SPEED (in seconds) (cont.)								
Load program	14	5	3		141	8	58	15
Load test file	78	24	14		61	36	36	15
BUILT-IN FUNCTIONS								
Math	7	6	8	9	6	9	9	9
Trig	0	3	7	7	0	4	7	7
Stat	6	4	4	5	4	6	6	6
Financial	0	1	1	4	6	2	2	4
Date	0	0	6	6	1	0	0	5
Logical	3	5	5	11	7	11	9	11
Special	1	1	1	3	4	3	2	4
Others	3	0	0	0	2	4	2	0

Appendix H
Bibliography

GENERAL (Chapters 1,2)

Flores, Ivan and Terry, Chris, *Microcomputer Systems.* New York: Van Nostrand Reinhold, 1982. 290 pp,

HARDWARE (Chapters 3-5)

Libes, Sol, and Garetz, Mark, *Interfacing to S-100/IEEE 696 Microcomputers.* Berkeley, CA: Osborne/McGraw-Hill, 1981. 322 pp.
Artwick, Bruce, *Microcomputer Interfacing.* Englewood Cliffs, NJ: Prentice-Hall, 1980. 341 pp.

COMPUTERS (Chapter 6)

Norton, P., *Inside the IBM PC; Access To Advanced Features And Programming.* Rockville, MD: Robert J. Brady, 1983. 275 pp.
WSI Staff, *IBM PC and XT User's Handbook.* Cleveland, OH: Weber Systems, 1983. 543 pp.

PROGRAMMING (Chapter 8)

Cooper, D., and Clancy, M., *Oh! Pascal!.* New York: W. W. Norton, 1982. 476 pp.
Cooper, D., *Standard Pascal: User Reference Manual.* New York: W. W. Norton, 1983. 176 pp.
Etlin, W. A., Gregor, and Folberg, *The MBASIC Handbook.* Berkley CA: Osborne/McGraw Hill.
Finkel, L., and Brown, R., *Data File Programming In Basic.* New York: John Wiley & Sons, 1981. 342 pp.
Grogono, P., *Programming in Pascal.* Reading, MA: Addison-Wesley, 1980. 363 pp.
Hughes, J., *PL/1 Structured Programming.* New York: John Wiley & Sons, 1979. 825 pp.
Hume, J., and Holt, R., *Better Basic For The IBM PC.* Reston, VA: Reston, 1984. 294 pp.

Kernighan, B., and Ritchie, D., *The C Programming Language*. Englewood Cliffs, NJ: Prentice-Hall, 1978. 228 pp.

Miller, A., *8080/Z80 Assembly Language; Techniques For Improved Programming*. New York: John Wiley & Sons, 1981. 319 pp.

Spracklen, K., *Z-80 and 8080 Assembly Language Programming*. Hasbrouck Height, NJ: Hayden, 1979. 168 pp.

Wirth, N., *Algorithms + Data Structures = Programs*. Englewood Cliffs, NJ: Prentice-Hall, 1976. 366 pp.

Wirth, N., *Programming In Modula-2*. New York: Springer-Verlag, 1982. 176 pp.

Xenakis, J., *Structured PL/1 Programming*. North Scituate, MA: Duxbury Press, 1979. 413 pp.

GRAPHICS (Chapter 13)

Foley, J., and Van Dam, A., *Fundamentals Of Interative Computer Graphics*. Reading, MA: Addison-Wesley, 1982. 664 pp.

Newman, W., and Sproull, R., *Principles Of Interactive Computer Graphics*. New York: McGraw-Hill, 1979. 541 pp.

SPREAD SHEETS (Chapter 14)

Castlewitz, D., *The VisiCalc Program Made Easy*. Berkeley, CA: Osborne/McGraw-Hill, 1983. 195 pp.

Henderson, T., Cobb, D., and Cobb, G., *Spreadsheet Software from VisiCalc to 1-2-3*. Indianapolis: Que Corporation, 1983. 336 pp.

Williams, R., *The Power of Multiplan*. Bellevue, OR: Management Information Source, Inc., 1982. 169 pp.

FOURTH GENERATION SPREAD SHEETS (Chapter 15)

Cobb, Douglas, *Mastering Symphony*. Berkeley, CA: Sybex, 1984. 378 pp.

Forefront Corp., *Framework: A programmer's Reference*. Culver City, CA: Ashton-Tate, 1984. 374 pp.

Harrison, Bill, *An Introduction to Framework*. Culver City, CA: Ashton-Tate, 1984. 378 pp.

Appendix I
Resources

List The Software Solutions Magazine for Business. Redgate Publishing Company 3381 Ocean Drive, Vero Beach Florida 32963; 305-231-6904.

Whole Earth Software Catalog ($18). Whole Earth Catalogue and Review, Gate Five Road, Sausalito, CA 94765.

Computer Graphics Directory ($80). Computer Graphics World, P.O. Box 21278, Tulsa, OK 74121.

The Software Catalog. Elsevier Science Publishing Company, 52 Vanderbilt Avenue, New York, NY 10017.

Dataguide. Technical Publishing of Dun and Bradstreet, 5 Kane Industrial Drive, Hudson, MA 01749; 617-562-9308.

Computer World Buyers Guide-Software. Computer World Communications, Box 880, 375 Cochituate Road, Framingham, MA 01701.

Date Sources ($30). Ziff-Davis Publishing Company, One Park Avenue, New York 10016; 212-725-3500.

All About Personal Computers, ($29). Datapro, 1805 Underwood Boulevard, Delran, NJ 08075.

All About 230 Microcomptuers; Datapro Reports on Microcomputers ($25). Datapro.

User Ratings of 125 Microcomputers; Datapro Reports on Microcomputers ($29). Datapro.

All About 171 PC Expansion Cards; Datapro Reports on Microcomputers ($25). Datapro.

All About 70 Electronic Spreadsheets; Datapro Reports on Microcomputers ($19). Datapro.

All About 92 Microcomputer Database Management Packages; Datapro Reports on Microcomputers ($19). Datapro.

All About 46 Portable Computers, Datapro Reports on Microcomputers ($25). Datapro.

All About 70 Microcomputer Word Processing Packages; Datapro Report on Microcomputers ($25). Datapro.

All About 148 Communications Software Package; Datapro Reports on Microcomputers ($25). Datapro.

How To Select Microcomputers for the Corporate Environment; Datapro's Management of Small Computer Systems ($19). Datapro.
Integrating Microcomputers in the Mainframe Environment ($19). Datapro.
All About 68 CAD/CAM Systems ($25). Datapro.
Guide to IBM PC Software ($19.95). Datapro.
Guide To Apple Software ($19.95). Datapro.
Guide To CP/M Software ($19.95). Datapro.
Intel Yellow Pages Software Directory. Intel Yellow Pages, (free) 3065 Bowers Avenue, Santa Clara, CA; 408-987-5057.
InfoWorld Report Card ($3.95). InfoWorld, 10060 Marsh Road, Suite C-200 Menlo Park, 94025; 415-328-4602.
Word Processing Industry Directory. International Word Processing Association, Maryland Road, Willow Grove, PA 19090; 215-657-3220.
Word Processing Glossary. International Word Processing Association, Maryland Road, Willow Grove, PA 19090; 215-657-3220.
How to Select Your Small Computer . . . without Frustration; Association of Computer Users, Box 9003, 4800 Riverbend Road, Boulder, CO 80301.
International Directory of Software ($145). Computing Publications Ltd. First Federal Building Suite 401 Pottstown, PA 19464; 215-326-5188.
Directory of Systems Houses and Computer Distributors; Technical Publishing, 5 Kane Industrial Drive, Hudson, Massachusetts 01749.

Illustration Credits

Source	FIG.	PAGE
Anadex, Inc.	4.3.6	91
	4.3.7	92
	4.7.4	107
Ann Arbor Terminals, Inc.	3.4.1	66
Apple Computer, Inc.	16.4.1	745
	16.4.2	745
	16.4.3	746
	16.4.4	747
	16.4.5	750
Copyright © Ashton-Tate 1984. All Rights Reserved. Framework and Ashton-Tate are trademarks of Ashton-Tate. Used by permission. 10150 W. Jefferson Boulevard, Culver City, CA 90230. (213) 204-5570	15.2.1	682
	15.2.2	683
	15.2.3	684
	15.2.6	688
	15.3.1	691
	15.3.2	692
	15.3.3	693
	15.3.4	694
	15.3.5	696
	15.3.6	697
	15.3.7	698
	15.3.8	699
	15.3.9	700
	15.3.10	700
	15.4.1	707
	15.4.2	708
	15.4.3	710
	15.4.4	712
Autodesk, Inc.	5.1.1	112
	5.3.8	124
	16.6.1	765
Calma Co.	13.1.7	534
Calcomp (California Computer Products, Inc.)	13.8.2	584
Diablo Systems	4.7.3	104
Electronic Imaging, Nov.-Dec. 1982	4.6.1	100
1. Flores, *Data Base*	9.1.1	329

Source	FIG.	PAGE
Architecture, © Van Nostrand Reinhold, 1981.	9.1.2	330
1. Flores, *Word Processing Handbook,* © Van Nostrand Reinhold, 1982	2.1.1	27
	2.2.1	27
	2.2.2	29
	3.2.1	53
	3.3.1	59
	3.4.2	68
	3.5.1	70
	3.5.2	73
	3.6.1	80
	3.6.2	81
	3.6.3	82
	4.2.1	86
	4.2.2	87
	4.3.1	88
	4.3.2	88
	4.3.3	89
	4.5.1	98
	4.5.2	99
	5.2.1	115
	5.2.2	115
	5.2.3	116
	5.2.4	116
	5.3.1	117
	5.3.2	118
	5.3.3	118
	5.3.4	119
	5.3.5	120
	5.3.6	122
	5.3.7	123
	5.4.1	126
	5.4.3	128
	5.4.4	129
	5.4.5	132
	5.5.1	136
	5.5.2	137

852 ILLUSTRATION CREDITS

	FIG.	PAGE		FIG.	PAGE
	5.5.3	137		14.7.18	679
	5.5.4	138	Carl Machover Associates	13.1.4	531
	11.2.1	390		13.5.3	555
	11.3.1	395		13.5.6	558
	11.3.2	396	Malibu	4.3.10	93
	11.4.1	399	Measurement Systems, Inc.	13.6.2	563
	11.4.2	401	Megatek Corp.	13.5.7	559
	11.4.4	404		13.6.1	561
	11.4.5	404	Motorola Semiconductor	6.2.1	158
	11.5.1	410	Products, Inc.	6.2.2	158
J. D. Foley and A. Van	13.3.5	545	NEC Information Systems,	4.7.1	103
Dam, *Fundamentals of*			Inc.	4.7.2	104
Interactive Computer Graphics,			P. Norton, *Inside the IBM*	3.3.2	62
Addison-Wesley, 1982			*PC: Access to Advanced*	6.6.4	188
GTCO Corp.	13.1.3	530	*Features and Program-*		
Hewlett-Packard Co.	13.1.1	529	*ming,* Brady, 1983		
	13.1.2	530	Qume Corp.	4.4.2	96
	13.1.5	532	A. Seidman, and I. Flores,	13.2.1	536
	13.6.5	566	*Handbook of Computers*	13.2.2	537
	13.7.2	569	*and Computing,* © Van	13.2.3	538
	13.8.1	583	Nostrand Reinhold, 1984	13.2.4	539
IBM (International Business	6.6.1	185		13.3.1	541
Machines Corporation)	6.6.2	186		13.3.2	542
	6.6.4	187		13.3.3	543
IDS Inc.	4.3.4	89		13.3.4	544
	4.3.9	93		13.4.1	546
M. Kiver and M. Kaufman,	**13.4.2**	**548**		13.4.2	548
Television Electronics:	13.4.3	549		13.5.2	554
Theory and Practice, Van				13.5.4	556
Nostrand Reinhold, 1983.				13.5.5	557
© Delmar Publishers, Inc.,				13.6.6	566
1983.				13.7.3	572
Lear Siegler Inc.	4.3.5	90		13.7.4	574
Lexidata Corp.	13.1.6	533		13.7.5	574
© Lotus Development	14.7.5	666		13.7.6	575
Corporation, 1984. Used	14.7.6	666		13.7.7	575
with permission.	14.7.7	667		13.7.8	576
	14.7.8	667		13.7.9	576
	14.7.9	668		13.7.10	577
	14.7.10	668		13.7.11	577
	14.7.11	669	Paul S. Strauss and James K.	13.5.1	553
	14.7.12	670	Rinzler		
	14.7.13	671	Summagraphics Corporation	13.6.3	563
	14.7.15	674		13.6.4	564
	14.7.16	675		13.7.1	568

Index

1-2-3, 658
  advantages, 659
  cell addresses, 659
  cell entry, 660
  characteristics, 658, 659
  commands, 660
  data base, 673
    actions, 674
      change field size, 675
      data query (*see* 1-2-3, data query), 675
      deletion, 674
      edit, 674
      insertion, 674
      posting, 674
      record expansion, 675
    format of SS, 673
      illustration, 673
    sorting, 673
      illustration of, 674
      key for, 674
      requesting, 674
  data query, 675
    criteria, 676
      compound, 677
    criteria range, 677
      illustration, 677
    functions, 678
    issuing command, compound, 677
    options, 676
    ranges, 675
      criterion, 675
      input, 675
      output, 676
    summary report, 678
      illustration, 679
  graph commands, 665
    bar charts, 665
      illustration, 667
      illustrations, 666
    data ranges for, 665, 667
    line graph, 667
      illustration, 668
    naming graphs, 672
    options, 665
    pie chart, 667
      illustration, 668
    printing graphs, 672
    Ranges for data, 669
      illustration, 670
      setting, 669
    recalculating, 672
    stacked bar charts, 665
      illustration, 667
    titles, 670
      illustrations, 671
    type, 665
    viewing graphs, 672
    written information, 670
    X labels, 671
      illustration, 671
    X-Y graph, 667
      illustration, 669
  graphs, 664
  key use, 660
  keystroke programming, 664
  macro, 664
  mixed references, 662
    absolute, 663
    automatic adjustment, 663
    examples, 662, 663
    mixed, 663
    relative, 663
  ranges, 660
    anchor, 661
      diagram, 661

854 INDEX (access time / assembly language)

1-2-3 (*cont.*)
  ranges (*cont.*)
    anchor (*cont.*)
      moving, 661
      naming, 662
      pointing, 661
    replicate, 662
      replaced with copy, 662
    requirements, 659

access time, memory, 163
accessibility, 41
accounting packages, 22
active cell, 600
active frame, 686
A/D, 180
address, 13, 30
addressability, 161
ALL, 450
alpha lock, 56
alphabet, 29
American National Standard Institute (ANSI), 61
analog to digital convertor (A/D), 180
answer mode, 82
antialiasing, 553
AP (application program), 44, 367
  choices for, 367
  consideration, 373
  documentation, 378
    extensiveness, 378
    guided lessons, 378
    importance of, 379
    installation guide, 378
    introduction to product, 378
    operator's manual, 378
    quality, 379
    tutorial, 378
    updates to, 379
    user aids, 379
      index, 379
  fixed, 367
  friendliness, 376
    detecting difficulties, 377
      remedying them, 377
    ease of invoking, 376
    error recovery, 376
    help recovery, 376
    help screens, 376
    problem prevention, 377
  modified, 368
  new releases, 373
  performance, 374
    advanced features, 375
    basic capability, 374
    extensiveness, 375
    responsiveness, 374
    terminal, 374
  programming of, 368
  programming them, 383
    contract programming, 385
    modify modules, 384
      assembly language, 384
      small patches, 385
      source code, 384
    small projects, 383
    turnkey systems, 386
  purchasing, 372
    alternatives, 372
  selection resources, 380
    books and manuals, 380
      specialty books, 381
    magazine reviews, 381
    need for, 380
    subscription services, 381
    trial packages, 382
      demo, 382
      friend, 383
      rental, 382
  support, 373
    extended, 373
    initial, 373
  tailoring, 370
    for PC, 372
    install routine, 370
      details of, 371
      for CRT, 370
      for keyboard, 370
      for printer, 371
  total package, 369
    characteristics of, 369
    operating environment for, 369
  transportable, 44
application package (*see* AP), 367
application program (*see* AP), 15
architectural graphics, 531
arithmetic logic unit (*see* ALU), 31
arm, 119
arrow, 61
ASCII, 30
ASCII code set, 53, 334
  table of, 53
assembly language, 307
  advantages, 308

(assignment / BROWSE) INDEX

disassembling, 308
  examples, 308
  what it is, 307
  why needed, 308
assignment, 279
attribute, 328
  name, 328
  value, 328
AUTO, 272
AutoCAD, 764

backspace, 56
backspace correction, 394
backup, 144
bank switching, 166
BASIC (*see also* BASICA, MBASIC), 278
  Advanced, 311
  array, 291
  branches, 286
  Cassette, 311
  conditions, 284
  dialects, 278, 291
    file handling, 293
    line numbers, 292
    symbolic names, 292
    translation mode, 293
  Disk, 311
  friendliness, 278
  I/O, 288
  input, 287, 289
  line numbers, 292
  loops, 287
    final value, 287
    initial value, 287
    variable increment, 287
  relations, 285
    table of, 285
  remark, 280
  running a program, 283
  saving programs, 283
  significance, 278
  statement, 278
    assignment, 279
      compound, 279
      simple, 279
    numbering, 280
    renumbering, 281
    type of, 278
  stopping a program, 284
  stopping the interpreter, 284
  subroutines, 286

  tables, 291
  true (*see* true BASIC), 318
  variable name, 279
BASICA, 311
  facilitations, 311
    abbreviations, 313
    editing, 312
    function keys, 311
    miscellaneous, 314
    screen actions, 314
  graphics, 316
  sound, 314
    BEEP, 315
    PLAY, 315
    SOUND, 315
  versions of, 311
batch files, 257
BDOS (basic disk operating system), 209
BEEP, 315
begin end, 298
Benchmark, 397
bidirectional printing, 102
BIOS (basic input/output system), 209
bit, 28, 332
bit map, 135
bit plane, 550
  array, 550
black on white, 67
block, 122
  and sector, 122
  skewing, 123
block mode, 52
blocks, 408
  copy, 409
  definition of, 408
  delete, 409
  highlighting, 408
  move, 409
  write, 409
boldface, 415
  kinds of, 415
booting, 209
  diagram, 210
  sign one, 211
  system loader, 210
  the loader, 209
branch, 14
break, 57
brightness, 547
BROWSE, 453
  activation, 454
  display, 454

BROWSE (*cont.*)
  editing with, 454
  scrolling for, 454
buffer, 36, 112, 174
bursting, 106
bus, 28, 33, 168
  compatibility, 182
  design, 160
    standard, 161
  PC boards on, 168
    activating, 169
    addressing, 169
    diagram, 168
business graphics (*see* graphics), 528

C language, 310
cabinet, 34
CAD (computer aided design), 535
Calc Star, 593
calendar program, 21
CAM (computer aided manufacturing), 535
caps lock, 63
carriage, 86
carrier, 86
cartography, 534
case, 300
cassette, 117
catalog program (public domain), 242
CATALOG, 244
cathode ray tube (*see* CRT), 64
CBASIC, 276
CCP (console command processor), 209
centering notches, 128
central processing unit (*see* CPU), 28, 157
character, 28
  code, 29
  nonprinting, 335
chassis, 32, 153
check sum, 83
chip, microprocessor, 155, 181
  6502, 155
  8088, 155, 181, 188
    revisions, 188
  MC68000, 155, 181, 743
    new, 181
      improvements, 181
  Z80, 155, 181
chroma, 547
clear, 57
Clipboard (Lisa), 748

CLOSE, 289
COBOL, 306
  discussion, 306
code, 29
  control, 54, 56, 336
  nonprinting, 54, 56
  set (see code set), 30
  standard, 56
code set, 30, 53, 333
  ASCII, (*see* ASCII), 30
  EBCDIC (*see* EBCDIC), 30
color, 547
  CRT (*see* CRT, color), 548
  packet, 549
  pallette, 549
  qualities, 547
  RGB, 547
  table, 500
color packet, 549
color table, 550
column stub, 600
command, 11, 31
COMMAND, 250
command file, 213, 269
command functions, 336
communicating, 35, 49
  with computer, 35
  keyboard, 35
  terminal, 36
communication, 9
  person/computer, 9
communication between computers, 78
  distance, 79
  emulation, 78
  host, 78
  master, 78
  need, 78
  networking (*see* network), 78
  parallel, 79
  peer, 78
  serial, 79
  slave, 78
compatibility, 11
compiler, 261, 265
  load module, 261
  machine language code, 261
  source code, 261
  steps in use (*see* compiling), 266
compiling, 266
  steps in, 266
    execution, 270

linking, 269
translation, 266
  details of, 268
  diagram, 267
compound selection, 461
compressed printing, 102
computer, 4
  applicability, 157
  as a professional, 6
  as alien force, 4
  as competitor, 4
  benefits of, 19
    kinds of, 19
    specific nonaccounting packages, 20
  brands of, 154
    compatibles, 155
    famous, 155
    look-alikes, 155
  catastrophe prone, 5
  category, 34
  chip, family, 159
      upward compatible, 159
  conceptual machine, 5
  decisions, 14
    branch, 14
  dedicated, 43
  incomprehensible, 4
  inside, diagram, 29
  intelligence, 10
  interconnection, 11
  lesser known, 156
  manufacturer, 161
  nature of, 3
    conceptual, 3
    electronic, 3
    machine, 3
    program driven, 3
    restructurable, 3
  package deal, compatibles, 155
  parts of, 32
  phases of operation, 13
    diagram, 13
    execute, 13
    fetch, 13
  portable, 156
  program, 7
    changing, 7
    commands, 8
  subsystem, processor, 11
  subsystems, 12
    control (*see* control), 12
    diagram of, 11
    memory (*see* memory), 12
    user friendly, 5
computer aided design (CAD), 535
computer aided manufacturing (CAM), 535
computer on a board, 175
computer system, 26, 729
  graphics (*see* graphics system), 762
  IBM PC (*see* IBM PC), 730
  IBM PC clones (*see* IBM PC), 730
  Lisa (*see* Lisa), 751
  Macintosh (*see* Mac), 740
  multiuser (*see* multiuser system), 753
  other brands, 154–157
  scope, 729
  purpose, 729
computerized system, 14
  components, 14
concatenation, 460
conjunction, 463
  example, 464
CONT, 284
control, interface, 31
control break, 515
control program, 205
  need, 205
control sequence, 77
control unit, 31
controller, 122
  disk, 122
COPY, 223
copy protection, 244
counter, 13
  instruction, 13
CP/M, 209
  booting, 209
  components, 209
CPU (central processing unit), 28, 157
  bus, 28
  chip, 157
    diagram, 157
    wafer, 158
  interface, 28
  memory, 28
  PC board, 160
    additional chips, 160
  processor, 28
CRC (cylic redundancy check), 172
  calculated, 122
  recorded, 122
criteria (dBase), 455, 456

cross-reference list, 269
CRT (cathode ray tube), 64
　color, 548
　　mask, 548
　　production of, 548
　　　diagram of, 548, 549
　　triad, 548
　flicker, 67
　monochromatic, 67
　persistence, 67
　　high, 67
　　low, 67
　phosphor, 67
　shape, 65
　size, 65
current access position, 551
cursor, 398
　blink, 74
　code, 61
　control sequence, 61
　　ANSI, 61
　counter, 73
　movement, 75
　　arrow keys, 75
　　left, 75
　　up, 75
　　repeat action, 75
　moving, 398
　position, 73
　reverse video, 74
　underline, 74
cut and paste (*see* blocks), 408
cyclic redundancy check (CRC), 121
cylinder, 119

D/A, 180
daisy wheel printer, 95
　petal, 95
　　selection, 95
　　　bidirectional, 96
　　　optimizing, 97
　petal register, 95
　petal table, 95
　print wheel, 95
　　alternatives, 97
　　configuration, 95
　　home position, 95
　　photo, 96
data, 15, 28, 326
　characters, 28
　description of, 326
　need for, 326
　representation, 332
　terms, 327
　　diagram of, 329
data base, 21, 436
　components, 437
　　data definition, 437
　　data entry, 438
　　index, 439
　　program language, 440
　　query, 438
　　report facility, 439
　　sort, 439
　　update, 438
　　　file, 438
　　　record, 438
　　utilities, 439
　data entry, 440
　　help, 441
　　prompt, 441
　　specifying, 440
　　　menu, 441
　　　mnemonics, 441
　introduction, 436
　mainframe, 436
　　applicatin, 436
　　DBMS, 436, 437
　small business, 437
　system, 440
　　dBase (*see* dBase), 440
　tiny system, 437
data file, 329
　activity, 332
　　batch processing, 331
　　　transaction file, 331
　　combined actions, 331
　　processing frequency, 332
　　random entry, 331
　　real time processing, 331
　　turnover, 332
　using, 329
　　diagram of, 330
　　maintenance (*see* maintenance), 330
　　retrieval (*see* retrieval), 330
　　update (*see* update), 330
data register, 174
date stamp, 442
dBase, 440
　APPEND, 445, 478
　　file, 479
　　record, 479

(dBase) INDEX

CHANGE, 481
  diagram, 482
collating sequence, 457
command files, 487
  extension CMD, 488
  invoking, 488
    DO, 488
    from OS, 488
  power of, 488
COPY, 485
  examples, 485
  options, 485
    delimiting, 485
    to ASCII file, 485
correction, 448
criteria (dBase), 455, 456
  collating sequence, 457
  compound selection, 461
    conjunction, 463
    denial, 461
    disjunction, 461, 462
    example, 463, 464
  concaternation, 460
  expression, 455
    definition, 455
    simple, 455
  FOR expression, 456
    example, 456
  numeric fields, 458
  partial values, 457
  relation, 455
  strings, 459
    extraction, 459, 460
    logical operator, 459
    upper case, 460
  upper case, 460
data entry (*see* data entry), 440
data stamp, 443
  example, 443
decisions, 498
  CASE, 499
  IF ELSE ENDIF, 498
    example, 498
  WHILE, 500
    example, 500
DELETE, 466
  file, 466
  record, 466
    multiple, 466
    using PACK with, 466
  deleting, 447

  need to PACK, 447
  particular records, 447
EDIT, 446
  control keys, 446
  editing, 446
  need, 446
entering data, 444
  supplying values, 445
  terminating session, 445
  USE file, 444
expression, 455
expressions, 455
file, 443
  display structure of, 444
  extension, 443
file creation, 442
  entering data, 444
  example, 444
  field specification, 443
  file name, 442
file structure, 444
  displaying, 444
file update, 477
FIND, 471
  attaching index, 471
  contrast with LOCATE, 475
  example, 472, 475
    DISPLAY results, 469
  multiple fields, 471
  value absent, 472
index, 468
  attaching, 468
  creating, 468
  FIND, 469
  updating, 468
input commands, 492
  ACCEPT, 493
    example, 495
  GET, 494
  INPUT, 493
  PICTURE, 496
    example, 497
  READ, 494
  RESTORE, 492
  WAIT, 492
INSERT, 477
  BEFORE, 477
  BLANK, 477
  diagram, 477
  positioning for, 477
language, 487

dBase (cont.)
  LOCATE, 473
    CONTINUE, 473
      end of file, 473
    criteria, 473
    example, 473, 474
      use of memory variables, 474
    scope, 473
  Loop commands, 500
  memory variables, 474, 491
    RELEASE, 492
    RESTORE, 492
    SAVE, 492
    STORE, 491
  MODIFY, command file, 488
    examples, 486
    STRUCTURE, 486
  NOTE, 489
  prompt, 442
    action, 441
    data, 441
  query (*see* dBase, retrieval), 455
  range, 452
    example, 452
  relation, 455
  RENAME, 467
  REPLACE, 479
    scope, 479
    selective, 481
  REPORT, 503
    action, 504
    example, 508
      listing, 509
    fields of, 505
    heading, 505
    setup, 503
      interaction, 504
    subtotals, 507
    totals, 507
    using, 506
      with NEXT, 506
  report programs, 514
    control break, 515
      sample loop, 515
    major break, 523
    minor break, 524
    multiple breaks, 520
      examples, 521
    multiple levels, 525
    partial report, 517
    printout, 518
  reports, 503
  retrieval, 448, 455
    compound (*see* dBase, criteria), 461
    introduction, 448
    LIST (*see* LIST), 449
    print during, 448
    serial, 448
    simple (*see* dBase, criteria), 455
    simple display, 448
  scope (*see scope*), 450
  screen commands, 488
    ?, 489
    @, 489
    ERASE, 489
    SAY, 489, 490
  sorting, 465
    example, 466
    invoking, 465
  strings, 459
  switches, 501
    examples, 501
    SET, 501
      table, 502
  time stamp, 442
  UPDATE, 483
    example, 484
  utilities, 477
DBPlus, 467
DDT, 230
debugging, 269
default drive, 212
DEFINT, 292
DEFSTR, 292
delete, 400
  content, 400
    affirm, 400
    cancel, 400
    example, 401
    highlight, 400
  geometrical, 400
  immediate, 400
  recall, 402
  reformat (*see* reformat), 404
demodulator (*see* modem), 81
density, 132
  bits per inch, 132
  bits per track, 132
  tracks per inch, 132

dependencies, 655
descender, 69
dial-up network, 82
digital to analog convector (D/A), 180
DIM, 291
direct command, 270
  examples of, 270
direct file, 350
  alter record in place, 353
  buffer for, 352
    put values in, 352
      with LSET, 353
  concept, 350
  creating, 356
    example, 356
      code, 357
        read and write records, 357
        write table, 357
      from streamed file, 356
        example, 356
  establishing, 351
    CBASIC, 351
    MBASIC, 352
  finding record, 354
    formula for, 354
    table for, 354
      complete, 355
      storing, 355
  maintenance, 361
    birth, 362
    changes, 361
    death, 361
    table rewrite, 633
  posting, 359
    BASIC, 359
    example, 360
  relative record number, 351
  retrieval, 363
  retrieval from, 358
    getting table, 358
      BASIC, 358
  use, 351
directory, 251
  commands, 255
  default, 253
  tree, 252
disjunction, 461
disk, 117
  appearance, 118
  arm, 119
  backup, 144, 149
  block (*see* block), 122
  care of, 148
  checking (*see* CRC), 121
  contents, 134
    allocation directories, 134
      bit map (*see* bit map), 135
    extent, 134
    file, 134
    file directory (*see* file directory), 135
    volume, 134
  controller, 122
  cylinder, 119
  data, 120
  density, 132
    bpi, 132
    double, 132
    single, 132
    tpi, 132
  double sided, 132
  drive (*see* disk drive), 117, 125
  drive selection, 146
  driver, 122
  formatting, 120
    program for, 120
  full, 148
  geometry, 125
  hard (*see* hard disk), 141
  holes, 128
    centering notch, 128
    index, 128
    protect notch, 128
    sector, 128
    spindle, 125
  layout, 138
  memory simulation of, 149
  mounting, 148
  multiple drives, 147
  purchase of, 147
  RAM, 149
  recording density (*see* density), 132
  rigid (*see* hard disk), 141
  sector, diagram of, 120
  seek, 119
    time, 119
  single sided, 132
  software, 123
    diagram, 124
  surface, 118
    heads per, 119

disk (*cont.*)
  surface (*cont.*)
    multiple, 118
    physical, 118
    recording, 119
    tracks per, 118
  timing, 119
    home, 119
    sector, 119
      diagram of, 120
    track, 118
  Winchester, (*see* hard disk), 141
disk controller, 112, 169
  addressing, 171
  clock, 173
  CRC (cyclic redundancy check), 172
  DMA (direct memory access), 171
  matching to drive, 169
  multiple drives, 171
  sector detection, 173
  serialization, 172
  track positioning, 173
disk drive, 127
  capacity, 133
  head access slot, 127
  head loading, 127
  operating, 129
    activating disk, 130
    inserting disk, 129
  positioning mechanics, 127
  specifications, 131
    summary, 133
  speed, 133
  timing, 130
    average, 131
    head load, 130
    latency, 130
    seek, 130
    settling, 131
    table of, 131
  transfer rate, 133
DISKCOPY, 223
diskette (*see* disk), 125
display, 36
DISPLAY, 453
display, buffer, 36
  capacity, 68
  cell, 69
  character creation, 73
    scan line, 73

character generation, 70
  figure, 70
character generator, 76
  graphic symbols, 76
column, 68
control, 77
  clear screen, 77
  highlight, 77
  insert blank, 77
control sequence, 77
counter, 72
  addressing, 72
DISPLAY, *criteria* (*see* dBase, *criteria*), 453
display, cursor, 71
  distinguishing, 71
  reverse video (*see* reverse video), 71
data entry, 74
  character register, 74
  flag, 74
  full screen, 74
  transmission, rate, 75
    in bauds, 75
definition, 69
  dot, 69
  undot, 69
driver, 77
fonts, 76
graphics, 78
layout, 68
  cell, 68
  diagram, 68
memory, 70, 72
  diagram, 72
  size, 70
memory mapped, 71
menu, 76
monitor, 36
DISPLAY, OFF, 453
display, procedure, 72
DISPLAY, prototype, 453
  range, 453
display, refresh for, 72
row, 68
DISPLAY, *scope,* 453
display, special marks, 77
  split screen, 76
  status line, 77
DMA (direct memory access), 171
document assembly, 428
  assembly instructions, 429

inserting variables, 429
output, 429
subdocument library, 428
dot, 69
dot matrix printer, 87
  carriage motion, 87
  character generator, 87
  character sets, 94
    downloading, 94
  characteristics, 92
  hammer register, 91
    filling, 91
  multipass, 93
    print sample, 94
  print buffer, 90
    external, 90
      diagram, 92
  print element, 88
    diagram, 88
    in position, 89
    photo of, 90
    print wires, 88
    shown printing, 89
  print grid, 87
    diagram, 88
  print samples, 93
  print wire, 88
    diagram, 91
drive, 119
  dual, 129
driver, 205
  availability, 206
  disk, 113, 122
  display, 77
  need, 205
  tailoring, 206
dual drive, 129
dumb terminal, 51
duplex, 82
  half, 82

EBCDIC, 30
ED (electronic document), 393
  creation (*see* ED creation), 393
ED creation, 393
  automatic scroll, 396
  backspace correction, 394
    with rub, 394
  status display, 393
  wraparound, 395

EDIT, 273
  commands, 282
    table of, 282
editing, 397
  cut and paste (*see* blocks), 408
  deletion (*see* delete), 400
  insertion (*see* insertion), 402
  positioning, content, 399
    context, 399
    express, 399
  positioning in text, 397
    cursor (*see* cursor), 398
    target character, 398
    target screen, 398
  search (*see* search), 405
  search and replace (*see* search and replace), 406
editor, 265
  line, 265
  screen, 265
electronic document (*see* ED), 393
elite, 413
emphasis, responsive display, 420
engineering graphics, 532
error listing, 269
escape sequence, 61
expanded printing, 102
extended addressing, 167
extension, 213
extent, 134, 135, 218
  multiple, 139
external storage, 27, 111
  data flow, 111
    diagram of, 112
    input, 112
    output, 112
    software, 113
  data units, 113
  importance, 111
  magnetic recording (*see* magnetic recording), 114
  software, disk driver (see driver), 113
    File Manager (*see* File Manager), 113
extraction, 460

FCB, 219
  location, 219
field, 328
  character, 341
  format, 340

field (*cont.*)
  name, 328
  numeric, 341
  type, 340
    character, 340
    integer, 340
    real, 340
    string, 340
  value, 328
file, 134, 328
  ASCII, 341
  creating, 138
  deleting, 140
  direct (*see* direct file), 338
  expanding, 139
  finding, 138
  large, 139
  random (*see* direct file), 338
  sequential (*see* streamed file), 338
  serial (*see* streamed file), 338
  space for (*see* file space), 339
  streamed (*see* streamed file), 338
  type, 329
    data (*see* data file), 329
    program, 329
    text, 329
  using, 140
file control block (*see* FCB), 219
file directory, 135
  allocation strategy, 136
  extentions, 135
  file names, 135
  hard disk, 144
File Manager, 112, 136
  allocation strategy, 136
  creating a file, 138
  deleting a file, 140
  expanding a file, 138
  large files, 139
  transparent, 136
  use of directory, 138
  using a file, 140
file name, 135, 213
  command file, 213
  extension, 213
file space, 339
  expanding, 40
  fixed, 339
fill, 554
fixed disks, 141
flicker, 67

floppy disk (*see* disk), 125
footnotes, 435
FOR NEXT, 287
FOR TO STEP, 288
form letters, 426
  envelopes, 428
  output document, 427
    considerations, 427
    printing, 427
  stencil, 426
  variable value list, 426
FORMAT, 231
format, 120, 409
  default, 409
    diagram of, 410
    example of, 409
  dot commands, 412
  embedded commands, 411
    mnemonics, 412
  emphasis, 415
    boldface, 415
    control sequence, 417
    printing characters, 417
      character count, 417
    requesting, 417
    underline, 415
  justification (*see* justification), 418
  long term, 409
    header, footer, 414
    setup, 414
    lines per inch, 413
      elite, 413
      pica, 413
    page numbers, 414
      altering, 415
    paper setup, 412
  menu, 410
    example of, 411
  mode, 410
  responsive display, 410, 419
    emphasis, 420
    justification, 420
    margins, 420
    page break, 419
  setting, 409
  short term, 410
  tab (*see* tab), 417
  tab line, 410
    example, 411
FORTRAN, 305
  advantages, 305

(Framework) INDEX

disadvantages, 306
Framework, 681
  container, 716
    display, 708
    need of, 717
  Create, 691
    display, 692
    frame parameters, 692
    frame type, 692
    options, 691
    Outline, 692
  data base, 709
    altering, 710
    data entry, 709
    file size, 712
    forms view, 711
      illustration, 712
      modifying, 712
    photo of, 710
    queries, 710
    selecting fields, 711
    setup, 709
    size, 709
    title lock, 711
  Disk, 690
    display, 691
    options, 690
  disk transfers, 689
    drive used, 689
    load, 690
    save, 689
      copy, 689
      move, 689
  display, 681
    photo, 682
  Edit, 693
    display, 693
    Undo, 693
  frame, 682
    contents, 682
  Frame, 695
    blank option, 695
    close and open, 695
    column option, 695
    display, 695
    graph type, 698
    drag option, 695
    label option, 695
  frame status, 688
  function keys, 686
    assignment, 687
    layout, 687
  Graph, 698
    data, 698
    display, 699
    graph type, 698
    redraw, 698, 699
    start graphing, 698
    graphs, 713
    replotting, 713
    steps in creating, 713
    types, 713
  integration, 681
  introduction, 681
  Locate, 694
    display, 694
    search, 695
    search and replace, 695
    sorting, 694
  menu choices, 690
    how to choose, 690
    options that prevail, 690
  navigation, 687
    general principles, 688
    numeric keypad, 688
  Number, 697
    display, 698
    recalculate SS, 697
  operation selection, 684
    menu bar, 684
    options, 685
  outline, 681, 683, 701, 715
    adding levels, 701
    default, 683
    entering data, 703
    expansion of, 684
    frame types, 701
    frame view, 715
    moving between frames, 701
    photo, 683
    printing, 716
      container (*see* Framework,
        container), 716
      entire outline, 716
      partial document, 716
    view, 715
    zoom, 703, 715
  Print, 699
    display, 700
    suboptions, 699
  printing, 714
    single frames, 714

Framework (*cont.*)
  printing (*cont.*)
    single frames (*cont.*)
      data base, 714
      spooling, 714
    requirements, 682
    screen content, 685
      active frame, 686
      diagram of, 686
      formula panel, 685
      frame path, 685
      level display, 685
      prompt line, 685
      status bar, 685
      trays, 686
    spread sheets, 707
      formulas, 708
      naming columns and rows, 707
      photo of, 707
      windows, 708
    tasks, 700
    word processing, 703
      editing, 703
        backspace correction, 703
        format commands, 704
          table of, 704
        startup, 703
    Word, 696
      alignment, 696
      display, 697
      emphasis, 696
      format, 696
free space, 135
friction feed, 102
full duplex, 51

games, 528
gap (*see* head), 115
gateway, 80
gigabyte, 40
golf ball, 86
GOSUB, 286
GOTO, 286, 450
grammar, 434
Grammatik, 434
granularity, 550
graphics, 526
  architectural, 531
  business, 528
    advanced applications, 529
      examples, 530, 531
    charts, 529

CAD/CAM, 535
cartography, 534
  example, 534
education, 532
engineering, 531
  example, 532
fill, 554
games, 528
high resolution, 531
host routines, 556
  object definition, 556
  rotation, 557
  three dimensional motion, 557
IBM PC, 583
  BIOS service, 591
  character graphics, 591
  graphics board, 585
    image memory, 587
    two port memory, 587
    two port memory, 586
  image display, 587, 588
  memory mapped video, 584
    problems and solutions, 585
  memory mapping, 588, 587
  text colors, 591
  text mode, 590
image creation, 551
  color, 552
  firmware, 551
  motion, 551
    absolute, 552
    relative, 552
  pixel by pixel, 551
  primitives, 552
  software, 551
image production, 540
  contrast of, 541
  raster scan (*see* raster scan), 542
  strokes, 540
    illustration, 541
input, 560
  classes of, 560
  conceptual, 560
    commands, 560, 561
    cursor keys, 561
    knobs, 561
  light pen, 565
    cursor feedback, 566
    use, 565
  mouse, 562
    photo, 563
    need, 560

tablet, 564
  use, 564
text, 567
  creating, 567
  extra image plane, 567
introduction, 526
low resolution, 628
medicine, 532
medium resolution, 628
menu driven, 568
  action, 570
  decription, 568
  implementation, 572
  photo, 568
  requirements, 571
  scenario, 570
    changing palette, 570
    color fill, 570
    straight line figures, 570
  sketching aids, 573
    drag, 576
    rubber band, 573
    rubber circle, 574
    rubber rectangle, 575
  submenu, 569
need, 526
output, 577
  culling, 579
  digital storage, 578
    data compression, 578
  photographic, 580
  plotter, 582
    photo, 583
  printing, 580
    dot matrix, 581
    ink jet, 582
    mixing pigments, 580
  storing commands, 579
pan, 554
primitives, 552
  circle, 553
  line, 552
    smoothing, 552
publishing, 533
report sketches, 532
shading, 559
state of the art, 527
statistics, 534
system, 535
  application, 540
  description, 535
  diagram, 536

hobby, 536
  diagram, 537
  levels of, 536
  management, 538
    diagram, 538
  professional, 539
    diagram, 539
  visual arts, 534
  window, 553
  zoom, 554
graphics system, 762
  components, 762
  diagram, 765
  I/O, 762
  purpose, 762
  software, 764
    AutoCAD, 764
    paint program, 765
  tablet, 763
    interface board, 763

half duplex, 52
hard copy, 387
hard disk, 141
  air cushion, 142
  backup for, 144
    alternatives, 145
    archive, 144
    selective, 144
    total, 145
  characteristics, 141
  checkout, 145
  considerations, 142, 143
  disk for, 142
  driver for, 144
  error detection, 145
    read after write, 145
  error prevention, 146
  file directory, 144
  specifications, 142
    table of, 143
hardware, 14, 27
  components, 27
  diagram of, 27
head, 115
  design, 132
    diagram, 132
  design of, 132
  diagram, 115
  gap, 115
  positioning, 115
    diagram of, 128

head (*cont.*)
  read/write, 115
head access slot, 127
hex, 332
  code, 333
hexadecimal, 332
highlight, 77
home, 57
horizontal pitch, 101
hue, 547
hyphen, 430
  hard, 431
  soft, 431

IBM PC, 184, 730
  AT, 192
  color graphics, 194
    devices, 194
    modes, 194
  compatibility, 731
    achieving, 732
    application program, 732
      achieving, 723
    hardware, 731
    levels of, 731
    OS, 732
      achieving, 732
  disk drive, 191
    AT, 192
  display card, 193
  expansion slots, 195
  expansion unit, 195
  graphics, 583
  hardware, 185
  importance of, 184
  keyboard, 192
    function keys, 193
    key placement, 192
    numeric keypad, 193
  marketing policy, 731
  memory, 187
    addressing, 190
      segment register, 190
    assignments, 191
    map, 191
  mode, 194
    A/N, 194
    APA, 194
  picture of, 185
  printer adapter card, 193
  ROM, 189
    chips for, 189
    contents, 189
  system board, 186
    expansion slots, 187
      picture, 187
    layout, 188
    picture, 186
  XT, 184, 185, 186, 187
IBMBIO, 250
IBMDOS, 250
IF THEN (BASIC), 284
if then (Pascal), 298
IF THEN ELSE, 285
image, 547
  digitizing, 547
  memory, 547
  storing, 547
index, 468
  connecting, 470
  creating, 468
  effect, 470
  updating, 470
  use, 468
    example, 463
index hole, 128
individual, 327
information management system (*see*
      data base), 436
ink jet printer, 94
input, 112
INPUT, 289
INPUT#, 290
insertion, 402
  command mode, 403
  open up, 403
    example, 404
  overtype, 403
    example, 404
  pushaside, 402
    example, 402
  reformat (*see* reformat), 404
  toggle, 404
instruction, 11, 31, 159
  cycle, 31
  set, 159
interface, 28
interleaving, 123
interpreter, 261, 270
  activating, 270
  mode, direct command (*see* direct
      command), 270

Modes, 270
  direct command, 270
  editing, 271
  execution, 272
interrupt, 176
  data request, 177
I/O block, 174
  diagram, 174

jaggies, 553
justicication, 101, 418
  kinds of, 418
  micro, 419

key, 55, 328
  alphanumeric, 55
    QWERTY, 55
  arrow, 60
  command, 57
    break, 57
    clear, 57
    home, 57
  control, 58
    escape, 57
  cursor, 60, 398
  function, 57
    programmable, 60
      downloading, 60
  multiplier, 57, 58
  numeric, 59
  prefix, 62
  repeat action, 54, 399
  shift, 55
  shift lock 55
  types of, 58
  universal, 58
key number, 62
key pad, 59
  numeric, 59
keyboard, 35, 49, 52
  action, 53
  alphanumeric, 55
  IBM PC, 62
    caps lock, 63
    case, 63
    control codes, 63
    graphic characters, 63, 64
    key number, 62
      diagram, 62
    special codes, 64
    two byte codes, 63
    table of, 65
  installation program, 61
  key arrangement, 36
    numeric key pad, 36
  layout, 59
    diagram, 59
  physical alternatives, 49
    built-in, 50
    in cabinet, 50
  purpose, 52
  QWERTY, 55
  requirements, 53

LAN, 80
language, 259
  formal, 260
  natural, 259
  programming, 260, 294
    factors to consider, 260
    properties, 294
      chopping it up, 295
      compactness, 295
      correcting errors, 296
      ease of learning, 294
      efficiency, 296
      file management, 296
      friendliness, 294
      readability, 295
  syntax, 260
laser printer, 100
  operation, 100
    diagram, 100
  price, 100
latency, 130
library, 266
light pen, 565
  cursor feedback, 566
line advance, 86, 105
  lines per inch, 105
  spacing, 105
  subscripts, 105
  superscripts, 105
line capacity, 81
line printer, 97
  print chain, 98
    diagram, 98
    motion of, 98
  printing, 98
    character buffer, 98
    completion, 99

line printer (*cont.*)
  printing (*cont.*)
    hammer activation, 99
      diagram, 99
    speed, 97
    transmitting print line, 98
    print buffer, 98
link program, 266
linkages, 651
linker, 266
Lisa, 742, 743
  active window, 746
  Clipboard, 748
    icon, 745
    use of, 749
  desktop, 745
    folders, 746
      frame (*see* Lisa frame), 746
  evaluation, 750
  hardware, 743
  history, 743
  moving folder, 747
  Scrapbook, 749
  screen, 747
  use, 749
    pads for starting APs, 749
    pasting, 749
  window, 746
    active, 746
    photo, 745
Lisa 2, 751
  software for, 751
Lisa frame, 746
  arrow in frame, 748
    moves ED in pane, 748
  box icon, 748
    for relative ED position, 748
    for scrolling, 748
  pane, 746
  title bar, 747
    for positioning frame, 747
LIST, 273, 449
  example, 449
    FILES, 452
      LIKE, 452
  present position (see present position), 450
  print during, 449
  prototype, 449
    print during, 449
  scope (see scope), 450

    STRUCTURE, 452
LLIST, 273
LOAD, 283
load module, 266
loading, 127
local mode, 52
Lotus 1-2-3 (*see* 1-2-3), 658

m-drive, 149
Mac, 751
  evaluation, 752
  hardware, 751, 752
  operating, 752
  photo, 745
  software, 752
macro, 664
MagicWand, 408, 412
MagicBind, 420
magnetic card, 116
magnetic recording, 114
  disk drive (*see* disk), 117
  medium, shape, 116
    diagram, 116
  principles, 114
    data storage, 114
      diagram, 115
    medium, 114
      substrate, 114
    read/write head (*see* head), 115
magnetic tape, 116
MailMerge, 427
mainframe, 34
maintenance, 330
  birth, 331
  change, 331
  death, 331
  streamed file (*see* streamed file), 347
managerial work station, 740
  approach, 741
  fallacies, 742
  implementation, 741
  theory, 740
margins, 420
mark, 82
master, 175
mating, 44
  operating systems, 44
MBA, 643
MBASIC, 270
  activating, 270
  commands (*see* command name), 272

(media choices / Multiplan) INDEX 871

numbering, 272
direct command, 270
  examples, 270
  editor, 270, 271
  listing a program, 272
  operation, 274
    diagram of, 274
  prompt, 270
  running a program, 272
media choices, 42
medical graphics, 532
medium, 40
  characteristics, 41
    accessibility, 41
    capacity, 40
    reliability, 41
    reuseability, 41
    size, 41
    speed, 41
memory, 30, 161
  address (*see* address), 30
  addressing, 161
  cell, 30
  chips, 162
  extended addressibility, 183
  PC board, 162
    layout, 162
  random access (*see* RAM), 30
  read only (*see* RAM), 31, 162
  volatile, 31
  what's in, 29
mesh figure, 559
micro, talking to mainframe, 37
  talking together, 37
microfloppy (*see* disk), 125
MicroPlan, 593
microprocessor (*see* chip), 181
MicroSpell, 433
minocomputer, 34
minofloppy (*see* disk), 125
Mini Model, 593
mixed mode, 275
  intermediate code file, 275
  operation, 275, 277
    diagram of, 277
  rationale, 276
mode, answer, 82
  originate, 82
modem, 37, 49, 81
  check sum, 83
  connection, 82

dial-up, 82
full duplex, 82
half duplex, 82
mark, 82
parity, 83
PC board, 177
protocol, 83
rates, 82
space, 82
tones used, 81
use of, 37
MODEM7, 241
modulator (*see* modem), 81
monitor, 36
  color, 37
  graphics, 37
motherboard, 33
  bus, 33
  slots, 33
mouse, 562
  photo, 563
MS-DOS (*see* PC-DOS), 245
Multibus, 161
Multiplan, 644
  cell address, 644
  cell selection, 644
  combining SSs, 652
    partial, 653
    requirements, 653
  commands, 648
    help, 648
    options, 648
      example, 649
      prompts eliminated, 649
      proposed response, 649
    selection, 648
  consolidation, 653
  cursor positioning, 645
  data entry, 646
    numbers, 646
    text, 646
  formulas, 649
    copying, 652
    entering, 650
      by pointing, 651
      no need to replicate, 651
    operands, 649
    operators, 649
    references, 650
      absolute, 650
      relative, 650

Multiplan (*cont.*)
  formulas (*cont.*)
    values in, 649
  link command, 654
    automatic linkage, 654
    automatic load, 655
    circular dependencies, 656
      diagram, 656
    external copy, 655
    load and link, 654
      options, 654
    multiple dependencies, 655
      diagram, 656
    storing worksheets, 654
    use option, 657
  load, 653
    partial, 653
  name command, 647
    if name exists, 647
  page scrolling, 645
  sort command, 658
    use, 658
multiprocessing, 759
  block diagram, 759
  description, 759
  master processor, 760
  operating system for, 760
  operation, 760
  pros and cons, 761
  requirements for, 760
  role of the master, 761
  spooling for, 761
multiprogramming, 756
  behind the scenes, 758
  block diagram, 757
  examples, 759
  hardware required, 756
  operating system, 756
    drivers, 756
  operation, 757
    log on, 757
    user protection, 758
  pros and cons, 758
  requirements, 758
  spooling for (*see* spooling), 757
multitasking, 754
  block diagram, 755
  description, 754
  examples, 756
  OS for, 755
  pros and cons, 756
  requirements of, 756
multiuser system, 753
  alternatives (*which see*), 753, 754
    multiprocessing, 759
    multiprogramming, 756
    multitasking, 754
  need, 754

nanosecond, 163
network, 78
  diagram, 81
  gateway, 80
  LAN, 80
NEXT, 450
nibble, 332
  hexadecimal, 332
numeric key pad, 36

object module, 266
off, 28
office layout, 530
offset, 123
Ok, 270
on, 28
ON GOTO, 293
1-2-3 (*see beginning of Index*)
OPEN, 288
operand, 13, 159
operating environment, 723
  alternatives, 735
  block diagram, 737
    components, 737
    illustration, 738
    input, 737
    intercourse, 739
    output, 739
  classification, 735
  multiple functions, 734
  problem, 723
    data compatibility, 734
  pros and cons, 739
    cost, 739
    results, 740
  windows, 736
    actions with, 736
operating system (*see* OS), 15
  compatible, 43
  overview, 199
order entry, 18
originate mode, 82

orphan, 419
OS (operating system), 199
　AP services, 219
　　identifying, 219
　　return code, 220
　　return to caller, 220
　booting (*see* booting), 209
　change drives, 216
　CP/M (*see* CP/M), 209
　definitions, 199
　delete a file, 216
　display file conent, 217
　example, 207
　file names (*see* file name), 213
　halt display, 217
　making requests, 211, 213
　matching computer system, 199
　　data, 202
　　diagram, 200
　　hardware, 200
　　user, 202
　mating, 44
　　diagram, 45
　nonresident service, 220
　　COPY, 223
　　description, 20
　　DISKCOPY, 223
　　PIP, 223
　　STAT (*see* STAT) 221
　nonresident services, 227
　overview, 199
　print console output, 217
　program space, 207
　prompt (*see* prompt), 202
　rename a file, 216
　resident, 204
　　components, 204, 209
　　control program (*see* control program), 205
　　driver (*see* driver), 205
　　map of memory, 208
　　　rationale, 208
　　ROM, 204
　resident services, 215
　　keying request, 215
　save a command file, 217
　sign on, 211
　starting a program, 213, 214
　system diskette, 203
　transient area (*see* TPA), 207
　utilities, 230
　　FORMAT, 231
　working system, 202
　　diagram of, 203
　outline form, 434
　overview, 3

PACK, 447
package deal, 154
package, application (*see* AP), 367
page break, 419
　manual, 419
palette, 549
　size, 549
pan, 554
paper bail, 86
paper feed, 105
　automatic, 106
　bursting, 106
　continuous roll, 106
　fan fold, 105
　manual, 106
parallel, 79
parity, 83, 121, 337
　error, 121
　odd, 337
parity bit, 121, 337
　invalid, 337
Pascal, 297
　blocks, 298
　　indenting, 299
　　using, 299
　features, 297
　procedure, 302
　　call, 304
　　definition, 302
　　parameters, 303
　relations, 298
　structure, 297
　types, 301
　　user defined, 301
　variables, 300
　　defining, 300
payroll, 18
PC board, 33
　analog to digital, 180
　clock, 169
　computer, 175
　　master, 175
　　slave, 175

874   INDEX (PC-DOS / printer motion)

PC board (*cont.*)
  console, 178
  disk controller (*see* disk controller), 169
  interface, 179
  modem, 177
    functions, 178
    modes, 178
    software for, 178
  on bus, 168
    diagram of, 168
  printer connector, 178
  video, 180
PC-DOS, 245
  batch files, 257
  COMMAND, 251
  components, 245, 246
    disk resident, 246
    RAM, 246
    ROM, 246
  directories, 251
    trees, 252
  history, 245
  memory assignments, 249
  resident components, 250
  start-up, 247
PeachTest, 403, 412, 422
people, 14, 16, 26
Perfect Calc, 593
peripheral device, 34
persistence, 67, 546
PERT chart, 531
phosphor, 546
  mixing, 546
pica, 413
pin feed, 103
PIP, 223
pitch, 101
pixel, 543
  multiple rels, 543
    illustration, 544
  single rel, 543
PL/I, 307
platen, 86
PLAY, 315
point, 651
population, 327
posting, streamed file (*see* streamed file), 344
POWER, 237

power supply, 32
  regulated, 33
preprinted forms, 429
  form stencil, 429
present position, 450
  GOTO, 450
    BOTTOM, 450
    number, 450
    TOP, 450
  setting, 450
    GOTO, 450
    SKIP, 450, 451
PRINT, 271
  literals, 281
  multiple variables, 281
  variables and literals, 282
print element, 86
printed circuit board (*see* PC board), 33, 157
printer, 27, 38, 84
  choosing, 108
    factors, 108
  cost, 109
  daisy wheel (*see* daisy wheel printer), 85
  dot matrix (*see* dot matrix printer), 85
  ink jet, 94
  laser (*see* laser printer), 85
  line (*see* line printer), 85
  maintenance, 109
    contract, 109
  motion in (*see* printer motion), 101
  need, 110
    application oriented, 110
  operating attention, 109
  print refinements, 109
  quality, 108
  ribbon (*see* ribbon), 107
  speed, 108
  terminal, 84
  types of, 38
  typewriter (*see* typewriter), 84
printer motion, 110
  direction, 105
  line advance (*see* line advance), 105
    friction, feed, 102
    pin feed, 103
      photo, 103
    tractor feed (*see* tractor feed), 103
  line advance mechanism, 102

paper feed (*see* paper feed), 105
print element advance, 101
  bidirectional, 102
  compressed, 102
  expanded, 102
  fixed, 101
  pitch, 101
    characters per inch, 101
  proportional spacing, 102
  variable, 101
    increment size, 101
ProCalc, 593
procedures, 14, 16, 26
program, 26, 258
  copy protection, 244
  creation, 261
  dependence on, 258
  entry mode, 264
    batch, 265
    terminal, 265
      editor for, 265
  evaluation of, 259
  introduction, 258
  mode of operation, 260
    compilation (*see* compiler), 261
    interpreter (*see* interpreter), 261
    mixed mode (*see* mixed mode), 275
  response time, 259
  source, 261
  starting, 214
  statement, 267
programmer, 26
programming, 26, 258
  steps required, 262
    data flow, 262
      diagram, 264
    document flow, 262
      diagram of, 263
prompt, 202
  action, 441
  data, 441
  dBase, 442
  OS, 202
Proofreader, 432
proportional spacing, 102, 420
protect notch, 128
protocol, 83

Q-bus, 161
query, 455

RAM, 162
  access time, 163
  bank switching, 166
  chip sizes, 163
  contrast of types, 163
  dynamic, 163
  expanding, 166
  package, 164
  PC board, 164
    boundary selection, 165
    configuration, 164
    disable, 165
    other chips, 165
    size, 164
  phantom, 165
  static, 163
RAM drive, 149
Ram Disk, 244
range (dBase), 452
range (spread sheet), 609
raster scan, 542
  color, 547, 549
    color table, color packet, 550
    image storage, 549
      color packet, 550
    qualities of, 547
    RGB, 547
  creating the image, 544
  CRT, 544
    diagram of, 545
    phosphors, 546
  diagram of, 542
  dot, 542
  example of, 543
  gun, 544
    deflection, 545
    diagram of, 545
    linearity, 545
    positioning the beam, 545
  image memory, 543
    pixels, 543
  intensity, 547
  resolution element (rel), 542
  retrace, 542
  scan line, 542
  synchronizing display, 546
  undot, 542
RBG, 547
read, 40
  disk, 40

record, 328
  key, 328
  streamed (see streamed file), 341
reformat, 404
  automatic, 404
  manual, 404
refresh, 546
  memory, 546
  register, 546
register, 12, 159
  instruction, 12
  status, 13
RENUM, 281
replace string, 406
replicate, 614
reports, 10
  printing, 10
reserved words, 298
resolution element (rel), 542
retrieval, 330
return, 56
reuseability, 40
reverse video, 72
ribbon, 107
  cartridge, 107
    photo, 107
  inked cloth, 107
    two color, 107
  multistrike, 107
rollover, 61
  multikey, 61
row stub, 600
rub, 56, 394
RUN, 272, 283

S-100 (bus), 161
saturation, 547
SAVE, 283
scope (dBase), 450
  options, 450
Scrapbook (Lisa), 749
screen (see CRT), 64
scroll, 398
  automatic, 396, 397
  backward, 398
  exclusive, 398
  forward, 398
  line, 398
  screen overlap, 398
search, 405

exact match, 405
extent of, 406
ignore case, 405
repeat, 406
reverse, 405
whole word, 405
wild cards, 406
search and replace, 406
  case, 407
  discretionary, 407
  last occurrence, 407
  multiple, 407
    global, 407
    number of, 407
  prompts for, 406
  repeat, 408
  replace string, 407
  search string, 407
  target string, 407
search string, 405
sector, 119, 120
  CRC, 121
  detection, 129
  diagram of, 121
  hard, 119, 120
  marker, 119
  soft, 120, 121
sector detection, 173
sector hole, 128
seek, 119
  time, 119
Select (WP package), 408, 412
semidisk, 149
sequential medium, 338
serial, 54, 79
serializer, 80
  diagram, 80
shading, 559
sheet feeder, 106
shift key, 55
shift lock, 55
sign on, 211
skewing, 123
SKIP, 451
skirt, 57
slave, 175
  layout, 175, 176
  need for, 175
slot, 125
smart terminal, 52

software, 42, 367
  application (*see* AP), 367
  application program (*see* AP), 44
  operating system (*see* OS), 43
sort, multiple fields, 467
sorting, 332, 465
SOUND, 315
source code, 261
source program, 261
space, 82
spacing, 105
  double, 105
  single, 105
spelling, 432
spindle hole, 125
spread sheets, 21, 593
  activation, 600
  actual spread sheet, 598
    diagram, 599
  basics, 597
  blanking 627
  border, 610
    controlling, 610
  calculations, 597
  cash flow model, 629
    cash flow, 631
    cash reserve, 635
    collections, 629
    disbursements, 631
    improving collections, 637
      uncollectable A/R, 638
    negative cash problem, 632
      interest rates, 634
      loan interest, 633
    other hypotheses, 639
    purchases, 631
    test more assumptions, 635
  cell entry, 602
    cancelling, 604
    commands, 604
    correction, 603
    formulas, 603
    numbers, 603
    text, 603
  changing column width, 612
  check reconciliation, 618
    diagram, 619
    problem, 618
    solution, 618
  classification, 642

  clearing, 606
  combination, 643
  commands, 604
    entering, 604
  conditional statements, 634
  copying portions, 609
  cursor, 600
    active, 601
    cell, 601
    direct movement, 602
    positioning, 601
      arrow keys, 601
  description, 594
    cells, 592
      entering data, 595
    pad, 594
  display spread sheet, 599
    active cell, 600
    column stub, 600
    diagram, 600
    moving, 602
    relation to CRT, 599
    row stub, 600
    status stub, 600
  effectiveness, 593
  electronic time sheet example, 615
    improving automatic calculations, 617
  entering boiler plate, 611
  exiting from, 605
  first generation, 642
  format changes, 612
    formula display, 613
    numbers, 613
    text, 613
  fourth generation, 680
    assessment, 722
      capabilities, 723
      complexity, 722
      recommendations, 725
      tutorial, 723
    candidates, 680
    Framework (*see* Framework), 681
    Symphony (*see* Symphony), 717
    windows, 681
  functions, 630, 639
    financial, 640
    logical, 641
    mathematical, 640
    range, 640
    table lookup, 641

spread sheets (*cont.*)
  functions (*cont.*)
    table lookup (*cont.*)
      example, 641
  introduction, 593
  layout, 598
    diagram, 598
  loading, 605, 606
  popularity, 593
  printing, 611
  range, 610
  recalculation, 632
  replication, 614
    adjustment, 614
    automatic adjustment, 618
    illustration, 616
  saving, 605
  second generation (*see* Multiplan), 642
  setting up formulas, 615
    illustration, 615
  status stub, 601
  text only, 607
    setting up, 607
    display, 608
  third generation (*see* 1-2-3), 658
    capabilities, 658
  title locks, 619
    both, 622
      illustration, 623
    horizontal, 620
      illustration, 621
    need, 619
    vertical, 622
      illustration, 622
  virtual spread sheet, 597
    size limits, 598
  ways to use, 595
  what if?, 628
  windows, 623
    and title lock, 626
      illustration, 626
    horizontal, 623
      illustration, 624, 625
    options, 623
    synchronize, 624
    vertical, 625
      illustration, 625
starting a program, 214
STAT, 221
status stub, 600
STOP, 283

storage, 8
  disk drive, 9
  external (*see* external storage), 111
  floppy disk, 8
streamed file, 338
  creating, 341
    BASIC, 343
  file space for, 339
  maintenance, 347
    appending records, 347
    at end, 348
    BASIC, 349
    batch, 349
    during copying, 348
    death and change, 350
  posting, 344
    batch processing, 345
      diagram, 346
    no match, 345
    one at a time, 344
      diagram, 345
  record retrieval, 343
    by key, 343
    BASIC, 343
    file review, 343
  sequential medium, 338
  storage, 39
  need for, 39
subdocuments, 425
  automatic assembly, 426
    document assembly (*see* document assembly), 428
    form letters (*see* form letters), 426
    preprinted forms (*see* preprinted forms), 429
  definition, 425
SUBMIT, 227
subroutine, 266
  library, 266
subscript, 105
SuperCalc, 598
superscript, 105
Symphony, 717
  communication, 722
  control, 719
    function keys, 720
    menus, 720
    services, 720
    settings sheets, 720
      changing, 720
      parameters, 720

data base, 721
goals, 717, 718
graphs, 721
requirements, 717
spread sheet, 721
task, 721
window, 719
  mobility, 719
  types of, 719
work processing, 721
work environment, 718
  five tasks, 718
  range for task, 718
  setup, 718
worksheet, 718
syntax, 260
syntax error, 266
SYSTEM, 284
system, audio, 152
  diagram, 153
  composite, 18
  computer, 152
    business, 153
      diagram of, 154
  computer (*see* computer system), 729
  computerized, 14
  extent of, 17
  integrated, 23
    multiple packages, 24
    single vendor, 23
      advantages, 23
      special requirements, 24
      truck routing, 24
system diskette, 203
system house, 766
  alternatives, 767
  description, 766
  OEM operation, 768
  selection, 768
  services, 766
    list of, 766
system loader, 210
  diagram, 210

tab, 56, 417
  clear, 417
  key, 418
  kinds of, 417
    center, 417
    decimal, 417
    indent, 417
    left, 417
    right flush, 417
    standard, 417
  line (*see also* status line), 417
  reset, 418
  set, 417
  set mode, 418
  setup, 417
  stop, 417
  use, 418
tables and charts, 435
teletypewriter, 84
terminal, 9, 27, 49
  functional alternatives, 51
    dumb, 51
    intelligent, 52
    smart, 52
  keyboard, 10
  mode, 52
  physical alternatives, 50
    built into computer, 50
    keyboard built in, 50
    separate, 50
  printer, 84
  screen, 9
  typical (photo), 66
time, access, 131
  average positioning, 131
  disk, 131
  head load, 130
  head positioning, 130, 131
  latency, 130
  settling, 131
  track, 118
track positioning, 173
tractor feed, 103
  adjustable, 103
    paper guide, 103
    sprocket holes, 103
  adjustment, 104
  photo, 104
transaction, 331
  file, 331
  record, 331
transfer rate, 133
transient area (*see* TPA), 207
truck dispatching, 19
True BASIC, 318
  branching, 324
  control statements, 321
  CASE, 320

True BASIC (*cont.*)
  control statements (*cont.*)
    IF, 321
    loops, 320
    example, 322
    introduction, 318
    language, 319
      matrices, 320
      substrings, 319
      symbols, 319
    mixed mode, 324
    subroutines, 323
turnkey system, 204
type, 300
typewriter, 84
  modified, 85
  parts of, 86
    diagram, 86
    print action, 86
    print element, 86
      diagram of, 87

underline, 415
undot, 69
UNIX, 310
update, 330
upward compatible, 159
utilities, 230
  CP/M, 230
  non OS, 236
    need, 236

valid statement, 267
var, 300
variable, 279
  name, 279
video display terminal (VDT), 49
virtual disk, 149
VisiCalc, 598
volatile, 31
volume, 134

widow, 419
Winchester drive (*see* hard disk), 141
window, 736
  as part of operating environment, 736
  graphics, 554
word processing, 18, 20, 387
  advanced features, 392

document creation (*see* ED creation), 391
editing assistance, 430
footnotes, 435
formatting (*see* format), 391
function selection, 389
  by menu, 389
    example, 390
    combination, 390
  from operation system, 389
grammar checkers, 434
hard copy, 387
hyphenation, 430
  automatic, 431
  computer assisted, 431
    hard hyphen, 431
    soft hyphen, 431
importance, 387
installing, 393
invoking the program, 393
need, 387
outline form, 434
portions of documents, 424
  blocks, 408
  phrase storage, 424
    defining, 425
    storing, 425
    using, 425
  subdocuments (*see* subdocuments), 425
printing, 392, 421
  format change, 422
    at print time, 422
    during printing, 422
  format suppressed, 423
  how much, 421
  paper setup, 423
    continuous forms, 423
    single sheet, 423
  printer setup, 423
  when done, 421
    restrictions on, 421
reformatting, 430
requirements, 388
  computer, 388
  printer, 388
  program, 388
  terminal, 388
spelling programs, 432
  checking only, 432

correcting, 433
full scan, 432
interactive, 432
tables and charts, 435
utilities, 392
editing (see editing), 391
WordStar, 390
wordwrap, 395

wraparound, 395
write, 40

Xerox Star, 742
XSUB, 230

zoom, 554

Sci Ref QA 76.5 .F47 1986
Flores, Ivan.
The professional
 microcomputer handbook

MAR 1 1 1986